Interpreting the Constitution

Interpreting the Constitution

Kent Greenawalt

OXFORD
UNIVERSITY PRESS

OXFORD
UNIVERSITY PRESS

Oxford University Press is a department of the University of Oxford. It furthers the University's objective of excellence in research, scholarship, and education by publishing worldwide.

Oxford New York
Auckland Cape Town Dar es Salaam Hong Kong Karachi
Kuala Lumpur Madrid Melbourne Mexico City Nairobi
New Delhi Shanghai Taipei Toronto

With offices in
Argentina Austria Brazil Chile Czech Republic France Greece
Guatemala Hungary Italy Japan Poland Portugal Singapore
South Korea Switzerland Thailand Turkey Ukraine Vietnam

Oxford is a registered trademark of Oxford University Press in the UK and certain other countries.

Published in the United States of America by
Oxford University Press
198 Madison Avenue, New York, NY 10016

Cataloging-in-Publication Data is available at the Library of Congress.
ISBN 978–0–19–975615–5

9 8 7 6 5 4 3 2 1
Printed in the United States of America
on acid-free paper

Contents

Preface

This third volume about legal interpretation covers a subject I have been interested in for my whole career and is somewhat related to the political philosophy on which I concentrated in my student days at Swarthmore and Oxford. Early in my teaching and writing, I tackled various aspects of constitutional law, especially those involving the First Amendment, and a good bit of my writing has been about that amendment's protection of freedom of religion and speech.

The main endeavor in this volume is to focus on general issues about constitutional interpretation, noting along the way how these relate to the subjects of the first two volumes. The connections to, and differences from, statutory and common law interpretation are most obviously important, but how constitutional interpretation relates to that of other disciplines and private texts is also relevant. I have provided fairly extensive citations to the earlier volumes, not because these are the most important writings on the subjects but so that readers who have an interest in a topic will be able to see my particular views more fully.

This volume attempts something that is relatively rare in constitutional interpretation, and it may well affect just what readers decide to cover and how they understand the last seven chapters. Virtually all writing about constitutional law is either about specific subjects or about interpretative strategies more generally. This book attempts both, with the first five chapters on the latter, and the following chapters on the former. Of course, all writing about interpretation includes specific examples, but when authors choose what illustrations to use to support their theses and to counter opposing views, that is hardly an assurance that the suggested general approach makes sense across the board. What this book attempts is to cover fairly broad subject matters in all or most of their important aspects. I believe this provides a much better test of what works and what doesn't, and of how different constitutional issues vary from one another. This should give readers a fairly solid basis to reflect on what approaches to interpretation they genuinely think are wise or misconceived.

Three aspects of this approach are important. The first is that the chapters on specific subjects are definitely not as well researched and comprehensive as would be a book or long article on the same topics. The effort here is not to provide an up-to-date, complete account of each, something that would be impossible even in the long chapters. Rather, the aim is to afford the reader a complete enough coverage to reflect on what interpretive strategies make sense.

The second aspect is that a reader who finds the book's length a bit threatening need not assume it is all or nothing. It would be quite feasible to assess the general themes by reading the first five chapters alone, or by reading those and one or two others that cover subjects in which a person has a special interest. This is not a book in which one cannot grasp the major points without reading all chapters.

A third point is that Chapters 6–12 portray many of my assessments about particular issues. Because some readers may be interested in the resolution of these issues, I have provided references to ones that I have addressed elsewhere. But the main reason for their place in this volume is *not* how specific controversies should be resolved, but what interpretive strategies make sense. A reader who disagrees with many of my particular suggestions about issues may nonetheless believe in interpretive approaches that resemble those supported here, and readers who agree with me about some specific resolutions may reject much of what I claim about interpretation. Nevertheless, I believe a genuine test of claims about how interpretation does and should proceed requires illustrations that cover broad ranges of constitutional issues, including the outcomes one finds persuasive. That is the overarching reason for this book's inclusion of chapters on various subjects along with appraisals of desirable approaches and outcomes.

My efforts on this book have benefited greatly from extensive scholarship on constitutional law and its interpretation. References within the book name many but not all of these scholars and their work. Comments given me on drafts and in other conversations with colleagues here at Columbia and elsewhere have also provided substantial assistance. Some of those scholars are Vince Blasi, Philip Bobbitt, Jessica Bulman-Pozen, Harold Edgar, Samuel Estreicher, Elizabeth Emens, Jeff Fagan, Robert Ferguson, Jamal Greene, Philip Hamburger, Bernard Harcourt, Paul Horwitz, Olati Johnson, Kent McKeever, John Manning, Tom Merrill, Gillian Metzger, Henry Monaghan, Jefferson Powell, David Pozen, Andrzej Rapaczynski, Dan Richman, Frederick Schauer, and Peter Strauss.

I could not have managed a book with such broad coverage without tremendous research assistance from those who have been students here. On the critical first five chapters, Amanda Meyer provided continuing research and editorial help over a number of drafts. Others whose similar contributions made chapters possible were Alex Blaszczuk, Ned Babbitt, Katherine Chen, Courtney Chin, Nate Crider, Dennis Fan, Rachael Hoare, Jon-David Jorgensen, Eric Johnson, Megan Larkin, Jared Miller, William Monks, Neema Nassiri, Andrei Popovici, Nicole Tortoriello, Peter Walkingshaw, Tali Yahalom, Georgina Yeomans, and Zhuoming Zhang.

Given that I still write by hand and do so unclearly in many instances, a crucial key to any productivity is the typing of drafts. Members of the Columbia staff, supervised by Caroline Lukaszewski, have done this quickly and carefully. The key figure, as with previous volumes, has been Katherine Bobbitt, who went over chapters and their stages of revisions, discovered missing and misspelled words, and made very perceptive editorial suggestions.

Finally, I am grateful to David McBride of Oxford University Press, who offered numerous suggestions about how to make chapters clearer and more readable. Helpful assistance at the final stage of production was provided by Molly Morrison and Cassie Tuttle.

My research work during the last three summers has benefited from the financial support of the Bernard H. Kayden Fund and the Madsen Family Research Fund.

Part I

GENERAL THEMES

Chapter 1

The Nature of Constitutions

Basic Questions about Their Interpretation

I. INTRODUCTION

How should a constitution be interpreted? Using a broad sense of "interpretation" that does not try to distinguish it from "application" or "construction," this book aims to provide an account that will prove interesting to both those who wish to learn about competing constitutional approaches and those already familiar with major positions. Any thoughtful approach to how constitutions should be interpreted depends significantly on their very nature. Beginning with that inquiry, this chapter then sketches various interpretive techniques and how one may evaluate them. Subsequent chapters undertake a deeper exploration of strategies of interpretation and their applications to a range of constitutional topics.

Although employing a few notable examples, the five chapters of Part I are basically concerned with general questions about how courts should interpret constitutions. The overarching focus is on the federal Constitution of the United States, with occasional comparisons to constitutions of individual states and other countries. Using a parable about the meaning and force of authoritative personal instructions, Chapter 2 initially suggests that multiple criteria figure in decisions about a person's responsibility to follow instructions. Recognizing significant differences between moral responsibilities and legal constraints, the chapter claims, nonetheless, that no single standard is appropriate for interpretive constitutional decisions carrying practical consequences. Chapter 3 explores the relevance of original understanding: how far what counts is text or intent, specific coverage or underlying substantive principles, and accepted strategies of interpretation; and whether the weight of various factors changes over time. The answer offered is that this depends significantly on the particular provision involved, that how one should determine original understanding does change over time, and that the basic importance of original understanding diminishes as the decades roll by. Chapter 4 treats other standards of interpretation, including precedents, modern understanding of the text, canons of interpretation, estimations of consequences, and adjustments to changing social conditions and fundamental values. Crosscutting these standards for courts are questions about how far the officials in other branches should employ standards of interpretation that differ from those apt for judges, and when judges should avoid decisions of issues altogether or afford substantial deference to the determinations of the political branches. Chapter 5 tackles complex puzzles about how much judges can rely on "neutral principles" or "objective" standards, concluding that these play a central role but cannot totally determine decisions in the most difficult cases. In all of these chapters, the inquiries are primarily normative—what is a sensible, desirable approach?—but no account of how judges and other officials *should* interpret can divorce itself from how they do interpret and how they are capable of interpreting.

The remainder of the book tests the conclusions of these chapters against specific constitutional issues that have arisen across a range of areas. The examination not only confirms generalizations made earlier, but it also demonstrates just how greatly interpretations of various provisions should and do differ from one another. Part II consists of a single chapter devoted to the significance of the ban on "cruel and unusual punishment" in the Eighth Amendment. That term, and its application over time, raise sharply and clearly a number of fundamental questions about how courts should interpret provisions that seem open-ended.

Part III addresses limits on the authority of particular government bodies. Chapter 7 considers allocations of power between the legislative and executive branches of the federal government and the troubling questions of how far courts should involve themselves when one branch acquiesces to exercises of power by the other or when disputes arise between the two branches. Chapter 8 addresses the distribution of power between the federal and state governments. It focuses mainly on the national government's power under the Commerce Clause, the Taxing and Spending Clause, and the Necessary and Proper Clause, paying particular attention to the 5–4 division on the Supreme Court over the status of the "Obamacare" healthcare law.

Part IV turns to various individual rights. Chapter 9 initially inquires whether "incorporation" of most of the Bill of Rights against the states is justified and then looks specifically at the part of the First Amendment dealing with freedom of speech and of the press. Chapter 10 discusses free exercise and nonestablishment of religion. Chapter 11 tackles aspects of constitutional protections connected to the criminal process besides cruel and unusual punishment, including the right to counsel, the prohibition of unreasonable searches, and the privilege against self-incrimination. Chapter 12 addresses equal protection.

Although the general theme in the chapters dealing with particular provisions is how the Supreme Court has and should approach their interpretation, I also analyze the soundness of certain competing positions about the range of substantive protections. Based partly on more extensive treatments in earlier articles and books, the account here is offered primarily to illustrate the urgent need for interpretation that is tethered to context and that varies depending on what subjects are invoked.

My belief is that the coverage in some detail of a wide range of provisions and issues provides a much more solid basis to assess more general claims about interpretation than does the offering of a few notable examples to support such claims or to counter competing positions. The discussion reveals just how difficult and controversial are the resolutions of many constitutional issues. It provides readers a basis for considering how their own assessment of desirable outcomes and interpretive standards compares with those defended here. Of course, even those whose appraisals of broad ideas of interpretation do not differ significantly from those I offer will almost certainly disagree about a number of the more specific recommendations; but those with a radically opposed sense of interpretation may discern nearly all of those recommendations as misguided. Much, much more could be said, and indeed has been said, about all of the topics of these chapters;[1] but the topics addressed here should assist readers to develop a reflective view of what forms of constitutional interpretation make good sense in a variety of contexts.

II. CONSTITUTIONS DISTINGUISHED FROM STATUTES

Although lawyers for many centuries have referred to an unwritten British constitution that influences what members of Parliament do and judges decide,[2] in modern times, we typically think of constitutions as being written and as representing supermajoritarian decisions. Such a constitution, like a statute, is an authoritative text, one designed to guide and constrain legislators, executive officials, and judges.[3] That judges are construing a document issued by higher authority distinguishes constitutional interpretation from common law interpretation, which is mainly based on decisions previously rendered by judges themselves and, to a lesser extent, on customary practices. The similarity of statutes and constitutions does not entail that whatever represents sound statutory interpretation applies to interpreting a constitution. Any such equation would be deeply mistaken. Many theories and arguments about each kind of interpreting resemble each other, and what is accepted in one domain can influence how the other is regarded; nevertheless, crucial differences render implausible any simple correlation.[4]

Key variations between statutes and constitutions concern (1) subject matters, (2) open-endedness of concepts, (3) the need for assessing competing interests, (4) difficulties of revision, (5) symbolic significance, (6) the primary addressees, and (7) different allocations of interpretive responsibilities. Each of these, briefly explained here, figures importantly in this book.[5]

A. Subject Matter

Constitutions have limited subject matters. Modern statutes cover the whole range of government involvements with citizens (including, in most of the United States, the entire scope of the criminal law),[6] and the common law deals with a wide variety of interactions between citizens. The typical constitution addresses two basic subjects: the structures of government and the core rights of citizens. At the time the Bill of Rights of the federal Constitution was drafted, these rights were conceived almost entirely as negative and as restrictions on government intrusions on the lives of its citizens.[7] In modern times, equality in crucial respects has become a central constitutional theme about how governments should treat people.[8] Modern constitutions may also require that governments guarantee certain minimal benefits to their citizens and assure that private businesses and persons do not engage in forms of discrimination,[9] but these matters are largely left to legislative decision in the United States.

The nature of the basic subject matters of constitutions affects desirable interpretive techniques. For many structures of government, a fundamental inquiry is whether courts are well placed to guarantee that other organs are observing their proper roles. A conceptual aspect of the inquiry is whether courts determining such questions fit well with premises of democratic government. A more practical concern for many particular issues is whether judges are well or ill equipped to undertake the balancing of interests concerning different branches of government that would be called for were an ideal standard of evaluation capable of being applied.

In the United States, as contrasted with most other countries, the inquiry about the judicial role has special dimensions because of what is commonly, if imprecisely, termed the separation of powers, and because of federalism. The separation of powers entails that the legislature cannot trespass on executive responsibilities and vice versa—issues that do not often arise in parliamentary, cabinet systems in which the executive is directly responsible to the legislature. Courts must face the difficult questions of how far they should assess claims of unwarranted intrusions or whether to leave it to the political branches to work out disputes about borders of authority.

The federal system confers on the central government, as well as each state, only limited authority. One *might* believe that the fact that Congress is composed of representatives of states provides a sufficient protection of state interests, and that courts need not worry much whether the federal government is overstepping its limitations. By contrast, some centralized constraint is definitely required against states trespassing on federal concerns and the powers of sister states. For this reason, it is hardly surprising that the original Constitution established federal law as supreme[10] and provided explicitly for federal judicial review of cases arising in states that involve claimed violations of that law.[11]

When we turn to individual rights, the considerations look different. A crucial reason why constitutions enumerate individual rights is the concern that the political sway of the moment or concentration on tactics to enforce the law may not adequately protect those individual rights. Executive officers may not be sufficiently attentive to rights if they believe that strategies, such as illegal searches, will help catch ordinary criminals or terrorists. And, when those asserting various basic rights are widely regarded as dangerous or detestable, judicial review may be needed to overturn legislative actions that fail to respect their rights.

B. Open-ended Provisions

Constitutions contain a combination of highly specific and open-ended concepts. The rules dictating that the U.S. Senate include two members from each state[12] and that a person must be at least thirty-five years old to be President[13] contrast with the Eighth Amendment's bar on "cruel and unusual punishment" and the First Amendment's ban on Congress "prohibiting the free exercise" of religion, or "abridging the freedom of speech, or of the press." The degree and kind of discretion constitutional provisions that are apparently open-ended should be taken to confer on courts are central concerns of constitutional interpretation.[14]

Those questions resemble ones raised about statutes cast in highly general terms. When legislators adopt statutory language that is not precise, interpreters can construe it in various ways. The open-ended language of the Sherman Antitrust Act, for example, has been taken as conferring on courts an interpretive authority similar to what they possess in the common law—allowing more flexible judicial responses than would be appropriate for most statutes.[15] Though not usually conferring quite as much latitude on its interpreters as the Sherman Act, much modern legislation does create wide-ranging authority for administrative agencies to interpret and implement general statutory directions.

C. The Need for Assessing and Balancing Competing Interests

Many common law doctrines and statutory formulations call for some weighing of the interests involved. What would otherwise be a prohibited degree of pollution might not be considered as such if the cost of stopping it would be excessive.[16] What counts as "negligence" in the common law of torts depends on what may be gained by taking the risk that is involved. Speeding that would be negligent if you were heading to a party would not be if you were carrying a severely injured person to a hospital. The formulations of "cruel" punishment and "unreasonable search and seizure" appear on the surface to call for similar assessments. The propriety of such an approach is less obvious with "abridging the freedom of speech," but everyone agrees that while publishing true factual information is nearly always protected, one cannot reveal the exact, otherwise secret, movement of United States troops in the middle of a war.

A weighing or balancing of values can take two different forms. One is that what would otherwise be a practical exercise of a right can be overcome in particular instances by strong competing considerations. That typically involves a kind of explicit balancing, whether or not a strong presumption is made in favor of the claim of right or the government practice. The other approach is to assess, perhaps implicitly, the range of contrary interests in defining the basic right, which, once determined, cannot be trumped.

Many modern constitutions, including Germany's and Canada's, include explicit standards for balancing.[17] How far American courts in constitutional cases should undertake such assessments is a central issue. Even if balancing strikes one as an intrinsically sensible approach, one may doubt how far courts can do that accurately and persuasively in individual cases. If Supreme Court Justices doubt the wisdom of undertaking such a balancing, they may defer to what a political branch of government has decided or develop fairly specific standards that restrict what government officials may do.

When individual rights are at issue, the usual supposition is that acceding to balancing will entail a reduction of the content of these rights. That indeed was the assumption in *District of Columbia v. Heller*, in which the majority declared a personal right to possess handguns in one's home,[18] rejecting Justice Breyer's dissenting argument for balancing.[19] But on occasion, the Supreme Court's regarding of balancing as intrinsically inappropriate or too difficult can actually narrow rights. A notable example involved the "free exercise of religion" in the 1990 case of *Employment Division v. Smith*.[20] Faced with previous decisions ruling that interferences with exercises of religion are unconstitutional unless the government has a compelling interest that cannot be achieved by less restrictive means, Justice Scalia, for the Court, relied partly on the impossibility of this balancing endeavor to conclude that the constitutional protection simply did not reach forms of religious exercise that were at odds with prohibitions not themselves aimed at religion. Thus, the Court held that the members of a Native American church enjoyed no constitutional protection to ingest peyote as the central aspect of their worship service, a practice that a fair balance of values would have protected.

D. Difficulties of Revision

Whereas statutes and the common law can be changed by the ordinary legislative process, constitutions may be difficult or easy to amend, depending both on the formal processes of revision and on political realities. The United States Constitution is very hard to alter. Doing so involves a complex process and typically requires heavy support within

Congress and three-fourths of the states. One powerful argument for less than rigid interpretation of key parts of the Federal Constitution is that with drastic changes in technology, social organization, and social norms, such flexibility is needed to keep the Constitution up to date—indeed, in some respects at least, to keep it workable.[21] A simple counter to this argument is that the amendment processes are specified; if things get bad enough, they can be used for reform. Another concern has to do with courts, and especially the Supreme Court. No single body can override what the Supreme Court has resolved about the Constitution. If Justices believe they have the authority to interpret the document in a flexible manner, this confers huge authority on a majority of the Court—five unelected officials, and this is an authority some regard as unacceptable in a modern liberal democracy, whatever the difficulties of formal amendment. And one might think that the rareness of amendments is actually tied to the Supreme Court's efforts to update constitutional content—that if the Court properly restrained itself to original understanding in some form, one consequence would be a reinvigoration of the amendment process, as citizens recognized the need to use that to accomplish necessary changes.[22] They might then either encourage Congress to employ the familiar standard process or pursue the alternative of using state legislatures to require Congress to call a convention to propose amendments.[23] Subsequent chapters suggest reasons to be skeptical about the likelihood of such a shift and what it might cover.

E. Symbolic Significance

Constitutions, especially those that have maintained themselves over time, may take on substantial symbolic significance, becoming part of what citizens rely on to identify the nature of their government and their society. Unless a person thinks the constitution is deeply flawed—as was the original document, which recognized slavery—she will regard this effect as overall healthy.[24]

The value of symbolic significance can be undercut by great length and specificity, by frequent changes in provisions, and by periodic replacements of one constitution by another. The U.S. federal Constitution now carries more symbolic significance than individual state constitutions not only because of its historic and patriotic association but also because federal power has become dominant, and most people see themselves primarily as national citizens. The length of state constitutions, the comparative ease of their amendment, and their replacements over time have also mattered. Some judicial flexibility may help to maintain the symbolism of the federal Constitution by making continuous amendment, or complete replacement, unnecessary. However, it is also true that too frequent judicial alterations, especially by a sharply divided Supreme Court, can reduce the power of constitutional symbolism by making observers feel that so much turns on the political preferences of particular judges.

Not surprisingly, many people take a divided view, accepting the symbolism in many domains, but attributing decisions they sharply oppose to misguided judicial arbitrariness.

F. Primary Addressees

Who count as the primary addressees of various legal norms? More precisely, who is meant to respond and in what respect? The common law and many statutes are largely designed to affect the behavior of ordinary people and businesses, letting them know what they should and should not do. Some statutes are mainly addressed to agencies, instructing them to set the standards private parties will observe. Still other statutes tell executive officials how they should behave, for example, what latitude they have to investigate whether terrorists are planning attacks. Although constitutions are created partly for public understanding, and citizens do, of course, claim constitutional rights, the provisions are directed mainly at public officials, telling them how to organize the government, carry out their responsibilities, and avoid infringing rights.

That the immediate subjects of most constitutional norms are legislative and executive officials does not by itself tell us who should be the main interpreters. Given that federal and most state courts cannot issue advisory opinions, legislators and executive officials must decide if what they are doing is constitutional before that question comes before judges. Legislators considering whether to set a penalty for a crime should determine whether it would be unacceptably "cruel and unusual"; and a police officer should not make a search he believes the Fourth Amendment bars as "unreasonable." Courts later review many of these judgments. Even when provisions are mainly designed to influence the actions of nonjudicial officials, courts can become the dominant interpreters by making final decisions about what the Constitution requires. The next section sketches the difference between these two aspects and its vital significance for constitutional interpretation.

G. Allocations of Responsibilities and Degrees of Deference

A crucial issue for constitutional interpretation is how much deference courts should give to the explicit or implicit interpretations of legislatures and executive officials. Within a federal system, an added complexity is that judges should grant less deference than they afford national officials when they consider whether officials in state governments have impaired the rights of citizens of other states. When the political officials whose actions are challenged are at the national level, one possible position is that the U.S. federal Constitution is directed mainly at Congress; therefore its interpretive judgments should predominate, and judges should override them only when constitutional violations are clear and extreme.[25] The opposite view is that interpretation is really the courts' business; that judges are both the ultimate and the most important interpreters. More persuasive than either of these simple approaches is a nuanced position that relies on variations among different constitutional provisions. For some, substantial deference to legislative, or executive, interpretations is warranted, either because the two political branches are largely to be trusted or because careful judicial review is impractical. Other provisions that courts are well suited to implement occupy a place in the Constitution precisely because the political branches need a genuine check. For these, deference is not called for. On such a basis, an observer may comfortably accept the prevailing judicial doctrines that Congress has much more latitude to exercise its authority to regulate interstate commerce than to impinge on expressions of opinion. The broad question of degrees of deference is central for judicial interpretation of all constitutions.

III. COMPETING STRATEGIES OF INTERPRETATION

How the U.S. Constitution should be interpreted is highly controversial in many respects. Individual Justices of the Supreme Court represent different outlooks, and prevailing views have shifted significantly over time. This book's primary aspiration is not to resolve debates about particular legal disputes of the moment, although some serve as fascinating examples, but to provide perspectives for understanding how and why approaches evolve and for assessing what approaches are sound. Any views about constitutional interpretation rest partly on judgments of political philosophy, given that much depends on conceptions of law, desirable political structures, and fundamental rights. Detaching one's stance about modern legal controversies from one's views about desirable interpretation is difficult, and most citizens, and even most lawyers, may assess the Supreme Court by whether particular results fit their own political predispositions; but the effort here is to avoid this as much as possible.

Engaging in such an effort does assume that one's endorsement of particular approaches to constitutional interpretation should not rest on whether, at a given point in time, with particular Supreme Court Justices sitting, those approaches will yield political results one favors. Frederick Schauer has raised the question whether it may not be sensible to use one's political convictions about socially desirable outcomes to guide whether one presently approves or disapproves forms of interpretation.[26] For a variety of reasons, which are discussed further in Chapter 5, this hardly seems promising. Were Supreme Court Justices to acknowledge in opinions that they reached important decisions on the basis of simple political preferences, they would compromise the Court's status. Were a scholar candidly to advocate that position, she would either need to accept a large degree of deception in judicial opinions or recommend a radical change in how opinions are written. Given these core difficulties, judges and scholars should both aim for approaches to interpretation that they think should survive short-term shifts in politics and membership on the Supreme Court.

The remainder of this chapter introduces various strategies of constitutional interpretation. The notion that these compete radically with one another fits the rhetoric of much debate about the legitimacy of what Supreme Court Justices do. But the realities of actual and sound practice are that Justices employ elements of different approaches in combination, in ways that may or may not be clear. As they relate to practical decisions, the serious normative and empirical questions one can ask about most competing strategies of interpretation are not "either-or" but "more or less."

The distinctions sketched here and examined in more depth in chapters to follow are: (1) original understanding versus evolving application; (2) text versus intent; (3) specific meaning of a provision versus broader principles; (4) avoidance and deference versus independent judgment; (5) great weight to precedents or new appraisals; (6) judges' reliance on community morality or their own political and moral judgments; and (7) development of open-ended standards or clear rules. Reserving for later chapters careful assessment of accounts of how judges should proceed in constitutional cases, the aims here are to clarify basic criteria judges may use and to offer preliminary evaluations. All of these criteria do have counterparts in statutory interpretation, but the striking variations between statutes and constitutions yield sharp differences in the wisdom of analogous strategies.

A. Original Understanding Versus Evolutionary Application

Whether they rely on the text or the intentions of the enactors, judges could determine the meaning of provisions and their applications on the basis of original understanding. The core notion, as with statutes, is that because certain people had authority to enact, *what* they enacted is determined by what they did, as this was understood at the time.[27] As with statutes, no one denies that original understanding is relevant, but arguments that it carries overarching importance are considerably weaker when the Constitution is involved.

Here are the reasons. Although as more documents become available and are carefully reviewed, and the ability to determine historical understandings about some particular issues increases, the changes in perceptions that occur over generations make it harder and harder as time passes for a modern individual to grasp just how those in a much earlier era perceived things. Further, social conditions and values change radically as centuries pass; thus, any assumption that the original understanding will apply sensibly and justly is much less warranted than with recent statutes. The difficulty of amendment makes enacting needed changes very hard when rulings that stick with original understanding ill fit modern society. Further, the symbolic character of the Constitution makes frequent amendments undesirable. With recent statutes, the legislators represent those to whom the statutes apply. The long-departed enactors of constitutional provisions do not directly represent modern citizens. And, for certain provisions, they did not fairly represent even the population of the time. When the original Constitution and the Bill of Rights were adopted, women were unable to vote, most blacks in the country were severely oppressed slaves, and often, only property holders and taxpayers had voting rights. When the key amendments were adopted in the 1860s after the Civil War, women were still unable to vote, and some male citizens remained unqualified to do so. A critic might respond that, despite these factors, which have been corrected by amendments, we have maintained what the original unrepresentative but wise officials did, so that should continue to control. However, most of the early Constitution has survived partly because of the difficulty of amendment, partly because abandoning it would be disruptive, *and* partly because the Supreme Court has departed from original understanding in many important ways. These realities strongly suggest that a degree of interpretive evolution over time is needed.[28] The serious questions arise over when that is desirable and what kinds of approaches contemporary Justices should take.

One possible way to reconcile the original understanding of enactors and readers with evolutionary interpretation is by a determination that the original sense of a provision, such as the bar on "unreasonable searches," was designedly open-ended to take account of changes in values and social conditions. Absent such reconciliation, modern judges may take the broad sense of such terms as central, even if those in 1791 saw the provision as mainly about specific applications.[29] So understood, such language authorizes courts to determine that novel practices fit within its terms, and that even practices once widely accepted, such as the death sentence for many crimes, may become unconstitutional.

A second form of reconciliation of somewhat evolving application with original understanding is broader. It claims that at that time, relatively flexible interpretive techniques were accepted, ones that might even allow later judges dealing with more specific language in provisions not to adhere to original views about particular practices or precise semantic content. I shall contend that original views about constitutional interpretation, even insofar as they are discernible, should not now be completely dispositive.

B. Text Versus Intent

What matters? Is it what the text of the document signifies to readers, or the intent of those who enacted it, or both? For statutes and constitutions, "textualist" Justices and scholars have emphasized reader understanding, but the distinction between that and enactor intent is much less sharp than it first appears.[30] This is even truer about the Constitution than in respect to statutes. The basic point, which no one now denies, is that people understand language in context. A crucial aspect of context is what those on the receiving end believe speakers or writers are trying to communicate. Thus, an informed reader of the Constitution would be aware of the historical context behind provisions and the problems that those with enacting authority aimed to address. The simplest and surest way to understand what people are communicating is what they tell you they are trying to do. Thus, even if one focuses overwhelmingly on how a reader understands a legal text, the communicated intentions of those who enacted the text will come in through the back door, *unless* a special reason excludes them. Of course, if communications to the public about intentions are lacking, as was initially true about the debates at the Philadelphia Convention that led to the proposed U.S. Constitution, readers will have to draw inferences based mainly on the text and its setting.

Are there plausible grounds to exclude reference to subjective intentions as a matter of principle?[31] One argument against using legislative history in statutory interpretation is that the structure of the Constitution precludes it. Unconvincing about statutes,[32] that particular argument is even less plausible in relation to the Constitution itself. Its drafters were assigned the authority to amend the Articles of Confederation. Given very serious concerns about how the country was functioning under the Articles, they decided something more radical was needed, so they exceeded their conferred authority, proposed abandoning the Articles, drafted a constitution, and specified a process of ratification. None of this itself would foreclose consideration of their subjective intentions. And documents like the Federalist Papers did indirectly convey to potential ratifiers in the states and to ordinary citizens ideas of what the Framers were trying to accomplish. Two stronger claims that actual intentions of the Framers are not crucial for the original Constitution rely on their treating their own deliberations as confidential[33] and on the nonuse of legislative history for statutory interpretation in England and in the newly independent states. One may infer from these facts a primary emphasis on text, as contrasted with subjective intent.

What should a focus on the Constitution's text entail? Because the Constitution is mainly directed at government officials, perhaps the relevant reader for most purposes should be a well-informed official rather than an ordinary citizen. Most structural provisions of the original Constitution are explicit, as are the words of typical statutes. But to understand much of the soon-to-follow Bill of Rights, one would need to be aware of the concerns about abuses in England and new states that gave rise to its protections. For guarantees of rights, the reading of nonofficials would be critical, but such readers could have a solid sense of what forms of search are "unreasonable" only by knowing what searches the enactors were likely to regard as unacceptable. This reality renders the line between reader understanding and probable enactors' intent so thin that it is nearly nonexistent.[34]

A central question about focusing on the text is what counts as the decisive time of understanding. For most statutes, one reason to rely on ordinary reader understanding is that, at least initially, it will reflect how people conceive the law that affects them. This reason carries somewhat less significance if the document is directed mainly at officials. More important, original reader understanding may represent a poor guide for how people *now* conceive a text. Perhaps present reader understanding should carry greater weight than what people happened to assume over two hundred years ago. Of course, if one focuses on modern readers, their understanding will commonly be influenced more by what the Supreme Court has decided than by what the text itself conveys. Despite objections to controversial rulings, a kind of acceptance often grows that the text effectively includes what has been authoritatively decided. Few now doubt that the Equal Protection Clause gives significant protections to women, although that was neither the original intent nor how readers would then have grasped the text.

When we turn to the significance of subjective intentions undergirding constitutional provisions, some special difficulties arise that are not typical for statutes. The most obvious is what significance to accord proposers in relation to ratifiers. Whether we are talking about members of the original Philadelphia Convention or members of Congress who have proposed amendments, how much should their intent count in relation to those who performed ratification within the states? These officials with different roles complicate concerns about possibly different intentions and undisclosed intentions. More particularly, the special status of the Philadelphia Convention might lead one to different conclusions than one would reach about Congresses that proposed amendments.[35]

A somewhat different issue is whether the priority of different levels of intentions and their relation to the text should develop over time. A standard view of intentions focuses on original understanding. If, as proposed in Chapter 3, the significance of original reader understanding should diminish as time passes, original *intentions* become a more important component of the original meaning that should count. And, if one aspect of a standard originalism that focuses on intentions is that the key is what most adopters (or key voters) perceived,[36] we have solid reasons, after a century or two, to give greater emphasis to what influential enactors with a deeper grasp of basic issues intended. (Chapter 3 explores this particular issue in respect to the views of Madison and Jefferson about the religion clauses.)

For the U.S. Constitution, we can completely disregard an approach to "intentions" loosely understood that is sometimes proposed for statutory interpretation. The idea that judges should ask what those with the ability to do so would now enact is vulnerable for statutes not only to the criticism that present legislators were not the actual enactors but also that discerning just what they would adopt is too hard.[37] Given the obstacles to achieving constitutional amendments, the multiple bodies involved, and the impossibility of pinning down what together they could do, the similar difficulty to guessing what potential amenders would do is overwhelming

Whether attending to reader understanding or enactor intent, one needs to remember that much more is involved than what they perceived as the coverage of a particular provision. For then, as now, three crucial questions are the relevance of a provision's overall purpose, the extent to which the objectives of the entire constitution should count, and what are the desirable interpretive strategies judges and other officials should employ.

C. Specific Meaning Versus Broader Principles

A critical question, whether one focuses on original text or intent or on what are now seen as acceptable practices, is the manner in which provisions are best understood when their coverage is at issue. Some provisions obviously convey, as intended, highly explicit standards. A thirty-three-year-old is not allowed to become President, however mature he or she, and others of the same age, might be. But some provisions in the Bill of Rights, as well as the Equal Protection Clause of the Fourteenth Amendment, *could* be regarded as general and open-ended, not only now but also when enacted, inviting changing applications over time. With respect to such provisions, it makes a big difference whether what is taken as crucial for the original text is its semantic meaning or its perceived applications.[38] If the terms of provision have a broad meaning and were regarded as open-ended when enacted, giving priority to original understanding can actually conform with evolutionary interpretation.[39]

A related point about specificity and generality concerns the relevance of the whole document. The specific provision on which a case turns matters greatly, but some theorists believe that with a constitution, perhaps even more than with statutes, the text of the whole document is important, and one provision should be interpreted in a way that fulfills the objectives of the whole.

D. Avoidance and Deference Versus Independent Judgment

Just how far courts should actually determine constitutional issues is not simple. Demands of standing and ripeness familiar to lawyers limit who can bring a constitutional claim and under what circumstances. But even when a plaintiff meets those ordinary requirements, the Supreme Court has declined to adjudicate certain kinds of issues. It is not always easy to discern whether the Court has ruled that the range of what other officials can do is simply unlimited, and therefore any act is constitutionally permissible, or the Court is genuinely declining to make a decision about constitutional acceptability.[40] But for some "political questions," the Court has clearly determined that it will not resolve whether a constitutional violation has taken place. About some matters, this approach is grounded in a textual assignment of responsibility to another branch, but for other subjects, what matters is the exceptional sensitivity or unmanageability of questions that judges would need to answer if they undertook to resolve the controversies involved.[41] Just how far this doctrine now extends is uncertain, and its proper range is debatable. A much more common concern arises when courts are going to make a final resolution: How much deference should judges afford the constitutional interpretations of other branches of the federal government? Although one might ask this question in general terms, it is better understood with respect to specific constitutional provisions.[42]

E. What Weight to Precedents?

As with other cases they decide in the United States and other common law countries, judges must assess how much weight to give constitutional precedents when they face substantial arguments for overruling or distinguishing what has been previously resolved. If one were an unstinting originalist about specific coverage, one might claim that precedents should carry no more weight than their persuasive power entails; but hardly anyone is this kind of unstinting originalist. Indeed, one might defend reliance on precedents partly by referring to their assumed authority in 1789. The practical question is whether precedents should carry somewhat less weight in constitutional cases than in other cases, given that no one is in a position to correct "mistakes" in the manner that legislatures can respond to perceived errors of statutory interpretation and can alter aspects of the common law that displease them.[43] The constitutional amendment process is too complicated and difficult to regard potential amenders as occupying anything like a comparable position.

Giving weight to precedents occupies a dual position with respect to evolutionary interpretations. On the one hand, once a precedent is in place, it supplants or reduces the significance of original understanding about the coverage of the text and represents a basic feature of evolutionary development. On the other hand, if courts become rigorously faithful to constitutional precedents, that can actually preclude otherwise healthy changes from the time the precedent is laid down. Any defense of an evolutionary approach to constitutional interpretation needs to explain how prior judicial precedents should be treated.

One must recognize in this context a sharp difference between the U.S. Supreme Court and lower federal courts, along with a similar difference between the highest courts of states and those below them. The prevailing assumption is that lower courts should always follow clear, recent precedents of the courts above them,[44] leaving to the higher courts the responsibility to follow or not follow what they have previously decided.

F. Reliance on Common Morality or One's Reflective Political and Moral Judgment?

Because constitutional cases, particularly those that reach the Supreme Court, raise deep political and moral issues much more often than do statutory and common law cases, the problem of how far judges should try to ascertain and rely on community sentiments, rather than implement their own reflective judgments about those issues, takes on special importance.[45] Of course, in discerning what the law explicitly provides and what it implies, judges must do their own assessments. But unless, like Ronald Dworkin, one takes a very broad view of what "the law provides" (one that for him actually includes independent moral judgments),[46] some crucial constitutional cases cannot be settled by reference to existing law. The argument that judges should not then undertake to rely overwhelmingly on community morality about specific practices is especially strong for guarantees that are designed to be a check on legislators and executive officials, who may well be responding to majoritarian points of view antagonistic to unpopular minorities. For judges, unlike individuals deciding what is morally right in their own lives, one crucial criterion is whether they believe that conclusions they reach will have persuasive power for other judges who are resolving similar legal disputes.

G. Open-ended Standards or Precise Rules?

Even if one sees some standards in the constitution as substantially open-ended, part of the task for interpreting courts may be to set precise rules that executive officials and other judges can follow. Although, as with the concept of "negligence" in common law, some operating constitutional standards can be open-ended, and allow a sensitive evaluation of particular circumstances in individual cases, judges may often conclude that more specific guidance is badly needed. An example of this approach is the "Miranda warning" in criminal investigations.[47] Since those approving the Fifth Amendment and original readers did not even have police interrogation in mind, and the text of the privilege against self-incrimination—that no one "shall be compelled in any criminal case to be a witness against himself"[48]—hardly sets out explicit restraints on police inquiries, the *Miranda* decision involves an undeniably flexible interpretation of that provision. But the rule the Court announces is highly precise, telling police and courts what the police must do and when. In the decades that have followed *Miranda*, the strictness of the rule's application during criminal trials has been relaxed to a degree, but the point here is that Justices may think both that a constitutional provision itself should be treated as somewhat open-ended and that the Court should lay down a very specific rule or rules.[49]

In the following chapter, we shall first explore a kind of parable involving private instructions. Its point is to suggest just how common it is in life to employ multiple criteria for discerning the "meaning" of instructions and the practical duties they impose. The second half of the chapter turns from private instructions to constitutional norms. It both notes very significant differences between these two kinds of guides and also suggests why multiple criteria are needed for interpreting constitutional provisions as well as ordinary instructions.

Chapter 2

Multiple Interpretive Criteria

I. INTRODUCTION

The thesis this chapter defends is simple, straightforward, and unstartling. It is, nonetheless, worth developing because much in judicial opinions and scholarly writing seems implicitly opposed to it.

The thesis is that a satisfactory account of how judges should resolve constitutional cases must be irreducibly pluralist. Over a range of cases, judges need to take into account a variety of factors in reaching decisions. For certain "easy" decisions, one interpretive standard may be sufficient, but across a range of cases, no formula can order these factors in a neat hierarchy, and no practically useful formula can assign the appropriate weight for each factor. Judges must, in difficult cases, consider the import of the language of particular constitutional provisions and the whole constitutional structure, various levels of intent and possible variations in intent among those who proposed and ratified provisions, the course of relevant judicial decisions, and how governing principles apply to the social facts of modern times. Not infrequently for the hardest cases, judges cannot avoid considering modern views about what is right and desirable and what is, they believe, actually right and desirable on the merits. For "hard" cases—"hard" exactly because one straightforward criterion will not resolve them—more than one of these standards almost inevitably comes into play. A more detailed exploration of interpretive criteria awaits later chapters; this chapter explains why each matters.

Abstraction and simplification are the essence of much theorizing. At their best, theories help us get a handle on otherwise indigestible reality. At their worst, theories obscure the complexity of that reality, comfortably disregarding what is inconvenient in the interests of conceptual purity or social objectives. Although legal theory is rooted in the richness of actual cases, the tendency of theorists to strive for soothing simplicity nonetheless infects it, especially as theorists reach higher levels of abstraction. Much writing about constitutional interpretation reflects this tendency, either by placing heavy emphasis on a particular standard for judges to employ or by emphasizing one or two criteria of decision in a manner that downgrades or disregards other relevant standards. This chapter seeks to show both that we cannot capture a judge's responsibilities by any single formulation and that elements of balance should serve as a counter to overwhelming emphasis on one or two interpretive criteria.

Before proceeding to the more rarefied atmosphere of constitutional theory, I begin with a relatively mundane choice that an individual given imaginary instructions must make. The illustration shows how various factors can play a role in many of life's decisions that involve faithfulness to a previously developed standard. Core problems are just how a recipient faced with a practical decision should understand a guiding standard, what he should do if the standard's implications are unclear, and whether he should ever override its clear implications. Central aims of the illustration are to show that multiple factors can be present even with relatively simple standards of direction and that, given the strength that various kinds of reasons carry in different contexts, no rigorous ordering of criteria will suffice for the difficult choices. The degree of detail about various factors in the example is somewhat cumbersome, but I believe that it is needed to show that choices in life are often not simple.

Because law differs in crucial ways from nonlegal directions and ordinary moral criteria, and because any "intent" underlying constitutional provisions involves scores of persons, an example of personal choice by itself proves nothing directly about constitutional interpretation, which must be responsive to a number of special considerations.[1] Nevertheless, I urge readers to suspend doubts about the parable's relevance until the chapter's second half, which connects its claims about multiple factors and the absence of a single hierarchy to how judges render constitutional determinations. Nothing in this chapter is meant to deny that numerous issues about constitutional interpretation are more complex than those posed by this example.

II. A PARABLE ABOUT INTENT, MANIFESTATION, COMMITMENT, AND DECISION

Faith, a widow unjustly convicted of a serious crime and soon to be transported to a remote penal colony for a twenty-year term, during which she will have virtually no ability to communicate with those back home, is legally permitted to designate a guardian for her five-year-old son, Samuel. Recognizing that she must otherwise relinquish legal control over his upbringing while she is away, Faith seeks a guardian who is sympathetic with her convictions about raising Samuel and will commit to fulfilling her aims. She chooses David, her brother, who responds that he will undertake the guardianship and carry out her expressed wishes if those do not contradict his values. Faith gets a friend to write up the terms, which are as follows:

> Samuel will live with David and his family or with another close relative, until he is eighteen. The little money left for Samuel by Faith will be used so that Samuel can become a skilled craftsman, such as a carpenter or tailor, or a clerk. David will decide which of these careers Samuel will follow on the basis of Samuel's aptitude, interest, and financial prospects. David will appoint as a successor guardian, if that is necessary, someone also willing to carry out these directions.

Understanding that they do not bind him legally, David agrees to comply with these terms, and Faith appoints him guardian. The fact that David is not legally constrained by the instructions means that he need not worry that a failure to fulfill their terms will lead a higher authority to cancel what would otherwise be a sound decision and to rebuke him for infidelity.

As Samuel develops, he shows a remarkable aptitude for reading and writing; he completely lacks manual dexterity. When Samuel turns twelve, David places him as an apprentice to a senior clerk within a legal firm. After three years, a few partners who become aware of Samuel's high intelligence, linguistic skills, and analytical powers advise David that Samuel should train to be a lawyer. Though this will cost David some additional money in the near future, the members of the firm are willing to help out; a legal career would greatly enhance Samuel's financial prospects over the long term. David must decide whether to allow and encourage Samuel to become a lawyer, recognizing that at some future day of reckoning he probably will need to justify his decision to Faith.

What follows is a thought experiment of how David might decide under a variety of assumptions. David must resolve how to understand the instructions in context, including what weight to give to broad purposes that may or may not be part of a shared understanding. He may have to decide what to do if the import of the instructions is uncertain and whether and when it could possibly be right to go against their sense.

A. What Does the Agreement Indicate?

Faith's instructions, taken literally, specify three particular careers, clerk, carpenter, and tailor, and a general category, skilled craftsmen. None of these include lawyers. But instructions need to be understood in the context in which they are given. As David knows, Faith, her immediate forebears, and her husband were all unskilled laborers and agricultural workers. Her instructions definitely reflect a wish that Samuel enjoy a career she perceives as better than those most familiar to her. The omission of any professions might reflect her failing to regard those as realistic options.

In reviewing how David should understand the instructions and decide how to act, we can imagine a variety of subtly different circumstances: (1) David and Faith might have shared an understanding not specified in the terms, but communicated when they reached their agreement, (2) Faith might have correctly assumed that David grasped her underlying purpose, though she did not communicate it at the time, (3) David might have perceived an underlying purpose, understanding that Faith was unaware of that, (4) David might have explicitly undertaken to fulfill Faith's broad purpose or, alternatively, only to carry out the agreement's terms, or (5) David might have learned of Faith's broader objectives only after committing himself to comply with her terms.

In deciding what to do, David begins with a sense of what the agreement's language actually meant to Faith and to himself at the time. If they both understood the same thing *and* that was communicated, either directly by the terms themselves or by accompanying conversation, that is how he must take the language. If Faith had then said, "I want my boy to do as well as he can," David could understand the agreement not to bar a legal career and even to implicitly favor it. On the other hand, if Faith, believing that lawyers are corrupt, had meant to exclude that career, David's permitting it for Samuel would depart from the agreement's terms. If neither Faith nor David communicated anything relevant on the subject, the terms of the agreement would provide David little help. He would need then to ask whether Faith's wishes expressed on other occasions were relevant or even determinate.

Suppose David realizes that Faith both has long held a strong anti-professional bias and knew that David was well aware of this. In that event, her failure to explicitly communicate that at the time of the agreement hardly seems relevant:[2] the agreement literally does not include a legal career, Faith intended that exclusion, and David understood this. If David realized that Faith had strong career ambitions for Samuel that she did not communicate when they agreed, he *might* conclude that the failure of the agreement's terms to include a legal career leaves him free to exercise his own judgment about that, but if she had previously told him that her primary aspiration was that Samuel do as well as possible vocationally, that may well be sufficient to be Samuel's guide.

The relevance of Faith's generalized purpose, known to David but neither contained in the agreement nor communicated at the time, raises a fairly subtle point about how "meaning" relates to "responsibility." A conceptual question is the meaning or understanding of the agreement; practically, David must ask how far he is bound by Faith's wishes. If David regards the language as essentially a vehicle for conveying her wish that Samuel achieve the best possible career, the way the literal language happens to point is comparatively insignificant.[3] If David takes his responsibility as carrying out Faith's wishes, he will construe doubtful language in accord with those wishes, thus taking the agreement itself as favoring a legal career. By contrast, were David bound to do only what he agreed to do under the instruction's terms, he would not take the agreement itself as embodying any underlying purpose that favors lawyering.

Thus, David's "interpretation" of the agreement will be largely grounded in what he believes he is bound to do. This connection is one illustration of why attempts to draw clear lines between "interpretation" and "application" and "construction" are problematic.

Both David's sense of responsibility and his interpretation could well have been affected by interchanges with Faith about what he was undertaking. If he had said he would be constrained only by the agreement's terms,[4] that would be quite different from his promising to do all that he could to carry out her wishes.[5]

What if David happened to be aware of Faith's overarching purpose, but he knew that Faith was not conscious of this awareness. Now it becomes more difficult to say that her wish is part of the agreement itself. But if David had actually undertaken to carry out Faith's wishes, these would still constrain him. That conclusion would not follow if David became aware of Faith's unexpressed purpose to favor the best career only after the agreement between them; if he would not have signed on to any instructions that included a possible career as a lawyer, he need not feel constrained by a contrary purpose he reasonably did not then perceive. This would be especially true if he undertook only to perform what was fairly communicated and then understood.[6]

These conclusions about David's responsibilities, some clear and some arguable, are not easily translatable to law. Moral obligations to perform agreements vary from legal obligations. The law needs conventions for resolving the force of authoritative instructions and undertakings to perform them. Since morality is without the formal sanctions of legal contracts, the meaning (from a moral point of view) and the moral force of any agreement are much more subtly modulated to the full relationships and precise understandings of the people involved. An agreement's "meaning" is closely related to the moral rights and obligations of those who are bound to comply. If mutually understood purposes fit an instruction's language, that points strongly toward making the indicated choice. By contrast, when the aims of the person giving an instruction differ from what its terms suggest, how the recipient should perform depends on the precise nature of the responsibilities he has undertaken.

B. Conditions of Uncertainty About What the Instructions Import

We have seen that how far David should adhere to the instructions' literal terms or carry out their underlying purpose depends significantly on communications and understandings at the time of their agreement, and that these factors also affect David's sense of what the instructions "mean." Two further practical questions are whether David could ever justify a decision contrary to how the instructions point strongly and how he should base his choice if the instructions do not point decisively in either direction. I begin with the second question, because its answer clarifies what might persuade someone to depart from an instruction's clear implications.

Suppose that when a partner asks him about Samuel's becoming a lawyer, David reflects that Faith was ambitious for her son, but distrusted and disliked professionals, and that she never addressed how she would feel about Samuel's being a lawyer. Although David understands that generalized intentions can definitely cover *some* unperceived applications,[7] he strongly believes that Faith would have needed further thought to resolve the question of a legal career, and he is unsure what she would then have concluded.

How is he to decide whether to encourage Samuel to become a lawyer? Should he focus on what he thinks is best, rely on the views of others concerned about Samuel's future, rely on something Faith may have indicated after the agreement, or try to delve further into Faith's wishes or the implications of her instructions when she gave them?

If the agreement and Faith's wishes are wholly unilluminating, David must turn elsewhere. His own strong view about what will help Samuel would count greatly, especially given his general duty as a guardian to promote his ward's welfare.[8] What about the views of other relatives? If they continue to have close relations with Samuel, their reactions could affect his life's quality. Thus, what actually *is best* for him could depend partly on their perceptions. And, if David has his own doubts about what is best, discussions with relatives might help him better understand Samuel or the values of legal practice. Even if not directly convinced by the reasons offered by other relatives, their sheer numbers and recognized wisdom might persuade him that they are probably right.[9] Whether David should give the relatives' views independent weight, apart from how far they persuade him, could depend on whether Faith conveyed a wish that the set of close relatives should bear responsibility for Samuel's upbringing, though legal formalities required a single guardian.[10]

Suppose by odd chance that Faith was somehow presently told that David needed to decide if Samuel should pursue a legal career, and she was able to communicate her wish to the contrary. If David saw his guardianship as a regrettable substitute for Faith's own decisions and did not write off her views as based on failures of information, he might well take her present wish as dispositive. But he might instead decide that Faith could not grasp enough about Samuel's recent life to make a conclusive judgment. He might also be moved by a notion that since he is investing time, energy, and expense in Samuel's upbringing, he has a legitimate basis to follow his own judgment, especially if he had told Faith that he meant to do that except when honoring her instructions.

Assuming Faith is now unable to express an opinion, David might try to delve further into the implications of the original instructions or Faith's wishes at that time, piecing together every scrap of relevant knowledge he can find.[11] However, if his commitment was solely to carry out the agreement's plain terms, that inquiry would have little point, and David would need to reach beyond the instructions.

Even if attempting a deeper investigation of Faith's instructions and wishes at the time, David might also consider independent sources, especially if his inquiry about Faith's intentions failed to provide a decisive resolution.[12] David would face a dilemma if he concluded that the instructions and their purposes pointed very slightly against Samuel's becoming a lawyer, but he and the other relatives were firmly convinced that that career would be best. Should he follow what he is convinced is a less desirable course, based on a highly uncertain judgment about the instructions' implications? Most people would believe not.[13] How might David later justify to Faith his allowing Samuel to become a lawyer? We can imagine the following conversation.

DAVID: Well, I allowed Samuel to become a lawyer because I didn't think our agreement resolved that question one way or the other, and I believed, for reasons *a*, *b*, *c*,. . . .etc., that that career would be best.

FAITH: But you said you would carry out my wishes. Even if the agreement didn't focus specifically on a legal career, why didn't you let my general wishes guide you?

DAVID: I really wasn't sure what your wishes were.

FAITH: You didn't have an idea?

DAVID: Not any idea clear enough to guide me.

In such a conversation, David would probably not acknowledge that his reflection on Faith's wishes themselves inclined him ever so slightly against a legal career,[14] but *were* David to admit this directly to Faith, he could rationalize his decision: "It just seemed mistaken to rely on such an uncertain signal when I was strongly convinced that the contrary course would be better."

We can conclude that other criteria, including his own and the relatives' views about what is best, will influence David if he finds that the instructions, with their purposes, fail totally to direct him or may point very weakly in a contrary direction.

C. The Use of Other Criteria When These Definitely Conflict with the Implications of the Instructions

Must David follow Faith's instructions if they provide a relatively clear signal for or against a legal career for Samuel? Let us assume that the instructions themselves and Faith's contemporaneous communications do not patently foreclose a legal career, but David's reconstruction makes him nearly certain that is what Faith actually wished. Even if David acknowledged to Faith that his basic responsibility was to be true to her wishes, one of four kinds of justifications might still lead him to have Samuel pursue becoming a lawyer.

The first, accepting a direct conflict, is straightforward. Conceding that his responsibility to fulfill Faith's instructions would preclude Samuel's becoming a lawyer, David could regard that decision as so unfortunate he should act otherwise. He might later say to Faith: "Yes, I know I promised to carry out your wishes, but when it came down to it, I just felt it would be desperately wrong to ruin Samuel's life. I'm sorry I broke my promise, but that seemed best."

A second, more complex approach would be to interpret Faith's wishes in a highly general way that rendered David's decision consistent with the instructions' most important component.

> "Faith wanted Samuel to have a secure, respectable career, without becoming greedy and unspiritual. A legal career is highly preferable on the first two counts to those she included. Her ideas about the nature of lawyers reflected misperceptions and overgeneralization. Given what I now know about the members of this firm and about Samuel's character, I am confident that had Faith been aware of those facts at the time of her instructions, she would have been pleased by the prospect of Samuel's becoming a lawyer. I am giving effect to her most fundamental preferences in light of all factual knowledge I now possess."

A third approach would rely on Faith's generalized wishes despite a perception that she would not now reach his conclusion. David reasons:

> "Even had I put all the present facts in front of her, Faith would still not have wanted Samuel to become a lawyer because she would have been incapable of understanding all the facts, and she has had an extremely stubborn prejudice against professionals. Nevertheless, her really basic concerns were for Samuel's happiness and spiritual welfare, and I see that these will be best served by his becoming a lawyer."

Whether such a disregarding of Faith's specific wishes and the actual terms of her instructions in favor of her general purposes could be cast as "faithful" to the agreement depends greatly on communications at the time. If Faith had accepted that David would rely heavily on broad purposes, he might well claim faithfulness; but that would not be possible if, instead, he had agreed to follow the instructions' actual terms.[15] Understandings about the basic quality of an instruction can affect whether decisions in tension with its specified outcomes can count as "fair interpretation" and implementation or clearly represent disregard.

A fourth approach comes yet closer to David's acknowledging that his choice directly conflicts with the instructions. He might claim a kind of implied exception for decisions that he deems to be gravely wrong, remarking to Faith upon her return:

> "Despite what else we said, I am sure neither of us really imagined that I should do something I thought would be hugely detrimental to Samuel's welfare."

The possible consistency of such a loophole with the instructions themselves would, again, depend significantly on communications at the time.

We can see that other criteria of decision *might* lead David to act contrary to the specific implications of the instructions. However, the greater his responsibility is to carry out Faith's wishes, embodied in the agreement, the more powerful the countervailing considerations would need to be in order to outweigh those.[16]

The force of Faith's communicated original wishes could be drastically affected if David could now contact her. If her present judgment *coincided* with his, that would end any obligation to keep to her original terms.[17]

Yet another factor that *could* cut against following the instructions is prior contrary decisions. Suppose, for example, that David allows Samuel to begin preparing for a legal career but then becomes convinced he has made a mistake about the force of the instructions. Assuming Samuel has embraced the pattern of life set by David's initial decision, David would require much stronger reasons to reverse the effect of that decision than he would have needed for an initial decision against the legal career. A similar logic would apply if a successor guardian reached the conclusion that David's initial decision had been mistaken. He would not suppose he could start from scratch and make every decision based solely on his own sense of the instructions.

D. Faith's Death

I want finally to consider one other variation. Suppose David is aware that Faith has died shortly after giving her instructions. Does the agreement still have force? So long as Faith is living, we conceive of her as having a legitimate and strong interest in what happens to Samuel.[18] Those who believe that one's spirit survives may suppose that death does not end one's stake in what happens among those remaining alive.[19] Whatever the rational power of this view,[20] on a deep psychological level, people find it hard to accept that the concerns of those they have loved or cared for are simply annihilated by death. Thus, the idea that promises to persons who have died continue to have force is partly grounded on a deeply felt sense that death does not end their stake in what happens. A subtler basis for this practice is that people who are presently alive now care a good deal what *is* to happen after they die. Any security they enjoy from believing they retain some control would evaporate if no one considered instructions from people who have since died as carrying any force.[21] Whatever the reasons, I assume David will consider the agreement as highly important even if Faith has died, though perhaps a bit less so than if she remains alive.

An interesting wrinkle on this variation concerns a possible successor to David. If David relinquishes his position with a firm insistence that the terms of the agreement be carried out, his successor will have an obligation to both David and Faith that continues David's responsibilities to Faith. But imagine that David has been a less faithful guardian and says to his successor, "Look, I promised Faith that I would carry out her instructions and would obligate my successor to do so, but frankly, I am disenchanted with them, and I don't really care whether you observe them." If Faith is still alive, the successor should conclude that his responsibility to carry out her instructions remains even if David has disregarded them. But if Faith has already died, the successor might consider himself freed of that burden. If this makes sense, an agreement to fulfill the instructions of someone who has since died may have more force for the person who agreed than for his successors.

In summary, we see that especially when instructions are less than clear, straightforward, and obviously pertinent to the choice to be made, both the responsibilities of actors and the senses of meaning of the agreements raise complex, related questions; and the choices that people subject to instructions must make often rest on a range of criteria, ones whose force varies and thus are not susceptible to simple hierarchy.

III. CONSTITUTIONAL INTERPRETATION

The task of judges interpreting a written constitution bears *some* resemblance to David's decision about Samuel's future. Setting out specific norms and reflecting more general purposes, a constitution often requires a kind of interpretation to discern its import. Judges and other officials who are determining how to fulfill their responsibilities according to the document must decide what factors count, including what weight, if any, to give to those removed from the document's straightforward instructions. Despite striking differences that stand in the way of drawing simple inferences from David's task to that of judges in constitutional cases—many of which *do affect the appropriate significance* of particular factors—judges applying the constitution fairly give weight to factors analogous to those influencing David, and these are no more reducible to a simplistic formula than they were for private instructions.

Although it is sometimes argued that judges who employ what scholars defend as a multifactor eclectic approach to constitutional interpretation need a "metaprinciple that mediates among conflicts,"[22] and a form of hierarchy has been proposed by Richard Fallon,[23] no rigorous hierarchy has been used by the Supreme Court, and none is really feasible.[24] Of course, judicial opinions, with their aim to persuade, are an unreliable guide to how strongly different factors actually have counted in a decision. Nonetheless, it is evident that a variety of considerations are given decisive force in different contexts.[25] Further, the status of compromises in resolutions and majority opinions precludes rigorous consistency for Supreme Court Justices who have competing views about interpretive techniques and what they entail in particular instances. But my claim here is even stronger; namely, that a single wise Justice, focusing only on what should count and not on how to persuade others, could still not come with any straightforward hierarchy because of the different force that similar factors carry in different contexts. One theme of this book is that not only judges but also critics do well to concentrate on particular provisions and issues, rather than accepting a grand scheme in which all fit together in some neat way.

To be a bit more precise, my claim here is not that how various factors should count in context necessarily lacks an objectively correct answer, or that no individual could consistently discover that, a matter I take up in Chapter 5; what I assert is that no verbal formulation could capture and convey the best approach. This difference can be illustrated by an example of what was once very important in my life; should one take a shot in a basketball game? In any particular context, these factors could be relevant: one's closeness to the basket, one's present or possible escape from defensive players, what teammates are then playing and whether they are in a good position to shoot, one's shooting ability on that particular day and one's confidence at that moment, the time remaining for a shot, the overall score, and the time remaining in the game. Even if a player could somehow be perfectly consistent and well guided in deciding when to shoot rather than to pass, no linguistic articulation could capture exactly how much each factor should count and when. Of course, one who is unguarded and next to the basket should shoot, and one at half court should not. But what natural language cannot do is provide a formula that reaches the most difficult choices with a precise answer. The impossibility of providing a clear linguistic formula often applies to the interpretation and application of constitutional provisions when judges are faced with their most difficult, debatable choices.

In what follows, the chapter first highlights differences between law established by authorities and morality. It then explores complexities involved in the notion of original understanding and contends that judges do and sometimes must rely on other criteria.

A. Differences Between Legal and Moral Constraints

In contrast to Faith's instructions to David, ordinary contracts and statutes create legal restrictions that require people to act in certain ways or risk adverse consequences. Judges themselves have a legal duty to adhere to the clear sense of legal documents, including most constitutions, even though no actual penalty typically falls on them if they fail to do so.[26] The line between legal duties and moral or political responsibilities is less clear when one talks about Supreme Court interpretations in the most difficult constitutional cases.[27] Theorists disagree about the precise domain of "legal" duty. Some see it as encompassing every aspect of interpretation of legal documents;[28] others conceive it as limited to matters that are already authoritatively settled in some way,[29] or as covering a portion, but not all, of yet unsettled issues. The jurisprudential debate about the exact scope of legal duty can carry rhetorical significance but does not itself answer the question of how judges should perform. Because this book's concern is what judges take into account and how they do and should decide, it makes no attempt to draw a precise line about which of the approaches it endorses are *required* by legal duty, but it does assume that none of them *violate* legal duty.

As with statutes and the common law, the responsibilities of a lower court interpreting the Constitution differ from those of a jurisdiction's highest court, even when a case is unlikely to be reviewed. The Supreme Court has announced that when it has determined a particular constitutional issue, other courts are supposed to follow its rule,[30] even if they regard it as mistaken and likely to be overruled. When lower courts face novel issues, they should probably afford Supreme Court precedents on related subjects more weight than the Supreme Court itself needs to give them.[31] The focus here is on how the federal Supreme Court, and highest state courts construing their state constitutions, should approach issues.

Legal interpretation distinguishes itself from many understandings of moral responsibilities by the law's need for concrete recognizable standards. Just how far such standards should dominate moral decisions is itself contested. Some people believe our reason, or instructions that come from God, tell us that we should never violate definite standards, for example, by lying, or committing one wrongful act to prevent a deeper wrong, or using artificial contraceptives. Competing views assign much more significance to particular circumstances and reject many claims that broad categories of action[32] are always intrinsically wrong.[33] One intermediate approach sees the ultimate standard of the morality of acts as contextual (e.g., does it promote the happiness of the greatest number?), but asserts that people commonly require more definite criteria to guide them.[34] For virtually all people, many moral choices do rest on a range of relevant factors that must be evaluated in context. A couple's choice of where to live needs to take into account the job each person will have, their income and expenses, the physical and social environments, the quality of the schools for their children, the psychological costs of dislocation from one home to another, and so on. No formula tells the couple exactly how much to weigh each factor.[35]

Whatever one concludes about the right grounds for moral decisions, individuals are the ones who must make them, and they do so on a number of bases. Although striking variations in moral approaches can produce social tensions, people in a liberal democracy accept that they will not agree with others about all their moral responsibilities and choices. Within the law's domains, greater consistency and coherence is needed. Although "official" enforcement is not always consistent, citizens and officials require clarity about what is legally allowed and what is not. Given their institutional setting, judges are limited in how they can acquire information; they are expected to decide on principled bases and to justify their important resolutions with reasoned explanations, which are partly designed to give guidance for future cases.[36] These special characteristics of courts affect what judges appropriately take into account and the weight they should give to a range of criteria.

B. Mutual Agreement or Subsequent Adherence

A radical difference between David's interpretation of Faith's instructions and modern constitutional interpretation involves the relation between those who formulate the authoritative document and those who interpret it. As with the agreement of two equal parties to a contract,[37] Faith and David had similar ability to determine the instructions' terms and to communicate what they entailed. With the possible exception of a present judge who earlier helped adopt a constitutional amendment, modern judges, by contrast, construe and apply terms that they had no involvement in formulating or approving. By swearing an oath to support and defend the constitution, those judges made a kind of agreement. Their understanding of that agreement when they took office, especially if articulated, might matter when they later defend themselves against claims that they are acting improperly;[38] but the bare responsibility to be faithful to the Constitution does not tell judges how to form their understanding of that. For modern interpreters of the Constitution, that is a key question.

C. Should Original Understanding Be Determinative?

The idea that original understanding should be determinative often relies on the premise that the proposers and ratifiers, representing a political supermajority, enacted constitutional law; what they enacted is what should count.[39] The ensuing analysis asks whether original understanding in some form should dominate constitutional interpretation, leaving for later chapters basic issues about how far the original intent of enactors should count in relation to how readers took their chosen language and perceived applications, and how far their specific language should dominate underlying principles and purposes.

A crucial initial question is the place of an original sense of how interpretation itself should take place. Put simply, a genuine, strict originalist, whether relying on intent or reader understanding, should be guided by the interpretive strategy explicitly or implicitly proposed when an authoritative norm is adopted.[40] To revert to our previous example, suppose Faith's instructions to David included: "See that Samuel's food, exercise, and other activities protect his health. Determine what is healthy in terms of developing knowledge and effects of different activities, and any changing conceptions about what it means to be healthy." If David later needed to decide whether Samuel's intake of sugar should be reduced, or whether his acute fears were a form of mental illness, he would be decidedly unfaithful to Faith's basic instruction if he asked only "would Faith have then believed high sugar affected physical health, and would she have seen mental problems as a health concern?" What this illustration shows is that an unqualified faithfulness to original understanding would give priority to the forms of future interpretation and application the instructions contain, rather than conceived notions at the time of what they specifically covered. An "originalist" can reject this conclusion only if he asserts that we cannot discern original interpretive strategies or that nonoriginalist reasons support focus on a different aspect of original understanding.

A common qualification to complete reliance on original understanding, which can apply to forms of interpretation as well as the coverage of specific provisions, concerns what has developed over time. If an interpretive approach has become solidly entrenched, a Supreme Court Justice might be hesitant to abandon not only the results it has produced but also the shared modern sense of how interpretation should proceed.[41] She might, on the other hand, believe that her overriding duty is to interpret the Constitution "correctly," say, according to original understanding, no matter how disturbing that would be to the legal system. Despite the flavor of some rhetoric, no Supreme Court Justice has rigidly adhered to an originalist position in respect to interpretive techniques or specific results, rather giving some weight to legal principles that have evolved over time and under various interpretive methods.

That much of the existing substance of constitutional law is not conveniently attributable to an original understanding is uncontroversial. All Justices take at least some of the law as "embedded," to use Chief Justice Rehnquist's term about *Miranda*'s doctrine regarding police practices,[42] and the status of stare decisis as a guide to interpretation is broadly accepted as either a supplement to original understanding or an aspect of it.[43] As Alexander Bickel once said, "as time passes fewer and fewer relevantly decisive choices are to be divined out of the tradition of our founding."[44] Although Justice Brennan's claim that "the genius of the Constitution rests ... in the adaptability of its great principles to cope with current problems and current needs"[45] is now controversial, no Justice has yet advocated a total disregard of all precedents that have reflected Brennan's view or claimed to be basing his or her interpretive techniques precisely on those accepted when a provision came into force.

A possible different form of qualification about unflinching adherence to original understanding involves decisions that conflict with the result to which a "proper" standard of interpretation leads. I have suggested that David might have resolved that the benefits of a legal career for Samuel were so great that he should actually break his promise to Faith. What should a Justice do who finds herself in a similar position—perhaps national security seems to demand a constitutionally forbidden practice, or the political branches have interfered with individual rights not covered by the Constitution in a manner that seems incredibly outrageous?

Should a Justice never override the result to which she would be led by the best techniques of constitutional interpretation or instead recognize that such situations might arise, though rarely? Whether such a choice will be needed depends heavily on whether the techniques of interpretation accepted by the Justice incorporate flexibility to respond to what seems just and necessary.

Whatever grounds judges actually use to decide, their formal opinions, designed to justify and persuade, will not acknowledge that they are disregarding a proper sense of what the Constitution provides in order to serve other values. As with the application of statutes,[46] and unlike deviations from the terms of trusts or wills,[47] judges do not say they are deciding against genuine constitutional meaning.

The question of possible deviation from ordinary interpretive practices touches the theoretical inquiry of what exactly counts as "interpretation." To briefly summarize a distinction sometimes drawn, does "interpretation," rather than including every legitimate ground of judicial decision, only concern criteria of decision that yield answers to what the document itself provides, leaving "construction" to address vagueness and gaps within the document that must somehow be filled?[48] Given the different levels at which a constitution can be understood and the complex variety of its provisions and purposes, anyone will find it hard to say where interpretation leaves off and something else like construction begins.[49] Both because of the ambiguity or vagueness of the very term, and because delineating what exactly counts as interpretation in any precise sense is so difficult, this book employs the term broadly, not casting competing arguments about what judges should do as ones about what is *really* true interpretation.[50]

Putting aside both the force of interpretive practices that have evolved over time and the possibility that judges should, on rare occasions, act against what their basic interpretive standards would indicate, should judges accept the original sense of standards of interpretation, whether that is derived from the text, from what enactors or ratifiers communicated, or from common assumptions at that stage of history?[51]

Four solid reasons stand in opposition to the idea that modern judges should be completely guided by any original sense of desirable interpretive practices. These include the limited insights of the constitution makers and people of the time, the near unworkability of such an approach for the entire document, extreme difficulties of ascertainment, and the weakness of any argument that, despite these problems, those adopting the constitution have claims of legitimate authority that control present interpreters.

Especially given the novelty of the U.S. Constitution, which was put in writing and seen as binding on all branches of the federal and state governments, people of the time, including those who adopted the document, could not have foreseen much of what has transpired since then. In their creation of the opportunities to add new provisions, the enactors, though consciously choosing not to make the process of amendment easy, almost certainly did not realize just how difficult it would prove to be. They lived in a much smaller nation, one with states whose conventions adopted the original constitution and whose legislatures shortly thereafter approved the extensive Bill of Rights. By far the most substantial subsequent amendments have been those after the Civil War; rebellious southern states were not included in the Congress that prepared the crucial Fourteenth Amendment, and its ratification was forced on them as a condition for their again being represented in Congress.[52]

Given the inevitable constraints on the visions of those in the late eighteenth century, about both the prospects of amendments and broader social changes, which have been much faster in the last two centuries than in virtually all earlier periods of history, it is highly implausible that their understanding of interpretive standards should control absolutely.

A huge difficulty, rarely acknowledged, would be raised by a genuinely consistent use of originalist techniques of interpretation. Constitutional provisions have been adopted at different times. Since the Constitution itself can be altered, presumably the understanding of adopters, or readers of the time, about how an amendment should be interpreted would trump whatever interpretive perspectives dominated when the original Constitution was enacted. On this assumption, strategies of interpretation for amendments *could* differ sharply from each other and from those attached to the original document.[53] With respect to individual rights, for example, Supreme Court Justices would need to assess how far understandings about interpretation at the time of the Fourteenth Amendment (which has been taken to make most of the Bill of Rights applicable to the states) differed from understandings seven and a half decades earlier.[54]

A more subtle question about new amendments and interpretation is whether these properly influence how older provisions should be understood. As a rough generalization, an originalist would not believe that a novel interpretive position about a narrow amendment should affect interpretation of unrelated aspects of the Constitution, but it might bear on how subjects closely related to broader additions should now be treated. On this theory, the Fourteenth Amendment might properly be taken to affect how the original Bill of Rights should be interpreted.[55]

The task of even ascertaining the original understanding of interpretive techniques, possibly including hypothetical intentions, presents yet another major obstacle. How should modern interpreters discern what the enactors or citizens generally understood on this score? The constitutional text itself fails to give direct guidance about interpretive strategies; if a textualist judge asks what readers then would have understood, that would depend largely on what readers believed the enactors were trying to do.[56] In contrast to David's relying on the intent of Faith and himself, the problem of determining intent, and even saying what "intent" means, is more troublesome for authoritative instructions issued by a large number of people. Persons who agree upon language may have different ideas of its scope. Although with lengthy technical statutes, one may assume a kind of implicit delegation to those deeply involved, that is less persuasive for the Constitution. In any event, assessing what exactly the central figures agreed upon about interpretation is very difficult.

A general concern about original understanding of the American Constitution that touches interpretation as well as the content of particular provisions involves the role of ratifiers. For a two-stage process of proposal by a central body (the Constitutional Convention or both houses of Congress) and ratification within states, one would usually suppose that the understanding of both groups counts similarly.[57] However, a special difficulty with assessing intent about interpretive techniques for the original Constitution concerns the downplay of the authority of the proposing convention and the confidentiality of its deliberations. When the ratifiers considered the original document, the deliberations of the proposing convention were confidential. The ratifiers had only the text, documents such as the Federalist Papers, and common assumptions of the time to infer how to regard the Constitution. Although all grasped that it represented a striking change from the Articles of Confederation,[58] and supporters urged that the Constitution did not expand the powers of the national government so far that the states would be submerged,[59] precise questions about forms of interpretation were far from a major focus. Alexander Hamilton did write in Federalist Number 78: "The interpretation of the laws is the proper and peculiar province of the courts. A constitution is, in fact, and must be regarded by the judges, as a fundamental law. It therefore belongs to them to ascertain its meaning, as well as the meaning of any particular act proceeding from the legislative body."[60] But comments like these hardly conveyed a precise sense of how judges should interpret the new Constitution, and that was far from the center of people's minds.

Whether one inquires about the intent of adopters or the understanding of the few members of the public who had any actual sense of legal interpretation, the best way to construct prevailing assumptions requires a focus on how judges in England and the newly independent states interpreted statutes and the common law.[61] This inquiry suggests that judges pay little or no attention to legislative history but that they did understand texts in historical context,[62] with some place for equitable considerations.[63]

Were one able somehow to discern a dominant approach to statutory interpretation and conclude that it heavily influenced views about constitutional interpretation, any simple transposition to desirable modern interpretation faces powerful objections. Given people's limited ability to foresee how long the Constitution would survive, how difficult it would prove to amend, and what radical social shifts would occur over the following 226 years, any simple assumption that constitutional interpretation should now replicate that for statutes prior to 1789 would be misguided. Against a possible response that original charters and state constitutions more nearly resembled the federal Constitution than typical statutes, the answers are that English authorities had issued the charters; and that state constitutions, which had existed only briefly, did not involve the complexities of the new federal document, with most not even being subject to judicial enforcement.[64] Past practice simply does not yield well-considered convictions about how the new Constitution should be interpreted.

A more subtle inquiry, resembling the question David put to himself about how Faith *would have regarded* a legal career if she were aware of the relevant facts, is what the enactors or readers would have regarded as appropriate interpretive practices if they had been better informed and had thought carefully about the topic. When a person asking a hypothetical question knows another's propensities and deals with simple facts, she can often reach a confident conclusion. But the task, and even the appropriate scope of the inquiry, become much harder if one must account for drastically changed conditions. Should the inquiry be: "How would an enactor have looked at this if, taken as he was, he was supplied with the relevant information?" or "How would an enactor who had adjusted to social changes have regarded it?" That those are not identical inquiries can be illustrated by the shifting views of people toward same-sex marriage. For much of my life, the idea of such marriages seemed nearly inconceivable for this society. If in 1958, someone had asked me what I would think about such marriages if everything took place that has in fact since transpired, I likely would have said, "This would still seem to me a misguided idea." But having lived through those events, and having myself changed in various ways, I now regard acceptance of such marriages as strongly desirable. Regrettably, no simple exercise tells us how to construct the person about whom one asks a hypothetical question that deals with major shifts in social life.

All of these problems yield powerful reasons not to be completely guided by an estimate of what enactors or people at the time conceived about constitutional interpretation. A possible argument to the contrary, put in terms of legitimate authority, is unpersuasive. Although most members of the society of 1789 did not even have the right to vote, one can still contend that, as far as their own *generation* was concerned, the adopters, with their representative capacity, were capable of binding others, especially officials who chose to accept positions and swore to apply the Constitution. However, because strategies of interpretation and expectations subtly shift over time,[65] someone who takes office more than 200 years after the Constitution was ratified may reasonably say that if her taking office commits her to any interpretive strategy based on its acceptability to her predecessors, it must be the strategy commonly accepted by people when she takes office, not that conceived at the time of adoption.

A number of the problems in discerning original understanding both about textual content and interpretation can be illustrated by the controversial case of *District of Columbia v. Heller,* which interpreted the Second Amendment to strike down parts of a District of Columbia law that forbade the possession of handguns in homes and required residents to keep other firearms "unloaded and disassembled or bound by a trigger lock or similar device," making them unavailable for immediate use.[66] In discerning and applying original understanding, the Court divided 5–4. Justice Scalia for the majority found an individual right that included a right of self-defense in one's home and that applies in modern times to handguns, the weapons people most commonly use for that purpose.[67] Justice Stevens' dissent contended that the original right concerned only protection of state militias and had no relevance for the District's law.[68] In a separate dissent subscribed to by the same Justices who joined Justice Stevens, Justice Breyer urged that even if Scalia's account of the original understanding was correct, one needed to balance the reasons for a restrictive law against the claims of a right, an exercise that he asserted would sustain the law.[69] When reading the rhetoric of Justices Scalia and Stevens, one's initial impression is that they are worlds apart in their assessments of the original understanding; but in fact, a great deal is not actually disputed. Their disagreement does not turn on any simple discernment of what people conceived in 1791.

The Second Amendment reads: "A well regulated militia, being necessary to the security of a free state, the right of the people to keep and bear Arms, shall not be infringed."[70] Much of what divides the Justices turns on the relation of the two clauses. The dissenters claimed that the right is all about protecting the militia; Justice Scalia, by contrast, downplayed the "prefatory clause" in favor of the "operative clause,"[71] which protected a "pre-existing right"[72] that was much broader in scope. No simple interpretive technique, as understood in 1791 or now, can yield a general answer to how an explanatory clause about purpose bears on its successor.

It takes a careful reading of the opinions to see important points about which the Justices apparently agreed. The fundamental reason the Second Amendment was adopted was to protect the "militia," preventing the federal government from suppressing political opponents by "taking away the people's arms. . . ."[73] The "militia," conceived as including all able-bodied men,[74] could be called up on short notice when needed. The right to "keep and bear arms" did include possession of weapons in homes by members of the militia during periods when they were not actively engaged in military endeavors.[75]

Since the weapons employed commonly for self-defense and hunting are no longer those primarily used in the military, and given the actual training of military personnel, the value of protecting arms possession so that individuals can be prepared to engage in military endeavors has greatly diminished, if not disappeared entirely, and probably does not apply to handguns.[76] Because many of the weapons used by military forces are exactly the sorts that create the greatest danger of multiple killings in the hands of mentally disturbed individuals, proposals to ban them flourished, if only briefly, after the tragic murders of young children in Newtown, Connecticut, in December of 2012.[77] Any practical objections to a law like the District's banning handguns must now be mainly grounded in nonmilitary legitimate reasons, such as defense of people's homes and families.

Whether we ask about ordinary readers of the time, as Justice Scalia's opinion emphasizes,[78] or about the enactors, we find it hard to say how they would have understood the amendment's language in the modern context. For Justice Scalia, the original amendment protected a right of self-defense that the federal government could not invade.[79] Of course, if someone can keep a weapon in his home, it will be available for self-defense, and various prior recognitions of a right to possess weapons had not focused on any militia. But would this constitutional language, applicable only against the federal government, with its specific reference to safeguarding a well-regulated militia, have been conceived broadly enough to protect a right to bear arms that actually bears virtually no relation to military use? Even had many people in 1791 conceived of a basic political right to keep weapons, they may well have considered the legal status of that possession as left to state governments. Would an enactor have thought: "We are creating a general right, though protecting the militia is our main concern," or, instead, "In certain contexts a broad legal right to bear arms may be called for, but we are concentrating exclusively on limits the federal government might impose to undercut the militia within states." This is really too subtle a question to expect that most enactors and fully informed readers would have perceived a clear answer. Certainly, we cannot now discern any such answer with confidence.

Closely related is a hypothetical question: How would people of the time, not imagining a gap between military weapons and weapons used in other ways, have responded to a particular claim to bear arms that bore no relation to an effective military? Although Justice Scalia is certainly right that the weapons protected need not be the exact kinds of weapons constructed in the founding era,[80] that does not tell us the status of possessing a weapon almost totally disconnected from military use.

An alternative way of reaching the Court's conclusion could rely on an understanding of "the right to keep and bear arms" when the Fourteenth Amendment was adopted. If the right was *then* conceived as one for individuals, and the later amendment is now properly seen as making most of the Bill of Rights applicable against states, then Justice Scalia's account would reflect the correct approach to the right's basic nature as applied to state restrictions.[81] Further, if the Constitution should be understood as a whole and in a way that makes judicial application feasible, rights vis-à-vis the federal government are sensibly seen as broadened by the scope of the understanding in 1868[82] (especially when that federal government is functioning in the District of Columbia like a city government within a state).

Whatever one concludes is the relevance of the Fourteenth Amendment for this problem, one needs to recognize that straightforward factual inquiries about the adoption of the Second Amendment resolve neither the issue of basic meaning nor exactly how its interpretation should proceed. Not surprisingly, the Justices almost certainly were influenced by their own views and affected by modern discourse about whether people should be able to keep handguns in their homes for self-defense. Reva B. Siegel has offered a powerful account of how the exact implications of original understanding that Justice Scalia presents are in large part a reflection of "the convictions of the twentieth-century guns-rights movement."[83]

The recognition of how little original understanding really settles here sharply raises the question whether a self-conscious balancing of interests is appropriate. People use handguns to protect themselves against intruders, but such guns are also used in anger against acquaintances and family members and to commit suicide; and in the wrong hands, these guns can also cause fatal accidents. According to various studies, ownership of a gun is twelve times more likely to result in the death of a household member than an intruder. Gun ownership is connected to a threefold increased risk of homicide in owners' households, and each year in the United States there are roughly 11,000 gun homicides and 19,000 gun suicides.[84] And in 2008 and 2009, not only were 5,740 children and teens killed by guns, but 34,387 suffered nonfatal injuries.[85] The wider availability of guns also makes them more easily accessible for criminals and complicates police decisions about whether someone might be carrying a weapon illegally.[86] On the opposite side, the ability of people to possess guns in their residences may help to deter criminal invasions of their homes and persons.

The Court's majority did not actually establish an absolute right. It did not rule that one may possess every possible kind of gun; it also said that gun registration is acceptable, guns can be denied to dangerous persons, and guns can be prohibited in sensitive places like government buildings.[87] Although rejecting explicit balancing, the Scalia opinion does rely on the fact that handguns are the weapons most commonly used in self-defense. This strongly indicates that people will have no constitutional right to have much more dangerous weapons, such as the assault weapons that were the focus of attention after the tragedy in Newtown. The approach that Justice Scalia uses provides some assurance that *a* reasonable balance will be struck, because it is highly unlikely that extremely destructive weapons will become those that most people want in their homes. Against Justice Scalia's contention that courts should not impede protecting rights by employing exercises in balancing,[88] Justice Breyer responds that Scalia's own approach weighs interests, although in a less transparent way.[89] If one really rejects *all* balancing, there is no obvious way to decide just how limits to the right to possess arms should be set—to what "arms" the right extends and which restrictions do not really impair the right to possess them. No investigation of original understanding can settle these complex questions, and we have no straightforward, originally understood or now agreed upon techniques of interpretation to resolve them.[90] Further, as subsequent chapters on specific topics show convincingly, exactly how any weighing of interests should take place varies with different constitutional provisions and with subsets of rights covered by provisions. As Gregory P. Magarian explains, it is certainly not the case that how courts assess gun regulations should match how they evaluate interferences with basic speech.[91]

IV. CONCLUSION

The bottom line revealed by the various impediments to total reliance on an original understanding about interpretive strategies and about the coverage of specific provisions is that these should not completely determine how judges interpret the Constitution.[92] What the analysis strongly suggests is that a variety of factors must be considered in deciding what is now the best overall approach to interpreting the Constitution. That does not entail that some original understanding about interpretation is necessarily irrelevant, only that it may be very difficult to discern and, even if perceivable, should not be conclusive. The discussion here has not mainly addressed how far original understandings should determine the scope of particular provisions, although the *Heller* case does illustrate problems with claims of unwavering compliance with that approach. One could conceivably conclude that because of the dangers of judicial lawmaking, judges should treat the original sense of the content of a particular provision as more conclusive than the original enactors might have.[93] But *Heller* shows just how difficult that exercise can be.

This brings us back to the relevance of David's possible decisions. These showed that in difficult applications of broad instructions in ordinary life, one would predictably take multiple factors into account, without any neat formula about how much each counts in particular circumstances. Despite the need for legal decision-makers to provide justifications for others and guidance to their successors, this book defends the position that with respect to the most fundamental matters of interpretation and application, judges' approach to the Constitution should not be—indeed, cannot practically be—so different. There are multiple standards that are relevant to how decisions should be reached; these often involve a subtle weighing not reducible to a formula, and at times, other factors can override the original understanding about content. The three chapters that follow further explain and defend these positions.

First, the complexities of original understanding and how much it should count are explored in more depth. Then, other criteria of interpretation are described and evaluated. Chapter 5 asks how far decisions in difficult constitutional cases can be made on "neutral" or "objective" bases, explaining different senses in which those terms are used and asking how realistic is an aspiration for objectivity in these various senses. The remaining chapters illustrate the theses of these initial five chapters with analysis of standards the Supreme Court has used for specific provisions in actual cases it has decided.

Chapter 3

Original Understanding

What Is Relevant and How Much Does It Count?

I. INTRODUCTION

Following the previous chapter's account of why original understanding is so hard to discern and why it would not make sense for courts to rely exclusively on that understanding, this chapter tackles a range of more specific issues. It urges that more than one kind of original understanding matters, that the significance of this understanding diminishes over time, and that the precise kind of understanding that counts most also changes with the passage of years. These inquiries strongly reinforce the basic claim that factors other than original understanding inevitably will, and should, play important roles in constitutional interpretation. The second half of the chapter is dedicated to a poignant illustration—a controversy over the meaning of the Establishment Clause of the First Amendment.

II. ORIGINAL UNDERSTANDING

As prior chapters indicate, the form—or forms—of original understanding that carry weight can matter. Different readers may perceive constitutional texts differently, and this ~~text~~ may or may not coincide with what the enactors intended it to convey. For interpretive purposes, the crucial readers might be ordinary or well informed. Among the enactors, those who were particularly influential and perceived basic principles more deeply might be afforded special importance, an approach defended in this chapter. As already noted, we can differentiate what those at the time of enactment conceived as specific applications of provisions from their semantic meaning and the general principles they embody. Further, original ideas about interpretive techniques could be critical; these could include flexibility over time and degrees of judicial deference to political bodies. The questions about how much various appraisals should count for constitutional interpretation track ones about the original sense of statutes,[1] but the best answers differ.

Whether or not they assign it overarching importance, everyone agrees that the original meaning of a constitutional provision matters, but that recognition does not by itself tell us what constitutes that meaning. To try to answer this question, we need to explore the significance of the chosen language, the understandings of the proposers and ratifiers, the various levels of intention and understanding, and the place, if any, for hypothetical estimations. Fundamental claims of the book are that comparative importance and overall weight of forms of original understanding depend on the provision at issue and how much time has passed since its enactment.

A. Understanding of Language and Intent of Enactors

As with statutory interpretation, central issues for considering constitutional content are how much the intent of the enactors should count in relation to the message sent by their enacted language and the level at which the intent or message should be understood.[2] In contrast to prominent originalist claims some decades ago that concentrated on enactors' intent,[3] most originalists now focus on reader understanding and, at least in theory, on semantic understanding as contrasted with expected application.[4]

Because the language of authoritative texts affects how people react, its relevance is undeniable, but for a number of reasons, discernible intents should also matter. When the implications of statutory and constitutional language are unclear, or obviously inapt for a particular situation, or the actual intent is to interfere with the rights of citizens less than the enacted language suggests, judges have substantial reasons to assign importance to the enactors' aims. Further, as the volume on statutory interpretation develops in detail,[5] focusing on how readers understand language does not itself eliminate the significance of enactors' intent. Because listeners and readers generally understand language in the context of what they believe speakers and writers are trying to say, they will also perceive authoritative communications in that way, barring some extraordinary reason to block that aspect from their minds. All these factors bear on the respective places of language and intent for the original meaning of both statutes and constitutional provisions. For the latter, additional factors play a role, and certain distinctive nuances touch the original Constitution of the United States.

Even though various claims about the Constitution's original meaning are straightforward, any comprehensive approach must take account of understood strategies of interpretation as well as practices the provisions embraced. The answers to these inquiries need not coalesce neatly. If the original view about interpretation concentrated on the broad meaning of terms, sanctioning shifts in understood content, then genuine faithfulness to the most fundamental original understanding would include evolving applications of particular provisions. Someone might reach this conclusion, but conclude nevertheless that judges should adhere to the original sense of substantive content because that approach promotes the rule of law, constrains judicial latitude, reflects the need for super-majoritarian collaboration to alter constitutional substance, and yields better judicial decisions in the long run. These grounds are offered by various originalists,[6] but if a Justice who relied upon them recognized that they did not quite fit the original sense of interpretation, she would be less than fully faithful to the original understanding.

In regard to the central issue, whether what matters is enactor intent or reader understanding, the Constitution proposed in 1787 presents a peculiar problem as to who count as the relevant enactors and readers. A simple modern assumption is that both the proposers and ratifiers of the Constitution enacted it, just as the members of one legislative house propose a statute and the other approves it. Interestingly, that may well depart from the original view. Influential members of the drafting Philadelphia Convention suggested that all they did was offer a proposal of no legal force and that the genuine enactors of the Constitution were the ratifiers in state conventions representing the people. In *The Federalist,* James Madison wrote that the Convention's "powers were merely advisory and recommendatory," that it "proposed a Constitution which is to be of no more consequence than the paper on which it is written, unless it be stamped with the approbation of those to whom it is addressed."[7] In a later speech within Congress, Madison rejected approaches relying on the intentions of the Framers, saying, "As the instrument came from them, it was nothing more than the draught of a plan, nothing but a dead letter, until life and validity were breathed into it, by the voice of the people, speaking through the several state conventions." To reach beyond "the face of the instrument," one needed to "look for it, not in the general convention, which proposed, but in the state conventions, which . . . ratified."[8] This approach was reflected in Chief Justice Marshall's opinion for the Court in the central case of *McCulloch v. Maryland* on the basic power of Congress and the "Necessary and Proper Clause," in which he wrote that the Philadelphia Convention had made a "mere proposal" and that the "whole authority" of the Constitution comes from the state ratifying conventions representing the people.[9] This restrictive sense of the interpretive significance of views at the Philadelphia Convention receives powerful support from the fact that no records of the convention were made available until well after ratification. (An alternate explanation of this is that members of the convention feared use of the records by opponents.)[10]

The rhetoric reads as if the members of the Philadelphia Convention were proposing a document in the sense that a private group might propose a bill for Congress to adopt. What would matter, then, would be the views of lawmakers, not those of the group's members. From a modern perspective, this analogy is deeply flawed. After all, the drafted Constitution itself set the terms that would count as a ratification. Although whether states could set conditions as part of their acceptance of the drafted constitution was a subject of some controversy, the prevailing assumption was that the ratifiers, unlike legislative bodies, had no authority to actually alter the wording of the document; they had to vote "yes" or "no."[11]

One wonders whether related political factors influenced minimization of the Convention's role. The Convention had vastly exceeded its designated authority to revise the Articles of the Confederation; it proposed a process of ratification that was radically different from the unanimous approval of state legislatures necessary to revise the Articles; and ratification by state conventions was portrayed as "The Consent of the People."[12] All of these reasons might well have led its delegates to downplay their own role in relation to that of ratifiers. Whatever the underlying bases, Philadelphia delegates hesitated to rely publicly on their knowledge of internal debates and adjustments. And early courts, as well as other officials, tended to refer instead to what happened at the ratifying conventions.[13]

The status of these conventions also raises the question whether the understanding of delegates counted for itself as a form of enactor intent or as a likely reflection of what general readers understood. At least some of the formulations of James Madison sound as if the ratifiers' understanding was critical because they represented the people, which could be taken either to infer that this constituted their authority or that what really mattered was what "the people" understood.[14] Whether this formal difference would actually affect interpretive practice depends largely on the degrees of knowledge and positions in society one attributes to the readers.

Exactly what "readers" should be imagined? When textualists such as Justice Scalia refer to "ordinary readers" and turn to dictionaries of the time to discern what words and phrases then meant, the crucial reader seems straightforward. But that is far from the truth. Consider the modern reader of no special capacity. He will not grasp the meaning of most words in an authoritative dictionary;[15] more particularly, the key words in technical statutes will be well beyond him. For such language, a sensible response is that the people whose work is in the relevant field are the ones who should count. For constitutional provisions, it may matter not only how well informed are the conceived original readers but also what positions they occupied.

Although not containing a large number of completely unfamiliar technical words, the Constitution does explicitly and implicitly refer to political structures, practices, and rights that would have been grasped by only a small percentage of the population. Modern Americans by and large understand relatively little about political and legal subtleties, and we have no reason to think most citizens were better informed centuries ago.[16] For judges to be actually "bound to follow" what the average citizen took the words of the Constitution to accomplish would be absurd. To render the reader approach attractive, one needs to hypothesize a very well-informed reader, and at least some originalists have moved to what has been referred to as a "stage three," in which a provision is taken to mean what "an idealized audience would have understood."[17] In conceiving such an audience, are we thinking of people of the time who were best informed *or* what ordinary people would have perceived if they became so informed? This could matter since, at any time, most of those who are actually highly familiar with political and legal processes may have had different values and outlooks than ordinary people.[18] Another complexity is raised by the fact that, whereas many statutes are directed at private citizens and businesses and their lawyers, most constitutional provisions, as Chapter 1 notes, mainly guide officials. For these, perhaps judges should take higher officials as the most relevant readers, ones whose understanding would have largely tracked that of delegates to the ratifying conventions. Of course, we need not, and should not, conclude that only one form of reader is relevant. The senses of private citizens and officials, including ones with an average grasp, as well as those highly informed, should all count to some degree.

With respect to which readers should matter most, individual rights guarantees may differ from allocations of government authority. For these,[19] what private citizens understood would be highly significant because they deservedly wanted to be able to act in the manner they took as protected. This would be particularly true if, as Justice Scalia claimed about the Second Amendment, a provision embraced a widely understood "pre-existing" right.

In this sorting out of enactors' intent and readers' understanding, the place of *The Federalist*, written anonymously by Alexander Hamilton, James Madison, and John Jay, is something of a puzzle. Although other writings may have been equally influential during the ratification process itself,[20] *The Federalist* became cited with increasing frequency over time.[21] Its essays reflect the understanding of leading delegates to the Convention; they are evidence of what the ratifiers—for whom they were written—understood; and they may also suggest what general, very well-informed, readers assumed. According to Chief Justice Marshall, *The Federalist*'s "intrinsic merit entitles it to this high rank (as a commentary on the Constitution); and the part two of its authors performed in framing the constitution, put it very much in their power to explain the views with which it was framed."[22] That does not reveal exactly why *The Federalist* account carries authority.

When we reflect on what judges should take as the comparative authority of reader understanding as compared with enactor intent, perhaps changes in social circumstances should make a difference. During the late eighteenth century, reliable records of how statutes and the Constitution were enacted were rarely available.[23] Judges lacking an ability to discern intents with accuracy would have a strong reason to concentrate on texts. When historical records became more complete and available, judges had a reason to pay more attention to the aims of enactors than they previously had done.

Of course, modern originalists broadly accept textualism for statutory interpretation despite the availability of committee reports and legislative debates. By disregarding intent, they decidedly depart from genuine originalism about interpretive methods, because during many modern decades, enactors and informed readers assumed that statutes and Constitutional amendments were to be interpreted in light of what legislators aimed to achieve. This reliance was then taken for granted, given the Supreme Court's consistent references to legislative intent.

The Fourteenth Amendment, and its relation to the original Bill of Rights, raises some distinctive issues about intent, text, and relevant enactors. Whether or not the Fourteenth Amendment should be taken to have made virtually all the Bill of Rights applicable against the states—a subject taken up in a later chapter—it was universally understood to place significant new restraints on state governments. As with other amendments, "enactors" would certainly have included Congress as well as the ratifying state legislatures, since congressional approval was the initial stage of an adoption process specified by Article V of the Constitution itself. Indeed, in practical terms, the understanding of those who drafted and approved the amendment in Congress would inevitably carry *more* authority than the perception of the ratifiers, since assembling an overall sense of ratifying legislatures is so difficult and since southern states were effectively compelled to ratify the amendment to retrieve representation in Congress. By the time of the Fourteenth Amendment, courts were also paying more attention to the intent of those who proposed and ratified the original Constitution and the following Bill of Rights than had judges after 1789. To summarize a far from simple record, "intent" then counted for a good deal more in relation to reader understanding than it had earlier. According to Jefferson Powell, "[b]y the outbreak of the Civil War, intentionalism in the modern sense reigned supreme in the rhetoric of constitutional interpretation."[24] This would mean that a completely faithful originalist would interpret the Fourteenth Amendment somewhat differently than the original Bill of Rights. Thus, even where the Fourteenth Amendment protects the same basic right as one of the Bill of Rights, not only might the later provision protect human activities the earlier amendment failed to do, but also the very process of interpreting could vary. A pure originalist might well have to conclude that the federal government is entirely free to restrict behavior, such as forms of speech, that is beyond state regulation.

The preceding analysis reveals clearly how a completely faithful and systematic originalist approach is radically at odds with practical realities. Although when facing a novel challenge to a statute, courts properly afford greater deference to Congress than to an individual state legislature, nevertheless they have strong bases to treat what are essentially the same provisions similarly for the state and federal governments, and to use interpretive strategies that do not depend completely on the date a particular provision of the Constitution was enacted. Reasonable interpretive strategies cannot be unqualifiedly originalist.

Final puzzles about original understanding, whether of enactors or readers, are how open-ended provisions should be treated. And what is the relevance of broader purposes underlying the specific provisions and the whole Constitution? Leading figures at the time of the writing of the Constitution, such as Madison, foresaw a fairly significant range of judicial development of unresolved and unperceived questions. Although Madison later wrote favoring "the propriety of restoring to the sense in which the Constitution was accepted and ratified by the nation,"[25] he did not regard particular provisions as highly precise, providing a clear answer to virtually every problem. In *The Federalist,* he observed that "[a]ll new laws, though penned with the greatest technical skill, and passed on the fullest and most mature deliberation, are considered as more or less obscure and equivocal, until their meaning be liquidated and ascertained by a series of particular discussions and adjudications."[26] Jack Rakove has summarized the view of defenders of the Constitution that if "reasonable explanations and predictions of meaning" were proved false by events or "ambiguities demanded resolution, intervening experience would provide the foundation for determining the course that the interpretation or revision of the Constitution should then take."[27]

According to Gordon Wood, within the colonies, "judicial discretion . . . abounded."[28] One might discount the relevance of that as being a product of political tensions, rather than convictions about interpretive methods. But Jefferson Powell has noted that the delegates to the Philadelphia Convention did assume a traditional process of interpretation in which judges, rather than being highly literalist, employed the "artificial reason and judgment of law."[29] When references were then made to the "intent" of a legal document, that was the "product of the interpretive process and not some fixed meaning that the author locks into the document's text at the outset."[30] Another reason why framers and ratifiers may not have understood terms to have coverage that was already fully determined was that many "were themselves decidedly empirical in their approach to politics."[31] As far as the Bill of Rights was concerned, beliefs in natural rights may have had a similar effect. Even those who thought that such rights were not themselves alterable may have conceived that understanding of them might increase and that the best means of implementing them could change.[32]

With regard to the question whether specific content or broader purposes and the aims of the entire Constitution should be afforded greater weight, Madison had written in *The Federalist* that less important parts of an expression "should give way to the more important part[s]; the means should be sacrificed to the end, rather than the end to the means."[33] In noting in 1819 that the Constitution permitted the creation of a national bank, Chief Justice Marshall carried forward this approach in *McCulloch v. Maryland,* writing that "we must never forget that it is a *Constitution* we are expounding," "intended to endure for ages to come," and "a fair construction of the whole instrument" focuses on its important objects.[34]

Exactly what was conceived in the founding era about language that has since been treated as highly open-ended, such as "cruel and unusual punishment," is less apparent. Enactors and readers might have regarded as central what were then understood to be specific instances of unacceptable punishments, or instead the semantic meaning of the term "cruel and unusual." If one asks what semantic meaning counts, is it the general sense of the term in ordinary usage or its plausible coverage as a constitutional constraint? Even if some people in 1791 regarded that phrase as referring to specific understood penalties rather than inviting later courts to respond to more modern sentiments, most enactors and informed readers by the time of the Fourteenth Amendment may have conceived "cruel and unusual" as forbidding many punishments that were accepted seventy-seven years earlier.

Whether one focuses on the enactors' "intent" or reader understanding at the time, it is hard to pin down what exactly were perceived as the right methods of interpreting constitutional provisions whose scope was not clear. Generally, given influential documents like *The Federalist Papers*, distinguishing what very able readers understood from what was agreed upon at the Convention is nearly impossible, though *some* unclear textual language may reflect specific compromises the Framers reached. Prevailing interpretive strategies and expressed views do indicate that actual subjective intentions did not occupy a central place, but the provisions, including the broad reference to Supreme Law, do not reveal some settled, relatively uniform sense of how particular texts should be understood. Professor Rakove has emphasized how complicated the inquiry about original understanding is, given "a bewildering array of intentions and expectations, hopes and fears, genuine compromises and agreements to disagree."[35] And Gordon Wood has noted that from the beginning, "contrasting meanings" were ascribed to the Constitution.[36]

Apart from the difficulties of discerning a precise original sense about constitutional interpretation, the novelty of the United States Constitution and its enduring significance over centuries would render it a grave mistake for judges and other officials to be held strictly to an original conception of interpretation, even were a shared one discernable. Whatever else one might expect from constitutional amendments, even dominantly originalist Supreme Court Justices would not be likely to interpret each provision exactly in accord with what techniques of interpretation were prevalent at that time.

Preceding chapters have suggested independent reasons not to rely completely on original understanding and not to take that understanding as based entirely either on reader's perception of the text or enactors' intent. Much of the rest of this chapter pursues these topics in further depth.

As Chapter 1 has emphasized, a critical difference between most statutes and many constitutions, including that of the United States, involves time. Statutes mainly operate within a constrained period after their enactment. Barring a sharp shift in technology or social values, the "readers" will not have changed greatly. But we have little reason to suppose that a reader of 1789 had the same sense of a vague constitutional provision as does a reader of 2015. Given that one basic reason to rely on reader understanding is to credit how people will actually react to authoritative instructions, the readers that should count most would be those now living.[37] A textual originalist may respond, "No, the ordinary civilian, or expert, reader sets the original understanding of authoritative texts and that simply constitutes their meaning." Absent a persuasive justification, that view strikes one as simply arbitrary dictation.

Given the difficulty of distinguishing early reader understanding from enactor intent, the practical relevance of the following conclusion is limited. But the long life of the federal constitutional provisions in the United States and the shifting sense of readers over time constitute reasons to afford the intent of enactors more weight in discerning original meaning than it carries in statutory interpretation.[38]

The importance of leaders (or key figures) in a voting body, as compared with other voters, is an important issue when judges consider the Constitution. Of course, the intentions of those centrally involved in the drafting and adoption of language will almost inevitably carry special weight since their expressed views inform other voters and are likely to be considered by informed readers as broadly representative. On the other hand, the notion that general members consciously delegate the meaning of a complex legislative text to those who developed its language has much less force for constitutional provisions, since their language is not so lengthy and esoteric, and all members can develop their own understandings.

The comparative weakness of the delegation concept does not itself resolve the intrinsic importance of leaders and followers, especially as affected by the passage of time. Perhaps judges will reach sounder conclusions if they follow the understandings of those who have thought carefully about a fundamental constitutional subject and worked on it extensively. The last half of this chapter urges that for constitutional provisions like the Establishment Clause, the passage of time not only renders original understanding less central to interpretation, but it also means that the original understanding that should count most becomes increasingly that of those with the clearest and deepest sense of what they were doing. The next section addresses a question tied to these issues, namely how far should conceived specific applications of particular provisions dominate their broader semantic sense and underlying general principles, including the overall import of the Constitution?

B. Specific Applications or General Principles as Guides

A central question about the original understanding of many fundamental constitutional provisions is whether what should be taken to matter most is particular applications or more general principles. This is not an issue with regard to highly specific constitutional language, such as the granting of two Senate seats to each state,[39] as its meaning and what it requires have not shifted over time, whatever the strength or weakness of contemporary reasons to protect smaller states.[40]

Provisions formulated more broadly raise the issue of specific applications versus the general sense of words and underlying principles. The original constitution provides that no state shall pass any "Law impairing the Obligation of Contracts."[41] The First Amendment dictates that "Congress shall make no law respecting an establishment of religion, or prohibiting the free exercise thereof; or abridging the freedom of speech, or of the press. . . ." The Fourth Amendment precludes "unreasonable searches and seizures."

How are such provisions to be understood if one gives priority to original meaning? This issue is sometimes cast as either/or—*either* applications understood at the time *or* what fits the language under modern conditions. Of course, assessing with confidence exactly the range of specific applications understood at the time is often impossible. When, as frequently occurs, Supreme Court Justices are unable to decipher a persuasive argument that original understanding points in one direction or another, they must rely on other criteria to resolve an issue, whether they acknowledge that or conclude (honestly or not) that their judgment fits the original understanding.

Beyond this practical obstacle, we can identify different levels of generality and how these relate to originally conceived applications. Statutes (or executive rules) may authorize: (1) government action that conflicts with specific applications of a constitutional restraint conceived when the provision was adopted; (2) novel forms of government action that so closely resemble originally forbidden ones that people of any era would see a constitutional provision's language as clearly covering it (for example, a novel, extremely horrendous punishment by torture would be "cruel and unusual"); (3) government behavior not then imagined but which would be reached by the general attitudes that underlay the constitutional restraint; and (4) forms of action that would then have been accepted but that we now regard as at odds with a provision's basic concept. An illustration of the last point, addressed in more detail in Chapter 6, would be capital punishment for a wide variety of crimes not involving the death of any human victim, such as counterfeiting, a practice widely accepted when the Bill of Rights itself was adopted.

As I have suggested, a "pure originalist" position would follow the level of original meaning according to the interpretive strategy that the enactors intended or readers then perceived. Given that courts had not then construed statutory language as restricted to applications that legislators probably had in mind, and that Madison and other key figures in the adoption of the Constitution recognized the ambiguities and incompleteness of any drafted language, this approach would not yield the conclusion that provisions were sharply restricted to specific applications then assumed. More significantly, given the endurance of the Constitution and changes in social facts and values, and the difficulty of amendments, especially if all that is involved is one particular out-of-date practice, courts should take as the most important original understanding of broadly worded provisions not what were then perceived as specific applications but the more general objectives.[42] Alternatively, courts could emphasize whatever aspect of original understanding makes the most sense and is most just. A correspondence between William Cushing, then chief justice of the Massachusetts high court and soon to join the U.S. Supreme Court, and John Adams, recently elected Vice President, conveyed a reliance on general objectives in their approach to how the state constitution's freedom of the press bore on the crime of seditious libel. Cushing suggested that even if in English law, truth was not a defense, the purposes of freedom of the press meant that it should be, and the state provision should be so construed.[43] After summarizing the letters between Cushing and Adams, Jefferson Powell has concluded that "[f]ounding-era lawyers did not view a constitution as a box the interpretive contents of which were fixed upon its drafting or adoption. . . . [C]onstitutionalists of the early Republic shared, universally to my knowledge, the conviction that at times the meaning of a provision required deliberation on what Cushing called 'the reason of the thing'. . . ."[44]

Two narrower questions about the force of original understanding are whether courts can appropriately approve novel exercises of power that limit rather than expand the range of protected rights and whether evolving applications should ever contradict the constitutional terms. One opinion by the Warren Court suggested that under the Fourteenth Amendment, individual rights could be expanded, but not cut back.[45] Whether one focuses on original understanding[46] or desirable development, any broad generalization of this position to all constitutional rights lacks a persuasive defense. Social changes may indicate that certain individual rights need to expand, and others to be more limited. For example, the original Constitution bars state impairments of the obligation of contracts. As Supreme Court cases have implicitly recognized, modern debtors may need forms of relief that would have been regarded as unacceptable restrictions on contractual rights when that provision was adopted.[47] We cannot simply assume that *all* individual rights may warrant further expansion but not narrowing.

Capital punishment sharply poses the trickier issue of the possible contradiction of original terms. Due Process Clauses of the Fifth and Fourteenth Amendments prohibit depriving a person of "life, liberty, or property, without due process of law"; their language unmistakably recognizes capital punishment as an acceptable penalty. Could it be consistent with this original understanding to bar capital punishment within states as unconstitutional?[48] This inquiry, explored in greater depth in Chapter 6, turns out to be less than simple. So long as the original understanding embraced *some* evolution of views on impermissible punishments over time, it fits with decisions that the range of acceptable capital punishment may differ now from what it was 224 or 147 years ago.[49] But that conclusion does not resolve the possible acceptability of complete judicial elimination.[50] If the Constitution stated "Capital punishment will be the (or a) penalty for murder," that could well be taken to represent an understanding that only an amendment could make its imposition always unconstitutional.[51] The actual language is not quite so direct. If only two states retained capital punishment as a matter of legislative choice, and even in those the death penalty was rarely inflicted—and then, always on members of disadvantaged groups—it could easily seem "cruel and unusual" or violative of due process or equal protection by a modern standard. Thus, the constitutional language does not absolutely preclude a resolution that all death penalties could be unacceptable; but it does make it much more difficult to argue that such a ruling would be in line with the original understanding so long as the federal government and most states retain the penalty.

A final question about levels of generality concerns whether one focuses on specific provisions or the Constitution as a whole. Chief Justice Marshall's opinion in *McCulloch v. Maryland* includes a famous articulation of attention to the broad document and its purposes, concluding that the Court's answers should comport with the Constitution's purposes unless the specific words "imperiously require" the contrary.[52] *Exactly* how much attention should be given to the broader constitutional document depends on the particular issue involved. Two arguments in favor of overarching attention to the specific provisions of statutes—that such language commonly represents compromises and that the judicial discretion entailed by reliance on broad purposes needs to be cabined[53]—have much less power for most constitutional provisions. Specific language does not commonly represent a compromise at odds with the Constitution's broader principles.[54] And, given the vagueness and breadth of many individual provisions, such as "abridging the freedom of speech," attending to the overall values of the Constitution hardly adds much to judicial discretion. Indeed, for a wide range of issues, whether the crucial original understanding is tied to a particular provision or the entire Constitution, judges are more likely to be restrained by a respect for settled precedents than by what they take as the specific original understanding, which is often uncertain.

C. Hypothetical Intentions and Understandings

A question about original understanding touched on in the last chapter is how far hypothetical intentions or understandings should figure into interpretation. One usually thinks of hypothetical *intentions* as just that: What would someone have intended if they had addressed an issue that they did not actually perceive? But the same question can arise with reader understanding: How would readers have conceived applications if they had considered problems that did not actually occur to them?

In two different respects, the line between actual and hypothetical intentions (and understandings) is less than sharp. The first respect concerns the closeness of an unperceived possible application to perceived applications. If a particular form of torture was plainly unacceptable, so also is its infliction by controlled electricity, a technology people of the time had not yet imagined. When the novel practice departs further from actually conceived applications, the issue of hypothetical intentions becomes more serious. Thus, one might ask whether people in 1791 would have regarded capital punishment as cruel and unusual if they had been aware of the infrequency with which it is now imposed and of changing perspectives on the preservation of life.

If hypothetical intentions should count (and it is hard to rule them out altogether),[55] it becomes a fundamental question just how judges should conceive the earlier people. As Chapter 2 suggests, one might ask: "If we provided these people with specific facts about the future, what would they have concluded?" or "What would people of their general outlook believe if they had lived in modern times?" The latter inquiry entertains more opportunity for changing outlooks and in form requires more creative thinking by the modern judge. That the two inquiries could lead to different outcomes is strongly suggested by the facts of an actual Supreme Court case.[56] A southerner whose language indicated that he was a moderate about race relations set up a park that was only for white persons. Roughly a century later, such parks were held unconstitutional. Would the man who donated the park have preferred that the park be closed or integrated? Given his actual convictions about racial separation, he might, even if informed about changes in overall attitudes, have opted for closure. But if we asked what would a person with his overall feelings about the races who was living in modern times prefer, that would almost certainly be integration. Of course, the more that modern judges rely on the broader outlooks of people of earlier times, rather than their more specific convictions, the harder it is for them to detach estimates of hypothetical intentions from their own normative evaluations.

III. REFLECTIONS ON MADISON AND JEFFERSON AND THE ESTABLISHMENT CLAUSE

The remainder of this chapter uses a familiar example to illustrate many of the complexities we have identified and to support certain proposed resolutions. Among the questions are these. How should Justices assess the original understanding of the Establishment Clause; how should the

Clause apply, if at all, to state and local laws through the Fourteenth Amendment; and should the standards and significance of original understanding alter as time passes?

In *Everson v. Board of Education*, the Supreme Court unanimously decided that the Establishment Clause of the First Amendment did apply to states under the Fourteenth Amendment's Due Process Clause.[57] The Justices were also united in adopting a stringent conception of the restraints that clause sets, partly captured by the phrase "separation of church and state." The Justices divided 5–4 on the precise issue of whether New Jersey could pay for the bus transportation of students attending parochial schools, with the majority ruling that such assistance was all right because it did not significantly aid religious education. Scholars and subsequent Supreme Court Justices have variously characterized the reasons the majority of the Court was willing to uphold that practice—and indeed, passages in Justice Black's opinion for the Court do point in different directions. But a central explanation is captured by his comment that "[n]o tax in any amount, large or small, can be levied to support any religious activities or institutions, whatever they may be called, or whatever form they may adopt to teach or practice religion."[58] Since the opinion goes on to acknowledge that the New Jersey law approached the "verge" of state power,[59] a reader can only infer that for Justice Black, more direct and substantial aid would not have been acceptable.

The related issues we shall examine are: (1) the basic idea of whether the Establishment Clause should apply to the states; (2) the heavy reliance on the views of Thomas Jefferson and James Madison; (3) the strict concept of nonestablishment, including the idea of "separation of church and state"; (4) what relevantly should count as the original sense of a provision as time from enactment elapses; (5) and how much the "original understanding" should now matter.

A. Incorporation of the Establishment Clause

Everson's majority opinion assumes without analysis that the Establishment Clause applies against the states as well as the federal government. That proposition is now solidly settled, despite occasional expressed doubts by individual Justices.[60] But the virtual certainty that the Supreme Court will not back away from this ruling has not eliminated scholarly debate over its soundness.

The decision that the Fourteenth Amendment makes the Establishment Clause applicable against the states depends on the more general proposition that the Due Process Clause of the Fourteenth Amendment renders the fundamental provisions of the Bill of Rights restrictive of state laws. By 1947, the time of *Everson*, the Free Speech and Free Exercise Clauses had already been held to limit states.[61] Thus, it might have seemed a simple extension to hold that the rest of the First Amendment, which begins "Congress shall make no law," warrants similar treatment. A subsequent chapter will sketch differing views over whether those adopting the Fourteenth Amendment really intended that most of the Bill of Rights apply to the states.[62] The focus here is on special questions about the Establishment Clause.

Two basic arguments against applying this clause to the states are that it was essentially jurisdictional, reserving power to the states, and that its concerns are institutional rather than related to the scope of individual rights.[63] The jurisdictional argument is that since the clause kept the federal government out of state business, it should never have been turned upside down to constrain states. When the Bill of Rights was ratified in 1791, roughly half the states favored religion in ways now regarded as at least weak establishments. Some influential members of Congress, most notably James Madison, who drafted the Bill of Rights, definitely opposed establishments in principle; other members, and many ratifiers within state legislatures, were undoubtedly comfortable with the degrees to which their own states favored one or more religions. Thus, the argument goes, the Establishment Clause assures that the federal government will not create a *national* church or otherwise interfere with state decisions whether or not to establish religion.[64] It follows that the Court was paradoxically wrongheaded to rely on the clause to restrict states.

This jurisdictional argument against incorporation is demonstrably unconvincing.[65] Although the clause was *partly* jurisdictional at the outset, leaving states free to establish religions, its language that "Congress shall make no law respecting an establishment of religion ..." also has clear implications for federal domains that were *not* subject to state authority. These included United States embassies abroad, the about-to-be implemented federal enclave of the District of Columbia, and fairly extensive federal territories. The national government could not have created a federal established church, such as England's Anglican Church, for these areas. By the time the Fourteenth Amendment was proposed and ratified, no state retained an established religion. Thus, by 1868, "no establishment" was regarded primarily as a basic principle of government and was not an allocation between different levels of authority. If, as is highly likely, the federal clause was *then* understood to embody such a principle, no special jurisdictional feature precluded its coverage extending to states.

The more tenable argument against incorporation is based on the clause's institutional character. If the Establishment Clause is essentially about relations between civil government and institutional religion, how can the Due Process Clause, a provision that protects individual rights, encompass it?

The answer is that supporters of nonestablishment have always perceived it as closely related to free exercise. Notably, Alexis de Tocqueville, in his famous *Democracy in America*, wrote in 1835 that, as a French visitor struck by the religious aspect of the United States, he questioned members of different sects including many clergy and was astonished "that they all attributed the peaceful dominion of religion in their country mainly to the separation of church and state."[66] Further, a central basis for nonestablishment is an ideal of nonpreference among adherents of different religions, an equality that might well be encompassed by both the Free Exercise Clause[67] and the Equal Protection Clause.[68] Had the Supreme Court ruled that the Establishment Clause did not apply to the states, courts would have needed to determine whether particular state measures that the Establishment Clause forbade to Congress violated the Free Exercise or the Equal Protection Clause. That approach would greatly multiply the complexities of review of state laws favoring religion, with very limited practical consequences. Acknowledgement that the Establishment Clause itself bears a sufficient connection to individual rights to be applied against states greatly simplifies judicial administration, a broad objective that has almost certainly influenced the Court's handling of the Fourteenth Amendment more generally.

B. Reliance on the Views of Thomas Jefferson and James Madison

Justice Black's opinion in *Everson*, as well as subsequent discussions of nonestablishment, relied heavily on the views of James Madison and Thomas Jefferson, a concentration that has been strongly criticized.[69] Just how far the conceptions of these two leaders should influence our present sense of the Establishment Clause raises crucial questions about the sort of original understanding that should matter most for general constitutional clauses of the founding and post-Civil War eras.

Why might the views of Madison and Jefferson carry particular weight? Madison, of course, was the original drafter of the Bill of Rights, which was adopted two years after the Constitution partly in response to concerns expressed by Anti-Federalists during the ratification process that the original document did not sufficiently restrict federal power. A key development toward nonestablishment had been Virginia's earlier rejection of a state tax to support religions, followed by its adoption of Thomas Jefferson's Bill for Religious Freedom, which, among other things, forbade requiring people to support any ministry. Madison had led the fight against the tax, and his *Memorial and Remonstrance* was the clearest, most eloquent public statement of principles of nonestablishment.[70] Jefferson, representing our government in France when the Bill of Rights was drafted, was the strictest separationist among the early Presidents, and in a now famous (but then obscure) 1802 letter to the Baptists in Danbury, Connecticut, he opined that the Establishment Clause built "a wall of separation between church and state."[71] Scholars disagree somewhat about exactly what Madison and Jefferson regarded as acceptable,[72] but the fundamental issue here is the significance their particular views should carry.

Three questions present themselves: (1) Should judges give primary attention to the actual (subjective) intentions of those who voted to enact or ratify the Bill of Rights, to what a reasonable participant in that process would have understood, or to the sense of readers of the time? (2) Should judges relying on those sources be guided mainly by originally understood concrete applications or more basic principles? and (3) Should judges assume that widely held original understandings about basic principles should determine semantic meaning and specific applications, or should they make present evaluative judgments about what best fulfills those principles in a just and desirable way?

Standard contentions, and the first part of the chapter, concentrate mainly on the first two questions. Whether one attends to most enactors or readers, giving huge weight to the views of Jefferson and Madison to interpret the original Establishment Clause is not warranted.[73] With seven states retaining forms of substantial aid to religions, and approval of the First Amendment by two-thirds of each house of Congress and majorities in three-quarters of state legislatures, many of those voting in favor did not embrace the outlooks of the two strongest proponents of strict separation.[74]

Questions about "specific applications" versus "abstract purpose" do connect to what weight the particular views of Madison and Jefferson should receive. An example of when a choice between foreseen applications and general principles could be critical would be a challenge to a modern law that criminalized blasphemy according to Christian conceptions while permitting what other religions would regard as blasphemy. Such a law would violate basic notions of nonestablishment, even if those in the founding era failed to recognize that implication.

Although it might initially seem that, since Madison and Jefferson were stricter than most of their contemporaries both about applications of broad principles of nonestablishment and the specific practices they would bar, their views should carry about the same weight whichever aspect was emphasized, two grounds suggest otherwise. The first relates closely to the premise of "incorporation." By the time of the drafting of the Fourteenth Amendment, the idea of "establishment of religion" had developed. Insofar as that amendment's proposers and ratifiers were influenced by views held in 1791, abstract principles almost certainly counted for more than the founders' generation's reactions to particular practices. Since by the 1860s all states had long since abandoned formal establishments,[75] enactors and readers of the Fourteenth Amendment were surely more consistently anti-establishment than officials and citizens had been when the Bill of Rights was approved. Because Jefferson's and Madison's general views were better known than those of most of the founders, they might well have influenced those who adopted and read the post-Civil War amendments and had a sense that the Fourteenth embraced key aspects of the Bill of Rights.[76]

In addition to the import of the later amendment lies an interpretive issue with deeper significance. Should judges treat the relevant abstract principles as simply strict or less-than-strict nonestablishment, or should they give weight to what conception now seems best for our society? According to the latter approach, not only may our modern understanding entail particular *consequences* that would not have been broadly conceived at the time of adoption, but the relevant underlying principles also might now look different.

Here is an illustration. Suppose that most of those who voted for the Bill of Rights and readers of the time did not think the government should support any particular church but that it was free to sponsor particular religious opinions, by, for example, engaging in specifically Christian public prayers, forbidding Christian blasphemy, and using the King James version of the Bible in all government ceremonies and in public schools (once these were created).[77] The accepted underlying abstract principles, let us assume, were that although nonestablishment entailed that American governments should not favor any specific church, they could, as representations of a Protestant Christian nation, properly reflect that outlook in many of their own actions.[78] A modern understanding of nonestablishment rejects this idea in two respects. Most obviously, given modern diversity, the government should not sponsor Protestant Christianity over other religious views. Further, we now see that expressions by the government itself of religious ideas are a kind of implicit, indirect favoring of the religious institutions that embrace these outlooks.

If a Justice believes that the focus should be on an understanding of abstract principles that represents the soundest grasp of a basic concept, she *might* well turn to Madison and Jefferson as having a truer sense of nonestablishment than did most of their contemporaries. Any approach of this sort, accepting the sense of original abstract principles that most fully realizes the true dimensions of a fundamental concept, can be challenged as no longer really relying on original intent at all. Before attempting to answer that challenge directly and asking how much original intent should now matter for provisions like the Establishment Clause, I briefly consider objections to the whole concept of "separation."

C. Strict Disestablishment and Conceptualization

In both the majority and dissenting opinions of *Everson*, closely connected with the reliance on Jefferson and Madison is the conclusion that disestablishment is strict, signaled by the use of Jefferson's phrase, a "wall of separation between church and state."[79] Powerful objections have been raised not only to the idea that the limits on government practices are this stringent but as well to the very terminology of "separation," a concept that some assert is quite different from "disestablishment."[80]

In practice, the Supreme Court has retained a "strict" approach in some domains, but not all. For decades, the Court carried forward the implications of *Everson* about financial assistance to parochial education, striking down subsidies that might genuinely aid religious education while approving fringe forms of assistance, such as the loan of secular texts and payment for implementation of government tests. But that approach shifted radically with the Court's approval in 2002 of a voucher plan in Cleveland, according to which parochial as well as other private nonprofit schools received substantial financial aid for the education of children from relatively poor families.[81] Although no longer imposing stringent restraints on financial aid to religions schools,[82] the Court has carried forward *Everson*'s underlying theme in regard to government sponsorship of religious beliefs and public school exercises.[83] Notably, public schools cannot engage in prayers and devotional Bible readings in classes and graduation ceremonies, they cannot post the Ten Commandments in all classrooms, and they may not teach "creation science" as an alternative to evolution. Similarly, cities and towns cannot erect crèches in a manner that endorses Christianity. Thus, governments, with very limited exceptions,[84] may not themselves endorse or sponsor religious ideas.[85]

Philip Hamburger has strongly urged that the founders did not think of "nonestablishment" as "separation" and that the growth of the latter idea has skewed interpretation of the Establishment Clause in a way that both departs from its roots and is unfortunate.[86] That critique substantially overstates the significance of this change in conceptualization.[87] To begin, no one has ever conceived a genuinely absolute notion of spatial separation. Churches receive protection from police and firefighters, are subject to regulations about the safety of buildings, and benefit greatly from exemptions from property taxes and tax deductions for donations. "Wall of separation" must be understood to mean a sharp divide only in certain crucial respects, most notably jurisdictional functions of governance. More broadly, the attack on "separation" underestimates the commonness of conceptual shifts and overestimates the practical force of a move to it from "disestablishment." The ways in which members of societies conceptualize their experiences and their worlds constantly alter through time. These changes almost always involve some adjustment of perspective, but the degree of adjustment varies greatly.

A different realm of constitutional law provides an illustration.[88] No one talked about a "right of privacy" in the late eighteenth century. The Fourth Amendment provided a protection of persons, houses, and papers against unreasonable searches and seizures; the Fifth Amendment protected people from being witnesses against themselves in criminal cases. Both provisions protect against the government's gathering information about one's life that one would prefer to keep secret. The idea that both protections involve a more general right of privacy connected the two provisions in an illuminating way, but has had only a limited effect on what exactly those two provisions were thought to cover.[89] By contrast, in some more modern conceptions, a "right of privacy" has been extended to a right to have an abortion, engage privately in sexual relations with other consenting adults, and possess pornography in one's home.[90] So conceived, the right includes engaging in a particular behavior, as well as limiting how officials acquire information. "Privacy" in this sense lies very close to "autonomy," carrying much broader implications than a mere restraint on information gathering.

Does the concept of "separation of church and state" radically alter the meaning of "disestablishment" or "nonestablishment"? Although eighteenth century ideas of nonestablishment were more limited than modern ones, this comparison alone tells us little about the particular influence of the concept of "separation," understood as concerning primarily the jurisdictional powers and functions of religious bodies and civil government. The coverage of "nonestablishment" would have changed over time even if that had remained the exclusive concept for analysis.[91] To try to develop a sense of the particular significance of "separation," we must estimate how "nonestablishment" would otherwise have developed. For aid given on a neutral basis to religious institutions performing secular functions, "separation" may well have greater bite than "nonestablishment;" but, as we have seen, the Court has moved away from powerful limits on such aid. When one thinks about school prayers or crèches in state buildings, the idea that government should not establish religion seems to have just as much force as the notion of separate spheres. The same is true for most other issues involving the state's relation to religion.[92] That the metaphor of "separation" has itself made a great difference in what the Supreme Court has decided until now is doubtful.

D. What Original Intent Should Count and for How Much?

What remains is reflection on how reliance on Madison and Jefferson relates to what should count as the crucial original understanding and its weight. For some critics, it is sufficient to condemn the Supreme Court's anti-establishment doctrine that (1) the heavy reliance on the views of Jefferson and Madison fails to represent the broad range of original positions, and (2) modern doctrine is more rigorously anti-establishment than were prevailing original views. These two conclusions are better seen as the beginning rather than the end of inquiry about what original understanding should now matter and what force it should carry.

Original intent can be important for reasons of political authority, continuity, and wisdom. As time passes in a constitution's life, the force of the political authority reason fades. For basic constitutional rights, understanding of abstract principles should count for more than beliefs about specific applications, and for a constitution that is difficult to amend, judges should treat original understanding with diminishing force.

The following analysis puts to one side the reality that if they followed a strict originalist jurisprudence, judges passing on state laws restricting rights would have to ask how matters were viewed at the time of the

Fourteenth Amendment in 1868, not in 1791 when the Bill of Rights was ratified. As I have mentioned, we rarely see a focus on these issues, even when originalist Justices are writing opinions.[93] This is partly because attention is given to the original enactors and readers; but the more basic reason may be that any constant splitting of hairs about what a freedom means vis-à-vis the federal government and what it means vis-à-vis the states would be awkward and confusing, if not unmanageable. Elaborating separate bodies of Bill of Rights law for the federal government and the states would further complicate the already arduous task of deciding controversies over fundamental rights, and citizens might feel a sense of injustice that what amounted to an infringement by one political authority would be acceptable coming from another.[94]

The crucial question of *whose* original understanding counts must be addressed not only by proclaimed "originalists" but also by everyone who takes original understanding as *a* significant component of constitutional interpretation.[95] Lying between the adopters' subjective intentions and reader understanding is how a "reasonable" enactor would understand the language of a statute or constitutional provision. This device appears to focus on legislative intent, but what it actually takes into account may fall closer to a knowledgeable reader's understanding, since such a reader would usually understand a piece of legislation as would a "reasonable" legislator.[96] For most of the issues treated in the rest of this chapter, it is not crucial whether one emphasizes adopter intent or reader understanding.[97]

With respect to what those who adopted or read the Bill of Rights assumed about the comparative importance of understood applications and broad principles,[98] one guide is the choice of general language. Of course, drafters would not have cluttered a constitution with every specific practice they wished to forbid, but had Madison or others wanted only to reach specific practices, they could have made more direct references to historical arrangements. Instead of language about laws "respecting an establishment of religion," they could have referred to "established churches" and perhaps to other specific forms of establishment. As we have seen, key enactors of the Constitution recognized that authoritative language definitely could not itself resolve all potential issues, and they were aware that interpretation of statutes tended to be fairly flexible. Knowing that the amendment process was not easy, adopters and readers of the Bill of Rights could not have contemplated a formal addition with every development in views about the right applications of the general concepts. Apart from its bearing on probable initial understanding, the difficulty of amendment, as Chapter 1 stresses, has independent significance. If a constitution endures over time, *and* it serves as a unifying force for a society, *and* it is difficult to amend, *and* it would lose some of its symbolic value if frequent amendments made it much longer and less coherent, judges have reasons to pay attention to more abstract principles.

Evident problems with sticking entirely, or mainly, to contemplated applications involve technological advances, other changes in the external world, and deep shifts in social values. The relevance of technical advances and undisputed changes in social practices is obvious. The adopters of the First, Fourth, and Eighth Amendments did not conceive of electronic media, electronic surveillance, or torture by electric shocks; and with regard to the Second Amendment, they were not considering radical changes in what constitutes the military. The relevance of changes in value, such as perceptions about the death penalty, is understandably more debatable.

With regard to religion and the state, we can perceive an alteration of both social circumstances and attitudes. Among other changes from 1791 are these. The choice of what religion to follow is now regarded much more as an autonomous choice for each individual. The number of Roman Catholics has increased dramatically (it is now the largest single denomination in the United States), and, partly because of changes within the Catholic Church itself, most Protestants now view it as one among many Christian groups, not as a distinctive embodiment of evil or source of tyranny. The number of Jewish, Muslim, Hindu, and Buddhist practitioners has become substantial;[99] and, although religion within the United States has failed to fade away as many social scientists once assumed it would, nevertheless, the percentage of citizens who profess atheism or agnosticism has risen.

Although pinning down ways in which the original understanding of free exercise and nonestablishment of religion fails to correspond with present conceptions is difficult, most citizens do not now think governments should teach Protestant Christianity as true. The Supreme Court has declared that religious tests of office within states violate the federal Establishment Clause;[100] and a prohibition of Christian blasphemy alone would now be regarded as an establishment.[101] If we value the extension of the Constitution over time, we have strong reasons to conclude that constitutional rights formulated in general language may now reach beyond originally conceived applications.[102]

As the prior chapters suggest, the premise that the political authority of the original adopters of the Constitution constitutes a strong reason to follow original understanding is itself unpersuasive. The enacting bodies that performed more than 220 years ago did not *represent us*, and had only the faintest glimmer of what we would be like. Moreover, the country within which the Bill of Rights was adopted not only had widespread slavery and subjected women to substantial legal disabilities, it was also composed of citizens who dominantly accepted some version of Protestant Christianity. Although one can fairly say that the actual written Constitution became and remains the foundation of our liberal democracy and that *it* enjoys political authority as a consequence, that alone does not tell us how it should be interpreted. On matters not clear from the text itself, modern citizens, with only the vaguest ideas about original conceptions, are more likely to be aware of recent and prominent Supreme Court decisions. Although some of those remain controversial, many, such as equal protection rights for women, have been widely and quickly accepted despite lacking support in original understanding. If it is the Constitution as a document and as interpreted in modern times that *now* has political authority, we can conclude that the original understanding should carry much less importance than it once did. In sum, the political authority argument for following that understanding weakens greatly as time passes, most especially for issues as to which the adopters would not have fairly represented large swaths of the modern population. That leaves interpreters greater latitude both to focus on what aspects of original intent *should* be given greater weight and to move beyond original understanding to other considerations.

A different possible reason to pay attention to original intent is continuity. If that intent figured prominently in the development of the substance of basic concepts and their prior legal interpretations, that constitutes a basis to maintain its significance. Michael Dorf has referred to this ground as "ancestral originalism."[103] Also, if a court applies a constitutional provision differently than was done in earlier cases, the judges' ability to show that they are corresponding with the broad principles envisioned by the adopters can be somewhat reassuring. A qualification about this kind of continuity, at least as it is perceived, recognizes that the main practical reassurance may come from a *rhetoric* of respect for original intent, which can vary from actual reliance.[104] Another more crucial qualification, explored further in the next chapter, is the continuity of legal doctrine for which judges aim within common law systems.[105] Although the Justices of the Supreme Court do regard themselves as freer to depart from prior constitutional case law than prior statutory case law (which is subject to relatively simple legislative "correction"), they nonetheless care about the continuity of following precedents, even when earlier decisions are seen to depart from original intent. Realistically, this sense of constraint both yields more continuity and is more limiting for Justices than an idea that original understanding should completely control.

Wisdom, which Dorf calls "heroic originalism,"[106] also is a possible basis for paying attention to original intent. The founders, so the argument goes, were an extremely gifted generation. They bequeathed to us structures of government that were uniquely suited for American democracy. We can trust the resolutions of these men more than our own less profound judgments. The force of this argument is seriously contested, and it certainly must be narrowed or qualified; but it has important implications for *whose* original understanding matters.

If one focuses on the wisdom of the adopters of the Bill of Rights, what they had in mind then should matter more than how a typical reader would have understood their language (if these differed). Moreover, when one talks about the wisdom of the founders, one is thinking mainly of political leaders, not ordinary members of the population or representatives in state legislatures.[107] This assessment can support giving extra weight to the leaders' views.[108]

Among the American founders, James Madison's *Memorial and Remonstrance* provided the fullest account of the values of nonestablishment. Madison went well beyond John Locke, whose ideas about natural rights were influential among the colonists. In contrast to Locke, who developed a voluntary conception of religion and religious liberty that could easily point toward nonestablishment but who did not actually reach that conclusion, Madison did come to that conclusion, providing a persuasive explanation of how nonestablishment implements the ideal of religious liberty. Especially since Madison was the main author of the Bill of Rights, drawing heavily from his understanding makes sense—even if for a standard political authority version of intent, one would have to consider all those who accepted his language but did not share his understanding.

This brings us to a critical aspect of the "wisdom" theory that shows it is only partially originalist. No one today would think the founders made correct judgments about all major subjects. Their views about relations of men and women, about the significance of racial differences, and about appropriate political rights for people who do not hold property are far out of line with dominant opinion today, not only within the United States but also within all liberal democracies. To conclude that the founders' intent should count because of their wisdom, one needs to do some initial screening, screening that cannot itself rest on original intent.

Conceding all of this, one may still believe that the main proponents of the Establishment Clause were deeply perceptive, not only in wanting to keep the federal government away from establishment but also in considering that nonestablishment was healthy within states. One may believe, further, that the founders were wiser in their general ideas than with respect to a practice that even they may have accepted out of habit, without adequate reflection on its conformity with fundamental general principles. One may also conclude that their wisdom about general ideas has more relevant application to modern conditions than their sense of acceptable practices in their particular time and place. With all of these (contestable) assumptions, we can conclude that it is entirely appropriate to give a place of prominence to the broad ideas of Madison and Jefferson in interpreting and applying the Establishment Clause.

Under this account, does original understanding really count for anything, or are Justices, relying partly on widely shared modern views or developed normative accounts by modern thinkers, basically deciding first what are sound principles and then ascribing them to some "wise" founder? The answer to this concern is fourfold. If a Justice can find no actual support in original understanding for what she believes are the soundest principles, she cannot honestly rely on support from that source.

Further, a Justice may think it matters for a final outcome whether such support exists. And an aspect of that support may not be only whether someone then expressed the "wise" view but also whether the holder of such a view was influential in adoption or understanding of the provision. Finally, for judges who do not have fully developed views about how a subject should be treated, they might find in writings like those of Madison an explanation that actually persuades them about what is the best conception. Thus, this "wisdom" approach still renders original understanding as genuinely relevant.

A summary of this section might be cast in the following way. A political authority basis to accord great significance to original intent fades over time, especially with a constitution that is designed to last, difficult to amend, and possessed of heavy symbolic significance.[109] The wisdom of the adopters may constitute a reason to follow their intent, but a conclusion about wisdom requires a nonoriginalist judgment about who was wise and about what subjects. Some focus on intent or original understanding may help provide a measure of continuity, but in many instances, continuity of constitutional decisions points away from a continuity that emphasizes original intent.

This analysis suggests that for the Establishment Clause, and other general formulations of restrictions on government adopted long ago, interpretations should give some weight, but not overwhelming weight, to original understanding, and the understanding that should mainly count is composed of the general principles of those who were influential *and* most fully grasped the underlying values involved.

IV. CONCLUSION

We have surveyed a range of questions about original understanding, attempting to develop an analysis that reveals how complex and debatable are many issues that are often treated by advocates as straightforward and one-sided. The fundamental positions offered here about the Bill of Rights and the Fourteenth Amendment are that original understandings matter but are not determinative, that the political authority and continuity reasons to follow original understanding diminish over time, and that what counts for basic provisions of the Bill of Rights are the abstract principles and wisdom of those who adopted them, not the precise applications then conceived by most enactors and readers. According to this approach, giving great weight to the understandings of Jefferson and Madison is warranted for the Establishment Clause, even if those reached beyond broadly shared conceptions at the time.

Chapter 4

Employing Multiple Standards

I. INTRODUCTION

Given the complexities about what constitutes original understanding and the reasons why reliance on it is inevitably limited in difficult constitutional cases, courts must also employ other interpretive standards, ones that in large part were themselves accepted at the founding. Examining major approaches, this chapter asks why, and how far, those standards make sense. The following chapter considers the possibility of an "objective" resolution of what criteria should be determinative, leaving for later chapters how these central issues bear on a range of major constitutional topics.

The multiple standards of interpretation, which reflect both actual and necessary judicial practice, vary in force for different constitutional provisions, and no single standard resolves all the problems raised by any provision.[1] Against the logical possibility that judges could line up standards in a neat lexical ordering, using an initial technique, such as the evident sense of the constitutional language, and turning to a second technique only if the first fails to resolve a case,[2] the reality is that more than one technique is often relevant at the same stage. Judges must then determine which criterion carries greater weight in a particular context. As Richard Fallon has developed, various kinds of arguments often support one another and can be fitted together in "constitutional coherence."[3] But when different grounds would yield conflicting outcomes, judges must determine which to follow. Fallon has suggested a hierarchy for such situations, although his account is far from rigid. For example, precedents rank only fourth but can still be extremely significant if the constitutional text and historical intent "prove indeterminable."[4] My own sense is that, as with statutory and common law interpretation,[5] the disparate force that arguments carry in varying contexts entails that we should not look for a consistent hierarchy. For example, lacking a clear priority between original meaning and the force of precedents when these conflict, Supreme Court Justices must decide which counts more in a particular dispute. However, it does not follow that claims about comparative weight are not accessible by reason. Many chapters of the book suggest why, in particular disputes, certain arguments do or do not have substantial force. Nevertheless, the interpretive criteria discussed here—precedents, modern textual understanding, canons of interpretation, accommodation to social change and independent value judgments, and deference—all play roles that are not reducible to a simple lineup.[6]

Although the standards this chapter treats differ from attempts to discern the original understanding about the substance of what a particular constitutional provision covered, each technique *might* be tied to an original sense of authorized interpretation, and it *might* be used only within a range of coverage limits set by the original understanding.

The idea of authorization is especially strong for open-ended provisions. A Justice might conclude that phrases such as "cruel and unusual punishment" explicitly encouraged judges to rely on the general principles the language reflects.[7] More broadly, the original understanding *could* be seen as embracing judicial respect for precedents and certain canons of interpretation, even if following these would diverge from specific applications perceived at the time of enactment. If a Justice who considered the relative novelty of a binding written constitution, the uncertainty about its endurance over time, and the difficulty of its amendment doubted that most enactors or informed readers had thought carefully about precise strategies of interpretation, or whether prevailing standards used for statutes should apply, she might pose a query about hypothetical intentions and understanding. She might ask: "If those enacting the constitution and its informed readers had, given their familiarity with the British judicial system, considered these matters with awareness of likely developments over time, what role would they have assumed for precedents and canons of interpretation?"[8]

A different function of original understanding could be to set limits on the use of other criteria of interpretation. A Justice might think she should not decide in a way that is definitely opposed to the original understanding about a provision's coverage.[9] Other bases of decision would then figure only in filling gaps or resolving instances in which the original sense is genuinely uncertain. A slightly different approach would be that one should only reach outcomes that *might* correspond with the original understanding, even if that could not be persuasively shown. The Justice could say to herself: "Because this result, supported by other powerful arguments, may possibly fit original understanding, I can reach it, although a slightly stronger originalist contention has been made for the contrary result."[10] In these various ways, original understanding could fulfill a special function, counting for more than one among a number of interpretive techniques.

Could someone believe that a particular approach to constitutional interpretation, however complex, is actually required by the Constitution itself?[11] That depends on what counts as "the Constitution." No original understanding, even if one puts aside variances among outlooks of the time, will yield an exact approach for judges in constitutional cases. Further, given massive social changes, one can hardly resist the conclusion that some shift in interpretive techniques over time was both highly probable and potentially healthy. If one conceives "the Constitution" not in some narrower sense but rather as including all of the interpretations judges now do, or should, employ, then the inquiry about what interpretive strategies it indicates becomes circular; whatever is deemed the best approach is attributed to the Constitution, not to some basic norm that reaches beyond the Constitution. That *could* include giving precedential force to whatever interpretive strategy is then dominant. Considering the infinite number of subtleties that concern how interpretation does and should take place, asserting that "the Constitution" *requires* the very best possible approach could be merely a way of saying that judges and others should aim to discern that approach. But to suggest that any judge fails in a clear duty whenever he does something different from the ideal approach would imply a misleadingly harsh judgment; by that standard, every Justice frequently "violates" the Constitution in one way or another. Whatever the extent to which the Constitution in some broad sense dictates appropriate strategies, it may certainly impose limits—not every conceivable approach is consistent with it. Whether one is referring to desirable standards or limits, one may well think that some potential strategies deviate only modestly from what is called for, whereas others are seriously flawed. For example, an originalist Justice might regard reliance on ordinary rather than well-informed readers as a relatively small mistake, whereas virtual disregard for original understanding would constitute a grave flaw. Those offering a critique of an approach to constitutional interpretation can explain how far they think it goes awry.

II. PRECEDENTS

The most straightforward nonoriginalist criteria judges use is precedent. Although they differ greatly over the degree of respect they owe them, every Supreme Court Justice believes that precedents count for something, even if they fail to conform with the original understanding about a provision's content. As with statutory and common law interpretation, precedents figure in two ways.[12] They are "controlling" when the facts of a prior case are indistinguishable from those the judges are considering *and* the stated rule of law of the earlier decision covers the new situation. Other precedents can persuasively point toward a conclusion without directly covering the case at hand. That force may be powerful, as illustrated by the unanimous opinion in *Brown v. Board of Education*.[13] Although the *Brown* opinion was limited to the status of racial segregation in education, the result and supporting reasons cast grave doubt on other forms of governmental racial segregation, many of which the Supreme Court subsequently struck down per curiam without even providing an explanation. On other occasions, precedents point only weakly in one direction or another.

As with precedents in other branches of law, neither the way to distinguish "binding" holdings from "nonbinding" dicta nor the importance of that distinction is simple. The three standard approaches to what counts as the holding of a case are: (1) the controlling rule of law stated by the deciding court, (2) the material facts as seen by the deciding court combined with the result it reaches, and (3) the prior case's material facts, with its result, as seen by the later court.[14] The third approach obviously gives judges more discretion to formulate the holding of a prior case in the manner they regard as wise; but in reality, all judges pay serious attention to how the precedent court saw the facts and stated its rule. The first two approaches differ from each other, but less than at first appears. The reason is that a clear sense of their stated rules helps reveal what judges have taken as material facts, and identifications of material facts shed light on a rule of law that is not precisely formulated. Deciding courts often do not limit themselves to one rule of law; rather, they state various rules that touch different aspects of the case or are cast at ascending levels of generality.

Apart from the complexities in discerning the holdings of particular cases, certain distinctions drawn between holdings and dicta are either inaccurate or difficult to draw in practice.[15] And when one considers Supreme Court precedents, the line is less significant than the simple categorization implies. The frequently stated notion that holdings, unlike dicta, involve whatever is "necessary to the decision" is inaccurate in two important respects. The first is when the prior decision rests on two separate rationales, neither of which is really required for the result; the second involves the force of the earlier court's interpretive techniques. If the Supreme Court determined that a penalty imposed for a cleric's inflammatory sermon violated both the Free Exercise Clause and the Free Speech Clause, those rationales would each be taken as aspects of the holding, although, given the two alternative bases, neither rationale itself would actually be "necessary" to the decision. By contrast, an interpretive strategy that a majority employs may well be *necessary* to a decision, given that a proposed alternative strategy could yield a contrary outcome, but Justices inclined to use different methods of interpretation do not regard the majority's interpretive technique as part of a holding that constrains how they should approach subsequent cases.

Were one to offer the circumscribed idea that at least in highly similar cases, judges should stick to the announced interpretive approach, the present answer is that those on the Supreme Court do not consider themselves bound to even this degree. This is patently clear when Justices continue to employ forms of interpretation that their colleagues consistently refuse to follow across the board. In principle, the Supreme Court could one day conceivably arrive at broad or narrow settled approaches to constitutional interpretation that members would properly regard as having precedential force not only for lower courts[16] but also for themselves.[17] However, given serious disagreements among the present Justices about how to interpret various constitutional provisions, the acceptance of some approach as like a binding precedent is highly unlikely in any foreseeable future.

For certain aspects of decisions and opinions, drawing the line between holding and dicta is very hard, and the distinction, both for lower courts and the Supreme Court itself, is less important than suggested by the standard formulation that holdings but not dicta bind the subsequent court.[18] With respect to the federal Constitution, Supreme Court decisions guide both federal and state courts. The Court accepts roughly eighty cases each year to decide, choosing which disputes to resolve, since it now has virtually no mandatory jurisdiction.[19] Justices often select disputes raising important issues that need to be settled.[20] Unlike most other judges, they almost always have an extended time to develop opinions with the help of law clerks. Partly because of compromises necessary to arrive at majority opinions, what they say about bases for decision and rules of law is not always clear, but the Justices recognize that what they announce about constitutional standards will be applied by other courts. If judges resolving common law cases often limit themselves to fairly narrow rules, that is not typically true for the Supreme Court. It often aims to provide guidance over a substantial domain, taking the opportunity to resolve troubling issues and frequently formulating rules that are broader than are necessary to resolve the cases before them. In *Miranda v. Arizona*, for example, rather than resting on the inadequacy of a particular warning, the Court laid down the exact form one should take.[21] Whether the *Miranda* rule is seen as holding or dictum, or something in between, its practical import was undeniable. The police were told what warning to give, and lower courts were aware that they could not allow confessions made absent that warning into evidence or they would be overturned by the Supreme Court. The *Miranda* warning had thus become part of the law of the Fifth Amendment.

Put generally, unless its comments are far removed from the subject of a case, what the Supreme Court states in a majority opinion as a constitutional rule will be taken as controlling by lower courts regardless of whether the Court's initial statement seems technically to be holding or dictum. Given the practical force of its announced rules, other judges and scholars talking about the Supreme Court's constitutional holdings are likely to focus on stated rules of law more than material facts.

What of the Supreme Court itself? Because the Court takes its own precedents as somewhat less constraining than courts usually regard their own statutory and common law precedents, the line between holding and dictum has less importance than for most courts addressing their own precedents.

When the Supreme Court faces precedents of its own that it now disfavors, it, like other courts, may distinguish or overrule them.[22] More than most courts, the Supreme Court probably needs to provide guidance about how far it means to abandon or maintain the coverage of its prior precedents; but sometimes, because of uncertainties or divisions among Justices, its opinions are less than clear on that score.[23]

III. MODERN TEXTUAL UNDERSTANDING

As prior chapters have explained, although "textualism" is commonly put forward as a Justice's or scholar's preferred form of originalism, what the text says to people here and now matters too. Indeed, if one focuses on the text providing guidance to citizens and officials about how they may behave, the way people presently understand the text matters far more than what someone grasped two centuries ago. And for modern people trying to understand constitutional provisions, distinguishing the text from what Supreme Court precedents have said about it is difficult. In contrast to most ordinary statutes, for which one could sensibly ask how readers would perceive texts if they were unaware of judicial decisions, the Court's resolutions about notable general constitutional provisions, such as the Free Speech Clause, heavily influence what people think the text entails. That reality generates one reason not to violate existing expectations based on prior decisions. It is true that when a decision is highly controversial, those objecting will resist the idea that the text entails what the Court resolved, yielding a sharp disagreement over "the text" between proponents and opponents of the decision. But such disagreements are unlikely to be mainly based on the explicit text itself. Although in some cases, Justices may worry that a result taken to strain the text beyond what is plausible could threaten the Supreme Court's legitimacy in the public's eyes, nonetheless, the greatest significance of a modern understanding of the text is its countering of any notion that original understanding should control completely.

IV. CANONS AND BROAD PRINCIPLES OF INTERPRETATION

Courts interpreting authoritative documents employ various "canons," general assumptions about how to understand statutory and constitutional language. These may be roughly divided into linguistic canons that concern the typical implications of language and substantive canons that concern how legal norms of various sorts should be treated. Among the linguistic canons is the premise that the inclusion of one thing is the exclusion of another[24]—"Dogs in this park must be on leashes from 9:00 a.m. to 7:00 p.m." means that we can let our dogs run free at other times. Another linguistic canon is that particular language should be read to have some effect, not merely to replicate what other language already provides. In a book primarily devoted to canons of interpretation, Justice Antonin Scalia and Bryan A. Garner divide what we may loosely call linguistic canons into ones that are semantic, syntactic, and contextual.[25]

Although these canons, subject to various exceptions and potentially outweighed even when applicable, are not typically the overriding bases of decisions, that does not mean that they are empty and without force.[26] They often point legitimately toward one reading or another, and they do carry some power. Constitutional analysis is subject to the same linguistic canons that apply to statutes. But, because constitutional language is generally more straightforward and more carefully drafted, these canons play less of a role in discerning its content.

Substantive canons, what Scalia and Garner call "Principles Applicable Specifically to Governmental Prescriptions,"[27] concern underlying premises for how provisions of statutes and constitutions should be understood. For example, the premise that federal statutes will not be assumed to apply abroad rests on a sense of our government's role in relation to other countries, not on general linguistic practices.

As far as terminology is concerned, the distinction between "canons" and other accepted principles for deciding cases is hardly clear. "Canons" are usually conceived of as possessing a general applicability; principles that apply to specific constitutional provisions, such as the standard that the government needs a compelling interest if it is to interfere with speech, are not commonly described as canons. Another distinction that can be drawn is between canons, which are concerned with fairly specific notions of language or substantive standards, and broader principles, such as the reality that "[n]o canon of interpretation is absolute."[28]

For judges interpreting the federal Constitution, we can identify certain accepted canons. The premise that standards of decision need to be comprehensible, turn on determinable facts, and be suitable for lower courts and government officials to administer applies to constitutional rulings as well as statutes. In this respect, a notable example of the force of the perceived need for an administrative standard is *Employment Division v. Smith*,[29] in which the Court rejected powerful free exercise arguments strongly supported by precedents and ruled that no free exercise right was available against general laws; its basis was that judges were ill equipped to weigh the strength of government interests against individual claims of rights when general legislation impaired the exercise of religion.

In addition to canons that directly relate to how constitutional provisions should be interpreted, various canons for statutory interpretation have a kind of constitutional basis, being grounded in values and structures that signify the appropriate roles of various government bodies.[30] Within this category are canons that federal laws should not be read to supplant state law unless that aim is clear, that statutes should be understood not to apply retroactively, and that penal statutes should be strictly construed. Identifying similar substantive canons for the Constitution itself that apply across the board is more difficult because the Supreme Court properly interprets various of its segments quite differently.

Notable suggestions scholars have made that the Constitution should be broadly interpreted from one general perspective or another might well be regarded as proposals for canons that should be adopted. Along these lines was John Hart Ely's widely discussed claim that the overall judicial perspective on the Constitution should be to protect fair political participation of disadvantaged minorities and to prevent majority discrimination against them.[31] This broad approach, for which Ely found support in the decisions of the Warren Court, would entail expansive constitutional interpretation of certain provisions restricting the political branches and very restrained interpretation in other respects. Had the modern Supreme Court been persuaded by Ely's approach, it would have found very few limits on Congress's power under the Commerce Clause and would have regarded the constitutionality of recent healthcare legislation as simple and straightforward.[32]

What we may regard as another proposal for a canon was Charles Black's suggestion that the Constitution should be taken as a whole, with each provision being interpreted in light of the implications of other provisions.[33] Insofar as Ely and Black found support for their proposals in existing constitutional decisions, they were offering canons or principles they took to be already largely implicit in the law, ones then guiding the Court even if not yet explicitly formulated.[34] What these exercises show more generally is that scholars, as well Justices, may discern not yet explicit canons from what the Court has been doing, or may recommend canons that set genuinely novel standards.

V. AVOIDANCE AND DEFERENCE

Among the approaches the Supreme Court and other courts take to certain interpretive issues are avoidance and deference. Avoidance occurs when, for one reason or another, a court simply will not resolve the underlying constitutional issue. When it defers, the court does actually answer the legal question posed, but in doing so gives substantial weight to the resolution made by another branch or branches of government, similar to the manner in which federal courts defer to statutory interpretations of administrative agencies concerning exercises of agency authority.[35]

We can identify at least five forms of avoidance. One of these is that a statute may be interpreted to avoid the need to decide a constitutional question.[36] Everyone agrees that between two equally persuasive understandings of a statutory text, courts should choose the one that conforms with the Constitution over the one that violates it. The strategy of avoidance comes into play when the more straightforward reading of the statute's text would present a constitutional issue, and the court chooses a different interpretation to avoid resolving that issue. Just how far courts should go in this direction is a matter of substantial disagreement.[37] One troublesome question is whether courts should disregard more obvious readings of statutes and dodge constructions that raise constitutional questions that the judges would resolve if avoidance was impossible. And, as we shall see in Chapter 8, disagreement can also arise over whether Justices should indicate that the more obvious reading would actually be unconstitutional, before turning to the reading they find more acceptable.

Four other forms of avoidance are these: a party may lack standing; the issue may not be ripe for determination; the determination of constitutionality may be assigned elsewhere; or the issue may be too sensitive or troublesome for the court to resolve. The following paragraphs sketch each of these briefly, leaving for Chapter 7 a further analysis of the last two categories, "political questions."

The Constitution gives the federal courts power to decide "cases" and "controversies."[38] This language has been taken to preclude advisory opinions. Thus federal courts, unlike some state courts, cannot respond to an inquiry from the legislature as to whether a proposed bill would be constitutional, and once laws are adopted, federal courts usually will not rule on their constitutionality before they are actually implemented.[39] Once that occurs, only those directly affected have standing to obtain judicial resolution of a legal issue. Outraged as I may be by what I feel is gross discrimination, unless I will suffer disadvantage, I do not have standing to sue. In regard both to standing and "ripeness," not all Supreme Court decisions rest clearly on what the Justices perceive as strict constitutional limits. Insofar as the Court uses prudential evaluation that reaches beyond perceived constitutional restrictions, Congress may extend standing to sue or authorize resolution at an earlier stage.[40]

For a few particular issues, the Supreme Court has determined that the Constitution itself assigns final determination to another political branch or that constitutional values preclude its involvement. These amount to "political questions," which the Court will not resolve. The logic may be either that any action by a "political" branch really comports with the Constitution or that this branch itself decisively determines the question of consistency. When it has declined to consider a constitutional challenge on the basis that the final decision lies with another branch, the Supreme Court has not always been clear whether it regards any choice by that branch as actually within its assigned constitutional power, or whether instead the Constitution confers on the other branch the determination of any such issue.[41] Two illustrations show the difference. (1) The executive branch decides which foreign governments to recognize; courts will not review these decisions, apparently taking any such choice as within the President's constitutional powers. (2) Congress makes the final decision as to whether a state has ratified a constitutional amendment.[42] Plainly, the Constitution does not actually authorize Congress to do whatever it wants; it could not legitimately count as a ratifier a state that has consistently voted negatively. Yet the courts will not review the resolution of Congress.

In the most difficult "political question" cases, the basis for judicial noninvolvement is more complicated than a straightforward conclusion that the Constitution assigns authority elsewhere. The Court may regard the facts needed to resolve an issue as too difficult to discern or too politically charged, or it may conclude that the Court's involvement could seriously embarrass another branch or interfere with the country's needed ability to deal with fellow nations. The range of "political questions" is an important and controversial issue regarding the separation of powers;[43] its present, uncertain scope is explored in Chapter 7.

When the Supreme Court *defers* in the sense I use here, it assigns a weight to what another branch has decided that goes beyond any intrinsic persuasiveness of that branch's reasons for its decision. Of course, the doctrine of precedent itself involves a kind of deference, but one that concerns lower courts following higher courts and courts respecting their own prior decisions. Here, the issue is judicial respect for the determinations of Congress, the executive, or state governments. (A similar question concerns how far one political branch should respect the decisions made by another.)

The most fundamental argument for deference is that the courts are really only secondary interpreters of the federal Constitution, which was mainly directed at Congress and the President and at state governments. James Thayer, in a famous essay that was once highly influential,[44] relied on this premise to infer that a court should declare Congressional legislation unconstitutional only if no reasonable defense could be made of the law.[45] Were such deference appropriate, it would follow that a member of Congress who voted against a proposed law because he thought it would be unconstitutional and who was then appointed to the Supreme Court might properly vote to uphold the same law in light of the deference he owed to Congress as a body.

We shall later examine this view in particular contexts, but it raises three general problems. The first concerns whether the original understanding of those adopting the Constitution, or of readers at the time, conceived the federal courts in this subsidiary role. A more practical problem is that if Congress does not think carefully about the constitutionality of a bill it adopts, the Supreme Court may end up sustaining a law that the Justices think is really not constitutionally permissible (though a reasonable argument can be made to the contrary) and that most legislators would have assessed similarly on reflection. Relying partly on more extensive discussions about constitutionality within early sessions of Congress, one might *hope* that if Congress possessed much more decisive authority about the status of its laws, it would exercise greater care about possible infringements of constitutional norms, but that development seems doubtful. The third problem concerns the variety of constitutional provisions and the inclinations and abilities of members of Congress. For claims that federal laws violate state authority, one might believe that since the citizens of the states elect its representatives,

Congress will fairly appraise state rights and interests.[46] But for provisions like those in the Bill of Rights, designed largely to protect individual rights—some exercised by members of unpopular minorities or dissenters—we should place less confidence in federal legislators who may pass unjust laws to satisfy popular will.

As Thayer does recognize, if federal courts should accord genuine deference to Congress, that should not extend to state legislatures.[47] The risk is that individual states, representing their own citizens, may impair the rights of citizens from other states. From the beginning, a clear function of the federal courts, with their jurisdiction in diversity cases, was to safeguard such rights, a role that would be difficult to fulfill if they gave generous deference to state legislatures on all kinds of issues.

Other bases for judicial deference can be the limited competence of judges to make necessary inquiries and the need for judges to respect and not offend other officials. Even when these factors are not strong enough for judges to totally avoid issues, they may lead them to undertake less than a wholly independent analysis of what other branches have done.

Appropriate degrees of deference, like many other interpretive strategies, definitely vary with respect to different provisions. Among the determinants are how far the legislature (or executive) can be trusted with respect to a subject, the extent to which judges are in a position to determine critical constitutional questions, how far courts can go to provide effective remedies, and the degree to which their involvement will not threaten the structure of our government. That the use of deference for interpretation may have much, little, or no force illustrates how the power of a particular interpretive technique can depend on the constitutional provision or issue before a court.

VI. RESPONDING TO SOCIAL CHANGES AND MAKING JUDGMENTS OF VALUE

The most controversial questions about constitutional interpretation involve how the Supreme Court should respond to changes in the nature of society and its values. Important aspects of these questions concern differences between provisions whose terminology is open-ended and those that are more specific, and how far Justices should be relying on their own judgments or those of experts or of the broader community. These issues sharply raise the role of courts in this particular liberal democracy. One perspective is that when a constitution that is very hard to amend endures over time, it must be brought up to date, treated as a "living constitution," and interpreted in an evolutionary way.[48] A competing view, explored in earlier chapters, is that unelected judges have no business overriding choices made by the representatives of the people who adopted the constitutional provisions. Yet a third perspective is that represented by James Thayer: except in extreme circumstances, courts should defer to other branches of government.

At least if the constitutional language is not at odds with the result, a novel application is most straightforward when new technology enables behavior, such as a novel horrible form of punishment, which was not conceived by people at the time of the Bill of Rights but clearly falls within the original connotation of "cruel and unusual punishment."[49] Whether electronic surveillance should be included within the Fourth Amendment's ban on unreasonable searches and seizures can also be seen as such an illustration, although using the language of "seizure" to cover simple acquisition of information is a bit awkward linguistically.

A less straightforward kind of change concerns the manner in which society is organized, as contrasted with simple technology. Such a change in the status of "militia" (once composed of able-bodied men not actually in military service) *could* easily have been perceived as critical to the coverage of the Second Amendment, as demonstrated by the discussion of *District of Columbia v. Heller* in Chapter 2. With respect to the Fourth Amendment, how far should the notion that arrests must be based on "probable cause," taken in ordinary circumstances to mean that criminal behavior comes close to being more probable than not, dictate when police on the street may "stop and frisk" suspicious individuals? Because cities have become much larger since the Bill of Rights was adopted, and tracking those who may commit crimes on public streets can be very difficult, the values underlying the Fourth Amendment may allow "stop and frisk" on the less demanding standard of "reasonable suspicion."[50] Although strong objections have been made about how police in many cities employ "stop and frisk," including assertions of racial discrimination and "profiling," the notion that traditional probable cause should not be required for all police stops is itself widely accepted.

When the primary changes are in values rather than external facts,[51] perceiving novel applications as fitting original understanding becomes more complicated. As explained in Chapter 3, one may conclude that the original provisions themselves authorized just such responses, but perhaps more important is the pragmatic reality that the constitutional order operates most effectively when the text is interpreted in light of the basic values of modern society. In this vein, one may see the Supreme Court's role partly as making decisions reflecting values that have developed over time. We have already looked at a number of changes in coverage that are easiest to explain in this way. An Equal Protection Clause, not originally conceived as barring discrimination against women or gay individuals, may now be interpreted to do so. The Establishment Clause should be regarded as barring the teaching of Protestant Christianity as true in public schools, although that was not widely thought unacceptable at the time of the drafting of the Bill of Rights or the Fourteenth Amendment.[52] Changes in perceptions of capital punishment also reveal shifts in value.[53] No one now believes that imposing death sentences for all the crimes that carried that possible penalty in 1791 is all right, and few object to the Supreme Court's rulings that death sentences may not be imposed for lesser crimes or on offenders under a certain age.[54]

In these various circumstances, the question arises whether Justices should make their own value judgments, rely on some set of community norms or expert opinions, or try to draw neutral implications from constitutional provisions and previous decisions. The next chapter argues that in many difficult cases, judges cannot plausibly rely wholly in some neutral way on legal materials. Clearly, a Justice should not decide based on a personal value, such as vegetarianism, that she knows is rejected by the vast majority of the population; but whether in hard cases she should, self-consciously, partly rely on her own convictions about what is just or desirable is debated.[55]

One aspect of cases not clearly resolved by existing legal materials is the likely consequence of alternative dispositions. Judges resolving hard, borderline issues often rely partly on estimates of the consequences of deciding one way or the other. The Supreme Court, 5–4, decided in the 2010 *Citizens United* case that free speech protects the rights of people and corporations to donate as much as they choose to organizations engaged in political advocacy, so long as organizations are independent of candidates running for office.[56] As a result, huge amounts of money were donated by some individuals and businesses to "independently" urge the election of Romney or Obama in 2012. Many, including myself, find this a truly distressing corruption of the electoral process. Let us suppose (almost certainly unrealistically) that a particular Justice would not have voted the way he did in *Citizens United* had he foreseen this outcome.[57] How should he have appraised that possibility? Community morality would not have provided the answer. If all experts agreed on what would occur, the Justice might have followed them, but if the "experts" disagreed or were uncertain, he would have needed to make his own judgment about whose estimations were most persuasive.

When we turn to judgments of value, including political morality, Justices undoubtedly *are* somewhat influenced by their own personal views. But whether that is healthy, and whether *self-conscious* reliance on those personal views is appropriate, are highly controversial matters. When community morality is divided or appears opposed to an underlying value of a constitutional provision, Justices must decide how far they should be guided by that morality. Insofar as they take community morality as a guide, they also need to determine what level is crucial—broad norms or specific applications. Neither task can be accomplished by a simple objective reference to the general population's moral views; both require some independent judgment. A thesis of this book is that Justices properly rely on some combination of broader views and their own appraisals when they face difficult judgments of value.

VII. INEVITABLE COMPLEXITIES AND VARIATIONS

A central purpose of this chapter is to demonstrate just how many variables go into an entire interpretive approach, how hard it is for anyone, judge or scholar, to formulate her own approach in more than vague terms, and why it is impossible to expect complete agreement across the board between even two Justices. Among the factors this and earlier chapters have suggested that judges must consider are the degree of deference to other branches; what elements they must consider in determining original meaning, and then conceived methods of interpretation; what level of generality to give primary importance; the comparative importance afforded to different original enactors and whether these should shift over time; the respect due to precedents and canons of interpretation; the relevance of shifts in social realities; and the ways to determine crucial questions of value. The place any Supreme Court Justice sensibly accords to these various factors depends partly on what constitutional provision(s) and particular issue(s) are involved. Given that with respect to these standards, the crucial question often is not either/or, or which comes first but involves matters of degree and comparative importance, it follows both that almost no one will be able to set out his own approach to interpretation in highly precise terms, and that no two judges are likely to follow exactly the same interpretive strategy, if that strategy is taken to include degrees of weight.

An overly simple illustration demonstrates this last point. Suppose, in contrast to a more complex reality, that two Justices could agree in a case that *only* original understanding and countervailing precedents count, and they are further coalesced on the kind of original understanding that matters and on what exactly is authoritative in the precedents. The original understanding points moderately in one direction and the precedents point moderately in the other. The two Justices are unlikely to have precisely the same view about exactly how strongly each factor supports the result it favors, or about how much weight to assign to the competing considerations. They *may* end up agreeing on the result, and one may join an opinion written by the other, but that does not mean their actual appraisals are identical. And such differences in degrees of weight to accord relevant factors can lead Justices sometimes to vote for opposite outcomes. The more complicated the relevant considerations become, the greater the likely divergences among particular Justices. Thus, even if we put aside the fact that opinions tend to marshal arguments for results, rather than candidly state the bases for decisions, the fullest possible articulation in a majority opinion could not realistically always capture the exact balance of considerations for any one Justice, much less for all joining members.

VII. "JUDICIAL ACTIVISM": WHAT IS IT AND IS IT ACCEPTABLE?

The various interpretive criteria judges use raises the question whether "judicial activism" is to be accepted or condemned. A crucial preliminary terminological concern is what constitutes "judicial activism." For some, the emotion-laden term evokes images of judges riding roughshod over the domains of political authorities and private citizens; for others, it connotes the needed protection of individuals against arbitrariness and abuse. Intelligent thought and discussion about concepts that provoke such passionate reactions is not easy. "Judicial activism" is so fraught with emotive overtones that those who attempt rational analysis may be best advised to steer clear of the term. But, whether or not the label is better avoided, so long as advocates of positions do refer to judicial activism, we need to understand its possible meanings. Doing so allows us to identify what divides those who disagree so strongly about judicial authority.

The opposite of being active is being "passive" or "restrained." For courts to be passive or restrained is to accept the judgments of others with political authority and to minimize their own power. No one advocates judges simply enforcing all their political wishes on the rest of society; no one claims judges should always accept what other public authorities decide. So the real problems come down to *how* active or restrained judges should be.[58]

In many cases, one can confidently say that a decision is more "activist" or "restrained" in a particular respect than a contrary decision would have been. The Court's ruling in *Brown v. Board of Education* was more activist vis-à-vis state legislatures than the alternative of accepting racial segregation, which then was dominant in the southern states. But whether the decision was, *simply put*, "activist" is more controversial. That depends on the implications of the Equal Protection Clause and prior cases. If *Brown* basically implemented what the Clause and prior cases explicitly or implicitly indicated, it was not activist with regard to the Constitution and precedents. Debates about whether particular decisions or opinions are unqualifiedly "activist" often obscure just whose judgment a "restrained" court would follow.

As the *Brown* case suggests, someone who says the Supreme Court is restrained or activist has in mind another political body or official whose power the Court either defers to or curbs. In most constitutional cases, at least three quite different comparisons are relevant. One is between the Court and either the political body that issues a challenged statute or regulation, or an official who performs an act such as an arrest that is claimed to be unconstitutional.[59] The second comparison is between the Court and what those who framed and adopted the constitutional provision had enacted. The third comparison is between the present Court and the established principles of its predecessors.

We can also identify at least four different though related respects in which judicial behavior may be considered activist. The first, the main subject of treatment here, involves the basic substantive decisions that courts reach. *Roe v. Wade*,[60] the case establishing a constitutional right to abortion, is strikingly activist in this sense. The Supreme Court then declared a right not envisioned by the Framers and original readers: it rendered invalid legislation existing in the vast majority of states, and it reached far beyond existing precedents. A different way in which a court may be activist is in the kinds of sources it brings to bear to reach a decision. If one thinks the real business of a court is to figure out what authoritative sources require—a subject addressed in the next chapter—a court is trespassing on the domains of legislators and the original Framers if it makes fresh evaluations of social desirability. Courts may also be activist in the breadth of their decisions. All agree that judges properly go beyond the narrow facts of a case and state a rule of law that covers like circumstances. What is controversial is the announcement of code-like standards to cover contingencies not really raised by the facts before them, as in *Miranda v. Arizona*,[61] in which the announced rules for police went well beyond what was needed to resolve the case. Yet another form of activism is when courts undertake systematic oversight of the performance of other branches of government—supervision over legislatures reapportioning, over school boards that have been directed to integrate, or over prison authorities who must improve prison conditions.

The discussion here concentrates on the United States Supreme Court and its employment of interpretive standards to reach substantive constitutional decisions that are arguably not for judges to make.[62] The easiest targets for critics are cases in which the Supreme Court overrides the conclusions of the political branches of government, departs radically from the holdings of earlier precedents, *and* stakes out principles of constitutional law not envisioned when provisions were adopted. *Roe v. Wade* and the *Miranda* decision were activist in all three respects. Another similar illustration is *Reynolds v. Sims*,[63] which established the "one person–one vote" approach of equal populations for election districts. The Court rendered invalid the composition of at least one house of virtually every state legislature. It did so in the absence of any precedents indicating that result, and it did so despite convincing evidence that the Framers did not consider malapportionment, at least in its ordinary manifestations, to violate the Equal Protection Clause of the Fourteenth Amendment.[64]

Debates over judicial activism can suffer from the misleading assumption that all assessments of activism and restraint are as simple as these three cases suggest. A further misleading assumption in much of our modern period is that the activist position is intrinsically linked with political liberalism, whereas restraint is the doctrine of conservatives.

When we think carefully about this second assumption, we recognize that earlier in the twentieth century, judicial activism was the instrument of political conservatives, who sought to protect private property and freedom of contract, and was the bane of liberals. A present antidote to any easy linkage of activism and political liberalism involves cases challenging preferences for racial groups previously discriminated against. Those with political authority, broadly including public universities, have established these preferences. The Framers of the Fourteenth Amendment, who themselves adopted the Freedmen's Bureau legislation and other measures designed to aid ex-slaves, did not object in principle to statutes providing special benefits for blacks. If it is "liberal" to be for such racial preferences, the liberal position in those cases shows greater deference both to other political authority and to original understanding than does the view that these racial preferences are constitutionally invalid.[65]

The complexity of varieties of activism and restraint is sharply raised by how one should characterize the position of someone like Justice Scalia, who believes that the Court should generally be faithful to the original text and understanding without giving great deference to the judgments of other branches of government or to precedents. In theory, at least, that position is activist vis-à-vis the decisions of modern political authorities and prior courts, but it is extremely deferential to the original understanding. To the contrary is the Thayer position that courts should overturn the decisions of political branches only in instances of the most patent and egregious violations of constitutional norms—a position that purchases deference to political authorities at the price of activism with respect to the original intent about substantive coverage. Some Justices, such as John Marshall Harlan, were relevantly constrained in regard to all three standards of evaluation,[66] but they, of course, had to face some situations in which restraint in one respect would be activism in another, as when precedents had departed from original understanding about the coverage of particular positions.

We are now ready to go to the heart of claims about why judicial activism is misguided. If the criticism of activist judges is more than rhetoric to challenge individual decisions that the critics happen not to like, it must rest on the claim that activist judges (1) are not faithful to the constitutional scheme in which they hold responsible and prestigious positions, and/or (2) undermine democracy, not only by producing undesirable individual results but also by sapping the vitality of majoritarian political processes.[67] These two basic claims against activism sound compatible, and indeed they often are; but a crucial difference exists between them.

The claim about faithfulness to the constitutional scheme relates closely to the notion of promises to perform their roles, made explicitly or implicitly, by officials to those who place them in power and to citizens generally. If the basis for defining judges' roles is the original constitutional scheme, as altered by formal amendments, then faithfulness to original understanding is central. This approach raises all the debated questions about what kind of polity it was understood that the adopters of the Constitution had established, how constitutional development was then conceived, and whether individual rights guarantees were taken to be strong bulwarks against dominant political forces. If individual rights were so understood, judicial activism vis-à-vis the political branches is warranted in connection with them. And, of course, if standards like "cruel and unusual punishment" were conceived to apply flexibly when the Bill of Rights or the Fourteenth Amendment, or both, were adopted, judges can be faithful to the original vision even when they establish specific rights not then conceived.

A different standard for conceiving the constitutional structure in which judges have sworn to play their part involves, as earlier analysis suggests, a more modern understanding of the nature of the Constitution and judicial roles. That guide for what judges should do is no clearer than the understanding at the time of adoption. Strands of activism and restraint are interwoven in our constitutional history; and powerful divisions exist in the present legal culture about the appropriate limits of judicial action with respect to many subjects. In any event, the important point here is that someone who asserts that for judges to be faithful to their role they must defer to the political branches, or rely on some version of original or modern understanding, must themselves present a persuasive account of values relevant for our liberal democracy.

The claim about activism undermining democracy, in contrast to that about an understood judicial role, is essentially a functional argument about fulfilling a central set of values. It asserts that judicial activity of the sort criticized will lead to bad consequences. Unfortunately, agreement on what consequences are worse than others is unlikely. When critics of activism point to the dangers of elites interfering with democratic decisions or departing from original understanding, their objection calls for an overall evaluation of the benefits and harms, including effects on political processes, of various degrees of judicial activity.

All judges, consciously or subconsciously, must work out for themselves some philosophy about the importance of fulfilling a role already defined, as compared with performing that role in a just and socially beneficial way. They must also, at least to some degree, assess how that role has actually been defined and what kind of performance will produce desirable consequences. These are the deeper questions about judicial roles that lie beneath the surface debate about activism.

Political opponents of the Supreme Court's most sensitive decisions have sometimes proposed both constitutional amendments and withdrawals of jurisdiction over particular kinds of issues. The failure of the overwhelming majority of such attacks perhaps provides some reassurance about the unlikelihood that political criticism of judicial practice will be converted into genuine legal restraint. But the troubling questions about how courts should behave that are raised by attacks on "judicial activism" will remain, as they must be, never fully resolved.

CONCLUSION

In its exploration of the variety of standards of interpretation used in difficult constitutional cases, this chapter has shown the actual complexity of many of those standards, the force of competing arguments for and against their use, and how these vary significantly depending on the kind of controversy involved. All these illustrate the book's fundamental theme that wise constitutional adjudication is not reducible to any simple formula that works across the board.

In the chapter that follows, we shall examine how far an aspiration for "neutrality" or "objectivity" is achievable for Justices and other judges who must determine difficult constitutional issues by taking account of a range of considerations.

Chapter 5

Neutral Principles or "Objective" Standards

Their Relevance and Attainability

I. INTRODUCTION

A central lesson of prior chapters is that no genuine strategy of constitutional interpretation is actually simple. Insofar as originalism in some form is portrayed as such, we witness either delusion or self-conscious deception. No Supreme Court Justice or thoughtful scholar really adheres to a single strategy. All agree that original understanding is relevant, and that precedents forming a law that has developed over generations should not be totally disregarded if they fit uncomfortably with an uncertain appraisal of original meaning. We are left with multiple criteria, though exactly how each figures is sharply disputed. Given that starting point, could someone believe in "neutral principles" or "objective standards" that might settle controversies about what are proper outcomes for cases? That is the subject of this chapter.

We need first to get a hold on the relevant meaning of "neutral" or "objective." Debate about "neutral principles" was largely generated by an influential lecture by Herbert Wechsler that criticized the Warren Court for not adhering to those principles in various cases, most notably the 1954 case, *Brown v. Board of Education*.[1] This critique generated vigorous responses. None of these actually contended that the Court had consistently complied with Wechsler's sense of neutral principles. Critics primarily argued that deciding cases on neutral principles was an unrealistic and undesirable aspiration.[2] Those who did accept "neutral principles" typically developed a concept that differed from Wechsler's.[3]

In the succeeding half century, the term "neutral principles" has faded in significance, but controversy remains over the extent to which judges can be "objective," in the sense of rendering judgments that do not depend on their personal outlooks. Although whether decisions can be "objective" constitutes a fundamental question about all forms of legal interpretation, it takes on special importance for many questions of constitutional law, especially those that reach the Supreme Court. Determinations of these issues are often less straightforward than those involving statutes; the relevant authoritative language is less determinate, and competing positions relate closely to opposing views about what is socially just and desirable, subjects on which Supreme Court Justices, like the rest of us, have strong convictions. The public perception that Justices are not being "objective" arises frequently with vital issues, such as the constitutional status of school prayers, abortion, gun control, and mandatory health insurance. That perception spreads and becomes more intense when, as recently, publicized divisions among Justices consistently reflect liberal and conservative political opinions. These "political outcomes" are all the more troubling because no legislature can "correct" them.

This chapter analyzes various ways judges, both in their actual bases for decisions and in their announced standards, could aspire to comply with objective standards or neutral principles. The degree to which such standards are attainable is central, but it is not the end of the normative inquiry. One might believe that an approach to constitutional issues that judges could actually manage would itself be undesirable or outweighed with some frequency by other considerations. And an approach judges cannot really achieve might nonetheless be worth aiming for. An illustration of this latter point would be a moral standard that each of us should give our own interests the same weight as the interests of others; incapable as we are of such assessments, perhaps we should still try.[4] My overall view is that complete reliance on neutral principles is not always possible, and that on occasion answers they provide may be outweighed by other considerations, but judges should generally seek to be guided by them. The following analysis does not treat as central what any particular Justice or scholar has claimed. But it does pay attention to Herbert Wechsler's distinctive thesis, partly because of my interest in this topic, which developed when I was a student of his powerful teaching, and partly because Wechsler is commonly mistaken to have asserted more than he actually did.

II. KINDS OF PRINCIPLES OF CONSTITUTIONAL DECISIONS

"Principles of decision" concern standards of judgment that reach beyond the facts and outcome of a particular situation. Thus, a person who is unsure whether she should stay home from work because she is seriously ill might reason that if friends with a similar ailment asked for her advice, she would definitely conclude that they should not risk their long-term health by going to work. This could give her a basic standard to apply to her own situation. References to such "principles" within the law can include (1) the specific rule used to resolve a case, (2) the interpretive standards supporting the court's approach, and (3) the underlying reasons for employing those standards. When one inquires what principles underlie a particular decision, one can focus on reasons the judges actually announced, reasons they probably relied upon but did not articulate, or different reasons that *could* support the result. Thus, for *Brown v. Board of Education*,[5] we can ask whether the Justices announced neutral principles, likely relied on such principles but did not state them in their opinion, or reached a result that others could defend by neutral principles, even if these differed from the bases the Justices themselves followed.

A central question about appropriate principles at the various three levels—specific rule, interpretive approach, and underlying bases of interpretation—is what breadth of coverage judges and scholars should conceive as needed. A quite separate issue is whether judges should definitely follow stated principles in subsequent cases.

Professor Wechsler's basic critique was that the Justices often failed to provide neutral principles; rather they failed to announce principles they would be willing to apply in all of the decisions they reached. When the Court employed summary judgments to reach outcomes that were less than obvious, they had failed to announce any principles at all.[6] In other cases, Justices had relied on reasons to which they would not usually accord a similar weight; in Wechsler's view, the focus in *Brown* on contested evidence about the psychological effects of school segregation on Negro students was of this nature.[7] In *Shelley v. Kraemer*,[8] which struck down the state enforcement of a private covenant to discriminate against blacks in the sale of property, the principle offered by the Court seemed obviously too broad, since it would bar state courts from carrying out the discriminatory terms of wills.

An aspect of Wechsler's thesis was that judges should provide principles that apply to circumstances beyond the particular facts before them, standards neither so narrow that they cover little else nor so vague that they are wholly indeterminate about other situations. Such principles help assure observers that judges are not reaching discrete outcomes just because they happen to favor them.

At its most minimal, Wechsler's approach is an obvious aspect of typical judicial exercises, especially when courts interpret statutes and the Constitution, rather than dealing with the common law. If the Supreme Court determines that it is cruel and unusual punishment to impose the death penalty on a minor, we assume that the Justices believe that no minor should receive that sentence. Although the Justices might later be persuaded to alter the rule, they think when they announce it that a general "neutral" application would be sound. In contrast to some common law cases,[9] judges rarely, if ever, properly decide a constitutional dispute on the basis of analogy without formulating any general rule. More common are standards that employ multiple factors, with a decision in one case providing very limited guidance about how non-identical cases will be treated.[10] An actual historical example was the Supreme Court's resolution that, based on a combination of connections of a privately owned restaurant to the government—including location in a public parking facility, space maintenance partly paid for by the city of Wilmington, and the reality that the restaurant served the public objectives of the parking lot—the restaurant's racial discrimination was attributable to the state.[11]

When judges and others rely in this way on multiple factors to reach a conclusion, estimating just how they will treat the absence of some of those or the presence of novel factors can be extremely difficult.

To say that principles in legal cases should have some generality with a range of clear applications does not itself determine how broad the generalities need to be and how much is properly left for resolution in subsequent cases. For virtually any stated principle, borderline cases or unforeseen situations may arise that will neither be clearly covered nor uncovered. If Justices state that racial classifications which disadvantage minority groups are unconstitutional, does their principle cover use of racial quotas in public housing that favor individual whites seeking apartments but are designed to promote overall integration? No simple application of the stated principle resolves that problem. And what should be done if temporary segregation in a prison is necessary to prevent racially motivated violence among prisoners? We cannot expect judges in an initial case of racial classification to resolve every related situation.

Whether asking a broad question or concentrating on a particular problem, judges and others may reasonably disagree about just how general and precise principles should be. Is "clear and present danger" an appropriate test in free speech cases if it plainly indicates that most speech is protected, that some is not, and that in close cases, multiple factors may come into play? Even when the constitutional provision is deemed open-ended, such as the bans on "unreasonable searches" and "excessive fines," perhaps courts should fashion from these more specific standards of judgment for actual controversies.

The inevitable reality that the projected coverage of a stated principle will not always be clear relates closely to another necessary limitation of any plausible thesis about "neutral principles." Even when a court states a rule that clearly covers certain situations, and the judges conceive the rule as properly applying to those situations, that does not preclude the court from subsequently altering or even abandoning the rule. When a new case comes before them, judges may be persuaded that situations covered by precedent's rule are actually different enough from the facts previously before them to warrant a contrary result. Or, the judges may even discern powerful reasons that should lead them now to abandon their earlier rule for all circumstances. These are issues about the force of precedents. Of course, if a court deviates from a stated rule too quickly and too easily, critics may guess that the judges did not really ever believe that the principle they first asserted was controlling. The discussion here is not fundamentally about when stated rules are properly altered in later cases. Rather, the concern is whether these rules, and the reasoning that supports them, are plausible principles accepted by the deciding judges in the first place.

One critique of an emphasis on applicable principles is that, as Mark Tushnet once put it: "New cases always present issues different from those settled by prior cases."[12] An assessment of this critique needs to distinguish among all new situations, new litigated claims, and new claims that reach the Supreme Court. If the principle of "no death penalty for minors" is so clear that no prosecutor ever seeks the penalty, then no subsequent "cases" involving that issue will arise; but that hardly demonstrates that the Court has failed to state a general principle that it believes should apply to situations covered by the principle. Similarly, the resolution of some issues by lower courts can be so straightforward given stated rules that they will never reach the Supreme Court. Even when litigators present a novel claim that is striking enough to lead the Supreme Court itself to consider revision of its announced rule, it does not follow that the initial rule was meaningless or unprincipled.

When considering how far we can rightly expect viable general principles from the actual opinions of the Supreme Court, we must take into account realities about candor, compromise, and the representativeness of opinions. In extremely controversial cases, questions concerning the proper degree of candor in Justices' opinions carry heightened significance. At the time *Brown* was decided, southern states with segregated schools also banned interracial marriages. Had *Brown* made it crystal clear that those laws were unconstitutional, the result would have generated even more controversy, conflict, and disruption than the huge amount it actually produced. Especially given the relatively few people directly affected by the marriage ban[13]—compared with the number of children in segregated schools—that concern *may* have led Justices to choose a narrower rationale tied to schools, even if they actually accepted a basic principle that would have precluded miscegenation laws.

Related to degrees of candor are the realities of compromise and the difficulty of accurately representing the views of judges joining majority opinions. In the United States, and especially in courts whose rulings guide lower court judges, garnering enough votes for a majority opinion is an important objective.[14] Attaining those votes can require papering over different senses of precise guiding principles,[15] thus failing to represent wholly those on which each member in the majority relied. Such opinions may even fail to articulate any fully defensible principle of decision. Judges and scholars disagree about just how far judges should accede to considerations favoring majority opinions by failing to announce defensible principles in which they actually believe, but we know that this happens with some frequency.

If we put aside these complications about candor and compromise in opinions, are neutral principles attainable? For the relatively narrow stated governing principle for a decision, the basic answer is "yes," with the minor qualification that it may not resolve borderline or unforeseen situations. The problem of basic attainability is much more severe when one turns from specific rules of decision to employed standards of interpretation and to the basic reasons underlying why those standards are employed. Mentioning the constitutional text, history, and precedent, Wechsler suggested that their "relative compulsion" should be judged, so far as possible, by neutral principles.[16] The idea that judges rely on neutral principles at every stage of the interpretive process would entail that when they decide a case on the ground that direct precedents should control unless blatantly at odds with original intent, they regard this interpretive strategy as applying to other kinds of cases. Of course, that would not preclude a judge from explaining why various criteria of interpretation carry different weight with respect to dissimilar constitutional provisions. And, as with specific rules of decision, announcement does not bar judges from reconsideration in light of new arguments or unforeseen circumstances. Nevertheless, general formulations of interpretative standards would typically reflect broad experience with cases in a range of areas of constitutional law. In this sense, interpretive principles on which judges actually rely in particular cases can be "neutral" standards they have used and plan to continue using in multiple constitutional contexts.

Unfortunately, the idea that principles should be neutral for every step of the decision-making fails to recognize how much more difficult this is for governing criteria of interpretation and for the reasons that underlie them than it is for particular stated rules. In fact, as earlier chapters reflect, at these levels, nothing like full achievement in linguistic articulation is feasible.

For interpretive criteria, three fundamental difficulties arise. The first involves how multiple criteria figure in situations in which no clear ordering works. No genuine, rigorous ordering is possible in constitutional interpretation, where history and precedents play such significant roles, along with the constitutional text and how it was originally understood. Without a definitive ordering, a judge determining the weight of two divergent factors in a particular instance must consider both the intrinsic importance of each *and* how strongly it supports a particular outcome.[17] If a judge believes textual language is usually more important than precedent but a text points only weakly in one direction and precedents decisively dictate the opposite result, the judge will follow the precedents.

For legal decisions as well as other contexts of choice, people are unable to formulate in any precise way degrees of intrinsic importance and respective weights. Few of us even have a carefully developed sense of each, as opposed to how importance and weight strike us as coming together in particular instances. Beyond the difficulty of attaining clear approaches in our actual perception, natural language does not allow us to achieve a precise expression of how exactly to make such calculations. Moreover, judges and others often find it hard to assess just how the balance will look in new situations. These difficulties are at least as great, if not greater, if one asks what are the exact reasons a judge should employ possible interpretive standards and what weight should be afforded each of these broader reasons. Unless one is insupportably simplistic, these reasons are bound to be rather vague and imprecise.

Actual majority opinions face two added obstacles. First, no two judges will perceive the balance of inherent importance and weight, and the underlying reasons for that balance, in exactly the same way. An opinion for five Justices cannot capture with precision the assessments of each. Second, the simple reality is that judicial opinions consistently overstate the perceived reasons for a result and understate opposing reasons.[18] Such opinions inevitably fail to reveal the exact degrees of importance and weight that judges have actually attributed to relevant factors. So long as judges follow this strategy of overstatement, they cannot accurately portray how strongly, and why, various underlying interpretive criteria will guide them in a broad range of cases.

The obstacle of limited candor is subject to the caveat that perhaps Justices *should* be more candid about the balance of considerations—an option discussed below. We must also recognize that impossibility of attainment need not entail that judges should not try. In explaining a personal decision that adversely affects someone you care for, you may try to sketch the relevant factors leading to the decision and how strongly they affected you, recognizing and acknowledging that although this is the best you can do, it is hardly precise. Judges can do something similar with considerations of legal relevance. Aiming to develop principles of decision—including interpretive criteria and their underlying reasons that reach other potential situations—is worth doing, even if full attainment is recognized to be impossible.

III. STANDARDS FOR ARRIVING AT FUNDAMENTAL PRINCIPLES

In regard to whether judges can rely on some "objective" standard to arrive at the fundamental interpretive approaches they use to decide particular cases and announce specific rules, we can quickly put aside two senses of neutrality that might conceivably apply to constitutional interpretation. First, such interpretation can proceed without choices of values,[19] and second, principles of decision cannot favor particular groups over others.[20] Many constitutional contests require resolutions between competing values. Whether the First Amendment protects various forms of "hate speech" involves a determination of how far the value of free expression trumps concerns about equality and psychological upset. The protection afforded hate speech in the United States is greater than in other liberal democracies largely because the Supreme Court has interpreted the First Amendment to afford a high priority to expression. Decisions about what counts as an "unreasonable search" often involve a conflict between the values of personal privacy and discerning possible unlawful actions by those whose privacy is compromised. Other constitutional provisions, on their face or as best interpreted, may favor some kinds of groups over others. The provision in the original Constitution that no state shall impair the obligation of contracts favors those who will benefit from the enforcement of contracts over those whose economic hardship makes it hard to comply. And the post-Civil War amendments may fairly be seen as aiming at equality for blacks, a conclusion that might lead a Justice to allow at least some racial categorizations involved in affirmative action.[21]

That principles of decision may involve judgments about conflicts of values and may favor certain kinds of groups does not tell us whether judges can derive these principles in some objective way and how far they should try to do so. What follows disregards judicial overstatements of supporting reasons and the inability of majority opinions to fully reflect how each judge determines her interpretive criteria; it asks instead how far an individual Supreme Court Justice can rely on objective criteria and whether she should attempt to do so for conceptualization and evaluation, as well as complex empirical estimates. Because the whole concept of "objectivity" or "neutrality" is far from simple, the treatment here first explores fundamental possibilities and then highlights the practical aspects of the debate over such standards for judges.[22] That debate largely comes down to how far judges are, and should be, constrained by factors outside themselves, ones that can be similarly evaluated by other judges.

A. Moral and Political Judgments

Before turning to judgments underlying legal decisions and rules, it helps to begin with judgments about what is morally required or morally desirable (though not required).[23] This discussion not only serves as an introduction to questions of legal judgment; it also directly concerns moral judgments that are intertwined with legal decisions and rules.

Philosophers disagree over whether moral norms are objective or subjective. They *could* be "objective" in the sense of established by an omnipotent God, even if accessible to humans only through faith. But the objectivity that matters for judges in a liberal democracy is whether human beings can arrive at correct moral norms by a process of reason. If moral outlooks develop only through personal experiences, those experiences vary radically, and reason is incapable of discerning which outlooks are really best, it follows that some moral norms that people hold and the judgments these yield will not be "neutral" or "objective" in the sense that counts.

What can a philosopher mean if he claims that objective reason can discover standards for what is *morally* required and desirable? He might think that ordinary humans who think carefully about a moral problem will reach the same conclusion, or that those who are able to set aside certain prejudicial attitudes will be able to do so, or that only a person with some ideal ability to reason would reliably reach the right conclusion. The last version does not suppose that actual human beings are consistently capable of discovering the right moral approaches by use of their reason. On this view, a person seeking objective truth may be doing the best he can to reason toward that, but realistically, he must acknowledge that his own reason, like that of all others, departs from the ideal and is flawed, and that other people, as able as he, and reasoning as best they can, will not infrequently reach different conclusions.

Does the intermediate version—that reason will provide answers if used conscientiously and with prejudices set aside—make a claim of greater practical relevance? That depends. If people cannot do fairly well to detach themselves from prejudices (or avoid prejudices), the intermediate version departs little from the claim that only ideal reason can discover moral truth. However, the "set aside" approach carries practical importance if people find that their prejudices are not too complex and difficult to identify and that they are capable of discounting their prejudicial inclinations.

The strongest version, a claim about actual humans reasoning, does urge that real people can reason their way to correct moral conclusions. This ability might be ascribed to ordinary people or only to the wisest among us. Someone who believes that real people can arrive by reason at correct conclusions may well acknowledge that certain of these conclusions can shift over time, as the nature of human society changes. For example, how the economy is organized could affect whether one who loans money does anything wrong by charging interest. But, within a historical context, people can reason their way to correct moral judgments. A claim about what reason can tell us may well include giving weight to the conclusions of others who have carefully considered problems. Much natural law argument is illustrative, resting on the premise that actual human beings, open to the insights of others, can reach moral conclusions about life on the basis of reason.[24]

Someone who is skeptical about how far reason can discern a proper morality for human beings in general might nevertheless believe that this is possible within a particular society. On this view, an important component of how one reasons to conclusions would be to determine what basic values are assumed and accepted within that society.

Whatever the breadth of one's inquiry, the relation of reason to moral judgment can better be seen as more-or-less, rather than either/or. Our reason does tell us that certain moral conclusions are objectively true for every human society. You should not intentionally kill an acquaintance simply because he has caused you minor irritation, or because your life would be slightly more pleasant if he were not around. And if you and your spouse live in a society with nuclear families, you have a responsibility for the welfare of children of yours that you have not put up for adoption. Rejecting these moral conclusions defies reason. But many moral judgments, whether offered universally or for a particular culture, are more debatable and harder to establish by reason alone. How much should a person leave in her will to her children and how much to charity? Even if many outcomes here would not be *immoral*,[25] some of these may be morally preferable to others. Intellectual reasoning about what we owe to the neediest, as opposed to what we owe to those closest to us, will not tell us just what outcome is morally best. Even when giving due respect to what has persuaded others, our reason alone fails to resolve many moral questions—often those involving the hardest moral choices. Perhaps, as I happen to believe, a full understanding of the nature of the universe and the place of human beings in it would reveal an objectively correct answer for each moral choice.[26] But for our purposes here, when the necessary understanding is beyond actual human capacity, the answers to troubling moral choices do not relevantly count as "objective" or "neutral." Rather, how people make these choices will inevitably rest not only on the force of objective reasons but also partly on subjective responses that include personal life experiences, which themselves differ in significant ways.

These conclusions about moral questions apply to the subset that constitutes issues of political morality. With respect to both particular issues about government involvement and more fundamental premises of political philosophy, some conclusions are objectively true. Does society need to restrain those who go about killing freely? Yes. Within a liberal democracy, does the government need to respect all citizens and treat them equally in some sense? Yes. But these answers do not tell us if the death penalty is *ever* desirable, or exactly how people should be treated equally, or how far equality should give way to other values. Despite the prevalence of reasoned arguments about both particular political outcomes and basic premises, reason alone cannot completely resolve all of these issues. Thus, when they focus on the place of law in human society and what particular laws are needed, even people who aspire to rely on basic premises that are shared within their political order[27] are bound to make certain judgments about debatable questions partly on "subjective" bases that cannot be resolved by ordinary, shared reason. The same will be true for judges, as well as others, if and when their determinations come down to reflective moral judgments about exactly what outcomes and political structures are best.

This conclusion does not by itself tell us how far people in general and judges in particular should *try* to rely exclusively on reason when they face moral and political questions. One could believe that society will be most fair and just if everyone tries to submerge personal outlooks in reason, and that when people do this, they may come closer to what ideal reason would suggest than if they self-consciously use any alternative method of decision, such as their basic intuitions.

B. Legal Judgments

The preceding discussion bears directly on the possibility of judges making objective decisions if they must, at least sometimes, rely on judgments about moral and political issues. An initial question is whether they should see themselves as guided by objective constraints that do not call for personal assessments of what is actually intrinsically most sound. Or do they sometimes properly rely on their own evaluations of morally just and politically desirable outcomes? In answer to claims of objective constraints that preclude such personal assessments, skeptics counter that reliance on personal judgments about these matters will inevitably occur and (or) that sometimes judges lack other sound bases in interpersonal reason to make more objective decisions. The serious controversy about judges is whether they do, and should, aim for bases of decision that are "objective" in a way that never rests on their best efforts at individual moral and political appraisals.

Three possibilities of such "objective" judgments that could underlie judicial decisions are worth examining. If the critical issue comes down to a question of fact, the answer seems more obviously objective than are many judgments of value. In modern democratic societies, we assume that for public resolution, the way to approach straightforward factual questions is by the use of reason.[28] One attraction of originalism, at least once the version of original understanding that counts is spelled out, is that it appears to pose an issue of fact: What did the adopters or the citizens of the time understand a constitutional provision to do?

A second possibility is a variation on the first. If judges must sometimes ultimately rest on judgments about moral or political desirability, perhaps they should rely on the community's judgments about these, either as a matter of principle or because doing so will help maintain public confidence in courts. That approach may appear to convert moral or political judgments into factual inquiries about what others believe.

The third possibility for objective decision-making is deriving conclusions from already-made authoritative value judgments. For example, whatever you personally may think is the relevance of the conception of embryos, suppose someone asks you: "For a society in which it is settled that human life that deserves protection begins at conception, does a pill that prevents a conceived embryo from attaching to the uterus do a wrong that does not occur when a pill prevents conception?" You can answer "yes." The bulk of legal reasoning is of this sort. Various legally established premises shared by judges are employed by reason to reach specific determinations of controversies.

In many instances, reasoning from precedents resembles that based on factual determinations about original understanding. Does the sense of the precedent's language reach the situation before us?[29] Even when reasoning from precedents goes beyond observing what language means in an ordinary sense, and a later court draws from values represented by earlier precedents, one could still regard this effort as largely factual,[30] discerning the broader implications of the prior decisions and the language judges had used to defend them.

Unfortunately, each of these possible bases of objective judgment involves complexities that undercut how far judges can rely on them without making independent judgments of value. For many "factual" questions involved in the context of legal interpretation, answers do not depend completely on simple estimates of whether particular events or states of mind occurred.[31] As Chapter 3 illustrates, an account of "original understanding" requires initial nonfactual judgment about what counts as the relevant original understanding(s)[32] and whether this changes over time. Judges interpreting the Constitution's original provisions must discern intents or understandings held more than 200 years ago by persons very different from ourselves. Beliefs and opinions at any particular time are interwoven with existing social facts, and any modern reconstruction is affected to some degree by our own convictions and interests.[33] The endeavor is made yet more difficult by the fact that in 1789, different individuals undoubtedly had different understandings of what particular constitutional language required or forbade.[34] Judges able to discern different understandings then face the question whether these all count equally or those of key figures count more, which is not an empirical question. This judgment requires an evaluation that the law fails to provide in any simple form.

One aspect of this evaluation is what judges should do about hypothetical intents. Given the vast changes in technology, social life, and social values, judges must sometimes ask: "What understandings would the founding generation have had if they had foreseen these circumstances?" Even if one regarded this question in principle as purely factual about what people would have concluded had they foreseen what has occurred within society, any judge will find it virtually impossible to think in those terms without interjecting her own sense of how closely the present situation resembles those her forebears had in mind. And judges also face the nonempirical question of how far to imagine the person of centuries ago having actually adapted over time to the new elements of our society. Both because of nonfactual elements and the extreme difficulty of key empirical questions, judges, as Chapter 2 illustrates about the Second Amendment, will commonly be unable to determine "original understanding" about serious contested issues in any straightforward, factual way. Of course, it may still be true that judges should try as hard as they can to rely exclusively on reason when they are making whatever judgments do come down to factual estimates.

Discernments of community morality raise similar problems. What exactly counts and for how much when people have different opinions? Do strong views count more than weak ones, careful views more than those formed thoughtlessly, the views of those directly involved in issues more than those of others, the views of leaders more than followers? Empirical inquiries do not answer these questions when community morality is unclear or divided. And even if a judge somehow resolves whose opinions count and for how much, she will sometimes find it hard to discern what exactly is the dominant view on a subtle question not covered by simple opinion polls. Of course, objective judgments about community morality *are* often possible. For example, community morality does not now condemn the eating of meat; and it is opposed to outright, flagrant racial discrimination. But for less well-settled issues, judges may have to construct community morality partly by nonempirical criteria or conclude that it is indeterminate.

A special problem about community morality for constitutional law concerns protections that are decidedly countermajoritarian. One cannot assume that present community outlooks should determine cases in which the claimed constitutional right rests on a premise that dominant views do not legitimate suppressing members of an unpopular minority or those who express strong countermajoritarian opinions. An easy illustration of the limits of dominant social views concerns whether the government should be promoting a particular religion. Even if most citizens within a state would approve of their government explicitly espousing the truth of Christianity, it hardly follows that Justices should interpret the religious clauses to allow this.

Analysis of how far judges can draw objectively from existing legal norms to decide cases and announce new norms is more complex. Frequently, this actual exercise is relatively simple. If multiple cases establish that speech may be suppressed or punished only if it creates a serious danger that illegal acts will soon follow, judges can use that norm to protect a kind of speech that has not been previously litigated but presents no such danger.[35] However, even in areas in which established broader norms yield many specific approaches, difficult borderline cases can arise, such as how far commercial speech should be protected in the same manner as other speech. And existing norms may not tell a Justice just how to interpret each constitutional provision formulated in an abstract way, a problem addressed in both earlier and later chapters. If "cruel and unusual punishment" warrants a fairly flexible interpretation, is that also true about the right "not to incriminate oneself?" Even when a Justice looks carefully at how other constitutional provisions are treated, he may find it hard to say exactly how a particular text should be understood if that is not yet settled or the existing approach is challenged.

Judges face a number of obstacles to using existing law to reach objective answers based on reason. The most obvious is determining which interpretive norms count and for how much. Do original understanding and given precedents lose force over time, and, if so, what degree of force do they retain? The norms of a legal system do not provide precise answers to these questions. Assessing the weight of various specific authoritative norms and the principles drawn from them can be incredibly arduous in hard cases. Even if an ideal judge could arrive at an objective answer by reasoning wholly from existing law, actual judges may be unable to do so. They may inevitably have to rely partly on other factors, including judgments about political justice and desirability.

Further, even if perfect judges were involved, it seems unlikely that they could resolve all borderline cases based on existing legal norms.

Some might respond that even though more specific legal norms cannot resolve all cases, a perfect judge employing all the principles and policies that one can draw from those norms would find an objective answer, and that actual judges should do the best they can to replicate the perfect judge. This sounds a bit like what Ronald Dworkin's Hercules could accomplish, but it is actually significantly different.[36] Although Dworkin does urge that nearly every legal case has a correct answer, and that in a sense the law itself provides that answer he also asserts that in arriving at and applying legal principles, an ideal judge must make some independent judgments about what is politically just and desirable. In that crucial respect, even the ideal judge is not drawing neutrally from existing materials. Under Dworkin's analysis, a correct answer to every case based on reason exists *only* if reason provides a correct answer to every moral question with political implications.[37] If one discounts this reliance on moral judgments as part of the law, existing law, even perfectly understood, contains some gaps.

A final obstacle to objectively correct answers based on legal materials is the possibility that—given changes in social relations and values, which might include an increasing understanding of what really is just—perhaps even perfect Justices who could come up with results and principles derived from existing legal norms would sometimes do better to deviate modestly from what those norms indicate and strike a new path.

A different question, but one of considerable practical importance, is how far actual judges should try to emulate a perfect judge who operates in a legal system with other perfect judges. The answer is far from obvious.[38] Perhaps real judges will do better if they do not try to emulate perfect performers as well as they can. To take an analogy from personal life, suppose an ideal human being would act best if she considers multiple factors when faced with moral choices and gives exactly the right amount of weight to her own interests. If real people both overestimate their own interests and are incapable of this kind of evaluation, they may do better to follow much more specific moral standards. The same may be true for judges. Especially given constraints on their time, actual judges might preferably employ relatively straightforward criteria or turn directly to their own best judgments about justice, rather than undertaking an impossible exercise of neutral assessment that takes account of every relevant legal standard.[39]

C. Groundings in Political Philosophy and Practical Circumstances for Arriving at Principles of Interpretation and Particular Results

Anyone considering the possibility of objectively correct constitutional interpretation must address the relevance of different governmental structures, different aspects of a constitution, and different stages of time and political context. The most troubling questions for this analysis concern the last inquiry, but the other two are also important.

Should courts adopt one mode of interpretation regardless of governmental structures and the nature of the Constitution? For example, might one say that any constitutional document should be understood in terms of what an ordinary or well-informed reader would think about the text? Prior chapters have strongly suggested that the nature of the government and particular constitution can make a great difference. If a constitution is very simple to amend and can be changed almost as easily as statutes are adopted, and if it has been altered with great frequency, its interpretation should resemble statutory interpretation. On the other hand, when the process of amendment is "cumbersome and complicated," it cannot be relied upon to make changes that reflect the majority will of modern times.[40] The fairness of the legislative process can also matter. If statutes are being adopted by those representing a distinct minority of the population whose interests are sharply opposed to those of the majority, as in the apartheid Union of South Africa, one might well recommend a reading of the constitution that would sharply limit legislative powers. One needs to assess interpretive strategies in light of a society's overall government structure, the nature of its constitution, and the range of opinions about the place of judges to arrive at what seem to be the best approaches to constitutional interpretation.

As other chapters demonstrate, desirable interpretive strategies can depend considerably on what provisions are involved. Within the federal structure of the United States, judicial review of claimed overreaching by the federal government into state affairs and executive trespasses on legislative responsibility are, and should be, quite different from the approaches to asserted violations of countermajoritarian guarantees of individual rights. What kind of approach judges should take may also depend on how well constitutional provisions seem to fit with a society's desirable progress over a long period of time. Recognition by judges in the 1840s that the historical development was inevitably away from the gross inequality of slavery could have been a reason to interpret the constitutional rights of slaveholders fairly restrictively. Belief now in a continuing movement toward equality of persons could constitute a ground to interpret the Equal Protection Clause expansively.

All of this brings us to a perplexing inquiry. Should judges or scholars rely on their convictions about the political setting of the present to adhere to or recommend general strategies of interpretation that they would reject if the political setting were different? Various scholars have suggested over time that the functioning of the Supreme Court has been essentially political,[41] a reality going back to Chief Justice Marshall, who was largely influenced by his acceptance of Hamiltonian federalism.[42] From this perspective, a proposal of what is "objectively" best would effectively concern desirable social developments. Frederick Schauer has suggested that this could be a basis for liberal Democrats who once favored judicial activism in one form or another[43] to now favor judicial passivity in similar respects.[44] Under such an approach, one's recommended principles of interpretation would be completely controlled by, and in one sense really a cover for, one's near-term political objectives. One would support the liberal Warren Court's activism, but decry any such activism by the conservative Roberts Court.[45]

We can begin by recognizing that it is impossible to imagine judges explicitly acknowledging that narrow political objectives drive their interpretive approach. When Justices write opinions explaining their techniques of interpretation, they do not indicate that these could change overnight if liberal colleagues were replaced by conservatives, or vice versa. If Supreme Court Justices announced that they were following this politically oriented understanding, interpretive techniques would essentially lose any intrinsic significance. The Justices would be candidly seeking to implement what they regard as promising political objectives. It is hard to think that this would be healthy for judicial review, since most people do not suppose judges should be the primary determiners of society's political aspirations.

This reality presents the question of what a scholarly recommendation of such an approach would amount to. One possibility is urging that judges, or at least Supreme Court Justices, could adopt this approach but not reflect it in what they say. A subtler version would be something like this: "We want judges to assume that their interpretive conceptions have a more permanent status, but we outsiders should support or oppose such conceptions based on the independent consideration of whether, given the present Supreme Court and political branches, the conceptions would now promote a just and desirable society." Of course, if the judges themselves, seeking more stable approaches that will last over time, are informed of why outsiders now support or oppose particular interpretive strategies, the outsiders' positions could hardly carry much intellectual force (though the mere fact of support could matter a bit).

These various difficulties confirm my sense that judges and scholars should aim for approaches they believe can be defended over time, whether the present Supreme Court—and the overall political ambiance—happen to fall on the liberal or conservative side. We should be thinking in terms of basic stages of history, or many decades. Perhaps the best approaches now are not those of 1830, but should be those that would have made good sense in 2005 and will continue to do so in 2025.

The most serious practical questions about bases of constitutional interpretation[46] are ones of degree, not exclusion or inclusion. Judges should largely rely on the objective criteria of existing legal norms, including text, original understanding and intent, precedents, and other settled principles of interpretation. In the most difficult cases, judges will inevitably end up relying to a degree on their own individual judgments—ones not mainly about narrow political issues, such as the desirability of universal healthcare, but broader principles, such as the appropriate scope of federal power under the Commerce Clause and taxing power. Whether judges should always *try* to decide on the basis of norms objectively derivable from the law itself is a critical subject of disagreement. If, as I believe, they should sometimes self-consciously rely on independent judgments not determined by existing legal norms, it can be debated just when this should occur. The most sensible practical position about constitutional interpretation is that Justices should recognize that in some difficult cases, their individual judgments will inevitably mix with external standards, and they should not worry too much about the degree to which each is involved or even try to develop a completely systematic theory of constitutional interpretation.[47]

Lurking in the background of all these issues is how far judicial opinions should reflect the manner in which judges actually do and should try to decide. Opinions in the most difficult cases commonly overstate not only specific supporting reasons but also the simplicity of necessary analysis and the degree to which the result is reachable based on objective factors. All of this can be partly a matter of self-persuasion—as when we decide in favor of a course of action, we tend to tell ourselves that the reasons for that decision are particularly strong. But one aim of opinions presenting the arguments in favor of a result as powerful, and not based on personal judicial reactions, is to enhance people's sense of judicial legitimacy and the fairness of the process. Dan Kahan has offered a powerful counterargument to this practice based on psychological research.[48] He argues that when the Supreme Court divides along ideological lines in a highly controversial case and attempts to make the case seem one-sided, it fails to respect the views of others about what really matters, and this produces the cynical response that Justices are engaging in obvious manipulation. It would be better, Kahan suggests, if uncertainties and the strength of counterarguments were honestly portrayed, thus giving due recognition to all those who feel strongly about a highly contested issue, such as abortion rights. Insofar as the view is persuasive, it presumably should lead to more honest accounts of the nuances of interpretive techniques, as well as narrower reasons for and against a particular decision.[49]

The thrust of Kahan's position is highly plausible, at least for the narrow segment of constitutional cases that draw great public attention. But Kahan's analysis focuses on oversimplification and overstatement of specific considerations, not the degree of emphasis on "objective" factors. It is much more doubtful whether candid acknowledgments that Justices are partly deciding based on their personal sense of desirable and just outcomes would improve perceptions of the Court. On this matter, Justices may do better to continue to emphasize the impersonal factors and, indeed, largely try to decide on the balance of those factors.

CONCLUSION

This chapter has explored many of the complexities of ideas that judges should decide in accord with "neutral" or "objective" standards. Even when one puts aside that in debatable cases opinions typically overstate the arguments for a result and that compromises are often needed to yield majority opinions, crucial difficulties remain, especially as one moves from stated rules to interpretive tactics and the reasons for those. It is possible for judges to aim to state rules that they see as applicable to other situations they cover, and they may more generally seek to do what is objectively right. But they cannot always rely completely on existing law; they cannot formulate grounds of interpretation and their underlying reasons in a precise linguistic formula that applies across the board; and no two Supreme Court Justices will have exactly the same perspectives on those matters. Thus, majority opinions in the hardest cases face not only the basic obstacles to precise formulations but the need to coalesce somewhat different outlooks.

What this chapter has claimed about objectivity and its limits, and what the prior chapters have urged about multiple and complex standards of constitutional interpretation that vary significantly depending on the provision and specific issues involved, is tested in the chapters that follow. They deal with a number of key provisions and structures and address a range of important constitutional issues. Although these chapters partly engage in support or critique of particular outcomes and of interpretive strategies used for distinctive constitutional provisions or issues, their overall objective is to demonstrate the complexity of what the Supreme Court must do in many hard cases, and even in deciding what issues are appropriate for judges to tackle and resolve. My hope is that this fairly detailed but far from complete analysis of different provisions and issues will strongly confirm the general themes asserted in the previous five chapters.

Part II

A POIGNANT ILLUSTRATION

Chapter 6

Cruel and Unusual Punishment

I. INTRODUCTION

Concentrating on a specific constitutional provision, the Eighth Amendment's bar on inflicting "cruel and unusual punishments," this chapter illustrates many of the fundamental complexities and plausible resolutions we have identified. The following two chapters focus on the distribution of political powers, whose interpretation varies in significant ways from the treatment of individual rights. Together, the three chapters demonstrate both how troublesome many crucial interpretive issues are and how practical considerations, often unspecified, play important roles in what courts actually do.

Part II of this chapter will explore what may be meant by the original understanding of "cruel and unusual punishments" and to what extent such original understanding should control. It discusses the time from which the relevant "original" understanding originates and whose understanding should matter. It then turns to bars on specific punishments and the role of proportionality between crime and punishment both historically and today.

There are seven central premises underlying this discussion. These premises overlap and intertwine, but they are touched on to varying degrees throughout Part II, and will recur throughout general discussions of Eighth Amendment jurisprudence. They are:

1. Even when a provision's language is drawn from existing documents, discerning a dominant original understanding based on enactor intent or reader understanding can often be extremely difficult or even impossible. Further, inquiry into just whose understanding should count and for how much yields no straightforward answer.
2. If one could discern an original sense of what practices the Eighth Amendment was meant to preclude, taking that as the main criterion for modern application would be extremely unproductive and unwise. The original sense of underlying values should count for more than specific foreseen applications. That emphasis is unambiguously reflected in what the Supreme Court has actually done.

One consequence of this approach is that *some* independent judicial evaluation beyond existing law is unavoidable.

3. How much deference courts should afford to the political branches, and how far those branches should see themselves as constrained beyond what courts will enforce, may be less for individual rights than distributions of power; yet, these questions do play an important part in how the Eighth Amendment is understood. A nuanced aspect of this is who exactly should receive such deference—present legislators or those over time; legislators in all states or those in a particular state?
4. Although past precedents exercise some constraint on present decisions, they have been far from controlling, and changes in the membership of the Supreme Court have been critical to some shifts in what the Court has ruled.
5. As the Supreme Court addresses different but related issues over time, its resolutions often do not fit together into a coherent set of principles. This reality is revealed by a close examination of almost any domain of constitutional law that individual Justices approach with highly varied perspectives, and it is especially notable in the Court's differential treatment of capital punishment and long prison sentences.
6. Courts developing constitutional principles are partly guided by what they can fairly ascertain and evaluate. This affects both what issues they tackle and how they address them.
7. Even if some differences in judicial assessment are not defensible according to basic principles, one may think that concerns about whether judicial involvement can work in a constructive way is a legitimate basis for treating somewhat similar concerns differently. This may be true both about *how* the Eighth Amendment is taken to apply in certain contexts and *why* the Supreme Court has declined to extend its coverage to subjects that fall within basic values the Justices have recognized. Particular resolutions and avoidances by the Supreme Court provide striking examples of how courts may be inclined to concentrate on issues they can fruitfully resolve, but end up with a range of determinations that do not fit well together.

In addition to the fundamental issue of how the Eighth Amendment's language should be interpreted flexibly in light of shifting social standards, we can identify a number of more particular questions about its range of coverage, both as originally understood and as now conceived. The Supreme Court's explicit and implicit answers to these questions reveal the varied perspectives of individual Justices over time as well as sensitivity to what issues are judicially manageable. Part III will address some of the most important particular questions about "cruel and unusual" punishment. These questions include:

1. To what extent is the proportionality of a punishment to the crime committed relevant in capital and noncapital cases?
2. Is the term "unusual" a criterion that must be independently satisfied for a punishment to be unconstitutional, the main technique for discerning what counts as "cruel," or one among various factors that, though not itself determinative, figures into what is unacceptably "cruel?"
3. Is legislative authorization central to what is acceptable punishment?
4. Does "unusual" refer to frequency of present use or to usage over time?
5. When judges make assessments of various punishments and their applications, should they rely entirely on external criteria or partly on their own independent judgments?
6. Does the acceptability of a punishment depend partly on the age or mental condition of the person convicted?
7. What bearing does the Eighth Amendment have on prison conditions and acts by prison guards?
8. When imprisonment is indisputably appropriate as a penalty, can the length of time and absence of possible parole raise serious constitutional issues?
9. For modern use, is what matters how often a punishment is authorized, prescribed in individual cases, actually imposed, or a combination of these factors? (This is a vital inquiry for capital punishment, which is authorized, but rarely carried out, in most states.)
10. Should it be unconstitutional to punish persons for a status, such as being a heroin addict, or for acts they cannot "control" if they have that status, such as using heroin?
11. Should it be unconstitutional to punish people for behavior they have no reason to think is unlawful?
12. Can unfairness based on race, gender, or class make the application of a punishment unacceptable?

These last three questions partly concern the possible reach of "cruel and unusual punishment" in relation to other constitutional safeguards like due process and equal protection.

Tackling particular issues about "cruel and unusual" punishment, the following discussion contains a sketch of historical evidence, an account of what the Supreme Court has decided, and suggestions about what might be desirable approaches; but all is mainly designed to reflect the book's broader themes. On certain questions, as we shall see, the modern Supreme Court has proved quite active; on others, it has not. One puzzle is how far these varying degrees of involvement make sense according either to fundamental principles or needs of judicial manageability.

II. ORIGINAL UNDERSTANDING AND ITS DEGREE OF CONTROL

As previous chapters have shown, in the controversy over the status of original understanding versus an evolving conception that responds to changes in technology, social organization, and values, even those who reject "originalism" as a doctrine accept that how a provision was originally conceived has relevance. As to what *counts* as the original understanding, the major divide between enactor intent and reader understanding is almost always hard to draw in practice, partly because of scanty evidence or significant disagreements about coverage, and partly because at the time, people may not have conceived what now has become a crucial problem. A yet more fundamental reason I have stressed for why enactor intent and reader conceptions tend to coalesce is that readers understand language in the context of what they take a writer to be conveying. This is particularly true when a reader considers authoritative language she understands to require the same behavior from many people, as contrasted with poetry that may aim to elicit quite different responses from individual readers.

Because the Bill of Rights was proposed by Congress and ratified by the states with relatively little debate, and because discussion of what the Eighth Amendment in particular entailed was not extensive, we have little basis to distinguish the intent of enactors from reader understanding. For both, most relevant evidence derives from the adoption of similar provisions protecting rights within states and from Anti-Federalist claims, made during the ratification process of the basic constitution, of the need to protect against federal abuses of power.

If one asks what kinds of readers are crucial, and how well informed they should be taken to be, the best answer depends partly on how a particular provision actually affects various classes of readers. If the provision protects the *performance* of a right, one might ascribe special significance to readers who plan to engage in what they take to be protected exercises, such as forms of religious worship or controversial speech. (As noted earlier, this reality also suggests that not only original but also modern readers should matter.) The Eighth Amendment also involves individual rights but does not similarly protect behavior from government interference. A person contemplating a criminal act might conceivably be influenced by the severity of the prescribed punishment, but that is quite different from criticizing official policy in the belief that one is engaging in protected speech. Thus, although the Eighth Amendment concerns the life and dignity of those punished, and their experience bears crucially on what is seen as "cruel," their reading of the provision's meaning probably should carry no special significance when compared with that of other citizens and of officials considering which punishments to prescribe.

Among the questions the Eighth Amendment raises about original understanding are ones that touch all of the aspects of the Bill of Rights that have been held to be selectively incorporated by the Fourteenth Amendment. Estimates about understanding at the time of the Fourteenth Amendment should be crucial. Whatever the persuasiveness of a broad "selective incorporation" approach, briefly addressed in Chapter 9, "due process" and "privileges and immunities" can fairly easily be read as protecting citizens against unjust punishments. In any event, the application of "cruel and unusual punishment" to the states is now firmly settled.

The idea of "incorporation" does not itself tell us how far those of the time of the Fourteenth Amendment assumed that what counted for rights rested on a content they then perceived or on the conceptions of 1791. Two special aspects of this question for the Eighth Amendment are that its language was itself drawn from even earlier documents, and that certain forms of punishment and the ranges of their applications had altered significantly between 1791 and 1868. One *might* conclude that this shift entails that forms of punishment permitted to the federal government should be "cruel and unusual" when imposed by states, or that either the original or later understanding should help determine what both the national and state governments can do. As earlier chapters have emphasized, perceptions in 1868 differed from those in 1791, *and* those who adopted and read the Fourteenth Amendment did not assume that Bill of Rights coverage against the states should be determined by 1791 perceptions. Because during adoption of the Fourteenth Amendment virtually no attention was paid directly to constitutionally unacceptable punishments, gauging a dominant understanding would involve asking what punishments people then deemed acceptable and how they perceived this kind of terminology in various state constitutions.

For the understanding in 1791, one needs to ask both what punishments were then regarded as unacceptable and whether the range of forbidden punishments was considered flexible over time. More particular questions are whether the language was taken to forbid only punishments that were seen as barbarous, or also those that departed from common law tradition and legislative authorization, and perhaps those that were out of proportion to the criminal offense.

The term "cruel and unusual" strikes a modern reader as quite open-ended. The sense of acceptable punishments has shifted radically in the last two centuries, and, especially given the harshness of our present penal system, we have little reason to suppose we have somehow reached the pinnacle of understanding or that our notions of acceptable punishments will be so perceived a century from now. Were courts now assigned the responsibility to preclude "cruel" punishments, we would assume that they could respond to developments over time, even if according deference to legislative choices.

Although the very nature of the terminology provides a strong reason for perceiving this temporal flexibility, conceivably people in 1791 saw that language differently. The narrowest understanding of the Eighth

Amendment would be that people then understood certain punishments as unacceptable, based partly on the 1689 English Bill of Rights and on state constitutions, and they regarded the amendment as declaring only those punishments out of bounds. On this understanding, an originalist Justice would discern what punishments were then seen as precluded, regardless of whether they now seem intrinsically atrocious or grossly out of line with the crimes committed. As stated, this formulation would need one modest, uncontroversial qualification for novel punishments that closely resemble those originally deemed unacceptable. If a particular form of torture was precluded, so also would be a new form of electronic torture similar in effect.[1]

One set of questions about the original understanding of the Eighth Amendment concerns its relation to similar language in the English Bill of Rights. The historical argument for a relatively narrow reading of "cruel and unusual punishments" rests partly on assertions about the sense of the English Bill, and more particularly its connection to the Titus Oates case.[2] Oates, an Anglican cleric, had fabricated the "Popish Plot" to assassinate King Charles II and had accused supposed plotters in an affidavit. Fifteen Catholics were executed as a consequence. When it became apparent that Oates had invented the plot, he was convicted of perjury at the King's Bench, over which Chief Justice Jeffreys presided. The death penalty was not available for perjury, but the court imposed life imprisonment, defrocked Oates, and authorized such extensive pillorying and whipping over time that death might well have resulted. When James II, the successor to Charles II, was replaced by William of Orange, Parliament enacted the Bill of Rights, including the provision on cruel and unusual punishment. Oates then petitioned both Houses of Parliament for relief. The responses are taken to constitute a revealing contemporaneous explanation of the punishment provision. Although the House of Lords declined to overturn the judgment, given Oates's grievous wrong, some of its members believed that the judgment was erroneous. A dissenting minority urged that affirming the judgment would violate the Bill of Rights, which barred punishments "contrary to law and ancient practice" and those that were "barbarous, inhuman, and unchristian."[3] The House of Commons voted to release Oates. In a conference with the Lords, its representatives urged that the sentence of life imprisonment lacked statutory authorization and precedential support and that imposing whipping so severe it was likely to cause death was "illegal and cruel, and of dangerous Example."[4] Remarking that it gave Oates's sentence "particular Regard" when it drafted the Bill of Rights, the House of Commons resolved that affirming it would violate that document.[5]

How should "cruel and unusual" be understood as it connects to the *Oates* case? Was the punishment imposed in essence too cruel to be acceptable, or did it generally lack standing in common law tradition or parliamentary authorization? A powerful obstacle to either of these views is that yet more horrible punishments, many involving components like those in Oates's sentence, continued to be imposed in England after the English Bill of Rights.[6] A more convincing account is that the punishment was out of proportion for the crime of perjury and was not contemplated by the common law or by statute *for that crime*.

Much more important for us than its original sense is how Americans in 1791 understood the English Bill and how far they took that to be controlling. In respect to readers and adopting legislatures, only those who were very well informed could have perceived the particular significance of the English document. The language of "cruel and unusual punishment" by itself hardly conveys nuances of English history, and a typical 1791 reader would not have said to himself: "I don't know about any earlier English document, but perhaps the language is drawn from one and tracks its understanding." Thus, one can assign substantial interpretive significance to the English Bill of Rights itself only if one assumes crucial "readers" or "enactors" were very well informed.

A central complexity about all of this is that language like that of the Eighth Amendment had been included in the Virginia constitution and then in the constitutions of eight other states. The exact words of these texts varied: some forbade "cruel *and* unusual punishments," others "cruel *or* unusual punishment," and two simply "cruel punishments."[7] Understandings when the Eighth Amendment was adopted presumably flowed much more directly from the sense of these recently adopted provisions than the English Bill of a century earlier. Any relevant influence of the English Bill would thus be largely indirect, having possibly affected to a degree what was understood in the individual states and about the Northwest Ordinance, which also contained such language. One argument supporting that the Eighth Amendment was originally conceived as covering only punishments that themselves were intrinsically barbarous is that the people of that time actually misconceived the English Bill in that way, based on influential writings about cruel punishments that did not accurately reflect the English position in 1689.[8]

How were the terms "cruel" and "unusual" then understood? One author has plausibly claimed that ordinary meanings of "unusual" at the time of the Eighth Amendment included "contrary to long usage" as well "uncommon," and that both the English Bill and the Eighth Amendment are best understood as precluding deviations from well-established usages.[9] Such an understanding can, of course, be a basis for evaluating both the intrinsic nature of penalties *and* their relation to the crimes for which they are imposed.

If "long usage" is assessed at the time of a modern court's decision rather than what was being done in 1791, this approach also allows a particular form of evolution over time. Given that the Eighth Amendment, like the English Bill of Rights, bars excessive fines and excessive bail, it is clear that adopters and readers of the time were familiar with notions of proportionality. Writing for the Supreme Court in *Solem v. Helm*, Justice Powell discerned a notion of proportionality as to punishment in the common law itself.[10] Anthony Granucci has urged that, although historically the basic sense of "cruel" as severe or hard did include a norm of proportionality, the ratification debates reveal that the enactors of the Eighth Amendment interpreted it to forbid "not excessive but tortuous punishments."[11] However, given the limited evidence of comments by a few ratifiers within states, one must be skeptical that these represented the sense of most enactors. Further, the explicit language about "excessive" fines and bail points toward a proportionality requirement for cruel punishments.[12]

Whether the English Bill of Rights or similar provisions in American states were deemed reflective of natural rights is also relevant to how they were probably conceived. Such a connection would point toward a coverage not restricted to what had, in the past, been taken as unjust punishments, including then accepted notions of proportionality. If certain penalties are so horrible that they always violate natural rights, others are sufficiently severe to offend such rights if imposed for very minor crimes.

The Eighth Amendment, like other constitutional provisions, raises the question of whether its constraint on other branches reaches beyond what courts will enforce. Since the English Bill was adopted by Parliament, largely in response to perceived abuses of the government prior to the Glorious Revolution, we can understand its restraints as directed at the monarch and Parliament itself, as well as courts. Even if judges were going to accept any penalties that received statutory authorization, members of Parliament might well have understood that they should not authorize new penalties that would be "cruel."[13] Given that the Bill of Rights was partly designed to preclude abusive exercises of federal power by Congress, its authorization would not have created automatic judicial acceptability of a punishment. That conclusion alone does not tell us whether legislators should perceive coverage as reaching beyond what courts will enforce.

However he might resolve the various complexities about the tie between original English understanding and what was conceived a century later by enactors and readers of the Eighth Amendment, a pure originalist who concluded that the language itself was not meant to be open-ended in application would accept the following premise: "Any punishment that was acceptable in 1791, and all new punishments that are not tightly related to punishments then deemed unacceptable, are permitted under the Eighth Amendment. *If* proportionality is relevant at all, it is to be judged by what were then seen as fair penalties for various crimes and offenders." This general approach would render the inquiry about forbidden punishment essentially historical. For federal penalties, the critical period would be around 1791; for states under the Fourteenth Amendment, it would be 1868.

A faithful use of this strategy would yield many results strikingly at odds both with what the Supreme Court has actually decided and with modern views about many punishments. Self-consciously inflicting physical pain by such penalties as flogging could be legally acceptable, as would capital punishment for a wide range of crimes that do not involve any actual physical harm to human beings, including armed robberies, thefts of horses, counterfeiting, and sodomy.

A strict originalist might defend courts giving the Eighth Amendment such limited significance by claiming that legislatures, juries, and the judges who actually impose sentences will protect against morally unacceptable punishments being employed, and that if things get bad enough, our country can always amend the Constitution. This possible approach would permit individual states to impose punishments that strike modern understanding as grossly unacceptable and highly unusual. Since such punishments are mostly inflicted on persons whom members of society view in a highly negative way, the political branches may not directly provide an adequate safeguard, and they are very unlikely to seek a constitutional amendment to combat occasional abuses. These are strong reasons to support more active judicial involvement.

A narrow originalist approach may be answered by rejecting its account of initial understanding, by challenging its underlying theory, or both. The first response is that what the Eighth Amendment did not allow was conceived more flexibly. The simplest argument for this is the amendment's language, taken by James Madison from the Virginia Declaration of Rights in 1776. The historical origin does not by itself tell us how flexibly the text's words were then understood, but whether a punishment is "unusual" can obviously vary over time, and perceptions of unacceptable cruelty also change, especially if such cruelty is seen as violating a natural right. *If* a more specific embodiment of prevailing attitudes had been intended, other language might have been chosen. Given that "excessive" effectively authorized judgments of some flexibility about fines and bail, why not regard "cruel" and "unusual" similarly? Two members of Congress did complain that the language was too vague, indicating that they at least inferred that it would leave more room for evolving interpretation than they wished. Grouping all of these factors together produces a fairly strong argument that acceptability under the amendment was not locked into existing practices. To grasp understanding at the time of the Fourteenth Amendment, one would look at how federal courts had been applying the Eighth Amendment and how state courts were treating similar language in their constitutions.

If an originalist maintains that, despite these complications, the conceptions in 1791 and 1868 were quite narrow, he must face the second level of response. If we *now* understand that conceptions of cruelty do change with time, and have some faith that what is usually involved is actual progress (not mere variations); and if the language of "cruel and unusual" punishment *now* seems to convey responsiveness to such developments, we can conclude that it should be taken to authorize judicial protection against unwarranted persecution of human beings who engage in acts that offend society. Since, as discussed above, we cannot realistically expect constitutional amendments to respond to unjustified punishments, courts rightly have some latitude to employ modern judgment about what is out of bounds.

The dominant modern doctrine (at least as to some matters) is that the Supreme Court will construe the meaning of "cruel and unusual punishments" according to "evolving standards of decency that mark the progress of a maturing society."[14] This doctrine should be regarded as possibly consistent with original understanding and, in any event, warranted by a developed understanding about what is desirable in a liberal democracy with judicial protection of individual rights.

III. SPECIFIC ISSUES AND THEIR RESOLUTIONS

When we examine more detailed aspects of what the modern Supreme Court has done, we quickly see strikingly major differences in how "activist" it has been about Eighth Amendment issues. Part of the descriptive explanation concerns when in time the Court has tackled different subjects; as with many other issues of individual rights, members of the Warren Court were more willing to push ahead in reviews of legislative decisions than most subsequent Justices have been. But we can also identify the influence of a restraint grounded in the sense that various issues would be highly difficult for judges to manage. This latter focus helps explain the Court's continuing hesitancy to involve itself in a range of topics that raise what should count as unacceptably "cruel" punishments.

A. Intrinsically Barbarous Punishments and/or Proportionality

As we have seen, the narrowest understanding of what "cruel and unusual punishment" covers is forms that are intrinsically unacceptable, regardless of a person's offense. In England in 1689, persons convicted of treason were hanged in public, taken down while still alive, disemboweled, and then beheaded and cut into four pieces.[15] Such a punishment would now be perceived as clearly beyond the pale, as would the severing of a part of a person's body, or the lesser infliction of flogging in public. This aspect of coverage is itself uncontroversial, but it raises the issue of how such an evaluation should be made. Assuming that judges should reach beyond the specific understandings in 1791 or 1868, they might rely on the presence or absence of legislative authorization, general assumptions about acceptability, conformance with prior practice, an independent evaluation resting on the goals of the criminal process and human dignity, or a combination of these criteria. An exploration of these various approaches is reserved for the section that treats evolutionary development.

Although John Bessler has concluded that most federal and state decisions about unconstitutional punishment during the nineteenth century in the United States involved the notion of intrinsic unacceptability,[16] John Stinneford's examination of cases suggests that nearly all of them between 1791 and 1865 recognized the relevance of proportionality requirements.[17] The Supreme Court decisively adopted that position in 1910.[18] Counting in favor of this conclusion is not only the openness of the amendment's language, including the clear standard of proportionality contained in the bar on "excessive" fines,[19] but also the indisputable truth that a punishment acceptable for murder might, in any natural sense of the words, be undeniably "cruel" and "unusual" if imposed for a parking violation.

John Stinneford's powerful argument that the original understanding did include a requirement of proportionality rests both on the relation of the English Bill of Rights to a common law tradition that barred excessive punishments, and on understanding in America in the late eighteenth century.[20] Stinneford refers to state statutes and constitutional provisions and to the arguments of Anti-Federalists during the constitutional ratification process that individual rights needed protection, arguments partly aimed at limiting the federal government to the restraints of the common law. He also notes that in two domains of state laws that restricted the behavior of persons—homicides that were committed by individuals and punishments of underlings, such as slaves and ship personnel, by those in authority—the phrase "cruel and unusual" was a synonym for excessive or disproportionate.[21] Given the deep moral wrongness of a punishment that is far too severe for the offense a person has committed, and the strong argument that the Eighth Amendment was actually understood to preclude such punishments, considerations of appropriate proportion are called for within Eighth Amendment jurisprudence. Certainly, no decisive argument about original understanding excludes them.

Could it possibly make sense to judge all penalties and their appropriate proportionality to committed offenses by perceptions of the late eighteenth century? For this, we face the obvious reality that views about forms of punishment have altered sharply over two centuries. One, but only one, reason for this is the development of imprisonment as the main form of physical imposition. In the eighteenth century, the aspiration of humane imprisonment extending over time was just beginning. Were imprisonment not a serious option, people might well think capital punishment more necessary than it is considered now, and also accept various direct inflictions of physical harm. What seems "cruel" as a form of punishment for what crimes depends partly on available alternatives.

The Supreme Court first established the constitutional relevance of proportionality in 1910 in *Weems v. United States*.[22] In the Philippines, then an American territory, Weems was convicted of falsifying a document going to the government; the crime was one of strict liability for which it was unnecessary to prove actual intent or even negligence. He was sentenced to fifteen years in prison, during which he was to be chained day and night at the wrists and ankles. Assuming that the amendment's broad wording embraced general principles, and that its proper applications were not limited to those actually perceived at the time of adoption, the Court resolved "that punishment for crime should be graduated and proportioned" to the offense.[23]

As following sections will describe in greater detail, the Supreme Court has actively restricted use of capital punishment. In a decision that rendered unconstitutional the procedures for capital punishment then applicable in every state, the Court ruled in *Furman v. Georgia* that a jury can impose death only after it has been given careful instructions about what to take into account.[24] The Court has since resolved that the death sentence cannot be imposed for standard crimes against individuals that do not involve the taking of someone's life, such as rape or armed robbery.[25] And, even for murder, capital punishment cannot be applied against minors or those who are mentally ill or disabled.[26]

In contrast to the death penalty, the Supreme Court has displayed great restraint to legislatures about lengths of time in prison, accepting virtually any sentence regardless of the crime, so long as the legislature has authorized that term of imprisonment. The one exception to this is that it has struck down life without parole for minors who have not committed homicide.[27]

This sharp dichotomy in treatment is impossible to justify in basic principle. If capital punishment is ever acceptable, how can it be "cruel and unusual" to impose that on a man who has committed multiple forcible rapes, and yet not be "cruel and unusual" to give a mandatory life sentence to someone who has stolen videotapes or three golf clubs? One *might* argue that judicial review of length of sentence is simply too difficult, but that argument does not hold up in extreme cases. Perhaps basic discomfort with capital punishment itself, and the Court's composition when it first seriously considered a challenge to the death sentence, help explain the radical divergence between its treatments of the death penalty and prison sentences; but there is no way that it really makes sense, a claim to which I shall return.

B. The Status of "Cruel" and of "Unusual"

A critical preliminary question about Eighth Amendment law is how "unusual" should relate to "cruel." Is each a separate requirement, does "unusual" provide the evidence for what is "cruel," or is it one among various factors in determining what counts as "cruel?" The linguistic question here bears some resemblance to the Second Amendment problem, discussed in Chapter 2, about how protecting militia relates to the "right" to bear arms.

Taken in a modern, literal way, the language specifies two independent requirements, that is, to be unconstitutional, a penalty must be both "cruel" and "unusual." A very cruel punishment would then be acceptable if employed frequently, and an unusual penalty would be acceptable if not cruel. This divergence apparently did not reflect the original understanding.[28] In light of the number of state constitutions that forbade "cruel *or* unusual" punishments, the silence about any critical difference between "and" and "or" during debates about ratification of the original constitution and adoption of the Bill of Rights implies that the two terms, "cruel" and "unusual," were then seen as closely related. Given the premise that acceptable punishments were embodied in the common law, the criteria for whether a punishment was cruel likely depended greatly on whether a harsh penalty was "unusual" within that law, as was Oates's sentence for perjury.[29] Although the degree of unusualness judges would require could depend partly on how cruel a punishment seemed, the inquiries about the two terms were apparently seen as interlocked. That account fits well what the Supreme Court has actually done; but its opinions have failed to provide any clear explanation of the relationship between the two words.

The remaining sections in this Part look at approaches Supreme Court Justices have used to determine what the Eighth Amendment precludes, and evaluates certain suggested alternatives. Given that "unusual" connects to what counts as "cruel," the question remains whether the Court should ever hold a punishment "cruel" by some independent standard.

C. Legislative Authorization and Prior Practice

Critical to determining the acceptability of a punishment are to what extent legislative authorization and prior practice should count. One reading of the English Bill of Rights is that it only permitted punishments established by the common law that were authorized by Parliament, but assumed that courts should accept any that Parliament did approve.[30] Given that the Eighth Amendment was designed to restrain the political branches, it was clear at the outset that congressional authorization was not by itself sufficient to validate a punishment challenged in judicial review. Whether federal law included common law crimes was unclear when the Bill of Rights was adopted;[31] in 1812 the Supreme Court settled that all federal crimes must be statutory.[32] Although some states retain common law crimes, virtually all modern challenged criminal sentences have been authorized by statute.

Since legislative choices provide some indication of prevailing social opinion, the question of how far such opinion should govern "acceptable" punishments bears on how much weight legislative authorization should carry in principle and how much deference courts should accord legislative choices.[33] Insofar as the Eighth Amendment is rightly seen as partly a constraint on a popular majority's not giving due regard to the rights of detested criminals, legislative views should carry reduced power.

A sub-question about deference is the extent to which courts should look at general coverage or particular applications. A penalty that may be all right for most offenders can be extremely harsh in certain instances. For example, in *Harmelin v. Michigan*, the Supreme Court upheld the sentence of life imprisonment without parole for someone with no previous arrests or convictions who had about a pound and a half of cocaine in the trunk of his car.[34] Even if such a severe penalty may be warranted for major operators in drug traffic, it is notably excessive for an addict who may well have been only a "mule" transporting the drugs. Yet the Court did not find a violation of the Eighth Amendment.

A different criterion of judgment about the acceptability of a punishment is prior practice under the law. Such practice could merely supplement deference to legislators as a guide to prevailing moral judgments. Yet if a Justice concludes that the ban on cruel and unusual punishments is largely meant to curtail the effects of temporary, ill-considered appraisals, she may take past practice as the most important standard, a position that John Stinneford has advocated.[35]

Within the United States, a very important consideration for both legislative authorization and past practice is whether an individual state or the country should be the political domain that counts. Stinneford criticizes a Supreme Court ruling that held Georgia cannot impose the death penalty for rape, given the state's consistent approval of that penalty over time.[36] However, the more compelling position is that prior practice in the whole country, federalist though it may be, should be what mainly counts. Given that no state other than Georgia then employed the death penalty for simple rape, Justices properly viewed it as no longer part of a widespread practice. This approach gathers added strength from the facts that the Fourteenth Amendment was adopted largely in order to constrain how states, especially those in the South, treated members of different races and that a continuing concern about unequal treatment has involved the severity of punishments given to blacks who commit crimes against whites.[37]

D. Evaluating Claims of Impermissible Sentences of Death and Imprisonment

Before tackling in more detail the Supreme Court's approaches to death sentences and imprisonment, I pause briefly over the distinction frequently drawn between "objective" and "subjective" criteria and the nature of independent judgment. As Chapter 5 explores, judges properly employing a kind of independent judgment are not simply relying on their "subjective" emotional feeling or personal reactions in the sense that one responds to the flavor of ice cream or the beauty of a sunset. They are *trying* to use their reason to reflect on whether a punishment really is "cruel" by a standard of correctness or of community morality. Although both legislative authorization and prior practice clearly count as "objective" criteria, neither actually eliminates independent evaluation. For legislative authorization, a judge must evaluate how much is needed and whether it covers all or only some specific applications. For *prior* practice, a judge must resolve what period of past time is both long enough and recent enough to authorize a punishment,[38] and determine how far practices in other states and countries may matter. A judge must also decide how much weight to accord legislative approval against prior practice when the two conflict. Since, as the previous chapter shows, no standard of this sort can be completely objective in the sense of determinable by external facts, the more neutral term of "independent evaluation" is preferable to "subjective" for cases that turn on the Justices' fundamental assessments of moral acceptability.

Although its precise elements are hardly clear, and it has neither been consistently employed nor accepted by all Justices, the prevailing standard for "cruel and unusual" since 1958 has been "evolving standards of decency." In *Trop v. Dulles*, which struck down a penalty of denaturalization for a soldier's desertion as contrary to human dignity, Chief Justice Warren's plurality opinion declared that the "not precise" language of the Eighth Amendment did not have a "static" scope. Rather, the "Amendment must draw its meaning from the evolving standards of decency that mark the process of a maturing society."[39]

The great majority of punishments ruled unconstitutional since the announcement of this standard have involved death sentences. The first of these, *Furman v. Georgia*, was decided in 1972.[40] By a 5–4 margin, the Justices held Georgia's death penalty statute unconstitutional, with each member of the majority writing a separate opinion. Justice Douglas believed the penalty itself was unconstitutional because it operates with discrimination;[41] Justice Stewart relied on capricious selection;[42] Justice White emphasized the infrequency with which the punishment is imposed;[43] and Justice Brennan urged that "calculated killing" is "uniquely degrading to human dignity."[44] Justice Thurgood Marshall, a former leader of the NAACP Legal Defense Fund, joined Brennan in finding the punishment itself unconstitutional. His announced general standard was whether people, if "fully informed," would find the death penalty unjust and unacceptable.[45] Applying this standard, which no judge could employ without using his independent judgment, Marshall concluded that death penalties did not really serve any legitimate purpose.

In requiring, at a minimum, that jurors or sentencing judges be given clear standards for when they might impose capital punishment, the Court in effect held invalid every state and the federal provision of the death penalty. The social consequence of the decision was actually increased support for the death penalty, with thirty-five states adopting revised laws to meet *Furman*'s requirements. The Supreme Court responded in 1976 in *Gregg v. Georgia*.[46] Upholding laws in three states as adequately guiding the judgment of those imposing the sentence, the Court relied partly on the sense of most Americans that the death penalty was "an appropriate and necessary criminal sanction."[47] *Gregg* effectively ended, at least for the time being, the likely success of any effort to have the Supreme Court declare the death penalty itself a violation of the Eighth Amendment, despite its abandonment in other Western democracies. Instead, a series of rulings have been handed down that have restricted the classes of convicted criminals on whom it may be imposed.

The Court has held that the punishment is barred for minors[48] and for those who are mentally disabled.[49] For ordinary offenses against individuals, it can only be used for homicide,[50] and its imposition then may not be mandatory, but rather requires a particular assessment of the offender.[51] Opinions reaching these conclusions have emphasized external "objective" criteria; but exactly what has been given weight differs, and certain decisions are impossible to explain, except in terms of the Justices' individual evaluations.

A key case is the 2005 decision, *Roper v. Simmons*,[52] in which the Court reviewed the death sentence imposed on a young man who, at the age of seventeen, had committed an especially disturbing murder.[53] Having earlier ruled that no one under age sixteen when he committed a crime could be sentenced to death,[54] the Court then in 1989 allowed a death sentence for a sixteen- or seventeen-year-old.[55] In 2005, *Roper* overruled that decision, with Justice Kennedy writing that the Court needed to determine "which punishments are so disproportionate as to be cruel and unusual" under "evolving standards of decency."[56] Justices must first review objective indices, in particular legislative enactments, and then "determine, in the exercise of our own independent judgment, whether the death penalty is a disproportionate punishment for juveniles."[57] Although twenty states authorized death sentences for juveniles, its actual imposition was infrequent, and no other country continued to give it an "official sanction."[58] A version of a prior practice approach might have supported the result in *Roper*, given the rarity of juveniles being sentenced to death, but the Court's disposition was impossible to justify if one assumes that legislative authorization is *the key* to unacceptability.[59]

For the mentally disabled, a similar conclusion had already been reached. Having ruled in 1989 that it was permissible to execute those who were "mentally retarded,"[60] the Court decided in 2002 in *Atkins v. Virginia* to the contrary, relying largely on a "national consensus" that was grounded partly in the fact that since the 1989 decision, sixteen states that had previously permitted execution of the mentally disabled had since prohibited it.[61] The Supreme Court has also restricted the kinds of crimes for which a death sentence may be imposed. After striking down its imposition for adult rape in 1977 in *Coker v. Georgia*,[62] the Court in 2008 extended this restriction to rapes of minors.[63]

An interesting peripheral aspect of the Supreme Court's relevant recent consideration of the death penalty is its review of how it is imposed, which has evolved over the years from hanging to the electric chair, to poison gas, to lethal injection.[64] In 2008, the Supreme Court, with two dissenters, rejected the claim that Kentucky's use of lethal injection violates the Eighth Amendment by causing unnecessary pain.[65] For the Court even to address this subject is remarkable. If one asks, "How much difference can it make to someone who knows he is about to be executed whether he suffers a few moments of avoidable pain?" the answer is: "Not a great deal in relation to all his other distress and suffering." By comparison, the undeserved suffering of someone sentenced to life imprisonment for a crime that warrants no more than a sentence of ten years would be extremely great. Prisoners more generally may be victims of unjust suffering if conditions within prisons are inhumane, or if various techniques, such as solitary confinement, have abnormally negative effects on their mental and physical stability. Nonetheless, when it comes to sentences of imprisonment, the modern Court's review has proved *much* more limited than for capital punishment. It has indicated that if prison conditions are unacceptably harsh[66] or prison guards are abusive,[67] the Constitution is violated, but its actual review of such matters has been highly deferential. By a 5–4 margin, the Court did rule in 2011 in *Brown v. Plata*[68] that California's prison conditions had become so inadequate that it had to reduce its number of prisoners by more than 30,000. But the Court, for the most part, has not carefully reviewed whether practices such as solitary confinement are acceptable.[69] When it has considered claims that prison officials are behaving unacceptably by not preventing obvious harms by prisoners on fellow prisoners, the Court has decided that one is liable under the Eighth Amendment "for denying humane conditions of confinement only if he knows that inmates face a substantial [excessive] risk of serious harm and disregards that risk by failing to take reasonable measures to abate it."[70] As Robert Ferguson has strongly urged, courts could well take a more active role in reviewing forms of punishment and official behavior.[71]

The Court has been even more restrained about the length of prison sentences. Although it did hold in 2010 and 2012 that juveniles cannot be sentenced to life without parole,[72] it otherwise has almost always accepted any length of sentence. In *Solem v. Helm,* decided in 1983, the Court did strike down as disproportionate a sentence of life without parole for a recidivist who had written a $100 check that was not backed by an account. [73] But eight years later, in *Harmelin v. Michigan,* the Court retreated in an opinion by Justice Scalia that denied that proportionality was an aspect of "cruel and unusual" punishment as originally conceived, and accepted life without parole for someone carrying a pound and a half of cocaine in his car.[74] In a concurring opinion, Justice Kennedy wrote that extreme sentences that are "grossly disproportionate to a crime" are forbidden; but drug trafficking was a great enough concern to make Harmelin's punishment acceptable.[75] In 2003, the Court sustained a mandatory prison sentence of twenty-five years to life for a repeat offender who had shoplifted three golf clubs.[76] Thus, the Supreme Court is now highly deferential to a state's legislative authorization of prison sentences, regardless of whether they deviate in length from sentences in other states and prior practice.

Finding a principle that both warrants fairly extensive restraint on capital sentences and grants such sweeping latitude about lifelong prison sentences is impossible. Any claim that judges cannot determine whether a prison sentence is too long fails. Whether their primary measure is treatment of the same crime in other states, treatment of similar crimes in the sentencing state, or prior practice, judges possess relatively objective bases for evaluation. If imposing the death penalty on someone who commits multiple rapes or armed robberies is unconstitutional, how can it be acceptable to sentence a woman to life imprisonment without parole for allowing a boyfriend to store a half-kilogram of cocaine in her attic?[77] A proportionality standard for imprisonment would not be too difficult to administer when the penalty is widely acknowledged as far too severe for the crime.

A possible counterargument is that judicial involvement over the length of prison sentences would demand too much effort to prevent only a few injustices. A full appraisal of this argument would require a sense of what standards courts could use and how often they would have to deal with claims that lack merit. A powerful consideration in favor of some judicial involvement is how unjust certain prison sentences can be, like the life sentences discussed above. All of this leads me to believe that more judicial engagement is badly needed, a conclusion supported by the fact that several state constitutions include provisions requiring that sentences be proportional to offenses.[78]

An important aspect of the wisdom of the Supreme Court's involvement concerns its likely effect on broader practices. The Court's recognition of individual constitutional rights often affects how officials and ordinary people see things. A broad right of free speech, for example, leads us to think that the government should not seek to impair most speech. Were the Court to declare even infrequently that some prison sentences are beyond the pale, citizens and officials might begin to care more about the fairness of what legislatures allow. The important need for reform is shown by Robert Ferguson's powerful book that reveals just how harsh our present practices are.[79] Not only does typical imprisonment fail to provide help to prisoners to reform their behavior, but also the number and length of sentences has increased drastically as a consequence of fear of crime. In the last three decades of the twentieth century in the United States, the incarceration rate rose by 500 percent, and it is now five to twelve times greater than in European countries and Japan.[80] Interestingly, one of those who has spoken out strongly for the proposition that "our punishments [are] too severe, our sentences too long" is Justice Anthony M. Kennedy, now the swing voter in many controversial Supreme Court cases.[81] Were the Supreme Court itself to begin to hold that various excessive sentences and unduly harsh prison conditions go beyond constitutional limits, that in itself would be only a small step toward the needed general reforms, but it could make a real contribution.

Whether one focuses on only the death penalty or includes sentences of imprisonment, the question of how disproportionate penalties should be assessed remains. Given that the objects of the criminal law include deterrence, retribution, incapacitation, and rehabilitation, should a state be able to select any one of these to justify the severity of its punishment? John Stinneford contends that the key should be the retributive basis of punishment: people should not be punished beyond what they deserve.[82] This conclusion, which need not imply that the main purpose of criminal punishment is retribution, only that punishments should not exceed levels of wrongdoing, is sound; but it does warrant a qualification for certain crimes. If deterrence is both very important and difficult, either because many people are inclined to engage in the dangerous behavior or because ferreting out offenders is arduous, the need to deter effectively may justify a stronger penalty than actual blameworthiness would indicate. One such example is slightly negligent driving by someone who has consumed just over the permitted amount of alcohol. Almost no one *always* manages to drive without falling into a degree of negligence, and many drive after drinking a bit more than their state allows; but if faulty driving results in a serious accident, a substantial penalty may be justified in order to discourage such behavior. However, apart from this kind of example, serious punishments should not be greater than a person's wrongdoing warrants.

When we turn to judicial methods of evaluation, both prior practice and legislative authorization should carry weight. A focus on prior practices provides a precaution against simply accepting what popular opinion temporarily supports,[83] and legislative authorization gives assurance of the views of the political branches. However, such authorization should not automatically be taken to cover every conceivable application—some of which legislators may not have had in mind. Independent judicial assessment, even beyond determining the needed thresholds of prior practice and legislative authorization, also has a place. Although moral appraisals and empirical evidence about the legitimacy and effectiveness of many forms of punishment are disputed, judges need not simply rely on their own personal reactions. They can properly afford substantial weight to assessments of relevant experts, such as the basic idea that juveniles, not having reached full maturity, are less responsible than adults, and that sentencing to life a drug-addicted "mule" who is carrying cocaine is unlikely seriously to deter other desperate addicts or the "kingpins" in charge of drug traffic.

A special problem about capital punishment is how the degree of acceptance should be assessed. A majority of states and the federal government now authorize capital punishment, but outside of a relatively few states, its actual imposition is rare. From 1976 to May of 2014, the federal government executed only three offenders, and in those years, sixteen of the states with capital punishment each had fewer than eight executions. Texas, on the other hand, had 515.[84] Exactly how a court should assess the degree of support for capital punishment is difficult because of these discrepancies. A sound approach would take into account legislative authorization, actual sentences, and actual executions. If the number of actual executions became very small or was limited almost entirely to one or two states, that by itself should be enough to declare the penalty unacceptable.

A broad interpretive question about the American constitution that has particular force for the death penalty and harshness of prison sentences concerns the status of international law and practice. One argument that capital punishment is unacceptable rests on its abandonment in nearly every other liberal democracy. For a strict originalist, this fact is completely irrelevant, and even those who accept a degree of evolution in what counts as unconstitutional may doubt how far sources outside this country should count. The answer is that they should certainly figure in any *independent* judgment reached by Justices since they do reflect the considered view of numbers of legislatures and populations.[85] And the idea that the United States is a member of a genuine international community should render the observance of standards widely accepted in other similar societies of modest relevance. One could reach a similar conclusion about prison sentences that are far more severe than what other liberal democracies authorize.

E. Status, "Uncontrollable" Acts, and Strict Liability

I now turn to areas in which the Supreme Court has refrained from what would be intrinsically plausible expansions of the Eighth Amendment. A half century ago, the Supreme Court tentatively embarked on a journey that could have implicated the Amendment in substantial domains of the criminal law, including acts over which a person has no "control," the insanity defense, and strict liability. The journey has ended without significant involvement by the Court.

The Court ruled in *Robinson v. California* that someone cannot be punished purely for a status.[86] California law had made being addicted to narcotics criminal, in theory covering an addict who had just moved to California for a treatment program and had never used narcotics in that state. The Court ruled with an opinion by Justice Stewart, one of the more conservative Justices on the Warren Court, that persons can be convicted only for criminal behavior, not for "status" alone.

What then of convictions for acts that are uncontrollable given that status? This issue was raised six years later in 1968 in *Powell v. Texas*, a case with potentially broad implications for both "cruel and unusual punishment" and "due process of law." [87] Leroy Powell was convicted in a county court under a Texas statute that made getting drunk in public a minor criminal offense. The defense claimed that Powell, who had been convicted of this crime about 100 times since 1949, suffered from the "disease of chronic alcoholism."[88] Although ruling that this was no defense, the trial court accepted "findings of fact" submitted by defense counsel that chronic alcoholism is a disease that destroys the afflicted person's willpower to resist the constant, excessive consumption of alcohol, that a chronic alcoholic does not appear in public by his own volition but under a compulsion, and that Powell was such a chronic alcoholic.[89] The Supreme Court affirmed Powell's conviction, 5–4, but five Justices actually accepted Powell's basic argument that one who engages in an act he cannot control because of an underlying condition should not be punished. For the plurality, Justice Marshall rejected this constitutional contention, expressing doubt that alcoholics lose a "voluntary exercise of ... will" over when and how much to drink.[90] Also evidencing more fundamental doubts about relying on the "compulsion" in this context, he suggested that civil commitment may not be better for alcoholics than minor convictions, which themselves may reinforce public attitudes against alcoholism and public drunkenness. Justice Fortas's dissent urged to the contrary, that is, that Powell's conviction did violate the Eighth Amendment because a person should not be punished if "the defined crime is a part of the pattern of his disease and is occasioned by a compulsion symptomatic of the disease."[91] Justice White, the fifth Justice voting to affirm the conviction, accepted the basic logic of Fortas's dissent but found the evidence insufficient to show that Powell's public drunkenness was an inevitable consequence of his alcoholism.[92]

One of the central interpretive disagreements in *Powell* was over the possibility of limiting the novel constitutional principle at issue. Justice Fortas wrote that an alcoholic could "be convicted for criminal conduct which is not a characteristic and involuntary part of the pattern of the disease as it afflicts him...."[93] Justice Marshall called this "limitation by fiat;"[94] if a chronic alcoholic cannot be punished for public drunkenness, how can he be punished for other antisocial acts caused by his drunkenness? Marshall also suggested that the rule proposed by Fortas would impel the court into defining an insanity test in constitutional terms.[95] Justice Black regarded its implications as even broader, namely that it would be "cruel and unusual to punish a person who is not morally blameworthy."[96]

Because the implications of much of the language of Justice Fortas's opinion are broad, it is instructive to explore how far they conflict with present law and whether one can identify considerations of utility, including problems of identifying those lacking control of what they do, as bases to set limits on the practical implementation of an approach like his. The kinds of excuses the Fortas approach might generate fall into two broad categories: claims that an act is compelled, that is, that the desire to perform it is not resistible; and claims that the actor was ignorant in some essential sense about the act.

1. Compelled Acts and the Insanity Defense

If an alcoholic is a "compelled" actor whose public drunkenness is not blameworthy and does not deserve punishment, neither retribution nor deterrence provides a core principle to treat all other "compelled" actions differently. Nevertheless, both the possibility that punishment is serving other utilitarian ends and the difficulty of identifying genuine compulsion could provide bases not to treat all kinds of compelled acts in the same way.

If, as Justice Fortas wrote, use is symptomatic of the disease of addiction, physical substances other than alcohol are similar. And one cannot really separate purchase and possession for one's own use from the use itself. Addiction, of course, is clearest when the body possesses a strong physical need for a drug, but since a chronic alcoholic's compulsion is not simply explained by physical addiction, a principle that covers his drinking would reach other forms of addiction that are significantly psychological. Although the difficulty of identifying whether someone is compelled by addiction to perform an act can vary depending on the drug involved, we have no reason to suppose it will be significantly harder for heroin and other drugs than it is for alcohol.

A conceivable utilitarian argument for punishing drug addicts, though not alcoholics, is that doing so may deter people from using narcotics in the first place or from becoming addicts once they are voluntary users. However, the practical force of this argument is sharply curtailed so long as addicts may be subject to lengthy civil commitment as dangers to themselves and to society. That could probably deter about as well as the threat of criminal penalties.

Looked at from the perspectives of retribution and individual deterrence, the dissent's principle in *Powell* would also imply some constitutional limit on tests of insanity. A person whose mental disease completely removes his capacity to resist an act is no more to blame for what he does than the alcoholic who succumbs to the urge to drink. Any attempt to distinguish these kinds of compulsions on the basis that "mental disease" is itself too elusive a concept for determining when someone is not to blame is unconvincing for three reasons. First, the concept that a person with an identifiable mental condition suffers from a disease is no more arbitrary than the notion that a compulsion to drink is a kind of disease. Second, all insanity tests now used already employ the notion of mental disease or disorder. Third, and most important, the crucial concern is not whether a condition is labeled a disease, but whether it produces a compulsion to act in a particular way.

The strict *M'Naghten* defense for insanity does not really fit with excusing chronic alcoholics for public intoxication. Under that test, a defendant does not count as insane unless he was "labouring under such a defect of reason, from disease of the mind, as not to know the nature and quality of the act he was doing; or if he did know it, that he did not know he was doing what was wrong."[97] This basic test remains the standard in thirty-one states.[98] Although approaches to the insanity defenses that excuse a person whose act is "compelled" by a mental disease are consistent with excusing "compelled" chronic alcoholics who know they are doing "wrong," that is definitely not true of a purely cognitive test. Yet when the *M'Naghten* standard, unameliorated by any version of an "irresistible impulse test," was attacked as violative of due process in *Leland v. Oregon*, the Supreme Court sustained it unanimously.[99] Justice Clark, writing for the majority, indicated that the science of psychiatry had not advanced far enough to *require* a departure from the right and wrong test.[100]

We can perceive practical arguments for retaining the *M'Naghten* rule even if chronic alcoholics should be excused. Since a finding of not guilty by reason of insanity is likely to result in indefinite civil commitment, we may assume that the defense is usually raised only for serious crimes, particularly murder, and the worry that responsible actors may hope to feign insanity is genuine. A different argument is that punishment of those who are not obviously completely out of their minds helps to satisfy outraged community feelings when someone who appears culpable commits a shocking crime. Although one could defend using the *M'Naghten* standard even while rejecting the punishment of chronic alcoholics for public intoxication, the principle of the *Powell* dissent, insofar as it is persuasive, does cast serious doubt on the tenability of a strict cognitive standard of insanity and should lead to a thorough reexamination of its grounds.

The Supreme Court's actual determination that the mental condition of an offender at the time of execution can render the imposition of the death penalty unconstitutional[101] could similarly point to a reexamination of *M'Naghten*. The Court's reasoning in *Ford* was that, as perceived in the common law, execution of someone who is insane does not deter and serves no retributive value and thus "offends humanity."[102] If this is true, can criminal punishment of someone who probably lacked control due to mental illness at the time he acted serve those objectives? That seems extremely doubtful. Of course, the need for isolation of those who seriously harm others remains, but for this, it may not matter much if commitment is civil or is to prison following a criminal conviction.

2. Acts That the Actors Do Not Realize Are Wrong

The theory of the *Powell* dissent is that it is objectionable to punish someone for an antisocial act performed by him but over which he has no real control. From the perspectives of blameworthiness and individual deterrence, punishing someone who supposes, after exercising all possible care, that the act he performs is socially beneficial and permitted by law seems just as objectionable, even though the actor turns out to be mistaken.

For crimes, or elements of crimes, that are framed in terms of strict or absolute liability, it matters not whether the defendant did everything in her power to conform her conduct or that of her "agent" to the law's requirements. Strict liability is common for public welfare offenses, such as building regulations, many traffic offenses, and the sale of adulterated foods; but it also applies to mistakes of fact with regard to certain other offenses. A man may be strictly liable if he misjudged the age of a female in a statutory rape prosecution, and an intervener in a fight may be guilty of assault if he reasonably, though mistakenly, believed the party he aided had a right to defend himself.[103] The felony-murder and misdemeanor-manslaughter rules represent a different form of strict liability, holding one who willingly commits a crime strictly liable for the consequence of death. This form of strict liability is consistent with a principle that an actor should be punished only if he is morally blameworthy, although the prescribed penalty may be disproportionate to his degree of blameworthiness.

Strict liability not only is common, but it also enjoys relatively long-standing acceptance by the Supreme Court.[104] While the opinions in *Powell* did not refer to those cases, the principle that would have excused Powell because he did not "deserve" punishment and could not be deterred applies equally to those who believe, after exercising all reasonable care, that they are performing lawful and desirable acts. The substantial arguments for strict liability are twofold: it makes people very careful, which is particularly desirable for certain activities, and it avoids the difficult endeavor of distinguishing culpable from nonculpable actors.

The argument about encouraging care has considerable force if one contrasts strict liability with liability based on purposeful, knowing, or reckless acts, but these are *not* the only alternatives. Punishment could be imposed for negligence or even for acts that do not meet some higher standard, such as "all care reasonably possible." Since an actor cannot be expected to do more than exercise "all care reasonably possible," strict liability can do little more in comparison with the use of that test than simplify identification of those to be punished, thus discouraging evasions of the law or carelessness by offenders who hope their willful disobedience or negligence will not be provable. An advocate of strict liability can urge that determining culpability is particularly hard for certain behavior or that making such assessments is too wasteful. We have little reason to suppose that the first hypothesis is generally true. Proving an actor's state of mind is common in the criminal law, and not even that would be required if culpability rested on an objective standard of negligence. The hypothesis that determinations of culpability are wasteful has greater force, given that it is always less efficient to allow a defense of nonresponsibility. That benefit, however, is not generally thought to outweigh the value of punishing only those found culpable. When speedy enforcement is essential and the consequences of "guilt" for an offender are minor, society has a sound basis to eschew the usual defenses in the interests of quick, cheap determinations. But this conclusion does not extend to more serious offenses. For these, genuine strict liability is a mistake.

In addition to strict liability, the dissenters' premise in *Powell* could have implications for negligence liability, when the actor, because of some incapacity, both lacked consciousness of any risk and was not to blame for that.[105] It could also cast doubt on the absence of a defense based on ignorance of law when a defendant was completely without fault for failing to know the law. In short, had the Supreme Court actually embraced the basic theory presented in Powell's defense, that might have led to the concepts of cruel punishment and due process being employed for constitutional review of significant aspects of the criminal law.

Why has the Supreme Court refrained from such involvement? Its backing away may partly be a consequence of changing membership, but it is also explicable in terms of a disinclination to get involved in the intricacies of the substantive criminal law. As with *Powell* itself, many similar appraisals could require difficult judgments about the effective operation of that law.

If we analyze these issues closely, I believe we can find *some protections* that would not create serious difficulties. For example, if strict liability is the basic standard, or ignorance of the law provides no defense, perhaps a person should have a right not to be convicted if she could establish by a preponderance of evidence that (1) by exercising all reasonable care, she could not have perceived the crucial facts on which liability is based or could not have discerned what the law provided, and (2) the act in which she engaged had no adverse social consequences given her well-informed judgment about the facts. At some time in the future, the U.S. Supreme Court, or state supreme courts, may enter some of these domains, but we can certainly understand the failure thus far as partly based on a judgment that such an entangling of the courts in supervising standards of criminal liability is too complicated to warrant such extensions of "cruel and unusual" punishment or due process of law.

F. Discriminating Enforcement

One might think a punishment is "cruel" if it is imposed almost entirely on members of a minority or on the poor, especially those who have happened to hurt upper- or middle-class whites. A person subject to capital punishment has a strong contention of unfairness if he knows that were he white, or his victims black, that sentence would almost certainly not have been imposed. But, here again, we have serious practical difficulties. Virtually no sentences are uniformly imposed, and individuals who are poorer and are members of minority groups may be likely, because of jury perceptions and less able legal representation, to be punished more severely. Courts cannot preclude every punishment that might have been lighter had the offender been of a different race or social class, and it is difficult, almost impossible, to say with certainty whether a particular punishment would not have been imposed had the guilty person been different in either respect.

Sex discrimination presents another problem for any such approach. If women tend to be punished less severely than men, should this provide a constitutional argument for any male offender against the punishment he has received? A further difficulty is that were any particular penalty, such as capital punishment, declared unconstitutional when imposed on members of one group, it would then not be fair to impose it on others. The Court's disinclination to get into this subject under the Eighth Amendment or Equal Protection Clause is thus understandable, even though it may sustain some serious injustices in the enforcement of the criminal law. As far as capital punishment is concerned, the unfairness in instances of its actual imposition is one strong argument for eliminating it altogether by statute or constitutional decision.

G. Active and Passive Domains

What we can see overall is that in certain regards, the Supreme Court has adopted a fairly flexible, evolutionary approach to the Eighth Amendment, but in the context of length of imprisonment and bases for criminal liability, it has been quite restrained, not tackling many results that are fairly seen as being at odds with modern conceptions of just punishment. These variations are at least partly explicable in terms of the complexities of constitutional interpretation and the hesitancy to enter domains in which particular determinations might be difficult and unlikely to have a significant effect on the general operation of our system of criminal punishment. Nevertheless, powerful arguments for greater judicial involvement with respect to the length of particular prison sentences is badly needed. Such involvement is also desirable in other areas as well.

CONCLUSION

The specific topics in this chapter provide strong support for many of the claims made in the general theorizing of its five predecessors. With "cruel and unusual punishment," we see how difficult it is to identify a dominant original understanding, or even to distinguish what enactors and readers might have perceived. We also understand why, in some domains, sticking with original understanding about specific practices would be greatly misguided, given changing social institutions and changing values. The Supreme Court has not here stuck with one interpretive strategy, and has failed to explain why it adopts radically different approaches to certain closely similar issues, such as grossly disproportionate prison sentences as compared with unjust capital sentences. Clearly, part of what is going on involves concerns about what assessments in individual cases judges will be able to make. If one looked at the range of Eighth Amendment law, one could not really identify with any precision a dominant interpretive strategy, and one easily sees multiple bases of interpretation that are affecting outcomes. In the chapters to follow, we will explore these complexities further in a range of constitutional domains.

Part III

ALLOCATIONS OF POWERS

Chapter 7

Federal Separation of Powers

I. INTRODUCTION

This chapter turns from the protection of a basic individual right to the distribution of political power within the federal government of the United States. Although commonly referred to as the separation of powers, that label is substantially misleading because many powers are shared rather than genuinely divided. The analysis here explores approaches to interpretation that have been, and should be, used in this broad area, which includes domestic political life, war powers, and agreements with foreign governments.

Along with the following chapter, which is devoted to federal and state authority, this chapter shows how issues about the distributions of power differ in specific respects from constitutional claims of rights, and it supports the book's central themes. No simple interpretative strategy suffices; the exact mix of strategies varies, depending on the provision and the particular subject involved. Judges need to be sensitive to society's historical development over time. They must also attend both to the kinds of issues they can fruitfully resolve and how they can develop standards that can best guide future decisions by judges and other officials.

A central way in which interpreting authorizations of power differs from enforcing basic restrictions on what the government may do concerns the role of the courts. Some controversies about whether an exercise of power is appropriate may never reach federal courts because of requirements of standing and ripeness. Courts refrain from deciding other issues because they regard them as political questions, assigned exclusively to other branches or too sensitive for judicial involvement. With respect to still other issues, judges accord great deference to resolutions by the political branches, especially when those seem to agree. Since overriding the other branches is especially difficult when judges undertake a functional analysis that weighs all relevant factors, advocates favoring greater judicial review are likely to be drawn to more formalist standards for specific issues.

Judicial restraint in its various forms when courts deal with the constitutional allocation of powers sharply raises the question how other branches should regard constitutional restrictions. As we saw in the last chapter, legislators might properly take the Eighth Amendment as imposing restraints about the length of prison sentences that courts will not enforce. The existence of constitutional limits on political branches that reach beyond judicial enforcement is of great practical importance for the distribution of powers because of practices of judicial avoidance and considerable deference to Congress and the President. How those other branches should conceive constraints receives more concentrated attention here.

Dichotomies between allocations of power and individual rights are not always stark and absolute. Claims about separation of powers do involve plaintiffs asserting legal rights, and one may believe that the distribution of powers helps to prevent tyranny.[1] But when a litigant asserts that only Congress, not the President, can restrict certain actions, he is not claiming an unassailable privilege to engage in that behavior,[2] and only rarely are concerns about political distribution tied closely to anxiety about tyrannical impairment of rights.

For assessing the places of original understanding and subsequent history, two features regarding the distribution of powers are especially notable. First, the Constitution set up structures of government different from those in preceding history—here, one cannot conclude that most vague or indecisive language simply referred to existing practices, a claim sometimes made about various individual rights. Second, the importance of historical development in this area has less to do with shifting community morality than novel structures of government and social relations that provide a powerful basis not to give too great a weight to original understanding about exactly how powers were to be distributed. Because what was created was unprecedented in many respects, enactors and people of the time could hardly have been confident about how things would work even then; and, of course, their foreseeing all the ways in which American society has changed over the centuries was outright impossible.

Before it focuses on controversies in specific substantive areas, the chapter explores the significance of nonjudicial constitutional restraints, comments on the relation between the degree of judicial involvement and the chosen form of interpretation, outlines the "political question" doctrine, and inquires about the proper balance in this domain of original understanding and historical development.

II. NONJUDICIAL CONSTITUTIONAL CONSTRAINTS

To appraise the role of constitutional law in constraining political actors beyond limits set by decisive judicial determinations, one needs to grasp why such constraints make sense, how they are best conceived, and how effective they may or may not be.

A brief reflection on "primitive" societies, nongovernmental bodies, customary international law, and certain historical constitutions helps reveal how legal constraints may exist without judicial enforcement. The best approach to when a "primitive" society first begins to create laws is that once clear rules of behavior are established with prescribed penalties for violations (imposed by the community or its leaders), these count as "law" although preceding the development of judicial bodies. Within many modern nongovernmental institutions, such as private law schools, certain rules exist that are seen to impose more than moral restraint, even though observance is left to the individuals themselves, or nonjudicial colleagues. For example, a professor must teach a course for a number of hours per semester, even if no judicial-like body determines her compliance. Were a person hesitant to speak of "law" when the government is not involved, the rule here is definitely "law-like," and it is the same as in state universities that are aspects of government.

Similarly, firmly settled aspects of customary international law are seen as "law" constraining national governments, whether or not judicial tribunals are available for enforcement. Finally, a number of historical written constitutions were not enforceable against legislatures. Nonetheless, they were properly understood as involving legal constraints on those legislatures.[3] In summary, if a society has adopted reasonably specific rules that members, including political officials, regard as having legal force, these constitute a kind of "law," whether or not judges enforce them.

Given this truth, it follows that judicial involvement need not be all or nothing. A legal system may include some rules that are subject to judicial enforcement and others that are not. (A constitution may also include, as does the Canadian constitution, intermediate circumstances in which courts can announce resolutions, but the legislature may override these by special procedures.[4]) In addition to legal restrictions totally unenforced by courts but part of the system of government,[5] courts may resolve other issues, but only after affording great deference to the judgments of political officials. In such instances, those officials may also need to perceive constraints beyond those that judges will impose.[6]

In asking whether constraints of these kinds exist, we must distinguish conceptual possibilities, actual understanding, and practical import. Although "legal restraints" *can* reach beyond what courts will actually enforce,[7] whether within any particular society those inside and outside the government *do* conceptualize constraints as "legal" is an empirical question. Insofar as the Office of Legal Counsel in the United States treats many restraints on presidential action as limits of constitutional powers, even though not subject to judicial enforcement, it engages in that conceptualization.[8] That alone does not tell us the scope of practical import. Do political actors use legal terminology because they understand possible inhibitions as genuinely "legal," or is this insincere rhetoric to justify decisions reached entirely on nonlegal political grounds?

Could one reject applying the idea that constitutional restraints reach beyond judicial involvement on the basis that the Constitution then represents only an "aspiration"?[9] The answer is "no." Given that another political branch may impose an effective penalty for what it takes as a trespass on its own powers, judicial noninvolvement does not entail that whatever the Constitution then says is *merely* a guide to a wise decision. Of course, absent judicial enforcement, an authoritative determination whether the Constitution has been "violated" may be lacking, but what is central here is how political actors do, and should, interpret and exercise their responsibilities. If a legislator considering excessive imprisonment for a minor crime said to herself, "Whatever prison sentence we impose actually satisfies constitutional requirements, but we should probably try not to be too harsh," she would be taking the Eighth Amendment as then providing only an "aspiration." But if she said, "We violate the Constitution if we impose an indisputably excessive sentence, although the courts will accept it," she would see the amendment as setting an actual restraint. Discerning how political officials genuinely conceive these matters will often be difficult, and no sharp line may distinguish a "strong aspiration standard" from an actual, though nonenforceable, constraint. But denying that officials may regard themselves as legally bound to comply directly with constitutional standards that courts decline to enforce, or under-enforce,[10] would be seriously mistaken.

Understanding that executive officials and members of Congress *may* consider themselves under constitutional constraints unenforced by courts does not, of course, tell us whether they actually take this view and, if so, whether their appraisal of their duties is reasonably balanced or indefensibly slanted toward whatever they would otherwise prefer to do. A person who reflects on possible dangers to the constitutional order needs to ask not only what crucial officials now perceive, but what future developments are likely and how those most threatening may be forestalled.

Exactly these questions have been raised about modern presidential power. Given the notable example of a memo from the Office of Legal Counsel during the administration of George W. Bush defending investigative techniques widely seen as constitutionally forbidden "torture," some have concluded that any nonjudicial restraints on the President are purely political, or that those within the executive branch do now, and will increasingly, interpret the Constitution to allow whatever the President and other leading executive officials are inclined to do. Bruce Ackerman has offered the most outspoken scholarly challenge along these lines. [11] He proposes combating this extreme danger to our constitutional fabric by a number of practical measures, the most important of which is the creation of a Supreme Executive Tribunal that would not be subject to presidential control. The tribunal, which would largely supplant the Justice Department's Office of Legal Counsel, would review proposed executive actions and issue legally binding rulings. Although compelling the President to adhere to rulings within the executive branch would itself involve a drastic change of doubtful constitutional validity, Ackerman urges that such a reform is necessary.

In an extended review of Professor Ackerman's book, Trevor Morrison responds to the basic concerns about the ineffectiveness of judicial involvement and the nonobjectivity of assessments within the executive branch itself.[12] Although the status of constitutional judgments made within the executive branch is more subtle and harder for outsiders to evaluate than whether the President complies with Supreme Court rulings, Dean Morrison notes multiple facts that cut strongly against the Ackerman position. On some important issues, the Office of Legal Counsel has concluded that the executive branch cannot constitutionally undertake what has been proposed. Its written reports do usually come out in favor of contemplated actions, but in many instances, initial negative evaluations are delivered orally, and proposals are then dropped or altered.[13] Finally, and perhaps most important, the value for the President of support from the Office of Legal Counsel depends on its employing, and being conceived to employ, standards of genuine evaluation, not merely writing briefs that favor any executive action. The Office's inclusion of civil servant lawyers who are not politically appointed reflects this tradition, and leaders of the Office are commonly concerned about how they will be perceived if they favor outrageous conclusions (such as those in the "torture" memos).[14] The White House Counsel's Office may be more one-sided in its evaluations, but it often adheres to what the Office of Legal Counsel has concluded, and many of its duties do not concern legal opinions.

Given Morrison's careful appraisal, the Ackerman challenge appears to be overstated, but there *are differences* between how the Office of Legal Counsel and courts approach issues. The Office tries to reflect its "best view of the law,"[15] but it may rely partly on special information not available to judges, and it gives a kind of precedential force to executive action precedents and its own past opinions. Further, when a proposed practice could easily be regarded as acceptable or not, the Office is likely to support it, and, unlike courts, part of its responsibility is to try to work out approaches that will constitute lawful ways to proceed.[16] These reasons do create risks that its opinions may become too one-sided, risks that Morrison suggests can partly be mitigated by publication of its written reports and by inclusion in those reports of accounts of preceding oral interchanges.[17]

A rather different question about how other officials should regard the Constitution concerns the force of actual judicial resolutions rather than non-involvement by courts. What should these officials do when they believe that the Supreme Court simply "got it wrong"? The idea that the

Court has reached a misguided conclusion can, of course, exist across the entire spectrum of constitutional issues. When legislators within a state consider passing a law that forbids early abortions, ones clearly protected by the governing cases, an advocate might argue: "The Constitution does not protect abortions, regardless of what the Supreme Court has mistakenly concluded." Such discussion is defensible, so long as the speaker is clear that he is contending that the Supreme Court has failed to understand the Constitution properly and that others should act upon this failure, even though the Court has final authority to resolve the crucial issues involved. In terms of political philosophy and practice, the question this problem involves is how much deference other officials should grant—not only to a court's resolution of a particular case but also to its announced constitutional rules. Unless such deference were common, the system would break down; it would be incredibly inefficient if officials with little hesitation acted against judicially set constitutional rules, litigants then claimed constitutional violations, and courts sustained the claims. A failure to follow a judicial ruling, especially one of the Supreme Court, would be particularly troubling to the overall system if a violation of a clearly established constitutional standard occurred in a manner that left courts helpless to respond effectively. However, granting that deference should almost always be accorded, its withholding on some vital issues may still be defended, especially if doing so might help the Court to change its mind.

III. JUDICIAL REVIEW

Closely tied to concerns about the effectiveness of constitutional constraints that are not enforced by courts are issues about how courts should perform. Although this chapter mainly concerns relations between Congress and the President, the status of judicial review is, of course, one aspect of the separation of powers. A fundamental preliminary question is whether the judiciary has any place reviewing the acts of other branches of the federal government. As we have seen, the Constitution itself explicitly provides federal judicial review of state actions claimed to violate federal law. Scholars have occasionally asserted that the Framers and ratifiers did not authorize judicial review of what was done by Congress and the executive branch;[18] but the balance of historical evidence is substantially to the contrary.[19] In *Marbury v. Madison*,[20] the Supreme Court established that it did have such authority, though it managed to do so in a way that did not practically interfere with what the presiding government was declining to do,[21] and Chief Justice Marshall's opinion did not reject the possibility that *some* constitutional questions might be left to the political branches.[22]

Whatever the original understanding, the authority of judicial review is firmly entrenched as an aspect of our constitutional law, one whose complete abandonment is really inconceivable. A partial answer to concerns about the nonrepresentativeness of federal judges is that, given their appointments by the President with Senate approval and the power of Congress to dictate the precise range of their jurisdiction, they are not wholly free of political control. The conclusion that courts appropriately review federal statutes and executive actions does not itself resolve just when and how judges should respond to contested exercises of power. Leaving claims that federal branches have violated the reserved powers of states for the following chapter, the focus here is on challenges to the allocations or modes of performance of powers that fall within the authority of the national government.

Issues regarding separation of powers break down into two main categories. The first involves the division of functions. Is any particular responsibility assigned to the legislature, the executive, the courts, or to a combination of branches? Central questions are how far Congress can prescribe allocations, and how far courts should decide these questions or leave them to Congress and the President. The second broad category concerns how any particular function is executed. For example, can Congress defeat a decision by the executive branch with a legislative "veto" exercised by only one of its houses? Although members of Congress can perform some tasks without formal legislation, that is required for others.

When judges and other officials reflect on allocations of power, the main values implicated are preserving conceived and healthy structures of government, rather than curbing unfair treatment of individuals. And the primary weight of historical practice here is not that it represents a particular moral vision but rather that its arrangements were not clearly settled by the constitutional document, or have achieved continuing acceptance over time.

The greater the concern that the political officials will go "off the tracks" if not checked, the more crucial judicial engagement may seem to be. Believing that judicial review is needed can underlie a functionalist reason for the Supreme Court to adopt formalist approaches to relevant constitutional constraints since these do not make outcomes depend on judges announcing that political officials have been misguided in what amounts to a subtle balance of relevant factors. After a period of strong withdrawal from separation issues, the Court has, in recent years, become more involved and more inclined to use formalist approaches both for interpretation and for its announced standards of application. Some of these standards have seemed insensitive to what should really be regarded as central. In general, more flexible standards in this domain may usually make the most sense, even if they entail less judicial oversight of what another branch has done.

IV. ALLOCATIONS OF POWER AND THE JUDICIAL ROLE

A. What the Text Resolves and Fails to Resolve

Although making some allocations and methods of performance clear, the constitutional text leaves many specific matters open. Section 1 of article I states, "All legislative Powers herein granted shall be vested in a Congress of the United States...." Section 8 sets out specific powers, such as "To declare War," "To regulate Commerce ... among the several States," and "To make all Laws which shall be necessary and proper." Other sections set various specific limits on how Congress may act. Without explicit "herein granted" language, which would imply the absence of any power not specified, article II vests the "executive Power" in a President. Section 2 states that the President shall be "Commander in Chief of the Army and Navy," can make treaties and appoint ambassadors and other officers with the "Advice and Consent" of the Senate, and can require the opinions of officers in executive departments, grant pardons, and fill vacancies during a Senate recess. Section 3 provides, among other things, that the President "shall take Care that the Laws be faithfully executed...." Although all of this language clearly assigns certain responsibilities, it fails to resolve many questions of detail about the respective responsibilities of Congress and the President.

Certain questions about the allocation of powers have existed from the beginning; others are the product of radical social changes. The war power illustrates both kinds. Louis Fisher has noted that, in contrast to the monarchial power to wage war, the Framers "allowed only Congress to loose the military force of the United States on other nations."[23] That does not by itself prescribe how the President was to respond if another country made a surprise military attack across the country's border, or a collection of political dissenters undertook a violent pillage in some isolated area of a state. And in modern times, with substantial United States troops stationed abroad, the country's commitments to protect allies, and the prospect of terrorist attacks, the notion that the President could never by himself, however briefly, authorize military deployment abroad is no longer tenable. A different issue is how far Congress may limit tactics the President might otherwise employ in military conflict. If the use of drone strikes to kill terrorists is legally justified, is that because Congress has authorized it or because it falls within the President's intrinsic powers?[24]

How the more vague provisions of articles II and III may best be construed is fundamentally different from the soundest approach to open-ended constitutional language about individual rights. For rights provisions, an originalist may discern either a reference to particular unacceptable practices, or the authorization of growth over time in response to developing conceptions of human rights and their implementation. Neither of these approaches is really an option for many uncertain aspects of separation of powers.

The structure set up for the federal government was unlike that in Great Britain or under the Articles of Confederation and was not quite like that in any of the new states.[25] Thus, although particular provisions may have been designed to establish specific divisions, no already-settled practice existed that the enactors or readers could implicitly have had in mind for aspects the text itself leaves unresolved. John Manning, developing a persuasive account of the original understanding that does not itself rest directly on whether one refers to enactor intentions or reader appraisals, urges that, lacking a shared sense of how exactly powers should be divided, the framers adopted a significant number of definite allocations and forms of practice that rested on compromises.[26] Because other aspects were not actually resolved, Manning believes that Justices should neither rely wholly on some general concept of the separation of powers *nor* conclude that the original document explicitly or implicitly settled all such issues.

Whether one concentrates on questions the original understanding appears to answer or leave unresolved, the relevance of historical practice and the appropriateness of avoidance or deference are somewhat different here than for guarantees of rights. The novelty of the structures in the original constitution not only makes discerning more specific understandings conveyed by highly general phrases impossible, it also creates powerful doubts that whatever resolutions were then conceived as sound were actually best, either in specific mandated practices or interpretive strategies to endure over centuries. For respective powers, the weight of developments over time depends primarily on changes in social organization, notably the development of political parties, the increasing involvement of government in regulating and supporting how people live their lives—a change that has radically increased the role of administrative agencies—and the drastic nationalization and internationalization of economic and political affairs.

B. Agreement or Acquiescence

A particular judicial concern that affects not only the weight of historical practice but also other bases for deference involves the apparent agreement or acquiescence between the political branches. When fundamental individual rights are stepped on, it does not usually matter much which organ of government is doing it and whether the other political branch approves. But when Congress and the President agree on who should perform an action that is clearly within the scope of the federal government, for a court to say that it knows better is more awkward. This is especially true given the practical force of many shifts over time. Are judges really in a position to second-guess what both political branches regard as a healthy allocation of power? Doubts about this, especially when they employ a functional approach, make it hard for judges to overturn settled practices accepted by both Congress and the President.

All of this confers a special importance on how far the two branches have agreed. The significance of agreement about powers, as well as the different status of basic rights, is illustrated by *Hamdi v. Rumsfeld*.[27] Finding agreement, the Supreme Court upheld the government's detention of a United States citizen as an enemy combatant aligned with the Taliban in Afghanistan, but it also ruled that due process required that he be able to contest the factual ground for his detention "before a neutral decisionmaker."[28] When agreement between Congress and the President is absent, judges are less hesitant to reach their own resolution. This was strikingly apparent in *Youngstown Sheet & Tube Co. v. Sawyer*, in which the Supreme Court refused to accept the President's argument that taking control of the steel industry before a threatened strike during the Korean War was needed to avert an impediment to the war effort.[29] This chapter's section on War Powers explores more subtle nuances in what constitutes actual agreement or degrees of acquiescence.

C. Political Questions

At the extreme end of judicial non-involvement lies the political question doctrine, according to which the courts do not attempt to resolve constitutional issues. Although employed in some cases involving claimed constitutional rights, the doctrine's main use has been with respect to the relative authority of different political entities. The doctrine's presently narrow scope is illustrated by the 2012 case of *Zivotofsky v. Clinton*.[30] Before we look at that case, it helps to divide "political questions" into three categories and to note briefly their historical development.

The simplest kind of political question involves decisions the Constitution leaves to political judgment, without imposing any legal constraint. Thus, the President may have the authority to recognize or not recognize any foreign government. Whatever his decision, it is constitutionally acceptable.

A second type of political question is constitutional constraints that the Constitution explicitly or implicitly designates for final decision to a nonjudicial branch. Thus, Congress decides whether a state has ratified a proposed constitutional amendment.[31] If it disregarded clear instances of ratification, it would violate the Constitution, but the federal courts apparently could provide no remedy.[32]

The third category of political questions involves subjects that are not obviously outside judicial authority. Barring a conclusion that the basic reasons against judicial involvement suggest an implicit constitutional assignment to other officials, a Justice may nevertheless decide that involvement would be unproductive and possibly damaging to the political order or to the Court.

Rachael Barkow has suggested that the original sense of "political question doctrine" was that it occupied one end of a spectrum of how far courts were meant to defer to the political branches.[33] As the doctrine developed, it became more prudential. It may now be reverting to something closer to the original conception but with a narrower understanding of limits on the judicial role.[34]

Historically, a majority or plurality of the Court has relied on the political question doctrine to avoid making an independent determination of whether a state government was not "republican" as required by the Guarantee Clause,[35] and of whether malapportionment in congressional elections violates equal protection.[36] The latter conclusion was overturned in *Baker v. Carr,* which provides the fullest account of bases for invoking the political question doctrine.[37]

Justice Brennan's majority opinion in *Baker,* determining that courts could consider equal protection challenges to malapportionment, identified six relevant elements that can produce political questions:

> a textually demonstrable constitutional commitment . . . to a coordinate political department; or a lack of judicially discoverable and manageable standards for resolving [the issue]; or the impossibility of deciding without an initial policy determination of a kind clearly for nonjudical discretion; or the impossibility of a court's undertaking independent resolution without expressing lack of the respect due coordinate branches of government; or an unusual need for unquestioning adherence to a political decision already made; or the potentiality of embarrassment from multifarious pronouncements by various departments on one question.[38]

A striking example of a circumstance in which a number of these factors would be in play—making it nearly unimaginable that a court would actually decide that the controlling statute and the consequence it directs are invalid—involves succession to the Presidency beyond the Vice President. Article II, section 1, gives Congress the power by law to declare which "Officer" shall succeed and act as President until a new President is elected. Congress has legislated that the Speaker of the House is next in succession. Akhil Amar has claimed that members of the legislative branch were not conceived of as "officers" in the sense that counts here.[39] One might regard the prevailing statute as a kind of subtle legislative invasion of the executive domain, if "officers" constitutionally meant only executive officials. Although the law does not rest on an actual historical practice, it is nonetheless impossible to imagine that, after tragic deaths, the Supreme Court would declare that a House Speaker who had taken over the duties of the President according to the statute was violating the Constitution. If judges tried to enforce Professor Amar's thesis, they would not only severely disrupt the government, but they would also have no clear basis to designate any particular executive officer as effective President, and they would issue rulings that might not be followed by those in power at the time. To avoid such an unsettling conclusion, a court might declare that individuals raising the claim lacked standing; if not, it would either rule that the issue, based on constitutional structure and practical considerations, is a political question in which the judges cannot get involved,[40] or it would defer to the judgment in the statute itself adopted by Congress and signed by the President.

Recognizing that this is an issue on which total judicial avoidance or extreme deference would almost certainly occur and be warranted, what can an outsider say about what is constitutionally required and allowed? She can, of course, follow Amar and conclude that the statute violates the Constitution, whatever view has been taken by each political branch and will be accepted by a court. Or, she can remark that the *present* Constitution, as understood by the people who matter, allows succession by the Speaker. Neither of these forms of rhetoric need be incorrect, but a thoughtful person would have some ground to choose one rather than the other. The label of unconstitutionality could provide a basis for Congressional reconsideration and repeal of the present statute in favor of the kind of designation of an executive official that earlier statutes provided.[41] The reference to "present understanding" would reflect how the sense of terms and the actual ways in which government operates can shift over time and might also imply that this is an inevitable and healthy aspect of perceptions of a constitution that endures. A full account of what the statute represents needs to be specific about how the political branches should perceive "officer" in this setting, and how that should affect judicial decisions.

A central concern with respect to political questions is whether judges can discern a manageable standard of decision. After *Baker*, decided in 1962, the Court went on to establish the "one person—one vote" standard of *Reynolds v. Sims*.[42] The underlying reason for this approach—which was definitely more egalitarian than was conceived for districting when the Equal Protection Clause was adopted—may have been that it is judicially manageable,[43] not requiring a sensitive judgment about when inequality of political representation amounts to unacceptable unfairness.

In the ensuing decades, the Court, rather than relying on political question avoidance, determined the constitutionality of the exclusion of Adam Clayton Powell, Jr. from membership in the House of Representatives,[44] and in other cases sent "signals that the doctrine was disfavored."[45] It did rule that it could not undertake responsibility for supervising state militia[46] and did not pass judgment on whether the Senate could impeach a federal judge based on the report of a fact-finding committee.[47] But in 2000, the Court took jurisdiction in the controversy over whether George W. Bush or Al Gore had won the key state of Florida in the presidential election.[48] In a helpful history of the political question doctrine, Rachel Barkow characterizes that case as "[t]he Nadir of the Political Question Doctrine and the Zenith of Judicial Supremacy."[49]

In the recent case of *Zivotofsky v. Clinton*,[50] the Court did not find a political question, and Chief Justice Roberts' opinion for the Court circumscribed what it treated as relevant to that issue. According to a congressional statute, someone born in Jerusalem (or his guardian) may, upon request, have "Israel" indicated on his passport as his place of birth. The United States government has declined to recognize that Jerusalem is part of Israel, rather than Jordan. When signing the relevant law, President George W. Bush declared that the "Israel" provision was an unconstitutional interference with the President's authority over foreign affairs, and the State Department has subsequently refused to comply with this aspect of the statute. The legal question presented to the Court was whether Congress has the authority to adopt the statute's requirements. Chief Justice Roberts wrote that such questions about the constitutionality of a statute are for courts to decide, that there was neither "a textually demonstrable constitutional commitment of the issue to a coordinate political department; or a lack of judicially discoverable and manageable standard for resolving it."[51] The Court, as a consequence, remanded the case for decision on the merits by the District of Columbia Court of Appeals.[52]

In a concurring opinion, Justice Sotomayor agreed with the result but expressed concern that the majority opinion did not attend to the other factors Justice Brennan had mentioned in *Baker v. Carr*.[53] Although one conceivable implication is that most present-day Justices do not care at all about those factors, that is almost certainly too hasty a conclusion—one that disregards what is special about the birthplace issue. Perhaps no one can assess precisely what degree of offense is done to Jordan and other Arab countries if "Israel" simply appears on a passport of someone born in Jerusalem, but the passage by Congress of the authorizing provision represents a much more telling acceptance of Jerusalem as part of Israel than does an actual passport designation, and if the State Department had been forced by a court to allow the designation, that would not actually have entailed any shift of the basic policy of the executive branch. In other words, whatever may have been the State Department's view, it is hard to see that the passport designation itself involves anything really momentous.

If one asks *only* about textual commitment to another branch and a discoverable judicial standard, the issue of the Speaker of the House succeeding to the presidency strikes one as no more complex than the birthplace designation. No obvious textual commitment gives to Congress the decision who counts as an "officer,"[54] and whether a legislator constitutionally qualifies is certainly as "discoverable and manageable" as most inquiries about original understanding. Yet presented with such a case, the Court would almost certainly invoke the political question doctrine if it did not otherwise avoid independent decision. This example illustrates why one needs to be hesitant to reach broad generalizations on the basis of the language of particular opinions. Although *Zivotofsky* and some previous cases do clearly represent a movement toward greater judicial involvement and a reliance on formal distinctions that contract the scope of the political question doctrine, only when subsequent cases arise that involve more charged issues will we see how far the Court will go in this direction. While I do agree with those who urge that virtual abandonment of the political question doctrine would "undermine the delicate constitutional balance of power,"[55] I also believe it is too early to assess whether this will occur.

V. THE POWERS AND METHODS OF PERFORMANCE OF CONGRESS AND THE PRESIDENT

Across the range of issues in which courts do evaluate the constitutional authority of Congress and the President and the ways they exercise their assigned powers, a pervasive question is how far the criteria judges use should replicate those guiding political officials. One of the particular issues that the chapter explores about the respective authority of Congress and the President is how far the President can reach international agreements by himself alone or with the majority of each house of Congress, rather than obtaining the two-thirds "advice and consent" of the Senate needed for formal treaties. A different issue is when the President can engage troops in military conflict without a formal declaration of war, or at least congressional approval. Domestically, key questions are what the proper practices of administrative agencies are and how far Congress may set controlling standards and actually involve itself. Before looking at these and other particular examples, we shall review various standards of evaluation.

A. Standards of Evaluation

Whether for the original or a modern "living" Constitution, an account of legislative and executive authority must include what is required, what is forbidden, and what is allowed but not required. Within the last category, if the President can do certain things so long as Congress remains silent, Congress may have the ability to terminate or control those actions since, given that when the President's power overlaps with that of Congress, legislation can typically trump a contrary executive practice.

The original understanding of the Constitution, which can matter here as with other constitutional issues, may seem to settle a question, point strongly or weakly in either direction, or leave it essentially unresolved. Defending judicial use of independent criteria to decide is easiest, of course, when the original or existing constitution points only weakly or not at all toward one outcome. As already noted, vague original language about novel respective powers cannot be taken to refer to already existing practices. Justices may believe that early exercises of power after the Constitution's adoption reflected a prior understanding or determined what the document itself left open. Historical practice may also count apart from any relation to original understanding, especially if it has become solidly established and reflects agreement among the political branches. One notable example of early practice settling things was President Washington's recognition of foreign governments. His exercise of this power became quickly accepted, although article II, section 3, of the Constitution, which says that the President "shall receive Ambassadors," does not specify who is to decide when a foreign government should be recognized. The Court decided in June 2015 that the scope of the recognition power overrode the conflicting congressional statute treated in the section on political questions which specified that, for a passport, birth in Jerusalem can be treated as in Israel, contrary to executive policy.[56]

Exactly what counts as acceptance by one branch of what another is doing need not be simple. Paying special attention to the President's allowing executive officials to testify before Congress while claiming a constitutional privilege that such testimony cannot be compelled, Eric Posner and Adrian Vermeule have suggested that what really counts is actual acceptance of a practice, not the President's rhetoric.[57] They grant that a verbal reservation should matter *if* the testimony is likely to be advantageous to him, since then the President has an independent reason not to preclude the official appearing as a witness. But *if* the testimony is to be damaging, the claim of privilege is not to be taken seriously. I think this oversimplifies matters. Because the President may wish to appear cooperative for a number of reasons—even if the specific testimony could be damaging in some way—he may honestly assert a constitutional privilege to prevent such testimony while actually allowing it. For this reason, consistent claims of constitutional authority can carry weight even if they are often effectively waived.

The dominant approaches adopted by major cases to the separation of powers have been classified as "functionalist" and "formalist." A standard formalist approach relies on what the text of the Constitution conveys, and lays down a specific standard for resolving discrete cases; a functionalist approach asks what allocation works effectively in existing social conditions without compromising the fundamental allocation of powers, and sets a more flexible standard for assessing particular claims. This typical connection of interpretive strategy to an announced standard for future cases is neither logically compelled nor always present. Formal interpretation, such as textualism, *could* produce a flexible standard for particular cases, and functionalism can yield quite specific criteria, as in *Miranda v. Arizona*. However, because a functionalist approach is ordinarily flexible about what practices it can allow and involves a weighing of complex considerations, judges find it harder to declare practices unconstitutional than when they adopt a formalist strategy. Problems with the latter are that it may rely on a dubious original understanding and can be insensitive to changing conditions. It turns out that most of the Supreme Court's formalist opinions have not concerned the division of powers among branches, but rather the way in which a branch performs delegated functions.[58]

Although some key opinions of Justices suggest that the original Constitution established a *general* standard of separation of powers which can be used to review various practices, John Manning's more nuanced account explains that compromises qualified genuine "separation" in numerous ways, strikingly, for example, in how statutes and treaties were to be adopted and high level officials were to be appointed.[59] For Manning, a court faithful to the Constitution should respect those compromises, while also recognizing that, as to certain other matters, the text allows subsequent resolutions based on whether practices have become accepted and are responsive to social developments over time.

A functional approach that gives weight to historical practice and to precedents[60] can be based on various foundations. One can understand the Constitution as itself developing apart from formal amendments. One possibility is to identify other forms of specific amendments. Bruce Ackerman suggested more than two decades ago that we should see the basic "constitution" itself as being altered by fundamental democratic changes;[61] but this interpretive approach faces the substantial obstacle of identifying just which democratic movements have been powerful enough to accomplish such changes and exactly what is the content of the new additions. These difficulties would be especially severe for courts, which would have to articulate precisely what political movements have effectively amended the Constitution and in what ways.[62] A less drastic, more viable sense of constitutional change rests on an understanding that is similar to common law development, a perspective that could serve a Burkean conservatism that values traditions and practices that have become settled over time.[63]

One functionalist critique of a judicial approach that relies heavily on the general "separation of powers" idea put forward by Madison is that a crucial claimed connection of "separation of powers" and a healthy system of "checks and balances"—in which each branch effectively curbs excesses by another—is not nearly as tight as is often assumed.[64] Regrettably, even the limited separation of functions the Constitution created is not necessarily effective in assuring the desired checking, and sometimes a mixing of functions may do so better. Courts need to focus on what really should count for an effective balance. One possible resolution, proposed by Thomas Merrill, is that Congress should be acknowledged to have effective authority to determine the divisions of functions, but courts should assure that genuine divisions do exist and that the political branches carry out practices in the proper way.[65] Daryl Levinson and Richard Pildes have suggested that a realistic approach to the respective powers of branches of government should take the alignment of political parties into account,[66] a factor that Curtis Bradley and Trevor Morrison say matters when one tries to determine how far one branch has agreed to or has accepted what another is doing.[67] This chapter returns to these proposed approaches when it examines particular issues.

Accompanying these questions about judicial approaches is how much deference courts should grant to what the other branches have done. With regard to the proper distribution of powers, courts almost always give some force to one branch's accepting or remaining silent about what another branch is undertaking.

For many issues about power allocation, the fact that modern conditions vary significantly from those at the founding undermines any proposal simply to carry out original compromises and to stick precisely to what was then conceived as a desirable separation. Perhaps the most striking development is the growth of the administrative state, which greatly affects both who performs functions and the manner in which those functions are performed. A subsequent section briefly explores a number of cases dealing with administrative agencies,[68] but their very existence demonstrates the obstacles to relying too heavily on the Constitution's text and original understanding. At the time of the founding, people perceived a clear distinction between the making and execution of laws. And the scope of the federal executive branch was very limited: concerned mainly with the collecting of taxes, it comprised a small number of people in just three departments.[69] Even then, officials who executed a law could not avoid some interpretation of it, but that limited exercise is quite different from establishing sets of rules that clearly reach beyond what a statute itself provides—a typical feature of administrative regulation.

In modern society, the federal executive branch, including administrative agencies, constitutes more than 2 million employees.[70] It would be would be impossible, or extraordinarily cumbersome, for Congress to try to adopt as statutes all of the levels of needed federal regulations. Congress thus delegates a great deal of rulemaking to administrative agencies. Although these rules must be "consistent" with authorizing statutes, they also represent independent judgments about what is desirable. In so surrendering their rulemaking power, members of Congress may occasionally wish to avoid taking stands on certain sensitive issues, but mainly they recognize that this delegation is the best way to develop a detailed regulatory system. Given that federal agencies also make quasi-judicial determinations about particular disputes, Professor Strauss's explanation, three decades ago, that these agencies exercise a combination of all three functions of the original branches is obviously correct.[71]

Given these realities, it would *not* make sense for the Supreme Court to dig in its heels and insist on sticking with the original compromises and understandings in light of the radically different modern social order. The gravity of such a mistake would be especially severe because of the general difficulty of enacting constitutional amendments and the near impossibility of formulating a precise division between what Congress itself should do and what it sensibly delegates to agencies. That such a division is not susceptible to simple formulation is partly confirmed by the failure of the Supreme Court, after two decisions in the 1930s that declared very broad delegations impermissible,[72] to subsequently police any line between permissible and impermissible delegations to agencies.

In contrast to disputes about basic allocations of power are those regarding how a branch decides to exercise a power it does possess. Insofar as one can generalize, the modern Supreme Court more readily involves itself in such concerns. In one important case, it suggested that even if Congress has authority to overturn an exercise of executive power, it is constrained in how it does so. Striking down a law allowing one House of Congress to "veto" certain executive decisions, the Court in *INS v. Chadha*[73] ruled that when Congress undertakes such actions, it must follow the normal requirement of bicameral approval and "presentment" to the President. The particular issue involved in the case, a veto of an Attorney General's ruling that a specific alien not be deported, may rightly be viewed as a quasi-judicial determination beyond the legislature's domain. But the Court's opinion was much broader, covering matters within the basic powers of Congress that have been delegated to the executive. In that respect, the Court failed to acknowledge a telling distinction and did not really consider how the best outlook on legislative functioning might have changed with administrative lawmaking.

An administrative ruling may simply implement an existing law or, in effect, adopt a "new rule" that clearly reaches beyond mere interpretation of an existing statute. Congress cannot enact new laws without following normal procedures; but one House, standing by itself, can *defeat proposed* legislative changes. Even if Congress assigns to the executive a broad power to make rules, why should it not similarly be able, by the disapproval of one House, to defeat novel regulations that create rights and duties not themselves contained in statutes? Of course, a formalist argument can be made that the assignment to the executive cannot be questioned, or that as soon as the agency acts, that *is* the law, rendering any congressional disapproval a "changing" of law. A more functional basis to reject single-house disapproval of genuinely new requirements is that distinguishing those from implementation of existing standards is simply too difficult. Nevertheless, from the perspectives of reasonable allocations of powers and appropriate "checks," allowing single-house disapproval of what would be, in effect, a new law seems eminently sensible.[74] Interestingly, a bill before Congress in 2013 aimed at this result with respect to some regulations. Under the bill, major executive regulations that would have a $100 million impact on the economy "shall have no force or effect unless a joint resolution of approval is enacted into law."[75] What the example of a "legislative veto" suggests is that changing structures could matter for performance of functions as well as allocations.

The sections that follow address specific areas of power distribution and some of the controversies that have arisen.

B. Treaties and Foreign Affairs Powers

Article II, section 2, clause 2 of the Constitution gives the President the "Power, by and with the Advice and Consent of the Senate, to make Treaties, provided two thirds of the Senators present concur"; he also needs the Senate's consent (but not a two-thirds approval) to appoint ambassadors. Why is only the Senate involved in treaty ratification, and why is a two-thirds majority required? The founders probably trusted the wisdom of Senators with longer terms more than members of the House of Representatives, and, given equal representation for each state, the two-thirds rule would prevent treaties that impinged unfavorably on a number of states.[76] Thus the northern states' representatives could not approve a trade treaty that would seriously harm the South.

The status of treaties presents a number of interesting, interrelated questions about the relation of the President to the Congress and the power of the federal government vis-à-vis the states. I first address three simpler, more straightforward issues: What constitutes the needed "Advice"? Can the President withdraw from a treaty on his own? And what is the status of treaty law vis-à-vis statutes?

The scope of the "Advice" requirement for treaties was resolved early. Whether the Framers and ratifiers conceived that the President should involve members of the Senate during the negotiations of treaties, that, from the beginning, has not been the standard practice. So long as the Senate willingly approves treaties reached without any initial consultation, a court will not say that something more was required. Given that the constitutional text is hardly explicit about what more—if anything—was needed, concluding that the Constitution, at least as it has developed, does not require prior "advice" is eminently sensible; and indeed the sense of "advice" at the founding may have conveyed less involvement than we would now conceive. Although consent to a set text hardly amounts to "advice" in the ordinary modern linguistic sense, given that the present approach was established early, in the Washington administration, one may surmise that may well reflect original understanding *or* fill in a gap left by the original document. In any event, it may be defended as simply working most effectively.

Whether the President can withdraw from treaties on his own without the approval of the Senate has never been decisively settled, but Presidents have done so on a number of occasions; and, given the extent to which changes take place in international relations, this is practically desirable on at least some occasions. When President Carter's termination of a mutual defense treaty was challenged, the Court of Appeals for the District of Columbia Circuit en banc upheld his unilateral power, and the Supreme Court dismissed the opposing claim as nonjusticiable.[77]

The Constitution, article VI, makes treaties, like federal statutes, parts of the "supreme Law of the Land," but it does not indicate their respective authority if they happen to conflict. Whether the President alone has the power to withdraw from a treaty obligation, a later statute adopted by Congress and signed by the President can definitely override what a treaty establishes for our domestic law.[78] It is less clear whether, absent an implementing statute adopted by both houses of Congress, a treaty can similarly cancel the import of a prior statute that is clearly conflicting. In part, this raises the question whether Senate approval can override a law in which the House of Representatives participated.

A more fundamental question about the treaty power is what behavior it may cover and whether other forms of agreement are similar in this respect. In *Missouri v. Holland*,[79] decided in 1920, the Supreme Court ruled that the Tenth Amendment protecting state powers did not apply to restrict the scope of treaties. So long as these treaties concerned "national well being," they could cover subjects otherwise reserved for states. (Although the continued validity of this approach was challenged, in a case decided in June 2014, the Court, as widely expected, resolved the case in much narrower terms, upholding the petitioner's claim that the statute barring the use of chemical weapons did not apply to her.[80])

The most substantial issue about the treaty provision is what else it allows. Sensible answers must depend partly on domestic political realities and the immense growth in international connections. The Constitution itself says nothing about other international agreements, but clearly, the treaty provision was meant to prevent the President from undertaking on his own any formal, binding international agreements that would alter the law within the United States. Presumably, a President could informally have agreed with a foreign nation about how the United States would act abroad, but one *might* have understood this provision as barring any formal agreements with other countries not made by the prescribed process. Whatever the original understanding, the practice has developed over time of the President entering agreements with foreign nations and obtaining the approval of both houses of Congress. Such approval involves a majority in each house but does not depend on a two-thirds vote in the Senate. If members of the Senate decisively rejected this approach, they could refuse to accede to such agreements.[81]

In recent decades, both houses of Congress have approved many international agreements. According to Oona A. Hathaway, from 1980 to 2000, 375 treaties were entered into as compared with 2,744 congressional-executive agreements,[82] which included all the undertakings with other countries in some important areas. For a court to rule that no such agreements are enforceable would be a strong interference with both political branches, especially considering Congress's undoubted power to adopt statutes that would effectively do most or all of what the agreements accomplish. Not surprisingly, the Supreme

Court, though not yet rejecting a specific challenge to such agreements, has indicated its acceptance of them.[83]

What remains unclear is the extent to which this form of agreement can substitute for a treaty and whether all or some of the most important international agreements must still be reached by the formal treaty process. Scholars have disagreed; some suggest complete interchangeability; others propose lines to be drawn. Their disagreement is partly reflective of competing views about how far original understanding should count in relation to modern conditions and arguable changes in basic constitutional structures.[84] From a practical perspective, given the widening scope of international agreements in the modern world, allowing slightly more than one-third of the Senate to defeat any undertaking this country has negotiated would be deeply unfortunate. However, especially given the fact that the Senate has actually adopted a declaration indicating that agreements limiting armaments or armed forces should be dealt with only by treaties, the most sensible view is that the two forms of international agreement are not yet totally substitutable for each other.[85] Nevertheless, whether a court would, or should, declare that any particular agreement approved by both houses of Congress falls into the category of what can only be done by treaty is extremely doubtful. Absent the likelihood of such a judicial ruling, the practical significance of the notion that only a treaty will do in some instances is that the President should accept this as a restraint on what he undertakes, one that Senate pressure or outright refusal to approve a different kind of agreement could "enforce."[86]

In regard to which circumstances, if any, should lead members of Congress and the President to conclude that treaties are required, the broad foreign affairs powers of a President who has congressional approval is highly relevant. Among the cases in which the Supreme Court has accepted an exercise of presidential authority is the 1936 case of *United States v. Curtiss-Wright Export Corp.*,[87] in which, relying on the President's extensive power regarding external affairs, the Court ruled that Congress, by joint resolution, could permissibly delegate to the President the power to prohibit sales of arms if that would promote peace in a region. In *Dames & Moore v. Regan*,[88] the Court accepted that the President, in response to the hostage crisis in Iran, had authority to nullify attachments regarding Iranian property, to order a transfer of frozen assets, and to suspend claims involving Iranian property pending in American courts. The Court determined that Congress specifically authorized the first two measures and that the general tenor of its actions constituted an implicit authorization of the third. If the President (on his own or with congressional authorization) could undertake the international consequences of what an actual agreement provides, and if Congress could adopt a law that carries the same domestic effects as the agreement, then the President and Congress together should be able to adopt such an international agreement without following the treaty process.[89]

That conclusion does not resolve whether such agreements should be able to reach into what would otherwise be reserved to states, as *Missouri v. Holland* provides about treaties. Probably the answer should be "no,"—such nontreaty agreements do not expand federal powers; but given the extent of modern federal authority both domestically and internationally, that limitation would carry very little practical consequence.

A somewhat different issue about treaties that are not self-executing is the President's authority to implement them. In the recent case of *Medellín v. Texas*,[90] the Supreme Court ruled against the President's authority to act on his own. President Bush aimed at compliance with the Vienna Convention, which provided that detained foreign nationals had the right to assistance of counsel from their countries. Not having been informed of this right, Medellín was convicted of murder and sentenced to death. Bush instructed Texas to meet the international obligation. The Court responded that, given a treaty that was not self-executing and given that Congress had not sought to enforce it in respect to states, the President lacked the power to do so on his own. The implementation of such treaties domestically is up to Congress, not the President.

C. War Powers and Congressional Authorization

Since the power to "declare War" belongs to Congress, the President has less range for autonomous determinations to engage the country in military conflict than he has for most subjects of foreign affairs. Despite this clear provision that denies a monarchical kind of executive authority to decide when to go to war,[91] none of this country's engagements since World War II have actually followed a formal declaration of military war, although acceptance by Congress has usually been sought at some stage.[92]

Among the questions about the use of armed forces are these: Are there circumstances in which the Constitution requires a formal declaration of war? To what extent can the President on his own commit United States armed forces to action and take other measures related to military conflicts? And to what extent can the President disregard what Congress has explicitly or implicitly provided for such matters? About all three questions, judges must face the fundamental issue of how far they should involve themselves, rather than leaving matters to be settled by the political branches.

For all-out wars such as the First and Second World Wars, a formal declaration of war *should* occur. Whether one is needed for more limited but sustained involvements, such as with the Korean, Vietnam, Iraq, and Afghanistan wars, is debatable. But such engagements are serious enough that Congress should need to agree to or accept what is happening. Congressional approval was obtained for all of these wars except the Korean War. Courts should probably not become involved except when Congress has actually rejected a military effort or set standards the administration has failed to follow, or when the executive actions not approved by Congress are interfering with aspects of domestic life in a manner beyond executive power.

Toward the end of the Vietnam War, Congress adopted a War Powers Resolution[93] that requires the President, when "possible," to consult with Congress before committing United States troops. Such a commitment was supposed to occur only after a declaration of war or statutory authorization, or in response to an attack upon the United States. Uses of armed forces are supposed to be terminated absent congressional authorization. When the Obama administration became involved to a limited degree in the conflict within Libya, the Office of Legal Counsel concluded, based partly on a historical practice, that prior congressional approval was unnecessary for such supporting efforts.[94] And although President Obama at one point sought congressional acceptance of a military response to the Syrian government's use of chemical weapons, he did not indicate that he lacked authority to act on his own.[95]

When courts have dealt with controversies involving the war powers, the presence or absence of congressional acceptance has proved important. In the classic case of internment of Japanese Americans, the Supreme Court relied partly on congressional authorization to uphold the practice.[96] In *Hamdi v. Rumsfeld,* a plurality construed Congress's Authorization for Use of Military Force Against Terrorists (AUMF) to respond to the September 11 terrorist attack as impliedly conferring authority to detain enemy combatants in Afghanistan.[97] By contrast, in the leading *Youngstown* steel seizure case, the opinion of the Court rested heavily upon and emphasized the absence of authorization by Congress. The concurring opinions of Justice Jackson and Justice Frankfurter additionally put weight on what they took as Congress's implicit prohibition of the kind of seizure of steel mills that the President undertook to prevent a strike potentially curtailing needed production during the Korean War.[98] As Jefferson Powell explains in a recent essay, Justice Jackson's opinion is remarkable in its candid acknowledgement of "the presence of conflict and the unavoidable uncertainties that accompany, or should accompany, momentous constitutional decisions." [99] Jackson wrote of the "practical advantages and grave dangers" of the "comprehensive and undefined presidential powers" impressed on him as a legal adviser to the President.[100] He went on to say that detached reflection on that experience probably influenced his views more than "conventional materials of judicial decision which seem unduly to accentuate doctrine and legal fiction."[101] And he expressed concern about the tendency of judges, like others, to confuse a power's validity with the particular cause for which it is used. As Powell emphasizes, such revealing, subtle explanations of what moves Justices in highly controversial cases is extremely rare. Much more recently, in *Hamdan v. Rumsfeld,* the Court declared specific executive provisions for trials by military tribunals as violative of the Uniform Code of Military Justice.[102]

What are probably the most important war powers issues in modern times, as David Barron and Martin Lederman develop in two articles, concern the degree of power Congress has to control what the President does if it chooses to exercise that power.[103] Whatever may be true for the kind of marginal assistance provided in Libya, or a limited military response to the use of chemical weapons, the basic war powers provision does strongly support the idea that our country should never be directly engaged in an actual war if that is contrary to a clear resolution of Congress. That restriction may appropriately be enforced by judges if requirements such as standing are met.

A different issue about the respective war powers of Congress and the President concerns tactics used during a conflict. Congress's power to "declare War" and the President's authority as "Commander in Chief" together hardly provide a clear textual answer to this question. In the country's early history, Congress authorized only limited military involvement, notably, the use of force by U.S. warships to seize armed vessels in a "quasi-war" with France. Congress's power in this respect was accepted by the Supreme Court.[104] In principle, Congress's 2001 Authorization for Use of Military Force against the terrorist organization responsible for the destruction of the World Trade Center is similar, although, whether this authorization applies to the use of military force against ISIS is neither obvious nor uncontroversial.[105] When Congress is authorizing something less than all-out war, it makes sense to allow it to set limits on what can be done. (Whether it has a similar authority to control executive determinations about strategies in full-scale wars is much more dubious.) On this basis, the President's decision to use drone strikes against leading members of al-Qaeda is primarily grounded on the effective approval by Congress of such a practice in the AUMF, not a unitary authority of the President's.[106] And, given that this is essentially an exercise of the war power rather than ordinary governance, the assurance of the executive branch in a white paper that due process will be followed is superfluous. This is particularly important because a decision by those in the executive branch about who should be targeted for killing, obviously without notice to those targeted, does not really amount to "due process" in its basic sense, which includes the chance of a hearing before an objective official.[107]

With respect to basic uses of military force, Congress and the President have accepted an approach that often does not require a declaration of war but does provide for review by Congress. Courts considering the respective range of authority of the two branches must somehow assess levels of agreement, acceptance, or rejection by the branch whose powers are arguably being stepped on. Curtis Bradley and Trevor Morrison point out in their perceptive analysis[108] that, in a genuine appraisal, a substantial difference exists between the executive and legislative branches. Even though presidents may not reject each perceived infringement, instead wishing not to offend Congress or agreeing to a bargain, they have a strong incentive to protect their office; and part of the responsibility of the Office of Legal Counsel is to consider whether Congress may be infringing on presidential powers. Congress, on the other hand, has much less incentive—or even opportunity—to register objections. A member of Congress is mainly concerned about re-election and the interests of her constituents. Since adopting formal resolutions or statutes takes concentrated effort, it is no simple feat for Congress as a body to register an objection to presidential practice. The members of Congress who belong to the President's political party, often a majority in at least one House, have a strong incentive not to interfere with or embarrass him. Especially when both houses are aligned with the President in a fairly coherent party,[109] the chances of strong resistance to presidential assertions of power are very slight.[110] In short, as Professors Bradley and Morrison urge, it is much simpler to discern presidential agreement or acceptance than to do so with Congress.[111]

The use of military force illustrates the different postures of Congress and the President. If the President engages in a conflict widely accepted as wise, members of Congress may hesitate to object that the engagement was unauthorized. On the other hand, if Congress seeks to restrict the President in a way he deems unacceptable, he may go ahead anyway, claiming an intrinsic power to do so.[112]

Just how far this analysis of what constitutes genuine acquiescence might guide courts raises difficulties both of actual evaluation and stated reasons. Desirable standards of judicial decision are often more restricted than a comprehensive appraisal. If Congress has remained silent in the face of a doubtful use of military force, judges are not well situated to assess the reasons why (which, of course, may be different among actual members). Whether courts should reach different decisions in otherwise similar circumstances because of the coherence and lineup of political parties is highly doubtful.[113]

More broadly, judges do not always state in their opinions their true appraisal of arguments for each side. Suppose that the President has been engaging in a practice long enough so that the Supreme Court is not willing to declare it invalid. Even if the Justices perceive that Congress has not *really* agreed to the practice or genuinely waived its own inherent powers, they may be tempted to write an opinion assigning responsibility for acceptance to both political branches. So long as they do not preclude subsequent restraints that Congress might enact, that rhetoric does not carry practical consequences. The idea of congressional acquiescence may be appealing to judges, even if the genuine basis for it is less powerful than they suggest.

D. Domestic Affairs

Questions about domestic affairs that concern the representative authority of Congress and the executive branch include the ability of Congress to allocate functions, its power to set standards for dismissal of executive officials, the degree of its permissible involvement in executive functions, and the manner in which it exercises the authority it does possess. A particular question about what the President may do concerns the range of his ability to make "recess" appointments that do not require the consent of the Senate.

With respect to the basic allocation of functions, the Supreme Court has recognized a broad power of Congress to determine the extent of executive authority. In large part, this acceptance represents a necessary response to the complexities of modern government and the value of administrative agencies. In two 1935 cases, the Supreme Court did hold invalid the National Industrial Recovery Act's sweeping and vague delegation to the executive to set rules to ease the economic depression.[114] But since that time, delegations of functions to administrative agencies have been so consistently upheld that the existence of any rule against nondelegation of legislative functions has been cast in doubt.[115] Also, with what has been regarded as explicit or implicit approval by Congress, the Supreme Court has accepted the performance within agencies of what would otherwise be the responsibilities of Article III judges[116] and has granted judicial deference to agency interpretations of statutes.[117] By contrast, when the Court has determined that an agency is acting in a way that is at odds with what Congress prefers, it has been more restrictive.[118]

As already noted, the blending of functions that occurs in administrative agencies is far removed from how the founders would have perceived most aspects of government and is one of the strongest examples of why it would be naïve or ill advised to believe that we should now simply implement the understandings of 1789.

How far Congress can set standards for the dismissal of administrative officials constitutes one issue about respective authority. Early on in the country's history, it was established that despite needing the Senate's approval to appoint high officials, the President could dismiss them on his own, on whatever grounds he regarded as adequate,[119] a sensible approach since things are unlikely to work well if a leading official has lost the President's confidence. In modern times, however, Congress has set standards for the dismissal of certain kinds of officials.

Issues about dismissal provide another illustration of how Congress and the President may respond differently to doubtful exercises of power by each other. Whether or not the original Constitution conceived that officials appointed with Senate consent could be dismissed on any ground the President chooses, actual senators need not have been greatly concerned, especially if the President had a solid reason to let someone go. On the other hand, once the President's power to dismiss was well settled, he did initially object to attempted congressional restraints, though, over time, Presidents have come to accept "for cause" requirements for dismissing principal officers of independent agencies.

In *Myers v. United States* in 1926,[120] the Supreme Court ruled that Congress could not require Senate approval for the President's removal of a postmaster. Although the Court's opinion emphasized that such decisions were the President's to make, subsequent cases upheld Congress's setting standards for the removal of officers of semi-independent agencies. In *Humphrey's Executor v. United States*,[121] the Court accepted the statutory requirement that members of the Federal Trade Commission could be removed only for "inefficiency, neglect of duty, or malfeasance in office." A half century later, in 1988, the Court sustained statutory limits on the Attorney General's power to remove independent counsels, casting the issue as whether the removal restrictions "impede the President's ability to perform his constitutional duty."[122]

In the 2010 case of *Free Enterprise Fund v. Public Co. Accounting Oversight Board*[123] the Supreme Court restricted the power of Congress to control removals from office, employing a theory that could have extremely broad implications. According to the statute being reviewed, the members of the Public Company Accounting Oversight Board (PCAOB) could be removed by the Securities and Exchange Commission only "for cause." A bare majority of the Court considered this requirement unconstitutional on the ground that, because members of the PCAOB were "inferior officers" of the S.E.C., whose own members could be dismissed only "for cause," the dual "for cause" limits interfered with the President's authority to see that laws are faithfully executed.[124] If the President believed that a member of the PCAOB required dismissal and the members of the S.E.C. disagreed, neither could the President get rid of the Board member nor could he dismiss any S.E.C. officers, since his disagreement with them over this would not be a cause for dismissal.

Whatever the merits of this particular judicial resolution, its theory of protecting the President's power to control the actions of inferior officers is extraordinarily expansive. Peter Strauss has remarked, "[O]ne easily finds hundreds if not thousands of government employees who can only be removed "for cause" by superiors who themselves can only be removed "for cause."[125] As Strauss points out, the strongest view of presidential authority would preclude any "for cause" restrictions,[126] but no Justice has adopted that position. In brief, it is very difficult to guess just how far all members of the majority will carry the logic of a rationale that seems to be both strikingly straightforward and insensitive to all the roles of different administrative bodies and their relations to the President.[127]

One interesting problem is that the majority's logic in regard to the distribution of federal powers extends to the allocation of federal and state authority. Various programs enacted by Congress, in which states may choose to become engaged, such as recent healthcare legislation, are implemented in large part by state authorities. On the view that it is the President's responsibility to see that all federal laws are faithfully executed, how can their implementation be assigned partly to state officials who are not under the President's supervision?[128] This question has no simple answer, but realism requires an understanding of how much more extensive federal powers are now than they were perceived in either 1789 or 1868. If a federal program provides heavy financial support in a domain that has for most of the country's history been left to states, Congress should not be required to make an all-or-nothing choice among complete noninvolvement, full replacement of the functions of state officials, and the subjection of all relevant state officials to presidential dismissal. The *Free Enterprise Fund* case provides an example of a rationale stated with such extreme breadth that it almost certainly will not be applied to every circumstance its language reaches. This leaves outsiders highly uncertain about both how far the Court will go in this direction and whether any narrower persuasive justification supports its initial decision.

When Congress has tried to involve itself, not just by setting standards but also in the actual performance of perceived executive functions, the Court's response has been more consistently negative. In *Metropolitan Washington Airports Authority v. Citizens for the Abatement of Aircraft Noise, Inc.*,[129] it struck down legislation that allowed Congress to veto decisions regarding a regional airport's authority. And when Congress set up a Federal Elections Commission to oversee federal elections with members appointed by the leader of the Senate, by the Speaker of the House, and by the President, the Court ruled in *Buckley v. Valeo*[130] that this violated the Constitution's Appointments Clause. In *Bowsher v. Synar*,[131] the Court held invalid a provision of the Gramm-Rudman-Hollings Act that centered executive powers on the Comptroller General, who could be removed only by impeachment or a joint resolution of Congress. These decisions reflect a sense that—even if Congress may allocate functions as it deems appropriate—when it seeks to exercise executive responsibilities, preserving the separation of powers is important.

The Supreme Court has also declined to accept certain congressional decisions about how its own powers and those of the President may be executed. A prior section of this chapter discusses *INS v. Chadha*,[132] a notable decision about how Congress must exercise its own functions. In holding that Congress could not authorize one House alone to override an executive decision, the Court declined to give effect to a well-established historical practice. More recently, the Court adhered to an original understanding of how government functions were performed in rejecting legislation allowing the President to make particular line-item vetoes, as contrasted with general vetoes of proposed laws.[133]

A fundamental question about cases involving the distribution and exercises of powers concerns the value of various forms of separation. Given that all three basic functions—legislative, executive, and judicial—are mixed within administrative agencies, and that checks by each political branch on the other may be as effectively achieved by certain combinations of functions as by divisions, it is doubtful that Congress's involvements beyond the passage of statutes should generally be viewed as negatively as the Supreme Court has treated them.[134] As in other respects, the Court should not rigorously and faithfully adhere to an original conception developed in a very different social environment (and based substantially on a Madisonian theory of checks and balances that may not have been strongly grounded even in Madison's own time).

In late June of 2014, the Supreme Court decided *National Labor Relations Board v. Noel Canning,*[135] which concerned the scope of the President's power— when the Senate is not in session—to make recess appointments, which do not require Senate confirmation. With respect to this important aspect of the allocation of federal power, the Court was unanimous on the resolution of the particular dispute, but sharply divided over both the extent of the President's power and what factors should count most heavily in resolving the key questions. Justice Breyer's majority opinion was substantially deferential to existing practice and flexible about how the meaning of particular terms should be construed in light of overall purposes. Justice Scalia's dissent was dominantly formalist with heavy reliance on original understanding and strong opposition to judicial adoption of standards that are unclear.

The case involved four basic issues about the Recess Appointments Clause, which grants the President power temporarily to fill up "all Vacancies that may happen during the Recess of the Senate. . . ."[136] The two issues over which the Justices divided were whether the Clause reaches intrasession recesses—that is, whether it covers recesses during the same session as well as intersession recesses—and whether it allows appointments when a vacancy arises prior to a recess but continues into a recess. On the broader reading, the President is able to make a recess appointment even if the vacancy occurs six months prior to a recess, he has sought approval of a nominee without success, and then the recess comes to pass. The two issues on which all nine Justices agreed was that what the Senate labels "pro forma" sessions, though genuine meeting and activity is very rare, do count as sessions, and that an appointment made in an intrasession recess of only a few days is not allowed. It was on this basis that all nine Justices ruled that the appointment of three members of the National Labor Relations Board had not been valid; a subsequent dispute resolution by the Board was overturned.

On the more fundamental questions, disagreement was sharp. Justice Breyer essentially concedes that the original understanding of "the Recess" was dominantly about intersession recesses; those recesses separated formal sessions, they were then typically the only kind of recess, and they often lasted for the majority of a year.[137] He also acknowledges that the most natural sense of "happen during" was actually "occurring during."[138] But he proceeds to conclude that in neither instance is the textual language decisive; rather, it is ambiguous. The word "the" in "the recess" need not refer to a single recess for a given session, and, had the original enactors and readers been aware that in time, intrasession recesses would increase greatly, they would have wanted constitutional language adopted to last for centuries to be construed in light of its overall purpose of permitting important vacancies to be filled.[139] As far as "happen during" is concerned, that also can include "continuing during," and given the time taken for Senate approval, it does not make sense to require that the vacancy actually occur prior to the recess.[140]

Justice Breyer explores historical practice over time with respect to both issues. Recognizing that early history has virtually no examples of intrasession recesses and appointments for vacancies that arise prior to a recess, he relies heavily on what has happened more recently, on the assumption by modern Presidents that they can appoint during intrasession recesses and for vacancies that arise prior to the recess. Important with regard to all of this is that although individual senators have objected to these exercises of presidential power, no formal opposition has been offered during the last three quarters of a century by the Senate as a whole or by a Senate Committee.[141]

Justice Scalia's basic position is that "the majority casts aside the plain, original meaning of the constitutional text in deference to late-arising historical practices that are ambiguous at best."[142] For him the majority would need both an "ambiguous text and a clear historical practice" to sustain its interpretation, but it lacks both.[143] With respect to the failure of the Senate formally to object to the broadening of the President's recess appointments power, Scalia expresses the concern that this approach will generally favor an unjustified expansion of executive power, citing Bradley and Morrison for the much greater difficulties of legislative houses to reach formal conclusions about these matters than for the President to do so.[144]

On the question of his disagreement with Justice Breyer over the "happen during" language, Justice Scalia, contending that the provision covers only situations when the vacancy arises once a recess has begun, did not need to address a common complexity about reader understanding, but his approach would raise that issue. He does say that Presidents can deal with vacancies that occur before recesses but continue into those recesses by appointing "acting officers" or calling the Senate back into session.[145] But is that sufficient to show that the original understanding was as crisp as he contends, or does a standard use of ordinary language here lead to a kind of absurd result that no one would intend?

Suppose, for example, an official died unexpectedly the night before the Senate went into a six-month recess, with Senators going to their home states and not easily reachable. In the most common usage, the vacancy did not "happen" during the recess, but if the President had no time to decide whom to nominate and then obtain Senate approval, it would be strongly counterintuitive to deny him the power to appoint someone to fill in for the deceased official. Asked about the Clause's language, would not most people respond, "Well, 'happen during' needs at least some flexibility here, given that the whole point is whether there is an opportunity for Senate approval." This is one example of how language often needs to be understood, and is understood by people generally, in the context of underlying purposes. If the President has had ample time to get Senate confirmation and failed to do so, saying that his recess power does not apply is much more plausible.

The *Canning* controversy is obviously somewhat related to the pressing practical concern that has flowed from the increasing use within the Senate of filibusters to prevent appointments not supported by at least sixty members. Although the Senate has adopted a novel rule to restrict this practice for most appointments,[146] the basic problem may well arise from other forms of blockage and delay by senators, especially when the Senate becomes dominated by a party opposed to the President. It is worth noting that neither opinion in *Canning* acknowledges this particular practical issue as bearing on how the "Recess" Clause should be understood; neither opinion treats the Justice's responsibility as countering this political standoff.

VI. CONCLUSION

This chapter has explored a range of particular issues about the separation of powers. These illustrate the sensitive concerns about how much judges should become involved when the respective authority of Congress and the President are in question. Clearly, these issues differ significantly from most claims about individual constitutional rights, and the role of judges is typically more deferential to what the political branches have resolved. Nevertheless, the basic divide between formalist and functionalist approaches, as well as distinctive interpretive strategies for different kinds of issues, spreads across the division of federal powers as well as other constitutional subjects.

Chapter 8

Federal Powers

I. INTRODUCTION

The federal division of powers between the national government and the states raises many interpretive issues that are similar to those involving the respective authority of Congress and the President, but the context differs, and this division is more complicated in certain ways. Among the controversial questions about contested powers of the central government and states are how much courts should involve themselves or leave resolution to political bodies, and whether, when they do deal with the allocation, they should focus on original understanding, a present sense of what the text entails, or modern economic and social realities. As with separation of powers, a basic interpretive issue is whether courts should rely on categorical approaches or make a more particularized assessment of relevant factors.

The responsibility of courts to strike down excessive assertions of power by states has never been in doubt. Given the provisions in the original Constitution that citizens of each state are entitled to "all Privileges and Immunities of Citizens in the several states"[1] and that the Constitution, federal statutes, and treaties "shall be the supreme Law of the Land, and the Judges in every State shall be bound thereby, any Thing in the Constitution or Laws of any State to the Contrary notwithstanding," [2] courts were required to determine if states violated valid federal laws or discriminated against the citizens of other states. Because state legislatures and executives are answerable only to citizens within their borders, courts have had no reason to assume that they have been adequately respectful of the rights of outsiders in a way that would warrant substantial deference. None of this has changed. What is less clear is how far courts should consider state actions as being implicitly "preempted" by federal statutes that do not directly apply or as being in violation of the constitutional assignment of interstate commerce regulation to the federal government, even absent controlling laws of Congress.

Whether courts appropriately resolve if Congress has infringed upon state authority is a genuine question. If courts should play this role, how far should they defer to Congress? And if Congress directly by legislation, or the executive branch by implementing regulations, can reduce what states are free to do, should courts at least require that statutes adopt clear statements to that effect?

Related to all of these questions is how the distribution of federal and state power should now be seen. When the Constitution was first implemented, the national government was very small,[3] and states dominated lawmaking that affected individuals. As the national economy has grown and become integrated, as citizens' movements from residence within one state to another have increased, as the country's involvement with other nations has drawn them closer and closer, and as the social sense that American citizens deserve forms of equal treatment has developed, the influence of the national government has increased tremendously. Although no one suggests that we somehow revert to the practical divisions of 1789, the problem remains just *how far* changing conditions should affect interpretation of the designated powers of the federal government.

A central issue about modern understanding is the value for states of domains of independent authority as compared with cooperative efforts in which they play a significant role in carrying out federal laws. Until recently, disagreement among scholars focused mainly on separate spheres, with some favoring judicial enforcement of "de jure autonomy" and others believing that it should be left to the political process to assure "de facto autonomy."[4] Now, a major competitor to each of these approaches is "cooperative federalism." Grounded in the extensive federal regulations that state officials now carry out, the claim is that states can often exercise power most effectively when they are thus involved, rather than wholly supplanted by federal regulation.[5] On this account, were courts to circumscribe too sharply federal power to control state officials, the end result could be more instances in which federal laws directly supplanted state action, thus leaving the states with less effective authority.

A peculiar feature of "cooperative federalism" is "uncooperative federalism," with states being able to alter or even undermine what a federal law is intended to do.[6] States can also protect the power of Congress by helping to ensure that the executive branch does not override its aims. How far one believes these notions about cooperative federalism should be accepted by courts can strongly affect what one regards as wise judicial resolutions. As in all areas, a thoughtful position on this depends heavily on what facts courts can assess and what categories and standards they can announce that will be both administrable and lead to desirable results.

This chapter focuses primarily on the powers of Congress to "regulate commerce with foreign Nations, and among the several States, and with the Indian Tribes,"[7] "lay and collect Taxes,"[8] and to "provide for the common Defense and general Welfare of the United States. . . ."[9] Much of what this language entails is straightforward, but the permissible boundaries of what Congress is allowed to do are vague, creating uncertainties about how it should perform, to what degree states are limited, and how courts should respond to legislative and administrative action. After providing a brief account of how the law developed before and during the New Deal and throughout the Warren Court era, I summarize a number of more recent decisions and controversies and finally discuss in more detail the Supreme Court's resolution of *National Federation of Independent Business v. Sebelius*,[10] which reviewed the central aspects of the Patient Protection and Affordable Care Act of 2010. The ways in which different Supreme Court Justices dealt with this most important piece of legislation adopted during Barack Obama's first term as President highlights many of the difficult interpretive questions.

II. CONGRESS'S AUTHORITY THROUGH THE NEW DEAL AND WARREN COURT

What Congress's power to "regulate commerce among the several states" most explicitly authorizes are laws regulating commerce that moves from one state to another, such as flights from Los Angeles to Chicago, or shipments of oil from Texas to Boston. Questions about the extent of what Congress may do fall mainly into the following categories: Does anything that moves from one state to another count as commerce? Can Congress regulate commerce within a state that relates closely to commerce among states? Can it regulate activities that precede or follow commerce? Can it choose virtually any objectives, or must its purposes be related to commercial activity? Can it require commercial acts of those who would prefer to abstain?

As a brief sketch of historical cases reveals, a continuing broader issue about interpretation is how far judicial answers to these particular questions should properly turn on matters of degree rather than clear, discrete categories, and how far courts should properly enforce what, in principle, the political branches should take as relevant standards. That the Supreme Court's responses have varied greatly over time has reflected not only radically changing social conditions and values and shifts in the dominant ideological perspectives of Supreme Court Justices but also the intrinsic difficulties of coming up with sensible, judicially administrable standards.

The Supreme Court early on disposed of regulation of traffic within a state that is really inseparable from interstate commerce, ruling in *Gibbons v. Ogden*[11] that New York's grant of exclusive rights to operate steamboats within its waters was at odds with a federal statute that authorized the entry of Gibbons ferries from New Jersey into New York.[12] In 1914, in what are referred to as the *Shreveport Rate Cases*,[13] the Court extended this principle to certain commerce that actually took place only within a single state, allowing the Interstate Commerce Commission to control railroad rates in order to preclude the favoring of internal state traffic over interstate traffic.

When reviewing activities less closely connected to interstate commerce, the Supreme Court's position shifted radically from an approach that restricted Congress to one that was highly permissive. In *United States v. E.C. Knight Co.*,[14] near the end of the nineteenth century, the Court ruled that the antimonopoly Sherman Act did not reach a monopoly for manufacturing sugar, because the Constitution did not authorize Congress to regulate manufacturing. This reliance on clear categories—manufacturing versus commerce—makes virtually no sense in terms of national economic life, given the extent to which a manufacturing monopoly destroying competition can interfere with "freedom in buying and selling articles" that affects people in every state.[15] The Court embraced another distinctive categorization in 1918, in *Hammer v. Dagenhart*,[16] striking down the provision in the Child Labor Act that prohibited interstate transportation of goods produced by companies that employed children under age fourteen or failed to satisfy conditions set for the work of those between ages fourteen and sixteen. The Court decided that since Congress lacked authority to exercise the police power left to states, its effort to "prevent possible unfair competition" was invalid.[17]

During the New Deal in the 1930s, the Supreme Court majority initially adhered to its categorical approach and invalidated regulations under the National Industrial Recovery Act that concerned working conditions set for New York's live poultry market[18] and for coal manufacture.[19] Justice Sutherland's majority opinion in the latter case remarked that it turned "not upon the magnitude of either the cause or the effect, but entirely upon the manner in which the effect has been brought about."[20]

Shortly thereafter, and following President Roosevelt's proposal to increase the Court's membership, the balance of the Court's position shifted radically. In *National Labor Relations Board v. Jones & Laughlin Steel Corporation*,[21] by a 5–4 margin, it upheld the pervasive regulation of labor-management relations against a challenge by a producer of iron and steel. Finding it unnecessary to decide whether the company's activities in interstate commerce brought the entire enterprise within a "stream of commerce," the Court ruled that Congress could protect interstate commerce from the "burdens and obstructions" that industrial strife in manufacturing operations could cause.[22] In *United States v. Darby*,[23] the Court sustained a ban under the Fair Labor Standards Act on shipping goods in interstate commerce produced by employees who received less than minimum wages or worked more than maximum hours. Given the ban on shipment, direct imposition of the standards themselves was also deemed appropriate in order to prevent unfair competition. The Court went yet further in *Wickard v. Filburn*,[24] approving a scheme of quotas for wheat production as it applied to a farmer who had harvested 461 bushels instead of his allotted 222 bushels, primarily for home consumption. The Court's logic was that growing too much wheat for home use would reduce the market demand for wheat and impair commerce. The approach adopted by these cases afforded Congress very wide scope to regulate direct and indirect effects on commerce as it saw fit, regardless of whether its primary objective concerned interstate commerce itself. Notably, the Court upheld the 1964 Civil Rights Act provisions that ban racial discrimination by any place of public accommodation whose "operations affect commerce"[25] and by any restaurant that offers to serve interstate travelers if a substantial portion of its food has moved in interstate commerce.[26] Clearly, the Act's main purpose was to prevent unjust racial discrimination rather than affect interstate commerce, but, finding a discernible connection to that commerce, the Court did not regard the law's primary objective as an obstacle.

In contrast to its authority to regulate interstate commerce, Congress's powers to "lay and collect Taxes" and to "provide for the common Defense and general Welfare" have always been seen expansively. Apart from article I's requirement that direct taxes be "apportioned among the several States,"[27] which was abolished for income taxes by the Sixteenth Amendment,[28] Congress's decisions on what to tax has been essentially unrestricted. It cannot, of course, impose taxes in a way that would violate constitutional protections of rights, such as singling out members of a particular religion for higher burdens. But state domains of authority do not curtail federal taxes designed to raise revenues. As a consequence, the main interpretive question for this power is how far what Congress has done really counts as a tax; resolution of this question played a prominent role in the Court's review of the 2010 Patient Protection and Affordable Care Act.

A central issue about taxing and spending is whether it matters if the legislative purpose is not really financial. In *United States v. Doremus*, in 1919,[29] the Supreme Court upheld provisions of the Harrison Act, which imposed an excise tax on the sale of drugs and which also required that such sales be made only to registered dealers, dispensing physicians, and persons with medical prescriptions. The law's obvious main purpose was to curb the sales of drugs, such as heroin, that were criminal within the states. The Court, nonetheless, sustained the indictment of a doctor for selling heroin to a "dope fiend," stating that "Congress may select the subjects of taxation and may exercise the power conferred at its discretion,"[30] and that courts cannot invalidate taxes on the basis of "supposed motives." Three years later, in *Bailey v. Drexel Furniture Co.*,[31] the Court did strike down the Child Labor Tax Act, which Congress had enacted after the Court's ruling that the commerce power could not support a prohibition on the interstate transportation of goods made by companies using child labor. The Court ruled that because the "so-called tax" of 10 percent of a factory's net profits was obviously designed to preclude the use of child labor, it lost its character as a tax and became "a mere penalty, with the characteristics of regulation and punishment."[32] In a case three decades later, however, the Warren Court sustained a tax imposed on those who accept bets, though the law raised a modest amount of money and required the tax collector to inform state law enforcement officials about who paid the wagering tax.[33]

The Supreme Court has long failed to indicate precisely what limits curb the use of the taxing and spending power to encourage or discourage behavior that Congress could not directly control. In *United States v. Butler*[34] in 1936, the Court did hold invalid the provision of the Agricultural Adjustment Act that taxed processors of agricultural commodities and used that money to subsidize farmers who restricted their production. Although the Court accepted Alexander Hamilton's view that the power to tax and spend for the national welfare was not "confined to the enumerated legislative fields committed to the Congress,"[35] the act invaded states' rights because it sought to control agricultural production beyond powers delegated to Congress.[36] Only one year later, however, the Court sustained a tax on employers that gave them a credit up to 90 percent of the tax if they paid into a state unemployment fund, the clear objective being to supplement state unemployment funds. Justice Cardozo wrote for the majority that it was not shown "that the tax and the credit in combination are weapons of coercion, destroying or impairing the autonomy of the states."[37] Pointing out that without federal involvement, states choosing generous unemployment support place themselves at an economic disadvantage, and noting that the statute coerced neither states nor individuals, Cardozo observed that if the concept of undue influence "can ever be applied with fitness to the relations between state and nation," the point at "which pressure turns into compulsion … would be a question of degree."[38] His opinion left open whether a federal tax could set conditions for states unrelated to matters fairly within national policy and power.

III. MORE RECENT DECISIONS AND MODERN ISSUES

A. The Commerce Clause

The modern Supreme Court has set certain restraints on what Congress can do under the Commerce Clause, although these have limited practical force and do not impair the huge expansion of actual federal power since the original enactment of the Constitution. In 1971, the Court upheld a federal statute making criminal "extortionate credit transactions,"[39] requiring no proof that the activity reached had an effect on commerce, so long as it was within a class that Congress could regulate. However, under Chief Justice Rehnquist, the Justices developed subject matter boundaries on what Congress can do under the Commerce Clause. In *United States v. Lopez* in 1995,[40] the Court held invalid a law making it a federal crime to have a firearm in a school zone. In contrast to Justice Breyer's dissent, which urged that guns could affect the quality of education and therefore commerce, a connection as significant as those that had sustained prior laws,[41] Rehnquist, acknowledging a lack of clarity in prior cases about just what was needed, stated that the proper test requires an analysis of whether the regulated activity "substantially affects interstate commerce. . . ."[42] Three of the five Justices in the majority suggested more categorical approaches. Justice Thomas, standing alone, would have returned to the original understanding that "commerce" is to be distinguished from manufacturing and agriculture.[43] Justice Kennedy, joined by Justice O'Connor, rejected the idea of reverting to a conception that would have fitted an eighteenth-century economy, but urged that certain areas of traditional state concern should be precluded from being taken over by the federal government.[44] These various opinions left the effective power and applications of any "substantially affects" test far from clear.

Five years later, in *United States v. Morrison*,[45] the Court struck down a federal law that granted a remedy in damages to victims of violent crimes motivated by gender. Chief Justice Rehnquist—again with four dissenters—wrote that Congress may not obliterate the distinction between federal and state powers, that gender-motivated violent crimes are not economic in nature, and that prior cases had upheld federal regulation of intrastate activity only if it was "economic."

Although their applications would largely overlap, a test of "substantially affects" differs analytically from one of "economic activity." A genuine requirement of "substantial effects" could bar some federal regulation of economic activities within states that have little effect on interstate commerce, whereas limiting regulation to economic activity might preclude federal restraint of some noneconomic practices, such as widespread violence against women or members of minorities, that could affect interstate commerce more than insignificantly. Although saying exactly what counts as "economic activity" may sometimes be difficult, that categorization seems more straightforward and susceptible to judicial application than determinations of what effects are great enough to be "substantial." However, applied without regard to indirect effects, it could preclude Congress from dealing with actual impairments of interstate commerce.

A standard proposed by Robert D. Cooter and Neil S. Siegel differs from both of these; they suggest that courts should ask whether the problem that Congress has addressed is one that calls for collective action.[46] In terms of the functioning of a federal system, this approach strikes one as sensible and capable of judicial assessment, even if it does focus more on the basic need for national action rather than any isolated constitutional provision. In this fundamental respect, it closely resembles Chief Justice Marshall's opinion in *McCulloch v. Maryland*,[47] which sustained the creation of a national bank by referring to a number of provisions whose effectiveness the bank could further—including both power over the taxing and spending and interstate commerce—and which interpreted the "necessary and proper clause" broadly to support legitimate means even if they are not indisputably required.

B. Impingement on Central State Functions

A different limit on federal authority concerns neither the particular subject matter nor the arguable source of federal power, but what are basic functions of state governments that need to be independent of federal control. Two ways in which such limits can arise is when Congress seeks to restrict state officers in the same manner as private citizens and businesses and when it actually demands that states enforce federal laws—what is referred to as "commandeering."

In the 1976 case, *National League of Cities v. Usery,*[48] the Supreme Court set what purported to be a categorical restraint on federal regulation of state and local governments, ruling that Congress could not, under its commerce power, apply the minimum wage and overtime provisions of the Fair Labor Standards Act to state employees "in areas of traditional governmental functions." Acknowledging that these wages and hours could affect interstate commerce, the Justices nonetheless held that setting the standards for state workers was within powers reserved to the states under the original Constitution and the Tenth Amendment, which reserves for states and the people powers not delegated to the United States. After roughly a decade of struggle with the boundary set by *National League of Cities*, the Court, 5–4 in *Garcia v. San Antonio Metropolitan Transit Authority,*[49] overruled it, holding that federal employment laws can apply to state employees. Writing for the majority, and declaring that drawing a distinction based on "traditional" or "integral" functions was both unworkable and unsound in principle, Justice Blackmun rejected judicial reliance on "*a priori* definitions of state sovereignty";[50] instead, the primary basis for assuring the role of states was the political process.

Among the four dissenters in *Garcia* was Justice O'Connor, who six years later in *Gregory v. Ashcroft* wrote an opinion for the Court that adopted a more nuanced approach.[51] The Missouri Constitution provided that state court judges had to retire at the age of seventy. The federal Age Discrimination in Employment Act of 1967 precluded such requirements generally, but it provided an exception for elected state officials and state appointees "on a policymaking level." The constitutional questions were whether Congress had the authority to forbid retirement age mandates for state judges, and whether Missouri violated the Equal Protection Clause by imposing such a requirement on its judges. A statutory issue was whether the federal exceptions for persons "elected to public office" and "appointees on a policymaking level" applied to judges. Missouri's judges were initially appointed; they were kept in office by retention elections that lacked any opposing candidate, but involved only a "yes" or "no" vote. Rather than decisively resolving the limit of Congress's power, the Court adopted a "clear statement rule." Because Congress's overriding of what the people of a state had included in their constitution about the qualifications for public officers "would upset the usual constitutional balance of federal and state powers,"[52] judges should not conclude that Congress intends this unless that is certain. Since it is debatable whether state judges count as officials on a "policymaking level," the statutory language was seen as too murky to conclude that Congress really intended the general prohibition on age retirement to apply to them. Among the four Justices who disagreed with the clear statement resolution, two thought the federal statute did exclude state judges,[53] and two thought it did not.[54] On the equal protection arguments, the Court held that retirement age requirements were generally acceptable and that judges differed enough from other officials to allow distinctive treatment. Most notably, except in extreme situations, no one is in a position to determine that a particular judge's age has so restricted his level of performance that he must leave office.[55] Even if one concludes that it is hard to prescribe specific state domains that are entirely outside congressional power, the requirement that intrusions on fundamental functions of state government be clearly stated is a wise judicial approach.

One domain in which the Supreme Court has held acts of Congress to be unconstitutional is when they demand that state officials enforce federal laws. In *New York v. United States*,[56] decided in 1992, the Court held invalid the part of a federal law that required states either to provide for disposal of low-level nuclear waste as stipulated or to accept ownership of the waste, thus subjecting themselves to potential liabilities. Justice O'Connor's opinion for the Court regarded the law as impermissibly coercive, in part because such a commandeering requirement would diminish accountability, leaving citizens without any clear sense of whether the state or federal government was responsible for failures to see that disposal of waste was effective. Five years later, in *Printz v. United States*,[57] the Court invalidated a part of the Brady Handgun Violence Prevention Act that effectively required state enforcement officials to implement a national background check system for weapons purchases. Rejecting a "balancing" approach, Justice Scalia wrote for the Court that the reasons given in *New York* against federal commandeering of state legislators applied to state executives as well.

IV. FUNDAMENTAL QUESTIONS ABOUT MODERN FEDERALISM

Just how courts should approach federal impingements on more traditional state roles raises basic concerns about how federalism should now be perceived, about what will best protect and promote its values, and about the appropriate role of courts.

Among the values commonly associated with federalism are these.[58] The distribution of political authority is healthy—preventing tyranny, protecting individual rights, and encouraging political participation. Having separate states with domains of authority promotes diversity, experimentation, and competition. People's senses of identity with their states help produce overlapping loyalties among citizens who also belong to more limited, potentially divisive forms of associations, such as religious, economic, and ethnic groups. Jessica Bulman-Pozen has recently emphasized the extent to which differences in political dominance at any time between many states and the national government allow individuals attached to political parties to associate with the party of their choice and pursue its objectives even when their party has lost in recent federal elections.[59]

Although the drafters of the Constitution were not really in a position to act based on comparative values of federalism and a simple unitary state (since the actual states would not have accepted the latter), they did make a deliberate choice to increase the powers of the national government over its areas of weakness under the Articles of Confederation. The Framers also believed in central values claimed for federalism, especially the preclusion of unfettered power in any political body;[60] and they understood that most citizens then identified strongly with their state governments.

The question of how far federalism really promotes the values ascribed to it connects closely to how we should now perceive its restraints. States within the United States are themselves essentially unitary. County, city, and local governments are generally subject to supervision by state legislatures. Yet many states enjoy substantial diversity within themselves, with citizens who often identify in part with their hometowns and participate actively in local government institutions and political parties. As someone who grew up in the New York suburbs and has spent most of his life in New York City, I am poorly equipped to evaluate the importance of local identification across the country, but clearly, many values ascribed to federalism may also be served, at least to a degree, by different levels of government in nonfederal structures.

Given the vast changes in economic life, social organizations, and social values, returning to an actual distribution of functions close to that in 1789, or even 1865, is really inconceivable. Yet, one might nevertheless believe that compromises reflected in original provisions should be carried forward, or that one or more core values of early federalism should serve as a guide. Corresponding with his position on the separation of powers, treated in Chapter 7 of this book, John Manning has proposed that the Supreme Court, as reflected in Justice Scalia's disclaimer in *Printz* of reliance on any particular provision, has relied too heavily on a broad conception of federalism without paying adequate attention to the specific compromises the document reflects.[61] Although acknowledging that comparatively open-ended provisions leave room for developing applications, Manning criticizes reliance on highly general formulations that lack specific textual support. As earlier chapters have explained, this kind of compromise-centered textualism Manning and others have advocated for statutory interpretation is inappropriate for any constitution that is very difficult to amend and endures over centuries.[62] The Supreme Court has rightly relied on a version of original understanding that looks mainly at an overall system of government, but that alone does not tell us just how such a sense of original understanding should be perceived and what weight it should carry.

In a notable 2012 book, Michael Greve urges an emphasis on the states as competitors, which he claims to be in accord with the overall structure of the original Constitution although not an explicit focus of its enactors.[63] Discrete provisions that effectively forced states to compete with each other include the Compact Clause, which bars agreements between states without the consent of Congress,[64] helping to preclude cartel arrangements.[65] As Ilya Somin points out, "competition" cannot rightly be regarded as the nearly exclusive original purpose behind federalism,[66] but that conclusion leaves open the weight that advantages of competition appropriately carry in a modern assessment of the values of federalism.

When one hears of "competition" versus "cartels," the former sounds obviously better. But it is crucial to consider what kind of competition or alignment is involved. If one state seeks to improve the health of its citizens in a manner other states are not yet ready to adopt, say, by restricting the size or content of soft drinks, or a state chooses to subsidize windmills that can produce electric power, these individual exercises are promising. But what of welfare for the poor? If the consciences of the citizens of state *A* incline them to give significant aid to the impoverished that well exceeds that of a neighboring state *B*, this could encourage the poor to move to *A*, while driving some of the state's well-to-do citizens to *B* to take advantage of lower taxes. Even if most people in most states approved in principle of helping the poor, the concern about impoverished outsiders moving in and rich insiders moving out could sharply curtail what measures seemed practically acceptable. This is the kind of circumstance in which state agreements or, more realistically, federal involvement, are needed to prevent a "race to the bottom" of what is actually desirable. Of course, a person who believes that, in principle, the poor should just fend for themselves may see this realm, like others, as an appropriate one for competition, which itself illustrates how much a person's overall social outlook can affect exactly what she perceives as healthy state competition. But financial aid to the poor is properly regarded as a field calling for national involvement in order to prevent debilitating state competition.

If one focuses on the benefits of exercises of political authority by modern states, judges need to ask what structures will best promote the values of federalism and what role courts should play. More specifically, should they emphasize states as fully independent governments or as participants in "cooperative" and "uncooperative" federalism? If preserving the independence of state officials from federal control is primary, then, when the federal government enters into a domain of regulation, perhaps it should act on its own, using those it hires to implement its requirements. Whether this approach was substantially enforced by courts or adopted by Congress, the consequence *could* be to reduce areas of federal involvement, given the practical unavailability of nonfederal officials to carry out all requirements of federal laws. But the primary effect could also be just the opposite in many areas. If Congress must not use state officials, it may simply appropriate money to hire new federal employees and displace states altogether from the activities it regulates. State officials do now carry forward the requirements of many federal laws. The overall effect of a significant judicial restriction on this structure is a complex empirical question, but a reduction on the power of states would be highly likely.

A related but somewhat different question is what forms of state involvement really promote federal values. Here, the way cooperative federalism operates becomes crucial. If all that the state officials are doing with federal laws is carrying forward their requirements, lacking any independence, it might be better to have them not under federal control so that, even if they are involved in fewer areas, they will have active authority in those domains. The defenders of cooperative federalism take a different view. They urge that when state legislatures and executive officials play a significant role in carrying out federal laws, they also have genuine influence on their effective content. Their ability to influence how the law is carried out rests both on the federal government's dependence on and integration with them, and on the source of power their state constituencies confer on them.[67]

Jessica Bulman-Pozen and Heather Gerken illustrate how states have been able to affect national standards they are implementing. The Federal Aid to Families with Dependent Children welfare program provided for state experimentation, authorizing waivers for state projects designed to promote its objectives. Wisconsin and Michigan used waivers to depart from the general national policy by requiring or strongly encouraging welfare recipients to seek work. Congress subsequently adopted a law that reshaped national policy in this direction.[68] With respect to the Clean Air Act, states were able to do less than the Environmental Protection Agency formally required, because the EPA depended on them for enforcement. States like California were also able to adopt more stringent requirements than were nationally established.[69] And when the USA Patriot Act required states to engage in investigations, detentions, and the sharing of intelligence, various states simply refused to engage in certain practices that they urged violated the federal and their state constitutions.[70] These significant forms of state involvement have allowed an influence that extends in time beyond a law's passage to its administration, something that would not have been possible had the federal government simply implemented these laws on its own. Of course, as I have noted, this kind of participation and influence, which could exist when cities and towns are designated to carry out laws adopted by state legislatures, does not depend distinctively on a federal structure of government. However, it definitely supports the notion that the federal government should not be precluded from engaging state officials in implementing its laws.

If a Supreme Court Justice were persuaded that "cooperative" and "uncooperative" federalism now play a highly valuable role in the way our country is governed, how might that affect her approaches to state authority? She might be less concerned about federal "commandeering" than if she saw state independence as more central,[71] and she might, when reviewing state laws, be disinclined to discern federal preemption unless Congress's aim to displace state authority is clear.[72] She might also conclude that what states themselves do should not often be excluded by the courts as violating the "Dormant Commerce Clause," rather leaving it to Congress to determine when state laws affecting commerce should be overridden.[73]

A key component about the appropriate role of courts for all of these issues is what judges can accurately discern and what standards of theirs can be adequately clear and socially desirable. One aspect of this inquiry is whether a restriction that courts set out will genuinely be effective. For example, one concern about an anticommandeering doctrine is that it will make little difference. Since Congress can use financial incentives or other benefits to encourage states to do what it wants, whether it can "compel" them to do these things is not very important.

A fundamental question about judicial involvement with respect to both separation of powers and federalism—one that reaches beyond the need for manageable judicial standards—is whether the political process itself provides adequate protection. A special argument about federalism is that Congress is composed of state representatives and thus can be taken to adequately protect state authority and interests. The persuasiveness of this argument could affect whether courts should ever overturn congressional statutes claimed to impair state authority; if not totally barring that possibility, should it at least lead to substantial deference and affect the particular forms of judicial review of federal statutes and their implementation? When a state act infringes on principles of fairness to citizens of other states or the powers of the national government, its legislators are not representing the citizens outside their states. But, as a classical essay by Herbert Wechsler emphasized, matters are different within Congress,[74] with members elected by citizens within their states. Is this sufficient to protect the interests of states, or does it at least provide a strong basis for judicial deference? Congressional representation of state interests must have been somewhat stronger at the founding when, for most people, state citizenship was more significant than federal citizenship, and members of the Senate were elected by state legislatures, a practice that was altered in 1913 by the Seventeenth Amendment.[75] Given national political parties, the strong sense of national citizenship, and the fact that most people care more about whether "government" does what they want than which part of the government has acted, Congress's protection of state interests has almost certainly diminished since 1789. And, of course, any such "protection" would never have fully safeguarded the interests of states whose citizens had a minority outlook not widely shared. In short, any simple assumption that Congress will always protect the values of state governments is not now persuasive.[76]

A rather different reason for not relying on political actors to protect federalism against intrusions is that state officials themselves cannot always be trusted to protect the underlying values of state independence.[77] Aware that citizens care more about what is done than about who is doing it, and are often ignorant of the exact distribution of responsibility between federal and state officials, state legislators and higher executives may be moved more by various narrow interests and national party loyalties than by wanting to protect the powers of their governments. And what they actually value for their states can differ from the underlying values of federalism; for example, wishing to protect themselves from competition from other states, they may favor a form of "cartel" over the value of independent decisions. If needed measures are bound to be controversial or unpopular, they may actually desire to have it look as if they are left without choice because of federal action. Such concerns could affect how far courts should involve themselves even when state officials go along with whatever federal statutes or administrative actions require.

Given all of these complexities, evaluating the desirable role of courts is quite difficult. As someone who is not an expert in this area of constitutional law, my sense is that, as elsewhere, broad simple judicial categorization is not the best answer. Judges need to be sensitive to the contexts of particular controversies and what measures they can usefully require.[78] The Supreme Court should not assume it has no role in protecting state domains. Requiring that Congress be clear when it intrudes on basic state functions makes sense, and so do some limits on how far Congress can interfere with these functions. But, in general, Congress should be able to decide what extensions of federal authority are warranted. The role of courts should be more active in reviewing administrative decisions that fall within the implementation of statutes.[79] And when neither federal preemption nor illegitimate state interference with interstate commerce is clear, courts should hesitate to invalidate state actions, leaving it up to Congress to respond.

V. THE SUPREME COURT AND THE AFFORDABLE CARE ACT

In late June of 2012, the Supreme Court in *National Federation of Independent Business v. Sibelius* (NF1B),[80] ruled upon central components of the politically controversial Patient Protection and Affordable Care Act (ACA) adopted during President Obama's first term. A majority of Justices surprised everyone who had guessed about probable results by the precise positions they took, and the divisions on the Court strikingly illustrated many of the dilemmas about interpretation of federalism summarized in the preceding sections.

The statute, the subject of intense partisan controversy and adopted without a single Republican vote, was designed to extend medical insurance to many persons not then covered, and to lower the rates for those whose preexisting conditions would otherwise entail higher-than-average charges. A basic provision was that insurance companies could not refuse to provide health insurance for individuals or charge persons with greater medical risks higher rates than they charge healthy people. The act also required that individuals under age sixty-five, and with adequate means, either purchase healthcare insurance or pay a "penalty" to the Internal Revenue Service. The logic of this mandate was that if those who were young and healthy chose to take the risk of not having insurance, what insurance companies would need to charge others would rise sharply, given that the ACA required those rates to include persons with pre-existing conditions. And no one really takes the full risk an absence of coverage might imply, since people suffering health emergencies are given treatment whether or not they have insurance and whether or not they can pay. Congress estimated that the average cost of family medical insurance is about $1,000 higher each year because of medical help given to people lacking insurance and unable to pay for their care.[81] Thus, requiring that healthy people pay for insurance could both get them to bear the cost of medical coverage they might actually receive and help to subsidize the costs of insurance for people at greater risk.

Costs for participating states were to be heavily borne by federal spending; although no state was required to get involved, those that declined were to lose all the federal assistance provided for existing Medicaid programs. In his opinion, Chief Justice Roberts notes: "Medicaid spending accounts for over 20 percent of the average State's total budget, with federal funds covering 50 to 83 percent of those costs."[82] Given this assistance, a state faced with termination would be extremely unlikely to refuse the funding and requirements of the new Act.

The Supreme Court needed to determine the constitutional validity of the "mandate" that individuals buy health insurance and of the condition that states must extend coverage or lose all Medicaid funding. Were they to find that one important provision was invalid, the Justices then had to decide whether simply to sever that provision from the Act or nullify the entire law.

The Justices were presented with arguments that the individual mandate was warranted by Congress's power under the Commerce Clause and its power to tax and spend. With respect to "taxation," a preliminary question was whether the Court should then even be considering the case, given that under the Tax Anti-Injunction Act, the validity of taxes can be challenged only if a person has paid and sues for a refund.[83]

The division on the central issues was this. Four Justices concluded that the individual mandate could be sustained under both the Commerce Clause and the Taxing and Spending Power. Four Justices concluded that the mandate was outside Congress's commerce power, and, given the statute as written, was not supportable as a tax. Chief Justice Roberts, the deciding vote, declared that the Commerce Clause could not support the requirement but that it was valid as an exercise in taxing, although the law did not count as a "tax" in a way that barred the Court's present resolution of its validity. With respect to the statutory prescription that states not extending their health insurance coverage lose all Medicaid support, seven Justices regarded this as invalid compulsion. The four Justices who believed that the individual mandate and the threat of states losing Medicaid funding were both unconstitutional also concluded that, if even only one of these provisions could not stand, the entire act should be declared invalid. The other five Justices determined that the ruling that states could not be coerced into the Medicaid expansion did not undercut other provisions.

Exploring these controversies reveals the complexity of certain central issues about federalism, including key disagreements about basic approaches and tenable judicial standards, and about what genuinely constitutes healthy federalism. It also reveals just how much can depend on the composition of the Supreme Court bench at a particular time. Although obviously critical for the status of healthcare, how the Court's determination in *NFIB* will affect future legislation and Supreme Court doctrine is much less certain. Given the Court's present division, whether constitutional limits will extend in the direction urged by the four dissenters or are constrained in favor of deference to congressional choices almost certainly depends on whether the next few appointments are made by Democratic or Republican presidents.

A. The Commerce Clause

Adopting a position with which the four dissenters fundamentally agreed, Chief Justice Roberts wrote that Congress's power under the Commerce Clause did not sanction the individual mandate provision. Employing a categorical approach rather than assessing the substantiality of effects, the Chief Justice concluded that the authority to "regulate" commerce did not include the power to require that people engage "in commerce to purchase an unwanted product."[84] Although individuals can be forbidden to perform acts with a negative effect on commerce, they may not be required to engage in acts that would promote commerce or a healthy economy. On this basis, Roberts distinguished *Wickard v. Filburn*, since its defendant had been forbidden to grow too much wheat. Even though the insurance mandate undoubtedly qualified as "economic" and would have had as much effect on interstate commerce as farmers growing wheat for their own use, the new law was not a regulation of "existing commercial activity," and upholding it "would open a new and potentially vast domain to congressional authority,"[85] because it impermissibly required a positive action. Part of the logic of the opinion was that if Congress could require individual acts that relate to commerce, its powers would be nearly unlimited, including requiring people to buy vegetables so they could be healthier.[86]

To reject the government's Commerce Clause argument, Chief Justice Roberts needed to address the Constitution's provision in article I, § 8 that Congress may "make all Laws which shall be necessary and proper" for exercising its powers. After all, if the mandate was a means to make the expansion of healthcare insurance by private companies feasible, why did that not make it acceptable as a way to promote commerce? As Roberts acknowledged, Supreme Court decisions had adopted an expansive reading of "necessary." In essence, if Congress regarded a means as called for, the Court had deemed that sufficient. The modern court had invalidated laws about guns in schools and violence against women that it found to be too remotely connected to commerce, but the connection of the ACA was much more direct. The Chief Justice's response was to rely on "proper." A means could be improper not only if at odds with a specific constitutional provision, such as the Free Speech Clause, but also if it violates the Constitution's basic division of powers and involves not a subsidiary means but a "great substantive and independent power."[87] This distinction had been suggested long ago in *McCullough v. Maryland*, [88] but the Court has rarely relied on it and its application in practice is hardly clear.[89]

The four dissenters in a joint opinion agreed with Roberts about the Commerce Clause and the limits of "Proper." They emphasized the "structural limits upon federal power," stating that to permit the mandate provision to stand would "extend federal power to virtually all human activity."[90] Since the dissenters did not actually join the Roberts opinion, and it is arguable, as I shall discuss below, whether Roberts should actually have reached this question, some have doubted whether the resolution reached by five Justices on the Commerce Clause counts as a holding.[91] As earlier chapters have noted, when the Supreme Court makes clear statements about legal rules, whether they are really holdings is not crucial because lower court judges do, and should, take them seriously; furthermore, the line between holding and dictum is hardly precise.[92] Although the subject is rarely discussed, a ground of decision shared by a majority of Justices who do not join a single opinion should properly be viewed as a holding. Indeed, in common law countries in which judges still mainly write individual opinions, discerning such agreements is the main way to identify a holding. On the point that his resolution about the Commerce Clause was not necessary to his decision, the answer is that if Roberts followed the order in which he thought he should approach the various constitutional issues, that is sufficient to make his resolution other than dictum.

Writing for the four Justices who dissented on this issue, Justice Ginsburg objected to a "rigid reading of the Clause [that] makes scant sense and is stunningly retrogressive."[93] She began with the premise that states cannot deal with the problem of healthcare insurance on their own, because the more generous states would attract the "needy and dependent" and impose extra costs upon themselves,[94] a conclusion strongly supported by the "disastrous" results[95] in the 1990s when some states required universal acquisition of insurance. Believing that a requirement that individuals purchase healthcare insurance was a proper means to help companies provide affordable policies for individuals with medical history, Justice Ginsburg stressed both the reliance on "actual experience" in prior cases and the respect judges should give to Congress when it enacts economic and social legislation.[96] Because all people need healthcare at some point in their lives, requiring payment at a particular stage, she contended, is unlike other activities in which individuals may choose never to engage. And given that healthcare is provided for those who are neither insured nor able to pay, the absence of an individual mandate would allow the uninsured to be assured of emergency help.[97] Under this scheme, they could also wait to purchase insurance until they are actually suffering illness or disability and still be assured that they will then be able to purchase that insurance at a modest rate. Because of this special relation of actual healthcare to insurance, Ginsburg urged that a decision upholding the mandate would not have the broad implications suggested by Chief Justice Roberts and the joint dissent. In neither the text of the Commerce Clause nor in prior cases did Ginsburg discern support for any sharp distinction between forbidding and requiring action; indeed, she found the line between regulating and requiring activity as far from simple. Since virtually everyone seeks medical care, requiring insurance could be seen as a regulation of that activity.[98]

Given what five Justices resolved about taxing and spending, the practical significance of the Commerce Clause ruling for future cases is unclear. But the division among the Justices clearly reveals sharply different approaches to the relative value of categorical versus context-sensitive appraisals and to whether judicial restraints on Congress's exercise of the Commerce power need to reach beyond specific constitutional limits, such as those in the Bill of Rights, and any requirement that commerce must be the subject of regulation. The Justices also have very different views about desirable relations between the national and state governments. If the practical consequence were to restrict how Congress can constrain individuals and states under the Commerce Clause, one effect may be to increase state influence on how federal programs are developed; but, as Abbe Gluck has pointed out, an "ironic" consequence may be that the national government will simply do more on its own.[99] No one now doubts that Congress properly imposes a social security tax to protect people when they retire; it could take a similar approach to extending healthcare, financing it out of a similar tax.

B. Taxing and Spending

Although the Affordable Care Act "required" that individuals purchase healthcare insurance and subjected those who failed to do so to a "penalty," the government argued that the mandate could be valid as imposing a tax. Since the four "liberal" Justices believed that the Commerce Clause supported the mandate, this became a crucial issue only for the other five Justices. The joint dissenters, resting heavily on how Congress itself had characterized its measure, concluded that the mandate should not be seen as a tax; if Congress wishes to invoke its power to tax, it needs to do so clearly.[100] Chief Justice Roberts, joined by the Justices who differed with him about the Commerce Clause, disagreed. Granting "the full measure of deference owed to federal statutes," he regarded the required penalty payments to the IRS as a form of tax.[101] Finding a "functional approach" in the prior cases, he wrote that this law differed from the Child Labor Tax struck down in *Bailey v. Drexel Furniture*,[102] by requiring only a payment that was not an "exceedingly heavy burden" and was generally less than the price of insurance. Further, the "penalty" did not include a scienter requirement that typically accompanies punishments; and it was collected not by the Department of Labor but by the Internal Revenue Service, which could not employ criminal prosecution for failure to pay.[103] Taking these factors into account, as well as the prediction that each year, roughly 4 million people "will choose to pay the IRS rather than buy insurance,"[104] one could see the law, like the tax on cigarettes, as both designed to bring in revenue and to discourage certain behavior. Roberts pointed out that other forms of federal taxation do encourage purchases, such as of houses and professional education. He rejected concerns that a broad interpretation of the taxing authority would give Congress a sweeping power since the ability to tax does not confer the same potential control over individual behavior as would the Commerce Clause; it can only require payment to the IRS, not impose direct penalties for actions, thus leaving individuals a genuine choice whether or not to engage in the taxed behavior.[105]

The approach of the Chief Justice to the tax question did not reflect any strong disagreement between him and the joint dissenters over what Congress *can* do. Agreeing that what are really prohibitions with genuine penalties cannot be simply justified as taxes, they differed over how explicit Congress must be to avoid a determination of unconstitutionality.[106] The dissenters would require Congress to make a clear statement if it wishes to invoke the tax power; the Chief Justice, on the other hand, believes that the Court should take a law as it can reasonably be understood, even if that sense is not the most obvious, when doing so will sustain its constitutionality.

The issue here differed from that in most cases employing standards of "clear statement" and "avoidance." These have concerned what behavior a particular law actually requires. Thus, if Congress really wants to insist that state judges not be forced to retire at seventy, which was the issue in *Gregory v. Ashcroft*, it must say so clearly.[107] And if one reading of what a law requires might make it unconstitutional, that is avoided in favor of an alternative without that consequence. The concern about the healthcare Act's individual mandate was Congress's source of power, not a conclusion of what it was actually requiring individuals to do. Although the point is debatable, I agree with Gillian E. Metzger and Trevor W. Morrison that if Congress definitely wants to set particular standards of behavior that are not themselves unconstitutional, courts desirably rely on a constitutional provision that can support the law, *unless* Congress has explicitly disclaimed any such reliance.[108]

One somewhat incongruous feature of the Chief Justice's avoidance approach was his conclusion that, although sustainable as a tax, the "mandate" did not count as one for purposes of when it could be challenged.[109] In terms of possible application of the Anti-Injunction Act, itself a statute, Roberts took Congress's designation to control. Although producing an odd combination, the distinction between the Act's label and how it may be construed to make it constitutionally defensible does make sense.

Of more general importance is the process of avoidance Roberts chose. The factual explanation *may* lie here in the possibility that the Chief Justice, initially disposed to vote with the dissenters, had drafted an opinion taking their position, but had then accepted the government's tax argument, because it persuaded him, or because he wanted to preserve the Court's institutional status, or both. With regard to interpretive doctrine, however, what is interesting is Roberts' explanation for resolving the Commerce Clause issue. According to what has been called "classical avoidance," courts would initially decide if what would otherwise be the most plausible interpretation would be unconstitutional.[110] If so, they would then avoid it in favor of a different construction that was acceptable. The modern approach has been more sweeping; courts have avoided interpretations that raise serious constitutional questions, typically without resolving whether the doubtful application would actually be unconstitutional.[111] This approach helps protect the edges of constitutional rights, especially in areas in which courts may be hesitant to declare that Congress has exceeded its powers. Had Roberts chosen this course, he could have indicated doubts about what the Commerce Clause authorizes and turned to the taxing power, while leaving unresolved just what Congress could permissibly do to regulate commerce.[112]

Given certain assumptions, I believe the Chief Justice did what was appropriate. If Congress definitely has mainly relied on one provision, and the Supreme Court can perceive a clear answer to how that reliance should be treated, the Justices properly address that first, before turning to whether another constitutional provision affords adequate support. If, on the other hand, the Justices, when first addressing the provision on which Congress mainly relies, are genuinely uncertain about the right result for that circumstance, or they doubt their ability to formulate a viable standard, they may do better to avoid that constitutional resolution. My own agreement with the Justices who regarded this as a legitimate regulation of commerce, and my sense that the "activity-inactivity" distinction is hard to draw and should not be central, leads me to conclude that the Chief Justice's not resolving the Commerce Clause issue would have been preferable; *but*, given his own appraisal of the substantive issues involved, his order of tackling them was not misguided.

C. The Loss of All Medicaid Funding for States Declining to Accept the New Coverage

This brings us to the aspect of the Affordable Care Act that contained Medicaid provisions establishing a new "essential health benefits package," and according to which involved states must cover all persons under age sixty-five with incomes of less than 133 percent of the federal poverty line. Unless agreeing to this extended inclusion, states were to forfeit federal support of existing Medicaid, which covers "pregnant women, children, needy families, the blind, the elderly, and the disabled."[113] The funding of that support is over 10 percent of most state revenues.

Seven Justices, including the four joint dissenters, regarded this threat of nonfunding as unacceptably coercive. Writing for Justices Breyer and Kagan on this point, Chief Justice Roberts quoted *Steward Machine v. Davis* for the proposition that "'when 'pressure turns into compulsion,' . . . the legislation runs contrary to our system of federalism."[114] In contrast to the result in *Steward Machine*, in which the 1937 Court had accepted a federal tax credit of up to 90 percent to encourage employers to contribute to state unemployment funds, the Chief Justice found the Medicaid funding condition to be over the line. Accepting the claim that the only purpose of the threat was to get them to expand healthcare dramatically, Roberts concluded that states were left with "no real option but to acquiesce. . . ."[115] In answer to Justice Ginsburg's dissenting argument that the old and new Medicaid provisions could be viewed as a single program that a state could either accept or reject, Roberts responded that the Act erected a new program, and the threat was to deprive funding of a well-settled existing program.[116] The joint dissenters agreed that Congress had designed the provisions so that "no state could possibly refuse the offer that the ACA extends."[117] Were this set of conditions not seen as coercive, Congress could "dictate policy in areas traditionally governed primarily at the state and local levels."[118]

Only Justice Ginsburg, joined by Justice Sotomayor, dissented on the issue of whether the pressure on states to accept the new program was acceptable.[119] She regarded the new program as an expansion of Medicaid, of a kind authorized by the earlier law. Justice Ginsburg was also sharply critical of the assumption that courts should determine whether a state has a "legitimate choice" or is being coerced. That inquiry "appears to involve political judgments that defy judicial calculation."[120]

Neither the Justices' opinions here nor previous cases make clear exactly how unacceptable compulsion is to be measured. What renders a condition on receiving money or avoiding taxes invalid? Should the courts assess the constitutional restraints in the same way as Congress, or should they grant considerable deference to Congress's judgment, or even abstain from enforcing relevant constitutional limits Congress itself should recognize?

The opinions for the seven Justices in this case reject any notion of either abstention or substantial deference on this point. They refer broadly to "coercion" and "compulsion" as if they are identical or loosely connected, but without really clarifying just how these terms relate to each other. Mitchell Berman has carefully developed an essential difference,[121] treating "compulsion" as involving a proposed program that a state really has no alternative but to accept, and "coercion" as an inappropriate form of pressure. As he explains, these two need not coincide. Were the federal government to attach fully reasonable and relevant conditions for use of an extremely generous offer of funds, these conditions, though perfectly appropriate, could put states under "compulsion," in Berman's terms, to accept. And if the government grants conscientious objectors to war an exemption from military service, but requires of them alternative civilian service, its condition amounts to compulsion; but since the whole draft involves compulsion, this condition for an exemption is fully appropriate.

On the other side, the government might use inappropriate pressure even if its moderate force does not compel acceptance. In *South Dakota v. Dole*,[122] the Supreme Court in 1987 considered a 5 percent reduction of highway funds for states allowing those under age eighteen to drink. The majority ruled that the reduction was obviously not coercive because it offered the states only a "relatively mild encouragement."[123] Justice O'Connor dissented on the ground that the connection between the drinking age and highway funding was insufficient to justify such pressure.[124] More straightforward examples of improper pressure are ones in which the government tries to condition funding on the waiver of an aspect of an individual's constitutional rights that are not directly related to the benefit conferred.[125]

Professor Berman's distinction is clear, but the terms "compulsion" to mean one is really left with no choice, and "coercion" to refer to the nature of the pressure,[126] do not fit ordinary usage. We do not think of a fantastic positive offer as compulsion, and "coercion" is not always bad. Although referring to coercion as imposing wrongful conditions, Berman does also recognize that what we think of as coercion may sometimes be justified.[127] This problem of terminology also entails questions about appropriate limits on Congress's power. Parents occasionally need to coerce their small children, and a military draft is undoubtedly coercive in requiring many men either to join the military or perform alternative service, yet both these may be proper exercises of power. Because of this fuzziness of terms, I shall use "improper form of pressure" as one side of the distinction and "no serious choice," representing incentives or adverse consequences so great that a person or state is left without a real choice, as the other side.

If we understand these two basic concepts, we can quickly grasp one of Berman's major claims: "compulsion" in his sense, that is, "no serious choice," is not enough by itself to render an incentive invalid. Arguably the crucial issue is, or should be, entirely about the form of a condition, however great its degree. If Congress uses a totally inappropriate incentive, that should be sufficient to condemn it. However, certain forms of pressure may be tolerable if they leave a free choice but not when they effectively dictate a result. On this view, the nature of pressure *and* its degree of strength could combine to render a condition invalid.

What constitutes inappropriate pressure? Perhaps the basic notion is that the condition set is not really related to the federal grant of funds. Thus, in *Dole*, we have O'Connor's argument that the drinking age is not related to highway grants. With respect to Medicaid, the argument can be that denying states funding for all Medicaid programs unless they subscribe to the new Act has no relation to the functioning and desirability of the programs that are now operating. Rather, the aim is simply to get compliance by an extreme threat. It is this approach that makes so much turn on whether the new program is separate from, or really part of, the old Medicaid program. When Congress sets up a single program of funding, it can, the Justices assume, require acceptance of all or nothing, leaving the states without a choice to accept one part and reject another. Berman tentatively disagrees with making the division of programs so important.[128] If one part of a single program is withheld simply in order to get acceptance of other parts, he thinks that pressure may be improper, and therefore unconstitutional.

This brings us to what seem to me the most difficult problems: What should count as improper pressure, and are courts in a position to assess that? Suppose Congress is responding to perceived irresponsibility and injustice that bears a relation to the states' use of federal funds. *Dole* and the Affordable Care Act both provide interesting examples. For the basic aim to save lives by funding better highways, the money of the federal government will be no less effective in states that allow eighteen-year-olds to drink than in those that do not. Indeed, the grants may carry the least public safety benefit in states with the most careful drivers. However, because drivers from eighteen to twenty-one are generally less responsible than older drivers, a state could increase its own highway safety by prohibiting that group from consuming alcohol. Could not the federal government reasonably take the view that the states that themselves act less responsibly to assure highway safety should receive lower grants than the states that are more diligent?

Is a similar view possible about the Affordable Care Act requirement of "all or nothing"? Berman himself suggests that it may be acceptable for the federal government to withhold healthcare assistance from states that refuse to cover victims of HIV/AIDS in a healthcare program meant for victims of specific diseases,[129] since that refusal would represent an unjust discrimination against certain citizens. But, on the same basis, could one not view the actual Medicaid provisions as precluding discrimination against single or childless citizens who happen not to fall within the previously covered categories? In brief, whether the federal government in allocating grants is responding with its conditions to a perceived irresponsibility or injustice, even within a domain essentially left to states, seems significant.[130] That is one reason the term "improper pressure" is preferable to "coercion," because an otherwise similar condition set may or may not be designed mainly to encourage states to be more responsible or less unjust.

That leaves two fundamental puzzles. First, is the degree of "free choice" at all relevant? The greater the degree of pressure, perhaps the more crucial its nature. So the extent to which choice is controlled is one relevant factor that courts should consider. Second, is anything like this approach really workable for courts, given their hesitancy to probe motivations, their deference to Congress, and the difficulty of assessing matters of degree? My tentative conclusion is that courts should properly get involved, but only in extreme cases—ones in which the kind of pressure to comply is completely inappropriate or appears to be both inappropriate and excessive. By these options, the healthcare Act posed a very difficult issue, but its condition on states might well have been treated as responsive to a possible form of discrimination.

VI. CONCLUSION

This chapter, along with the one before it, has explored a number of issues involving divisions of governmental authority. Although these raise some basic questions of interpretation like those focused on in prior chapters, they also reveal aspects that are special, most notably a number of circumstances in which courts may need to avoid constitutional issues or accord substantial deference to choices made by Congress or the President, and the special difficulties of judges undertaking a functional weighting of relevant factors when they undertake a determination of Congress's authority concerning a distribution of powers, as contrasted with its possibly violating individual rights. The limits on how far original understanding should control interpretation are starkly illustrated by radical changes of government structures since the founding.

Beginning with the First Amendment, the following chapters explore the dimensions of a range of issues about individual rights.

Part IV

INDIVIDUAL RIGHTS AND NORMS OF EQUALITY

Chapter 9

Freedom of Speech and the Press

I. INTRODUCTION

Returning to issues about individual rights directly protected by the Constitution, this chapter first addresses briefly the basic notion that the Fourteenth Amendment "selectively incorporates" most of the Bill of Rights, and then concentrates on First Amendment safeguards of speech and the press. Chapter 10 focuses on how those amendments protect free exercise and nonestablishment of religion.

A. Selective Incorporation

Before engaging protections of rights concerning speech and religion covered by the First Amendment and criminal process rights governed by the Fourth, Fifth, and Sixth Amendments, the puzzles and values of "selective incorporation" require a brief explanation.

According to prevailing Supreme Court doctrine that has become widely accepted, the Fourteenth Amendment selectively incorporates most aspects of the original Bill of Rights, requiring states to respect those rights.[1] This approach supplanted earlier decisions that the Amendment did not make such rights applicable against the states.[2] Before adopting incorporation, the Supreme Court had ruled that the Amendment did protect certain fundamental rights against states, such as not to suffer a coerced confession, but these did not reach as extensively as the coverage of the provisions in the first eight amendments.[3] With selective incorporation, the coverage is taken to be full; the coverage is also treated as essentially the same for the federal government and states, a conclusion that does not follow automatically.

We can first ask how well selective incorporation fits with the constitutional text and original intentions. The Fourteenth Amendment provides that states may not "abridge the privileges or immunities of citizens," deprive anyone of "life, liberty, or property, without due process of law," or deny persons "equal protection of the law." Equal protection, dominantly aimed at barring unequal treatment of black citizens, many of whom were freed slaves, plainly does not incorporate many individual rights that states may have declined to afford anyone. The "due process" language may be a bit vaguer and might plausibly cover rights such as the privilege against self-incrimination. But two substantial obstacles stand in the way of finding textual incorporation here. First, "due process" does not seem to cover a range of substantive rights, such as possessing guns, worshipping as one chooses, and speaking freely. Second, the same due process language is in the Fifth Amendment; no one then conceived that all the rest of the Bill of Rights was redundant rhetoric because "due process" provided the only necessary guarantee. If one is looking just at the constitutional text, the "privileges or immunities" clause appears the most promising basis for incorporation; but its specification of "citizens" rather than "persons" raises a serious problem about its range of coverage.[4] The fact that the Supreme Court has relied on the "due process clause" is basically a consequence of its ruling in 1873 that gave privileges or immunities a very limited, implausible coverage.[5]

If one turns from the text to adopter intent and reader understanding, there is substantial disagreement over the relation of the Fourteenth Amendment to the Bill of Rights.[6] Some of the leading advocates of the amendment did have an expansive view of its coverage,[7] but beyond the protection of freed slaves and other black citizens, there was hardly a consensus about what exactly it was designed to reach. As with many basic constitutional issues, fixing on a specific and shared intent is impossible; and the understanding of readers, whether general or well informed, would be no more determinative.

How does the "selective" element conform with the text and intentions? Certainly neither provides a clear guide about just which rights are incorporated and which are not, but one might see the Amendment's general language as failing to reach rights that were not then, or are not now, seen as fundamental. Thus, to take an example, many states did not provide grand juries for individuals in the mid-nineteenth century; and, since grand juries are cumbersome and tend to do whatever prosecutors want, demanding all states to have them might be wasteful and unwise, and not required by the original sense of the Amendment. Of course, "selective incorporation" does require a range of judicial determination about what rights really count, and this was one ground on which Justice Hugo Black defended "total incorporation."[8]

Does it follow from "incorporation" that a faithful originalist will perceive the same limits on states as the federal government? The basic answer is "no." For an originalist, what counts for the Bill of Rights itself is the understanding in 1789–1791. For the Fourteenth Amendment, by contrast, the perceptions of enactors and readers at the time of that enactment are what should matter. Having a developed view of the scope of various rights, their notion of "full protection" would not simply have replicated the sense of the late eighteenth century. Although, as Chapter 3 notes, it is conceivable that some enactors or readers imagined that what an amendment was making central was the understanding at the time of the Bill of Rights, that idea is much too refined to be plausible. It also disregards the degree to which the promoters of the post-Civil

War amendments distrusted the founding generation, which accepted slavery.[9] For a genuine originalist, what should be "incorporated" by the Fourteenth Amendment is how the various rights covered by the Bill of Rights were then taken; this would include what strategies of interpretation were deemed appropriate after the Civil War.

Given this obvious conclusion, why is it that the Supreme Court, despite most of its rights cases being claims against state governments, rarely refers to the understanding in 1868 of the protections contained in the Bill of Rights? And why does it almost always treat the constraints on the federal and state governments as the same?

Jamal Greene has argued persuasively that the failure of Reconstruction, the lack of figures of the time who were as notable as the leading original Framers, and the absence of clear principles with definite applications are three reasons why originalists have tended to disregard understandings at the time of the Fourteenth Amendment.[10] This disregard is not defensible in principle.

Treating the constraints on the federal and state governments in the same way makes great practical sense. It simplifies to a degree what are, in any event, often complex inquiries. Although courts might afford more deference to the national Congress than a single state legislature in assessing the scope of a protected right, they would find it hard to justify to citizens that the Bill of Rights requires states to respect rights that clearly do not apply to the federal government, because the perception of protections expanded in decades before the Civil War. Seeing the understanding of the later amendment as working backward to alter how the first eight amendments apply to the federal government is a sensible approach to the overall constitutional structure.[11] But, as Ryan Williams has shown, with respect to substantive due process, that correlation is not derivable from what enactors (or readers) were actually assuming when the Fourteenth Amendment was adopted.[12]

A final issue about "selective incorporation" is the role of Congress under the Fourteenth Amendment and how that relates to its original power. The Supreme Court has, over time, granted Congress increasing power to control activities within states that can affect interstate commerce; it has not supposed that Congress can actually determine what constitutes a state infringement of federal constitutional powers or rights. Under section 5 of the Fourteenth Amendment, Congress has the power "to enforce, by appropriate legislation, the provisions of the article." This language clearly confers on Congress the power to forbid practices that will inevitably lead to violations, but can it also expand on what the Supreme Court has cast as the range of violations? This issue, closely tied to when courts should afford deference to Congress, is not really resolvable by the text and original understanding. The Supreme Court's basic approach at this stage is fairly restrictive. In *City of Boerne v. Flores*,[13] the Court held that under the Fourteenth Amendment, Congress could not interpret the Free Exercise Clause as demanding more than the Court had most recently stated, even though Congress's approach in the Religious Freedom Restoration Act had replicated what had been the Court's prior free exercise doctrine; further, Congress could forbid behavior only if it was fairly closely tied to the judicial account of violations.

Although the chapters that follow touch on changes in understandings between the Bill of Rights and the Fourteenth Amendment, they take "selective incorporation" for granted and assume that settled applications will be the same for the states and national government.[14]

B. Freedom of Expression

As drafted, the First Amendment came third, but the failure of states to ratify the first two proposed amendments put it first.[15] That final categorization strikes one as apt, given the absolute centrality in a liberal democracy of freedom of expression and of religion.

A central aspect of the actual and desirable development of constitutional protection of freedom of speech and the press is the complexity of what is involved. What communications count as speech, and, among these, are there sharp differences in value? What reasons might the government have to restrict speech that are strong enough to survive constitutional challenges? How crucial are the nature and breadth of a restrictive law's categorization, the line drawn between what is accepted and what is not? Claims about freedom of speech arise in an incredible variety of circumstances, ones in which the force of the underlying fundamental values differs strikingly. Many of these variations are especially hard to pin down and classify.

These realities lead to a number of descriptive and normative conclusions, ones that strongly support the book's overall thesis that interpretive approaches do and should vary not only with respect to different constitutional texts but also with the particular kinds of controversies covered by a particular provision. No single doctrine, or even a few doctrines, of what is constitutionally allowed and what is not can fit the range of issues about free expression. Sensible approaches must take into account perceived social conditions and how far fundamental values underlying the basic right are in play.

As this chapter reflects, judicial opinions do not provide a clear, systematic account of what is involved in free speech standards and applications. Free speech doctrine has been regarded by scholars as "maddeningly complex,"[16] as employing "slippery and hard to apply categories,"[17] and as constituting "one of the most complicated and confusing areas in constitutional law."[18] A theme of this chapter is that, given the multiple values that underlie freedom of expression, the fact that both the comparative relevance of different values and their total force varies greatly with distinctive contexts, and the reality that individual Supreme Court Justices do not agree about these values, we should not be surprised that the opinions in leading cases do not yield a coherent, persuasive account of all that is going on.

Prior chapters have explored the many reasons that can lie behind a failure of majority opinions to provide a careful analysis of what is at stake. Here, the difficulty of capturing subtle but important differences among situations is especially important. As in other areas, a central divide is between formalist and functionalist interpretation, between categorical and *explicit* balancing approaches.

In its efforts to afford appropriate importance to relevant factors and to provide standards that courts are capable of applying, the Supreme Court has drawn distinctions between the core aspects of free speech and "low-value" speech and between content-based limits and other limits on what is communicated. For solid reasons, it grants the political branches the least deference when restrictions curtail speech based on its content within categories of high value. As with a number of other individual rights, one issue about the right of expression is its relation to equality. Do the government's efforts to regulate or promote expressions treat similar communications equally? Does it matter whether the aim of a restriction is to contribute to equality? On this latter point, Justices have disagreed sharply when it comes to donations to political speech.

Much of this chapter is devoted to particular kinds of expressions and how the Supreme Court has or has not protected these. Specific topics are: (1) the clear and present danger test, (2) antigovernment speech, (3) the revealing of secrets, (4) special protection of the press, (5) soliciting or encouraging criminal behavior, (6) "fighting words," (7) hate speech and insults, (8) lying, (9) defamation, (10) invasions of privacy and emotional distress, (11) obscenity, (12) commercial advertising, (13) content distinctions, and (14) content-neutral restrictions.

A thoughtful evaluation of how these topics have been and might be treated requires a sense of what constitutes "speech," its values, and the force of countervailing considerations. I tackle these rather complicated inquiries before moving to the specific topics, aiming to provide bases to understand and evaluate judicial approaches. As in other domains, the status of original understanding is important. A summary of that, and of premodern historical development, precedes a theoretical assessment of how we can understand free expression. Together, these provide a striking example of why the original understanding about acceptable government restrictions should not determine modern application of general provisions.

Although this chapter hardly provides a systematic account of all that this part of the First Amendment might cover and should cover, it does attempt to clarify some aspects that are rarely explicit in judicial opinions and to suggest certain approaches to particular issues that are not in line with presently prevailing doctrines. However persuasive is this effort to provide an account that seeks clarity and coherence, while respecting crucial complexities, we must never forget that Justices aiming at majority opinions and constrained by respect for precedents do not have the latitude of a single individual scholar to try to pull things together in a more or less systematic way.

II. ORIGINAL UNDERSTANDING AND PREMODERN HISTORY

The First Amendment provides that "Congress shall make no law … abridging the freedom of speech, or of the press; or the right of the people peaceably to assemble. . . ." The Supreme Court may be seen as having implemented the basic values underlying the amendment, but the original understanding of what it was specifically meant to protect has disappeared almost totally from modern doctrine. Multiple cases provide far more expansive safeguards against government interferences than were conceived then or were understood when the Fourteenth Amendment, which the Court has taken to apply the First Amendment to the states, was adopted.[19]

Prior restraints are the one topic for which the original understanding has been carried forward. During the sixteenth and seventeenth centuries, the English crown was able to censor the content of printed works and to deny licenses for their publication.[20] After that practice was abandoned, William Blackstone in his 1769 Commentaries, which were widely influential in the United States, wrote: "The liberty of the press [concerns] laying no previous restraints upon publication[s] and not in freedom from censure for criminal matter[s] when published."[21] As we shall see, the Supreme Court has been sharply restrictive of government efforts to preclude publications; but it has also stretched protections far, far beyond this. Justice Hugo Black did claim that the amendment itself provided absolute protection for freedom of speech, but no actual historical evidence supports this.[22]

What historical scholars have mainly debated is what the conceived status was of "seditious libel," an issue that is tied, as Chapter 3 notes, to the level of generality at which freedom of the press was understood.[23] Under the English common law, a person was criminally responsible for "the intentional publication, without lawful excuse or justification, of written blame of any public man, or of the law, or of any institution established by law."[24] Whether the First Amendment left this subject wholly to legislative choice, or allowed the crime but required that truth be a defense and that a jury determine guilt, or precluded seditious libel as a federal crime, is far from clear. In England in the seventeenth and eighteenth centuries, enforcement against seditious libel was only sporadic, but most objections to the ban there and within the American colonies were that truth should be a defense and that the jury should resolve not only the fact of publication but also overall guilt or innocence. In a famous 1735 case in which John Peter Zenger, a New York journal publisher, was charged with seditious libel, the judge refused to rule that truth was a defense, but the jury disregarded his instructions and declared Zenger "not guilty."[25] As with many other constitutional issues, the realistic answer about original understanding is almost certainly that neither the Framers and enactors nor informed readers had a common and clear sense of exactly how the Amendment related to seditious libel.

In 1798, Congress, under the Federalists, adopted a "Sedition Act," which made it criminal to write or publish "false, scandalous, and malicious writing or writings . . . against the government of the United States, or either House of the Congress . . . , or the President . . . , with intent to defame [them] . . . or to bring them . . . into contempt or disrepute; or to excite against them . . . the hatred of the good people . . . , or to stir up sedition. . . ."[26] The act was enforced against individual and newspaper supporters of the Republican Party. The Supreme Court did not pass on the act, but convictions were upheld by lower federal courts and by three Supreme Court Justices sitting on circuit.[27] The Act expired in 1801, and President Thomas Jefferson pardoned all those who had been convicted; Congress subsequently repaid fines on the ground that the Act was actually unconstitutional. A century and a half later, in 1964, the Supreme Court stated that the challenge to the validity of the Sedition Act "has carried the day in the court of history."[28]

Although some other speech controversies had arisen over the next century,[29] the Supreme Court in 1907, in an opinion by Justice Holmes, indicated in *Patterson v. Colorado* that the First Amendment's protection of freedom of expression covered only prior restraints.[30] Not until the First World War did the Court tackle major free speech issues. In 1917, Congress adopted the Espionage Act, which made it criminal to willfully "cause or attempt to cause insubordination, disloyalty, mutiny, or refusal of duty in the military or naval forces" or "obstruct the recruiting or enlistment service of the United States."[31] In 1918, Congress added a Sedition Act under which saying anything disloyal about the government or encouraging resistance to the war effort against Germany was criminal.[32]

In 1919, the Supreme Court, with Justice Holmes writing the opinions, upheld three convictions under the Espionage Act. The cases are especially significant both because of the formulated standard of review and how it was applied. In the first case, *Schenck v. United States,*[33] without explicitly rejecting what he had written in *Patterson,* Holmes noted that the amendment may go beyond prohibiting prior restraints. He also provided the first use of the "clear and present danger test," which he arrived at by reference to his earlier reflections on the law of criminal attempts.[34] He remarked that "[t]he question in every case is whether the words are used in such circumstances and are of such a nature as to create a clear and present danger that they will bring about the substantive evils that Congress has a right to prevent."[35]

In contrast to the manner in which Holmes and other Justices later developed the test, its modest degree of protection in early 1919 is largely revealed by the nature of the publications involved. Schenck had agreed to help print and circulate an antiwar tract to those called to military service. The leaflet talked of a "right to assert your opposition to the draft," suggested that a failure to assert those rights would help to "deny or disparage rights," and urged, "You must do your share to maintain, support and uphold the rights of the people of this country."[36] Assuming that the statute required an illegal purpose, Holmes discerned from the content of the pamphlet that its aim and tendency was to interfere with recruiting, and this satisfied the clear and present danger test.

The actual language that defendants in the other two cases had used was significantly less explicit. One had published articles favorable to Germany, which called those who resisted the draft "technically ... wrong" though "more sinned against than sinning."[37] In the third case, the defendant, a highly prominent socialist leader named Eugene Debs, had made a speech in which he blamed the war on the ruling classes and praised some draft resisters. He exhorted the audience, "Don't worry about the charge of treason to your masters; but be concerned about the treason that involves yourselves."[38]

Together, these cases reflected a clear willingness to find a criminal intent from language that is far from explicit and to discern an adequate danger in any likely impairment of legitimate government objectives. As Section IV on clear and present danger describes below, within nine months, Justice Holmes's approach became more demanding, a striking shift that eventually yielded a radical invigorating of First Amendment protections.[39] For some years, the majority of the Court abandoned Holmes's formula in favor of a much less rigorous standard;[40] but that did not endure. During the 1930s and subsequently, "clear and present danger," was applied strictly and became the basic approach for not only subversive advocacy but also a whole range of free speech issues. Partly because of the expansion of First Amendment protection, the general acceptance by leading political figures and by citizens of sharp criticisms of government actions, including military involvement, has grown tremendously. During World War I, nearly 2,000 individuals were actually indicted under the Espionage and Sedition Acts.[41] During subsequent wars, virtually no one has been prosecuted for even the strongest criticisms of government policy;[42] one is substantially at risk only if he specifically urges criminal behavior.

III. SPEECH AND ITS VALUE

Any interpretive approach to the First Amendment requires a sense of what constitutes "speech" and "the press" and of the values that warrant their special protection. The simple premises that speech typically involves the communication of ideas and sentiments and that "the press" concerns publications do not themselves tell us just what the First

Amendment reaches and how. Is it limited or not to expressions that concern the general society and its political life? What is the status of verbal and written communications that depart from an ordinary sense of "speech"? Is there any protection of physical acts, such as flag burning, that may express opinions in a nonverbal form? Does "the press" refer only to those professionally involved in publications? Given modern technology, particularly the ability of ordinary people to engage in electronic communication that can reach a global audience, is there any clear line between ordinary speech and publication? After noting the values that lie behind speech and justify its constitutional protection, this section addresses these questions.

A. Consequentialist and Nonconsequentialist Values

A range of values are served by persons being able to express themselves. Although the line is hardly sharp, some of these values are tied directly to consequences; others depend on a normative judgment about what is intrinsically right or good.[43]

The most familiar argument for freedom of speech is that open discourse helps us to discover truth. In his book *On Liberty*, John Stuart Mill urged that if the government can prevent communication, it may suppress ideas that are true, and that even false ideas promote a re-examination that vitalizes truth for people.[44] For Mill, relevant truth covered values as well as empirical facts and concerned matters of not only social importance but also personal life. No one claims that people grasp the truth on each occasion they are exposed to it, but over time, open discourse may promote acceptance of what is true and rejection of what is false. This fundamental assumption about freedom of speech, expressed in powerful opinions of Justices Holmes and Brandeis among others,[45] has been challenged in various ways. Facing the force of these challenges is a vital component of assessing the value of free speech in modern times.

One author blithely asserted in 1984 that "the assumption of the existence of objective truth is crucial to [the] classic marketplace theory, [and] almost no one believes in objective truth today."[46] Quite the contrary, every sane person believes in objective truth. Did it rain last night in our town? Did Barack Obama receive more votes in the 2012 presidential election than Mitt Romney? Is the earth round or flat? Such questions have correct and incorrect answers, ones most people discern when information is freely available. Some people do deny that questions about values have objective answers, but even here, as Chapter 5 suggests, certain assertions about what is good or bad seem definitely right. Is it desirable for a person to be constantly in excruciating pain? Is it appropriate to kill anyone whose looks do not appeal to you? The answer to both questions is "no." Since many questions of value connect to judgments about the quality of lives, information about people's positive and negative experiences can help us arrive at judgments about value.

The serious question about objective truth is not whether it ever exists, but rather how far free expression promotes its understanding. For some aspects of what is true for people, such as what tastes good to them, communication may add little to personal experience. And some communications are mainly aimed at objectives other than revealing truth; advertising, for example, typically presents at best a partial truth to persuade people to act in a certain way, often appealing to non-rational feelings and perceptions. On the other hand, with regard to scientific facts and what happened historically, extensive communication may be vital to persons grasping what is true. Given both the reality that some communications are not designed to convey truth and the grossly unequal ability of people to communicate effectively in the "marketplace" of ideas, one may wonder whether government oversight can promote truth better than unregulated speech and press.

A central question about how well freedom of speech leads to people understanding truth, as compared with government suppression or involvement, is whether the government can be trusted to decide what speech to suppress or promote. With respect to political topics, suppression almost inevitably concentrates on opinions contrary to government policy. Among the most important connections of free expression to discovery of truth is revealing abuses of official authority,[47] a benefit that government suppression would certainly undermine. The knowledge that an active, inquisitive, free journalism may reveal such abuses can also help to deter some of their happening. On subjects such as scientific knowledge, those in the government may not be particularly well suited to determine what is true and what is false. Bases like these make it easy to conclude that free expression is preferable to government censorship for the discovery of truth overall. That, however, leaves open the harder questions of whether and when government is warranted in promoting more equality of discourse in areas such as political campaigns, in conveying particular needed messages, such as the dangers of smoking, and even in suppressing messages, such as cigarette advertisements, that demonstrably lead people to harm themselves.

If the discovery of truth is a basis for free speech that focuses on those who receive communications, one must also consider the value for people of being able to express their opinions and emotions. This is a crucial component of developing a sense of dignity and autonomy.

As Vincent Blasi has argued persuasively, the exchanges involved in a culture of free expression can help to build "good character," including the traits of "inquisitiveness, independence of judgment, distrust of authority, willingness to take initiative, perseverance, courage to confront evil, aversion to simplistic accounts and solutions, . . . self-awareness, . . . empathy, . . . and respect for evidence."[48] Lee Bollinger has emphasized how much freedom of expression can also promote tolerance of the opinions and behavior of others who are unlike ourselves.[49]

One aspect of the discovery of truth is that free expression reveals the conditions of people and what they care about, thus contributing to an accommodation of competing interests and to social stability. People communicating their needs and desires increases the chances that these will be taken into account. Of course, a "free communication market" can reflect an imbalance that favors the rich, the powerful, and the articulate over the poor, the powerless, and the inarticulate. But most forms of government suppression are unlikely to produce a more accurate account of the range of citizens' desires and interests. The benefits of free expression contribute to fulfilling the underlying assumption of liberal democracies that the basic choices of citizens should determine what a government does.

Some scholars, notably Alexander Meiklejohn and Robert Bork, have urged that the First Amendment's free speech and free press clauses protect only communications about public affairs.[50] Given the difficulty of drawing the line at which matters are public, the importance for government of broad aspects of citizens' lives, and the fundamental values of free communication in many domains, no restriction to public affairs is warranted;[51] and the Supreme Court has mandated a much broader scope of coverage. But this does leave open whether protecting speech about political subjects is especially important. A core value of the Amendment is to protect free political discourse, and, as Robert Post has shown,[52] a special focus on this feature could affect how one perceives some of its applications. With political subjects, one can distinguish between the values of citizens arriving at correct or sound conclusions and their being able to participate freely in political life.[53]

A fundamental question that arises for political and other discourse is what is the government's proper role. The First Amendment is most obviously implicated when the government suppresses private speech. On many matters, we assume that government bodies can express points of view, though they cannot instruct people which candidates to support. A perplexing issue explored in a later section is just how far the government can determine financial support on the basis of views that private individuals or companies express or agree not to express.

Among the claimed values of freedom of speech that are not directly consequentialist is the notion that its very existence acknowledges that people should be seen as autonomous and rational, and recognizes their dignity and equality. For someone who accepts a social contract theory that government properly rests on the consent of citizens, with powers limited to what individuals cannot adequately protect for themselves, free expression can be seen as a basic right that people have not surrendered to their governments.

Three important truths concern these collected values underlying free speech. Their force varies with different forms of expression, and the degree of tension among them depends on the particular government practices involved. A more subtle point is that although many of these values are also served by practices other than free communication—and this has a bearing on what should count as "speech"—an overlap of values that underlie it and other human activities does not undercut the special status of speech.[54] The weight of particular values, or their combinations, can be greater with respect to speech; so also can the danger that government involvement will impair those values.

B. What Constitutes "Speech" and "the Press"?

Tied to underlying values are questions of what has counted, and should count, as "speech" and "the press" for the understanding and application of the First Amendment.

I say relatively little here about "the press." When the First Amendment was adopted, it covered not only writers and publishers of newspapers and magazines but also all of those who wrote and published books and manuscripts. A crucial question the specific section discussing "the press" addresses is whether the First Amendment itself affords special protections to those who communicate to the public as a profession, or at least allows the government, whether by statute or executive decision, to grant them distinctive privileges.

With respect to the boundaries of "speech," some distinctions may be too subtle for judges to use them as standards of inclusion and exclusion. One issue about the First Amendment's range of coverage is whether, either as a matter of original understanding or desirable modern application, it should be conceived as reaching only particular classes of speech.

"Speech" in any ordinary sense covers assertions of fact and value—not only those about general truths but also about personal preferences and expectations. As the prior section claims, although allowing competing perspectives on important public issues and the checking of government abuses are major reasons for freedom of speech, it hardly follows that only political utterances should be protected. Speech that is not explicitly political often has political implications. For example, views about the morality of sexual relations between people of the same gender can matter greatly for whether someone believes same sex-marriage should be authorized, and, if so, whether various religiously based exemptions should be granted. Even more important, people frequently communicate about aspects of their lives that are not political. Of course, were governments never to concern themselves with such topics, we would need no constitutional protection. But legislatures may be tempted by popular outrage to suppress unfashionable views about how people should live, including the sexual relations of themselves and others. Although political messages do raise special concerns, that is not a ground to restrict the First Amendment to them.

Similarly, the protection of free speech is not limited to "acts of expression" that "are addressed to a large (if not the widest possible) audience."[55] Whether a communication is private should sometimes affect its degree of protection; but many personal communications with family members, close friends, and colleagues are extremely important for what people understand about themselves and others. No reason justifies excluding them from constitutional coverage.

Whether something counts as speech does not depend on a speaker's motivation. Ordinary people, as well as political candidates, sometimes say things just to help others understand, but often they are furthering a direct personal interest. That objective alone does not disqualify what they say as protected speech. But if a person communicates a fact, such as a lock combination, *simply* to produce a practical consequence, one may doubt whether that should count as relevant speech since it has nothing to do with the values of freedom of expression.

Lies about facts and insincere assertions of values pose harder questions. One may initially wonder whether people have any legitimate interest in saying what they do not believe is true. But we sometimes say things that are less than true to protect the feelings of others, or to not reveal aspects of ourselves. Although personal decisions about whether it is morally acceptable to speak other than the truth as we perceive it can be difficult, the government should not have a free rein to control all statements understood by their speakers to be false. Additional practical reasons for why this is so are that the line between truth and falsity is not always clear, the inquiry about what a speaker actually believed can often prove nearly impossible, and the prospect of such an inquiry could itself discourage people from saying things they actually believe but recognize are highly unpopular. All of this is *not* to say that falsity and lying never matter; in some domains, the government properly attaches negative consequences to false statements.

The concept of free expression includes various forms of artistic communication not formulated in words, such as sculpture, painting, photography, ballet and modern dance, and instrumental music. These expressions are designed to enrich people's lives, and many of them do communicate understandings of facts and values. Once we recognize that protection must extend beyond linguistic communication, we need to address the reality that all of us, by bodily movements, facial expressions, and ordinary activities, communicate with each other. If I frown, that may equate to "I'm a bit angry about that." If I play tennis, I implicitly convey the message that this is a good way to spend one's time and that I have agreed to play by the rules. If almost all we do communicates something, how can any line be drawn about what counts as constitutionally protected speech? The short answer is that the government can forbid and regulate behavior that is not primarily communicative.[56] It can, for example, forbid suicide, even though some people considering that action may wish to convey a message to those who have hurt them, and the very act of suicide strongly affects how others think and feel. This short answer does not, by itself, tell us whether the government can forbid nonverbal behavior, such as burning flags, precisely because that behavior almost always conveys a hostile message. Nor does it settle whether a person who communicates a message by violating a government prohibition not itself designed to discourage expression has any valid free speech claim. A later section explores these sorts of cases.

Forms of communication that are not primarily designed to express facts, values, and feelings, such as words of agreement, promises, offers, and instructions, raise vital issues about the boundaries of speech. By such utterances, persons commit themselves to perform acts and/or impose on others a duty to act. Although merely defending the moral acceptability of breaking a law constitutes a genuine act of expression, we do not so regard an agreement to commit a crime or an offer of money to someone to kill a rival. Although no judicial opinion has carefully explained how the line is drawn, criminal law reaches all sorts of verbal and written utterances that are not considered speech.

As a general category, we may classify these as "situation-altering utterances" that actually change social settings.[57] Such utterances, very broadly understood, include expressions of fact and value, and ordinary factual assertions, such as a wife conveying to her husband her awareness of his unfaithfulness, that also change social settings. Nevertheless, from the point of view of protecting free speech, ordinary communications are critically different from those that are dominantly commitments to performing nonverbal acts.

Categories that are more difficult to classify are threats and inducements, and requests and encouragements. Suppose a father says to an adult child, "If you marry a Protestant, I'll give you financial support; if you marry a Catholic, I will disinherit you." If the father is *only* reporting what he would do in any event, he is giving a factual warning. If the father would not have responded in these ways had the child, without the father's knowledge, previously married a Catholic, and his *sole* object is to alter the child's likely behavior, this amounts to a kind of situation-altering utterance. But, of course, the same aim to affect behavior may accompany a warning about a response one might make even in its absence. An outsider will rarely be able to discern that the *only* or *overriding* reason for such a warning is to manipulate another's behavior.

Although requests and encouragements do not commit speakers or listeners to perform behavior in the manner of agreements, promises, and instructions, they do change social settings to a degree. It is difficult, for example, to simply walk away from a blind woman if she hears your footsteps and asks that you help her cross the street. Just how far the First Amendment should apply to requests and encouragements presents a difficult question, one sharply raised when one person encourages another to commit a crime.

With this initial exploration of the values of speech and press and how that may affect coverage of the First Amendment, the chapter turns to specific aspects. This survey reveals just how multifaceted and complex the law is regarding freedom of speech and of the press. Most of the approaches the Supreme Court has taken to various problems make good sense, but the opinions often fail to provide a clear explanation for distinctions drawn. The analysis here aims partly to assess why a particular level of protection is or is not warranted; but in relation to the larger themes of this book, what follows mainly illustrates the need of courts to respond to context and not to assume that one categorical approach will be right for a broad range of different practices and problems.

Most of the following sections concentrate on particular kinds of communication, but those on the clear and present danger test, content discrimination, and content neutrality focus on constitutional standards that cut across a range of speech. I begin with "clear and present danger," originally formulated in connection with antigovernment speech (a topic treated in Section V), but then extended much more broadly.

IV. THE CLEAR AND PRESENT DANGER TEST

In 1919, in *Schenck v. United States*, the Supreme Court in an opinion by Justice Holmes first formulated the clear and present danger test.[58] The test requires judicial evaluations in context of the dangers that speech will produce wrongful behavior. As applied in that case and its companions, the test provided little protection for expressions that could encourage young men to violate the draft law in wartime. Nine months later, in what actually represented a radical shift, Justice Holmes employed the test in *Abrams v. United States*[59] to dissent from the majority's affirming of convictions under the 1918 Sedition Act. The defendants in the case had called for a general strike to discourage interventions against Russia's revolutionary government; they were charged with inciting resistance to the war effort against Germany and trying to hinder prosecution of that war. Holmes wrote that no one could suppose that the 5,000 leaflets created any immediate danger to the war effort. He asserted that for a legitimate prosecution, there needed to be a "clear and immediate" danger and an emergency that would not allow competing speech to correct the efforts of inflammatory rhetoric.[60] The *Abrams* dissent itself did not acknowledge that Holmes had altered his sense of the right approach, and one relying simply on his opinions in *Schenck* and *Abrams* might surmise that he consistently saw the test as highly speech-protective, affirming the conviction in *Schenck* only in order to get his conservative colleagues to accept the approach. However, Robert Post has suggested that he reformulated the standard because the Espionage Act of 1918, unlike its predecessor, directly prohibited language;[61] and Thomas Healy has persuasively demonstrated that Holmes's view did change, largely as a consequence of interactions with Learned Hand, Harold Laski, and Felix Frankfurter.[62]

The *Abrams* dissent initiated the version of "clear and present danger" that was highly speech-protective, and that test grew to dominate First Amendment jurisprudence, albeit in somewhat different formulations over time. After Holmes dissented in *Gitlow v. New York*,[63] he joined a dissent by Justice Brandeis in *Whitney v. California*,[64] a case upholding a California conviction of someone who helped to organize a group to engage in forbidden advocacy. In eloquent passages, Brandeis wrote of the value of speech for human development and political freedom. Suppression is warranted only if a danger is imminent: "If there be time to expose through discussion the falsehood and fallacies, to avert the evil by the process of education, the remedy to be applied is more speech, not enforced silence."[65]

Among the questions about the "clear and present danger test" are these: What is the relation between an actual clear and present danger and what the speaker intends? Is the magnitude of the danger important, or do only its probability and immediacy matter? Is "presentness" independently relevant, or is it an objective test of probability?[66] The Brandeis opinion in *Whitney* indicated that the relevant danger did have to be imminent, that it needed to concern "immediate serious violence" (a danger of criminal trespass would not suffice), and that the test could be satisfied if the violence "was to be expected or was advocated."[67] In sum, the test was put forward as one in which judges had to evaluate contexts, but they were to do so in a manner highly favorable to protection and demanding a powerful competing public need to sustain a restriction.

In the 1930s and 1940s, the Supreme Court as a body broadly expanded First Amendment protection with reference to "clear and present danger." In *Herndon v. Lowry*,[68] decided in 1937, the majority referred to the test in overturning the conviction of a Communist Party organizer in Georgia for inducing others to join a combined resistance to the lawful authority of the state; there had been no evidence presented that he had actually urged revolutionary violence or distributed the revolutionary literature that had been found in his possession. In *Hartzel v. United States*, during World War II,[69] the Court overturned a conviction under the Espionage Act of a man who wrote articles denouncing the English and the Jews and urging conversion of the war into a racial conflict. A plurality adopted the position that one could not merely infer an intent to cause forbidden consequences absent definite proof. In *Cantwell v. Connecticut*, in 1940, the Court held that someone who was not personally abusive, but expressed highly controversial religious views, could not be punished for breach of the peace; he had not raised a "clear and present menace to public peace."[70] And in *Bridges v. California*,[71] the Court ruled that the absence of a clear and present danger precluded a punishment for contempt of court. In contrast to the California Supreme Court's ruling that a publication with "a reasonable tendency to interfere with the orderly administration of justice" was unprotected, Justice Black's opinion cast the clear and present danger test as "a working principle that the substantive evil must be extremely serious and the degree of imminence extremely high before utterances can be punished."[72]

During the height of the fear of Communism in 1951, the Supreme Court in *Dennis v. United States*[73] retreated sharply from the standard formulation of clear and present danger when it sustained convictions under the Smith Act for advocating the overthrow of the government by force or violence, and for conspiring to engage in such advocacy. At the trial, Judge Medina had charged the jury that the defendants must be found to have intended to cause overthrow as speedily as circumstances would permit. Regarding the clear and present danger test as an issue of law for the judge to apply, he determined that its conditions were satisfied. For the court of appeals, Judge Learned Hand, whose earlier views about the need to protect speech had influenced Justice Holmes's conversion, declined to treat the phrase "clear and present danger" as a "rigid rule." Rather, judges must "ask whether the gravity of the 'evil,' discounted by its improbability, justifies such invasion of free speech as is necessary to avoid the danger." Since the Communist Party was disciplined and secretive and occupied a worldwide position, its members' advocacy of violent overthrow met this test. For a plurality of the Supreme Court, Chief Justice Vinson adopted the Hand formulation.[74] Justices Frankfurter and Jackson also voted to affirm, but objected that judges were not in a position to discern what events were likely over an extended period of time. (The reality that, in retrospect, the actual threat of a domestic Communist overthrow of this government was decidedly minimal supports this skepticism.) Justice Frankfurter favored rejecting the clear and present danger test in favor of ad hoc balancing, an approach that would allow greater suppression of speech. In subsequent cases dealing with Communist Party membership, the Court proved somewhat more protective, deciding in *Scales v. United States*[75] and *Noto v. United States*[76] that only "active" members who shared the party's illegal purposes could be punished.

If *Dennis* represented an obvious retreat from the standard clear and present danger test, substituting an approach that judges could not possibly have applied with confidence, the Warren Court, in *Brandenburg v. Ohio*,[77] came up with a formulation that was more protective of speech than any of its predecessors. The case involved the conviction under a state criminal syndication statute of a speaker at a Ku Klux Klan meeting. Although the organization historically had opposed equality and sometimes undertaken violence against blacks, evidence was lacking that the speaker had urged the commission of any crime. The Supreme Court's unanimous reversal was not surprising, but its per curiam formulation of the relevant test was. The " 'constitutional guarantees' of free speech and free press do not permit a State to forbid or proscribe advocacy of the use of force or of law violation except where such advocacy is directed to inciting or producing imminent lawless action and is likely to incite or produce such action."[78] The not infrequent judicial practice of disregarding precedents without saying so was carried to an extreme in *Brandenberg*; the Court actually suggested that *Dennis* was consistent with this approach, but that was clearly false.

According to *Brandenberg*, lawless action must be imminent and must be *both* intended and objectively likely. This is a very stringent speech-protective approach, one judges should not find too difficult to apply.[79] The harder questions are whether it actually provides too much protection to speech when it does apply and what are the circumstances when neither it, nor a somewhat less constraining clear and present danger test, should apply. As subsequent sections will suggest, in a variety of circumstances, communications should receive a lesser degree of constitutional protection or none at all. Dealing with these strikingly different situations is a major challenge for all viable approaches to interpreting the First Amendment, since these need to afford due recognition to its underlying values. But for the main areas of its coverage, the clear and present danger test is a basic First Amendment test, one that conveys a standard of assessment that allows consideration of competing interests but in a manner that is both more viable and better protects constitutional values than would an "ad hoc" balancing approach.

V. ANTIGOVERNMENT SPEECH

Formulated in response to convictions for criticisms of government policies that might have encouraged forms of illegal behavior, the "clear and present danger test," as expanded, has essentially precluded punishment for speech that challenges government activities. One can be sharply critical of a military effort or other government program, and even imply that people who break the law in a protest against it may be justified. Such speech cannot be punished under a federal or state statute that resembles the 1917 Espionage Act. In the 1973 case of *Hess v. Indiana*,[80] the Supreme Court applied the *Brandenburg* test to hold that a participant in an antiwar demonstration who shouted "We'll take the fucking street later!" could not be punished for disorderly conduct. These words were not likely, the Court said, to cause imminent disorder. Very likely, the relative unseriousness of the crime and the likelihood that the defendant's shout would have no effect (except perhaps to reduce potential violence at that moment) influenced the Justices; but given that "later" for the speaker almost certainly implied the same day, the time between the rhetoric and any feared consequence was hardly very long. In 1982, in *NAACP v. Clairborne Hardware Co.*,[81] the Court overturned the conviction of a demonstrator in Mississippi who, urging a boycott of merchants engaging in racial discrimination, said that if "we catch any of you going to any of these racist stores, we're gonna break your damn neck." Given the profound national commitment to "debate on public issues," the Court concluded that the "mere advocacy" of violence at a later time was protected speech.

It is instructive to compare these cases with a 1969 decision of the First Circuit involving what was perhaps the most notable prosecution of those who protested the Vietnam War.[82] Benjamin Spock, a famous pediatrician, and William Sloane Coffin, then chaplain at Yale University, had signed an antiwar proclamation, "A Call to Resist Illegitimate Authority" (the Call), which stated, inter alia: "Many of us believe that open resistance to the war and the draft is the course of action . . . most likely to bring an end to the war," and "We will continue to lend our support to those who undertake resistance to this war." Overturning the convictions because the trial judge had improperly put special questions to the jury, the court of appeals also ruled that Spock could not be convicted for conspiring to counsel violation of the Selective Service law because the evidence did not clearly establish that he accepted the illegal aspects of the Call. A jury could, however, convict Coffin, who had joined a statement that characterized the Call as a way of aiding, abetting, and counseling against subscription. The court's logic was that if public advocacy included both legal and illegal components, a participant could be punished only if he clearly subscribed to the illegal aspects. Under the *Brandenburg* test, announced just weeks prior to the decision in *Spock*, a person's explicitly encouraging illegal activity, as Reverend Coffin had done, would not seem by itself to be enough for a conviction. Rather, the government would have to show that draft resistance was then so substantial and the signers so influential that the Call would be highly likely to lead to immediate violations of draft laws. That showing would have been quite difficult, given the likelihood that an actual draft resister is moved by a combination of factors.

Not surprisingly, the threat of terrorism has led the present Supreme Court to draw back from *Brandenburg* and other cases protecting antigovernment speech, as they relate to membership in antigovernment organizations. In *Holder v. Humanitarian Law Project* in 2010,[83] the Court sustained a conviction under a federal statute that forbids "material support" of a designated terrorist organization. In contrast to the earlier *Scales* case dealing with Communist Party membership, the Court in *Holder* ruled that when people give "material support," it is unnecessary to prove that they intend their support for illegal as well as legal purposes. The *Holder* decision is troubling in that it allows the government to forbid people from supporting legitimate political objectives when the organization they assist is also pursuing illegal purposes. On the other hand, if an organization is engaging in both nonviolent political activity and terrorist acts and uses its money for both, when someone donates substantially for the nonviolent aspects, that frees up other money for terrorism. Further, unless someone is actually involved in planning or performing the illegal acts, it may be very hard to prove that he wanted his financial support to include those. In sum, if an organization is demonstrably carrying out extremely serious criminal acts, it is reasonable to forbid its being given financial assistance, at least if the donor is aware of what the organization is doing. However, the government should carry the burden of showing that an organization's activities are highly damaging and that the donor must have been aware of the criminal behavior in which it is engaged.[84]

People who engage in antigovernment speech may find themselves constrained by the government in ways other than criminal punishment. A government employee does not have the freedom to say anything that a private citizen might; comments that could impair the efficiency of public services can lead to discipline or dismissal.[85] More recently, allowing a district attorney's office to discipline a deputy for a memorandum he had written, the Court indicated that expression that is part of a government worker's job may be subject to regulation.[86] And, although such employees cannot be required to swear that they are not members of an organization with a purpose to overthrow the government,[87] narrower loyalty oaths are acceptable. More broadly, individuals outside government can sometimes be compelled to answer questions about involvement with groups whose purposes include illegal objectives.[88]

VI. THE PUBLICATION OF SECRETS

Criticizing government policies is one thing; revealing what the government legitimately has kept secret is another. Does the First Amendment bear on the revelation or publication of secrets? Based on what the Supreme Court has ruled so far, no one working for the government has a First Amendment right to reveal secret information, regardless of whether he believes that doing so is in the national interest. In *Haig v. Agee*[89] in 1981, the Court sustained the revocation of Agee's passport. A former employee of the Central Intelligence Agency, Agee had disclosed the names of CIA officers and agents. A year earlier, in *Snepp v. United States*, the Court had said that the CIA could condition employment on promises not to reveal information about the agency.[90] One recent illustration of the absence of any constitutional right to disclose secret information was the conviction of Army Private Bradley Manning for violating the Espionage Act by releasing thousands of classified State Department documents about highly sensitive matters.[91] Reflecting the same view are the efforts of the Obama administration to bring Edward Snowden back into the United States to stand prosecution for his revealing the government's extensive surveillance of communications inside and outside the country, undertaken to combat terrorism.[92] Few have suggested that what these men did was constitutionally protected. And even if one believes, as many do about Snowden's disclosures, that they served the public interest, imagining how judges could assess whether he exercised a constitutional right is extremely difficult. According to what the Supreme Court has said, persons outside of government who are involved in violating the law to acquire secret information are also unprotected. Thus, if a newspaper publisher pays someone to break into the Pentagon to acquire secret military information or bribes a person like Snowden to make secret files available, he would lack First Amendment protection.

The publication itself is different. In *Bartnicki v. Vopper*, in 2001,[93] the Court ruled that statutes forbidding wiretapping could not be applied to a radio station that broadcast a tape it knew was from an unlawfully intercepted telephone call, given that it did not participate in the illegal act. The leading case considering whether an entity that was not directly involved in wrongdoing has a right to publish secret information involved the Pentagon Papers. After the New York Times and the Washington Post had published some of the documents Daniel Ellsberg had given them, the government filed suit to prevent further publication.[94] The case proceeded quickly through the lower courts. The Supreme Court granted review and reached a resolution quickly—too quickly, some of the Justices believed. In a per curiam opinion, the Court ruled that the government had failed to carry the "heavy burden of showing justification for the imposition of . . . a [prior] restraint." Each Justice wrote an opinion, some of which were joined by colleagues. For Justices Black and Douglas, the bar on prior restraint was absolute. Justice Brennan acknowledged that precluding the publication of information about secret troop locations would be acceptable, but that prior restraint could not be grounded on conjectures about uncertain consequences. Justices Stewart and White believed that some of the documents might impair the national interest but that the government had not carried the heavy burden that could justify an injunction. Justice Marshall relied on the absence of any statute authorizing the executive to preclude such publication. The three dissenting Justices favored more of a balancing test and judicial deference to the executive judgment about the threat to national security.

Although no Supreme Court case has settled on what basis criminal punishment could be imposed *after* the publication of confidential data, the flavor of the opinions in the *Pentagon Papers* case suggests that, though the burden would not be quite as great as that needed for a prior restraint, the government would need to make a powerful argument about potential harm to national security, or some other crucial interest, to punish the publishing of material of broad public concern. Geoffrey Stone has suggested that the government would need to prove that the press knew (a) it was publishing classified information, (b) that the publication would be likely to produce imminent and serious harm, and (c) that it would not meaningfully contribute to public debate.[95] Although Professor Stone is right to suggest that the social importance of revealed material should play a central role in whether publication can be criminally punished, were the harmful consequences of publication obvious, immediate, and extremely severe, that should be sufficient for punishment even if the public learns something of value. This could be true, for example, about revealing secret troop movements (for which even prior restraint may be warranted) and for the publication of the names and activities of our spies in a hostile country.

VII. THE PRESS

Does the press have a special status, and, if so, to whom does the label apply? This question actually has four dimensions. The first is whether the First Amendment itself affords rights to the press and its members that are not possessed by ordinary citizens. Second, can statutes or executive policies afford special privileges for the press? Third, may the government regulate forms of the media in special ways designed to enhance their contribution to the public? Finally, how should the government draw the line between the press and others? Courts might need to make that distinction for direct constitutional claims, and the political branches may do so to promote wise policies on acceptable bases. When the latter occurs, courts may have to review the way the legislature or executive has defined "the press."

The question of whether the press has special constitutional status was presented in *Branzburg v. Hayes* in 1972.[96] A newspaper reporter who had written about drug activities had refused to reveal to a state grand jury the identities of persons involved. The Supreme Court, by a 5–4 margin, rejected his claim of First Amendment protection. It held that the press possesses no special constitutional right to gain access to information and that press members have no special claim to refuse to testify.

Justice White's opinion gave considerable emphasis to the "practical and conceptual difficulty" of defining who exactly would qualify were such a constitutional privilege recognized. Justice Powell joined the Court's opinion but made clear in a concurrence that a reporter might have a valid claim to safeguard sources if the grand jury investigation was not in good faith, or if the information he would provide related only tenuously to the investigation or did not concern a legitimate need of law enforcement. Three of the four dissenters in *Branzburg* urged that a reporter should be able to withhold such testimony unless it clearly related to a probable violation of law and was urgently needed, and the same information was not otherwise available. Justice Douglas favored an even more absolute protection of the reporter's silence.

The specific designation of the press in the First Amendment might seem to imply a special constitutional protection, but the original language was almost certainly referring to all published materials, not simply those of newspapers and magazines; and both line-drawing problems and how to balance competing interests present substantial obstacles to judicial creation of privileges not available to other citizens who disclose information and express their views. Since *Branzburg*, the Supreme Court has not established constitutional rights that are limited to "the press."[97]

Concerning access to information, the Court has held some restrictions challenged by newspapers to be unconstitutional. Notably, it has declared invalid various laws and court orders that have authorized closures of trials and of examinations of prospective jurors.[98] Both the fundamental nature of public trials and the First Amendment figured in these determinations, but the Court drew no line between access for the professional press and access for general members of the public.

It does not follow that the political branches should avoid drawing that distinction. Most obviously, members of the press can attend presidential press conferences and have access to military locations that are barred for other citizens. And as far as a privilege of members of the press not to reveal sources, forty-nine states and the District of Columbia have adopted such laws. Although governments cannot favor some members of the same media over others,[99] a general privileging of the press by taxing it less than other businesses is also apparently acceptable.[100] Allowing statutes and executive actions to grant certain special benefits to the press makes good sense, whether the First Amendment should be construed to directly provide these or not.

A number of difficult questions arise if the government seeks to regulate branches of the media in the public interest. Up to the present, a sharp distinction has been drawn between constraints on publishing media and those on radio and television. In 1974, the Supreme Court unanimously struck down a Florida law requiring that newspapers publishing a critique of a candidate's character or record allow him or her to print a reply free of charge.[101] Five years earlier, it had upheld the Federal Communication Commission's regulations of the broadcasting industry to implement a "fairness doctrine,"[102] under which broadcasters were required to discuss public issues and present them in a fair way and to give those personally attacked a chance to respond. An aspect of the Court's logic was that the number of broadcast channels was limited. In 1994, noting that most cable operators have a monopoly, the Court accepted a rule of the Cable Television Consumer Protection and Competition Act that required cable systems to devote a portion of their channels for transmissions by local broadcast stations.[103]

Given the small number of operating newspapers in most parts of the country, the vast expansion of television channels, and the ability of ordinary citizens to reach strangers through electronic communication, the sense that broadcasters may be much more restricted than newspapers because of their limited number is no longer plausible. One might still believe that because some broadcasters have an overarching influence nationally, they do need special constraints.

A different defense of the striking variation in treatment has been offered by Lee Bollinger.[104] If we can see value in both the government's allowing unregulated free communication and its setting certain standards that will serve the public interest in acquiring important information and being exposed to a range of views, then perhaps it makes sense to be guided by each of those opposing principles in different domains, even if the basis for distinguishing between the two domains is unpersuasive. Whatever one concludes about desirable policy and the appropriate role of courts, a real tension exists between the principle that the government should not control communication and the belief that some regulation helps to assure that highly influential public communication is not dramatically one-sided and does not descend to a low level that serves appetites for coverage of matters that may be trivial for the lives of citizens and for society.

VIII. SOLICITING AND URGING CRIMINAL BEHAVIOR

If one simply looks at what the written opinions of the Supreme Court say, one might wonder what relevance the First Amendment has for ordinary criminal activities and communications about them. In many respects, the practical answer is that "free speech" is then irrelevant, although some borderline situations are not so clear.

As the section on the coverage of free speech indicates, much communication connected to crime does not qualify. When one participant is instructing another about how to open a bank vault they are robbing, this does not count as speech, nor does an agreement to commit a crime. The law forbids criminal conspiracy, and someone can be punished for having agreed to commit a crime that will not actually occur until months later. There is no requirement of "imminence" or "presentness" here.

What if no agreement exists, but one person simply urges another to commit a crime? Suppose that a nephew of a wealthy woman says to a niece who resides with her, "You know, if our obnoxious aunt died, we'd both never have to worry about money again. When you go sailing with her three months from now, push her off the boat and make sure she does not get back on." The Model Penal Code section regarding the crime of criminal solicitation covers someone who, with the purpose of promoting a crime's commission "commands, encourages or requests another person to engage in specific conduct that would constitute such crime. . . ."[105] Under that section, and the law in actual jurisdictions, what the nephew says to the niece is criminal. Is there a First Amendment issue?

It helps first to distinguish what I will call simple solicitation from the kind that includes a "threat" or "offer" (one that is not just a statement in advance of how one will naturally respond). Suppose an acquaintance tells a worker in the Defense Department, "Show me the files on anti-terrorist activity; if you do, I'll give you $10,000." Or, "If you don't, I'll see that you lose your job." As explained earlier, such threats and offers are designed to be situation-altering. They put the recipient of the communication in a setting that did not previously exist. Although a minor altering of circumstances can occur when a solicited individual would just prefer not to disappoint the speaker, that alone does not change what will objectively occur to the listener if she does or does not perform the requested act. Thus, a solicitation without an offer or threat comes much closer to ordinary communication.

Does it matter if such a solicitation occurs in private? I have asserted that "free speech" definitely includes private communications; but that context can be relevant, especially if what is communicated is not a subject of public discussion. Part of the basis for protecting speech is that it can be countered by opposing points of view, and that this is far preferable to suppression of opinions regarded as mistaken. This is why the "immediacy" of danger is so important; others lack time to respond effectively with contrary opinions. None of this applies to one person urging another in secret to commit an ordinary crime for personal advantage. Not knowing about the solicitation, others are not in a position to respond.[106]

In three connected ways, even private "encouragements" to commit ordinary crimes relate to freedom of speech. It may sometimes be hard to draw a line between encouragement and disinterested advice. First, if the speaker, rather than actively trying to get the listener to do something, is merely giving advice about the best choice, she is making a statement of fact and value covered by the basic reasons for free speech. Second, the speaker's words may not reflect a definite criminal objective. The words themselves may be ambiguous; they may seem to approve commission of a crime, but that may not be what she actually intends.[107] And even unambiguous words may not reflect a genuine purpose. People often speak in stronger forms than what they genuinely want to happen. Finally, people's sentiments and plans can shift radically in fairly short spaces of time. A person just deeply hurt by what she takes as harsh treatment might at that moment really welcome the offender's being injured seriously, but she may well change her mind within hours or days. A genuine encouragement to another to commit a crime may be withdrawn long before the crime itself would occur.

These reasons, which connect to free speech, should lead to hesitancy to punish pure encouragements unaccompanied by offers or threats. But I do not believe they should preclude such punishment altogether. Rather, the degree of constitutional constraint should depend on the kind of crime encouraged, the speaker's motives, and the setting of the communication. Free speech values are hardly involved at all, if, as in the nephew example, the speaker in private and for his own benefit solicits a crime that has nothing to do with the welfare and justice of society. Here, probably the First Amendment should not be considered directly applicable, even though sensible criminal law would not punish a speaker unless he definitely intends to encourage the crime's commission, rather than engaging in overheated rhetoric or expressing temporary frustration.

When the solicitation is both public and ideological, it can have substantial expressive value, and it is open to being countered. Such a solicitation should not be punishable unless the speaker urges commission of a serious crime in the very near future and it is reasonably likely that the speech will contribute to commission of the crime. Although such an approach can be formulated in different ways, this essentially fits a strict version of the clear and present danger test, as formulated in *Brandenburg v. Ohio*.

The intermediate circumstance of private, serious, ideological encouragement is more difficult. Such communications do have substantial expressive values. But often, when a speaker communicates privately with one or two listeners who are close acquaintances, she is aware that likely carries more influence than someone who addresses a broad audience at a public meeting; and others will be unaware of exactly what has been urged. Relevant cases do not make clear how far such encouragements are protected by the First Amendment, but I believe they should not be punishable unless they present a significant danger of criminal harm. This would constitute a more relaxed standard in terms of the gravity and likelihood of the crime and its temporal connection to the speaker's utterances than is needed for public ideological solicitation. One may, of course, question whether such nuances are appropriate and manageable for courts. But these kinds of cases do not frequently arise. The categorization between public and private is manageable if not precise, and judges should be competent to make the necessary assessments.

IX. FIGHTING WORDS

According to Supreme Court doctrine, "fighting words" do not enjoy the protection given to ordinary speech. Just what should count as fighting words and why they should be unprotected proves not to be so simple. Analysis here relates closely to that for insults and epithets covered in the following section.

In *Chaplinsky v. New Hampshire* in 1942,[108] the Supreme Court reviewed the conviction under a state statute of a member of Jehovah's Witnesses who had been warned by a city marshal to "go slow" with his proselytizing that was disturbing a number of listeners. Chaplinsky told the marshal: "You are a Goddamned racketeer" and "a damned Fascist and the whole government of Rochester are Fascists or agents of Fascists." The Supreme Court held that among the classes of speech that are not constitutionally protected are "the insulting or 'fighting' words—those which by their very utterance inflict injury or tend to incite an immediate breach of the peace."[109] The words used by Chaplinsky were "epithets likely to provoke the average person to retaliation, and thereby likely to cause a breach of the peace."[110]

The notion that "fighting words" are special raises the following questions. Are such words without speech value? Is their key component that they are likely to cause the average addressee to fight? Should it matter whether the actual addressee is likely to fight?

It helps initially to distinguish among various uses of fighting words. Within a particular culture or subculture, certain utterances may be clearly understood as a direct challenge to engage in a fight. Thus, when one man says directly to another, "You are a cowardly bastard," he may be inviting a fight, and if the listener instead retreats, he may be assumed to be a coward. I am putting aside this form of fighting words, assuming they can be identified, because, as they constitute offers to engage in illegal action, they are situation-altering utterances.

A different use of fighting words (which can, of course, be combined with the first) has the primary objective of hurting the listener. Just as physical attacks can injure, verbal assaults can cause serious pain. Of course, typical verbal abuse also expresses opinions and sentiments;[111] but one may reject the conclusion that this qualifies it as speech on the basis that if the overarching purpose is simply to injure, the state appropriately intervenes.

This leaves us with "fighting words" that express upset and anger. If one person shouts at another, "You are a fucking son of a bitch," he may be mainly expressing his tremendous hostility and frustration—even if he recognizes that his words may hurt or provoke a fight, that is not his primary objective. Concluding that such words really fail to be "speech" does not make sense, given that, had the speaker expressed the same sentiments more calmly in acceptable language,[112] his words would undoubtedly be protected.[113] Although the difficulty of distinguishing words that are mainly expressive from those that are primarily designed to injure and/or to provoke a fight might lead one to accept suppression, we cannot simply dismiss the idea that such words have any communicative value.

If we reflect on Chaplinsky's own comments, it is extremely unlikely that he wanted to provoke an actual conflict with a city marshal who was accompanied by the police. And if he did partly seek to hurt the marshal's feelings, what he was mainly doing was expressing outrage that his behavior, rather than that of the members of his audience who had assailed him, was being curbed.[114] Given that Chaplinsky's comments were undoubtedly expressive, does it nonetheless make sense to punish him because his words may lead to violence and are likely to cause the "average" addressee to fight? This question starkly poses who counts as the average addressee, whether it should matter if the actual addressee is similar, and, if that does matter, what differences should and should not be taken into account.

Suppose a strong man who is twenty-five years old addresses highly provocative words to another young man, or to an elderly gentleman who is eighty-five years old, or to a middle-aged woman, or to a ten-year-old girl, or to a public official. None of the last four potential respondents are likely to fight. The public officer will probably see his position as precluding that response;[115] the other three will simply be disinclined to a physical conflict, realizing that they could be hurt by trying. In brief, if one asked about how particular words would affect most human beings to whom they *might* be addressed, the answer is that probably none would cause a majority to respond by fighting. But perhaps "average addressee" should be taken to mean those to whom such words are likely to be directed, and perhaps abusive words may be spoken most often by one young man to another.

If the genuine concern is about preventing fights, should the average addressee or the actual addressees be crucial? A strong argument exists that public officials should be able to restrain themselves and not to take things as personally as those in private relations. But what of the middle-aged woman, child, and elderly man? Even if an actual fight is not likely, it strikes one as unacceptable that such individuals could be subject to abusive language that would not be protected if aimed at a vigorous young man.

This comparison strongly shows why the genuine concerns about such language involve *both* its hurtful qualities and its propensity to provoke violent responses. The existence of that propensity for some recipients is, among other things, a measure of how upsetting words may be for all of those who are objects of such scorn. If prevention of actual fighting tips the balance for why such speech may be prohibited, both its injurious effects and fairness of treatment should allow punishability even if the actual addressee is unlikely to fight because of his or her physical characteristics. These are complexities that judicial opinions have yet to address with any precision.

X. HATE SPEECH, INSULTS, AND EPITHETS

The puzzles about "fighting words" lead us into the more general topic of hate speech, insults, and epithets that may offend and injure even if they are unlikely to produce immediate violence. Should the government be able to forbid such speech because of its harm? About this genuinely troubling question, the constitutional doctrine in the United States is more protective of the range of such speech than is any other liberal democracy.

Insults or "hate speech" may be about an individual's qualities or those of a group. "You are a cheating, lying bastard," or "Those dirty kikes will steal every chance they get." The words may be spoken to an individual or a group that is the object of the insults, or to others who are not themselves being cast down. An example of the latter would be when a leader of the Ku Klux Klan speaking to his own group severely insults an individual "black" leader, such as Martin Luther King, Jr. or Barack Obama, or denigrates all persons regarded in this society as blacks.[116] Finally, some persons regard harsh criticisms of particular perspectives about life as a kind of hate speech or insult of members of a group accepting those views.

I shall say just a word about this last category. Although some Muslim countries do forbid criticism of Islam, within the United States, that is clearly understood as covered by freedom of speech (and religious exercise). People are free to express their opinions about what is true or false, sound or unsound, even if their views are sharply opposed to what others believe. The only serious First Amendment question about such speech is what the authorities may do if its expression within the challenged group seems likely to produce a hostile response. I shall return to that issue.

When words are seriously insulting to persons or groups and are not cast simply in terms of honest statements about the activities in which others engage and about the values people should accept or reject, three reasons might support a government prohibiting them. As with "fighting words," two of the concerns are about violent responses and deeply felt injuries. A third concern about group epithets is their long-term effect. Especially when they are directed against segments that are already at a disadvantage, such as blacks within the United States, the communications can enhance already existing, unjustified prejudices, and they can affect the members of the groups themselves in ways that reinforce their inequality. Writing about racist remarks, Mari Matsuda cautions, "The negative effects of hate messages are real and immediate for the victims . . . [who] have experienced physiological symptoms and emotional distress ranging from fear in the gut, rapid pulse rate and difficulty in breathing, nightmares, post-traumatic stress disorder, hypertension, psychosis, and suicide."[117]

The risk of a violent response is obviously greatest when abusive remarks are made to those being insulted. However, a basic concern about racist speech in the United States and anti-Semitic speech in Germany is that its delivery to nonmembers of the group can increase the chance of subsequent violence against members. The concern about emotional injury is also most direct when listeners themselves are being insulted, but individuals and group members can also be deeply hurt when they learn that they are being denigrated by comments made to others. The dangers of group epithets creating emotional injury over the long term may be just as great, or greater, when these are offered to those who do not belong to the group. Such concerns have led many countries to forbid hate speech directed at the qualities of vulnerable groups. The United States has been different.

In 1952 in *Beauharnais v. Illinois*,[118] the Court, by a 5–4 margin, affirmed the conviction of the president of the White Circle League who had distributed a pamphlet that was seeking to forestall "the further encroachment, harassment and invasion of white people . . . by the Negro." The pamphlet went on to say that if preventing "the white race from becoming mongrelized by the negro will not unite us, then the aggressions, . . . rapes, robberies, knives, guns and marijuana of the negro, surely will."[119] Justice Frankfurter wrote for the Court that individual libel was a common law crime not protected by the First Amendment and that a state is also free to punish group libels directed at "designated collectivities and flagrantly disseminated."[120] Since *Beauharnais,* the Court has been much more protective of speech that is insulting.

In *Cohen v. California*[121] the Court overturned the conviction of a young man for wearing a jacket in a courtroom that read "Fuck the Draft." Justice Harlan wrote that the jacket did not involve a personal insult and that no evidence had shown that it was likely to provoke a violent response. In a series of cases, the Court declared that statutes directed at offensive language were overbroad and vague.[122] When considering a planned march by members of the National Socialist Party wearing uniforms and swastikas in a town whose population was mainly Jewish and included survivors of Nazi concentration camps, the Supreme Court overturned the state court's refusal to review whether it should stay a trial judge's injunction against the march. The state court had to grant the stay or review the requested injunction under strict procedural safeguards.[123]

In 1992, the Court decided the important case of *R.A.V. v. City of St. Paul.*[124] A young white man had burned a cross on the lawn of a black family—such cross burning being a common symbolic threatening form of expression engaged in by the Ku Klux Klan. He was convicted under a city ordinance that forbade displaying that symbol or another that one knows or has reason to know "arouses anger, alarm, or resentment in others on the basis of race, color, creed, religion or gender. . . ." Four Justices believed that despite some narrowing language of the Minnesota Supreme Court, the statute was still overly broad. Justice Scalia for the five-member majority relied on quite a different ground, one that I believe is seriously misguided. His ground was that even if the statute had been adequately narrowed to "fighting words," and even if R.A.V.'s cross burning qualified, nonetheless, the statute was unconstitutional because drawing a distinction among kinds of fighting words violated a rule against content-based regulation. Any restriction must treat all fighting words equally.

Without doubt, many content distinctions are rightly viewed as unacceptable. A state could not forbid anti-Catholic speech and allow anti-Mormon speech, but drawing a line based on subject matter content is somewhat different. If legislators reasonably judge that fighting words or gross insults concerning race, religion, or gender are much more damaging to individuals and threatening to society than such words that focus on personal characteristics or political association, they should be able to draw that distinction. The relevance of such categorization is especially strong if one reflects on what sorts of insults are likely to cause severe psychological injury and contribute to long-term social harms.

In *Virginia v. Black*,[125] a 2003 case, a majority of the Court, while striking down a Virginia cross-burning statute on other grounds, did indicate that a state could forbid a particular form of intimidating speech, such as cross burning. The majority, including Justice Scalia, regarded this as not the same as a distinction based on the kind of message conveyed. If, in fact, cross burning in the United States is almost always connected to racial intimidation, this difference does allow a kind of indirect focus on at least one form of that destructive speech.

Hate speech and group epithets pose some of the most troubling questions about free speech protection. If one were addressing such expression from a standpoint of wise policy, much depends on the history and culture of the society involved and the likely effectiveness of enforcement. For Germany, a restriction on hate speech directed at Jews is plainly warranted. In terms of practical consequences, perhaps general limits on hate speech will actually be mainly used to punish what members of already unpopular groups assert, or will simply reduce the publicness of communications that will continue in private and pose serious dangers. Perhaps open expression of hate engenders opposing speech that better counters it than does legal restriction.

Although the matter is certainly debatable, given the diversity of American society and the fundamental tradition of open discourse, as well as the difficult tasks of enforcement officials and judges drawing lines, restrictions of hateful speech are properly limited to something resembling the coverage of a well-formulated "fighting words" approach. Within such an approach, the purposes of the speech and the context in which it is uttered need to be taken into account. Speech should be punishable only if it is designed to injure or threaten and is likely to have that effect. In accord with the Court's ruling in *Virginia v. Black*, legislators sensibly single out particular forms of threatening speech. Contrary to the *R.A.V.* ruling, they should also be able to draw certain categorical lines that focus on the most harmful forms of communications that are not themselves constitutionally protected.

An interesting variation on issues about insults and epithets concerns special social settings, such as universities and workplaces. Of course, absent government regulation, private organizations can regulate what their members say without constitutional restraint. But state universities do not have this latitude, and the federal government has adopted laws that constrain speech within private places of work.

Many universities have internal standards that forbid discrimination and harassment. An example of a broad formulation along these lines was the University of Michigan Policy on Discrimination and Discriminating Harassment. It made persons subject to discipline who verbally stigmatized "an individual on the basis of race, ethnicity, religion, sex, sexual orientation, creed, national origin, ancestry, age, marital status, handicap, or Vietnam-era veteran status" if their speech involved an implied threat to someone's academic efforts or participation in university activities, or carried a "reasonably foreseeable effect of interfering" with these efforts or activities, or created "an intimidating, hostile, or demeaning" environment.[126] A federal district court determined that the Michigan policy was constitutionally overbroad and too vague.[127]

Universities have a legitimate interest in protecting their students from outright discrimination and open hostility. But they also have a core function of promoting honest expressions of opinion. If they decide to restrict what students sometimes may say, they should not curtail genuine convictions expressed in classrooms and in informal conversations outside class. They may appropriately ban both insults directed at others with the intent to injure them, and repeated negative comments made to fellow students who have made clear they do not wish to be subjected to them.

In contrast to the university issue, the Supreme Court has dealt with workplace harassment. The law concerning that has grown mainly out of the federal Civil Rights Act, Title VII, which prohibits discrimination by race, religion, national origin, and sex.[128] An employer is responsible if the harassment is by upper management, or if it fails to counter harassment by coworkers. According to the Supreme Court, the statute applies if the conduct creates an abusive working environment, even if it has not affected an employee's psychological well-being.[129] Clearly, no First Amendment problem is generated if impermissible harassment applies to a boss's telling a subordinate that unless she has sex with him she will lose her job. Speech questions arise only if what is involved are assertions of fact and value.

One might argue that the working environment is special, that people are there to work, not engage in speech. But that would disregard the fact that most people spend the majority of their waking hours outside their dwellings at work and that they communicate often with coworkers about what matters to them. The First Amendment clearly applies to government regulation of what is said at work. However, because workers are not free to leave whenever they hear remarks that trouble them, a solid basis does exist to limit everything that might be said in public. And bosses are in a special category. If they convey the message to subordinates that they will be unlikely to receive equal treatment, such comments should count as forbidden harassment. Thus, if a man says, "I know from experience you women are not really up to doing this work adequately," that is ostensibly an expression of opinion. But any woman at whom the remark is directed will assume she will not be treated the same as a male colleague. When remarks are made by coworkers, neither attempts to "put down" colleagues nor repeated negative remarks offered to those they hurt should be protected, but honest opinions expressed in other contexts should be. Again, these issues illustrate the difficult problem of line drawing and show how context affects the way other social values need to be measured against freedom of expression.

XI. LYING

What is the First Amendment status of outright lies, statements that the speaker knows are false? That lies in certain circumstances are punishable has long been established. A person can be guilty of fraud if he makes false statements in order to acquire money or some other advantage. Lying under oath is the crime of perjury. Persons can also be punished for claiming to represent the government or for making false statements to those in the government about official matters. Various Supreme Court opinions have suggested that knowingly false statements are simply outside the protection of the First Amendment, the basic idea being that these do not serve the purposes of free expression. As the section on speech values explains, the more complex truth is that people sometimes have good reasons to say what they are aware is not true. Still more important, if all lies could be punishable, unpopular comments that speakers actually believe might be considered by others to be lies, and prosecutors might go after controversial figures for the wrong reasons.

In 2012, the Supreme Court determined in *United States v. Alvarez*[130] that the First Amendment does protect most lies against government punishment. Xavier Alvarez had falsely claimed in a public meeting that he had received the Congressional Medal of Honor. He was prosecuted for violating the Stolen Valor Act, which aimed to protect the integrity and purpose of military decorations and medals. Despite this plausible reason for the statute, six Justices ruled that Alvarez could not be punished. For the plurality, Justice Kennedy acknowledged various circumstances in which lies are punishable, but rejected the notion that false speech always lacks protection.[131] Because the statute was cast in terms of the content of speech, and its coverage did not fit into a "traditional" unprotected category, the standard of review was "exacting scrutiny."[132] Although the government's interest in protecting the integrity of its medals was significant, that objective could be achieved by countervailing speech and by a government database listing all actual Medal of Honor winners. Kennedy concluded that no "clear showing of the necessity of the statute," required by strict scrutiny, had been made.

Given that three dissenters believed that the conviction should have been affirmed, because the statute's objectives could not be adequately achieved by other means, the swing opinion was actually that of Justice Breyer, joined by Justice Kagan. Breyer rejected "strict scrutiny" in this context, opting instead for "intermediate scrutiny" or "proportionality."[133] He favored a more precise balancing of the purposes of the law and its degree of interference with speech. Largely because the statute covered a wide range of military awards and reached what is said in not only public meetings but also purely private communications, Breyer concluded that the risk of chilling expression was significant. As drafted, the statute was too broad; a "more finely tailored statute ... [could] achieve its important protective objective."[134] When we put the Breyer opinion and the dissent together, we see that five Justices do think a valid statute could criminalize outright lies in public settings about the award of important medals. And one doubts whether any Justice who deals with laws directed at outright lies of some public importance will really apply "strict scrutiny" in the manner that is highly protective of the communications involved.

Alvarez is notable not only because it makes clear that ordinary lies are within the protection of the First Amendment but also because it shows just how difficult formulating and applying the best judicial approach can be when the government has a special interest in protecting the truth. My own sense is that for outright lies in public settings that do impinge on government interests, Justice Breyer's approach is appropriate.

XII. DEFAMATION

For most of American history, it was assumed that First Amendment protections did not reach defamation, that is, false statements that damage a person's reputation. Exactly when an injured person could recover was left to the tort law of libel (written statements) and slander (oral remarks). This changed a half century ago in the landmark case of *New York Times v. Sullivan*.[135] A published advertisement appealing for funds had contained some inaccuracies about civil rights events and police responses. These included claims that Montgomery, Alabama, police had "ringed" a college campus (they had been there in large numbers) and had "padlocked" the dining hall, and that Martin Luther King, Jr. had been arrested seven times (the actual figure was four). L.B. Sullivan, a city commissioner who supervised the police, claimed he had been libeled by the false accusations concerning the police. Roughly 35 copies of the *New York Times* had been distributed in Montgomery County, 394 in Alabama as a whole. Without showing any pecuniary loss, Sullivan was awarded $500,000 damages by the jury.

Had the Supreme Court simply let the judgment stand, the use of defamation claims in southern states to combat publicity supporting civil rights was a near certain consequence. Given the "profound national commitment" to "robust debate" on public issues, Justice Brennan wrote that the law should not deter people from criticizing public officials, and he specified that a public official can recover damages for a falsehood relating to official conduct only if "he proves that the statement was made with 'actual malice'—that is, with knowledge that it was false or with reckless disregard of whether it was false or not."[136] No doubt concerned that an Alabama judge and jury might find liability under any prescribed standard, the Court also ruled that Sullivan could not recover on these facts, both because no adequate proof had suggested "actual malice" and because any libelous statements were not really about him. In a case four years later the Court specified that the recklessness needed for recovery was "a high degree of awareness of [probable] falsity."[137]

A more divided Court in the meantime extended the "actual malice" approach to "public figures" who were not actually officials.[138] With two Justices for more protection and four for less protection, Chief Justice Warren wrote the key opinion, which relied on the role of public figures in resolving important public issues and on their ability to gain access to the media to defend themselves. The Court later declined to extend the same protection to a libeled person who was not a public figure, but it declared that even then, states cannot allow liability without fault, and that, unless actual malice is shown, compensation must be limited to actual injury rather than include punitive damages. In 1985, the Court 5–4 narrowed the range of the latter requirement,[139] allowing punitive damages without actual malice for an inaccurate statement that a company had filed for bankruptcy, because that was not a matter of public concern.

What general lessons can we draw from these defamation cases? The importance of the First Amendment on damage awards is clear. Especially given the fact that the torts of libel and slander can apply to statements believed by speakers to be true, excessive punitive damages could restrict open discourse about controversial subjects. Given the aim to avoid speakers and the press being deterred from healthy expression by the threat of financial loss, the Court needed to set standards that citizens can comprehend and judges can clearly apply. Exactly how far damaging statements about people should be protected and what the precise standards should be is debatable, and perhaps those defamed should at least have the opportunity to establish what is untrue, even if barred from recovering damages. Nevertheless, the Supreme Court's approaches are sensitive to what is at stake concerning free expression. What they show, among other things, is that this subject, like many others, requires standards that are particularly suited for itself, ones that do not apply to free speech issues in general.

XIII. INVASIONS OF PRIVACY AND EMOTIONAL DISTRESS

Two other bases for tort recovery that typically flow from communications are the invasion of privacy and the intentional infliction of emotional distress. With respect to each of these, the Supreme Court has resolved that the First Amendment constrains when recovery can occur. Reviewing an award of damages for invasion of privacy to a father after a television report of a prosecution for rape and murder named his deceased daughter as the victim, the Court declared that truthful publication of what is already on the public record cannot be made actionable.[140] Although whether in this instance the public benefited from broad publicity that included the victim's name is certainly doubtful, the Court's resolution involves a sensible and administrable standard. What should be done when information is not already available to the public is more difficult. Given other free speech doctrines, publications of genuine public concern are protected even if they contain embarrassing information about individuals.

When information about the private lives of ordinary citizens is spread simply in order to satisfy readers' curiosity, tort recovery should be available. Although such information not only may satisfy people's unhealthy curiosity but also may provide some insight into the nature of our society and the qualities of particular behavior, the value of not having some aspects of people's lives exposed to a wide audience entails that broad publication of such information that lacks genuine public interest should be actionable.[141] With respect to just how far First Amendment protection should reach here, it is worth noting that the United States strikes the balance between protected speech and privacy further in favor of speech than do other liberal democracies.

Considerations about the tort of emotional distress are similar. Although that tort is phrased in terms of "intentional infliction," recovery has been allowed on the basis of highly likely harm of which the speaker was probably aware, even if causing harm was not his objective. In *Hustler Magazine v. Falwell*,[142] the Supreme Court reviewed recovery for publication of an acknowledged fictional interview that cast the prominent minister, Jerry Falwell, in a negative light. Because the magazine made no claim of truth, the jury rejected recovery for libel but awarded a judgment of $150,000 for emotional distress. The Supreme Court reversed, ruling that when public figures and public officials are involved, one expects criticisms that may be emotionally upsetting; tort recovery is then permissible only if false statements about what is really true are made with actual malice.

As with invasions of privacy, just how far the First Amendment protections should reach is not easy. Matters are further complicated by the development of electronic communication. Not only may professional journals publicize information, one private person can divulge secret facts about another or engage in emotionally hurtful comments that are accessible worldwide. At least when people are aiming at a broad audience and lack a reason of public concern to divulge highly private facts or to offer comments sure to cause emotional distress, tort recovery should be permitted.

A different kind of publicity was presented in *Snyder v. Phelps*,[143] in which the Supreme Court reviewed picketing by members of an antigay Baptist Church on public land about 1,000 feet from a church holding a funeral service for a veteran. The picketers had signs saying "Thank

God for Dead Soldiers" and "Fags Doom Nations." The father of the dead soldier, who had seen the signs while driving to the funeral but had not learned their content until a later news broadcast, had been awarded substantial damages for the intentional infliction of emotional distress. The court of appeals reversal was upheld by the Supreme Court on the ground that such expression about matters of public concern could not be treated as tortuous. Justice Alito dissented based on the infliction of "severe emotional injury . . . at a time of intense emotional sensitivity."[144]

The distance between the picketing and the church, and the way in which the father actually learned of the content of the signs, make it uncertain just how the Justices would resolve a fundamental issue that could have affected the outcome of this case. The death of those closest to us is a tragic and deeply upsetting experience for all people. In the particular settings outside private dwellings in which we honor and remember those who have died, we expect and need moral support and the absence of disturbance. The limit on genuine free expression is minimal if the government, in one way or another, forbids self-conscious interference with the emotional needs and sensitivity of those who are grieving together on these special occasions. Certainly, a parent who has lost a child who was a soldier will be extremely upset if picketers right in front of the church have signs saying "Thank God for Dead Soldiers." The government should be able to limit highly disturbing messages pushed in the faces of those gathered at funeral services to remember, honor, and pray for loved ones and friends who have died. In this special circumstance, context should permit an exception to standard free speech protection. *If* the Court takes *Snyder v. Phelps* as precluding *any* such exception regarding speech of some public relevance made at a public place, that would be a serious mistake, although most people's sensitivity to the grieving of others might reduce the practical effect of any uncompromising protection of such expression.[145]

XIV. OBSCENITY

A form of communication that has consistently been held to be outside of First Amendment protection is obscenity. What has changed radically is what qualifies as obscene and whether the lack of protection makes a practical difference. Until the middle of the twentieth century, a publication could count as obscene if isolated passages had a tendency "to deprave and corrupt those whose minds are open to such immoral influences. . . . "[146] Under that standard, significant literature, such as D.H. Lawrence's *Lady Chatterley's Lover* and James Joyce's *Ulysses*, had sometimes been successfully banned. In 1957, the Court in *Roth v. United States*[147] ruled that to constitute obscenity, material must go "substantially beyond customary limits of candor" and be "utterly without redeeming social importance."[148] After *Roth*, a plurality occupying the

Court's center adopted a threefold test requiring (1) a dominant appeal to a prurient interest, (2) patent offensiveness that affronts community standards about sexual descriptions or representations, and (3) an utter lack of redeeming social value.[149] In 1973, a majority adopted a version of this standard, qualifying the third component so that "taken as a whole," the work does "not have serious literary, artistic, political, or scientific value."[150] Given increasing cultural acceptance of openness about sexual activity and the widespread availability in electronic communications and elsewhere of sexually explicit material, the absence of constitutional protection for obscene material no longer matters much, except with respect to child pornography. Nevertheless, why obscene representations fall outside of free speech and how to categorize them remain interesting questions.

Among various possible bases for nonprotection are these. Such sexually explicit material comes close to actual physical stimulation because it is overwhelmingly intended to generate sexual satisfaction, not communicate ideas.[151] Relatedly, those who distribute obscene material are not really communicating; they are simply trying to profit from people's (mainly men's) sexual inclinations. Obscenity may convey an immoral attitude about sexual relations, and its consumption can lead people away from loving respect for spouses and partners. Many obscene items also send a message that women are mainly sexual objects who do not warrant respect as individuals.[152] As these various claims indicate, one cannot say that obscenity conveys no message, even if it is true that its conveyers and its consumers care little about that. Any full explanation of noncoverage must rest on an assumption that negative factors are powerful enough to warrant placing this form of communication beyond constitutional protection. Again, we see that conclusions about coverage and noncoverage, and the drawing of relevant lines, can rest on the nature of a particular form of communication.

The Supreme Court has upheld convictions under both a state statute banning material that depicts "sexual performance" by children under age sixteen[153] and a federal law that extends to apparent depiction of minors even if actual children were not used.[154] In a 2010 case, the Court declined to extend this exception to depictions of animal cruelty.[155]

Overall, the Supreme Court remains willing to recognize that for some communications, the speech value is slight enough and the likely harm serious enough to deny First Amendment protection; but these categories are decidedly limited, and the protection given to most speech is extensive.

XV. COMMERCIAL ADVERTISING

With regard to commercial advertising, the Court has moved from the position that it lies outside First Amendment protection[156] to invalidating various restrictions on truthful advertisements. In 1976, in *Virginia State Board of Pharmacy v. Virginia Citizens Consumer Council*,[157] emphasizing the value for people of accurate information, the Court ruled that a state may not forbid pharmacies from advertising drug prices. At the same time, it acknowledged that various forms of regulation of commercial speech are acceptable and that such speech warrants "a different degree of protection" than noncommercial communication.[158] In 1980, when striking down a ban on electric utility advertising to promote the use of electricity,[159] the Court offered a four-part analysis: (1) Is the speech about lawful activity and not misleading? (2) Is the government interest substantial? (3) Does the regulation directly advance the government's interest? (4) Could the interest be served by a less restrictive measure? If the answer to the first question is "yes," a regulation fails unless it serves a significant government interest in a way that could not be achieved with less restriction.

In the ensuing years, the Supreme Court has declared invalid a number of regulations of commercial advertising, including a prohibition on advertising the price of alcoholic beverages,[160] and a federal rule that exempted compounded drugs from the standard requirements for approval by the FDA, but only if the providers did not advertise the drugs.[161]

Under present doctrine, truthful commercial advertising enjoys substantial protection but, in contrast to most other communications, a government can prohibit advertising that is false or, even if not untrue, deceptive or misleading.[162] It can also compel certain disclosures.[163] And such advertising may generally be subject to restrictions not allowed more broadly. When faced with a city ordinance forbidding advertising on billboards, a measure designed to improve traffic safety and the city's appearance, the Supreme Court held it valid for commercial advertising but invalid as applied to noncommercial advertising.[164]

As with other kinds of "low-value" expression, the Court has needed to take due account of the interests at stake in determining the boundaries of protection and providing an administrable standard. For advertising, as well as obscenity, hate speech, and other forms of expression, both judges and commentators may reasonably disagree about just how this should be done; but clearly, a sensible approach depends significantly on the kind of speech involved.

XVI. CONTENT DISTINCTIONS

A central categorization in First Amendment law is between content distinctions and content-neutral regulation. The fundamental idea is that when the government forbids or regulates speech on the basis of its content or message, that poses the greatest threat to free expression. A consequence, as the *Pentagon Papers* case reflects,[165] is that actual laws and attempted executive restraints of this sort are subject to strict standards of judicial review. This core assumption about heightened review of content-based regulation is uncontroversial, but a number of variations make the existing law and desirable approaches a bit more complicated.[166] These include the difference between distinctions based on viewpoint and those based on subject matter. Other questions are the extent to which practices generally regarded as outside of free speech protection may involve content distinctions and the relevance, if any, of those distinctions for unprotected or less protected speech. Important practical issues include how far the protection against content regulations applies to expenditures of money by private persons and companies, and what restraints exist on what government institutions themselves may do, including their supporting of private expressions.

The most obvious form of content distinction concerns viewpoints. The government cannot allow speech offering one viewpoint and forbid speech asserting a competing position. It cannot favor speech that promotes its interests and its views of a healthy social order, and suppress the opinions of opponents. That viewpoint discrimination is judged according to the strictest scrutiny is uncontroversial.

It is worth noting, however, that some of the limits on the range of protected speech that we have reviewed do, in a sense, involve particular forms of viewpoint discrimination. These are allowed in order to prevent specific harms that flow from particular communications. If I strongly urge someone to commit a crime, I may be guilty of criminal solicitation. If I urge him to refrain from breaking the law, I am not punishable.[167] If a person castigates a member of a racial minority in the harshest language, he may have used forbidden "fighting words" or engaged in workplace harassment. If he praises the same person in complimentary language, he cannot be sanctioned. In brief, certain of the permissible limits on speech that we have reviewed do partly involve expressed viewpoints whose opposites are protected.

A different form of content discrimination involves subject matter, allowing free speech about some topics but precluding it for others. With respect to most conceivable regulations of private speech, the government can no more forbid expression because of its subject than its particular viewpoint. An obvious qualification to this general approach concerns subjects that are regarded as having less expressive importance. The government can forbid obscenity and can regulate what is portrayed in commercial advertising. Although this special treatment could conceivably be defended as serving a compelling interest,[168] the fact that these communications relate much more weakly to the basic values of free expression is more important.[169]

In other contexts, communications that can be important for the welfare of recipients are something other than a free expression of personal views. Doctors and lawyers are professionals with special responsibilities; they have undertaken what are, in a sense, public roles. Although the government cannot forbid their expressing a range of outlooks in nonprofessional settings, it can regulate the kind of information they convey to patients and clients.[170] A doctor can be sanctioned if she tells her patient to do what the wider profession has decided is clearly unjustified and highly dangerous; a lawyer cannot inform a client that he would be right to break the law because it is unjust and he is unlikely to be caught.

Perhaps the hardest question about content discrimination is whether it should be permitted within categories of communication that, taken as a whole, are regarded as outside the First Amendment or as warranting only limited protection. In *R.A.V. v. City of St. Paul*,[171] the Supreme Court indicated that strict scrutiny applies, and content distinctions are effectively foreclosed, even for expressions that would not warrant protection if treated as a general class. An earlier section suggests that this conclusion is mistaken.[172] If we assume, as did the Court's majority, that all "fighting words" may be prohibited,[173] and we understand that the practical task of distinguishing fighting words from less inflammatory communication is hardly simple, allowing a state to concentrate on the kinds of epithets that cause genuine harm makes sense, rather than requiring that it forbid all or no fighting words.

Justice Scalia's majority opinion does present an argument that concentrating on fighting words about race, religion, gender, and so forth can produce unfair inequality, a form of viewpoint discrimination, in interchanges. A person calling "papists" misbegotten could be punished, while someone calling "anti-Catholic bigots" misbegotten could not. That either of these expressions would actually qualify as fighting words is itself highly implausible, but one can imagine examples of such asymmetry—for example, a racial bigot calls a man a "dirty nigger," and he responds, "you are a fucking Nazi." But even if the application of this kind of anti-discrimination ordinance would occasionally produce viewpoint discrimination, that is far from its main thrust.

Notably, the Court's opinion in *R.A.V.* does not fit with its approach to workplace harassment. If some elderly male workers harass women based on their gender, the employer must respond or be liable. If women harass the men because they are old and ugly, the employer need do nothing. Workplace harassment law clearly is content-based. If potential viewpoint discrimination is a sound basis for striking down St. Paul's ordinance, the same logic applies to any rules against workplace regulations that specify prohibited forms of harassment. This conclusion strongly supports the view that any line like that drawn in *R.A.V.* requires more careful analysis, and I believe it also tells us why for "fighting words," the "all or nothing conclusion" is misguided.

The most perplexing questions about content distinctions involve forms of government involvement other than prohibitions of private communications. Most obviously, the government itself can issue statutes and other official documents that express particular points of view. The constitution is properly understood as precluding some forms of official expression, such as the desirability of voting for Democrats in the upcoming election;[174] but on most subjects, the government is not precluded from adopting or rejecting outlooks about desirable social and political life.

The tricky questions arise when the government is dealing with the expressions of others, as it does with libraries, auditoriums, financing, and courses and student activities in schools and colleges. In most of these areas, some distinctions based on content are inevitable, but judicial decisions have hardly made clear just which of those are appropriate and why.[175]

In all of these domains, government officials properly evaluate the quality of what is written or spoken. When public libraries decide what books to buy and keep, when officials invite speakers and plays to public auditoriums, when state universities determine tenure of faculty members, and when public grants are given to artists or writers, evaluations of the quality of content are necessary. In most of these settings, officials should not favor or disfavor persons because they like or dislike their particular views. When that form of content discrimination has obviously happened, it is properly regarded as constitutionally unacceptable.

A major problem with this conclusion is how judges can possibly draw the line between assessments of quality and rejections of unpopular points of view. This is not only a problem for judicial review of officials' motivations, but it also can touch the officials themselves. I was recently asked to review for possible publication an essay defending a position I have long thought was clearly wrong. I declined, partly because I doubted that I could fairly distinguish my appraisal of the quality of the analysis from my negative view of the conclusion. If someone thinks a position taken is outrageous or antisocial, she will be hard put to conclude that the account is of high quality. Given this impediment, and the added problem of having judges determine what has actually motivated such decisions, Erwin Chemerinsky's recommendation that courts should require that officials use clear standards that are as specific as possible and that do not discriminate on the basis of the ideas expressed is a sound approach.[176]

When it comes to public schools, the government's latitude should be somewhat greater. Clearly, teachers can be forbidden from conveying within classes messages that are strongly opposed to accepted public values; they cannot, for example, recommend that students smoke marijuana or engage in racial discrimination. And when it comes to schools, for librarians to ask whether the messages conveyed in books conform with what the school is trying to teach is more appropriate than when those who run general public libraries pick books because they fit public norms.

The treatment of student organizations presents another issue about public educational institutions. One assumes that a state university cannot forbid participation in a student organization based on its ideology unless the organization's purpose, say, inflicting harm on another group of students, gives it a very powerful reason to do so. What is trickier is what criteria the university may use in determining funding. In cases that have arisen, that question has been interrelated with claims about free exercise and nonestablishment of religion and about the status of anti-discrimination norms. In *Rosenberger v. Rector & Visitors of University of Virginia*,[177] the Court, 5–4, ruled that nonestablishment concerns were not sufficient to support the university's content-based rule against funding publications that are primarily religious.[178] Subsequently, the Court, again 5–4, determined that a state could not forbid the Boy Scouts from revoking a scoutmaster's position because they learned he was an "avowed homosexual."[179] Requiring that an organization keep as a leader someone whose life was being lived in a way that is at odds with the norms of an organization was said to violate its First Amendment rights as an expressive association. In 2010, however, the Court, 5–4, sustained a refusal by Hastings College of Law to formally recognize and financially aid a chapter of Christian Legal Society. In violation of a university rule that organizations may not discriminate on the basis of religion or sexual orientation, the chapter required members and officers to sign a "Statement of Faith" and not to engage in "unrepentant homosexual conduct."[180] The four dissenters in an opinion by Justice Alito saw this as a "political correctness" violation of free speech;[181] Justice Ginsburg's majority opinion emphasized that government has greater latitude in "limited public forums" than other environments and that the indirect pressure created by nonfunding does not raise the same impairments on free association as prohibitions and outright requirements.[182]

The divisions on the Court and the different contexts in which governmental educational institutions may disfavor groups that promote views that the government itself could not adopt (i.e., religious claims), or that engage in practices that are at odds with norms of nondiscrimination, illustrate the complicated nature of these issues.[183] A full analysis demands consideration of religion clause values and equal protection as well as freedom of expression and association. But the Court is right to treat a refusal to fund as subject to less strict scrutiny than an outright bar, and to be more accepting of forbidden limits on membership than bars on expressions of controversial views.[184]

Crucial questions about government involvement that is content-based but viewpoint-neutral concern political campaigns. Two obvious competing considerations are these: (1) people should be able to express themselves on matters of public importance, and this includes decisions to spend money in order to publicize their views; (2) in a fair political process, opposing political candidates should have roughly the same ability to communicate to the voters, and it is unhealthy if a candidate who achieves office sees his past and future success as dependent on satisfying the wishes of particular rich donors. The details of the present constitutional law on this subject are both complex and highly controversial.

The Supreme Court has thus far upheld federal and state restrictions on the amount of money people can give to individual candidates,[185] and it has permitted public financing of campaigns designed to produce greater equality.[186] On the other hand, the Court has moved strongly toward precluding restrictions designed to promote campaign equity. In 2008, it treated as unconstitutional restrictions on candidates' use of their own money.[187] In 2011, in *Citizens United v. Federal Election Commission,*[188] by a 5–4 margin, it overruled a 1990 decision[189] and held invalid a federal law prohibiting corporations and unions from using general treasury funds to advocate the election or defeat of candidates. Although a corporation has not yet been afforded a constitutional right to directly donate money to a campaign, it can now spend millions of dollars to support a candidacy. Given the virtual impossibility of assuring that those representing a candidate do not communicate what kind of support would be beneficial, the line between donation and "independent" support is distressingly thin in practice, and the consequence of the Court's decision is to give those controlling wealth an even bigger clout in the political process than they had previously, creating conditions in which an uneven balance in campaigns becomes both more common and more severe.

As Kathleen Sullivan has explained,[190] a central aspect of what divided the Justices in *Citizens United* is what is most important about freedom of expression. If one emphasizes freedom of participation fully, the Court sensibly regards any government constraints with suspicion. On the other hand, if one gives emphasis to people's being fairly exposed to competing positions and making judgments as balanced as possible when they vote, government efforts to discourage gross inequality make good sense, especially given the realistic concern that an elected official may be anxious to please a major donor, whether or not that serves the public interest. Another crucial aspect here is whether corporations should be treated like individuals.

In the spring of 2014, in *McCutcheon v. General Election Committee,* the Court took another step toward eliminating barriers on financing, striking down the part of a federal law that limited the total amount of financial support one could give to all the candidates in an election.[191] Without resolving whether the somewhat less rigorous standard than strict scrutiny should be maintained for such restrictions, Chief Justice Roberts, writing for a plurality, determined that the government's reasons were inadequate.[192] Under the *McCutcheon* decision, someone may contribute the maximum amount to every Republican or Democratic candidate in a federal election.

All of this is both highly sensitive and extremely controversial, but everyone should recognize that important constitutional values include *both* people's freedom to express themselves and participate, and fairness of a political process that will best aid people to make wise decisions and curtail legislators' self-interested concessions to major donors.[193] Corporations, like individuals, should be able to express their views about substantive political issues, but a restraint on what they spend on campaigns makes sense in light of the need for a fair process, and the fact that the expressive rights of corporations should be regarded as less powerful than those of individuals and non-profit organizations. People can reasonably disagree about just how the balance of maximum free expression versus fairness in the political process needs to be struck, but I believe *Citizens United* goes considerably too far in the first direction.

XVII. CONTENT-NEUTRAL RESTRICTIONS

The last part of this chapter briefly touches on circumstances in which the government sets restrictions that are content-neutral about expression, at least formally.[194] Some laws not themselves cast in terms of communication may be broken by people wishing to convey a message. The most notable case on this subject is *United States v. O'Brien*,[195] in which the Supreme Court reviewed the conviction of a young man who had publicly burned his draft certificate in protest against the Vietnam War. Given that the law had already required registrants to keep the certificates in their possession, the relevant section of the law, which covered one who "knowingly destroys" his certificate, was in fact adopted in response to protests. The Court nonetheless treated it as not directed at expression. "[E]ven on the assumption that the alleged communicative element in O'Brien's conduct" made the First Amendment relevant, the Court found the conviction justified. The standard it announced was that a law must further a substantial government interest not related to suppressing expression, and that its effect on First Amendment freedoms must not be greater than is essential to further that interest.[196] This actual formulation is fairly protective of the kind of speech in which O'Brien engaged, although the Court's finding that the government had met that standard was not. The Court has similarly sustained application of laws forbidding public nudity, even when claims are made that expression is involved, as in nude dancing.[197]

As far as existing law is concerned, it is worth noting that the *O'Brien* test is in severe tension with the Court's approach in *Employment Division v. Smith* to the free exercise of religion,[198] which allows a neutral law to be applied across the board without granting violators who are engaging in religious exercises any balancing test whatsoever. The fact that it is nearly impossible to see why use of peyote as the center of a worship service can be barred without judicial assessment of what is at stake, yet burning draft cards calls for such an appraisal, makes one wonder what the status of *O'Brien*'s logic is with the present Court's majority. *Employment Division v. Smith* creates serious doubt about exactly when, if ever, the Court will continue to "balance" circumstances in which neutral laws affect expression.

When the Supreme Court addressed a flag desecration statute two decades after *O'Brien*, it determined that the law was actually designed to suppress expression and therefore could not sustain a conviction of someone who had been protesting the policies of the Reagan administration.[199] The Justices reached a similar conclusion a year later in regard to a new federal statute, despite its having been drafted to avoid the implications of the previous case by stating that the aim was to protect the flag's physical integrity.[200]

As the prior section indicates, one issue that has arisen about "neutral applications" of laws not themselves directed at expression concerns the application of laws forbidding discrimination against groups that claim their practices constitute forms of expression. Before sustaining in 2000 the argument of the Boy Scouts that, given their right of expressive association, New Jersey could not forbid them from dismissing a scoutmaster who was an "avowed homosexual,"[201] the Court had rejected a similar claim to exclude women by an organization that promoted the ability and interests of young men.[202] Acknowledging a right to associate for expressive purposes, the Court found that Minnesota had a compelling interest in combating gender discrimination and that allowing young women to become members would not significantly interfere with the organization's expressive purposes.

Yet another issue about content-neutral rules is the accessibility of public forums. The government may apply reasonable time, place, and manner constraints;[203] but it cannot preclude access to public spaces, and it cannot favor some messages over others. In regard to distinguishing between kinds of messages, the Court held invalid a ban on demonstrations close to public schools that did not cover picketing of schools involved in labor disputes;[204] but a slender majority upheld a city's allowing commercial advertisements but not political ones on its streetcars and buses, a distinction a plurality regarded as a reasonable way to avoid appearances of favoritism and impositions on a captive audience.[205]

Although it may be impossible to state precisely how various reviews of expression in conflict with content-neutral laws should be resolved, a court needs first to assess that the law is not obviously aimed at discouraging expression and then to undertake a more relaxed form of scrutiny than applies to constraints on expression itself. This is what amounts to the roughly described "two-tier" approach to free speech cases.

As Geoffrey Stone explained some years ago, an intermediate form of balancing is generally appropriate if the "neutral" law involved is not actually aimed at discouraging expression.[206] Unlike a "clear and present danger test," content-neutral balancing neither requires that other government interests give way nor undercuts claims of free expression by a highly deferential approach. Some form of intermediate review is wise when the government is not seeking to restrict speech and the value of free expression is less strongly compromised. For certain kinds of laws, the courts may develop categorical approaches that reflect competing values. For others, a more particular balancing may be necessary, one that focuses on the degree of restriction on expression, the substantiality of the competing government interests, and whether these could be served by means less intrusive on expression.[207]

XVIII. CONCLUSION

This chapter has covered a wide range of free speech issues, emphasizing their distinctiveness, outlining existing treatments, and suggesting sound resolutions. This specific examination reveals many domains in which what the Supreme Court has decided, and what makes sense in our liberal democracy, are miles and miles away from the original understanding of enactors and readers about the actual coverage of free speech protection. And this is true even if one focuses on 1868 when the Fourteenth Amendment was adopted rather than 1791.We have looked at a variety of forms of expression, some of which contain much more speech value than others, and some of which raise special reasons for governmental regulations. What all of this demonstrates is that even in one particular realm of constitutional rights, no uniform, simple approach to interpreting coverage can work. Context matters greatly, and judges need to be responsive to a broad variety of vital considerations, as Burt Neuborne urges persuasively in *Madison's Music*.[208] Insofar as First Amendment law is criticized for being unclear, imprecise, and controversial, we can fairly see that this is largely the consequence of genuine complexities, ones that render straightforward and consistent analysis very difficult, especially with a Supreme Court that is sharply divided and has changing membership.

Chapter 10

The Religion Clauses

I. INTRODUCTION

A second central aspect of the First Amendment is its treatment of the government's relation to religion. Originally, Congress was forbidden to enact any law "respecting an establishment of religion, or prohibiting the free exercise thereof;" and that bar now applies to states. As Chapter 3 explains, since roughly half the states in 1791 had practices that we would presently regard as establishments of religion, many members of Congress and state ratifiers undoubtedly viewed the Establishment Clause as mainly precluding federal interference with state practices, not as a principled rejection of all levels of government doing what amounted to establishing religion. Chapter 3 suggests why, given shifts in outlooks by the time of the Fourteenth Amendment and the connections between free exercise and establishment, taking Establishment Clause limits to apply to the states now makes sense. That view, adopted by all nine Justices in the historic 1947 case of *Everson v. Board of Education*[1] and solidly entrenched in subsequent decisions, is taken as a settled premise in this chapter.

Both religion clauses are aimed at promoting religious freedom, precluding the government both from interfering with religious beliefs and activities and promoting a particular faith. For many conceivable government practices, such as Congress proclaiming the truth of Protestant Christianity, the two clauses point in the same direction. But certain circumstances generate a tension between them. Various acts of government, such as affording exemptions to those with religious convictions from nondiscrimination mandates, may accommodate "free exercise" but also to a degree may "establish" religion by favoring it. A central inquiry about the two religion clauses is just how they should be fitted with each other in various contexts. With respect to exemptions, how far is the government constitutionally required, or permitted, to excuse religious practitioners from ordinary legal requirements, and, if it does so, must it also extend exemptions to persons with similar nonreligious bases? A different issue is when, if ever, governmental financial assistance to religious bodies is warranted as promoting free exercise and, if so, whether nonreligious groups must receive similar benefits. When the activities of government officials are involved, how far does free exercise protect their acts of religious worship and their use of religious justifications for what they do, and how far should nonestablishment preclude or discourage those practices?

Having written extensively about the content and application of the religion clauses,[2] I here concentrate on issues that raise fundamental concerns about appropriate interpretive approaches. The chapter first covers basic Establishment and Free Exercise problems and then turns to central controversies about how the relationship between the two clauses should be understood.

II. NO ESTABLISHMENT

The Establishment Clause was adopted to preclude the national government from sponsoring or promoting any particular religion and from interfering with state practices about religion. In addition to requiring that the federal government allow states to treat religious institutions and practices as they saw fit, the Clause barred "establishment" in purely federal domains, such as the District of Columbia, Western territories, and embassies abroad. Clearly, the national government could not anywhere create a genuine established church, such as Great Britain's Anglican Church, which was the country's official religion, received substantial government support, and had its practices partly dictated by parliamentary laws. The novel language of the First Amendment reaches beyond formally establishing a church to cover any laws "*respecting* an establishment of religion," thus barring laws that move in the direction of establishment. How should judges and other officials determine whether laws that assist a particular religion or religions are actually unconstitutional, given the vagueness of the term "respecting"? This puzzle had limited practical relevance as long as the clause restricted only the federal government, which initially exercised a fairly narrow range of powers. But with the application of most of the Bill of Rights to the states, and with the much greater involvement of federal and state governments in the lives of citizens, the question of what laws cross the border of permissibility has emerged as very important.

A. Financial Assistance

Most of the establishment cases decided by the Supreme Court have involved the granting of financial assistance for activities that are significantly religious. In its first major establishment case, *Everson v. Board of Education*,[3] the Supreme Court, in an opinion by Justice Black, not only failed to address directly how the Fourteenth Amendment Due Process Clause protection of individuals could incorporate a clause mainly restricting government relations to institutions. It also assumed that those who adopted the Establishment Clause itself accepted the perspectives of James Madison and Thomas Jefferson, which was most unlikely in 1791 given the support of religion in various states. (Chapter 3 defends both this incorporation and an approach that is fairly strongly antiestablishment, but recognizes that neither conclusion follows simply from the origins of the First and Fourteenth Amendments.)

Having embraced the basic antiestablishment perspective, the *Everson* Court sustained what amounted to a kind of marginal assistance to parochial education. New Jersey had adopted a law that required school districts providing transportation to public schools also to pay for transportation to nonprofit private schools. In the particular district involved, only children attending Roman Catholic schools, presumably the only eligible schools in that locale, were benefiting from this financial support. The Court divided 5–4 over whether this degree of aid was permissible. Four dissenters would have struck down the New Jersey law, relying on Madison's basic notion that any financial support to religion is objectionable because it violates the right of taxpayers not to support religions in which they do not believe.[4] Justice Black, for the majority, sustained the financing of busing, but his opinion's language embraced severe restrictions on what was allowable.

Black's opinion contains two theories which, as has long been recognized, often point in contrary directions. In one passage, he wrote that the "Amendment requires the state to be neutral in its relations with groups of religious believers and nonbelievers; it does not require the state to be their adversary. State power is no more to be used so as to handicap religions than it is to favor them."[5] This approach, which has taken on increasing importance in ensuing decades, seems to allow the same government support of activities, such as for hospitals and adoption agencies, whether carried on by religious or nonreligious groups. If, however, one genuinely tries to discern the force of Justice Black's *Everson* opinion and the Court's position, this neutrality passage is *not* central. Black also wrote that neither a state nor the federal government "can pass laws which aid one religion, aid all religions, or prefer one religion over another.... No tax in any amount, large or small, can be levied to support any religious activities or institutions, whatever they may be called, or whatever form they may adopt to teach or practice religion.... [The Establishment Clause] was intended to erect 'a wall of separation between Church and State.'"[6] Addressing the specific issue before the Court, the opinion remarked that New Jersey could not "contribute tax-raised funds to the support of an institution which teaches the tenets and faith of any church."[7] The actual law "approaches the verge" of the state's constitutional power[8] but was valid because it protected and benefited the children attending the school in the manner of police and fire protection and other public services. Not every Justice in the majority may have embraced this very restrictive language, but, when one takes into account the four dissenters, one inevitably concludes that most Justices viewed states as highly constrained as to how far they could financially assist parochial education.

For the following half century, the Court continued to take a restrictive view of permissible aid to parochial schools, although its rhetoric and acceptance of certain modest, indirect forms of assistance reflected a degree of flexibility. In *Board of Education v. Allen*,[9] two decades after *Everson*, the Court sustained the state's lending free textbooks to students in nonpublic schools, so long as those books had been designated for use in public schools or approved by the public board of education. With Justice Black, *Everson's* author, dissenting sharply, Justice White emphasized that the benefit went to the parents and children, not the school, and that the state may assist sectarian schools in performing the public purpose of secular education.

Three years later, in *Lemon v. Kurtzman*,[10] the Court struck down the statutes of two states that authorized payments for parts of the salaries of teachers of secular subjects in private schools. In both states, the vast majority of schools covered were Roman Catholic. Emphasizing the close connection of the schools to the Catholic Church, Chief Justice Burger's opinion announced a threefold test for Establishment Clause cases. A law must (1) have a "secular legislative purpose," (2) have a "principal or primary effect ... that neither advances nor inhibits religion," and (3) not foster "an excessive government entanglement with religion."[11] Preceding his announced standards, the Chief Justice had acknowledged that the right lines of demarcation were "blurred, indistinct, and variable," not a "wall,"[12] and that the proper lines could only be "dimly perceive[d]."[13] Not doubting the laws' secular purpose, the Court found it unnecessary to determine their principal effect, because the measures the statutes adopted to assure that assistance went only to secular teaching involved an "excessive entanglement." Given the schools' ties to the Catholic Church and the number of nuns and other Catholics teaching there, the states' needed degree of investigation and supervision to assure nonreligious use of their funds would unacceptably involve the government's being too closely connected to the practices of religious organizations. Since a clear implication of the opinion is that, had the laws *not* authorized substantial oversight of how the funds were used, they would have failed the effects test, it followed that states seeking to help pay the salaries of parochial school teachers were unable to avoid invalidation under one of the *Lemon* standards.

The *Lemon* opinion treats "divisive political potential" as "entanglement of yet a different character,"[14] one that can arise when benefits going to only a few religious groups intensify political divisions along religious lines. Although Burger presents divisiveness as a nearly independent element of entanglement, its significance has diminished in later opinions. This is hardly surprising. A concern about political conflicts along religious lines may constitute a basis for nonestablishment, but judges who are hardly well situated to estimate the degree to which particular assistance creates that risk cannot employ that criterion as a central basis for acceptance or disapproval.

The three central elements of the *Lemon* test are themselves hardly clear and decisive forms of categorization. They do not explicitly authorize a balancing of relevant factors, yet their application definitely involves assessments about which reasonable judges may differ. Reference to a "principal or primary effect . . . that neither advances nor inhibits religion" requires an estimation of how far the secular effects dominate the influence on religious practices. And "excessive" entanglement necessitates an implicit evaluation of how far the need for government oversight generates undesirable involvement with religious endeavors. "Secular purpose" is more straightforward, but whether that appears even to exist may depend on just how dominant a religious purpose seems to be. In 2005, an opinion for the Court referred to an "ostensible and predominant purpose," perceived by an "objective observer."[15]

Whatever one concludes about the precise formulations in the *Lemon* test, they represent a typical variety of constitutional standard, calling for attention to specific criteria that do not simply involve direct application of textual language nor a comprehensive weighing of all relevant factors, but still leave for judges in many cases enough uncertainty in application to produce competing assessments of whether government action is permissible.

A particular puzzle about the *Lemon* test is how it fits with self-conscious concessions to religious practices, such as allowing members of the Native American Church to use peyote as the center of their worship services. As we shall see when we turn to free exercise, the *Lemon* formulation does not capture well what is, and what should be, the law about such matters.

On the same day it decided *Lemon*, the Court, in a 5–4 decision, upheld federal construction grants given to church-related colleges and universities for facilities that were not to be used for sectarian instruction or religious worship.[16] According to Chief Justice Burger's plurality opinion for four Justices, these institutions were not "pervasively sectarian" in the manner of Catholic parochial schools, given that college teachers are less likely to mix religious messages with secular topics, and college students are less impressionable and susceptible to religious indoctrination. As a consequence, much less supervision was needed to see that religious aspects did not infect use of the facilities for secular purposes. Five Justices actually did not perceive higher education aid as so different from that involving schools; four voted to reject the federal program; the fifth, Justice White, believed that both that and the aid to schools in *Lemon* were acceptable.

During the next decade, the Court upheld assistance to religious colleges and universities in the form of construction bonds and grants based on numbers of students. In one of these cases, Justice Blackmun's plurality opinion summarized the factors that could lead to the conclusion that colleges are not "pervasively sectarian."[17] Exactly when anything crosses the line between being modestly of a certain character to being pervasively so is vague. It follows that the inquiry a secular court would need to make into religious understandings and practices to determine if a particular educational institution was too sectarian would be far from simple, though perhaps using the "pervasively sectarian" standard is acceptable to distinguish most religious colleges from most parochial schools without any intensive individual investigation.

While sustaining aid that benefited colleges, the Court continued to strike down forms of assistance to parochial schools, including grants to repair facilities, the provision of auxiliary services such as counseling and remedial education by public school personnel within private schools, and tuition reimbursement for low-income parents. It did permit the lending of textbooks, the supplying of standardized tests, and the provision of diagnostic services.[18]

Between 1980 and 2002, the Supreme Court moved unevenly toward a more permissive approach to aid. In *Mueller v. Allen,*[19] in 1983, Justice Rehnquist, who had been dissenting in cases denying aid, wrote for the five-member majority upholding a Minnesota statute allowing parents to deduct from state income taxes their payments for tuition at private schools, 95 percent of which were sectarian. The opinion relied on the fact that any aid to schools came indirectly through parents' choices and that the law was facially neutral. Although many expected a radical shift toward permitted aid after *Mueller,* in 1985, the Court struck down two programs authorizing state payments to teachers from public and private schools to conduct after-school "remedial" and "enrichment" courses in the private schools.[20] A member of the majority in *Mueller,* Justice Powell shifted to the other side in the 1985 cases. This allowed Justice Brennan to write for the Court that the program in Grand Rapids, Michigan, could aid religious instruction and entail a "symbolic union of church and state,"[21] and that New York City's system to prevent religious instruction failed the entanglement test. Although eight Justices voted for the same results in these 1985 cases that they had supported in *Mueller,* Justice Powell's contrary conviction proved crucial.

Subsequently, the court upheld the application of a program for vocational rehabilitation of the blind to aid someone studying to be a pastor at a Christian college[22] and also sustained public funding of a sign language interpreter helping a deaf child at a Catholic high school.[23] The Court then reviewed its invalidation of New York City's program to have public school teachers provide after-school programs within private schools.[24] With the Court's composition having changed significantly, Justice O'Connor, a dissenter in the original case, wrote for the majority that such teaching would not amount to a symbolic union of church and state or aid religious educational functions. Since public school teachers would not be inclined to teach religion, the city did not need to undertake pervasive monitoring. O'Connor treated "entanglement" not as a separate test but as an element of impermissible effect. Although calculating the precise practical significance of this conceptual move is impossible, it appears to reduce the comparative weight of entanglement considerations. This illustrates how the exact formulation of a test can both be affected by the way judges wish to apply it and itself influence future coverage.

In 2000, in *Mitchell v. Helms,* [25] the Supreme Court, taking a more permissive position than it had previously,[26] upheld the use of federal funds for local agencies to lend educational materials and equipment to private schools. In a concurrence for herself and Justice Breyer, Justice O'Connor supported the result on the basis that what was involved was not a direct monetary subsidy and that no real danger existed that the instructional materials would be diverted to religious uses.[27] Justice Thomas's opinion for a four-Justice plurality, by contrast, adopted a radical shift in how financial assistance should be addressed. His dominant theme was "neutrality" in terms of equal treatment. So long as nonreligious aid is offered to a broad range of groups regardless of their religious affiliation, it is permissible even if religious groups are the main beneficiaries *and* aid is actually diverted by them to religious purposes. Such a diversion would not violate the Establishment Clause because it would not be attributable to the government. Whether the wide scope of Justice Thomas's opinion will eventually be accepted by a majority is not yet clear; if adopted, it would permit extensive aid to schools in virtually any form.[28]

A special element of the Thomas opinion is its sharp rejection of any "pervasively sectarian" standard. Calling that standard "not only unnecessary but also offensive" and asserting that "born of bigotry, [it] should be buried now," Thomas urged that courts should not be "trolling through a person's or institution's religious beliefs."[29] In assessing the persuasiveness of this sharp attack on the "pervasively sectarian" standard, we cannot rule out the possibility that anti-Catholic attitudes affected some judges and others who have supported it. However, the particular conclusions about Catholic parochial schools were based substantially on how their own documents described their aspirations. Realistically, the degrees of sectarianism in educational institutions with religious connections do differ significantly, and the closer the intertwining is of religious and other educational elements, the more likely it becomes that any aid will assist the religious aspects. For these reasons, a "pervasively sectarian" standard is hardly irrational given Establishment Clause principles. However, the Supreme Court has never been precise about how the border of "too sectarian" would be determined, and, were the standard used to evaluate individual institutions, it would, as already noted, require extensive examination of religious beliefs and institutional practices, an entangling endeavor for secular administrators and judges. Because of that difficulty, courts should *not* employ "pervasively sectarian" to assess particular recipients of aid,[30] but the disinclination to use that standard should depend on this kind of evaluation, not any simple condemnation that it was produced by bigotry.

The Supreme Court's most important modern Establishment Clause case, *Zelman v. Simmons-Harris*,[31] which was decided in 2002, upheld a program of substantial assistance for education at religious schools. Although the division of Justices was 5–4, one cannot imagine the Court returning to anything like the *Everson* perspective. The sense that religious schools are overwhelmingly Roman Catholic and that these strongly inculcate that religion has diminished with the growth of other religious schools and the sharply decreasing number of nuns and priests available to teach at Catholic schools. Antagonism toward Roman Catholicism as a religion has also lessened greatly, in large part because of changes within the church itself. Finally, once the Court has approved substantial assistance, as it did in *Zelman*, it would be very hard to step backward and invalidate programs created in reliance on its own ruling.

The *Zelman* case involved an Ohio program designed to aid education for low-income families in Cleveland, a city in which the schools had "[for] more than a generation . . . been among the worst performing public schools in the Nation."[32] Parents of children in private schools received vouchers for as much as 90 percent of tuition up to $2,250, which they made payable to the schools. To be eligible, schools could not discriminate on the basis of race, religion, or ethnic background, and they could not "advocate or foster unlawful behavior or teach hatred of any person or group on the basis of race, ethnicity, national origin, or religion."[33] During a recent year of operation, 82 percent of the participating schools, enrolling 96 percent of the benefiting students, had had a religious affiliation. In addition to the private school tuition program, the state had also tried to improve the city's education by funding community schools that local school boards ran and magnet schools that emphasized particular kinds of subjects.

Chief Justice Rehnquist's opinion for the Court relied on the program's neutrality with respect to religion, the secular objective of the assistance, and the range of choices available to parents whose decisions to send children to religious schools would be "genuine and independent."[34] Justice Souter's dissent emphasized that the degree of aid flowing to schools far exceeded that in any previous case, and that the maximum amount of tuition rendered the program less than neutral because religious schools operating on lower budgets could benefit in a way most nonreligious private schools could not.[35] He worried about increasing state control of religious perspectives, including the anti-discrimination provision[36] and the specific "hatred" restraint upon what schools could teach about differing religious beliefs and groups. Souter also noted a concern developed more fully in a dissent by Justice Breyer, that religious divisiveness may be produced by a scramble for public money.[37]

How should the Court be dealing with financial assistance that goes directly or indirectly to religious schools? That question poses fundamental issues about how the Establishment Clause should be viewed and the respective values of formal and contextual approaches. A preliminary question is whether schools should be treated differently from other institutions with religious connections. That hospitals, adoption agencies, and private welfare organizations can receive funds for activities that do not directly promote their religious ideas is well settled. Are religious schools essentially similar, or does teaching that is related to religion more closely connect to what churches themselves largely do, promoting particular religious ideas and practices? For those who take the latter view, the concern that taxpayers should not have to provide financial support for the promulgation of religious doctrines, an idea that traces back to James Madison's Memorial and Remonstrance,[38] may lead to a conclusion that legislatures and courts should sharply limit aid to religious education.

If one starts with the premise that government aid should not be going directly toward the promotion of religious ideas, that by itself does not resolve critical issues about the right judicial approach. Is the main concern what the government formally provides, what it seeks to do, or what the actual effects will be? As in *Zelman*, the government's approach may be formally neutral and carry forward a legitimate secular objective, and the direct assistance may go to families, not religious institutions. But the overwhelming amount of aid that ends up in private schools is going to religious schools.

Under a contextual approach, what matters could include the percentage of funds that goes to religious schools, the extent to which these funds promote religious activities, whether parents have a genuine free choice about where to send their children to school, how much the government is encroaching upon what the schools choose to do, and whether the prospect of aid is likely to cause religious divisiveness. Earlier chapters have explored competing benefits and drawbacks of formal and contextual standards of decision; but religion poses a special problem with the latter. Not only may a particular assessment be debatable, but the court's engagement in it may itself constitute an undesirable government involvement with religious practices. This concern, which affects the desirability of any standard of "pervasively sectarian," also relates to determinations of when the percentage of aid going to religious schools becomes too high, exactly how far money indirectly assists religious elements, and to what extent government conditions may impair the freedom of religious schools. One cannot put aside the last concern on the ground that no school need participate in a program, because schools are under considerable pressure to conform to conditions if the resulting aid is significant, and the whole society has an interest in the government's not being too closely intertwined with religious practices.

These various concerns are lessened if courts accept formally neutral programs so long as aid does not go overwhelmingly to religious schools, parents have some genuine choice, and the conditions set by the government do not severely impair what the religious schools aspire to do. This is apparently the approach in *Zelman*, although it does seem to me that Justice Souter raises a genuine concern that the program is not "neutral" in effect if secular schools are almost inevitably more expensive and thus less likely to accept students supported by limited government funds.

A sharper variation of the issue of choice would occur if a state adopted a similar program that applied to a small school district in which the only private school was of a particular religious denomination. That parents' only choice would be between public and religious education might not be troubling if the public schools were excellent, but the pressure on parents would be great if the only private school afforded an education far superior to that in the public schools. Using government funds in such a circumstance would create serious establishment problems, including what kind of "neutrality" should count. With its confidence that Cleveland parents did have a genuine choice, the *Zelman* Court was able to avoid this problem.

One important issue about financial assistance to religious schools is whether states can, by constitution or statute, impose stricter limits than those derived from the federal Establishment Clause. In fact, a majority of states do have such restrictions in their state constitutions, commonly referred to as Blaine Amendments. Although the Supreme Court has upheld one application of such a restriction, their status in other contexts has yet to be resolved. I postpone discussion of this problem for the section that addresses conflicts of free exercise and no establishment values.

B. Tax Exemptions

Key forms of actual financial assistance are tax exemptions. In contrast to direct grants of government money, these have been accepted since the country's origin and play a critical role in the financial survival of churches and other religious groups. Relevant organizational exemptions take many forms, most notably from state property taxes and taxes on income connected to religious functions. Relief is also given indirectly by deductions from taxable income for individuals who contribute to religious organizations. Narrower special concessions include a cleric not having to count as income the church's provision of a parsonage in which to live.

Although exemptions may have financial effects similar to those of grants, two core differences matter. In principle, the government's imposition of a tax represents a kind of interference or involvement with religious activity, and the failure to demand money is a form of nonengagement. A practical concern about taxing church property is how it should be evaluated—according to its use as a church, or according to its market value? Under the latter approach, which makes good sense for most assessments of property, a church in the middle of a commercial part of a city with surrounding skyscrapers might be forced to move because the property tax is very high. And if officials assessed value according to use as a church, should they estimate what another church would pay for the property or calculate in some other way? Whatever their formal approach, assessors might be influenced by their views about particular religious groups. These concerns generate substantial reasons for the government not to be involved in estimates of the value of church property.

That the Establishment Clause does not preclude substantial exemptions was solidly established in 1970 by *Walz v. Tax Commission of New York*,[39] which upheld exemptions from property taxes required by the state constitution. For the Court, Chief Justice Burger emphasized that these exemptions constituted a reasonable response to the dangers of government involvement with religion. Only Justice Douglas dissented.

The serious practical questions about the constitutionality of tax exemptions concern their breadth. One absolutely clear point is that such exemptions cannot directly favor some religions over others; they must be neutral in that respect. In *Larson v. Valente*, discussed below in Section III on free exercise, the Supreme Court struck down a Minnesota law that imposed more onerous requirements on religious groups that raised most of their money from nonmembers. Less clear than equal treatment of religious groups are the circumstances in which nonreligious and religious groups must be treated similarly. The exemptions reviewed in *Walz* extended to a range of social service organizations. Although Burger's opinion rejected the idea that a church property exemption must depend on what social services it provides, the Court did not determine whether a law could grant exemptions to religious groups and not to secular organizations that provide social services or conduct meetings of members to reflect upon fundamental issues about reality and human life. A rigorous neutrality approach would bar such classifications, but historical understanding and the premise of free exercise could support them. In the final part of this chapter, I address the complex issue of when, if ever, exemptions that relieve individuals and groups from obligations other than taxes are properly restricted to religious claims.

C. Government Messages

A core aspect of nonestablishment is that the government cannot advocate particular religious beliefs and practices. Although when early states accepted general principles of nonestablishment, the fundamental soundness of Protestant Christianity was still assumed in many public schools and in other settings, the government is now barred from asserting that any one religious outlook is correct. And, as settled by a 1961 case,[40] the government cannot require officials to take an oath that includes a belief in God.

The modern practical problems concern less direct connections and forms of practice that may be regarded as very mild support. Among these issues are how the lines should be drawn between the permitted and the forbidden, and whether judges need to make certain accessions to public sentiment that they properly decline to explain in these terms, a question posed by the status of "under God" in the Pledge of Allegiance.

1. Devotional Practices in Schools

Many of the earliest and the most important cases about government involvement with religious messages have dealt with devotional practices, teaching, and uses of space within public schools. In 1962 and 1963, a decade and a half after *Everson*, the Supreme Court held that the Establishment Clause bars school-sponsored prayers and Bible readings. In *Engel v. Vitale*,[41] the Court decided that New York's public school classes could not begin the day with a nondenominational prayer including "Almighty God," which had been composed by the State Board of Regents. A year later, in *Abington School District v. Schempp*,[42] it reached the same conclusion about Bible reading, a practice it regarded as indisputably religious. In this case, Justice Clark announced for the Court the first two prongs of what became the standard Establishment Clause test laid out in *Lemon v. Kurtzman*: "there must be a secular legislative purpose and a primary effect that neither advances nor inhibits religion."[43] Although these decisions about prayers and Bible reading did not affect the country in the profound way of *Brown v. Board of Education* or *Roe v. Wade*, they did rule out practices engaged in by many schools and were decidedly unpopular among large groups of citizens.

Three decades later, the Court, 5–4, extended the school prayer ban to graduation ceremonies[44] and after that to football games.[45] Among the prayer cases, graduation is the most troublesome issue because some students and parents feel that acknowledging the place of God is important at profound stages of their lives. But the problem remains that graduation prayers both endorse a religious view and cannot fit the religious views of everyone.[46]

A less straightforward issue about prayers concerns the moment of silence in public schools authorized by most states. In its only full consideration of that practice, the 1985 Supreme Court struck down an Alabama law because the legislature had specifically amended an existing authorization of silence for "meditation" to include "voluntary prayer," which the bill's sponsor urged would encourage prayer.[47] This was sufficient to persuade six Justices that the law lacked a secular purpose. However, given the concurring opinions of Justices O'Connor and Powell, a majority was clearly willing to accept most moments of silence.

O'Connor indicated that such a law would be all right if it did "not favor the child who chooses to pray" or convey the message that the child "should" pray.[48] This exact language is doubly obscuring. If only silence is involved, no child will be practically favored or disfavored by what she is doing with her mind and emotions. And, if students are aware that the moment of silence in this context[49] is basically designed to allow and even encourage prayer, they would rightly see it as promoting prayer even if not given the message that they "*should*" pray. Thus, whether this amounts to an endorsement of prayer is not resolvable by the two simple criteria Justice O'Connor offered. The real issue should be seen as whether this opportunity, created largely to allow a form of prayer, should be accepted because it does not represent a particular religious view or impose any outlook or practices on students. If one believes, as I do, that this degree of accommodation to religious desires is appropriate, it undercuts the apparently simple standard that government practices within schools may in no way favor religion.

2. What May Be Taught

Although public schools may not promote the truth of religious doctrines, they can, and should, provide students with information about the crucial place of religious understandings in the history of human societies; they can also include religious texts as examples of literature, and use religious compositions in music classes and performances. Although discerning what amounts to approval of religious doctrines is not always simple, drawing such a line is necessary if schools are not to obscure or minimize the role religion has played in human history.

Two questions complicate the notion of exactly what counts as religion and what to do about teachings at odds with religious views. In most circumstances, saying whether a particular perspective is religious or not is simple, but there are exceptions. In *Malnak v. Yogi*, the Third Circuit had to determine if a course in Transcendental Meditation was religious.[50] Its answer was "yes," and in a concurring opinion, Judge Adams developed a threefold test that looks at concerns with fundamental questions, claims to comprehensive truth, and formal signs and practices like those of accepted religions.[51] This chapter does not delve into what exactly counts as religion and how courts should determine that, but that categorization is needed for both the Establishment and Free Exercise Clauses, and no single criterion suffices, given the wide variety of beliefs and practices perceived as religious. Elsewhere, I have defended an analogical approach that considers how far a wide range of factors that combine in what is typically religious are present in what is disputably religious.[52] No approach to this issue is perfect, and one cannot deny that in practical applications, officials and judges may end up favoring more widely accepted religious views. Nonetheless, for most circumstances, this flexible approach works better for unfamiliar minority religions than no test at all or a single factor test.

Different issues about religious perspectives are whether public schools violate the Establishment Clause if they do not teach material because it offends religious views, or if they instruct students about religiously based options without endorsing them. Obviously, a school cannot be constitutionally barred from all teaching that is at odds with any religious perspective. To take extreme, silly examples, schools could not be foreclosed from teaching the earth is round if a few people still believe God made it flat, or from teaching about likely future consequences of various practices, such as air pollution, if some believe God will bring the earth to an end in one month. The important question is whether states or individual schools may decide not to teach certain subjects because they convey claims of truth that many religious persons deny. In 1968, in *Epperson v. Arkansas*,[53] the Supreme Court held that an Arkansas law that forbade teaching that humans descended from lower orders of animals was an unconstitutional implementation of a particular religious view. Two decades later, it held that teachers who teach evolution could not also be required to teach creation science since that would constitute an advancement of religion.[54]

To what extent views that connect to religious perspectives should be offered to students presents a complex set of questions with which the Supreme Court has yet to grapple.[55] Two important variables are the degree to which what a school course presents is grounded in objective criteria of truth and how far those criteria can provide answers. Perhaps to oversimplify slightly, natural science is based on objective criteria; there is, for example, hard empirical evidence that the world has existed for millions of years and that life on Earth has developed progressively. Thus, a simple version of creationism that God created the world in six ordinary days a few thousand years ago is not really a "scientific" alternative. It does not belong in a science course, and if it is put there, it is the advancement of religion in opposition to science. However, science cannot tell us why anything exists at all. Nor can it prove that natural evolution explains all human development without any degree of involvement of "intelligent design" any more than a doctor could show decisively that a person's recovery from serious illness involved no degree of divine intervention. Teachers in science courses appropriately indicate limitations on what science can actually establish. More controversially, they should also be able to indicate briefly various competing views, including religious ones, on the unprovable matters.

For school subjects lacking a solidly based objective way to determine what is true, presenting religiously based options is defensible, in contrast to including creation science in biology. Suppose a course covers moral views about how people should live their lives. In that context, excluding all reference to religious perspectives would be troublingly slanted. A teacher might meet this concern by explaining that although she covers only nonreligious perspectives, many people believe proper moral behavior is closely tied to religious premises. Or, she could describe certain religious perspectives (so long as she does not promote any one of them as true). Neither of these approaches should be seen as violating the Establishment Clause.

3. Indirect Assistance and Use of Facilities

Different connections between public schools and religions involve the use of school facilities and other indirect assistance. In its second important Establishment Clause case, the Court in *McCollum v. Board of Education*[56] held invalid a "released time" program under which teachers of various religious faiths taught classes once a week in public schools to students whose parents wished them to attend. Other students were required to stay in school for that period, effectively in a study hall. Justice Black wrote the Court's opinion that, given the use of public facilities, the cooperation of school authorities with the interfaith council, and the fact that pupils "compelled by law to go to school for secular education were released in part from their legal duty upon the condition that they attend religious classes," the practice violated the Establishment Clause. Four years later, in *Zorach v. Clauson*,[57] the Court shifted ground when presented with a similar system in New York in which excused students went to religious classes off school premises. Parents still had to choose between sending their children to religious instruction or keeping them inside a public school classroom in which no actual teaching was taking place. With Justice Black dissenting, Justice Douglas, who subsequently became the most separationist of the Justices, wrote an opinion for the Court that looked favorably on efforts to encourage religious instruction that did not prefer any particular denominations. He compared this accommodation to allowing individual parents to have their children excused from school for special religious occasions. Of course, when schools grant such individual requests for religious and nonreligious occasions, ordinary class instruction does not stop; disregarding this difference, the Court accepted the state's use of compulsory school attendance to indirectly encourage religious instruction.

Issues about the use of faculties, when coerced school attendance is not involved, concern whether any particular forms of religious activity are constitutionally foreclosed, and, if not, whether the state may choose to make its facilities available only for nonreligious purposes. As the law has developed, the Court has permitted religious activities of all kinds and has not allowed those to be disfavored in relation to nonreligious counterparts. In 1981, the Court struck down a rule of the University of Missouri that registered student groups could use its facilities for other purposes but not religious worship or teaching.[58] Nine years later, it sustained a federal statute under which public secondary schools receiving financial assistance had to provide equal access for religious and nonreligious groups.[59] The Court subsequently considered the denial of school facilities to a group wishing to show a film series addressing family life from an evangelical Christian perspective. The application of New York's law according to which school boards making space available to private groups were not to include those with religious purposes was unanimously held in this context to be invalid viewpoint discrimination.

In 2001, the Court reached a similar conclusion about a Good News (Christian) Club for children ages six to twelve that wished to meet in an elementary school building right after school.[60] For the majority, Justice Thomas rejected the argument that religious worship and proselytizing are relevantly different from ordinary speech, and held that the exclusion was unacceptable viewpoint discrimination. In emphasizing that parents could freely decide on their children's participation, Justice Thomas did not address the possibility that small children, aware that friends and classmates would go to a religious club after school, might feel an incentive or even pressure to do likewise, and that this could yield permission from parents not wanting to upset their children. In contrast to the Court's ruling, I believe public school authorities should have the latitude to decide whether to avoid the risks of such pressures on small children and their parents.

When presented with the denial of university finances to student publications that "primarily" promoted or manifested particular religious beliefs, the Court also concluded, here 5–4, that the Establishment Clause could not justify this viewpoint discrimination,[61] even though the consequence was that public university funding would be used to convey a particular religious message. These various cases illustrate the tension between ideas that freedom of speech and association should not depend on content, and "establishment" concerns about government promotion of religion and pressures on people, especially children, to become involved in religious practices. The Court has consistently treated the value of equal ability to communicate as dominant, so long as the government is not directly endorsing a religious message.

4. Government Communication

A different form of government involvement with religion is what it, or its officials, communicate directly. The Establishment Clause imposes no actual restrictions on what officials may say, although, if legislators make clear that they are passing a law to serve a religious objective, the law will likely fail the "purpose" component of the *Lemon* test. In special settings in which persons are not free to go where they wish, notably prisons and the military, the government may actually pay for chaplains and provide religious services.[62] Based largely on continued historical acceptance, the Supreme Court has upheld the hiring of chaplains to open legislative sessions with prayers, and in 2014, accepted prayers to open town meetings that were specifically Christian, rather than nonsectarian.[63]

The primary issues that the Court has faced about government speech have involved various religious texts and symbols in public places. For many of those cases, the dominant approach has been an "endorsement" test, which, as the next section explains, presents fascinating questions about how what really matters relates to a test's desirable judicial formulation. In at least one setting, the endorsement test also raises the question whether the Supreme Court should, in effect, occasionally fail to apply a test according to its terms because a mild concession to competing public opinion is socially preferable.

The primary controversies over actual texts have involved displays of the Ten Commandments in public schools and in state office buildings. Not until 1980 did the Supreme Court decide a dispute over this use, perhaps because long-standing practices reflecting a Christian perspective had only recently begun to seem problematic. In *Stone v. Graham*,[64] the Court struck down a Kentucky statute that required public schools to post the Ten Commandments in every classroom. Given the sacredness of the text, the law's purpose was "plainly religious."[65] A sharply divided Court reached a similar conclusion in 2005 regarding the display of the King James version of the Ten Commandments on the walls of Kentucky county courthouses.[66] Although the counties had responded to an earlier challenge by including nonreligious texts, such as the Bill of Rights, and had posted an explanation of how the Ten Commandments provided a moral background for these, the Court's majority still found that the primary purpose violated neutrality by advancing religion. Justice Scalia, who himself has never accepted the appropriateness of a secular purpose test, wrote for the four dissenters that an adequate secular purpose was present. With two of the other dissenters agreeing, he also rejected the basic notion that the state needs to be neutral about religion.

In another case decided at the same time, the Court permitted a monument inscribed with the Ten Commandments on the grounds of the Texas State Capitol.[67] Four dissenters considered the monument, with "I AM the LORD thy God" in especially large letters, as conveying a religious message.[68] With eight of the Justices voting the same way in the Texas and Kentucky cases, Justice Breyer's shift determined the outcome. He acknowledged that the text in Texas had a religious message, but believed it also had a historical and moral one.[69] Given the presence of the monument for forty years without controversy and it being surrounded by other nonreligious monuments, Breyer did not believe people regarded it as a detrimental favoring of religious beliefs; and a striking down of the monument might well exhibit a kind of hostility toward religion that would generate disputes about other displays and cause the very divisiveness the Establishment Clause was designed to avoid.

Other cases the Supreme Court has decided have involved religious symbols, Christmas crèches, a Chanukah menorah, and a cross. In *Lynch v. Donnelly*,[70] the Court allowed a crèche in a Christmas display owned by the city and erected in a shopping center. Chief Justice Burger's opinion for the Court rejected a strict application of the *Lemon* test. It suggested various bases for acceptance, including the secularity of the display as a whole, the historical acceptance of this kind of support or endorsement of religion, and the slight magnitude of any support of a religious perspective. Justice O'Connor, concurring, first proposed the "endorsement" test for reviewing such practices,[71] a standard we shall examine shortly. In the next case involving public displays, the Court held that a crèche could not stand alone on the Grand Staircase of the County Courthouse, but a Chanukah menorah could be placed next to a Christmas tree outside a government building.[72] Seven Justices voted the same way about both displays, four believing that the government appropriately recognizes the role of religion in society, and three concluding that the displays impermissibly showed a favoritism toward particular religions. The swing voters, Justices Blackmun and O'Connor, did not believe that the menorah, standing next to the Christmas tree, was conveying a religious message.

In a religious symbol case that presented a different kind of issue, the Supreme Court ruled that when Ohio allowed a wide range of unattended displays in its Capitol Square, the regulating board improperly refused to allow the Ku Klux Klan to erect a cross.[73] Doing so constituted an impermissible form of content discrimination as to speech.

During the last decade, the Supreme Court considered two cases involving displays with religious significance that were not resolved in terms of the religion clauses. In *Pleasant Grove City v. Summum*,[74] a city park displayed a donated monument of the Ten Commandments. When a minority Gnostic Christianity group wanted to erect a monument with what it considered an alternative "true" version of those commandments, the city refused. The group claimed a violation of its freedom of speech, not relying on the religion clauses. The Court treated the dispute under the Free Speech Clause, rejecting the claim that displaying a monument with one point of view and refusing to accept a competing perspective was content-based discrimination. Its reason was that the existing display was a form of government speech, and the government was not required to present views contrary to its own speech. When one puts this case together with those allowing some government displays of symbols with religious significance, a consequence of the result is that advocates of competing religious perspectives may be disadvantaged.[75] Taken by itself, this is regrettable; but it follows from the premises that the government may display some texts or symbols that have both secular and religious significance and that, unless it is open to private displays in general, it need not accept each proposed display for government property. Nevertheless, courts should be able to engage in enough review of officials' actions to see that cities are not obviously trying to promote one religious view over another.

Salazar v. Buono[76] involved a display of a cross in a national park to commemorate soldiers lost in World War I. After the park service declined to allow a Buddhist display there, a district court issued an injunction against continued display of the cross, a decision upheld upon review by the Ninth Circuit. Congress responded by transferring the property holding the cross to the Veterans of Foreign Wars. Because the government had not appealed the Ninth Circuit's ruling on the government's displaying the cross, the Supreme Court considered only the transfer and did not resolve the underlying issue. Justice Kennedy's plurality opinion did indicate that the display of the cross was constitutional because it was embraced as a war memorial with the transfer of land. As Christopher Lund has noted, one cannot think of a cross as purely secular; its significance as a memorial for those who have died is not detached from its core religious significance. Thus, accepting government displays entails a conclusion that the secular significance in context dominates the underlying religious meaning.[77]

Given the sharp division in the Supreme Court over when public displays with some religious significance are acceptable, and the absence of any clear standard guiding what is permitted and what is not, no one can predict with confidence what will be allowed in the future. However, noting that the key figure in the outcome of these cases has become Justice Kennedy, and that Kennedy has favored a "coercion" test over one of "neutrality" or "endorsement," Frederick Gedicks perceives the Court as moving toward acceptance of "government use of religious symbols and worship" that are broadly representative of the Judeo-Christian tradition.[78]

5. The Endorsement Test

In many of the leading cases involving displays of texts and symbols, the "endorsement" test has provided the key standard. This is not surprising, given that for some time, Justice O'Connor's vote for one side or the other was usually critical. Although this test has also been referred to in other Establishment Clause contexts, it has not really replaced other formulations outside of displays of texts and symbols. It has been mainly regarded more as an alternative to the *Lemon* test than an application of it.

The basic core of the endorsement test is clear, and it aptly bears on the permissiveness of displays. The government should not be conveying the message that it endorses a particular religious view. What is less clear is exactly how such a test should be formulated and applied. In her concurring opinion in *Lynch v. Donnelly*, Justice O'Connor proposed the test as "a clarification of our Establishment Clause doctrine." The Clause "prohibits government from making adherence to a religion relevant in any way to a person's standing in the political community."[79] The government may not endorse or disapprove of religion, sending "a message to the nonadherents that they are outsiders" and a "message to adherents that they are insiders."[80] For the audience, a statement's content depends both on the speaker's intention and the "objective" meaning in the community. With regard to the moment of silence in *Wallace v. Jaffree*, O'Connor asked whether an objective observer acquainted with religion clause values and the text, legislative history, and implementation of a statute would perceive an endorsement.[81]

Four crucial questions about the endorsement test are: (1) Does an "objective observer" approach capture what really matters? (2) How far should the perceptions of adherents and nonadherents count? (3) What kinds of insider and outsider messages are unacceptable? (4) Should even a mild, widely accepted, broad endorsement be declared invalid?

Although Justice O'Connor once criticized a "subjective" test of people's reactions on the basis that it would mean that if some passersby would perceive an endorsement, a display would be precluded,[82] this is a non sequitur. One could ask either how most people react or qualify an inquiry into actual perceptions with a test of reasonableness. If the main concern governing endorsement is how people feel they are being regarded, a form of subjective test is more directly relevant than an objective one, especially if the objective text is cast in terms of degrees of knowledge that few ordinary people will possess.

What may really be at stake here is what a court, especially an appellate court, is capable of doing. If the basic test concerned the reactions of ordinary people, these could vary in different communities, and it would be difficult for a higher court, especially the U.S. Supreme Court, to determine that a local district court judge had failed in her assessment. This problem would be especially worrisome given that citizens in many localities may regard clear support of the dominant religion as a good thing. In summary, one can defend an objective approach, despite its detachment from the actual human reactions that are central to endorsement. It is worth noting that under an objective approach that employs a fully informed observer, distinguishing "purpose" from "effects" would be unlikely since such an observer would not perceive an endorsement if he concluded that the government had no aim to endorse.

Whether we are talking about an objective evaluation or actual reactions, whose responses are crucial? Perhaps adherents and nonadherents will see things differently. When I was a public school student, we sang Christmas carols in the central hallway during the two weeks before Christmas vacation, and the older students put on a Christmas pageant. I did not perceive any of this as a school endorsement of Christianity, but I now wonder how my Jewish companions felt. Adherents may take various symbols for granted that nonadherents perceive as communicating a message that they are outsiders. If the central concern is that the government not convey messages of endorsement, the probable and reasonable reactions of those who may feel they are being cast as outsiders should carry special weight.

Justice O'Connor's reference to "standing in the political community" might be taken to refer to whether one considers oneself an equal citizen or equally accepted within the social community. We can conceive of a government message that conveys: "You are entitled to all the rights and privileges of a citizen, but we want to let you know your views are perverse and at odds with the sentiments of our community." Under a proper endorsement test, it should be enough that the government is effectively casting nonadherents as social outsiders.

"Under God" in the Pledge of Allegiance strikingly raises the issue whether any endorsement test should be strictly applied and how candid judges should be when they explain their reasons for a ruling. The Pledge of Allegiance was adopted by Congress in 1942; in 1954, "under God" was added, in order, according to the sponsor, "to contrast this country's belief in God with the Soviet Union's embrace of atheism."[83] In 2004, the Supreme Court reviewed a Ninth Circuit decision that the inclusion of "under God" in the pledge said in public school violated the endorsement test.[84] The Supreme Court managed to avoid a decision by determining that the noncustodial father who challenged the law lacked standing. Among the three Justices who reached the merits and voted to uphold the practice, Chief Justice Rehnquist treated reciting the pledge as a patriotic exercise that did not involve expressing fidelity to any particular faith.[85] Justice O'Connor, exploring the issue in some detail, considered the Pledge an act of "ceremonial deism," which commemorates the role of religion in our history and solemnizes occasions, rather than invoking divine provenance and endorsing religion.[86]

O'Connor's stated position on this is extremely unconvincing. She said that no particular religious view is being endorsed, but clearly, the existence of a single God is asserted, a view at odds with those who believe in multiple gods or are atheist or agnostic. And, whatever one might conclude about adults who handle money that says "In God we Trust," or who recite the Pledge of Allegiance, this controversy involved the Pledge being said every day in public school elementary classes. One cannot expect third graders to say to themselves, "'Under God' here is not really an assertion that God exists. It is a historical reference and solemnizing form of speech." Justice O'Connor is explicit that there "are no *de minimis* violations of the Constitution—no constitutional harms so slight that the courts are obliged to ignore them."[87] But, in truth, one cannot escape the conclusion that having elementary school students recite the Pledge as part of the school day will be perceived by those children who do not simply utter the words without thinking as asserting the existence of a single, beneficent God. That such perceptions do occur was confirmed in a seminar of mine in which an atheist student spoke about how the Pledge's being recited in school made him uncomfortable and feel like an outsider.

Given public acceptance of the Pledge, its long-standing use, and the mildness and breadth of its endorsement, we can certainly understand the Supreme Court's hesitancy to bar it from public schools. We can also understand that it would be hard to draw an explicit line between mild and unacceptable endorsements. Perhaps what makes the most sense practically is acceptance of very modest endorsements when other values are substantially served,[88] although this position raises the general question of whether, in their opinions, Justices making minor qualifications in standard approaches should be explicit or, instead, should be less than candid and articulate what are ostensibly sharper boundaries, even if they fail to stick to them.

III. FREE EXERCISE

The basic principle underlying the Free Exercise Clause is that the government should not interfere with people's liberty to decide what they believe about religion and to engage in religious practices. Of course, not every religious practice is accepted; a state will treat religious sacrifice of human beings as murder, but it must, at a minimum, have some secular reason to forbid forms of religious worship. In a world in which many people die each year because of their religious affiliation,[89] the United States is fortunate that its serious free exercise issues arise over marginal questions about the proper role of a government committed to religious freedom. The most perplexing of these questions concern when exemptions from valid laws are constitutionally required, left to legislative choice, or constitutionally forbidden because they discriminate in some form. Before focusing on exemptions, we look at simpler forms of free exercise rights.

A. Compelling and Targeting Religious Practices

Government is not permitted to compel profession of belief, to target practices because of their religious elements, or to discriminate among religions. In *Torcaso v. Watkins*,[90] the only modern case that involved a forced expression of belief, the Supreme Court held that Maryland could not refuse to allow a man to become a notary public because he refused to declare his belief in God. The basic idea underlying this decision may also be discerned in *West Virginia Board of Education v. Barnette*,[91] in which the Court, overriding an earlier case, declared that Jehovah's Witnesses had a general First Amendment right to freedom of conscience to have their children in public schools excused from a compulsory flag salute. Justice Jackson wrote for the Court: "If there is any fixed star in our constitutional constellation, it is that no official ... can prescribe what shall be orthodox in politics, nationalism, religion ... or force citizens to confess by word or act their faith therein."[92]

A targeting of religious practice was presented by *Church of the Lukumi Babalu Aye, Inc. v. City of Hialeah*.[93] The Santeria religion included rituals in which various animals, such as chickens, pigs, and sheep, were sacrificed and usually consumed by members of the religion. Faced with plans to create a Santeria house of worship, Hialeah adopted ordinances prohibiting animal sacrifice, while continuing to allow kosher slaughtering, private slaughtering of a small number of hogs or cattle per week, hunting, and the killing of animals such as dogs and cats not used for food. Writing for the Court, Justice Kennedy concluded that the aim and effect of the law was to suppress the central element of Santerian worship. A law that restricts "practices because of their religious motivation . . . is not neutral and it is invalid unless it is justified by a compelling interest and is narrowly tailored to advance that interest."[94] Although one might quibble about the exact formulation of this standard,[95] the basic constraint is indisputably sound.

A harder question about targeting is when a law is probably adopted because of religious practices, but its direct effect is to limit a harmful consequence of a dangerous practice. In various southern states, members of small charismatic Christian groups—building on a passage in the gospel of Mark about Jesus's appearance after the Resurrection[96]—handle poisonous snakes and drink poisons. Some of these states have adopted laws against handling poisonous snakes; most do not single out religion. Given that few people handle poisonous snakes *and* the vast majority who do are not hurt, a state's passing of such a law is almost certainly a response to the religious practice. In these states, equally dangerous activities, such as skydiving and boxing, are allowed. However, protecting human life by forbidding a dangerous activity is a legitimate secular objective. Even if legislators act partly because a particular religious view seems odd and indefensible, so long as what they do is plainly a means of genuinely protecting life and health, and their prohibition is formulated in general terms, a court should not declare that the law itself violates free exercise unless it *obviously* would not have been undertaken had the religious activities been assigned a value similar to that of other equally dangerous activities that are permitted.[97]

A different kind of treatment involves disqualification of clergy for public office. Although early in the country's history such laws were not uncommon, and they might be seen as promoting separation of church and state, the Supreme Court held in 1978 that the only such remaining law, Tennessee's, violated the free exercise clause by discriminating against clergy.[98]

Explicit discrimination among particular religions is obviously unconstitutional. In *Larson v. Valente*,[99] as already noted, the Court applied this principle to invalidate a Minnesota law that relieved all religious groups from certain reporting requirements, except those groups that raised more than 50 percent of funds from nonmembers. Since the dangers of fraud might increase when funds are coming largely from solicitation of nonmembers, the line drawn did not completely lack a secular rationale. But the legislative history adjusting statutory language indicated a clear design *not* to curtail major religious groups; and the final act reached only the unpopular minority Unification Church, colloquially known as the "Moonies." That was enough to lead most Supreme Court Justices to treat this as a "suspect" denominational preference that failed the compelling interest test.

B. Religious Exemptions

Whether laws should include religious exemptions is sharply controversial. A law that is adopted by a legislature requires certain behavior from most people: should it, or must it, create an exception for those whose religious convictions and practices are at odds with the law's demands?

The Supreme Court's first major case dealing with a free exercise claim not to be subject to a particular legal restriction involved a Mormon's 1878 challenge to his conviction for having engaged in polygamy.[100] At this stage of history, male members of the Mormon faith were considered under a religious duty, circumstances permitting, to practice polygamy. Leaving no doubt that it regarded polygamy as a despicable practice condemned by all civilized nations, the Court's primary basis for its decision was the sharp line it drew between belief and action. Relying heavily on Thomas Jefferson, the Court portrayed the original understanding as: "Congress was deprived of all legislative power over mere opinion, but was left free to reach actions which were in violation of social duties or subversive of good order."[101]

In its first application of the Fourteenth Amendment as incorporating the Free Exercise Clause, the Court in *Cantwell v. Connecticut*[102] softened the belief-action dichotomy. Overturning the conviction of a Jehovah's Witness for solicitation without having obtained a certification, it ruled that a state could not designate an administrative official to determine if a cause was religious. Regarding free exercise and free speech as closely linked here, the Court declared: "[T]he [First] Amendment embraces two concepts, freedom to believe and freedom to act. The first is absolute, but in the nature of things, the second cannot be. Conduct remains subject to regulation for the protection of society.... In every case the power to regulate must be so exercised as not ... unduly to infringe the protected freedom."[103]

Having two years earlier denied the claim of an Orthodox Jewish clothing store owner that he should be free of a Sunday Closing Law,[104] the Court in 1963 reached a high-water mark for free exercise rights to religious exemptions in *Sherbert v. Verner.*[105] A Seventh-Day Adventist claimed that the state violated her rights by denying her unemployment compensation because she refused to work on Saturday, her Sabbath. According to South Carolina's law, persons could get such benefits only if they were "available for work," and an administrative commission determined that Sherbert had not qualified. Although Justice Brennan's opinion for the Court did refer to a distinct provision favoring workers who were conscientiously opposed to working on Sundays, the opinion's main emphasis was not on religious discrimination. Rather, if a disqualification from benefits burdens someone's free exercise of religion, that may be justified only by a "compelling state interest in the regulation of a subject within the State's constitutional power to regulate."[106] Finding no showing of a danger of spurious claims, and expressing doubt that evidence of such a risk could justify forcing someone to choose between the loss of benefits because she follows her religion or working despite her religious beliefs, the Court sustained Sherbert's claim.

As we shall see, both the formulation and the application of the "compelling interest test" in this context have figured in controversies over how claimed religious exemptions should be evaluated and what legal standard is best for that.

One crucial point in this respect is difficulty of application. If, as later formulations indicate, it takes a "substantial" burden to set the test in motion, how do other officials and judges determine whether a burden on religion is that great? And what is enough to make the government's interest "compelling"? The latter evaluation is especially tricky if what judges are really doing is comparing the degree of interference with religious exercise against the government's need—counting an interest of a certain force as "compelling" if its impairment of religion is modest but not if it is very great. Another element of the test is how strictly to view whether the government can accomplish its compelling objectives by less restrictive means.

A special concern about this overall test for free exercise protection is that its application by secular officials requires too great an involvement with religion when assessing the force of religious claims. One aspect of this worry is that in practice, the test may disfavor unpopular minority religions, but this difficulty is not crucial, given that the obvious alternative of no required exemptions is still less favorable for minority religions.

A second major point concerns the special character of the free exercise "compelling interest test." The judicial use of the test in this setting has never really fit with how it is employed in its two main areas. One of these, as we saw in the last chapter, is when the government directly interferes with free speech. The other, treated here and also in Chapter 12, involves outright discrimination against groups on dubious grounds. Formulated in cases reviewing active interferences with freedom of expression and racial discrimination, the test has been close to impossible to satisfy, being used to strike down legislation and administrative actions that were highly suspect.

The exemption cases are different. The law being reviewed is not itself "suspect," and the claim that is being made is that a person or group deserves special treatment not afforded to others. The government is contending only that it should be able to treat everyone the same way under a valid law. Not surprisingly, neither the Supreme Court nor the lower courts have applied the "compelling interest test" in exemption cases with the rigor employed for challenges to racial categorizations disfavoring minorities and direct interferences with speech. Realistically, this version of the test has really been an "intermediate standard of review," somewhere between "rational basis" and an "extremely demanding" test of government action. That was perhaps most clearly demonstrated in the Supreme Court's denial of a claim by an Amish employer not to pay Social Security taxes. The employer urged that forced payment violated his religion and did not serve the public interest in assuring the financial security of former workers since all of his employees were Amish, and the Amish do not believe in accepting such benefits from the government.[107]

Even though its application of the compelling interest test—and that of lower courts—was not stringent in this context, the Supreme Court has been inclined to employ a broad sense of what qualifies as a religious claim. In 1970, a plurality interpreted the Selective Service Act exemption from the draft for objections based on "religious training and belief" very expansively, to include someone who rested his claim on strong personal convictions.[108] Nearly two decades after *Sherbert v. Verner*, the Court made clear in *Thomas v. Review Board*[109] that for a constitutional claim, a person's religious conviction against a form of work did not have to be based on a broadly shared premise of a religious denomination. A Jehovah's Witness who was unwilling to help make weapons was denied a layoff when he was moved to a department making turrets for tanks; he then resigned. Chief Justice Burger's opinion for the Court quickly rejected the state court's strange conclusion that Thomas's objection was not religious, even though he might have been struggling with his beliefs and not been able to articulate them precisely. "[R]eligious beliefs need not be acceptable, logical, consistent, or comprehensible to others in order to merit First Amendment protection."[110] A court's narrow function was to examine an individual's own convictions. In terms of fairness to the persons claiming religious objections to certain forms of work or days of doing work, this approach is definitely sound, but it does require either nearly blanket acceptance or a careful examination of what an individual person claims to believe.

The major Supreme Court decision sustaining a free exercise exemption claim not involving unemployment benefits was *Wisconsin v. Yoder*.[111] Amish parents objected to complying with a state law requiring attendance at school by children who were fourteen and fifteen years old. They believed that after eighth grade, children needed to develop skills of manual work and self-reliance within the Amish community and should not be taught values that conflict with their religion. One expert had testified that high school could harm Amish children psychologically, and that requiring their attendance could eventually destroy the community as it existed.[112] Despite the clear secular value of children attending high school, the Supreme Court upheld the religious claim. In answer to the state's argument that teenagers needed to attend high school to become "self-reliant and self-sufficient participants in society," Chief Justice Burger responded that the Amish had proved to be a successful social unit rejecting ordinary public welfare, whose members had a "valuable vocational" training that would prevent them from becoming burdens on society even if they left the community.[113] Further, the effective functioning of the community answered the claim that more education was needed for them "to participate effectively and intelligently in our democratic process."[114]

Notable features of the *Yoder* case are these: (1) the Court did not really answer one of the state's bases for compulsory education; (2) the result appears to depend substantially on special characteristics of the Amish; (3) the Court effectively accepted a significant reduction in a young person's freedom of choice, at least as understood in one plausible way; and (4) the Court clearly distinguished the force of this religious claim from any nonreligious claims.

In terms of the first feature, the Amish do not participate in any typical way in the political process, and their way of preparing teenagers for life within their community does not train them "to participate effectively and intelligently in our democratic process" in the ordinary sense. Self-reliant withdrawal is not active participation. Without quite saying so, the Court implicitly decided that the value of preparing individuals to participate actively in ordinary political life was not a sufficient basis to counter the religious convictions and practices of the Amish.

The number of young Amish men and women who leave the community historically has been about 20 percent.[115] Suppose that a relatively new religious group with otherwise identical views did a much poorer job of training their own youngsters, that 80 percent left the denomination, and many of these ended up being supported by public welfare. The acceptability of parents in this group depriving teenagers of education after eighth grade would seem strikingly less, and in *Yoder*, the Court did emphasize the coherence, community, self-reliance, and competence of the Amish. Thus, the decision rests significantly on the quality of this religious group in ways that extend beyond the sincerity of its religious outlook. Under such an approach, secular officials and courts considering a possible exemption must appraise carefully just how a religious group functions.

If we assume that the teenagers leaving school agree with their parents, one might nonetheless say that they have not reached a level of maturity at which they really understand possible options and can make many fundamental choices. Thus, the state could urge that further education is needed to give them the liberty of other citizens. The problem here is that the very exposure to competing views and a highly diverse culture could undercut the kind of deep adherence to their own community that most Amish children develop. Thus, the *Yoder* Court implicitly had to decide whether the intense interests of a close-knit religious community outweighed an increase of free choice conceived as a more fully informed assessment of alternative ways of living.

No doubt partly because of the value of education and the risk of fraud by a parent who, for basic economic reasons, chooses to have a child stay home and help out with the parents' work, the Court, referring to Henry David Thoreau, stated that one whose choice for such a life "was philosophical and personal rather than religious . . . does not rise to the demands of the Religion Clauses."[116] Thus, in contrast to the draft cases in which Justices stretched the classification of views as religious, here, the Court explicitly stated what views would fall outside this classification and thus fail to receive similar constitutional protection.

In 1990, the Supreme Court radically changed direction and shifted away from the compelling interest test for most exemption claims. *Employment Division v. Smith*[117] involved members of the Native American Church who ingested peyote as the sacramental center of their worship services. In contrast to some other states, Oregon had no legislative exemption for its prohibition against taking peyote. Although the state did not enforce the law against religious users, it did refuse unemployment compensation to two workers who were dismissed from a private drug rehabilitation organization for ingesting peyote in church services. After the Oregon Supreme Court determined that the failure to provide an exemption violated the federal Free Exercise Clause, the U.S. Supreme Court ruled to the contrary, despite the absence of evidence that this use of peyote had harmful effects or somehow spread to unsupervised private use. The result would have been very hard to reach under either a genuine compelling interest test or intermediate scrutiny, given the centrality of peyote for religious practice and the lack of evidence of harm.[118]

Writing for the Court, Justice Scalia rejected the compelling interest test, instead ruling that if a law is not directed against religion and applies generally, a person or group has no free exercise right to violate it; an "individual's religious beliefs [do not] excuse him from compliance with an otherwise valid law prohibiting conduct that the State is free to regulate."[119] Justice Scalia's opinion not only represents a wholesale rejection of what was then prevailing doctrine, but it also contains a good deal that is troubling and difficult to defend.

The heart of the opinion is that courts should not have to decide when religious claims are strong enough to triumph over state interests of variant strength. If the state really had to show a compelling interest to cover religious motivated conduct, that "would be courting anarchy."[120] Against the argument that the compelling interest test might be invoked only if the prohibited conduct was central to a religion, Scalia responded that judges cannot appropriately determine the importance of various religious ideas in different religions. The strong preference here for a relatively formal test that does not involve the assessment and weighing of considerations in context fits a consistent theme of Justice Scalia's jurisprudence. What is different from most of his constitutional opinions is the absence of reliance on original understanding. Scalia's opinion is clear that legislatures, though not required, can choose to grant religious exemptions. By leaving such decisions to the political branches, the Court was accepting the reality that dominant religions could end up better off than minority religions, especially unpopular ones.

For example, historically, when laws against the use of alcohol have been adopted, exemptions have been made for religious use in communion. Yet drinking a small amount in a service, which may lead some participants to seek more later, poses risks to human welfare that are similar in one respect to the ingestion of peyote at issue in the *Smith* case.

Justice Scalia's treatment of then prevailing law is impossible to defend except as a strategic device that rejects the basic principles on which prior decisions were based without really saying so. He notes that the Supreme Court has not often ruled that free exercise requires that legal prohibitions contain religious exemptions; but his survey of the law does not include what had happened in lower federal courts and state courts after *Sherbert v. Verner.* As far as readers of his opinion can tell, many courts and executive officials may have made accommodations to religious practices because of *Sherbert*'s fairly robust free exercise doctrine (one which, as noted, has never been applied as a highly stringent compelling interest test).

Scalia's efforts to distinguish *Sherbert* and *Yoder* carry him into stated positions that are impossible to defend. With respect to *Sherbert,* Scalia treats unemployment compensation as special, accepting the result in it and subsequent cases, but not applying their formulated standards more broadly, or resolving whether what is special about the facts of these cases might apply to other kinds of situations. Another exception Scalia identifies to the general approach of allowing legislatures to determine exemptions is "hybrid claims," the joining of free exercise with other constitutional claims. Scalia treats *Yoder* as involving hybrid claims of free exercise and parental rights.

What are the problems with this hybrid approach? We need first to distinguish two kinds of situations. Of course, if another constitutional provision, such as free speech, can alone yield a right that cannot be infringed, the assertion of a free exercise claim will not be dispositive, and the result of a *Smith* test unfavorable to such claims will not lead to a different result. But the situation Scalia is imagining is one in which each claim carries some weight, and together they are strong enough to generate the constitutional right. As an actual explanation of *Yoder,* this is weak. The *Yoder* Court did not emphasize any general parental right not to have children go to school, and it explicitly rejected the idea that any similar nonreligious claim could possibly succeed; its overwhelming emphasis was plainly on religion. Later decisions often try to accommodate previous cases whose opinions do not fit comfortably with the new results by reformulating their rationales, but the hybrid approach's problems are much more severe than its mere lack of congruity with *Yoder.* It is anomalous in three different respects.

If two constitutional provisions can combine together to generate an actual specific right, how can we be sure that one of these will never be strong enough by itself to create a right? Scalia's opinion provides no analysis of how one could conclude that in the kinds of circumstances when a hybrid claim could succeed, a free exercise claim alone will *never* be sufficient.

A practical problem with the hybrid standard is how to determine if another provision counts as being "in play." Why, for instance, could not group religious worship be seen as also involving freedom of association? Scalia's opinion does not get into how judges are to determine when the threshold of hybridness has been passed, and this has indeed proved a puzzle for judges of other courts.

Yet another practical problem is the ill fit of the hybrid approach with the basic logic of *Smith*. If a court needs to rule whether two constitutional claims together generate a right, it must determine the strength of each. The overarching rationale in *Smith* is that the difficulties of the needed contextual assessments of a compelling interest test are beyond what should be expected of courts in constitutional adjudication. That logic also applies to assessments of the weight of the religious claims when these happen to be joined by other constitutional claims. Thus, a diligent use of the hybrid approach would narrow the range of cases in which courts would have to make assessments Scalia regards as inappropriate, but it would not eliminate them.

All of these reasons leave highly uncertain just what role the extremely dubious "hybrid" proposal played in *Smith* itself, whether courts should genuinely seek to implement it, and, if so, whether they should limit its use to cases closely similar to those treated in *Smith*. These are questions the Supreme Court has yet to resolve or clarify.[121]

A crucial issue that Scalia's opinion understandably does not address is when the legislative granting of some exceptions may make it unconstitutional to fail to grant religious exemptions as well. That question carries considerable importance for the actual breadth of the *Smith* approach. While sitting as a judge on the Third Circuit Court of Appeals, Samuel Alito wrote the court's opinion in a case that held that if Newark allowed police officers to have beards for the medical reason of preventing a harmful skin condition, it also had to provide an exemption from its "no beard" rule for Sunni Muslims who regard themselves as under a religious obligation not to shave.[122] Alito's opinion does not get into whether the strength of the need for the exemption the legislature has chosen to grant matters. Were an exemption provided only to those for whom a standard restriction would threaten their lives or physical ability to function, that should not yield a required extension to religious claims. Thus, as long as *Smith* remains the law, whether a free exercise claim succeeds because of the grant of a nonreligious exemption should depend on the strength of reasons underlying that exemption. Of course, if one believes, as I do, that *Smith* itself accords inadequate respect to free exercise claims, one may welcome the broad use of other exemptions to constrain the breadth of its application.

With respect to the Free Exercise Clause, *Employment Division v. Smith* represented a radical, largely unpopular change that remains the present law. However, its practical significance has been decidedly limited because of federal and state legislation and state constitutional interpretation. In each of these ways, the scope of free exercise claims has been increased from their minimal force in *Smith,* and thus far the Supreme Court has perceived no Establishment Clause objections to such extensions.

Three years after *Smith,* Congress, with near unanimity, adopted the Religious Freedom Restoration Act (RFRA).[123] As a preface toward its articulated standard, Congress stated that "the framers ... [recognized] free exercise of religion as an unalienable right," that laws 'neutral' toward religion may burden religious exercise," that religion should be burdened only by satisfaction of a compelling interest, that this was a workable test for courts, and that *Smith* "virtually eliminated the requirement that the government justify burdens on religious exercise. . . ." The Act's purposes were "to restore the compelling interest test as set forth in Sherbert v. Verner, 374 U.S. 378 (1963) and Wisconsin v. Yoder, 406 U.S. 205 (1972)," and to provide a claim or defense to persons whose religious exercise is substantially burdened by government. The formulated test prohibits a "substantial burden" on the exercise of religion unless the government can demonstrate a compelling interest and is using the least restrictive means.

Although both its purposes and formulated standard represent Congress's unambiguous rejection of *Employment Division v. Smith,* the statute's language presents a puzzle about how it should be interpreted. Prior to *Smith,* the Supreme Court had applied much more relaxed standards than compelling interest for denials of exemptions in the military[124] and in prisons.[125] Since the statutory language contains no such exceptions, one might take it as actually broader in coverage than the Supreme Court's pre-*Smith* approach. The more important issue is how to understand the formulated test: Did Congress mean the highly stringent compelling interest test used in other contexts, or the "intermediate" standard of review that courts had actually employed? Given the strong reasons why in this context it does not make sense to employ a standard that is virtually certain to sustain a constitutional claim against legislation or official practices, the RFRA standard is rightly seen as roughly the same as the less strict approach of the Supreme Court and other courts after *Sherbert* and *Yoder.*

Two possible challenges to RFRA were that it unconstitutionally favors religious claims over nonreligious ones and that its application trespasses on the range of state authority. The federalism problem turned on the scope of Congress's power to "enforce" the Fourteenth Amendment. Could Congress effectively expand the scope of free exercise coverage by disagreeing with the Court's interpretation, and, if not, how far could it justify extensions as means to prevent undoubted violations courts would not be able to discern? In *City of Boerne v. Flores,*[126] the Supreme Court rejected both possible justifications. Congress had to accept what the Court had ruled about the coverage of the First Amendment as applied to the states through the Fourteenth. "Legislation which alters the meaning of the Free Exercise Clause cannot be said to be enforcing the Clause."[127] Nor could RFRA be regarded as genuinely remedial for possible violations, because the breadth of what it required "reflects a lack of proportionality or congruence between the means adopted and the legitimate end to be achieved."[128]

The Court's striking down of RFRA as it covered states and localities did not address whether the act properly applied to actions of the federal government and whether similar state laws were acceptable. Given that *Smith* itself had explicitly assumed that state legislatures could provide protections of religions practices beyond those guaranteed by the Free Exercise Clause, no authority suggested that Congress could not do the same for matters of federal law. In *Gonzalez v. O Centro Espirita Beneficiente Uniao do Vegetal*,[129] the Court did apply RFRA to yield nonapplication of the Controlled Substances Act and instead require the permitted importation of a tea containing a hallucinogen used by a small sect as communion.

In 2000, Congress adopted the Religious Land Use and Institutionalized Persons Act (RLUIPA),[130] which employed standards like those in RFRA. The application of this Act to states rested on the bases that the federal government supplies financial support for state prisons, and that decisions about religious use of property affect commerce and are sometimes made in a manner that reflects religious discrimination. The act's prison provision was upheld in 2005 against an Establishment Clause challenge in *Cutter v. Wilkinson*.[131] In its formulation of a standard of review, the Court emphasized that "context matters" for the compelling interest test and that "due deference" was to be given to prison officials acting to maintain order and safety.[132] Although the Court did not directly address whether the prison section of the Act improperly invaded state powers, almost certainly if most Justices believed Congress had done so, they would not have ruled as they did.

In a major decision about RFRA, the Supreme Court in 2014 ruled 5–4 in the *Hobby Lobby* case that the Act did apply to for-profit closely held corporations, and Justice Alito treated its tests of "substantial burden" on religion exercise, "compelling interest," and "least restrictive means" in ways that were favorable to religious claimants."[133] Although the actual holding of the case was quite narrow, Alito's opinion did regard RFRA as significantly broader than pre-*Smith* free exercise law regarding exemptions.

A minor concern about Free Exercise law and legislation that protects religious beliefs and practices is *Lemon*'s test of "secular purpose" and "primary effect ... that neither advances nor inhibits religion." A substantial majority of the Supreme Court has made clear that the purpose and effect of accommodating religious beliefs and practices are not themselves unconstitutional. One *could* call these aspects of a law "secular," but the purpose is not an ordinary secular one, and the effect could be seen, in a sense, as advancing religion. The truth of the matter is that these standards, developed for circumstances in which the government is directly involving itself in religious practices or symbolism, are not well formulated for the discretion of legislatures to exempt religious believers from certain requirements. No majority opinion has stated this disjunction clearly, though it has been addressed in a concurring opinion.[134] However, the basic permissibility of many forms of accommodation is plain, despite their tension with a literal reading of *Lemon*'s "secular purpose and effect" test.

A long-standing assumption about exemptions from ordinary laws forbidding discrimination or limiting the bases on which individuals can be dismissed from their employment has been the "ministerial exception." The basic notion is that religious groups can choose their leaders according to their religious understanding and that the government will not interfere. When anti-discrimination laws have not explicitly provided such an exception, courts have typically read one in. Where the ministerial exception stood after *Employment Division v. Smith* was not entirely clear. On the one hand, the logic of *Smith*'s basic approach that a general law need not provide a religious exemption would appear to make it possible to forbid religious groups, like other organizations, from choosing their clerics on the basis of gender or race. On the other hand, for public officials and courts to get involved in why ministers and priests are being hired or dismissed would be to entwine the government with religion in a highly troubling way, a large aspect of what the *Smith* Court aimed to avoid.

In 2012, a unanimous Supreme Court, in *Hosanna-Tabor Evangelical Lutheran Church and School v. Equal Employment Opportunity Commission*,[135] ruled that the "ministerial exception" remains a crucial aspect of the religion clauses, that its content is broad, and that, when it applies, it decisively bars government involvement. The dispute involved not an ordinary cleric but a "called" teacher at a religious school who, after theological study at a Lutheran college, had become a "Minister of Religion, Commissioned." Cheryl Perich's teaching in elementary school included a religious class four days a week, as well as a number of other subjects. After becoming ill with narcolepsy, she began a school year on leave. When she sought to return that winter, the principal responded that someone had been hired to fill her position for the rest of the school year; he also expressed doubt that she was ready to return. When Perich refused to resign and showed up for work despite being told that the school no longer had a position for her, she was fired. The congregation of Hosanna-Tabor voted to terminate her employment based on her "insubordination and disruptive behavior." Perich filed a complaint with the EEOC charging that she had been dismissed in violation of the Americans with Disabilities Act. The church responded that she had been fired for a religious reason—that her threat to sue violated the belief that Christians should settle disputes internally.

The case presented three issues. (1) Does the ministerial exception still apply? (2) If so, how broadly does it reach, and, in particular, does it cover a teacher at a religious school with the status of Cheryl Perich? (3) If so, how far can officials and courts involve themselves in what are the actual grounds of dismissal, if it is claimed that the asserted religious basis was a mere cover for a nonreligious ground? The Supreme Court relied on history, going back to the Magna Carta, the original understanding of the First Amendment, and various cases precluding government involvement in disputes between groups within churches, to conclude that "[b]oth Religion Clauses bar the government from interfering with the decision of a religious group to fire one of its ministers."[136] Although this was its first case involving a claimed "ministerial exception" to anti-discrimination laws, the Supreme Court agreed with the uniform view of courts of appeals when it granted the exception. *Smith* was distinguished on the basis that it involved regulation of "outward physical acts."

Without adopting "a rigid formula," Chief Justice Roberts wrote for the Court that, given all the aspects of her employment, including her formal status as a "minister" and her religious teaching, Perich counted as a minister for purposes of the exception.[137] On this point, two concurring opinions took positions opposed to each other. Justice Thomas urged that civil courts should accept any "religious organization's good-faith understanding of who qualifies as its minister."[138] Under this approach, if a religious group genuinely regards all of its members as ministers, it could dismiss any of them from a job and be protected by the ministerial exception. Justice Alito, joined by Justice Kagan, claimed that the exception should not depend mainly on a designation as minister. Rather, courts should ask if personnel are performing key functions, including conducting worship services or ceremonies, or serving as a messenger or teacher of the faith.[139] Taking the Roberts opinion for the Court along with the other two opinions, the formal title carries some significance but is not the only critical factor. The functions performed are highly important. It follows that context can make some difference for whether the ministerial exception applies, an assessment courts can make without getting into the details of just how important a religious group regards its various practices.

Chief Justice Roberts did note that the Court's decision did not resolve whether the ministerial exception would apply to claims of breach of contract and tortuous conduct,[140] but its application in the discrimination context was absolutely preclusive in two ways. Although Perich no longer sought reinstatement, back pay and damages were also barred since they would be a penalty for terminating an unwanted minister. And Perich's claim that the church's asserted basis for dismissal was "pretextual ... misses the point of the ministerial exception ... [which] ensures that the authority to select and control who will minister to the faithful ... is the church's alone."[141]

Particularly because the opinion fails to offer an explanation of its absolute rejection of a "pretextual" exception to the ministerial exception, one wonders whether, in furtherance of its understandable aim to protect religious autonomy, the Court's language does not reach a bit further than it should. It makes perfect sense that no church should be required to keep a genuine minister it seeks to dismiss. However deplorable the reasons for dismissal, a cleric is not likely to be very effective if rejected by his or her congregation. Whether reinstatement would ever be acceptable for someone in a position like Perich's if the religious organization lacks any genuine religious basis for dismissal is more debatable, although simply precluding that remedy when the ministerial exception applies makes sense. But suppose the person fired offers highly plausible evidence that the real ground for dismissal had nothing to do with religious practices and convictions, and the church is unable to present even a remotely tenable counterargument. Should she not then at least be able to recover damages? In principle, the ministerial exception should not preclude such a recovery; however, these circumstances may be so rare that it is undesirable to invite litigation and judicial assessment of such claims. In that event, an absolute rule barring monetary recovery, no matter what kind of minister is involved and no matter how outrageous her dismissal appears to be, is warranted, but only on the basis of considerations of administrability.

IV. TENSIONS BETWEEN FREE EXERCISE AND NONESTABLISHMENT, AND RESOLUTIONS

In the subjects and cases we have looked at, we have seen some contexts in which free exercise and nonestablishment point in the same direction, including when government favors some religions over others. In other contexts, the clauses may suggest different conclusions. For example, the bar on religious worship and practices within public schools may preclude what many parents and students would regard as desirable exercises of religion. For some of those circumstances, courts may be able to apply a relatively straightforward standard, such as the rule that public schools may not promote particular religious practices. Like every rule, this one has debatable borders, such as moments of silence and Christmas symbols, but most of its coverage is clear. For determining which religious exemptions may violate the Establishment Clause, it is much harder to conceive of workable standards that do not come down to matters of degree. Three crucial aspects of exemptions are whether particular practices are being singled out for them; when, if ever, religious reasons may be distinguished from other grounds of decision; and when exemptions impose unacceptable burdens on others.

The Supreme Court considered the last of these questions in *Estate of Thornton v. Caldor, Inc.*[142] in 1985. Connecticut had adopted a law granting employees an absolute right not to work on their chosen Sabbath. Because it took no account of the burden on employers and fellow workers, and because it contained no exception for circumstances in which a person's Sabbath fell on a key day of his employment (such as a school teacher whose Sabbath was Friday), the Court ruled that the statute went "beyond having an incidental or remote effect of advancing religion. [It] has a primary effect that impermissibly advances a particular religious practice."[143] (The Court did not rely on the added fact that the language of the statute allowed a person to take his Sabbath as a day off, even if he had no objection in religious conscience to attending an early service and working the rest of the day, but preferred to avoid work on that day for family reasons shared by many others.)

Justice O'Connor wrote a concurring opinion not only emphasizing the absoluteness of the exemption but also claiming that by singling out of a particular belief and practice and by failing to accord "similar accommodation to ethical and religious beliefs and practices of other private employees,"[144] the law conveyed endorsement of Sabbath observance. O'Connor distinguished Title VII of the Civil Rights Act, which requires only reasonable accommodations and extends to "all religious beliefs and practices rather than protecting only the Sabbath observance."[145]

It would be unfair to take Justice O'Connor's opinion as ruling out every exemption that applies to a particular practice, but it is worth asking whether that would make sense. The answer is "no." If a statute is worded generally in the manner of the Civil Rights Act, RFRA, and RLUIPA, it is up to an employer or government official to decide initially whether a particular claim for an exemption should be granted. If a dispute remains, a court must resolve the issue. Given that people can reasonably disagree about the wisdom of some possible exemptions, legislatures should be able to say that in certain instances, they are appropriate. Thus, we have had exemptions from military draft laws and a federal requirement that hospitals not insist that doctors and nurses perform abortions. So long as an exemption has a reasonable scope, legislatures should be able to focus on particular practices, as well as across-the-board standards. One prominent recent example of when this consideration is desirable is when state legislatures adopting same-sex marriage, or responding to judicial determination of such a constitutional right, consider what, if any, exemptions from involvement should be granted to those opposed in principle. Another such example is just how the federal government should treat employers whose religious convictions oppose granting insurance for contraceptives.[146]

When we turn to whether a "burden" of an exemption on others is too great—a question that can arise both in constitutional review of legislation and the applying of an open-ended standard such as "reasonable accommodation"—the answer may not be straightforward. When the legislature has specified just when an exemption from ordinary requirements must be granted, the court's role in assessing the law's constitutionality is to determine whether the law strikes a reasonable balance of key values. If a statute contains a general standard, judges must decide whether, in particular circumstances, an exemption should be granted. Courts resolving this issue cannot avoid a context-sensitive evaluation. It is important in this respect that even Justice Scalia—and other Justices who reached the result in *Smith* partly because the prevailing free exercise standard was too indeterminate and required too much sensitive evaluation—nevertheless had accepted Congress's dictation of essentially the same standard in RFRA.

Perhaps the hardest theoretical question about exemptions is the relationship between religious and nonreligious bases. There are two straightforward approaches, each of which, in my judgment, is misguided. The first is: "Religion is special, and recognized to be so by the Free Exercise Clause. Of course it is all right to limit an exemption to religious claims." The second counters: "Favoring religion is unfair and a form of establishment; religion must be treated in the same way as otherwise similar claims." Under the second approach, not all *wishes* have to be treated similarly since the state need not extend a Sabbath exemption to someone who wants to go to baseball games, but it must treat all claims of conscience similarly. Although the question of what claims should be recognized for exemptions is often a matter of legislative judgment, my focus here is on constitutional limitations.

Present doctrine definitely allows treating religion specially in various circumstances. *Wisconsin v. Yoder* strongly suggested that a nonreligious claim to take children out of school would not succeed, and the Court has cast no doubt that both RFRA and RLUIPA appropriately focus on religious claims. Accepting legislation of that kind does not in itself tell us whether nonreligious claimants might have a valid constitutional argument to be treated similarly, but it does indisputably treat as acceptable a legislative accommodation that focuses only on religion.

Some scholars have claimed, nonetheless, that it should be regarded as constitutionally unacceptable to grant special concessions to religion. This position warrants a careful contextual examination. Among the relevant considerations are whether otherwise similar nonreligious claims that courts can assess are likely, what message an exemption will send, and what is the precise scope of the exemption that a person or group receives. Analysis of these various factors strongly suggests that legislatures sometimes should treat religion as special and sometimes not, and that courts should regard a failure to include nonreligious claims in certain circumstances as unconstitutional.

The argument for equal treatment is especially strong when a form of speech or military service is involved. With respect to speech, we have seen that the Supreme Court treated a tax exemption limited to religious publications as a forbidden establishment,[147] and it regarded the failure of the University of Virginia to treat religious publications like other student journals as unconstitutional.[148] When the state is encouraging or discouraging forms of expression, it generally makes sense not to allow categorization according to religion. A similar conclusion should apply to military service, although no specific provisions like the Free Speech Clause is at hand. Young people can develop pacifist convictions for nonreligious reasons. Draft boards, and officials reviewing the claims of those now in the military to be excused from further service because they have become pacifist, have a chance to ask questions and evaluate an applicant's sincerity. That the Supreme Court effectively extended the statutory definition of religion in *Seeger* and *Welsh* was no doubt responsive to this concern; and I believe Justice Harlan's concurrence in *Welsh* rightly regarded an exclusion of nonreligious pacifists as unconstitutional.

However, it would be mistaken to generalize broadly from these two illustrations. For some other situations, it is hard to imagine an equally forceful nonreligious objection to a requirement, and even if one can conceive that such an objection could occasionally arise, administration that takes account of that may be impractical. Kosher practices require that animals to be eaten be killed in a certain way; if this does not conform to ordinary legal standards, can we conceive of a similarly powerful nonreligious reason for an exemption? A person who objects to treating religion specifically might concede that it is all right to do so if we really can imagine no parallel nonreligious view. The troublesome issues arise when a parallel nonreligious view is conceivable but rare and difficult to assess, and when extending an exemption may convey an undesirable message. Three relevant examples concern confidential communications to clergy, Sunday employment, and same-sex marriage.

The law provides protection for doctors, lawyers, and clerics by not requiring them to reveal confidential communications, but at least in many jurisdictions, the protection is more absolute for clerics. Others may be required to report such things as plans to commit crimes, gunshot wounds, and abuse of children, but since 1215, the Roman Catholic Church has imposed an absolute duty on priests not to break the seal of confession, and violators may be excommunicated.[149] Even if one can conceive of a lawyer or doctor who believes that for some reason she has an absolute duty of conscience not to reveal what the law requires, such individuals must be rare. It thus makes sense to provide a more absolute privilege for at least some clerics than for other professionals.

When we turn to work on Sunday, we can conceive of someone whose sense that he must spend time with his children is as strong as the religious conviction of others that God's instructions or religious worship preclude Sunday work. But a great many people would prefer not to work on Sunday. If the privilege not to do so is opened up to all of those with objections in conscience, how is an employer or a judge to decide when a genuine moral reason, such as spending time with one's family, amounts to a conscientious objection? And if the exemptions were extended in this way, how would a worker feel who would greatly wish to have Sunday off and would be able to do so on the basis of seniority had not exemptions been granted to others? He may not particularly like the fact that religious exemptions are afforded, but he is likely to resent more those junior employees whose reasons are otherwise like his, but who further claim their reasons are so strong they cannot in good conscience work on Sunday. All of this supports limiting such an exemption to Sabbath observers.

Another consideration is in play regarding same-sex marriage. Again, it would be very hard to assess the force of a nonreligious claim that one cannot accept such marriage; but the message sent by an exemption also matters. If a state means to convey that gay people are equal citizens with a right to get married, granting some exemption to those with religious beliefs that God has intended only marriage between men and women may be framed as a concession to the state's interest in not interfering too much with religious practice. But an extended exemption, as has been granted for abortions, may seem to imply more doubt about the basic principle of equality as it applies to these marriages. Extending the exemptions, thus, could undercut to some degree the most fundamental message of the equality-based law. Although we might wish matters to be simpler, both for legislative choice and constitutional permissibility, context bears on whether an exemption is properly limited to religious claims.

Another element is the extent of a privilege, an issue raised by *Hosanna-Tabor*. Perhaps nonreligious organizations devoted to conveying messages should also have some extra degree of freedom to decide who will be their leaders, a freedom not available to ordinary employers making decisions about hiring and dismissing those who work for them. But whether nonreligious organizations (except those actually devoted to promoting aspects of gender and race equality) should have the ability to discriminate on the basis of gender or race is highly doubtful. Further, the absolute protection given the choices of religious bodies in hiring and firing ministers, even in the face of overwhelming evidence that any claimed religious basis is pretextual, should not be extended to employment by nonreligious groups. Thus, with regard both to whether any other groups should receive a comparable exemption from antidiscrimination laws *and* to what the precise scope of such an exemption should be, it is mistaken to assume that nonreligious grounds of individuals and organizations must, or should, always be treated equally to religious ones.

Whereas religious exemptions provided by legislators, or deemed to be required by state constitutions, arguably promote and protect free exercise at the price of relaxed nonestablishment, the precluding direct or indirect financial assistance to individuals and organizations to serve uses that are both public and religious could be seen as furthering nonestablishment at the price of free exercise. Of course, *if* the state's financing of religious schools or providing religious instruction are deemed to be forbidden by the Establishment Clause, they cannot also be required by the Free Exercise Clause. But that conclusion alone leaves open whether states, and perhaps Congress, may reach further in the direction of nonestablishment than the federal constitution requires. Just this issue was posed in 2004 by *Locke v. Davey*,[150] involving the state of Washington's program to provide financial assistance to college students, but not if they were pursuing "a degree in theology." After *Zelman v. Simmons-Harris*,[151] which accepted extensive aid to parochial schools, it was fairly clear that Washington *could* have treated all college students equally, regardless of what they were studying, so the Establishment Clause did not require the exclusion. In a surprisingly one-sided decision, the *Locke* Court ruled 7–2 that the state of Washington's choice was permitted, not constituting a violation of free exercise by disfavoring religious activity. Chief Justice Rehnquist's majority opinion referred to a "play in the joints" that left it up to the states to decide whether to pursue nonestablishment beyond what the federal constitution required.[152]

Since most states have "Blaine Amendments" in their constitutions that are stricter than the Supreme Court now requires about not aiding parochial schools, or religious institutions more generally, the question of state latitude has considerable importance. Since the opinion in *Locke v. Davey* is specifically concentrated on ministerial education and provides little guidance about how exactly courts should be determining when the pursuit of nonestablishment might violate the Free Exercise Clause, one cannot discern what would now be seen as the limits on state flexibility to do what impinges negatively on religious practices. However, together with the permissibility of religious exemptions, both states and Congress are left with some range of decision about how to treat religious practices and institutions without violating either federal religion clause, and within at least part of that range, they may do so without having to satisfy a compelling interest test.[153]

V. CONCLUSION

Although the religion clauses present a number of particular tensions and complexities, largely derived from the need for government not to involve itself in matters of religion, many issues of standards of interpretation are similar to those reviewed in earlier chapters. There are especially powerful reasons here to avoid discrete evaluations that require deep examination of specific beliefs and practices, but regrettably, many crucial issues do not lend themselves to standards that resolve certain cases in a simple or general way. As elsewhere, contextual evaluation of circumstances is frequently needed, although here, courts should generally rely on individual factors that are discernible without a searching investigation of particular beliefs and the comparative importance of various religious elements.

Chapter 11

Criminal Process

The Right to Counsel, Unreasonable Searches and Seizures, and the Privilege against Self-Incrimination

I. INTRODUCTION

Many of the guarantees in the Bill of Rights, now applicable against state and local authorities through the Fourteenth Amendment, concern the criminal process. Most of those, unlike the bar on cruel and unusual punishments, provide protection for innocent citizens as well as those who have committed crimes, and restrain how far the government is permitted to intrude upon persons' lives in order to prevent crimes and solve those already committed. This chapter considers three of those rights. The basic right to counsel concerns the operation of processes to determine guilt of those formally accused of criminal acts. The ban on unreasonable searches and seizures, by contrast, is about tactics of investigation, protecting people against sweeping intrusions into their domains of privacy and confidentiality. The privilege against self-incrimination operates at both levels. As initially conceived, it concerned formal proceedings, but now also carries significance for police questioning. And, under the doctrine of *Miranda v. Arizona*,[1] the right to remain silent also embraces a right to counsel at this earlier stage.

The analysis that follows focuses on a number of broader themes developed in earlier chapters and shows that, as we have seen in other contexts, the application and relevance of particular interpretive approaches varies among these three criminal process rights. One question, of course, is the status of original understanding: how relevant could it be, how much should it be seen in relation to basic conceptions or specific applications, and how far should it guide decisions? I shall urge that a fundamental shift in values undercuts how far the Sixth Amendment right to counsel should be taken as originally understood, that changing technology renders the specific applications of the Fourth Amendment bar on unreasonable searches and seizures little help for many modern issues, and that a similar conclusion holds for applications beyond formal criminal processes of the Fifth Amendment against self-incrimination. With regard to legal assistance by counsel, the dominant original sense was that the government had to allow it, not provide it. In modern times, the notion that a person without money being tried for murder can do without a lawyer strikes us as incredibly harsh and unacceptable, and is contrary to a mass of Supreme Court decisions; but that is where the original understanding would lead. With unreasonable searches, much of the problem concerns modern electronic devices that, in one way or another, provide crucial sources of information. People in 1791 simply did not conceive such a vast technological advance, and the best one can do in respect to their perceptions would be to ask how their fundamental sense of privacy protection would apply to modern communications. Changes in values and technology may not have altered the basic idea that people should not be forced to incriminate themselves, but in 1791 there were no organized police forces. Thus, the application of that privilege to their investigations presents problems not then conceived.

One may believe that the values originally underlying these amendments remain highly relevant, although the modern right of provided counsel reaches well beyond any basic original sense of what defendants are entitled to. With regard to the privilege against self-incrimination, genuine uncertainty and disagreement exist over its justification. Of course, as the preceding First Amendment chapters reflect with respect to forms of "hate speech" and the "free exercise" status of religious acts that violate neutral laws, every fundamental right generates differences both over how it should apply at the borders and over how its various underlying values should figure; but often, as with the rights to free speech and free exercise, people agree about the basic core and underlying rationales. That this is less true about the privilege against self-incrimination and the bar on unreasonable searches affects disagreements over their ranges of application and over the remedies that should flow from violations.

Given that original understanding is unable to resolve many constitutional criminal process rights, judges must, as in other domains, rely on criteria such as precedents, acceptance over time, and judgments of what is just and desirable. Because criminals are not widely popular and legislators do not commonly rush in to provide protections if courts limit suspects' constitutional rights, consistent judicial deference to legislators and law enforcement personnel is not appropriate here. However, when it comes to estimations of vital concerns about safety, such as how to preclude terrorist attacks, judicial deference to "experts" may be unavoidable.

As with many other areas, multiple values underlie specified rights, and satisfying maximum claims of protection can conflict with public interests. In light of the crucial needs to deter serious crimes and solve those that are committed, the conflicts are strikingly obvious for both the rules limiting searches and those forbidding compelled self-incrimination. How far courts should bend standards and accept the judgments of those trying to protect the broader society is a deeply troubling question.

Crucial interpretive issues for all constitutional provisions are how far judges should weigh sets of considerations, and, if so, explicitly acknowledge that in their opinions. Closely related is how far particular rights should be regarded as absolute. Although the original sense of these terms within the Fourth Amendment is not clear, "unreasonable search and seizure" and "probable cause" seem to suggest a kind of weighing of considerations, though without specifying just when and how various factors should count. The Fifth and Sixth Amendments read as if they are unqualified, but, as we shall see, competing considerations have played a role in when and how these rights have been applied. For each right, we can imagine alternative understandings that would provide fuller safeguards but which the Supreme Court has declined to adopt.

As with other constitutional provisions, to assure reliable implementation and enforcement, the Supreme Court tries to announce standards that lower court judges and other officials can effectively apply. Conceptually, clarity of a standard does not always coalesce with simple administrability. For example, the Fourth Amendment "stop and frisk" standard of "reasonable suspicion" is clear enough in principle, but discerning its absence is very hard for judges, especially since the accounts given by the police who have made "stops" provide the bases for judicial estimation. Perhaps more than with any other constitutional protections, the ability and willingness of ordinary officials, here police officers, to carry forward set constitutional standards is critical. Not only are clear guides necessary, officers must accept them, rather than twisting the facts to support misbehavior and make judicial identification of violations nearly impossible. Judges are often incapable of assessing just how high the probability was that a particular person committed a crime or whether the police were genuinely questioning someone to acquire broader information or elicit an admission of wrongdoing. These difficulties are especially great when the police are less than candid about details.

For all constitutional claims, one question is what should happen if it succeeds. Often the answer is straightforward: if a punishment is unconstitutional, it cannot be imposed (or continued); if one has a free exercise right, one can engage in the religious behavior involved. Sometimes, a deep concern about a workable remedy may lead courts not to get involved; this, as we saw in Chapter 7, is one basis for the political question doctrine. A special dilemma arises with the privilege against self-incrimination and the ban on unreasonable searches. The most obvious remedies for violations may be civil damages, but if these are not effective, what should courts do? The exclusion of evidence obtained directly by an illegal act or gotten as a "fruit of the poisonous tree" will benefit mainly those who are guilty of crimes. That "remedy" may seem out of proportion to the magnitude of the wrong done to them; and it does not directly help those who suffered violations that failed to produce harmful evidence. Further, the remedy may or may not be perceived as actually being required by the Amendment itself. Is it nonetheless appropriate for Justices to mandate such remedies as constitutional requirements if they believe they are needed as effective deterrents against misbehavior?

A distinctive aspect of criminal process rights is how far the government should, and must, notify people who might exercise them. It may be healthy for the government to educate people in respect to free speech and free exercise, but doing so is not a constitutional requirement. For the privilege against self-incrimination and right to counsel, as these apply prior to formal processes, the issue of required notification is a vital aspect.

With most constitutional rights, we see obvious differences between formal rights and actual effects. A person with a highly unpopular point of view may know he has a right to speak his mind in a public meeting, but he may remain silent because he does not want his neighbors to shun him. With respect to searches and self-incrimination, the relation of formal right and likely effect is both more subtle and arguably more central to how the right should be understood. Even when a person asked to consent to a search or respond to police questions is aware that she has a right to say "no," she may want to appear cooperative and not to have police infer likely guilt from a refusal. A defendant at a criminal trial has a similar incentive, recognizing that whatever they are told, jurors may think a guilty person is much more likely not to testify than someone who is innocent. Should these realities play an expansive role in how the right should be understood, or is suffering this kind of consequence a reasonable disadvantage for those who choose to exercise the right?

Although like most constitutional rights, those concerning criminal investigations are distinctively about relations between citizens and their governments, I shall suggest that analogies to private relations can help clarify what would seem to be appropriate and inappropriate behavior, and that these conclusions should carry some weight in how the specified constitutional rights should be understood.

As with the prohibition of "cruel and unusual punishment," criminal process rights are partly related to notions of equality. This idea heavily influences a modern sense of the right to counsel; and a frequent criticism of police use of "stop and frisk" in New York and other cities is that it is employed mainly against the liberty of young members of minorities freely to walk the streets. As with capital punishment, how far these concerns about inequality should affect a right's formulation is troublesome.

A final introductory note about these three aspects of the criminal process concerns the language of the Fourteenth Amendment and the place of "selective incorporation." In contrast to free speech and free exercise of religion, and the right to bear arms, for which the textual language of "privileges and immunities" fits much better than "due process of law," the rights related to criminal investigations and trials are properly conceived as involving due process. With respect to such rights, the Supreme Court during the first half of the twentieth century required states to observe minimal standards not as rigorous as those that applied to the federal government, in effect, treating "due process" as more flexible than specific constraints of the first ten amendments. Although the modern Supreme Court has not applied the federal right to be indicted by a grand jury to the states, and has allowed the requirements for state jury trials to remain more flexible than those governing federal trials, in respect to the three subjects of this chapter the Court has determined that states are subject to the same restraints as the federal government. In other words, "selective" (not covering every aspect of the Bill of Rights) "incorporation" (containing the same content) applies to these rights.

A plain textual argument is in severe tension with this incorporation of criminal process rights. The existence of a "due process" clause within the Fifth Amendment strongly suggests that enactors and readers of the time would not have regarded all the more specific protections of the Bill of Rights as demanded by due process itself. A conceivable response is that by the time of the Fourteenth Amendment, due process was viewed more inclusively as embracing most of those protections; but, in truth those adopting or reading the Fourteenth Amendment were not thinking in exactly this way. What may be easier to defend is the idea that the Fourteenth Amendment, with its combination of clauses, "due process," "privileges and immunities," and "equal protection," together embraced federal criminal process protections. The equal protection clause could figure in an argument that these guarantees were a needed safeguard against gross inequalities in respect to race that extended to criminal prosecutions. As Chapter 9 explains, a pragmatic approach to incorporation relies not on a specific original understanding, but on the desirability both of states providing these protections and of federal courts having a uniform standard of evaluation for federal and state cases.

II. *THE RIGHT TO COUNSEL*

Rather than examining the numerous nuances and details that are aspects of the Sixth Amendment's right to counsel, this chapter concentrates on certain central features of how it is now conceived, asking what these reflect about constitutional-interpretation strategies in general and about distinctive aspects of this right. The primary subjects covered are (1) the provision of counsel to indigents, (2) the right to refuse counsel, (3) the circumstances in which the right is in play, and (4) the range of a requirement of effective assistance. These topics reveal the importance and the difficulty of characterizing the core values underlying the right and the impossibility of relying overwhelmingly on original understanding. They also illustrate the debatability of how much deference judges should accord, and to whom, what obstacles they face for fact-specific evaluations, and what account they should take of practical concerns not directly within their control.

A. Provision of Counsel to Indigents

The Sixth Amendment provides that in federal criminal cases the accused has the right to "Assistance of Counsel for his defense." Exactly what constituted a right to counsel at the time of adoption is not susceptible to a simple answer. In England prior to the American revolution, the common law allowed misdemeanor defendants to use retained counsel but did not accord this right to felony defendants.[2] During the eighteenth century courts began to permit felony defendants to use retained counsel, but only to argue points of law.[3] For treason cases, a statute provided that not only could an accused use counsel in his defense, he could have one appointed upon request.[4] Within the colonies, the scope of a right to counsel varied, with some providing appointed counsel in capital cases.[5] After the Declaration of Independence, in some states, constitutions included a right to counsel; in others, legislative enactments provided it.[6] Although some states did grant appointed counsel in capital or felony cases,[7] most did not include such a right in their constitutions or statutes. Whatever formal right existed at trials, before the Bill of Rights the criminal process operated largely independent of counsel, with many suspects admitting their guilt or incriminating themselves in preliminary hearings.[8] Although the historical data are somewhat murky, the Sixth Amendment, which gives the right to counsel's assistance in "all criminal prosecutions," was almost certainly taken by enactors and readers as granting a right to retain counsel, but not to have the government provide a defense lawyer in a broad range of cases.

The uncontroversial core of the Sixth Amendment's right that the government cannot bar assistance of counsel for defendants in criminal proceedings remains. In respect to the federal government and states supplying counsel for those who could not afford to hire one, a radical shift in what the Sixth Amendment has been taken to require has taken place after its adoption and the later passage of the Fourteenth Amendment.

According to present doctrine, if a defendant cannot afford to hire counsel in the most important circumstances covered by the right, the state must provide one, either by compensating a private attorney or using government "public defenders." The relevant circumstances include all prosecutions for felonies and those for misdemeanors resulting in sentences of imprisonment. A federal statute in 1790 provided for the appointment of counsel in capital cases, but this was not then seen as a constitutional requirement. In 1932, in *Powell v. Alabama*,[9] the Supreme Court did rule that due process required that counsel be provided for indigent defendants in capital cases unable to defend themselves adequately. Six years later it held that the Sixth Amendment required appointment in noncapital federal cases,[10] but in 1942 in *Betts v. Brady*, it ruled that in noncapital state cases, counsel needed to be appointed only if the absence of counsel would offend "fundamental ideas of fairness and right."[11] This holding was overruled in *Gideon v. Wainwright* in 1963, which employed the "incorporation" approach and determined that counsel must be provided in all felony cases.[12] All nine Justices concurred in this result. Its rule was later extended to misdemeanor cases involving an initial prison sentence or a commitment to prison based on a violation of conditions of probation.[13] Because the Court has declined to expand the rule to cover all crimes for which imprisonment is an authorized sentence,[14] the present approach effectively necessitates an initial determination of a likely sentence prior to trial.[15]

The most basic point about provision of counsel is that the prevailing doctrine is not derivable from, or consistent with, any straightforward account of original understanding. The best one could do in those terms is to urge that members of the founding and civil war eras were fundamentally concerned with fairness in the criminal process, that the adopters of the Fourteenth Amendment valued equality highly, and that at both times appointed counsel was provided within some parts of the country. We now grasp that genuine fairness at criminal trials and rough equality when individuals face the prospect of being subjected to serious criminal punishment do entail that counsel should be there to help. Since only the most fervent libertarians or incredibly strict originalists would doubt whether the Constitution as now understood should include this protection, it provides a powerful example of why changes in social understandings and values should yield protections broader than those original conceived.

That counsel should sometimes be provided for the substantial percentage of defendants who are indigent[16] does not by itself tell us just what criminal prosecutions should be covered *or* what should count as genuinely adequate assistance. Two points are obvious. Counsel should not have to be provided for every violation of law. Although I may pay counsel to help me contest a parking or speeding ticket, concluding that taxpayers should bear that cost if I cannot does not make sense. Reasonable arguments can be made about just what crimes deserve coverage, but the Supreme Court does have to draw the line somewhere, either in terms of clear categories or the circumstances of particular cases, or both. The present doctrine relies for this issue on the clear categories of felony prosecutions and those for misdemeanors that lead to imprisonment.

A much more complex concern is the overall effect of a right to counsel. The higher the cost of a criminal trial, the more likely a prosecutor is to try to bargain for a guilty plea. Given the severity of penalties in the United States, the prescribed or possible punishment for many crimes is a good deal more severe than the actual offenses really warrant. This allows a prosecutor to offer a lesser offense or reduced penalty for a guilty plea that will be much less than the maximum that he might seek, but will be at least as severe as the offender deserves. As a consequence, a person charged may make a self-interested calculation to plead guilty, even though the resulting sentence is not lenient by any objective standard. Guilty pleas are obtained in the vast majority of criminal cases. During a period some decades ago, the percentage of guilty pleas for crimes rose from 60% to 95%.[17] Thus, few defendants actually have trials at which counsel assist them. Most may plead guilty only after consulting counsel, but that is far from the same as having an expert who might break down a prosecutor's case or help establish innocence. Even an able counsel who thinks she *might* win at trial may advise an accused not to take the risk of losing if he is offered a much reduced sentence to plead guilty. Consequently, only a small minority of defendants who end up in jail were actually helped by counsel at a trial. Since public defenders in most states are overburdened and private lawyers do not receive adequate compensation to provide genuinely extensive assistance in complex cases,[18] lawyers themselves have some personal incentives to recommend guilty pleas.

Could the guilty plea "problem" be dealt with? A court or legislature might resolve that no one can be convicted without an actual trial. Alternatively, it could establish that the penalty after conviction at trial must not exceed what was offered in a "plea bargain," thereby eliminating the incentive of potential defendants to plead guilty in order to receive a lesser sentence. Either of these alternatives would greatly enhance an effective right to counsel but also be very expensive. It would also almost certainly reduce enforcement of parts of the criminal law, as the government strove to save resources by not pursuing some convictions. Expense and less enforcement constitute strong reasons for legislatures not to adopt either of these more absolute protections, and, along with the absence of any clear constitutional bar on plea bargaining, they may help explain its wide judicial acceptance. Another possible approach would be for courts to carefully screen prosecutorial discretion about what crime to charge and what to seek as a sentence, but judges have understandably not chosen to take on this review of decisions within the executive branch.

B. The Choice to Be Pro Se

The choice of an accused not to consult with, or be assisted by, counsel raises fascinating questions, which fortunately have limited practical importance. Given the nuances of legal knowledge and trial experience, it is widely assumed that virtually no persons formally accused who make this choice benefit by a more effective defense. This reality raises two stark and related questions. What is the basic nature of the right to counsel? Should trial courts and appellate judges approach waiver with a simple approach or contextual evaluation?

The Sixth Amendment does not explicitly say that anyone can choose to refuse counsel, but the nature of most rights is that a person may decide not to exercise them, or, put differently, that one aspect of the right is to not undertake its positive exercise. Thus, freedom of speech includes a right *not* to express one's opinions; freedom of religious exercise includes a right *not* to engage in worship. If the Sixth Amendment is seen substantially as about a person's autonomy to decide about how best to proceed at trial, then her choice should be determinative. In 1975 the Supreme Court decided in *Faretta v. California*[19] that a person has a constitutional right to voluntarily and intelligently decide to proceed without counsel. The three dissenters denied any constitutional basis for this holding. Relying partly on the federal Judiciary Act of 1789, which gave defendants a right to self-representation, they contended that this showed members of Congress did not perceive the Constitution to provide that privilege.[20] But their main point was that the right to counsel is designed to assure fair trials, not to enhance irrational choices of persons accused.

Tied to this issue of basic value is the question of whether a state must or should evaluate the competence of a defendant to choose a waiver. In 1993 the Supreme Court held that the constitutional standard for competence to waive counsel, and also to plead guilty, is the standard for competency to stand trial;[21] but in *Indiana v. Edwards* in 2008,[22] it ruled that a state *may* determine that someone able enough to stand trial is not adequately competent to refuse the aid of counsel. Of course, the more one emphasizes fairness at trial in relation to autonomy of choice,[23] the stronger the argument becomes that the state should have this ability. Given that people with very severe mental disorders may be tried and do not qualify as insane under the *M'Naghten* standard, as described in Chapter 6, allowing state courts to conclude that *some* defendants should not be able to deny the assistance of counsel makes good sense. However, both prosecutors and courts should afford substantial weight to a person's basic freedom of choice. The nature of such an evaluation means that a federal court reviewing the constitutional status of a particular request for self-representation will rarely be in a position to override the decision of a state court either way.

3. When Does the Right Apply?

One set of questions about the right to counsel is when it applies: at what stage does it arise; when must the government allow an accused's own counsel to be present or provide counsel for the indigent; and when does the right end? One crucial answer to the first inquiry involved an expansion of the practical right, its extension to arrested suspects who are to be subjected to police interrogation. This protection, established by *Miranda v. Arizona*,[24] is conveyed to the suspect in the *Miranda* warnings. Since this stage precedes the formal criminal process, the Sixth

Amendment itself does not cover it. Although consulting with a lawyer prior to interrogation may help protect the later value of assistance by counsel at trial, because *Miranda* derived that protection from the accused's privilege against self-incrimination, discussion is reserved for the next section.

Putting aside the police interrogation safeguards, when does the right to counsel come into play? Rejecting the competing idea that this happens only at a stage at which the government has a lawyer present, the Supreme Court held that it "attaches" at the beginning of any formal process.[25] Thus, when an arrested man was brought before a magistrate who listened to evidence of his guilt, set bail, and confined him to jail until a surety bond was posted, his right to counsel should then have been recognized. As a concurrence by Justice Alito emphasizes,[26] the Court's ruling does not establish that the state must provide counsel for every interaction after which the right has attached; that assistance is required only at "critical stages."[27]

Exactly what counts as a "critical stage" is certainly debatable and demands a judgment not directly provided by the Sixth Amendment. However, because judges can rely on how processes work within a jurisdiction, they need not carefully investigate individual circumstances.

For eyewitness identification procedures, the Supreme Court has held that the right to counsel applies to post-indictment lineups,[28] but not those held before indictment.[29] This combination is hard to justify in terms of adequate protection against lineups that may unfairly influence a witness to identify the suspect. The right to counsel has also been held not to apply to photo examinations, although in those settings something may occur that would be treated as a due process violation.[30] Subsequently, the Court rejected a per se rule, which would have excluded all evidence derived from an improper photo examination, regardless of the reliability of resulting testimony. Reasoning that any such deterrence benefit was outweighed by the negative consequence of not having the jury receive reliable evidence, the Justices instead adopted a "totality of circumstances" approach to this due process issue.[31]

The "end" of the right to counsel concerns appellate procedures and subsequent challenges to convictions, as by habeas corpus. For such processes, anyone who wishes to hire counsel for help may do so; the issue is whether and when counsel must be provided. Obviously the government cannot be expected to pay for counsel for an interminable set of meritless challenges to a conviction. The real issues are whether at *some* stage after conviction, a basic right to provided counsel remains, and whether such a right exists if a convicted person's essential claim is obviously substantial (for example, newly discovered DNA evidence reveals that an unrelated person almost certainly committed a murder for which the claimant was convicted).

The Supreme Court's approach to post-conviction counsel has been affected by its prior conclusion that the Constitution itself establishes no right to appeal a conviction.[32] That decision has not yet been overruled despite the existence of appeal as of right in every state as well as by statute for federal cases. Although the Court has not discerned a Sixth Amendment right of provided counsel for appeals, it has reached that conclusion on the basis of a combination of the Due Process and Equal Protection Clauses.[33] If those who can afford to pay lawyers have a right to use counsel, it would be unfair and fundamentally unequal to preclude the indigent from that assistance. Thus far, the Court has not extended this constitutional right to further appeals that are discretionary and to subsequent challenges;[34] it has not yet ruled that counsel must be provided even in settings when a person's claim appears very powerful, notably when newly discovered evidence indicates his innocence.[35]

The Court's approach to cases on appeal may be challenged as lacking clarity about the precise roles of due process and equal protection[36] or on the basis that equality is really an empty concept because everyone should get what they otherwise deserve.[37] Neither of these challenges is substantial. One may believe that there are significant reasons to treat people differently, but the fact that they are equal in some sense can outweigh those reasons. Thus, saving money is a reason for the government to allow counsel but not provide it; but the status of two persons accused of similar crimes weighs against nonprovision for the indigent.[38] And if basic fairness—having a genuine chance to develop arguments on appeal—and equality *both* count in favor of state provision of counsel, then, for reasons earlier chapters explore, sorting out the exact force and relation of two such reasons need not be simple.

D. Effective Assistance

If counsel is constitutionally required for those who wish it, it follows that wholly incompetent, inadequate counsel that fails to provide adequate[39] protection at trial does not really satisfy the basic right. How should a court engaging in constitutional review approach this question? That depends partly on just how the basic right is seen, and on the court's ability to evaluate particular circumstances. Also at stake are the appropriate degrees of deference by courts generally to the judgments of lawyers for defendants and by federal courts to state court determinations they review.

Whatever approach might be adopted, it is clear that the government cannot assure genuinely *equal* representation across the board. A billionaire can spend millions to use the most able lawyers and to finance their extensive investigation of all possibilities. Only by forbidding the affluent to hire counsel of their own could the government come close to achieving equality; this egalitarian approach is now inconceivable and would rightly be viewed as itself unconstitutional. This simple illustration shows how the value of equality can carry some force, but not dominate all other considerations. The most that can be hoped for is competent counsel with adequate resources and available time, not government provision of the best conceivable assistance. On this score, the overworking of public defenders and inadequate compensation for assisting private defense lawyers are serious impediments. If these obstacles are great enough, courts might constitutionally impose requirements of greater aid,[40] but thus far they have become constitutionally involved only in the adequacy of particular representation.

The Supreme Court's approach to that has been that assistance is not inadequate unless counsel obviously failed to take steps that one would expect from a competent, conscientious lawyer, *and* the consequence of this failure was prejudicial to the defendant.[41] Thus, the Supreme Court held in one case that a lawyer's failure to explore one possible ground for mitigation at a sentencing hearing for a man who had pleaded guilty to "three brutal stabbing murders" and other crimes did not constitute a failure and did not prejudice the imposition of the death sentence.[42] It held in another case that when a lawyer failed to examine documents he knew the prosecution would use during sentencing, he did not exercise "reasonable competence."[43]

This approach involves assessing a lawyer's behavior according to what would have been a reasonable choice at that time, but also looking at the consequences of a failure in terms of what actually occurred after the fact. The first component here is obviously right—even the best strategic judgments can turn out to be mistaken after the fact. A lawyer's competence cannot be judged by whether each of his or her choices ended up with as favorable a result as a different choice might have produced. Reviewing the question of actual prejudice in the result is less straightforward. If the right to counsel is fundamentally a right to a fair process, one might see an evaluation of the outcome as beside the point when the defendant's lawyer has failed to perform his duty.[44] On the other hand, if the basic right is not to be unfairly convicted and sentenced, the effect on outcome is highly relevant. A sensible way of mixing these two views would be to say that actual satisfaction of the right to counsel does not depend on outcome, but that the remedy of reversing the outcome does.

A rather different, though related, issue is whether appellate courts are really in a position to evaluate all the circumstances of individual situations. This, of course, is a major concern across the entire range of constitutional interpretation. How much should depend on the totality of circumstances, how much on simpler categorizations? What is special here is that these circumstances are ones that judges themselves are very well equipped to evaluate, depending as they do on the records and arguments concerning trials and sentencing hearings, matters within the professional experience of the great majority of judges.

Despite the theoretical appeal of the Court's basic approach to counsel's effectiveness, its practical significance has been limited. Out of a great number of claims of inadequate counsel, few have succeeded,[45] given both deference to lawyers' choices and the questionable deference a federal statute requires for federal habeas corpus review of state determinations.[46] Virtually the only claims of counsel incompetence that have succeeded in federal courts have involved the death penalty,[47] another illustration of how the Supreme Court and other judges are much more sensitive to possible misapplications of the death penalty than to even very lengthy terms of imprisonment.

III. *THE PRIVILEGE AGAINST SELF-INCRIMINATION*

The most basic coverage of the Fifth Amendment, which provides that "no person . . . shall be compelled in any criminal case to be a witness against himself," is obvious; a defendant cannot be physically forced to testify, or convicted or jailed for refusing to do so. But in many broader respects the proper scope of the right is debatable: just when does the right come into play; what count as violations; what are the consequences of violations; what are the effects of its exercise by a defendant or suspect; and what steps should be taken to guarantee the right? As with other provisions, courts must consider the status of original understanding, decide how much weight to give competing interests, and determine whether decisions should rest on discernible categories or evaluations of particular circumstances. In contrast to the Fourth Amendment's prohibition of "unreasonable searches and seizures," the formulation of the privilege against self-incrimination does not implicitly invoke a weighing process. It is, rather, cast in categorical terms: one can never be "compelled" to incriminate oneself. Yet, as we shall see, whether one focuses on original understanding or modern doctrine, many questions about exact coverage and consequences have been resolved partly in terms of the power of competing values.

A. Range of Coverage and the Original Understanding

Given the language of the Amendment, one might surmise that the right bars only outright compulsion at actual criminal trials. The content of "compelled" is a core question about the original sense; but two crucial facts show that a broader coverage than trials was then understood. When the provision was adopted, the English practice that criminal defendants, though permitted, even strongly encouraged, to speak, were not *allowed* to testify under oath still prevailed in American courts. This entailed that a *right* not to testify under oath at one's trial would have been of minimal significance. Even more important, many of the crucial determinations of guilt occurred at preliminary proceedings, showing that the right extended at least to pretrial formal proceedings. And historically the right developed in England at least partly as a protection against sweeping inquiries concerning heresy and sedition by the English

High Commission, which had required suspected persons to swear to tell the truth.

Three related questions about original understanding concern the roots of the privilege, the underlying values it reflected, and its perceived coverage. For some time, the prevailing historical understanding was that the privilege developed in common law courts as a consequence of John Lilburne's "notorious agitation" against the Star Chamber, and the abolition of it and the High Commission which followed. Both of those bodies, in contrast to ordinary criminal proceedings, did require people to take oaths to answer criminal charges.[48] More recent historical scholars have been persuaded that the core of the privilege derived from broader European practices and those of ecclesiastical tribunals in England[49] and that, far from operating on the basis of any full scale right to silence, preliminary proceedings and trials for serious crimes in both England and the American colonies relied heavily on the answers of those accused to claims about their misbehavior.[50] Tied to all this was an effective absence of any role of counsel in those proceedings; it was up to magistrates and judges to protect the legal rights of suspects.[51]

Although some state constitutions in the new nation provided a privilege against self-incrimination, this apparently did not then affect ordinary practices. In part, emphasis on the privilege derived from prerevolutionary concerns about invasive procedures employed by England against the American colonies,[52] but it was not seen as a sweeping natural right to remain silent without any inference of guilt being drawn. Rather it was regarded as barring a suspect from being physically forced to speak and from being compelled to swear an oath to tell the truth—such swearing then being seen as a critical compulsion based on God's authority.[53]

Related to the accounts of original understanding are central questions about how the privilege should now be regarded. Should it be seen as a basic right to remain silent or a bar on improper methods of interrogation?[54] Should criminal procedures rest heavily on what the accused says or on the prosecution itself establishing guilt?[55] At the time of adoption of the Fifth Amendment, prevailing practice did not involve a sense of a fundamental right to remain silent; rather it depended heavily on how those accused responded to allegations—one study showed that 69% of suspects in New York City's Quarter Sessions confessed at preliminary examinations.[56]

Within the nineteenth century, the constitutional privilege apparently played little role federally and within states. Rather, common law practices continued without reference to the constitutional provisions. But as the nineteenth century progressed the significance of the privilege expanded; this was largely the consequence of a fundamental development of criminal processes in which defendants received the aid of counsel, and the government was taken to have the burden to show guilt.[57] Also, the basic logic of the privilege shifted; in 1886, *Boyd v. United States* notably relied on a rationale that the privilege protected "the sanctity of a man's home and the privacies of life."[58]

Two questions about the privilege are whom does it cover and when. While sitting as trial judge, Chief Justice Marshall ruled in 1807 that a witness before a grand jury could employ the privilege to decline to answer whether he had copied a document on Aaron Burr's orders.[59] Thus, "any criminal case" clearly included formal proceedings prior to trials, and the privilege was available to witnesses who were not themselves being prosecuted. That conclusion does not itself resolve whether the privilege also reaches investigations that are not yet formalized. Those with a specific original understanding almost certainly did not even consider this, since organized police forces carrying on intensive investigations did not exist at that time.[60] That, in itself, would hardly be a sufficient reason to conclude that the privilege should now have no application to police interrogation, contrary to the landmark case of *Miranda v. Arizona*.[61] Although the original sense of the privilege did not touch police investigations, the possibility of using broader underlying values as a guide raises the puzzle just how those values were then seen and how we should now perceive them. Given the prevalence then of suspects being expected to give an account of what they had done, one would conclude that if asked, people who were told about the future growth of police forces, would not have objected to some police pressure to speak, short of physical coercion.

B. What Are the Core Values?

With most constitutional rights, the basic underlying values are fairly straightforward, though controversy exists over their respective weight and the relevance of certain peripheral values. The difference with respect to the privilege against self-incrimination is well captured by a leading casebook on criminal procedure that calls it a "doctrine in search of a theory" and remarks that in contrast to other constitutional rights, "[t]here is no agreement on the privilege's purpose; indeed, some writers challenge the idea that it should exist at all."[62] Among the possible underlying values are protecting the innocent, avoiding sweeping unjustified investigations and arbitrary prosecutions, preventing abusive methods of discerning guilt, safeguarding individual autonomy, and recognizing a right that people have not to bring about their own punishment.[63] If we go back to the original development of the right in England, concerns about unrestrained inquiries by the Star Chamber and High Commission regarding religious and political commitments, and about behavior that should not have been criminal at all, may have been significant. But these concerns are now mostly protected by other constitutional rights, and the privilege against self-incrimination has always reached beyond their coverage. At its minimum, it was seen as foreclosing physical torture to produce testimony and any requirement that criminal suspects actually swear an oath about what they say they did.

By including the privilege in the Fifth Amendment, Congress made part of the federal constitution what had developed initially as a common law right, and was included in many early state constitutions.[64] In respect to modern conceptions, as well as original understanding, it matters greatly how one understands the values the privilege reflects. Especially when one focuses on courts, the perceived values have significantly affected when the privilege has been seen in play and what have been the consequences of both its exercises and its violations.

The difficulty of grasping the underlying values and of developing thoughtful opinions about their implementation can be aided by comparing analogous moral appraisals in settings not involving the government. I shall sketch two of these comparisons, concerning close friends and employer-worker relations, and ask whether the government's role drastically changes one's evaluations. These comparisons suggest what may be a moral basis to remain silent and what consequences appropriately follow. They also can aid reflection on whether the privilege against self-incrimination should be seen mainly as a right to silence, and, if so, just how that should be conceived.[65]

Agnes, who shares an apartment with her close friend Betty, cannot find a bracelet of hers. Should she question Betty whether she stole the bracelet, and, if she does, how should Betty respond? If the overwhelming likelihood is that Agnes merely misplaced her bracelet, questioning to explore Betty's possible guilt would reflect an unjustified distrust, and Betty might appropriately respond that she is offended and refuse to engage in the conversation. On the other hand, if Agnes has substantial reasons to think Betty may have taken the bracelet—for example, a friend has told her he saw Betty's sister wearing an unusual bracelet just like hers—her questioning Betty would be perfectly proper and Betty should see it as such.

If Emily, the owner of a gourmet market, wonders if some food has been taken, should she confront each of her fifteen workers to see if any are guilty? Although an employer may have an acceptable range of inquiry that is broader than that of a close friend, she also should be affected by just what evidence she has that any particular worker may have been taking food. And Walter, a worker, offended like Betty if subjected to intense questioning without any real evidence he has done a wrong, *might* reasonably refuse to answer, although that could cost him his job.

With these examples, how might Agnes and Emily fairly respond to silence, and would other techniques of investigation be more appropriate? If one estimates only pure probability, silence in any of those situations would seem to increase at least slightly the probability of guilt. However outrageous questions may be, an innocent person may be more likely to respond than a guilty one. But given solid reasons why Betty and

Walter would have *not* to respond if no significant evidence exists that they have done wrong, any strong inference of guilt would be unwarranted. However, when evidence against them is already substantial, innocent persons will almost always respond (unless they owe it to someone else to preserve a secret), whereas persons who did wrongs might hesitate to make their guilt clear or to get trapped in obvious lies. Thus, the legitimate inference from silence becomes much stronger when prior evidence of wrongdoing is substantial.

Related to all this are possible alternative techniques to discern the truth. Should Agnes decide to enlist a friend of Betty's who will deceive her into thinking he totally approves of her possible theft and would like to participate in the next one, and who will then report Betty's response? That strikes one as showing much less respect for Betty's autonomy than if Agnes asks her direct questions. The same conclusion would apply if Emily enlisted an "undercover agent" to deceive workers into admissions. In brief, in many human situations, when substantial evidence exists that a person has done wrong, the most respectful approach is to ask direct questions, *and* an inference about guilt is a natural reaction to a refusal to respond.

Does this all change if what is involved is a criminal trial or interaction with officials who are engaging in a criminal investigation? One might believe that a person has a stronger moral basis not to respond, even in the face of substantial evidence, if what is at stake is likely punishment as a criminal. But, as in informal settings, if substantial evidence is presented against someone, his declining to answer does commonly make his guilt seem at least somewhat more probable. The reality that jurors draw such an inference creates a substantial incentive for defendants to testify, and most do so.

In terms of reasonable inferences, silence during police investigations should count for less than silence at trial. Of course, by the time of a trial, a defendant faces substantial evidence of guilt. If he can counter that, a response would be natural and, barring recognition of a special right to remain silent, people would expect that.[66] At the earlier stage of police investigation, a suspect may doubt the presence of substantial evidence of his guilt, he may worry that open discussion will disclose aspects of his life that he wishes not to reveal, and he may fear that the police will attribute to him things he did not actually say.

When one considers alternative techniques of investigation, for government officials themselves to undertake deception so that a suspect believes he is talking to a sympathetic friend rather than an enlisted informer seems less respectful of autonomy than direct questioning, just as it does in the informal settings. That a strategy respects a person less does not, of course, establish that legally it is also forbidden. Perhaps compelled self-incrimination is just not involved, and this indeed fits the prevailing constitutional doctrine. When a person talks to someone who seems to be just a friendly acquaintance, he does not realize that what he says connects to a likely criminal accusation or possible conviction, he does not sense that he may be incriminating himself, and his comments do not involve any perception of a "criminal case." On the other hand, it would not be absurd to suppose that the government is secretly but effectively "compelling" him to be a witness against himself for criminal charges yet to be brought. Insofar as direct questioning seems fairer to a suspect than certain other strategies of determining his activities, one could see this as a basis either to extend the privilege against self-incrimination to cover forms of deception or to curtail the existing constitutional right to permit more explicit incentives for suspects to speak.

With this preliminary explanation of when guilt-focused questioning seems warranted, and what are appropriate responses to silence, as well as how direct questioning compares with deceptive methods of eliciting admissions, we turn to more specific issues and how these may be affected by judgments about basic values.

C. The Content of the Privilege, When It Applies, and Consequences of Invocation and Violation

Certain Supreme Court resolutions of the scope of the privilege against self-incrimination follow from an understanding of the basic text; others clearly involve an evaluation of competing considerations. In both categories, only some of the boundaries that have been set fit well with a moral assessment of comparable private situations.

In respect to the fundamental privilege not to give formal testimony that could be incriminating, two obvious points are worth noting. First, innocent persons, as well as guilty ones, can properly invoke it. Suppose that Daniel gives his friend Richard a ride to the bank, unaware that Richard is going to steal money there. Asked about any connection to Richard's crime, Daniel might plead the Fifth Amendment, believing that he would find it very hard to persuade others that he both drove Richard and was completely ignorant of the planned theft.[67]

The second point is that when anyone explicitly invokes the privilege, the government is rarely in a position to say she has done so improperly, since knowing exactly what a person speaking honestly might reveal is typically impossible. As Chief Justice Marshall wrote in regard to the witness before the grand jury that indicted Aaron Burr, if any direct answer might implicate him, "the witness must himself judge what his answer will be. . . ."[68]

Although an ordinary witness may answer some questions and then invoke the privilege when a new question threatens self-incrimination, a defendant at his own trial is differently situated. He need not testify at all, but once he chooses to do so, he is deemed to have waived the privilege. He cannot answer some questions and refuse to answer others; and once he does testify, he opens himself up to cross-examination.

1. Practical Effects

A particular feature of the privilege as conceived in the United States is highly questionable in its basic principle, but it *can* be defended in terms of likely practical effect or as needed in response to an aspect of what defendants' testimony generates at trials. The Supreme Court established half a century ago in *Griffin v. California* that neither prosecutors nor judges may tell jurors that they can draw any inference of guilt from a defendant's declining to testify;[69] and it later ruled that defendants have a right to have jurors instructed that they are not to do so.[70] These outcomes lie in tension with normal inferences, illustrated by the examples involving private persons. Although a guilty defendant may well testify and an innocent one may not, a natural inference is that a person who committed a crime is more likely to remain silent than one who is innocent. Especially if a defendant is faced with telling evidence that she might well rebut if she gave her own account, in principle should her silence be able to count at least a little in whether "guilt beyond a reasonable doubt" has been established?

In respect to underlying bases, if one saw the privilege itself as precluding any negative effect from silence, then barring any inferences would make sense. But if the right, while protecting against a person's bringing about her own conviction, allows others to draw completely natural inferences, then perhaps jurors should not be told they are precluded from doing so. In fact, the United States' constitutional rule about this is stricter than the practice in any other common law country.[71] In a recent concurring opinion, Justice Thomas, joined by Justice Scalia who had urged a similar conclusion in 1999,[72] claimed that *Griffin v. California* should be overruled.[73] Relying partly on the reality that at the time of the founding defendants were encouraged to give unsworn testimony and that adverse inferences were accepted if they refused to do so, Thomas argued that even when the privilege is explicitly invoked, that should not preclude the drawing of an adverse inference from silence.

Principle alone cannot resolve the issue of instructions about inferences; practical realities also matter. Whatever they are told, jurors are likely to view a defendant's refusal to take the stand with suspicion, and, consciously or not, to draw negative inferences from silence. With their lawyers perfectly aware of this, many defendants at trials do testify.[74] One could defend the instruction about *no inference* on the basis that it discourages jurors from drawing a much stronger inference than is really warranted, and is needed because judges may not be capable of conveying effectively to jurors that they could appropriately give some weight, but only a little, to a defendant's silence. Whatever one thinks about a judge's instructions, the concern about jurors drawing too great an inference does powerfully support the rule that prosecutors cannot argue that jurors should infer guilt from silence, since a prosecutor making such an argument would almost certainly emphasize just how telling silence is.

A further practical basis for the present approach to instructions is that the prosecution can introduce a defendant's criminal record if she testifies. Were the law ever to shift toward allowing judges to inform jurors that they may draw an inference from silence, fairness to defendants would demand that they not be faced with the choice of having their whole criminal record introduced or having their silence taken as evidence of guilt. (A possible exception to excluding that record would be to allow introduction of its aspects that directly suggest that the defendant's particular testimony has been untrue.) These two practical reasons supporting an instruction of "no inference" do reflect how such considerations may inform what are desirable legal standards. Nonetheless, for judges to tell jurors to avoid totally what it is perfectly natural, and what in terms of underlying principles may well be appropriate, is nonetheless troubling.

Another issue about the privilege that raises concerns both about underlying values and practical implications is the government's obtaining testimony from witnesses by granting immunity. If the privilege represents a fundamental right not to reveal criminal behavior, which could cause intense embarrassment and social rejection, then immunity should not be able to cancel it. If, however, the privilege concerns protecting people from having to contribute to their own criminal convictions, then an adequate grant of immunity suffices. When one reflects on a person having to testify under a grant of immunity, that hardly seems worse than providing highly damaging testimony that hurts close friends and loved ones (other than a spouse) who have committed crimes, a compulsion indisputably allowed. Moreover, a person who has himself done a serious criminal act may be regarded as lucky to escape conviction even if he must admit what he has done. Perhaps most important, grants of immunity can be very effective in solving crimes that involve many people and in penalizing those mainly responsible. Not surprisingly, the Supreme Court has long accepted compelled testimony under a grant of immunity.[75] To be effective, the immunity rightly extends beyond mere use of the testimony itself. Although not requiring absolute protection in respect to the acts admitted, the Court has ruled that neither the testimony nor its fruits (independent evidence that might be obtained as a result) can be employed against the witness.[76] This does not provide an absolute practical safeguard against investigators secretly and indirectly using the testimony to uncover evidence, but courts can properly set a strict standard on the prosecution to demonstrate that that has not taken place.[77]

In the historic case of *Boyd v. United States*,[78] decided in 1886, the Supreme Court ruled that the privilege against self-incrimination was closely connected to the bar on unreasonable searches. It held that persons could not be required to produce invoices that would support government seizure of imported property and yield possible criminal penalties for fraud. In the ensuing years, the Court backtracked with respect to papers. Organizations are not protected by the privilege,[79] and people can be required to submit mandatory records.[80] Susceptibility to merely civil penalties such as forfeiture is not by itself reached by the privilege, and the Supreme Court has largely left it up to Congress and state legislatures to determine what counts as genuinely civil and criminal.[81] Given the crucial importance of business records in various kinds of cases, the Court's not protecting people from having to submit them is hardly surprising.

The status of more private documents is not so clear. Whether the act of producing them itself is testimonial can depend on whether the government was already aware with "reasonable particularity" of the subpoenaed materials when it sought their production.[82] Within this broader question is the issue concerning the proper status of electronic documents. The Eleventh Circuit Court of Appeals decided in 2012 that a defendant did not have to decrypt his hard drives for the government because "decryption and production ... would require the use of the contents of Doe's mind and ... that ... would be tantamount to testimony by Doe...."[83] A contrary conclusion was reached by a federal district court in Colorado.[84] Nicholas Soares has urged that the current jurisprudence about the privilege against self-incrimination is ill equipped to deal with evolving technology and that more attention should be paid to the original conception that an individual should not be "compelled to provide ... information, in whatever form, that could be used to incriminate her."[85]

2. Investigatory Settings

This brings us to what is the most important modern development in the privilege against self-incrimination: its application to investigatory settings that precede formal proceedings. For much of the twentieth century, the Fifth Amendment was not held to apply against the states. In relation to the federal government, only those confessions involuntary under a common law standard were considered barred by privilege against self-incrimination.[86] In 1936, the Supreme Court held that the Due Process Clause renders a voluntariness requirement applicable to states.[87] In 1964, it ruled that, given incorporation by the Fourteenth Amendment, the privilege against self-incrimination itself applies against the states.[88] Two years later, *Miranda v. Arizona*[89] established that the privilege reaches police investigations when a suspect is in custody. The case set specific requirements for informing suspects of their rights that were stricter than then existed in any state.

When a person has been arrested, he must be told that he has a right to remain silent, that if he does speak, anything he says can and will be used against him in court, that he has a right to counsel, and that the government will provide counsel if he cannot afford to do so. If the suspect says he wants to remain silent, he cannot be questioned; if he asks for counsel, he cannot be questioned until he is advised by counsel. Chief Justice Warren's opinion for the *Miranda* Court expressed the concern that inappropriate police pressures, which, by this time in history were primarily psychological rather than physical, were generating too many confessions. The Court's opinion made clear that a waiver of the privilege must be clearly stated and that it cannot be presumed on the basis of a person's silence after receiving the warnings.[90]

Should custody be the key factor for the onset of the privilege? Warren's opinion formulates the criterion as when an individual is "in custody at the station or otherwise deprived of his freedom of action in any significant way."[91] At least if the privilege is regarded as a person's fundamental right not to incriminate himself, the crucial stage might seem to be when the police focus on a person as a suspect, since admissions made prior to custody by suspects who are ignorant of their rights also seem troublesome. Perhaps the pressure to speak may then be somewhat less intense, but the strongest counter to drawing the line in terms of degree of suspicion is that despite occasional uncertainty about exactly when the border to custody has been crossed, judges are much more capable of making that determination than discerning exactly when a person became a serious suspect.

The Supreme Court in *Miranda* did not rule that its required warnings and the exclusion from evidence at trial of a person's statements made after violation of the Court's standards were actually demanded by the Fifth Amendment itself. Rather, after stating that "we cannot say that the Constitution necessarily requires adherence to any particular solution,"[92] the Chief Justice wrote that the warnings and necessary waiver were prerequisites to the admissibility of statements in evidence "in the absence of a fully effective equivalent. . . ."[93]

When *Miranda* was decided, some feared that it would seriously impair law enforcement. That has not occurred for at least two reasons. By far, the most significant concerns the psychology of suspects and, at least to some degree, the suspects' reasonable sense of likely reactions by those who wish to interrogate them. Although most lawyers, if consulted, would typically recommend silence, given that answers to police questions will more often hurt suspects than help them, what is a suspect likely to think when he receives a warning that he understands? He typically will say to himself—especially if he is not a seasoned professional criminal—"If I remain silent and ask for counsel, they will assume I have something to hide and am probably guilty." On top of this reaction, the suspect may also worry: "If I insist on counsel, they will investigate me with more intensity than if I can give an account (true or not) that seems to establish my innocence." Many of those so inclined do not grasp how damaging statements may be if they can later be proven to be untrue, or happen not to fit a theory of defense that might be presented at trial. As a consequence, most suspects waive their rights to silence and to counsel at this stage, even if it would have helped to assert those rights.[94] This can hurt not only persons who committed crimes whose guilt might be hard to prove but also persons who are actually innocent, or who are on the border between innocent and guilty, whose statements may imply wrongdoing. Without a doubt, damaging statements to the police increase the pressure on a defendant to agree to a plea bargain, rather than risking a trial.

Two possibilities to provide greater actual protection would be to require that counsel actually be present for all police interrogation of suspects in custody or that all questioning that is done while suspects are in custody be recorded. Requiring that counsel always be present would be expensive, would impede many investigations, and might be intrinsically inappropriate for persons who wish to admit their guilt or who actually have solid grounds to quickly show their innocence. Many legislators and judges must believe that affording this greater protection, mainly helping persons who have committed the crimes of which they are suspected, would go too far.

The recording of all interrogation, which is already done in some jurisdictions,[95] is a much simpler added protection, allowing judges to review what actually took place during warning and questioning, rather than having to rely on what the police say happened.

A second reason *Miranda* has not seriously interfered with law enforcement is that instead of putting overt pressure on suspects in various ways, interrogators have largely pursued other strategies that are similarly effective. These include winning the confidence of a suspect and assuring her that they want to help her and are on her side;[96] and misleading suspect *A* about various crucial facts, such as that a co-participant *B* admitted his involvement in a crime but said that *A* was the one primarily responsible.[97]

These strategies raise the question whether crucial deceptions that produce incriminating statements should be regarded as violating the privilege. I have suggested that the government's use of secret informants to elicit admissions by deception hardly seems morally preferable to asking direct questions with an acknowledgment that a failure to respond may lead to a possible inference of likely guilt. Viewed linguistically, trickery is not quite the same as compulsion, and courts have understandably not extended the privilege to cover deceptive strategies that do not generate perceived pressure upon suspects to talk.[98] However, it would not be absurd to see admissions obtained by deception that makes a suspect think a key acquaintance is putting the primary blame on her as close enough to compulsion to warrant the same treatment.[99]

A third reason *Miranda* has proved less earthshaking than many initially thought is that the Supreme Court in the ensuing years has been somewhat more permissive about admitting evidence than the original opinion implied it would. Notably, the Justices have admitted statements that were voluntary but made in the absence of adequate warnings to impeach a defendant's actual testimony at trial, deciding that that exclusion is not necessary to make the right effective.[100] And when time elapsed from when a person did invoke the privilege, and from when he had been released from custody, the Court allowed questioning following another warning.[101]

In connection with effective waivers, the Court has relaxed the standard announced in *Miranda*. Rather than requiring the police to get a waiver that is clearly explicit, the Court indicated in 2010 that "[t]here is good reason to require an accused who wants to invoke his or her right to remain silent to do so unambiguously."[102] And in *Salinas v. Texas*, decided in 2013, the plurality stated that "we have long held that a witness who desires the protection of the privilege . . . must claim it at the time he relies on it."[103] The waiver of the privilege "need not be knowing."[104] Thus, a suspect who received an adequate warning and did not really respond or was vague will be unable to claim that he did not actually waive the privilege.

3. What Constitutes Self-Incrimination?

Interesting issues concern what exactly counts as self-incrimination. The Court has ruled that taking blood samples or obtaining other physical data such as fingerprints or DNA is not covered by the privilege.[105] Such facts do not involve any testimony or mental exercise by a suspect. Certain components of routine inquiries, such as a suspect's name and address, his birthday, and his provision of a signature, have also been held outside the privilege,[106] although these do involve mental exercises and a person could fabricate his signature in various ways.

The privilege does preclude the government from requiring that an accused submit to a psychiatric examination and then using what he said at sentencing,[107] but that protection does not apply for defendants who claim they were insane or subject to extreme emotional distress.[108] The growth of cognitive neuroscience technology has raised the concerns that physical information about the brain may reveal aspects of a person's character, as may various kinds of responses not directly related to indicating what a person has done. Scholars have suggested that current Fifth Amendment doctrine is in conflict with insights of neuroscience and that an expansion of what counts as self-incrimination is needed.[109] As with a number of other aspects this chapter has covered, someone who sees a tension between the present scope of the privilege and other circumstances that are somewhat similar may favor either an expansion that covers those circumstances *or* a reducing of the limits on government encouragement of actual speech by suspects and a formal allowing of jurors to draw inferences from silence.

In its formalist approach, the Court has decided that the privilege does not apply prior to the government's attention to the person who becomes a suspect. Thus, when a defendant was tried for murder and claimed that he acted in self-defense, the prosecution was allowed to show that he had not come forward after the shooting to provide that explanation.[110] That decision is seriously at odds with the notion that a genuine right to remain silent constitutes the basic value on which the privilege is grounded. Suppose one kills in self-defense, as George Zimmerman successfully claimed that he did in his highly publicized trial in 2013 over the death of Trayvon Martin. If no one witnesses a shooting or otherwise identifies the person who did it, for the shooter to come forward claiming self-defense runs the risk that others may believe he did the shooting, but for different reasons. That would clearly be a basis to invoke the privilege if a person were already in custody and asked about the shooting. If a person should not by his own statements be forced to risk criminal penalties, is not the same concern present if the law presents him with the choice of initially coming forward on his own, or having his failure to do so later undercut his claim of self-defense? Given that the exact limits of permissible self-defense differ among jurisdictions and that their applications to actual events is sometimes less than obvious, coming forward could undoubtedly create a genuine risk for some of those who believe they did act in self-defense. Perhaps the best that can be said for the Court's ruling that a person must take that risk is that the need to know when people have been killed is great, and that the slight risk to a shooter who genuinely acted in self-defense is remote enough that it will rarely affect his or her possibly reporting what happened.

One notable qualification to the coverage of the privilege is that, as all states require, those in automobile accidents must remain at the scene,[111] even though doing so involves an effective statement by them that they were involved and may subject them to criminal penalties for their driving. In a case raising that issue, a plurality of Supreme Court Justices said the conduct of remaining was neither testimonial nor incriminating; Justice Harlan, whose vote was necessary for the result, relied instead on an explicit balancing approach in which the concern about possible self-incrimination was overridden by the need for traffic safety. The centrality of competing values also helped produce nonapplication of the *Miranda* standards when a mother resisted a court order to produce a son who was in her custody.[112] And when police, prior to any warning, had questioned a man in a supermarket about the location of a gun he had had with him, the Court relied on a "public safety" exception to the *Miranda* requirements.[113] As the opinion explains, because the Fifth Amendment does not contain a "reasonableness" standard like that governing searches and seizures, officials can proceed without a warning only when the need to get crucial information involves saving human life or satisfying some other highly compelling reason.[114]

4. Noncriminal Consequences

A troubling question about the privilege is how far the government can respond to its invocation in ways other than criminal proceedings, such as firing its own workers who invoke it. After some sharp divisions in the 1950s and 1960s,[115] the Supreme Court apparently settled upon the following principles.[116] The government cannot dismiss an employee simply because he invokes the privilege against self-incrimination. If the government grants him immunity from criminal prosecution, it can then fire him if he refuses to answer relevant questions about his work. It can also fire him if he testifies about corruption or dereliction of duty under a grant of immunity. But if the government declines to grant him immunity, it cannot "penalize" his refusal to respond by terminating his employment.

I have suggested that if an employee presented with substantial evidence of his wrongdoing fails to offer an explanation of his performance of duties, termination of employment is a natural response. The government's indulgence in this natural response should not by itself be considered an unconstitutional penalty on the exercise of a right to silence, or an impermissible form of compulsion to testify that is taken to "compel" the answers of those who fear that consequence.[117] However, this generalization is subject to caveats. The government should not be able to fire employees who invoke the privilege in proceedings unrelated to their employment.[118] Nor should government employees have to respond to every fishing expedition concerning possible wrongdoing. (Perhaps this principle should be relaxed for high-level officers with very important government responsibilities; they carry special responsibilities to preserve the openness and integrity of government operations.[119]) Finally, although a practice of dismissal based on particular circumstances seems appropriate, statutory requirements of automatic dismissal are unacceptable. Such an inflexible mandate smacks of an intent to force testimony rather than preserve the fitness of the workforce; the government-as-employer needs to be able to make the kind of individuated response to exceptional circumstances that one would expect from an ordinary employer.

IV. *UNREASONABLE SEARCHES AND SEIZURES*

Although the Fourth Amendment protection against unreasonable searches and seizures raises questions similar to those regarding the privilege against self-incrimination, how they have been and should be treated differs considerably. The Fourth Amendment is not only cast in terms that seem to direct assessments of actual circumstances, these are unavoidably necessary if the protection is taken to apply broadly. This reality does not itself resolve just how its boundaries of coverage and the consequences of violations should be assessed. One particular concern is how to treat developments in communications that allow acquisitions of information in manners that only loosely resemble an ordinary search. What follows explores both specific issues about the Amendment's applications as well as its relation to the Fifth Amendment.

The Fourth Amendment reads in full: "The right of people to be secure in their persons, houses, papers, and effects, against unreasonable searches and seizures, shall not be violated, and no Warrants shall issue, but upon probable cause, supported by oath or affirmation, and particularly describing the place to be searched, and the persons or things to be seized." Aspects of the text itself could lead to differing conclusions about which searches are unconstitutional; and—perhaps more than with any other part of the Bill of Rights—how courts should treat developing technology and engage in a weighing of relevant factors have become central concerns. The answers depend partly on how far the protected values are being undercut and on what courts are capable of doing. Among the more specific questions are these: (1) What constitutes a "search" and "seizure," and what is the connection between those? (2) What is the status of warrants and when, if ever, should they play a prominent role in searches and seizures? (3) What does "probable cause" consist of, and to what extent does "reasonableness" depend on that or other factors? (4) How far should competing public needs figure in assessing the scope of Fourth Amendment rights? (5) How much should concerns about equality of treatment matter, an issue raised by the law of "stop and frisk"? (6) What remedies should follow violations, and, in particular, should reliable evidence be excluded? Although at earlier stages, the right to be free of unreasonable searches and seizures was perceived partly as a protection of property against government interference, in modern times, it has come to be regarded primarily as the safeguarding of personal privacy and autonomy. Disagreement is mainly over when those interests are sufficiently in play to justify affording the constitutional protection.

A. Original Understanding and Its Relevance

Within recent decades, historical scholarship has indicated that, despite certain definite objectives, the original understanding of the Fourth Amendment was indecisive or did not address issues that later became important. What is clear is that a predominant objective was to forbid general warrants and related "writs of assistance" that authorized widespread searches without specific evidence of wrongdoing.[120] The employment of such warrants by Great Britain's customs officers, among others, had aroused intense objections within the American colonies.[121]

Where uncertainties and disagreements arise is over the Amendment's possible application to warrantless searches and arrests, the status of the reasonableness requirement, and the content of probable cause. Tied to these particular questions is how far practices of criminal enforcement were covered by the "due process" clause of the Fifth Amendment rather than the Fourth Amendment.

Since the language conveying the right to be free of "unreasonable searches and seizures" precedes the warrant requirement, it reads as if it sets a more general standard, and that, indeed, is one account of its content, rendering warrantless searches and arrests subject to a standard of reasonableness.[122] A contrary view is that this language merely referred to specific forms of search regarded as unacceptable. On the narrowest view, the Amendment addressed only general warrants for searches of houses and "was primarily intended to set minimum standards for the issuance of noncriminal revenue search warrants," without "any significant bearing on criminal arrest and search authority and especially on warrantless arrest authority."[123] This view does not necessarily entail a lack of constitutional protection for criminal arrests and searches since the Due Process Clause may have been conceived as including restrictive common law doctrines about when these were permitted.[124] A broader sense about the Fourth Amendment is that it was also aimed at multiple-specific warrants for searches and arrests and at nocturnal searches and no-knock entries,[125] leaving unsettled the status of searches incident to arrest.[126] With regard to "probable cause," there was apparently no agreed upon sense of just what degree of probability was needed and what evidence was necessary to establish it.[127]

As with other provisions, these uncertainties render overarching reliance on the original understanding about specific practices an undesirable, even impossible, interpretive strategy. But two other features are even more important here. One we have reviewed in other contexts. On a genuine originalist approach, a Justice considering challenges to state practices would need to determine how the search and seizure language in the federal and state constitutions was understood when the Fourteenth Amendment was adopted. We have no reason to suppose that views about what practices were restricted were then identical to those dominant in 1791, or that the extent to which enforcement of the criminal law was then seen as covered by "due process" without regard to the language of the Fourth Amendment had remained just the same.

The other consideration involves changing structures within society and government. One crucial difference is that organized police forces did not exist when the Bill of Rights was adopted.[128] If regulation of warrantless searches and arrests was not a major concern then, it hardly follows that the same is, or should be, true now. And, of course, more broadly, given the novel ways in which human information is now shared and maintained, it would not make sense to conclude that the amendment is simply irrelevant for all of these.

These realities support the general positions taken in this book that, especially with provisions that contain open-ended language, the aspect of original understanding given the most importance should be what were taken as the underlying general principles and purposes, and that even at this level, that understanding should constitute only one criterion of interpretation. It is both interesting and instructive that scholars who differ about specific dominant understandings when the Fourth Amendment was adopted basically agree that what should now mainly carry weight is the kind of fundamental protections that it was designed to afford.[129] That position contrasts with that taken of Justice Scalia,[130] and articulated in some majority opinions of the Court,[131] which also accepts a broad application of the reasonableness standard, but first relies heavily on the common law up to 1791 to discern whether a type of search was clearly allowed or disallowed by the original amendment.[132] If no definite answer emerges, what then follows is an ad hoc balancing version of "reasonableness" that does not afford special weight to the more fundamental values underlying the Fourth Amendment, and may, as applied, provide inadequate protection.[133]

B. Searches and Seizures and Their Relation

In what follows, I will disregard the possibility that the original sense of the Fourth Amendment did not really concern criminal law enforcement and assume, as has long been well established, that the Amendment's language bears directly on that. Given this premise, what precisely should the Fourth Amendment be taken to cover? The language referring to "person or things to be seized" obviously covers arrests as well as ordinary searches for evidence, but that alone does not tell us what counts as an arrest, a search, or a "seizure," or what the precise relation is between impermissible searches and seizures.

Although textual language of "unreasonable searches and seizures" is not exactly explicit about whether both a search and seizure are needed for the amendment to come into play,[134] the two elements need not be present together. The amendment can apply if a search does not involve a seizure, or an arrest is made or property seized without any search. However, if the government, unrelated to possible criminal proceedings, seizes the yacht of someone who has failed to pay taxes, that, by modern understanding, does not involve the Fourth Amendment.[135] Whether there can be searches not even aimed at possible "seizures" depends on how these terms are understood. Conceptually, one *might* think that wiretapping or acquiring information from confidential text messages involves searching without any contemplated "seizure" of the kind covered by the amendment. Interestingly, when the Supreme Court held in *Olmstead v. United States*[136] in 1928 that the Fourth Amendment did not apply to wiretapping absent any physical trespass because speech is not property, it still did apparently assume that had a trespass occurred, the acquired evidence of a communication would be a seizure. Of course, since *Olmstead*, the Court has adopted the principle reflected in Justice Brandeis's dissent,[137] considering the heart of the Amendment as concerning not property but a "right to be left alone"—that electronic surveillance, with or without trespass, is relevantly a search and that the listening to or recording of a conversation counts as a seizure. Given all of this, virtually any search is aimed at some kind of seizure.[138]

A more recent problem involves the acquisition by the federal government of vast information about who has sent messages to whom and when they have done so.[139] The assumption is that no one will look into the content of the messages unless a positive reason arises to do so. What is involved does seem to be a kind of "seizure" (assuming that the information is not given "voluntarily" by those with the power to do so), but the government could contend that until it seeks more substantial information about a communication, no "search" is involved. Given the sweeping data that are being acquired, the better perception would be that minimal seizures and searches are involved, even if the practice, and the degree of secrecy, are regarded as acceptable in light of threats of terrorism.

C. Relation to the Privilege Against Self-Incrimination

Among the questions about what counts as unacceptable "searches" and "seizures" is how the protection against unreasonable searches relates to the privilege against self-incrimination. One inquiry is what values underlie the two protections. Both can be seen as protecting people's privacy and autonomy, as safeguarding them from being compelled to provide the evidence for their being seen as criminal, and as precluding government invasion of private domains absent a compelling reason. Although the core privilege against self-incrimination is formally cast absolutely, unlike the language of unreasonable searches and seizures, this does not preclude seeing the two as related and finding borders of coverage where each might apply. Notable in this respect is when the government aims to seize possibly incriminating private documents or uses an informer armed with a recording device to obtain admissions of guilt.

In 1886, the Supreme Court decided *Boyd v. United States*,[140] a fascinating case that closely linked unreasonable searches to the Fifth Amendment. In what was actually only a proceeding to have plate glass forfeited because it had been imported illegally, the government required the importers to submit the invoice showing the value of the glass. The Supreme Court determined that the statute authorizing such a demand was unconstitutional because it violated the Fourth Amendment to compel "production of a man's private papers to establish a criminal charge against him, or to forfeit his property."[141] Justice Bradley's opinion purported to rely significantly on English history and took the key value of protecting people's property as the basis to discern what the Framers regarded as unreasonable searches. In condemning "this forcible and compulsory extortion of a man's own testimony or of his private papers," Bradley remarked that "the Fourth and Fifth Amendment run almost into each other."[142] In response to the argument that the terms of neither Amendment covers civil cases, Bradley wrote: "We think (the proceedings) are within the spirit of both."[143] According to *Boyd*, compelling someone to submit papers effectively required him to be a witness against himself. This made "unreasonableness" turn on the categorization of what a person was required to do, not a low probability of finding incriminating evidence.[144] In a comment at odds with what a strict texturalist would contend, Justice Bradley adhered "to the rule that constitutional provisions for the security of persons should be liberally construed. A close and literal construction deprives them of half of their efficacy and leads to the gradual depreciation of the right, as if it consisted more in sound than in substance."[145]

Although dictum in a 1921 case indicated that the *Boyd* rule applied to forms of property besides documents,[146] the Supreme Court in the same year began to unravel both the actual coverage of *Boyd* and the assumption that the Fourth and Fifth Amendments are so closely linked. It ruled then that the government could seize any property actually used in the commission of a crime,[147] and, over the next half century, it reduced the possible linkage of the two amendments in various ways. In 1928, rejecting Justice Brandeis's dissent based on a right to silence, the Court in *Olmstead*[148] allowed wiretapping, absent physical trespass, to acquire information that could be used as evidence. When it later abandoned *Olmstead*, the Court regarded the use of illegally obtained evidence as violative of an exclusory rule to enforce the Fourth Amendment, not as itself an infringement of the right to silence.[149] In 1967, the Court rejected its earlier distinction between materials that are only evidentiary and those instrumental in a crime, ruling that searches and seizures and uses at trial were appropriate for both.[150] A decade later, when upholding a summons to obtain from his lawyer records made by a defendant's accountants, the Court remarked that the Fifth Amendment does not "prevent the otherwise proper acquisition or use of evidence which, in the Court's view, did not involve compelled testimonial self-incrimination of some sort."[151] Shortly thereafter, extending an earlier ruling that corporations could not invoke the privilege against self-incrimination,[152] the Court permitted seizure under a warrant of a person's private business papers.[153] What has not yet been decisively resolved is whether the Fifth Amendment protects individuals from being compelled to produce personally made business records,[154] and whether searches seeking personal diaries in which people describe their experiences and feelings are permissible.[155] For the most part, however, the Fourth Amendment is not now seen to overlap significantly with the Fifth, and few physical items, if any, are absolutely protected against searches and uses in evidence.

Certain activities, such as the employment of informers who may record what is said to them, are in tension with the values that underlie both amendments. The discussion of the Fifth Amendment has indicated how use of informers may be seen as deception designed to get people to incriminate themselves. From the perspective of the Fourth Amendment, the continuing use of a deceptive informer is arguably a much greater invasion of a person's privacy than a simple physical search. Yet, under present doctrine, this practice is not subject to the restraint of either constitutional provision. The concern about informers is especially acute when they infiltrate organizations known to be opposed to governmental policies, as happened during the era of civil rights and opposition to the Vietnam War, when J. Edgar Hoover headed the F.B.I. If members of organizations suspect an informer may be in their midst but have no idea who he may be, their internal communications can be sharply curtailed, substantially undercutting freedom of expression and association. Although exactly how constitutional standards should apply is debatable, the widespread use of secret informers can pose a great enough threat to constitutional values that its immunity from constitutional review seems mistaken.

D. Warrants: Their Role and Exceptions

As the section on original understanding indicates, the Fourth Amendment is not explicit about the fundamental relation between warrants and reasonable searches; and it is uncertain whether the original purpose of the warrant clause was simply to bar general warrants[156] or also to require that officials obtain specific warrants in some circumstances. On the former account, whether an ordinary search was reasonable would not have turned at all on whether the police had simply failed to get any warrant. Whatever its historical accuracy, the Supreme Court has rejected that position and decisively resolved that getting warrants is the norm for ordinary searches.[157] The logic of this approach is that a judgment by a magistrate helps assure that a search is really justified. Especially given uncertainty about original understanding, the practical value of warrants and the force of authoritative precedents should be the main guides as to when warrants are required.

Their genuine effect is not easily demonstrable. Applications for warrants (or their equivalents) are almost always approved, whether an ordinary judge is making a determination about a typical search[158] or an administrative tribunal is passing on a government petition to undertake comprehensive antiterrorist surveillance.[159] This is hardly surprising, given that before its issuance, no one has an opportunity to contest the granting of a warrant, and those seeking to make the search are the ones offering the facts for review. Further, magistrates issuing search warrants may often not consider carefully whether the searches are really justified. Although William Stuntz has suggested that the standard reasons given for warrants—including a neutral, detached decision-maker and the prevention of unconstitutional searches—are much less compelling than is often supposed,[160] nevertheless, the very need for officials to make the effort to assemble and assert the facts and to persuade a judge that the vague standard has been met do constrain, to a degree, the law enforcement personnel who must seek authorization. And, as Stuntz suggested, pre-search warrants can counter the post-search inclination of judges to assume that any finding of incriminating evidence must mean probable cause was present.[161] Whatever its weaknesses, the warrant requirement does help protect the privacy of citizens.

Given the amount of time a police officer must take to formulate an application for a warrant and to receive approval, it is obvious that one cannot always be required. With respect to ordinary searches, the crucial criteria involve safety and possible destruction. When making an arrest, an officer needs to assure himself that a suspect is not carrying a loaded gun or other weapon that he might then use. And if someone becomes aware that his apartment may soon be searched for forbidden drugs or evidence of a criminal act, he is highly likely to destroy or remove the evidence. When they possess a solid basis to believe that a suspect has this sense, the police need to enter and search immediately. Less obvious is when the likelihood of a suspect's destroying evidence is slight enough and his right to have his privacy protected is forceful enough so that a warrant must be obtained, problems the Supreme Court has addressed on various occasions.

A peculiar question about warrants is the kinds of circumstances in which they are never required. One thinks, for example, of searches when one enters the country, is flying on a commercial airplane, or is stopped in one's automobile. I shall treat these shortly in relation to the limits on requirements of probable cause.

Another particular issue about warrants is the extent to which they are, or should be, required for arrests. Obviously, if police perceive someone they suspect at the scene of a typical crime, they may arrest without a warrant. Although warrants are sometimes issued for arrests, most arrests occur without them. In 1966, for example, within New York City, 366 of 171,288 arrests were made under warrants, that is, 1 out of every 468.[162] Although the language of the Fourth Amendment contains no explicit difference of treatment for arrests and searches, the main original concern was about searches grounded in general warrants; warrantless arrests for felonies were apparently then an accepted aspect of the common law.[163] At least as to "crimes" within an officer's view, the Supreme Court has extended this acceptance to the most minor of offenses, including an arrest for the failure to wear a seat belt.[164] Since the "offender" was a mother in her car with small children, arresting her on the scene caused serious inconvenience and was acknowledged by the Court to reflect "extremely poor judgment." But the Justices, 5–4, declined to adopt a case-by-case approach, rather than formulating a categorical rule.[165]

Whether a warrant is ever constitutionally required for an arrest is not settled.[166] This issue would be presented if officers neither viewed the crime nor arrived at the scene shortly after its commission *and* there was little fear that the person suspected would attempt to escape the jurisdiction. Although these circumstances might be seen as too unusual to justify special treatment, requiring a warrant then would fit with the basic principles governing searches. And it is highly doubtful if a warrantless arrest should be accepted in cases like that involving the seat belt, when no reason of any force exists actually to arrest someone, even if she is technically guilty of violating a minor restriction.

E. Reasonable Searches and Arrests and Probable Cause

Perhaps the most important Fourth Amendment coverage issues concern what the requirement of probable cause amounts to and what constitutes an "unreasonable" search or arrest when "probable cause" is not the main criterion. The latter question involves two components: Does some action count as a "search" or "arrest," and, if so, how should reasonableness be assessed? These problems implicate the extent to which judges should employ general categorical standards or undertake particular evaluations, a question prominent in many areas of constitutional interpretation.

1. Probable Cause

What is "probable cause?" In *Brinegar v. United States*, the Supreme Court said that probable cause was present for an arrest when officers had "knowledge" and "reasonably trustworthy information" of "fact and circumstances" that are "sufficient in themselves to warrant a man of reasonable caution in the belief that an offense has been or is being committed."[167] In reviewing a search in *Illinois v. Gates* in 1983, Chief Justice Rehnquist wrote for the Court that information needed to provide "a fair probability that contraband or evidence of a crime will be found in a particular place."[168] What degree of probability does such language suggest and what sort of information is needed?

This language I have quoted is hardly precise about the needed probability. Along with the very term "probable cause," the formulation in *Brinegar* connotes "more probable than not," but the phrasing in *Gates* is less demanding, and the Rehnquist Court explicitly indicated that the standard does not require more than 50 percent.[169] The fact that a high percentage of searches pursuant to warrants do produce incriminating evidence[170] suggests that those who apply for and issue them are guided by at least a notion of substantial probability. But it can hardly be doubted that in actual practice, the seriousness of a crime and the need for immediate action can matter. For example, if reliable information suggested that there was one chance in five that a man who was definitely planning to leave the country in a few hours had brutally murdered an entire family, we would expect the police to arrest him. And after the bombing at the Boston Marathon in April of 2013, the sweeping investigation involved detentions and searches based on far lower probabilities than "more probable than not."[171] Any sensible enforcement of the law must respond to the varieties of criminal acts, either by allowing a somewhat flexible standard of probability for "probable cause" or carving out circumstances in which "reasonable" searches and arrests do not require that. Sherry Colb has urged that the Amendment's "reasonableness" standard should explicitly take into account the seriousness of crimes involved and the degree of invasion of a person's privacy.[172] Although judges may hesitate to say they are responsive to such differences, not wishing to encourage officers to accept lower levels of probability whenever they regard crimes as serious, acknowledging that at least in extreme instances of seriousness and triviality these underlying values bear on what counts as probable cause, as well as what is reasonable, would be desirable.

The Supreme Court has shifted its position on just how information offered for warrants should be evaluated. Especially for drug crimes, lots of critical information is supplied by informants, either ones known to officers or anonymous ones. Two fundamental concerns are how reliable such information is and whether officers may fabricate "informer information" to support a search they believe would be productive but for which they do not yet have an adequate basis. In a 1969 decision, the Court rejected a "totality of circumstances" approach for warrant applications that rely on informants, instead calling for information about an informant's reliability and the grounds for his knowledge.[173] But in *Illinois v. Gates*, the Court not only relaxed the needed probability, but it also rejected the need for strict adherence to this two-pronged standard, rather treating reliability and bases of information as relevant factors in applying the "fluid concept" that requires "assessment of probabilities in particular factual contexts."[174]

Even under this more flexible approach, the claimed reliability and bases of information figure in an assessment, and what is involved may still be more than a simple objective probability estimate. Suppose an anonymous informant contacts police and, without indicating how he knows this, accuses a man of a serious crime and states specifically where particular evidence will be found. Given the absence of any basis to assess the informant's reliability and the grounds for his conclusion, the police presumably could not get a warrant.[175] But how often do people "inform" the police in this way, and how often, when they do so, are they substantially accurate? I doubt that reliable data exist about this,[176] but my own guess would be that when such an informant's claimed information is fairly detailed, it may well be true more often than not. The reliability approach suggests that courts are genuinely concerned about assuring the objective bases of warrants and preventing fraud (by informants or police), as well as assessing actual probabilities.[177] When it comes to how reviewing courts should themselves consider probable cause, the Supreme Court has indicated that they should accord deference to the judgment of magistrates who issue warrants,[178] but not to police decisions to engage in warrantless searches. The latter part of this differentiation wisely encourages the use of warrants; and deference in borderline situations to magistrates' conclusions is appropriate, but if that deference becomes too great, the practical effect of rules about probable cause is sharply reduced.

2. The Borders of Search and Relaxed Probability Requirements

The Fourth Amendment does not constrain the acquisition of information absent a relevant search; and, if for some reason, a search can be carried out with a lower level of probability, the "reasonableness" requirement does not necessitate a showing of probable cause. Some of these exceptions to "probable cause" fit ordinary understandings, whereas others are grounded on a weighing of public needs versus intrusions on privacy.

When an officer is located appropriately and happens to perceive criminal behavior or evidence of a crime, he may, of course, act on the basis of what he sees or hears even though no prior information led him to that discovery. Simply seeing something, without more, is not a search. Whether a similar conclusion is sound if investigators have located themselves in specific public places hoping to find evidence of criminal activity is more debatable. For example, officers may look through a suspect's windows at what is taking place within his dwelling, or observe what is transpiring in a greenhouse by flying over property, or use electronic equipment to measure the heat being generated from the inside of a building, or comb through someone's garbage. Investigators may also undertake a standard kind of search on physical property owned by a suspect but not closely connected to his dwelling. These forms of observance all raise issues about the borders of the coverage of the Fourth Amendment.

Here is how the Supreme Court has dealt with them. Simple visual observance from public property does not constitute a relevant search.[179] However, by a 5–4 margin, the Court ruled that the use of a thermal imager to measure the heat coming from a suspect's home, in order to ascertain whether he was employing high-intensity lamps to grow marijuana indoors, counted as a search covered by the Fourth Amendment.[180] Joined by four colleagues, Justice Scalia, referring to the *Katz* case on electronic eavesdropping, wrote that the privacy protected by the Amendment was affected by advancing technology and that the crucial test was whether society would recognize an expectation of privacy as reasonable.[181] The Court had previously ruled that, although people may subjectively regard what they put in their garbage bags as private, their placing those bags on the street, accessible to animals, children, and scavengers, to be picked up by garbage collectors, precludes any objectively reasonable expectation of privacy.[182] Thus, the police can examine the contents of typical garbage without regard to the Fourth Amendment.

The legitimacy of observation by the "naked eye" from 400 feet in the air was upheld 5–4 in *Florida* v. *Riley*.[183] Eight Justices did not regard the height of the helicopter, used to discern the growing of marijuana in a greenhouse, as relevant; they disagreed about whether the owner had a reasonable expectation of privacy. Justice O'Connor, concurring, rejected the claim on the basis that the helicopter was "at an altitude at which members of the public travel" with some regularity.[184] In terms of expectations of privacy, this hardly seems relevant, since ordinary travelers are not staring down at greenhouses to see if some illegal crop is being grown.

Given the Amendment's reference to "houses," the Court has not extended its coverage to "open fields," regardless of what steps an owner has taken to isolate the public from that property.[185] "Curtilage" surrounding a home carries a reasonable expectation of privacy; a barn roughly fifty yards from a fence that circles a residence does not.[186] Exactly what counts as a search reached by the Amendment is not easy to say in some of these borderline circumstances; but the guiding criteria may best be what are reasonable expectations of privacy.

A rather different basis for nonapplication of the ordinary standards of the Fourth Amendment is when "special needs" are taken to justify searches and arrests that do not satisfy any probability standard.[187] The most straightforward of these is that according to present doctrine, police can search someone they have arrested, regardless of whether he is probably carrying a weapon or evidence he might destroy. Officials in schools can search the lockers of students for forbidden drugs.[188] Customs officers can undertake searches of individuals and of what they carry. And all passengers on commercial flights are subject to at least a limited examination of their persons and bags. Customs and airport searches are widely accepted, although they may cause inconvenience and some embarrassment, and the vast majority of those searched have nothing to hide.

The airline example sharply illustrates the effect of public needs and also reveals a subtle aspect of how these are perceived. In a case involving passengers of a bus at a stopover who were asked by police to consent to searches, the Supreme Court assumed that such consent was necessary.[189] Why are buses different from airplanes? We rightly think of airplane security as mainly designed to protect against terrorist bombing and hijacking of planes. These are genuine risks to lives and safety. But statistics show that in modern times, air travel is much safer not only than ordinary automobile driving but also than travel on trains and buses.[190] Very likely, were there no airport security, the percentage of passengers' lives lost in airplane flights would still be less than those lost in bus transportation over a similar mileage. Does that matter? The truth is that people feel more at risk on planes, that the large number of lives lost when a plane is destroyed is deeply disturbing to us all, *especially* when that is a consequence of an intentionally destructive act. And the fear of terrorism is understandably much stronger than its actual addition to our ordinary risks of harm. Even if one puts aside the risk that a hijacked airplane may be used to kill nonpassengers, as in 9/11, our human perceptions and sense of community are strong reasons to accept airport examinations, as expensive and as time-consuming as they are. Although neither the Supreme Court nor lower courts have provided an agreed upon explanation of just why airport security is special,[191] these reasons make it unthinkable that judges will decide airport inspections must be curbed or genuinely consented to. And these reasons may well support somewhat similar examinations on subways and other public transport with respect to which security is a genuine concern.[192]

A notable exception to ordinary Fourth Amendment requirements includes national security surveillance by the federal government. Aimed at assuring the nation's safety against foreign threats, rather than discerning outright criminal behavior, that surveillance has been much more extensive than could possibly be justified by ordinary constitutional standards.[193] Partly as a concession to general privacy values, the government has not used data acquired by its extensive surveillance for criminal prosecutions. Recent revelations of the extent to which the federal government acquires information about persons within the United States as well as abroad have raised sharply how far present practices should be restrained by judicial constitutional doctrine, as well as congressional statutes.

A basic interpretive question that concerns "reasonable" (and implicitly at least the probability needed to satisfy "probable cause") is how courts should assess relevant factors. In some cases, the Supreme Court, as Justice Scalia has urged, has employed what amounts to "ad hoc balancing" of government interests against intrusions on individuals.[194] Given the hesitancy of judges to declare that asserted needs to enforce criminal prohibitions are not substantial, this approach has been criticized as not being responsive enough to the basic values underlying the Fourth Amendment and as insufficiently protecting individual privacy.[195]

F. Stop and Frisk and Equality Concerns

The major category of circumstances in which arrests and searches require a level of individual probability less rigorous than "probable cause" are instances of "stop and frisk." What distinguishes these stops from standard searches and arrests is not that the public need for any particular stop is overwhelming; it is that the intrusion on individual autonomy and privacy is much reduced. Given that, and the fact that were police unable to stop on less than probable cause, suspicious people in public places, especially in large cities, could often simply walk away without even being identified, the Supreme Court has adopted a standard of "reasonable suspicion,"[196] which requires a significantly lower probability than ordinary probable cause. In principle, this seems an appropriate balancing of public need versus degree of privacy invaded; but is "reasonable suspicion" really enforceable? An obvious problem is that very few people who are stopped, who have nothing to hide, and who walk free after a few minutes, are going to challenge what the police have done. Those on whom incriminating evidence is discovered will be hard put later to convince anyone that "reasonable suspicion" was lacking, especially since it is the police who will indicate what was the basis for their assessment. The consequence is that in terms of actual judicial enforcement, the "reasonable suspicion" standard has had relatively little effect,[197] although its formulation may restrain conscientious police officers and has occasionally been used by courts to declare particular stops invalid.[198]

A troubling aspect of this reality is the manner in which some police practice actually takes place. The right to stop is not restricted to very serious crimes; police can act on suspicions not only that young men are carrying dangerous weapons but also that they may possess a small amount of an illegal drug. And, in New York and other cities, it is a pervasive complaint that police discriminate in whom they stop, with much more restriction of African Americans and other minorities than of whites. That issue was a major concern in a prominent 2013 case in which New York City's practice of stop and frisk was challenged.[199] The challenge was upheld and reforms mandated;[200] newly elected Mayor Bill de Blasio decided to drop the appeal and accept the reforms as needed.[201] According to District Court Judge Shira A Scheindlin, a careful evaluation of police records indicated that "the City adopted a policy of indirect racial profiling by targeting racially defined groups for stops based on local suspect data."[202] This amounted to "intentional discrimination based on race."[203] A central question this case presented is how police may or may not use a person's racial identity in deciding whether to make a stop.[204] With respect to terminology, the inappropriate use of racial criteria is commonly cast as "racial discrimination"; thus, the practical question about what use of racial criteria is improper here can be cast as what should be seen as such "discrimination" in this context.

If members of minority groups are disproportionately involved in crimes of violence and carrying concealed weapons on the street, is it constitutionally acceptable for a police officer to take account of a person's race in deciding whether to make a "stop"? Between January 2004 and June 2012, New York City police officers made over 4.4 million stops; 52 percent of these were of blacks, and 31 percent were of Hispanics. Blacks constituted 23 percent of the population; Hispanics 29 percent. Only 10 percent of the persons stopped were white; whites are 33 percent of the population. Of course, some lack of correlation between stops and the races of the total population would derive from the concentration of the police in high-crime areas, a practice everyone accepts. The city, with a written policy that prohibits racial profiling, defended the actual statistics on the basis that they fairly reflected the percentages of criminal suspects. Noting the absence of "evidence that law-abiding blacks or Hispanics are more likely to behave *objectively* more suspiciously than law-abiding whites," Judge Scheindlin concluded that the city's "defense *against* a charge of racial profiling" was really "a defense *of* racial profiling ... not a race-neutral explanation for racial disparities in NYPD stops ... [but] itself a *racially biased explanation*."[205] In her view, "[t]he Equal Protection Clause does not permit race-based suspicion."[206]

A core issue raised by the disagreement between the city and Judge Scheindlin over what could constitute acceptable bases for stops and frisks is whether it is ever acceptable to give direct weight to someone's race in circumstances other than when actual suspects of crimes have already been racially identified. More specifically, is it ever plausible that a person's race could affect whether the probability of criminal involvement has exceeded the standard for "reasonable suspicion"? And, if so, should the police be able to take aggregate data about race and crime into account in deciding whether to stop and frisk an individual? These *are* different questions. Even if an "objective" basis may exist to take race into account, having law enforcement practices exclude that data may nonetheless be both desirable and best seen as constitutionally required.

The controversy over stop and frisk can be illuminated by comparisons with private reliance on race and other group characteristics, which illustrate the difficulty of relying on "objective" criteria and discounting prejudices, the problem raised by the absence of independent information, and the worry about how those viewed negatively will take the implicit message sent to them. The private examples also suggest how reliance on race is strikingly different in important respects from reliance on gender and age and why, when government officials openly engage in that practice, what is conveyed is especially powerful and disturbing.

Imagine that Michael, a middle-aged, well-dressed white man, is walking along a city street late at night and sees three noisy, poorly dressed strangers in their early twenties walking toward him. He realizes that chances are slight, but he worries that he might possibly be constrained and forced to turn over money. He considers crossing the street to assure his safety. If Michael were aware that the rate of "muggings" made by young black men is three times higher than by young white men, would it be wrong for him to cross the street if the approaching strangers are black, even if he would not do so if they were white?

If we ask a similar question about gender and age, the answer seems straightforward. Both women and men reasonably fear that men are much more likely to engage in violent confrontations than are women[207] and that men over sixty are much less likely to be violent than those between fifteen and twenty-five. Were Michael to have crossed the street only if approached by young men, almost no one would say he had engaged in gender or age "discrimination."

Is race different? Historically, attitudes of members of the dominant white race about blacks have been more pervasively negative than attitudes of men about women and of mature persons about younger ones. Michael's estimates of how gender and age relate to dangerousness are likely to be more dispassionate than those about race. Of course, none of us are capable in making such personal decisions of being *completely* objective, especially if we are experiencing strong emotional feelings such as physical fear and if we possess deep-seated prejudices we cannot put aside. When it comes to race, not only is our cultural heritage a problem, but also the closest we can come to objective evaluation is itself based on statistics about crimes, which are much affected by whom the police suspect, investigate, and arrest.[208]

The actual consequences of the cultural setting provide a possible basis for Michael not to cross the street. When members of a minority recognize that they are being treated differently based on negative judgments about their qualities, they commonly feel put down and insulted.[209] The approaching three young blacks might well experience Michael's crossing of the street as a kind of symbolic "put-down" that makes them feel a bit like alienated outsiders.

These concerns do not themselves yield the conclusion that a private person like Michael is doing something immoral or engaging in racial discrimination *if* he crosses the street. Were he challenged as having done wrong, Michael might respond, "I didn't know the precise chance of being stopped by black youths as compared with white ones, but the danger, slight as it was, was sufficiently greater to justify my crossing."

As we turn from moral assessment of private action based on highly limited information to legal norms for stop and frisk, the standard for evaluating police practice does not depend on an officer's subjective appraisal, but on whether an "objective" basis supports his action.[210] When suspicious movements and appearances (such as might suggest carrying a concealed weapon or the "casing" of a jewelry store for theft) are adequately classified, the membership of someone in a group *could* affect the objective probability of criminal behavior, and might do so in a way that would bring the overall likelihood above the threshold needed to justify a stop. This can be illustrated by artificial figures.

Suppose a city has 80,000 young male residents; of those, 20,000 are minority blacks and Hispanics, and 50,000 are white. Among these two groups in a relative time period, the percentage of minorities who commit the kinds of crimes that lead to stops is 6 percent and the percentage of whites is 2 percent. Further, when undertaking to commit crimes, half of these in each group by their movements and demeanor act in ways that are observed by police officers and might lead to stops. Among those who are innocent of such crimes, only one in twenty engages in similar movements, and this percentage is the same for innocent minority members and whites.[211] If we add these figures together, it turns out that of the 20,000 members of minorities, 600 guilty ones have displayed such movements and demeanor, and 940 innocent ones have done so. Among the 50,000 whites, 500 guilty ones and 2,450 innocent ones have acted similarly. If a police officer sees a young minority male acting in this way, the chances are slightly less than 39 percent that he is committing or about to be engaging in some crime. For whites, the percentage is 17 percent. Thus, under an objective measure, the race of a person acting somewhat suspiciously *could* affect the probability of criminal involvement and might even elevate the level of likelihood over a threshold appropriate for a stop. Of course, a similar, less controversial conclusion would be true about gender and age. A young man engaging in suspicious movements would be more likely to be doing something wrong than a woman or an eighty-year-old man.

Does it follow from analysis that the law should recognize and accept the use of racial criteria as one element of what would justify stops and frisks? The answer is "no." Because of the severe risk of reliance on prejudices, because of statistical data about crimes that does not objectively reflect actual rates of commission, and because of the destructive consequences for the young members of minorities who suffer the humiliation of stops, police departments would better develop standards that are wholly independent of race. Further, given the difficulty for individuals of knowing just how far they are relying on objective truth rather than personal feelings, the importance of police training and supervision, and the impossibility of judges assessing just what did move a particular officer to action, a conclusion that the Constitution requires use of nonracial criteria for ordinary "stops" would be sound.[212]

G. The Scope of Searches, Especially After Arrests

For searches police are allowed, what is their proper scope? The simplest examples involve searches pursuant to a warrant. There is a rule, though not enforced by exclusion of evidence,[213] that absent a reason to think doing so will be dangerous or lead to destruction of evidence, those executing a warrant must knock and announce their presence, offering a resident time to open the door.[214] The search is then limited in the area it covers and the form it takes. If the warrant specifies that a suspect has a large stolen painting in his living room, the police could look in other rooms where the painting might have been moved; but they could not comb through a tiny desk drawer in hopes of finding evidence of some other crime.[215] Of course, if the police just happen to see strong evidence of another crime in "plain view" while carrying out a valid search, they may seize that. The border between merely seeing and engaging in a further search without probable cause was raised when police, carrying out a search for weapons, saw stereo equipment, which they turned over to discern serial numbers that would allow them later to determine if the items were stolen. The Supreme Court, with Justice Scalia writing for the majority, treated this simple physical examination as itself an extra search, not a mere perception, and held that it violated the Fourth Amendment.[216]

Related questions are raised by the scope of searching after valid arrests. When an arrest is made, police may search a suspect to make sure he does not possess a weapon or destroy evidence he is "suspected" of carrying. Although the acquisition of personal physical evidence, such as a blood sample, does not invoke the privilege against self-incrimination, it does constitute a search.[217] For the extraction of blood, which involves a significant invasion of the body, police need good reason to believe it will show an illegal level of alcohol while the suspect was driving, or some other incriminating fact.[218] With respect to certain other information, police are allowed to acquire it from all suspects. They can demand that a person reveal his identity and can search his belongings if he refuses.[219] And it is well established that police are permitted to fingerprint all those they arrest.[220] This acquisition of physical evidence is regarded as a "reasonable search" because it aids identification without seriously intruding further on the privacy of a person who has been arrested.

This brings us to a significant recent case that divided the Supreme Court.[221] Alonzo King had been arrested in 2009 for assault, having menaced a group of people with a shotgun. A DNA sample was taken by applying a "buccal swab" to the inside of his cheeks. His DNA was subsequently discovered to be that of a man, whose identity was unknown at the time, who probably had committed a rape in 2003. When King was subsequently convicted for that rape, he challenged the acquisition of evidence through the DNA sample in 2009.

The majority of the Court, in an opinion by Justice Kennedy, treated the taking of the sample as a form of identification, not so different from the gathering of fingerprints, assisting officials in knowing exactly whom they have in custody, including any past criminal history. That can be helpful in determining a suspect's bail and assuring his availability for trial. Given that Maryland law authorizes the collection of samples only when arrests are for serious crimes, and that it limits the information to be gathered from the DNA to identification, Kennedy concluded that the balance of considerations strongly favored the minimal intrusion on privacy of taking samples, and was therefore "reasonable" independent of any probability of showing guilt in a particular instance.[222] Kennedy also noted the value of collecting DNA samples both for discerning those guilty of previously unsolved crimes and for clearing innocent persons who have been suspected of or convicted for those crimes, but he did not emphasize these benefits.[223]

Justice Scalia's dissent,[224] when compared with the majority opinion, reflects both the status of competing conceptualizations and the complexities of striking needed balances. Scalia's conceptual point is that what was involved here was not typical identification. Since the DNA sample was taken on April 10, could not be tested under Maryland law until the arraignment days later, was not uploaded onto the state's database until July 13, and was not matched to the earlier sample until

August 4, the process hardly served identifying a suspect in the ordinary sense. Moreover, the very comparison of the sample with items in the "Unsolved Crime Collection" showed that the objective was to possibly assist with an unsolved crime.[225] Unlike all other standard inquiries and examinations at the time of arrest, as well as the basis for other "special needs" searches, the whole point here of acquiring and submitting the DNA information to the general collection was to learn if a suspect was actually guilty of a crime other than the one for which he was arrested. Scalia regarded this objective as simply precluding an exception to Fourth Amendment requirements.[226]

On the balance of values, Justice Scalia relied partly on the fact that for people actually *convicted* for serious offenses, the taking of DNA samples is not in dispute. Thus, upon a conviction for assault, King's sample could uncontroversially have been taken and used. Thus, precluding samples from being taken and used after arrest and prior to conviction would not greatly undercut law enforcement, especially since innocent person are the ones most likely not to be convicted.[227]

Interestingly, both the majority and dissenters here take categorical approaches, not dependent on the circumstances of individual cases. Although it is both true that what Kennedy takes as ordinary identification objectives *could* be served and that simple fingerprinting does sometimes link a person to an earlier unsolved crime, nonetheless Scalia is persuasive that the main object here was not ordinary identification, and that the aim of possibly discerning separate criminal acts differs from the primary reason for other information acquired at the time of arrest.

Despite this conclusion, if this is a practice that is highly valuable for accurate law enforcement, it seems worth the modest intrusion on privacy. On the issue of balance, two aspects are troubling about the Scalia position. The first is that those who are not convicted of a "serious crime" include suspects who are actually guilty, but who avoid conviction because of insufficient evidence, or receive grants of immunity for testifying against others, or who, after a bargain, plead guilty to a lesser offense. And requiring a timing delay until conviction is itself troubling, since one use of DNA evidence is to show that someone else who has been suspected, or even convicted, is not guilty. An innocent person should not have to wait two extra years until the real culprit is convicted of another crime and his DNA evidence is then brought to bear.

There are various nuances to all of this that the majority does not tackle, such as whether the use of the sample and its retention over time should be analyzed separately from its acquisition. It also does not ask if it matters that given the high percentage of members of minorities who are arrested, the store of information about them will be particularly great. Nonetheless, the case provides a striking illustration of competing possibilities and assessments: My own view is that, given the need for accurate resolution of serious crimes, the majority's disposition is preferable, even if its analysis seriously oversimplifies the "identification" connection and makes the balance of considerations appear more one-sided than it actually is.

H. Varieties of Consent

This section considers two forms of consent. Simple consent occurs when the person in control agrees to a search. In basic principle, consent to a search is like the agreement to answer questions. A person is free to waive her constitutional right. A slight analytical difference, without practical consequence, is that when one freely waives a right to silence, he is not "compelled" to incriminate himself, so the Fifth Amendment does not apply, whereas consenting to a search does not render what follows other than a "search," but rather makes it "reasonable." What matters practically is how voluntariness is to be assessed and whether, in particular, the officers involved need to give a clear warning.

The Supreme Court's resolution has been that warnings are not required for consent to searches that police could not otherwise make.[228] Its rationales are that searches do not connect to fair trials in the way that self-incrimination does and that searches with consent are a common practice of law enforcement that detailed warnings would seriously impede. As a consequence, in contrast to the *Miranda* standard, the key to any consent search case is whether the person did voluntarily agree—"a fact to be determined from the totality of all the circumstances."[229] Not surprisingly, this restraint has proved very slight. If a person orally agrees, how is an officer or judge to determine whether that was really "voluntary?" And what should even count as "voluntary?" As noted with respect to police questioning, people want to appear cooperative, not indicating likely guilt by saying "no." Even with full warning, most suspects answer police questions, and many people "consent" to searches, even when these are likely to produce damaging evidence. Among other possibilities, they may assume the police will go ahead whatever they say, and that appearing cooperative is better than resisting. Given all this, requiring that police give *some warning*—such as "I can't make this search unless you consent; may I go ahead?"—would provide a minimal protection and not be too cumbersome.

The second "consent" question is more complex. How should the practice be regarded when one party to a conversation allows the police to listen, or keeps a record of what is said after having undertaken that he will give that to the police. I believe the prevailing judgment that this does not present a Fourth Amendment problem is regrettable; what is needed is an evaluation of what genuinely protects privacy in context.

Frequently, one party to a conversation uses an electronic means to record or transmit the conversation without the knowledge of the other. Not only may the police wish to assure an accurate account of a conversation with an informer, but also a victim of extortion or parents of a child who has been kidnapped may wish to have the police hear what is being said. In still other settings, one party to a conversation may want an accurate record for possible future use, but without any intent to hurt the other participant, or even to disclose in the near future what has been said. President Nixon's recording system in the White House presumably fit into this category.

Is any intrusion on privacy involved in those practices? Even when the person making the recording does not intend to harm another participant or disclose more broadly what she has said, a subtle alteration in the conditions of the conversation has occurred. The other participant might choose her words more carefully or even refrain from expressing some ideas if she knew that what she was saying was being reproduced in semi-permanent form. Indeed, these very reasons help explain why the person making the recording does not inform his conversational partner.

Given that an informer or secret agent is already deceiving the other participant about the basic conditions of a conversation, does the electronic transmission or recording really add to the intrusion upon privacy? In providing a complete and accurate account of what has been said, it may, in some circumstances, actually protect the person conversing with an informer by assuring that she will not be convicted on the basis of the informer's lies or misconceptions about what she said. This fact has led some critics to conclude that, so long as informers may function, no good reason exists to restrict their use of electronic devices. On the other hand, when we speak confidentially, we may rely partly on the evanescence of our words and our ability to claim that we have been misquoted or misunderstood if our companion discloses our thoughts more broadly than we wish. One thinks in this connection of whether the owner of the Los Angeles Clippers, Donald Sterling, would have made his racist remarks if he knew his female "friend" was recording them; and we can be almost certain he would not have done so if he was aware that she, or another, would make them public.[230] The presence of a recording or transmitting device eliminates much of the protection of limited dissemination, and, beyond the presence of the informer himself, definitely creates an added threat to privacy.[231]

Whenever it has faced the question squarely, the Supreme Court has held that the recording or transmitting by an informer or government official of a conversation unknown to the other party to a conversation presents no constitutional problem. Many observers thought that after the Court's expansive treatment of the Fourth Amendment regarding telephone surveillance in *Katz v. United States*, it would hold that a court order was required for this practice. But in *United States v. White*,[232] its latest decision on the point, it rejected that argument 5–4. The narrowness of the margin, as well as an eloquent dissenting opinion by Justice Harlan, did however demonstrate the seriousness of this constitutional issue of privacy.

One may ask how this practice differs from (1) someone turning a recording over to the police that they had no role in encouraging, or

(2) with advance police involvement, forwarding a confidential text sent by a suspect. In the first instance, the government is not "searching"; it is merely receiving information someone has chosen to provide. Such information is, of course, a fundamental aid to determining criminal activity. The second instance comes closer, but here, the suspect is fully aware that he has provided material that *could* be given to someone else. In that respect, what happens is similar to an informer simply telling the police what was said in a conversation. Although even if a designed use of informers is not seen as encouraging self-incrimination—a point discussed previously—it could be seen as a form of search covered by the Fourth Amendment. When informers allow the police to listen or make a recording with their knowledge, that enhances the intrusions on privacy, transforming what a person assumes are merely temporary, fleeting communications to a trusted acquaintance into undeniable content that may injure him. It would require no stretch of the concept of "search" to conclude that the government here is intruding on someone's private life to obtain hard evidence. And my own judgment is that this activity should be allowed only upon some determination about its possible success. Otherwise, innocent or guilty, supporters or opponents of the government, we have no guarantee that our private comments in oral conversations are not transmitted in hard form to those who may hurt us.

I. Electronic Communication and Storage

Exactly how the Fourth Amendment should be seen as applying to modern electronic communication and the storage of information on computers and on the servers of Internet service providers (ISPs) involves a set of questions not simply answered by the text, original conceptions, or existing Supreme Court doctrine. What is clear is that with the vastly increasing importance in people's lives of these forms of communication, just how far the government can acquire information matters greatly, a reality brought home sharply by Edward Snowden's revelations about the National Security Agency's mass surveillance of telephone records and the release of documents revealing the agency's tracking of emails.[233]

Without attempting to deal with nuances in just how the amendment should apply to these various kinds of government investigations and uses,[234] a task for which I am particularly ill equipped, this section does highlight some central questions and suggests possible answers. The basic questions are these: (1) What should count as a covered search and a covered seizure? (2) What degree of probability should be needed and how narrow should the focus of attention be? (3) Does it matter if what is reviewed is held by the person whose communications are being investigated or by an independent entity? (4) Should prior judicial approval be required?

If the government is seeking information about possible illegal activity and those working for the government are not merely observing what is accessible to the general public, that should count as a search. Given that the government's mere acquisition of records of what telephone calls were made, as contrasted with their content, has been held not to raise Fourth Amendment issues, a similar division might make sense for Internet communications.

Whether copying or just observing conveyed messages amounts to a seizure is not clear. Orin S. Kerr has noted that in *Arizona v. Hicks,* which held that the moving of equipment did constitute an illegal search, Justice Scalia stated for the Court that "the mere recording of the serial numbers did not constitute a seizure."[235] If a search itself is illegal and yields evidence that a prosecutor seeks to use at a trial, perhaps it does not matter whether that evidence has been "seized" within the terms of the Amendment; it may be excluded from use simply on the basis that it was produced by an unconstitutional search. In any event, the language in *Arizona v. Hicks* is hardly precise in its implications, and the wiretapping and eavesdropping cases do not make a "seizure" depend on a physical acquisition.[236] In referring to the "mere recording," Justice Scalia did not clearly address whether the recording *after* an illegal search did amount to a seizure. In *Katz v. United States,* Justice Stewart, one of the Warren Court's more conservative Justices, wrote that the government's using an electronic listening and recording device attached to a public telephone booth to listen in on a suspect's conversation "constituted a 'search and seizure' within the meaning of the Fourth Amendment."[237] What was crucial was the invasion of privacy, not whether anything was taken away. If, following an illegal search, the recording of, or even listening to, a telephone conversation can be a "seizure," no basis exists for treating the copying, or even reading, of a written electronic communication differently.

With respect to the degree of probability needed to search electronic data for ordinary crimes, the traditional approach to the standard of probable cause seems apt.[238] Whether it is appropriate for officials to comb through personal electronic equipment held by a person being arrested is a harder question the Supreme Court is now addressing. National security concerns raise special difficulties. Especially if the intrusion on any individual's privacy is minimal, the needed probability will be much reduced if the government's concern is terrorism or other national security worries.[239] But the scope of investigations should be limited to what is practically necessary to obtain the specific information.[240]

Given that vast amounts of private information regarding individuals' lives are now stored with companies that make electronic communication possible, the law should focus on whose privacy is intruded upon, not who happens to hold the information.[241] Combing through a company's storage, with or without its consent, is not like looking in one person's apartment for information that someone else has committed a crime. Rather, the relevant analogy is to telephone use. A person making a telephone call is able to do so only because of a telephone company;

yet, intercepting the message invades the privacy of the caller, not the company. And the same would be true if the company happened to keep recordings of all the calls made on its system.

For ordinary crime investigations, warrants would be appropriate to the degree they are needed in other contexts.[242] For national security matters, prior review may be made by independent administrative agencies rather than judges.[243]

In sum, the Fourth Amendment clearly does apply to governmental investigations of modern electronic communications and their storage; development of just how it reaches those data will be a very important aspect of the evolving law of "search and seizure."

J. Exclusion of Evidence

A final question about unreasonable searches concerns appropriate remedies. A person subject to an illegal search can, of course, sue, but such suits are uncommon.[244] Someone who perceived a close connection between unreasonable searches and the privilege against self-incrimination might view exclusion from evidence at a criminal trial of what an illegal search has discovered as dictated indirectly by the right to silence. But barring that conclusion, which the modern Court has decisively rejected, why should such evidence be excluded? If a person commits a serious crime, and persuasive evidence of that is discovered, however unjustified the intrusion on his privacy has been, that is quite different from whether he deserves to be convicted. Nonetheless, in the famous case of *Mapp v. Ohio*, the Supreme Court held that an exclusionary rule applies to both the federal government and the states.[245] Since no such exclusionary rule was common when either the Fourth Amendment or the Fourteenth was adopted, *Mapp*'s conclusion has no support from any original understanding. For the Supreme Court, the logic has been not that this is directly and absolutely required by the Constitution itself, but rather that it is the only effective way to enforce the protection against unreasonable searches. This reality means that although in direct application the exclusion of evidence mainly assists guilty persons who are receiving a benefit they may not really deserve,[246] the indirect effect of the rule is to restrain law enforcement in a manner that also protects innocent citizens again unwarranted intrusions on their lives.

Since the underlying reason for exclusion is deterring constitutional violations, that the more conservative Justices who have followed the Warren Court have qualified it in a number of ways is not surprising.[247] Evidence illegally obtained can be used to impeach a defendant's testimony.[248] Because the aim of the rule is to deter police misconduct, the Court has also allowed a "good faith" exception; evidence can be admitted if police reasonably acted on a warrant issued by a magistrate, so long as the application for the warrant did not include fraud and the magistrate's decision was not obviously wrong.[249] Thus, even if an appellate court, with its limited deference to the magistrate's judgment, concludes that probable cause did not exist, the evidence may still be admitted. This exception for reasonable police action has not yet been extended to ordinary warrantless searches, though it has been applied to a negligent bookkeeping error that led an officer reasonably to believe that there was a valid warrant.[250] When one combines all of these qualifications of the exclusionary rule with the Supreme Court's ruling that a state prisoner who had an opportunity to litigate Fourth Amendment claims in the state courts may not get federal habeas corpus relief on the basis that evidence should have been excluded on this ground, the *Mapp* rule may now provide very limited restraint on what states can actually do.[251]

K. Automobiles and the Fourth Amendment

I have postponed for this final subsection a brief account of how the Fourth Amendment has been applied to automobiles. A number of the issues previously examined arise in that context, and the efforts to draw appropriate lines reflect both sensible bases and the difficulties of distinguishing what is reasonable from what is not. Cars involve a technology not in existence when the Fourth and Fourteenth Amendments were adopted—they move very quickly, their operation can be highly dangerous, and people's sense of privacy within their cars is substantially less than within their homes. All of these factors have figured in when the Supreme Court has accepted automobiles being stopped and has permitted searches pursuant to that stopping. In the section of self-incrimination, we have already reviewed acceptance of the requirement that drivers of cars in accidents remain at the scene, although this could lead to criminal proceedings. In dealing with stops and searches of automobiles, the Supreme Court has made limited reference to specific understandings when the Fourth and Fourteenth Amendments were adopted. In sustaining an automobile search in 1925, Chief Justice Taft did rely partly on the assumption of early Congresses that "moveable vessels" were not covered.[252] Apparently, when the Fourth Amendment was adopted, there was no discussion of its possible application to horse-drawn carriages.

An obvious point about stopping and searching modern cars is that when police have good reason to suspect that a car is carrying stolen or forbidden goods, they can stop and search without acquiring a warrant. By the time it took to obtain a warrant, the car might well be out of range or had the goods removed from it.[253] The important practical questions about stopping now arise over the selectivity of which cars to stop and over the stopping of all cars passing a certain location.

On most highways in the country, the majority of cars are exceeding the speed limit. On the New Jersey Turnpike, for example, for which the posted speed limit ranges from 55 mph. to 65 mph., well over 95 percent of the drivers of cars exceed the limit if there is no traffic delay or inhibiting weather. People assume that they will not be pulled over for speeding unless they are going even faster than other drivers, and exceeding the specified limit by more than a few miles per hour. Thus, judged by the formally prescribed law, the traffic police have a probable cause justification for stopping almost anyone. That could lead to undoubted unfairness of two varieties, and what may be regarded as a third. If the speed limit is 65 miles per hour, and the police stop a driver going 70 mph. while letting numerous other drivers pass by going 75 mph., and they do so without any explicable reason, or with a reason that bears no relation to why people should be stopped, that would be plainly unfair. The second, related, concern has arisen in connection with the New Jersey Turnpike, where, over time, a high percentage of drivers stopped were members of minorities. As with "stop and frisk," this condition itself can raise the question what counts as relevantly discriminatory. If the stops were genuinely *for speeding*, and were made on all those exceeding a certain speed, correlations of race, gender, and age would be irrelevant to who was relevantly guilty. That would depend on how fast particular cars were traveling. Perhaps because reviewing why any particular driver was really stopped is so difficult, judges have had limited involvement in circumscribing the stops and ticketing of those who technically violate the written law, whether or not they exceed the speed of most drivers. In New Jersey, the main efforts to curb discriminatory criteria have been made instead by those within the political branches.[254]

The third, arguable, form of unfairness is officers stopping drivers for speeding because they think those drivers may be guilty of another crime, one that can be discerned as a consequence of the stop. It is arguably unfair to arrest someone for a "crime" one would otherwise let pass because that person may possibly be guilty of a different, more serious crime. Perhaps the reasonableness of any such arrest depends partly on the probability of commission of the more serious crime; but courts are in a poor position to determine just why the arrest was made for the less serious one, especially since the police can say, "The more serious crime possibility was just an *extra* reason why we acted." In 1996, the Supreme Court, with Justice Scalia writing the opinion, ruled that the Fourth Amendment reasonableness requirement does not make actual motivations for stops relevant.[255]

A discrimination concern like that for "stop and frisk" can arise when the stopping of cars takes place because of the possibility of non-driving crimes. Here, connections with racial status, age, and gender may also be objectively supportable. Although few are troubled by the use of age and gender in this context—few men over 65 and few women are stopped because they are suspected to be carrying loads of heroin—the use of race is a concern. Suppose a higher percentage of members of a minority than of the overall population are involved in a form of criminal activity. If large numbers of members of that race who are completely innocent are stopped on the highways because of that percentage, that is genuinely troubling; but, given their difficulty in assessing the real reasons for individual stops, judges may be ill suited to deal with this problem according to the Fourth Amendment and Equal Protection Clause.

What is the probability needed for a valid stop and search? If what is involved is the stopping of individual drivers for likely traffic offenses, the violation should definitely be more probable than not, and usually it is virtually certain. In cases involving stops because of suspicions of other crimes, the Supreme Court has typically spoken in terms of "probable cause," but we must assume that here, this standard is somewhat flexible. If it is thought that there is a fair chance that a particular driver is carrying a kidnapped child or the body of a murder victim, the police must be able to stop the car even if they do not suppose guilt is close to more probable than not. Police and courts may take a fairly relaxed approach here to probability even for less severe crimes, given that cars may be employed to remove evidence and perhaps even the suspects themselves.[256] "Reasonable" search has not been explicitly accorded a generally relaxed standard by the Supreme Court for individual suspects driving cars, along the lines of the "reasonable suspicion" for "stop and frisk," but in a 2000 case rejecting a checkpoint stop of all autos to discern which ones might be illegally carrying drugs, the Supreme Court opinion of Justice O'Connor did state that "stops can only be justified by some quantum of individualized suspicion."[257] That sounds like a much more relaxed standard than probable cause.

In certain circumstances, the Court has approved systematic stopping by roadblocks of all cars passing a particular location. This is, in effect, one category of a "special needs" exception to ordinary Fourth Amendment requirements. The Court in 1976 approved stopping cars at a permanent checkpoint on a highway leading away from the Mexican border, balancing the interests and determining that the need for such stops is great enough to warrant them.[258] It similarly sustained roadblocks employed to check drunken drivers.[259] More recently, it accepted stopping drivers to ask about their possibly witnessing a hit and run accident committed at that place and time a week earlier.[260]

When the Court ruled in 2000 that such stops could *not* be used to stop traffic in illegal drugs,[261] it reasoned that the checkpoint approach was not a proper way to acquire evidence for ordinary criminal investigations. Does this case square with the Court's earlier rulings, considering that drunken driving and assisting illegal immigration are also criminal? Drunken driving is distinguishable because it concerns highway safety and forbidden conditions for driving. And although one might say that using a car to carry a drug is like using one to carry an illegal immigrant, nevertheless cars seem more central for transporting people into the country, *and* the need for checks close to the border is crucial for effective enforcement. Thus, the Court's limitation of when systematic stops can substitute for "individual suspicion" was both sensible and consistent with earlier cases.

The Court has struggled with the more complicated question of just what scope of search is appropriate when a car is stopped because of a suspicion of criminal activity. If the driver is stopped only because of speeding or other simple traffic violations, one that leads only to a ticket and not an arrest, the police may perceive evidence of other criminal activity, but they cannot search to find it.[262] But matters are different if the stop involves a probability of other criminal activity. Although the logic that a search without a warrant is needed because the car can be moved does not really apply if the driver is arrested and the car taken to police headquarters, nonetheless, the Supreme Court has declined to establish a warrant requirement for that setting, not wishing to complicate law enforcement in a way that fails to yield significant added protection to privacy.[263]

The trickiest questions have involved the permissible extent of searches. From 1977 to 1981, the Court did not allow searches without warrants of a locked footlocker that had been taken from a train to a car,[264] a suitcase that had been taken from an airplane to a car,[265] and a recessed luggage compartment.[266] In 1982, it upheld the search of a package containing drugs, distinguishing that from closed containers such as luggage about which people have a greater expectation of privacy.[267] In 1991, the Court determined that the permissibility of searches applied to all containers about which probable cause was satisfied.[268] In 1999, in *Wyoming v. Houghton*,[269] the Court accepted searches of possessions of passengers as well as of a driver who, after a stop for speeding, was seen to have a hypodermic syringe that he acknowledged he used to take drugs. Justice Scalia's opinion noted that passengers, like drivers, have reduced expectations of privacy when they transport property in cars.[270]

This logic, as well as the range of cases, raises the question how far relaxed requirements follow from the special mobility of cars, a kind of exigent circumstance, and how far they follow from reduced expectations of privacy. On the latter point, one really wonders if most people truly feel less of a sense of privacy about what they take in a car from what they carry with them while walking or have in their living room or office. Cars are special, but just how far different reasons support relaxed requirements, and exactly how far this relaxation should go, are not easily answered questions. The difficulties of developing a precise rationale for special treatment for cars and of drawing convincing lines about particular kinds of objects within cars help explain why the Supreme Court's efforts in this domain are hard to put together in a coherent account. Of course, a different reason is that, in general, the Supreme Court has, in the last few decades, drawn back from earlier approaches to Fourth Amendment protections.[271]

V. CONCLUSION

This chapter has explored a large number of specific issues, a great many of which are subjects of serious disagreements over appropriate resolutions. Some of these strikingly illustrate the importance of context and the strong need to give weight to competing considerations. As in many other areas, original understanding is unrevealing about many crucial issues, it has not been taken as central in important decisions, and it could not provide a sensible basis for much modern interpretation. Here, as elsewhere, the exact strategies of interpretation depend both on particular provisions and the nature of the specific problem, A constant concern is the extent to which judges should aim for clearly discrete categories or engage in evaluations of individual circumstances. Sometimes, one approach or the other seems definitely more sensible, but often, there is no clear answer to which is better.

Chapter 12

Equal Protection

I. INTRODUCTION

This final chapter on a specific constitutional clause concerns the Fourteenth Amendment's provision that "No state shall . . . deny to any person within its jurisdiction the equal protection of the laws."[1] As the chapters on the religion clauses, the Free Speech Clause, "cruel and unusual punishment," and criminal process show, for various provisions in the original Bill of Rights, especially as now interpreted, equality is an important value. But no actual language about equal treatment is to be found in the Constitution prior to the Fourteenth Amendment. Given the original document's protection of slavery, and the unquestioned subordinate status of women, this absence is not surprising.

The Equal Protection Clause was designed and understood to assure certain equal rights for freed slaves.[2] Were a Justice faithfully to stick to the original understanding of coverage, assessed either by the intent of most enactors or the sense of readers, most differences in treatment according to gender or sexual orientation could in no way be subject to its terms. This reality about "equal protection" sharply raises for any version of strict originalism cast in terms of covered practices, whether limiting the clause now to racial categorization would really be best. Relatedly, with respect to race, should all categorizations then regarded as acceptable now be treated as such, an issue posed by racial segregation within public schools?[3]

These specific issues raise the broader question regarding what level of generality of original understanding should matter. Judges may identify specific forms of unequal treatment deemed improper, the particular group or groups whose claims of equality were being protected, a broader sense that could reach similar groups and forms of inequality, and a general principle that people who count equally should get equal treatment. Of course, if one takes the last idea as the key, developing conceptions of unacceptable differentiations properly underlie a flexible interpretation of the clause's content.

Although judges and scholars have considered whether the Equal Protection Clause, in its original understanding, is consistent with a ban on racially segregated schools, as well as whether the entire amendment incorporated provisions of the Bill of Rights,[4] relatively little has been written about exactly what level of generality was then taken as appropriate for constitutional amendments and how that would bear on the Equal Protection Clause. Almost certainly, a primary reason is that no particular widely accepted answer is discernible. Given that the Amendment followed the intense controversy over slavery and the terrible toll of the Civil War, one would guess that most of those voting for Fourteenth Amendment and readers, informed or not, perceived the Equal Protection Clause, though applying to all states, as mainly designed to help achieve aspects of equality for former slaves in the South. But someone looking for broader conceptions could find support in the stances of some abolitionists.[5] Notably, John Bingham, who actually as a key committee member moved the main content of section 1 of the Fourteenth Amendment in Congress,[6] had previously claimed that the Constitution, including the Due Process Clause in the Bill of Rights, "is based upon the EQUALITY of the human race" and that each state must "protect each human being within its jurisdiction in the free and full enjoyment of his natural rights."[7] For anyone who both took this perspective and recognized that conceptions of natural rights grow over time, a developing and flexible interpretation of the Equal Protection Clause (and other language in section 1) would be perfectly appropriate. Awareness of just how widely this broad perspective was shared by enactors and readers could bear on desirable interpretation of the clause, but any clear assessment is extremely unlikely; more important, as earlier chapters contend, original understanding should not determine the level of generality at which open language in the Constitution is now taken.

In regard to race, gender, religion, nationality, and sexual orientation, we can identify five different kinds of categorizations. The first, obviously the main focus of the clause originally, was explicitly unfavorable treatment by governments of members of a group that had suffered unequal status in the past. Second, a different form of law involves explicit separation, which may or may not obviously imply a sense of superiority and inferiority, and effectively disadvantage one of the groups. Third, a law neutral on its face may operate negatively for members of a disadvantaged group. Fourth, a law may actually favor such a group, and that preference may or may not promote equality. Such laws are commonly labeled "affirmative action" or "reverse discrimination." With regard to these four basic forms of classification, questions also arise about the extent to which governments can enforce or forbid private individual choices to engage in them. Finally, a group characteristic may be taken into account in arriving at a judgment that itself is, or is supposed to be, essentially independent. We have briefly reviewed a regrettable form of that in Chapter 6; the death penalty is more likely to be imposed on a black defendant than a white one, especially if he has killed a white person (although determining whether race has affected the penalty in an individual instance is virtually impossible). A different use of race, treated in Chapter 11, is by police officers trying to discern who has committed or is about to commit a crime, when they exercised their "stop and frisk" powers. Can they properly take into account that certain crimes are more likely to be committed by members of racial minorities?

The following sections tackle forms of categorization and their coverage. More general treatment of appropriate levels of review and interpretive strategies are saved for the end of the chapter.

II. RACIAL CATEGORIZATION

Shortly before the Civil War, the Supreme Court held in *Dred Scott v. Sandford* that, given the Constitution's guarantee of the "property" of owning slaves, Congress could not, as it tried by compromise to do, forbid slavery in the northern federal territories.[8] That highly controversial decision, which was directly at odds with claims of abolitionists that Congress clearly had such a power, and even that the Constitution itself barred slavery in the federal territories,[9] was one of the events that led to the Civil War. At the war's end, the Thirteenth Amendment was adopted, forbidding slavery and involuntary servitude. Many southern states replaced slavery with "Black Codes," which forbade blacks from pursuing some occupations, owning property, testifying in court, and breaching employment contracts. After adopting a Civil Rights Act, Congress proposed the Fourteenth Amendment and made its ratification, which ultimately occurred in 1868, a condition for southern states to rejoin that body. Two years later, the Fifteenth Amendment forbid denial of the right to vote based on race or previous servitude.

The Equal Protection Clause clearly made unconstitutional the kinds of formal denials of equal legal rights found in the "Black Codes" (and barred by the Civil Rights Act) that precluded blacks from being able to contract and to own property.[10] In 1879, the Court took a somewhat more expansive view of coverage, sustaining a black defendant's claim that the ineligibility of blacks for jury service denied him equal protection.[11] Seven years later, it extended protection to members of another minority group, ruling that the administration of an ordinance that required laundry operators to get permission to function in wooden buildings had violated Equal Protection because permission had been granted to virtually all others but not to Chinese operators.[12]

After the withdrawal of federal troops from the South in 1877, which ended the era of Reconstruction, southern states began to develop more rigid and pervasive laws segregating members of the two races, including in public facilities such as buses and railroads. In *Plessy v. Ferguson*, in 1896, the Supreme Court rejected the claim of a passenger, who said he was seven-eighths white and that he could not constitutionally be prosecuted for refusing to leave the coach reserved for whites.[13] According to the Court's opinion, any "assumption that the enforced separation of the two races stamps the colored race with a badge of inferiority" was fallacious. If that was a consequence of the law, it was "because the colored race chooses to put that construction upon it."[14]

This appalling appraisal totally disregarded both the history of racial differences in the United States and the standards by which persons were categorized. In all of the southern states, one needed to be much more than one-half white to count as "white."[15] Thus, a great many persons, such as Plessy, who were more white than black (if one calculated on the basis of their predecessors) were classed as colored, relegated to facilities for nonwhites and not permitted to marry whites. If someone who is three-fourths white goes to a school for blacks and can marry someone who is 100 percent black but not someone who is 100 percent white, the underlying design is patently clear: to protect the purity of the dominant, superior, white race. This classification *cannot* fairly be seen as equal treatment of races, a point to which I shall return when we look at same-sex marriage.

Although *Plessy* itself did not include any such guarantee, according to the doctrine developed in subsequent cases, acceptable racial separation needed equal facilities.[16] In actual practice, facilities were typically unequal, and schools for blacks were often pitifully inadequate. The Supreme Court struck down a form of inequality when it held invalid a state law providing for legal education of whites within the jurisdiction and the payment of tuition for blacks outside the state.[17] In 1950, it required that a black student be admitted to the University of Texas Law School because the state law school for blacks was not equal.[18]

In its historical 1954 decision of *Brown v. Board of Education*, the Warren Court unanimously declared that racially segregated schools are unconstitutional.[19] The Chief Justice's opinion relied primarily on the psychological harm that occurs to black children. "To separate them from others of similar age and qualifications solely because of their race generates a feeling of inferiority as to their status in the community that may affect their hearts and minds in a way unlikely ever to be undone."[20]

Given that eight northern states had racially segregated schools and five others excluded black children from public education when the Fourteenth Amendment was adopted, *Brown* is at odds with the original understanding about accepted practices, yet virtually no one now thinks the result was mistaken. Of course, if we ascend the level of generality, casting the original aim as creating equal opportunity and taking into account how important education is to a person's success, the clause properly requires genuine equality in education, which, partly for psychological reasons, cannot be achieved by school segregation.

The result in *Brown*, though resisted in southern states for many years, was widely accepted by those who believed in racial equality. The Warren opinion, however, came under criticism, most notably by Herbert Wechsler in his famous essay on Neutral Principles, discussed in Chapter 5. The essence of Wechsler's critique was that the focus on psychological harm gave it a centrality that it would not have been given for most constitutional issues and that, in reality, the psychological harm for a black student placed among hostile white students could be even greater than that of being separated.[21] The approach also failed to resolve what would be the status of other forms of racial segregation, such as a bar on "interracial" marriage. (I add the quote because a woman who was three-fourths white could marry a black man but not a white man.)

This criticism of the opinion in *Brown* sharply raises what Supreme Court Justices should aspire to, and what we outsiders should expect and hope for when cases are intensely controversial. In *Brown*, the Justices aimed to speak about segregated education with a uniform voice; when Justices aspire to render a single opinion despite disagreement over nuances, producing a rigorous and sharply analytical explanation is extremely difficult. And, one would guess that, not wanting to generate even more hostility than the decision itself was bound to do, the Justices hesitated to make clear that all basic forms of state racial segregation, including a ban on interracial marriage, were unconstitutional.[22] Finally, when it comes to psychology itself, the Justices undoubtedly recognized that racial segregation *does* treat blacks as inferior and is so perceived. Even if some individual black students might suffer more from being among hostile whites, the expectation and hope was that over time, the psychological benefits of integration would outweigh any temporary negative effects. Putting all of these elements together, one can grasp why Chief Justice Warren may have written what he did, and one may even believe it was strategically wise under the circumstances. That, of course, depends on whether concerns about public reactions can properly lead to less in the way of analytical clarity.

On the same day it decided *Brown*, the Court also declared that the District of Columbia could not maintain racially segregated schools.[23] Given the absence of any Equal Protection Clause that applies directly to the federal government, and the pervasive racial inequality at the time of the Bill of Rights, this result was not easily justified by any simple original understanding or plain meaning of constitutional text. But, of course, it was undeniably sensible in terms of justice and wisdom. From these perspectives, one could not defend acceptance of federal racial discrimination foreclosed to states or the judicial adoption of a different standard of review. A plausible basis in general constitutional theory for this conclusion is that later amendments should be taken to bear upon, and even alter, the content of earlier provisions.[24]

The implementation of *Brown v. Board of Education* was notable in ways that bear both on how judges should perceive basic constitutional rights and on the extent to which appropriate remedies may depend on effectiveness as contrasted with simplicity. In the year following its substantive decision, the Court ruled on *Brown*'s enforcement.[25] It remanded cases to lower courts to ensure that school authorities carried out desegregation. Remarking on the national importance of the decision, and implicitly acknowledging its controversiality, Chief Justice

Warren wrote: "Full implementation of these constitutional principles may require solution of varied local school problems."[26] The district courts were to assure that public school systems undergo a transition to become racially nondiscriminatory and admit students who were parties in *Brown* "with all deliberate speed. . . ."[27] The "all deliberate speed" phrase, along with the rest of the opinion, in context definitely permitted some delay. One implication, clearly at odds with usual "remedies," is that some individual litigants would never themselves directly benefit from their declared right. A black who was in tenth or eleventh grade when *Brown II* was decided might well finish high school without an opportunity to enroll in a school that was no longer restricted to whites. Nonetheless, especially given the fact that these individual plaintiffs were predominantly representing a broader movement toward equality in which the National Association for the Advancement of Colored People was a dominant player, the Justices understandably regarded practical workability—with some precaution against racial violence and extreme hostility—as more important than whether schools immediately had to become fully integrated and whether all the particular young men and women who were parties actually became enrolled in previously white schools. The Court's language was challenged by some as actually encouraging continuing hostility and resistance and making ultimate implementation harder rather than easier. Who can say whether insistence on more immediate compliance would have been preferable practically? The answer to that puzzle might well have depended on what state and locality was the focus. Whether an alternative would or would not have been more effective for implementing integration safely, *Brown II* shows that in extreme cases, practical concerns can affect the scope and timing of remedies as well as substantive legal conclusions.

Although racially blind school districts might seem the simplest form of remedy for segregated schools, that approach would have itself reflected serious injustices. Notably in southern states, extensive racial segregation controlled where people could live. Even fairly drawn districts after *Brown* would have resulted in total separation or great imbalance in the racial composition of schools. Moreover, unless the shape of a district looks very peculiar, as do many present congressional districts, judges would find it hard to discern if local officials had taken race into account in drawing district lines.

For much of the period after *Brown*, the Supreme Court left decisions about particular remedies up to the lower courts. It did, however, get involved in response to a governor's order that the Arkansas National Guard deny entry to black students scheduled to enroll in an all-white school, holding unanimously that the students could not be deprived of their constitutional rights.[28] In 1964, Congress adopted a Civil Rights Act that gave the Attorney General authority to institute suits for desegregation and also made that a condition for state schools to continue to receive federal funding.[29] The Court subsequently ruled that a simple "freedom of choice" plan was not sufficient to alter a segregated school system.[30] In *Swann v. Charlotte-Mecklenburg Board of Education*, in 1971, it stressed the importance of flexible remedies and approved a district court plan that involved busing students outside their neighborhoods and doing so on the basis of racial criteria.[31] This entailed that a remedy for past and existing racial discrimination could properly rely on racial criteria to correct an unjust imbalance. Although this use of race is analytically distinguishable from what is commonly called "affirmative action," its underlying logic bears on how those practices should be viewed.

The Supreme Court has never held that de facto segregation must be corrected, and in many northern cities, striking variations in the racial composition within public schools continue. Although, at the time of the Fourteenth Amendment, some northern state laws required that schools be segregated by race, that was no longer true by the time of *Brown*. Racial imbalance by then reflected the racial composition of areas within which people lived. Of course, prior discrimination contributed largely to where people resided, but residential school districts were not treated as unconstitutional. Thus, northern states have been under no constitutional requirement to increase racial integration within their public schools. However, in the *Swann* case, the Justices did indicate that when housing patterns have caused a kind of de facto segregation, school boards *may* respond by assigning students to schools according to their race in order to promote a better balance.[32]

Brown and the decisions supporting its implementation did not formulate a special standard of review for racial cases. But when, more than a decade after *Brown*, the Court finally struck down Virginia's ban on interracial marriage, it announced in *Loving v. Virginia* that "the Equal Protection Clause demands that racial classifications, especially suspect in criminal statutes, be subjected to the 'most rigid scrutiny.' "[33] As with respect to freedom of speech, such scrutiny requires that the government have a very powerful interest and that this interest could not be served effectively in some other way. Particularly given the underlying purpose of the Fourteenth Amendment, only an exceptionally strong argument would permit a governmental racial classification that explicitly, or in likely effect, disadvantages members of a minority. When might the government now have such an argument?[34] The Supreme Court decisions make clear that a general practice of racial segregation within prisons is not permitted,[35] but if a violent racial conflict engaging a large percentage of a prison population occurred, prison authorities might be able to authorize temporary racial separation in order to reduce violence and save lives.

Exactly what constitutes a "racial" classification is debatable, but what matters is the form of review that a law distinguishing among groups receives. In *Korematsu v. United States*, in which the Supreme Court during World War II sustained the removal from the West Coast of persons of Japanese ancestry, who were then placed in detention centers, Justice

Black's opinion for the Court referred to the legal restriction as curtailing "the civil rights of a single racial group." [36] Shortly before *Brown v. Board of Education*, the Court held that the systematic exclusion of persons of Mexican descent in a Texas county was to be treated in the same way as more typical racial discriminations.[37] In 1987, the Court interpreted the Civil Rights Act adopted during Reconstruction as barring discrimination in employment against Arab Americans; this constituted "racial discrimination that Congress intended § 1981 to forbid, whether or not it would be classified as racial in terms of modern scientific theory."[38] Although the Supreme Court has never made clear exactly what counts as "racial" as contrasted with other group characteristics, social perceptions are more important for Equal Protection than pure physical differences.[39]

Much harder issues are posed by how the courts should treat actions that are by themselves "neutral" but have the effect of promoting racial separation or resisting integration. In *Washington v. Davis*, the Court rejected a claim by black applicants to a police force that the personnel test discriminated against them because its measuring of verbal ability, vocabulary, and reading comprehension was not closely related to the skills necessary for police work.[40] The Court declined to apply the constitutional compelling interest test to statutes and administrative practices designed to serve neutral ends. Although a discriminatory purpose *could* exist without being on the face of a statute, disproportionate impact did not itself call for scrutiny of how closely the standard chosen for hiring was related to what persons needed to function effectively on the job. The Court reached a similar conclusion in *Village of Arlington Heights v. Metropolitan Housing Development Corp.*, when it sustained a zoning regulation in a mainly white, upper-middle-class suburb that had the effect of disadvantaging members of minorities.[41] Although the plaintiff did not have to show that an action was solely motivated by a discriminatory purpose, actual proof of such a purpose was required, and that was found lacking. In 1991, the Court found permissible a prosecutor's refusal to have Latinos as jurors, given the assertion that bilingual jurors would find it hard to accept the official interpretation of what Spanish-speaking witnesses said.[42] In *Palmer v. Thompson*, the Court held, 5–4, that a city council decision to close municipal swimming pools after a court order that they be integrated did not violate the Equal Protection Clause.[43] The majority regarded an investigation of purpose based on actual motivations as improper. Given that the closure so closely followed the order to integrate, one effect of the council's decision was to send the clear message to blacks that many whites did not want to be in swimming pools with them.

Washington v. Davis, the *Arlington Heights* case, and *Palmer v. Thompson* pose important issues about how far practiced realities should affect desirable judicial review of statutes and administrative actions. A sensible starting point is that a genuinely neutral standard, perceived as such, is not unconstitutional simply because members of a minority group fare worse on the average than do others to whom the standard applies. But that does not resolve problems created by concealed motivations, mixed and unconscious motivations, and public perceptions. In *Palmer*, for example, it was obvious that the city council did not want whites and blacks in the same swimming pools. Conceivably, the dominant fear was physical violence. But given past segregation, one cannot avoid inferring that council members did not want integration, and that is how outsiders would have understood their action.

The issues posed by the *Davis* and *Arlington Heights* cases are more complex. Dominant motives that are unlikely to be expressed explicitly are extremely difficult for courts to discern. In a legal culture that bars government racial discrimination against blacks, government officials are not likely to say that is exactly what they are doing. A more subtle point is that individuals are not always aware of exactly what motivates them or the comparative importance of motives they do perceive.[44] Thus, someone living in a white upper-middle-class neighborhood might say to himself, "I'd like to continue living close to people with healthy incomes and social status," not acknowledging even to himself that a preference to be with whites and not blacks is involved. And if he is perceptive enough to recognize that feeling, he may underrate its influence because he believes racial prejudice is immoral.

One considering these various factors cannot avoid concluding that courts requiring explicit proof of racial discrimination will end up accepting many rules and practices that are in fact so motivated, consciously or unconsciously, at least in part.[45] That is a powerful basis to support a somewhat more expansive form of review that would analyze the strength of independent reasons for what the government has chosen to do, or would give considerable weight to the cultural meaning of a practice, that is, how it is broadly perceived,[46] or both. Although the prevailing cultural meaning may often be difficult to discern, it would have resolved the *Palmer* case, and Charles Lawrence has analyzed how it could have produced results contrary to those the Court reached in *Arlington Heights* and *Washington v. Davis*.[47]

Different issues are raised when those acting for the government directly rely on racial criteria but for reasons that may be independent of racial discrimination. The Supreme Court has held that prosecutors, even in making peremptory challenges, cannot exclude people from jury service because of their race.[48] Although a stricter sentence imposed on a defendant because of his race is also clearly improper, the inability of reviewing courts to ascertain when that happens renders this form of racial discrimination effectively immune from review.[49] When it comes to assignment of police officers, investigations, arrests, and stop and frisk, both acceptable connections to race and desirable degrees of judicial involvement are debatable, as Chapter 11 indicates. For many aspects of these practices, both the Equal Protection Clause and the Fourth Amendment ban on unreasonable searches and seizures, are relevant.[50]

A different issue about the Equal Protection Clause concerns the power of the federal government to forbid private discrimination. In 1875, the Supreme Court declared that Congress's enforcement power in the Fourteenth Amendment did not include the authority to forbid private discrimination,[51] and in 1883, it held invalid the public accommodations provision in the 1875 Civil Rights Act.[52] However, as Chapter 8 of this volume indicates, the expansion of Congress's power under the Commerce Clause and its Taxing and Spending Power are adequate for it to reach a great deal of discrimination by private companies and persons.

What of the judicial enforcement of private agreements or directions to discriminate? In *Shelley v. Kraemer*, which preceded *Brown*, the Court held that it was unconstitutional for a court to enforce a racially restrictive covenant.[53] Although Chief Justice Vinson's opinion failed to articulate the need for distinctions and how they might be drawn, plainly some legal enforcements of private discrimination must be acceptable. If a person leaves less to a child because she married someone of a different religion, the state's enforcement of the will does not count as an establishment of religion or infringement of free exercise. And if a man tells a woman to leave his apartment because of her race, she does not have a right to stay. If she adamantly refuses to leave, he may enlist the aid of the police to remove her, and she may be guilty of criminal trespass. Certain kinds of decisions are really up to individuals on virtually whatever basis they choose; for the government to give effect to those decisions does not mean it is acting improperly. On the other hand, a contract that requires private discrimination is designed to force someone to act that way even if he is disinclined to do so. And restrictive covenants attached to property are even more troublesome. If a private community has such a covenant, and I want to buy property there, I must sign on even if I would prefer to have the property without the restriction. Thus, these covenants can be self-perpetuating as long as even a small minority of the owners of the properties covered want to adhere to them. In this context, government enforcement is not just carrying out someone's private wishes, and the danger to genuine legal equality in life is much more threatening. When one considers these varieties, one sees that the issue of the government's relation to private discrimination involves complexities and that a constitutional approach needs to respect these and to strike appropriate balances.

III. AFFIRMATIVE ACTION AND RACE

A crucial question about modern equal protection law is how far the government may engage in affirmative action designed to benefit members of a group that has previously suffered disadvantage. In connection with race, plausible bases can be offered for radically different positions. If one genuinely relied on original understanding about specific practices, programs that favor blacks would almost certainly be regarded as acceptable, given that Congress in 1866 adopted a Freedmen's Bureau Act that provided educational assistance for newly freed blacks and protected blacks who had occupied certain abandoned lands. The Act was adopted over President Johnson's veto and despite arguments that Congress should not assist "a portion of the people, discriminating against all others. . . ."[54] Were one to emphasize the historic and modern needs to help those who have suffered from racial discrimination directed at themselves or their forebears, one might conclude that state and federal governments may assist blacks and other persecuted minorities as they think best. The opposing view is that racial classification is itself undesirable and unjust and should not be perpetuated—that regardless of which group benefits, any law or government practice that classifies by race should be subject to strict scrutiny. The modern Supreme Court has formally adopted the latter position, and it has been embraced by Justices who generally rely on original understanding without any real explanation of how their stance on affirmative action fits their broader constitutional approach.[55] In practice, as we shall see, strict scrutiny in the affirmative action context is not quite as strict as the approach to classifications that harm racial minorities.

Because the issue of affirmative action poses sharply how the Supreme Court should arrive at constitutional standards of review, and because in this instance the opposing considerations are strikingly powerful, I shall first sketch the core arguments for the competing approaches. The basis for fairly strict review in modern times is straightforward. Classifying people by race is generally undesirable. Doing so implicitly encourages people to think in racial terms and to organize in that way, undercutting an overall aim to reduce, or even eliminate, the extent to which a person's race is central to his or her life. More specifically, those who do not get a job or other benefit because of their race may resent both the use of racial criteria and those who are chosen in their place. Moreover, identifying genuine "affirmative action" could sometimes be difficult. If within a locality the majority of legislators are members of a racial minority, or an organized interest group of such members exercises extraordinary political power, are measures favoring those groups genuinely designed to promote equality or simply to reward those with political weight? This could be an extremely hard question for a court to answer.

The arguments in favor of affirmative action rely on justice and practical consequences. Without doubt, the present position of many blacks in this country is partly the result of governments' unjust treatment of their predecessors. Both in terms of compensating for past harms and promoting a presently fair distribution, justice as a value can support affirmative action. Of course, if the favorable treatment is available to all blacks, some who benefit, such as recent immigrants, may not have suffered because of previous discrimination within this country. And, for some benefits, such as college education, the blacks receiving them may not be those whose forebears suffered most. Nonetheless, the vast majority of those who benefit from affirmative action could point to previous unfair treatment of themselves or their ancestors.

A more sweeping argument against such justice claims is that injustices happen all the time; governments should look forward, not be in the business of constantly reviewing and trying to rectify past wrongs. As a general approach, this position makes sense, but in this country, we should regard as special the extreme injustices done to American Indians and to blacks. Those to African Americans, which continued powerfully after the end of slavery and well into the twentieth century, are the subject of the cases discussed in this section.

When one considers justice and affirmative action, the treatment of remedies for illegal discrimination warrants comparison. If a government body or private employer has discriminated against blacks in hiring, the remedy is not limited to those individuals who have unfairly been denied jobs. This makes good sense, both because people who know they will be rejected are not likely to apply in the first place and because those who did apply two or three years ago may now have other jobs they will not leave. As a consequence, the remedy for past illegal discrimination typically includes hiring members of the disfavored group who were not themselves previously rejected by the agency or company involved. If this reaction to previous illegal behavior is sound, affirmative action as a response to general treatment, such as racial segregation, does not seem so different.

The "utilitarian" argument for affirmative action is that it can help produce a genuine society of racial equality by aiding more members of minorities to achieve significant positions in society. To take an obvious example, the admission of blacks with lower academic qualifications to colleges and graduate schools, a practice that began in the late 1960s when few blacks had had precollege education comparable to that of many whites, has undoubtedly contributed to their increased percentage within the professions and among government officials. This increase helps provide more role models for what careers young people may envision, undercuts simple racial stereotyping, and contributes to a multiracial community life, both within the educational institutions and the broader society.

The strength of both the justice and utilitarian arguments for affirmative action does shift over time. If we ever achieve an integrated society in which members of minorities are fully accepted and cease to suffer disadvantage, the utilitarian ground will have disappeared and the justice considerations will become weaker and weaker. My own view when this issue first became prominent was that the arguments in favor did provide sufficient support for affirmative action, despite the legitimate concerns about the negative aspects of racial categorization. Because of these negative aspects, and the problem of continuing categorizations that can lose their desirability over time, or were even designed to favor groups with local power, I supported a form of review that was intermediate, one that looked carefully at the claimed basis for treating members of minorities favorably.[56]

In most respects, the actual course of the Supreme Court's law has been quite different. Notably, it is much more restrictive about what constitute acceptable justifications. In its first affirmative action case, the Supreme Court upheld employment preferences for American Indians in the Bureau of Indian Affairs, relying on the unique status of Indian tribes and the need to make the Bureau more responsive to its constituents.[57] The Court's next case, like a number of those that have followed, involved a preference for blacks at state institutions of higher education. In this initial review, *DeFunis v. Odegaard*, the Court declined to reach the merits. The plaintiff, a young white man who had been ordered admitted by the district court, was about to graduate from the University of Washington Law School, thus rendering his constitutional claim effectively moot.[58] Justice Douglas did reach the merits. Although highly critical of schools basing their admissions primarily on college grades and scores on the Law School Admission Test, Douglas urged that any direct use of racial criteria was unconstitutional, regardless of whether those defending this use can claim that it serves a "compelling interest." He saw such a standard as itself "a stamp of inferiority" on those who were admitted on that basis.[59]

Four years later, a sharply divided Court resolved a similar dispute involving the University of California at Davis. In *Regents of the University of California v. Bakke*, the opinion of Justice Powell proved to be crucial for its disposition and for the developing law, and, I believe, created a significant gap between dominant purposes of institutions and the purpose permitted by the Court's constitutional interpretation.[60] The medical school had set up a special admissions program for "disadvantaged" students that in practice benefited only applicants who were members of minority groups, including "Blacks," "Chicanos," "Asians," and "American Indians." Each year a specific number of places were set aside for those chosen by the special committee that administered the program. Bakke, a white male who was denied admission, had a grade point average and scores on the Medical College Admissions Test that were higher than most of those admitted in the special program.

Four Justices concluded that Title VI of the 1964 Civil Rights Act, which provides that no person "shall, on the ground of race, color, or national origin, be excluded from participation in, be denied the benefits of, or be subjected to discrimination" under programs receiving federal financial aid, barred the use of racial criteria for medical school admissions; these Justices did not reach the constitutional issue.[61] Five Justices, including Justice Powell, did not believe that the statute precluded constitutionally permissible means to remedy unequal treatment of minorities.[62] They relied largely on what supporters of the legislation sought to achieve, and Justice Powell noted that the key term "discrimination" is "susceptible of varying interpretations."[63] Among these five Justices, all but Justice Powell found the admissions program constitutionally permissible. According to them, when racial classifications were designed to further remedial purposes, neither a rational basis nor a compelling interest test was appropriate. Rather, a program "must serve important government objectives and must be substantially related to achievement of these objectives," an intermediate level of scrutiny that had been used for gender discrimination cases.[64] Given the handicap that past discrimination placed on the education of minorities, the use of a race-conscious admissions program to remedy those effects was a sufficiently important objective.

Justice Powell differed in two crucial respects. Based on the lack of a principled basis to draw a line between classifications warranting heightened scrutiny and those calling for a more permissive level of review, and the "perception of racial classifications as inherently odious," Justice Powell rejected the comparison to gender classifications in favor of stricter scrutiny.[65] Preferring persons only on the basis of race amounted to unconstitutional discrimination, but attainment of a diverse student body was a permissible goal for higher education, one that furthers a compelling state interest.[66] While race cannot be used as a definitive criteria, it can be taken into account, and academic freedom, "a special concern of the First Amendment," grants universities the latitude to make their own judgments about selection of their students.[67] Thus, although the Davis program was unlawful, a more flexible approach considering an applicant's race would not be.

Although at that stage, no one could be certain whether the Powell approach would prevail over time, especially given the fact that four Justices had not even reached the constitutional issue, it did set the boundary of what was then permitted. This boundary had two ironic features. Especially notable was this: most educators who believed in affirmative action were moved greatly by a sense of justice and the social desirability of a more equal society, as well as by the benefits of diversity within their institutions. It would have taken extraordinarily legalistic faculty members or administrators to block out all the reasons Justice Powell's opinion regarded as improper constitutionally and to ask themselves, "What should we do if internal diversity is our only objective?" The Powell standard effectively allowed programs to be sustained for the reasons of diversity even if that was actually only one, and perhaps not their main, objective.

The other irony was that effective diversity in education depends significantly on intercommunication. At that point in our history, members of minorities often felt more comfortable with other members of their group. As a consequence, an increase in minority admissions, which created communities of members of those groups, did not necessarily increase intercommunication with whites outside of class. In any event, had schools really treated diversity as their overriding object, they would have investigated how far particular minority applicants did interact with persons outside their group. As far as I know, this never became a major criterion of admissions. Despite these deficiencies, Justice Powell's position later became dominant for the Court.

In the year following *Bakke,* the Court upheld the private use of racial criteria in hiring,[68] despite the language of Title VII of the Civil Rights Act of 1964, which not only makes it unlawful to "discriminate" because of race, but also contains more specific language forbidding classification of "employees ... in any way which would deprive ... any individual of employment opportunities ... because of such individual's race...."[69] Part of the basis for the decision was that it would be difficult for courts to make the legitimacy of using racial criteria depend on whether an employer had previously engaged in illegal discrimination.

A year later, in *Fullilove v. Klutznick*, the Court upheld a statute requiring that when they were granted federal funds, local public works projects had to use at least 10 percent of their grants for minority business enterprises.[70] Two other Justices joined Justice Marshall, who wrote that such assistance was consistent with the stance he had taken in *Bakke,* accepting what the medical school had done in that dispute.[71] In an opinion joined by Justice Powell, Chief Justice Burger wrote that Congress acted appropriately based on evidence that minority businesses had been excluded from public contracting opportunities;[72] Justice Powell added that the addressing of prior discrimination constituted a compelling interest.[73]

In *City of Richmond v. J.A. Croson Co.*, the Court ruled 6–3 against a local program that resembled the federal set-aside that had been sustained in *Fullilove.*[74] Noting that the majority of the Richmond City Council were themselves black, Justice O'Connor, applying a standard of strict scrutiny, concluded for the plurality that remedying the effects of past societal discrimination did not constitute a compelling interest. For the Court's majority, she stated that Richmond's provision that minority group subcontractors get 30 percent of the amount of each contract was not narrowly tailored to achieve the city's objective of increasing minority participation. In 1995, the Court's majority in an opinion by Justice O'Connor established that federal decisions using racial criteria were subject to the same strict scrutiny that applied to the City of Richmond.[75] Remanding the case to the court of appeals, which had employed a more relaxed standard, she wrote that racial classifications, whether they favor or disadvantage members of a minority, "are constitutional only if they are narrowly tailored measures that further compelling governmental interests."[76] Given this approach, which involves a strict approach to formal racial categorizations even when they are designed to redress prior discrimination and reduce present inequalities, governments are unable to take many steps that could further those objectives.[77]

In 2003, the Court returned to racial criteria in university admissions in two cases involving the University of Michigan. The Court held invalid the college's system of awarding specific points toward admission based on race, a practice that made race decisive for almost all minimally qualified minority applicants.[78] However, the law school permissibly took racial diversity into account as one relevant consideration in a process that relied on an evaluation of each applicant's entire file.[79] Writing for the Court, Justice O'Connor explicitly endorsed Justice Powell's approach "as the touchstone for constitutional analysis of race-conscious admissions policies," and the Court held that that supported the law school's practice.[80] In an unusual passage that reflects changing race relations in the United States, O'Connor stated that the core purpose of the Fourteenth Amendment to do away with racial discrimination entailed that "race-conscious admissions policies must be limited in time." She concluded, "We expect that 25 years from now, the use of racial preferences will no longer be necessary to further the interest approved today."[81]

When the Supreme Court in 2012 agreed to review the use of racial criteria for the admission of undergraduates at the University of Texas, many expected the Court to rule that any use of race was no longer acceptable. The Court, however, did not take that step, instead holding that the Court of Appeals had been too deferential to the university and had failed to apply the required strict scrutiny.[82] According to Justice Kennedy's opinion for the Court, judges properly afford a degree of deference to a university's judgment that diversity serves its educational mission, but when it comes to whether the means chosen is narrowly tailored to that goal, "the University receives no deference."[83] Since Texas had adopted a law according to which all those who finished in the top 10 percent of their high school classes are granted automatic admission to any public state college, the university would need to show that race-conscious admissions were needed in addition to this program to achieve desirable diversity.

In a 2007 case, the Court reviewed the use of racial percentages to fill public schools in Seattle, which had never undergone legally authorized segregation, and in Jefferson County, Kentucky, which had previously been under a desegregation decree that had been dissolved in 2000.[84] A five-member majority held that calculating enrollment according to percentages of minorities and whites was impermissible. Four Justices, in an opinion by Chief Justice Roberts, adopted a more restrictive approach to when race might properly be a factor than did Justice Kennedy, who concurred in the judgment. Based both on this case and Kennedy's opinion in the *Fisher* decision, we may surmise that his is now the crucial vote on whether use of racial criteria to promote diversity and equality will be treated as acceptable.

My own view coheres with that of those who have constituted a minority since *Bakke*. Intermediate rather than strict scrutiny would be the better standard, once judges reach the preliminary conclusion that a categorization is genuinely designed to promote racial equality. Although the majority formally uses "strict scrutiny" for all racial categorizations by government, it remains true, even given the Court's scolding of the court of appeals in *Fisher* for being too permissive, that the centrally located Justices are more accepting of racial categorizations that are aimed at achieving equality than those disfavoring minorities. This reality, along with other illustrations, poses the question of just how the Supreme Court should approach standards of review. Should it be explicitly more flexible than the three standards—rational basis, intermediate scrutiny, and strict scrutiny—suggest, should it apply each of those standards in a more uniform way, or should it continue to use a rhetoric that seems less flexible than its actual practices. This fundamental issue is tackled at the end of the chapter.

Special questions about the government's use of racial criteria arise in connection with voting districts. These concern not only what categorization is involved and whether that may foster or fetter the interests of victims of past discrimination but also the boundaries of federal and state power and the right degree of judicial deference to Congress.

Although the original Constitution leaves determinations about eligible voters to the states, the Fifteenth and Nineteenth Amendments explicitly forbid denial or abridgement based on race or gender, and the Equal Protection Clause of the Fourteenth Amendment has been construed to have various applications to voting. Most important, *Reynolds v. Sims* established the one person one-vote principle for the population of districts,[85] and other cases have forbidden poll taxes[86] and restrictions that exclude those who do not own property within a district.[87]

The situation with race is rendered complex by the fact that using racial criteria to define the borders of districts can be a means to improve or curtail the political say of a minority group. It is clearly unconstitutional when lines have been drawn or voter qualifications established in a way that is definitely designed to disenfranchise blacks. Thus, the Supreme Court invalidated an Alabama law that set boundary lines excluding almost all black voters from the city of Tuskegee,[88] and it also struck down a provision of the Alabama Constitution that disenfranchised those guilty of misdemeanors involving moral turpitude, determining that the dominant motivation was to keep blacks from voting.[89] More generally, the Court indicated in 1993 that districting that is race-neutral on its face but clearly designed to separate races is unconstitutional absent a strong justification.[90]

When districts are drawn in a way that corresponds substantially with the racial character of residents, the initial inquiry is whether strict scrutiny is appropriate. In contrast with the suggestion in *Village of Arlington Heights*[91] that if plaintiffs show discrimination to have been a "substantial" or "motivating" factor, defendants then would carry the burden of showing that the law would have been enacted absent that factor, the

Court has indicated in voting cases that strict scrutiny applies only if "race was the predominate factor motivating the legislature's" districting decision.[92] Although the Court has not explained exactly why a special approach is called for in voting cases, one obvious factor is that in our culture, residential racial decisions are often related to what "communities" people feel themselves a part of, and drawing districting lines according to social communities makes sense. Also relevant is the fact that sometimes drawing lines that take account of race may protect minorities from being swamped in nearly all districts and ending up underrepresented.

A crucial component of the regulation of race and voting has involved the federal Voting Rights Act, initially adopted in 1965, and reauthorized and supplemented in 1970, 1975, 1982, and 2006.[93] Section 2 of the Act applies to all states and forbids abridgment of voting rights on the basis of race or color. Sections 4 and 5 were different. Founded in a coverage formula based on a low percentage of voting in 1964 in nine states and also applying to some counties that had used tests or devices for voting regulation, those jurisdictions could change voting procedures only with prior federal "preclearance." The Supreme Court initially upheld the law as a legitimate way for Congress to enforce the Fifteenth and Fourteenth Amendments.[94] One implicit aspect of this conclusion was that an attempt to comply with the federal statute by using racial criteria to ensure that a law did not have the effect of abridging a minority's voting rights might well satisfy the compelling interest test, a conclusion to which six Justices subscribed in 2006.[95]

However, in 2013, by a 5–4 vote, the Court, in *Shelby County, Alabama v. Holder*, held sections 4 and 5 of the 2006 law to be invalid, because the conditions that made its provisions acceptable had ceased to exist.[96] Thus, although Congress had re-enacted the law after fairly intensive assessment of its effects and the continuing danger of discrimination, a law that singled out particular states and counties for federal oversight of their underlying right to set voting requirements and districts could not survive on the basis of categorizations made in terms of what was true a half century ago. Justice Ginsburg's powerful dissent relies heavily on how often the federal review has proved necessary and on Congress's conclusion, with substantial bipartisan majorities, that such review was still needed and that the original criteria of categorization still covered the areas in which discrimination remains a threat.[97] Ginsburg argued, among other things, that Congress should have been given substantial deference in its determination of how best to enforce the post-Civil War amendments.

That the voting cases have produced such a lack of precision, as well as a split among Justices, is hardly surprising. Not only is it hard for judges to determine how dominant is the use of racial criteria and whether a particular districting helps or hurts a minority, voting districts do not really entail particular individuals benefiting or losing, as they would if admission or employment partly depended on one's race. And both the proper degree of deference to Congress's judgment of needed enforcement and the importance of the basic rights of states to set voting requirements are also involved. The special considerations involving voting, as well as affirmative action, help illustrate how special complexities of particular kinds of issues can affect what interpretive strategies are, and should be, used.

IV. GENDER CLASSIFICATIONS

Apart from race, the major classification in the country's history that have treated groups unequally have been according to gender. Four important differences distinguish these from racial inequality. The most obvious is that when the Equal Protection Clause was adopted, neither enactors nor readers assumed that gender distinctions were precluded. Notably, women could not vote or serve on juries, they typically surrendered control of financial resources when they married, and they were barred from certain occupations. Second, that women and men are physically different makes it much easier to accept "segregation" in who participates in many athletic activities, and the reality that most sexual attraction and activity occurs between members of opposite genders bears on whether having separate bathroom facilities is all right. Third, women have never been regarded as inferior in the sense that many whites regarded blacks. In a sexist culture, women may have been widely seen as lacking important skills that men generally possess, but they were also seen as performing critical functions in family life, and as warranting loving affection. This is not to say that women did not feel subordinated by how the law and social norms regarded them; but the subordination was not as total as that conveyed to nonwhites. Fourth, although historically crucial classifications distinctly treated women worse than men, many modern classifications that benefit some women and disadvantage others are aimed at redressing aspects of inequality, but may do so in a way that actually helps perpetuate prevailing social patterns. How to deal with such classifications presents an issue not often involved in racial classifications. (A preference for whites in acquiring public housing designed to encourage integration could be viewed as somewhat similar.)

Apart from obvious physical differences, an underlying question is to what extent variations between most men and most women are the product of particular cultures or are more deeply embedded, and whether this matters. Opinions about what causes the differences themselves are sharply divided. Realistically, it would be foolish to deny that culture can be and is hugely significant. That is demonstrated by what women are doing vocationally in comparison with a century ago, and by how men and women now widely regard each other. But it would be overly simplistic to conclude that all is culturally relative. To take a psychological aspect closely related to a physical difference, is it "natural" that women feel closer attachment to, and responsibility for, newborn babies? Given the profound effect that pregnancy has on a woman's emotions, the months in which her offspring develops within her may affect her sense of the relationship after birth.

If one estimates that, in general, mothers will feel a closer attachment to babies than fathers, and that this is probably not just a consequence of culture, should that matter as far as the law is concerned? The conclusion does not necessarily follow. For example, if a couple is divorcing and a dispute arises over who will have custody over their six-month-old baby, the general law could take the following approach. The custody determination should be based exclusively on individual characteristics, including time and resources, as well as emotional connection to the child, not on a parent's gender. Even if the overall result is that in 90 percent of such disputes, primary custody goes to the mother, the judge should make his or her decision independent of that. This issue illustrates the general question of whether the law and officials should take direct account of what are arguably embedded differences between men and women.

The Supreme Court's initial approach to gender classifications was highly permissive. In the 1873 *Slaughter-House Cases,* which sustained a statute establishing a single-company monopoly against a Fourteenth Amendment challenge, the Court expressed doubt whether the Equal Protection Clause reached anything other than racial classification.[98] The next day, in *Bradwell v. Illinois,* it upheld the state's refusal to license a woman to practice law.[99] Justice Bradley, who had dissented in the *Slaughterhouse Cases,* wrote in an often quoted concurring opinion that the "natural and proper timidity and delicacy which belongs to the female sex evidently unfits it for many of the occupations of civil life." The function of women, according to the "law of the Creator" was to fulfill the offices of wife and mother.[100] Subsequently, the Court upheld denial of a right to vote[101] and a statute prohibiting the employment of women in factories for more than ten hours a day.[102] As late as 1948, it sustained a law that a woman could not be a bartender unless she was the wife or daughter of the male owner.[103]

Not until 1971 did the Supreme Court actually invalidate a gender classification. In *Reed v. Reed,* it reviewed a state law according to which, when an administrator needed to be appointed for the estate of someone who had died without a will, and a choice was to be made within any particular class of otherwise equal claimants (e.g., a son and daughter), "males must be preferred to females."[104] Although this rule did simplify the workload of probate judges, Chief Justice Burger's opinion for the Court regarded the preference for members of one sex as "the very kind of arbitrary legislative choice forbidden by the Equal Protection Clause. . . ."[105] The Court ostensibly used the deferential "rational basis" test it had employed for nonracial claims of unfair treatment; in reality, its review was stricter than when it had addressed ordinary economic and social issues.

Two years later in *Frontiero v. Richardson*, the Court struck down a federal law that allowed a male member of the military to claim his wife as a dependent automatically (thus acquiring a greater housing allowance and medical benefits) while, by contrast, requiring that a female member wanting to receive these benefits show that her husband depended on her for over half his support.[106] Justice Brennan, joined by three colleagues, wrote that gender classifications, like racial ones, should be subject to strict scrutiny.[107] Justice Powell, joined by two other Justices, agreed with the result but explicitly did not join the assertion that all classifications based on gender were "inherently suspect" and needed close scrutiny. He found it unnecessary to reach that question in order to resolve the dispute.[108]

In *Craig v. Boren*, three years later, Justice Brennan did announce for the Court a standard of review significantly stronger than "rational basis."[109] For classifications by gender to be sustainable, they "must serve important governmental objectives and must be substantially related to achievement of those objectives."[110] This intermediate level of scrutiny is more accepting than a strict compelling interest approach, but it does involve genuine oversight. In the case, the Court struck down a law that between the ages of eighteen and twenty-one, females but not males could drink 3.2 percent beer. The fact that young males were much more likely to engage in drunk driving than females failed to provide a sufficient basis for the law, given that even among males, only 2 percent had been arrested for that.

In the years between *Frontiero* and *Craig*, the Court had sustained a property tax exemption for widows and not widowers on the basis that that was a response to uneven opportunities in the job market.[111] It also approved a federal statute that provided women in the Navy a longer period to achieve mandatory promotion, given their nonparticipation in combat.[112]

In the highly controversial case of *Geduldig v. Aiello*, the Court declined to strike down a California law that excluded from insurance coverage for disabilities those produced by pregnancy.[113] Although clearly the provision affected only women, the Court's majority did not regard it as discrimination according to gender, in part because nonpregnant women were treated the same as men. This is, in itself, a totally unsatisfactory justification given that only women were subject to the disadvantage. What is a harder question is whether pregnancy could be seen as special because usually it is the result of voluntary choice. The dissent by Justice Brennan did note that the voluntary choice of male circumcision was not excluded; but his basic position was that any classification by characteristics inextricably linked to one's sex are discriminatory.[114] If it is right that pregnancy is by far the most important medical condition that is acquired by choice, *Geduldig* raises a genuine problem about what should count as classification by sex. In deciding this, should courts assess whether broader attitudes about gender differences are probably affecting relevant legislative decisions? In a 2012 case, Justice Ginsburg, who was, of course, a major leader in promoting gender equality before she became a judge, urged that *Geduldig* be overruled.[115] She was joined by only three colleagues.

In reviewing a law that formally disadvantaged males, the Supreme Court in 1982 ruled that Mississippi University for Women could not exclude men from its school of nursing.[116] The Court stated that the exclusion tended to perpetuate the view that nursing was exclusively for women. The Court subsequently determined in *United States v. Virginia* that the Virginia Military Institute could not exclude women, rejecting claims that the benefits of single-sex education and the suitability only for men of the harsh methods of education the Institute employed justified exclusion.[117] Virginia had responded to a previous ruling of the Fourth Circuit Court of Appeals by creating a separate educational program for women interested in joining the military. The Court did not accept this program, which emphasized military education less and used cooperative techniques, as satisfying the equality requirement. Neither of these cases, nor any other, has declared that public education can never separate males from females.

When other particular classifications have been claimed to rest on genuine differences between men and women, the Court has sustained many, but not all. In 1981, it accepted the limiting of draft registration to men, given the exclusion at the time of women from combat duty.[118] The same year, the Court accepted a statute that made a male guilty of statutory rape if he had consensual intercourse with a female under eighteen years old.[119] The logic was that because the young woman might become pregnant, punishing the participant who did not bear that risk was appropriate. With respect to the consequences of sexual intercourse outside of marriage, the Court also accepted a state statute allowing only the mother of an illegitimate child to sue for its wrongful death, unless the father had undertaken formally to legitimate the child.[120] It also permitted the mother of an illegitimate child to allow adoption without notifying the biological father unless he had met statutory conditions.[121] However, the Court had previously held unconstitutional a law that across the board required only the consent of the mother, not the father, for adoption of a child born out of wedlock.[122] These cases obviously involved the underlying question of how far the state can take account of the facts that biological mothers are more intimately involved with babies than biological fathers, *and* that a significant percentage of biological fathers outside of marriage are not closely connected with either the mother or the child.

The difference between biological mothers and fathers has also been a relevant factor in statutes concerning citizenship. In *Nguyen v. Immigration and Naturalization Service*, the Court sustained a law according to which a child born abroad to unmarried parents was automatically a citizen if the mother was a citizen who had lived in the United States for a continuous year, whereas, if only the father was a citizen, the child became one only if the father agreed in writing to provide support and obtained formal recognition of his paternity before the child turned eighteen.[123] The specific circumstances of the case were these: the father, conclusively proved to be so by a DNA test, was an American citizen; the mother was a citizen of Vietnam; the boy, born in Vietnam, had been raised in the United States by his father from the age of six. The son was convicted of a felony at the age of twenty-two and was subjected to a deportation proceeding, at which time the father obtained an order of parentage. By a 5–4 margin, the Court sustained the statute and the rejection by the Board of Immigration Appeals of the son's claim to citizenship. As a general approach, given the historical uncertainties about the actual parentage of claimed fathers and the closer relations of most mothers to children born out of wedlock, the statute makes some sense; but its application here was so harsh that the Court might better have ruled that an exception was required. If someone is undeniably the father and has raised the child in this country from the age of six, treating his interest in the child's attaining American citizenship as weaker than that of a biological mother is seriously unfair. This conclusion suggests a strategy that the Court has rarely, if ever, pursued in this area. If a gender distinction is generally acceptable, but seriously unjust in a particular application, perhaps a court should not strike down the statute itself but rule that equal protection requires an exception to its coverage.

In a more recent nationality case, the Court reviewed a statutory provision that governed whether a child born abroad to unmarried parents could be given citizenship at birth.[124] If the mother was a U.S. citizen who had lived in the country for a year, this was possible, but if the father was the U.S. citizen, he had to have lived here for ten years, five of them after the age of fourteen. Since the father had been only sixteen at the time of birth, he was not old enough to meet the statutory requirement. Divided 4–4, with Justice Kagan not participating, the Court in an unsigned per curiam opinion affirmed the court of appeals decision upholding the statute. Based on her approaches to other issues, one would guess that Justice Kagan would not favor similar sharp divisions in the treatment of male and female parents.

A 1977 case involving financial benefits illustrates the sorts of circumstances in which some women and men benefit and some women and men do not. Under a federal program, widows received survivors' benefits based on the earnings of their late husbands; a widower, on the other hand, got the benefits only if one half of his support had been coming from his wife's earnings.[125] Four Justices regarded this as unacceptable discrimination against female workers; Justice Stevens concurred on the basis that the widows who actually benefited from not having to show their dependency were ones who least needed the money, and thus could not fairly be treated more favorably than the male widowers.[126]

By contrast, the Court, in a per curiam opinion, upheld a provision in the Social Security Act that treated men and women differently for purposes of calculating benefits on the basis of average wages.[127] Women were allowed to exclude a greater number of years of lower earnings than were men. The Court's logic for sustaining the difference was that it "operated directly to compensate women for past economic discrimination."[128]

These various cases about gender discrimination illustrate two fundamental points. The first is that given the constitutional text of Equal Protection and the underlying value of equality, distinctions drawn on the basis of gender differ significantly and often require careful evaluation rather than the application of a simple, uniform standard. The variations involved are related to those between racial discrimination and genuine racial affirmative action, but are somewhat more complex. The second lesson, one clearly illustrated by different categories of speech in Chapter 9, is that the interpretive approaches for a single constitutional standard rightly vary if the kinds of practices and social contexts involved differ significantly. Although blacks and women were undeniably victims of long-standing discrimination, what judges should do to further the constitutional value of equality is not necessarily the same for both groups.

V. SEXUAL ORIENTATION

As gender lines powerfully illustrate, social conceptions of unjust classifications shift over time. Given a somewhat flexible approach to Equal Protection, these changes affect both judicial standards of review and what practices are declared impermissible constitutionally. Within the last four decades, we have experienced a strong change in general attitudes toward sexual relations between persons of the same gender and same-sex marriage. That has significantly affected what the Supreme Court has done, most notably ruling 5–4 in late June 2015 that the Constitution protects same-sex marriages and requires every state to provide them.[129] Although Justice Kennedy's majority opinion, sharply attacked by the dissenters, rests most heavily on the thesis that the due process clause assures that people can exercise fundamental rights and that these include marriage, it also relies on equal protection, treating the two protections as closely related. Because this book was already in its very final stage of review when *Obergefell v. Hodges* was decided, it does not undertake a full analysis of the case, rather concentrating on what preceded its predictable outcome.

To set the background for this discussion, it is worth noting the Court's "rational basis" treatment of most legislative classifications and its development of other levels of review that more nearly resemble those based on race or gender. In the latter context, the crucial inquiry is what has been, and should be, the principled basis for heightened scrutiny.

For most economic and social classifications, the Equal Protection Clause has little significance. Courts assess these according to a "rational basis" test that comes very close to acceptance without review, given the high degree of deference accorded both to legislative purpose and chosen means. In the 1955 case of *Williamson v. Lee Optical*, the Court passed on a statute that did not allow opticians to fit old glasses within new frames without a written prescription by an ophthalmologist or optometrist; the law exempted from the requirement those who sold ready-to-wear glasses.[130] Although such a law appeared mainly designed to protect particular economic interests of one group over another, the Court found it supported by the legislature's possible appraisal of the health value of eye examinations. In answer to the argument that from that perspective the exception for sellers of ready-to-wear glasses did not make sense, Justice Douglas wrote for the Court that the Equal Protection Clause covers only invidious discrimination, that "the legislature may select one phase of one field and apply a remedy there, neglecting the others."[131] In *Minnesota v. Clover Leaf Creamery Co.*, the Court in 1981 upheld a law that allowed the sales of milk in nonreturnable containers that were paperboard but not those that were plastic.[132] Despite claims that the object of the law was to benefit the local dairy and pulpwood industries, and that the line drawn did not serve its purported environmental purpose, the Court responded that judges need not be persuaded about the correctness of such evaluations, which are left to legislative judgment. Under such a level of review, discerning an actual violation of equal protection is nearly impossible.

Among the classifications that have explicitly received a higher degree of scrutiny are those based on alienage and wealth. In *Sugarman v. Dougall*, for example, the Court subjected a New York law that broadly excluded aliens from civil service positions to "close judicial scrutiny," it concluded that the law was not cast narrowly and precisely enough for the purpose of assuring an identity between the government and its citizens.[133] With regard to wealth, the Court has held that a person cannot be denied the right to vote because of a failure to pay a poll tax,[134] and we have seen in Chapter 11 various efforts have been made to assure a fair criminal process for the poor. However, in general, it is not unconstitutional for governments to charge for services that will be harder for poor people to pay for. The Court, in *San Antonio Independent School District v. Rodriguez*, has also sustained state methods of financing public education that rely on local property taxes and are bound to generate better public schools in wealthier districts.[135] Given the central role of education in creating the prospects for one's life, the competing perspective that states should have to strive not to make the quality of a child's public schooling depend heavily on her parents' income has considerable appeal. A Supreme Court Justice could build both on *Brown v. Board of Education* and cases precluding different treatment based on wealth to conclude that laws rendering the quality of public schools dependent on the wealth of a local community violates equal protection, a conclusion actually reached by the four dissenting Justices in the *San Antonio* case.[136]

At the time of the founding, homosexual acts were subject to serious criminal penalties, including in some states a possible death sentence. And most states formally maintained criminal penalties through much of the twentieth century, though actual enforcement became rare. In this historical context, same-sex marriage was a nearly inconceivable notion, and the idea that gay people should not be discriminated against held little popular sway. Yet here was a group of people who were a clear minority and had long been treated as inferior in an important sense. In the famous footnote 4 of *United States v. Carolene Products Co.*, which itself used a relaxed rational basis test to sustain a distinction among milk products, Justice Stone wrote that more stringent review might be needed for statutes directed at religious, national, and racial minorities because "prejudice against discrete and insular minorities" may seriously undermine ordinary political processes.[137] A question this raises about sexual orientation is to what extent homosexuals fall within the kinds of classes conceived in *Carolene Products*. A broader issue is how far that footnote has provided the best criteria for heightened scrutiny.

In *Lawrence v. Texas*,[138] decided in 2003, the Supreme Court overruled its 1986 decision in *Bowers v. Hardwick*[139] and declared that a Texas statute forbidding oral and anal sex between persons of the same gender was unconstitutional. Although relying primarily on the concept of substantive due process, thus not permitting the state to turn around and prohibit all oral and anal sex, Justice Kennedy's opinion for the Court did connect the guarantee of liberty to equality of treatment. He wrote: "When homosexual conduct is made criminal by the law of the State, that declaration in and of itself is an invitation to subject homosexual persons to discrimination both in the public and in the private spheres."[140]

The Supreme Court has yet to hold that governments must always treat homosexuals equally to heterosexuals, but its rulings move strongly in that direction. In *Romer v. Evans* in 1996, the Court reviewed an amendment to the Colorado Constitution that was adopted by popular referendum in response to laws in municipalities, including Boulder, that barred discrimination on a number of bases, including sexual orientation.[141] The state's constitutional amendment provided that neither the state nor its localities could forbid discrimination based on "homosexual, lesbian or bisexual orientation, conduct, practices or relationships."[142] The dissenting Justices contended that since states could reasonably aim to protect traditional cultural values of family life and did not need to preclude discrimination based on sexual orientation, a state constitution could provide that legislators may not bar that.[143] For the majority, Justice Kennedy relied on both the narrowness of the classifications covered and the breadth of kinds of anti-discrimination laws that were forbidden, to conclude that discrimination of an "unusual character" was involved. Given the absence of an identifiable "legitimate purpose or discrete objective," the amendment "classifies homosexuals not to further a proper legislative end but to make them unequal to everyone else."[144] Thus, the Court, without explicitly adopting heightened scrutiny but employing a rational basis approach in what was definitely a less than deferential way, concluded that the Equal Protection Clause was violated.

On the fundamental question of what should count as suspect classification for equal protection purposes, homosexuals are different from racial minorities in certain respects. One is that the typical basis for less favorable treatment concerns actions rather than one's intrinsic nature. However, given the reality that persons consistently engaged in homosexual activity almost all have strong sexual inclinations that differ from those of the majority, the line between status and action here seems almost trivial, especially since the actions do not directly harm others. Certainly gay people have been a minority subject to historic discrimination, although a traditionalist *might* claim that this was warranted to protect the quality of family life. Homosexuals are, of course, not as easily identified as members of racial minorities and women, and thus can often avoid unfavorable treatment by concealing their sexual inclinations; but this hardly bears on whether heightened scrutiny is appropriate for laws explicitly providing less than equal treatment. Finally, some have claimed that because homosexuals tend to be well off economically and have political clout, special constitutional protection is not needed. But if a group is a relatively small minority, the personal status of many of its members is hardly an assurance that it will receive fair treatment.

In recent years, a number of states have adopted laws allowing same-sex marriage, and in some states, their highest courts have held that limiting marriages to persons of opposite genders violates either the federal Equal Protection Clause or an analogous provision in the state constitution. A number of decisions by federal courts of appeals reached similar conclusions about the federal Constitution, preceding the Supreme Court's 2015 resolution to that effect. In June of 2013, the Supreme Court reviewed an amendment to the California Constitution and a federal statute that raised issues closely resembling those in *Romer*. In both cases, it managed to avoid a determination whether such marriage constitutes an actual right under the Equal Protection Clause or substantive due process, although four dissenting Justices definitely rejected such a right.

Hollingsworth v. Perry involved the constitutional amendment in California.[145] The California Supreme Court had initially held that limiting marriage to opposite-sex couples violated the state constitution. A ballot initiative called Proposition 8 was adopted that constitutionally defined marriage as a union between a man and a woman. Affirming a decision of the federal district court, the Ninth Circuit Court of Appeals held that the amendment violated the federal Equal Protection Clause, which it precluded anti-discrimination legislation in the same manner as in *Romer v. Evans*.[146] The United States Supreme Court avoided a decision on the merits; state officials had not appealed the decision below and the proponents of the amendment who sought to defend it lacked standing because they were not ordered to take or refrain from any action.

The second case involved the federal Defense of Marriage Act (DOMA) adopted in 1996. Prior to the adoption of same-sex marriage in any state, Congress had provided that for the broad purposes of federal regulations and benefits, the words "marriage" and "spouse" cover only legal unions between a man and a woman. In *United States v. Windsor*, the Court passed on the claim of a widow of a same-sex marriage recognized by New York law who had been charged $363,053 in federal estate taxes that would not have been required of a surviving opposite-sex spouse.[147] The Second Circuit Court of Appeals had explicitly applied intermediate scrutiny to review the law, determining that homosexuals qualified as a "quasi-suspect class." Given the history of discrimination, the absence of any relation to contribution to society, the existence of a discernible characteristic that defines a discrete minority, and a political power that may be significant but not adequate to prevent pervasive discrimination,[148] the court of appeals declared the federal law unconstitutional.

On review, the Supreme Court reached the same result, but the opinion by Justice Kennedy took a somewhat different approach. Kennedy emphasized the extent to which the federal law undercut the traditional authority of states to regulate marriage and family life, but found it "unnecessary to decide whether this federal intrusion on state power is a violation of the Constitution because it disrupted the federal balance."[149] Rather, the law was invalid for seeking to injure the very class New York sought to protect. The House Report talked of "moral disapproval of homosexuality."[150] The Court found that the main purpose of the law was to "impose inequality," not to serve legitimate government objectives.[151] Quoting the 1973 case of *Department of Agriculture v. Moreno*, in which the Court had invalidated a restriction that barred households containing unrelated individuals from participation in the food stamp program,[152] Justice Kennedy said that " 'a bare congressional desire to harm a politically unpopular group cannot' justify disparate treatment of that group."[153] The Court concluded that the federal law violated the equal protection aspect of the Fifth Amendment's Due Process Clause. The four dissenters regarded the law as well within federal authority to determine what counts as marriage for the national government and to do so based on the traditional concept of persons suitable to marry each other.[154]

The writer of a number of majority opinions dealing with classifications that reflect a negative view about homosexual relations and same-sex marriage, Justice Kennedy is now the key member of the Court for how these cases turn out. Not surprisingly, he authored the majority opinion holding state preclusion of same-sex marriage as unconstitutional.

Both the present treatment of gender discrimination and same-sex marriage illustrate the open-endedness of standards like Equal Protection; they also support the view that original understanding about specific practices should not be the overriding technique of constitutional interpretation.

VI. LEVELS OF REVIEW AND INTERPRETIVE STRATEGIES

In raising broad questions about how it should be interpreted and applied, the Equal Protection Clause is similar to other constitutional provisions, but some of the particular aspects of it are not widely shared. The individual rights we have reviewed in prior chapters primarily involve bars on government interference with forms of activity or safeguards against unjust intrusions in people's lives. Although equal treatment figures as important for various provisions, only the Equal Protection Clause is fundamentally about equality, not what behavior the government can prohibit or encourage. That makes categorizations the central subject for analysis. What kinds of categorizations does the clause genuinely reach? Need those be explicit, or are implicit purposes and effects sufficient? Among the categorizations that count, what level of review is appropriate to determine whether they are justified? Apart from its evident purpose to achieve equal treatment in various respects for freed slaves, the Equal Protection Clause itself provides no textual guidance about how courts should approach these questions. As Jamal Greene has written about the Fourteenth Amendment in general, "[it] represents a commitment to a series of principles rather than rules or even standards, and principles often do not lend themselves to definitive application."[155]

As we have seen, the Supreme Court's formal approach has been to employ three basic standards of review: rational basis, strict scrutiny, and intermediate scrutiny. In reality, the application of each of these standards varies, and Justices are more deferential to legislative choices in some instances than in others.

Although the rational basis test in form allows the conceptual possibility that virtually any form of classification might violate Equal Protection, the way that test is usually employed renders the clause effectively inapplicable as far as judicial review is concerned. The courts afford legislatures extreme deference for ordinary economic and social statutes. A theoretical point that is rarely noted is that if a genuine rational basis is needed to satisfy equal protection, and promoting the financial position of a political supporter does not qualify, legislators considering such measures should ask themselves whether they would be violating equal protection, even if they are confident that whatever they do will be accorded judicial deference and accepted. In contrast to allocations of government powers discussed in Chapters 7 and 8, the subject of nonjudicial official perceptions of equal protection is rarely discussed, although even with more stringent forms of review, legislators could, and should, consider themselves restrained beyond likely judicial enforcement. An example would be when a legislator is aware that a court is likely to accept a basis for a proposed statute, but the legislator herself finds that ground completely unconvincing and is inclined to vote in favor only because the statute will also serve a purpose, such as preserving the whiteness of a neighborhood, that would lead to invalidation if it were the exclusive and obvious purpose. In this setting, a conscientious legislator might vote against the bill because she recognizes that the purpose that moves her is not constitutionally appropriate.

In the remainder of this section, I will disregard the extent to which legislators and executive officials should regard themselves as constrained by Equal Protection beyond the level of judicial enforcement. I will also assume that the use of the genuinely relaxed rational basis approach is essentially equivalent to nonapplication of the clause. I will focus on forms of categorization that need some more stringent form of judicial review.

The earlier sections of this chapter show why one single standard of review for all equal protection challenges would not be wise.[156] At the other side of the spectrum would be an approach that does not rely on mediating standards and considers each equal protection challenge in light of the basic values underlying the clause. Something close to this strategy was endorsed by Justice Stevens, who criticized the three-tiered judicial scrutiny as too rigid and arbitrary.[157] Unfortunately, the heightened degree of sensitivity to different circumstances that an "unmediated" review would allow would also carry substantial disadvantages. Even when Supreme Court Justices agree on what standard of review is called for, they often disagree about the outcomes that follow. Were most of the Justices to abandon more specific guiding standards in favor of an overall assessment of how relevant values bear on the dispute before them, almost certainly the range of disagreements would increase. And, whether or not that would be true, that kind of approach provides extremely limited guidance for lower courts and legislators, beyond telling them that they should not accept laws that are indistinguishable from what the Supreme Court has declared invalid.

Although it would not necessarily follow from a disclaimer of reliance on a particular level of review, there is also a risk that "balancing" of competing considerations could undercut the desirable degree of judicial emphasis on basic values. We have seen with respect to freedom of speech, free exercise and nonestablishment, and criminal process rights that certain laws and practices are properly declared invalid even if a plausible argument is available that, on balance, they would promote social welfare or community contentment. The Equal Protection Clause similarly represents fundamental values that should not be outweighed by many plausible assertions of competing considerations. As Alexander Aleinikoff has observed, what was really involved in the *Bakke* case was a dispute over whether Equal Protection was fundamentally about "colorblindness" or helping blacks achieve equality, not whether, on balance, the medical school's admissions standards were desirable.[158] Although

Aleinikoff's basic criticism of ad hoc balancing is forceful, two qualifications are needed. The first is that a constitutional provision often involves more than one basic value, and these sometimes come into conflict. This chapter has defended the view that countering the effects of past injustices against blacks and eventually eliminating racial categorizations are both properly seen as values underlying the Equal Protection Clause. The second qualification is that extreme needs of social welfare are rightly taken to justify departures from the basic values that underlie particular provisions. A free speech example is that the publishing of true information about secret wartime troop movements that are taking place is not a First Amendment privilege. A hypothetical example in this chapter is that a temporary segregation of prisoners by race may be an acceptable response to extremely violent and extensive racial conflict within a jail.

If the Supreme Court properly uses discrete standards of review, just what should those look like when decisions must be made about covered categorizations and degrees of scrutiny? I shall address in turn explicit categorizations, formally neutral laws and practices that cause differential effects, and standards of assessment once it is determined that a categorization is, or may be, covered.

For explicit categories, we can start with race. If blacks and whites are treated differently, the Equal Protection Clause comes into play. The same is true if the categorization closely resembles that, for example, disadvantaging Americans of Chinese or Arab descent. The serious questions arise when we look at other forms of unequal treatment, lines drawn according to gender, sexual orientation, age, or disability. As the chapter shows, what Equal Protection is taken to cover has developed over time. William Eskridge has developed a substantial account of how the reach of Equal Protection and other clauses has been the consequence of identity based social movements.[159] Of course, a Supreme Court Justice does not rely directly on the existence of a movement; rather, she will consider the intrinsic force of the values claimed and the degree of their public acceptance. Thus, with respect to same-sex marriage, it has mattered how many states have provided it, how broadly people accept it, and whether its recognition is called for by a wide understanding of the value of equality. Michael Dorf has suggested that other constitutional provisions, even ones whose connection to Equal Protection is less than obvious, should be an important guide to what categories are subject to serious review.[160] Viewing the Constitution as a whole in this way makes good sense, but when another provision is peripherally relevant, Justices will still need to be guided by what they take as underlying equal protection values, and sometimes these properly reach categorizations, such as sexual orientation, that are not mentioned in the federal constitution. Although whether a particular categorization should receive careful scrutiny will sometimes be debatable, this degree of uncertainty is an acceptable cost of interpreting equal protection in a manner responsive to modern conceptions of equality.

A more perplexing question is what approach courts should take if laws do not formally categorize in a particular way, but may be motivated or widely perceived as doing so, or have negative effects on members of disadvantaged groups. Clearly the Supreme Court has been correct in not treating every law about which such an argument might be made as demanding careful review, but, as previous sections have suggested, it could desirably be somewhat less deferential to proffered neutral justifications, be less demanding that actual proof be shown of discriminatory purposes, and be more sensitive to widespread cultural understandings of what laws are doing. Were it to moderate its stance in this way, the consequence would be somewhat more stringent review of laws whose underlying objectives are less than obvious.

Once a law or executive practice qualifies for review beyond relaxed rational basis, the question is what form that review should take. Some classifications, such as those disadvantaging or segregating racial minorities, warrant highly stringent review, the kind of "strict scrutiny" that applies to most impairments of speech based on its content. This chapter has resisted the view that genuine affirmative action, seeking to redress injustice and promote equality, deserves such scrutiny, although courts should not simply accept every claim that a law has this objective. The Supreme Court's actual position lies somewhere between an intermediate approach and the strictest form of review; it says "strict scrutiny" applies, but is somewhat more deferential and accepting than it would be if a classification preferred whites over blacks.

For various forms of classification, including at least some involving gender, an explicit intermediate standard is most sensible. Under such a standard, a court should neither begin with a strong presumption against a law, sustaining it only if overwhelmingly powerful reasons exist to override equality values, nor assume on the contrary that any plausible argument in favor of the law is enough to sustain it. In their process of assessment, courts should give heightened importance to basic constitutional principles as compared with other asserted social benefits, and their degree of deference to legislative judgment should depend somewhat on the kind of law and the circumstances of its enactment.

It is evident that for many individual Justices and for the Supreme Court as a whole, their disposition of cases is not consistent with the three basic standards of review being uniformly applied. Although the aspiration for greater precision and consistency is legitimate, it is less important than responses that are sensitive to particular contexts. It probably would be helpful for Justices to acknowledge explicitly that formulated standards of review are generalizations that themselves do not specify all the nuances that are relevant for particular evaluations, and further to say that these nuances are often not susceptible to precise formulations, particularly in majority opinions that capture the views of Justices who are almost certainly not treating relevant factors identically.

CONCLUSION

This chapter has explored vital issues concerning Equal Protection. It has analyzed approaches to specific issues, and suggested some alternatives. However, as with other chapters, the overall theme is the complexity of relevant considerations and irreducibility of what counts to simple formulas.

Conclusion

The last seven chapters have dealt with particular provisions and subject matters covered by the United States Constitution. Although offering various critiques and suggestions, their prevailing themes are that interpretation of a Constitution that is difficult to amend rests on multiple standards whose significance varies, depending on what provisions and issues are involved. These are, of course, overarching claims of the more general first five chapters. We can roughly divide the later chapters into ones dealing with allocations of political authority and individual rights, although the nature of the individual rights involved varies, and that itself affects actual desirable interpretation.

Distributions of government power involve relations between the national government and states and the assignment of functions within the federal government. In both of these respects, the original Constitution did not simply replicate structures that already existed—what it set up was significantly novel. Given radical changes in relations between governments and citizens in all liberal democracies since the late eighteenth century, including increasingly close national and international ties, we cannot expect present constitutional interpretation about what branches of government can do to replicate the structures of 1789. Most notably, the national government now has much greater scope, and administrative agencies perform critical roles in the federal government and the states, roles that actually involve functions of all three branches of government. They not only implement statutes, they adopt novel regulations with coverage they regard as wise, and they make quasi-judicial resolution of disputes. These developments make it not only unwise but also impossible to leave unaltered the precise ranges of political authority conceived at the time of the founding.

The allocations of powers present special problems of interpretation that differ from those for individual rights. Notable among these are how far courts should defer to what other branches of government have decided and how far those branches should regard themselves as legally constrained beyond what courts will enforce. Although one can perceive certain questions about deference as across-the-board—for example, should courts defer to Congress because the Constitution was addressed mainly to it?—the argument for substantial deference is much stronger with respect to *some* allocations of power.

That individual rights guarantees were, in effect, adopted as limits on overstepping by legislators and executive officials generates a powerful argument against broad acceptance of decisions of theirs that arguably infringe those rights. This is especially true given both the concern at the time of the original Constitution that states might not treat citizens of other states equally, and the overriding aim of the Civil War amendments to assure that states, especially those with a history of slavery, would treat African Americans fairly.

Three crucial differences concern the allocation of powers. The simplest argument for deference is that because states elect members of Congress, what Congress resolves should not be seen by courts as infringing on state powers. At least in modern circumstance, this is not a convincing basis for judges to afford complete acceptance of claimed infringements on state powers, but it does provide a reason for some deference to Congress that does not exist for a claim that a state legislature has transgressed on federal authority. Within the federal government, the strongest argument for deference is that when the Congress and the President agree, courts should be very hesitant to override their resolutions. As Chapter 7 explains, identifying agreement or acquiescence is not always simple, but it is definitely present sometimes. And even when genuine acquiescence is doubtful or clearly absent, leaving resolution of certain matters up to the political branches may be wise. If, for example, it is arguable that the President has exceeded his authority as commander in chief, perhaps the main source of restraint should be left to Congress.

Closely related to the question of deference is whether there are areas in which courts should simply not involve themselves, because the Constitution is best understood as assigning a final decision to a political branch, or judicial involvement would be insensitive to very important practical considerations. Chapter 7 provides the example of whether an "officer" who may succeed to the Presidency can include a member of Congress. Once the House Speaker takes over as President, according to the prevailing statute, for a court to say that simply doesn't fit what "officer" means in the Constitution would be so seriously disruptive that such a determination is almost inconceivable. Although the "political question" doctrine can apply to some issues of individual rights, its main significance, as in this example, concerns allocations of governmental responsibility.

Tied to the ranges of deference and political questions is how far should the political branches view their constitutional limits as going beyond judicial assessments. Without doubt, political officials can, and sometimes should, conceive their authority under the Constitution as more constrained than what courts will enforce. How far legislators and executive officials actually regard themselves as so constrained, and how effectively this works, are practical questions. But as Chapter 7 suggests, that such constraints can exist is conceptually clear, and evidence supports the claim that the President has taken many seriously.

Five of the last seven chapters are about individual rights, but the kinds of rights vary in important ways, and these support differences in interpretation. Freedom of speech and of religious exercise involve rights to engage in behavior that is of central importance in a liberal democracy. Especially for freedom of speech, it makes a difference whether a person's form of expression connects significantly to considerations of public concerns or involves an honest declaration of one's beliefs and feelings, or, like commercial advertising or suggestions of how to commit a crime, is only remotely connected to those subjects. As Chapter 9 demonstrates, the interpretive strategies the Supreme Court has sensibly used depend significantly on whether the expression involved lies close to the core values underlying protection. With religious exercise, how far that can be constrained depends on whether it does a significant harm that is independent of an evaluation of the persuasiveness of the religious position involved.

Equal protection and nonestablishment of religion largely concern a different variety of right, barring on government treatment of some people and organizations differently from others. As Chapter 12 describes, a crucial question about equal protection is how far it should be understood to preclude differential treatment that was taken for granted when the Fourteenth Amendment was adopted. That it now covers discrimination against women has become widely accepted, and we have also seen an evolving approach toward differences in treatment that depend on the gender of sexual partners. This is one of the many areas in which some response to changing social understandings and values is called for.

The hardest questions about establishment of religion involve what the government itself can do—how far can it convey particular religious views. Here, a critical tension exists between a historical tradition that has included forms of government expression reflecting the dominant Christian religion and the basic idea that if the government promotes one religion, it is treating others unfavorably. As Chapter 10 urges, we cannot return to the early nineteenth century, when government's effective acceptance of Protestant Christianity was an aspect of public schools. But the precise limits on governmental expression now are not easy to settle.

The other two chapters, related to the criminal process, are about yet different kinds of individual rights than what private behavior is protected. The limits on searches and seizures and police violations of the privilege against self-incrimination require that effective notice be given to officers of what actions they are allowed and forbidden. Clarity of standards is then especially important. The right to counsel is now partly invoked to avoid self-incrimination but mainly concerns fairness of the process for those accused of criminal activity. Here, we see a radical shift from the founding about how far those unable to afford counsel must be provided one. Virtually no one believes that right should now be regarded as outside constitutional protection because it fails to conform with original understanding.

Freedom from "cruel and unusual" punishment concerns government treatment not of suspects but of persons convicted. Here, warning in advance seems less significant than careful evaluation of what is acceptable. Given the punishments of 1791, a return to all practices accepted then is unimaginable. A much harder question is whether the Supreme Court's careful assessments of bases for capital punishment is reconcilable with its nearly total acceptance of any statutorily authorized length of imprisonment. I have suggested the answer is "no."

The early chapters of the book explore a variety of senses of original understanding. The subsequent chapters demonstrate decisively what the first five chapters claim—namely that what the Supreme Court has done, and should do, is not simply to try to follow faithfully what either the actual enactors or readers, or imaginary objective enactors or readers, would then have understood as applications of provisions or as the linguistic meaning of the words in particular provisions. When a constitution is hard to amend, interpretation that responds to changing social structures and values is needed, and exactly what kind of interpretative strategy is called for depends on what kind of issues judges must resolve. The only viable approach that makes central original understanding is one that starts from the premise that the founders or readers then recognized, or that the prevailing interpretive approaches then accepted, evolution over time, especially for provisions cast in general and open-ended language.

The rest of this conclusion relates the claims made in this book to the themes of the first two volumes. I will start with statutory and common law interpretation, since the connection to these is obviously closest. In much of this volume, I have compared interpretation of a Constitution that is difficult to amend with many crucial general, open-ended terms to typical statutory interpretation, pointing out a number of reasons the methods of interpretation should not be identical.

Of course, in many respects, constitutional interpretation falls closer to interpretation of statutes than to other interpretive endeavors in law. The central reference is to an authoritative text issued by persons with public authority. Courts must sometimes consider what to do if apparent specific applications are in tension with purposes, which themselves can be understood at various levels.[1] There are multiple bases for decisions, carrying different weight in different contexts. Just as coherence with other statutes is one basis for statutory interpretation, judges try to treat the Constitution as a coherent document. Judicial opinions about the grounds of decision in difficult cases are often less than completely candid, in part because majority opinions may smooth over varying understandings, but also because judges often try to make results seem to depend more heavily on standard legal sources than their views about what will work best or conforms with their political philosophy. Insofar as original intentions and original understanding matter, similar perplexities are raised about exactly whose and what intentions are relevant and how one should construct the relevant readers—should they be ordinary or well informed, members of the majority or people most affected by a law?[2] For statutes construed by administrative agencies, the question of judicial deference bears some resemblance to whether courts should defer to how branches of the government understand the scope of their constitutional authority. In the United States, the Justices of the Supreme Court have not reached agreement about exactly how to interpret either statutes or the Constitution.

Despite these commonalities, constitutional interpretation for many reasons has been, and needs to be, different from that involving typical statutes. Among the most important reasons is the procedure of revision. So long as the existing legislature can revise or repeal a statute, that is a strong reason for judges to concentrate on its original coverage, a reason that does not apply to the United States Constitution, which is very hard to amend and neither has, nor should have, hundreds of provisions that deal with particular details.

Another important difference concerns common terminology. Statutes usually contain considerable details with technical words and phrases, ones that most legislators do not even read. These are important bases to accord status to crucial legislative history developed by committees responsible for the statutes. The language of constitutions is much more accessible and widely read, and the argument that many of those who enact their provisions are in some way "delegating" responsibility to the drafters is much less viable. That does not mean, of course, that those who vote for provisions, and outside readers, are indifferent to the aims of the drafters. The general truth that people understand language largely in terms of what they take speakers to be trying to say is relevant for both statutory and constitutional interpretation. What differs are the implications of this similarity for how much independent weight to give to what is portrayed during the drafting process itself, as compared with other sources for grasping the goals behind provisions. Because with original constitutions and amendments, those voting to approve provisions and other citizens have a realistic opportunity to read and develop an understanding of their own, what one group of those who are involved have perceived as the meaning of language carries less significance.

Three other aspects of the American Constitution are also important in this respect. One is that the drafters' debates were not even available to those voting in the ratifying conventions, and the drafters downplayed the significance of their role. More generally, given two distinct stages of constitutional adoption or amendment, we have much less assurance that those proposing provisions and those ratifying them will have similar outlooks than is true for the two houses of Congress voting for a statute after a Conference Committee report.

A third aspect, which concerns the passage of time and the nature of provisions, is relevant both for the place of "legislative history" and all aspects of original understanding. With precise provisions being applied not long after adoption, judges sticking to what the drafters specifically intended makes sense. For open-ended provisions applied over centuries under changing conditions, this is not workable. This observation does apply to some statutes, such as the Sherman Antitrust Act, but it is much more widely relevant for key constitutional provisions. This passage of time is also a reason not to accord overarching importance to original reader understanding of ancient provisions, since what modern readers believe they mean carries great importance, even if their views are formed partly on the basis of subsequent historical practice and judicial decisions.

These variations between typical statutes and many constitutional provisions support interpretation of the latter that are more flexible, give less emphasis to original intent and understanding, and are responsive to changing political and social structures and shared values. In early chapters on statutory interpretation, I strongly resist the notion that judges interpreting statutes are exclusively "faithful agents" of the legislature, since they properly take into account various considerations that do not really fit that role.[3] Nonetheless, the notion of "faithful agency" is a very important component of how judges interpret statutes. For the Constitution that has existed over centuries, "faithfulness" to the original enactors, or to those with the capability now to amend, is much less central. Were one to believe that Supreme Court Justices should be "faithful" in major constitutional cases, it would need to be to the basic structures of government and underlying values reflected in provisions.

All this brings much constitutional interpretations closer than standard statutory construction to common law interpretation. For many of the provisions that are interpreted flexibly over time, precedents, in both their stated rules and treatments of particular circumstances, play a prominent role. The Supreme Court gives considerable weight to what has been previously decided, but it also feels free to depart from or overrule prior cases. How the common law has been understood and how judges have developed it have changed over the centuries.[4] Given this, as well as shifts in techniques of statutory interpretation, we should not be surprised that constitutional law interpretation has not remained fixed. For Justices to attempt to discern and adhere rigorously to interpretive methods accepted when any provision was adopted would not be sensible.

One of the chapters on the common law develops in detail reasoning by analogy and its place in decisions, a subject about which scholarly disagreement is sharp.[5] Without going into all of the subtleties covered there, I will note six different uses of examples in judicial decisions, in part because failure to recognize how these vary is one reason for conflicting views about analogy and because in constitutional decisions, one kind of reliance is very rare, if it happens at all. When courts face novel issues, examples from prior cases or hypothetical illustrations can aid the process of discovering a good resolution, can assist persuasion, and can be seen as representing the law. These uses are undisputed and uncontroversial. Examples may also serve as a basis for decision and actual confidence in a result. They can provide a helpful key to understanding a rule cast in broad terms. If a stated rule is very general and rather vague, it may not really provide an independent standard that carries much beyond the examples, which may be the real rationale for a decision when judges find themselves unable to formulate a helpful rule.

In some common law cases, the reliance on analogous examples may even be the overwhelming ground for a novel resolution of common law duties and rights, either because the majority opinion does not formulate a general rule that really amounts to more than a vague encompassing of the examples, *or* because, absent a majority opinion, judges agree more on examples than any stated rules. The first of these alternatives is almost never present with the Supreme Court's resolution of constitutional issues. Any opinion will state one or multiple governing standards, partly to give direction to lower courts and partly because the idea of enforcing the Constitution seems to call for this. Nonetheless, for many decisions, the actual outcomes of prior situations play a prominent part, especially when the prevailing legal standard is one that takes into account multiple elements and their weight. And when those in the majority are divided in their accounts of prevailing constitutional principle, observers could, as with the common law, conclude that what an actual decision stands for is best explained in terms of actual or hypothetical outcomes.

The main relation between much constitutional and common law interpretation is that judges consider what rights and duties fit best with preexisting law *and* with developing evaluations of what is just and wise in light of changing social circumstances and values. Of course, deciding what is a "cruel and unusual" punishment is vastly different from how far contracts should be interpreted in light of the signers' intents; but both will take into account prevailing values and what is administrable. As with common law, higher courts must consider what specific standards of interpretation are workable for judges and what rules of acceptable behavior give adequate notice to affected persons about what they can and cannot do. For the common law, a major concern is what private persons and businesses will understand and use efficiently; this is a ground not to give too much weight to intentions not reflected in the terms of contracts, since doing so could create opportunities for fraud and too much uncertainty about obligations. With many constitutional standards, those who mainly need to know what they can and cannot do are officials. That objective does provide a reason not to adopt a constitutional standard of behavior that involves a weighing of multiple factors; but sometimes, such a standard seems better than any alternative.

Given the need for higher courts to provide workable standards not only for those subject to legal restraints but also for judges and juries, the Supreme Court often seeks categorical approaches that rely on information they can discern. Frequently, this provides a genuine protection of a claim of right, but as we saw with respect to the acceptance in *Employment Division v. Smith* of impairments of religious exercise that result from a neutral law not directed at religion, sometimes the search for an administrable standard can limit rather than protect constitutional rights.

The connection between constitutional interpretation and the interpretation of private legal texts such as contracts and wills, which is treated in Volume I, is more attenuated than the ties to statutory and common law interpretation. With contracts, the dominant aim is to carry out what two or more private individuals or businesses have agreed to do; with wills, the objective is to fulfill what someone who has since died has specified. In both cases, concerns about uncertainty and the risk of fraud lead to special emphasis on what is actually written, as against other evidence about what writers may have intended. In contractual relations the reasonable reliance of one party on a contract's words also matters greatly. The bases for relying on text rather than intent are different when those with general authority establish standards to control the future actions of millions of people for decades or centuries.

In all of these domains, it does make sense to interpret particular language in context, at least if the context is clear. The chapter in Volume I on wills describes a notable English case in which the court had to determine if the deaths of a husband and wife had "coincided" if both died in a ship sinking from which no passenger survived.[6] The majority's very narrow sense of "coincide" as strictly simultaneous almost certainly did not fit either the husband's probable sense of the term or his broader objectives. With respect to the contracts, I use a hypothetical example of what "during its season" should mean for a soccer team and a player from abroad if generally that term covers training and exhibition games, but the team was fully aware that this player was committed to playing in Europe until America's regular season started.[7] Eyal Zamir has urged that judges give more emphasis to trade usage, fairness, and reasonable expectations, in comparison with contractual language, than they may acknowledge.[8]

With constitutions, no question about crucial context concerns the perspective of one or two particular individuals, but what language conveys does depend on why it is being used. A sharp illustration of this, described in Chapter 7, is the provision (article II, § 2(3)) that the President may fill vacancies "that may happen during the Recess of the Senate. . . ." Vital questions resolved by the Court in 2014 were what relevantly counts as a "recess" and whether a vacancy that occurs well before a recess may be filled if Senate approval of an appointment has not occurred.[9] But on a much narrower question, context indisputably seems relevant to how "happen" must be understood. If the Senate recess begins at 5:00 p.m. on November 30, it should not matter if an official with three years left on her term dies at 6:00 p.m. on that day or 4:00 p.m., even if, according to the standard linguistic use of "happen," only the 6:00 p.m. vacancy does so "during" the recess. Since a President cannot appoint and get Senate approval within an hour after an unexpected death, "happen" here must be given at least some degree of flexibility to satisfy the whole basis for recess appointments. In many areas of constitutional interpretation, context makes a difference, but there can be disagreement about what counts as that context and what effect it should have on how a provision is treated.

In occasional situations with private texts, context can actually override what specific language clearly provides. An example about wills was when the testator's language left money to a stranger, Robert J. Krause (with his correct address); the court concluded that he meant the benefit to go to his close friend Robert W. Krause.[10] In constitutional cases, courts do not rule that a provision's language represents this kind of outright mistake.

With contracts, and to a lesser extent wills, the way a court construes an unclear provision is occasionally affected by public policy or by what events have transpired since the document was written. If one way of reading a particular aspect of the document now seems severely at odds with its overall objectives or with public values, that constitutes a reason to adopt a feasible alternative. Such judgments figure more extensively when courts must interpret and give effect to the language of trusts that have force for many decades, and when specific language has become at odds with overall purposes, courts may explicitly deviate from what it specifies.[11] For constitutional provisions cast in general terms and applicable over centuries, events after adoption and public policies figure much more significantly than with ordinary wills and contracts, but judges do not acknowledge that they are actually altering what a provision says.

Among the topics treated in Volume I are informal instructions and instructions to agents. These often create for recipients the need to make decisions about how specific language relates to general purposes and what to do when unexpected events arise. Both prior volumes, as well as this one, use examples of such instructions as illustrative analogies to considerations that bear on legal interpretation. Although persons who are acting as legally constrained agents subject to instructions are in a fiduciary relationship that requires them to fulfill their supervisor's objectives,[12] no such simple overriding aim limits Justices in constitutional cases, and Chapter 2 of this book provides an example of how a child guardian subject to instructions that are not legally binding might place the child's welfare over the import of what he has been told to do.

A theme of Volume I is that in many respects, interpretation in other disciplines, the philosophy of language, and general theories of hermeneutics bear more on constitutional interpretation than the reading of statutes and common law development. This book confirms that thesis; it also illustrates again the relevance and limits of insights drawn from general theories and disciplines outside the law. Although these may illuminate certain possibilities and occasionally provide actual guides, they really are not much help in resolving genuinely debatable questions about how constitutional, or other legal, interpretation should proceed.

One insight is that people at a later time are incapable of understanding exactly what those who communicated decades ago had in mind or how a reader or listener would then have taken what was said. That provides a genuine caution about simple claims of originalist constitutional interpretation but does not by itself tell us whether or not this is what interpreters should try to do as best they can. Philosophic disagreement over whether the basic core of meaning for ordinary communications is what the communicator meant to convey or what the ordinary receiver understands is itself probably never fully resolvable,[13] but even if it were, it would not follow that the answer to that question is how judges should determine what language adopted by hundreds of enactors should be taken to entail for officials and affected citizens centuries later, a topic whose nuances are addressed here in Chapter 3.

Whether concentrating on law, as does Aharon Barak,[14] or more generally, like Hans-Georg Gadamer,[15] a general theory of hermeneutics can be plausible only if it is cast as a fairly high level of abstraction and allows different factors to carry importance for various interpretive exercises. A theory formulated in this way could, as the conclusion to Volume I suggests, end up recommending priorities almost entirely consistent with what one who remains skeptical about a general theory recommends. This book does not offer a single theory that applies to all constitutional interpretation. One might say it does suggest that Justices should interpret the constitution according to the force of its language, basic and desirable government structures, as well as conceptions of rights, that take account both of historical understanding and what is a just recognition of how the government should treat people and of human equality. But such a formulation does not carry us very far about desirable approaches to particular provisions and issues.

Controversies about the content of literary and musical compositions illustrate some possibilities, but their character varies radically from constitutional interpretation. Writers try to use language that others will grasp, but they may or may not seek to stimulate varying responses by different readers. To say that the reader of every fiction and poem must attempt to grasp exactly what was in the mind of the writer is arbitrary.[16] And it may actually be beneficial for people to be offered multiple interpretations, ones that may aid them in various aspects or stages of their lives. For example, one might interpret the behavior of Alyosha in Dostoyevsky's *The Brothers Karamazov* somewhat differently depending on whether one wanted to see the novel as realistic about human motivation, as profound as possible morally, as maximally aesthetic, or as best reflecting what the author intended.[17] Perhaps no single perspective here is really better than the others.

Similarly misguided is the idea that any performer must aim to capture as precisely as possible how the composer conceived the sounds of his music—which would effectively preclude playing seventeenth-century pieces on twentieth-century instruments.[18]

Legal interpretation is sharply different from that for literature and music in its general application. A judge cannot say, as might a critic about *The Brothers Karamazov,* "I think that, whatever the author had in mind, it is insightful sometimes to see Alyosha as a saint-like figure, and other times as an ordinary person who has various good qualities and weaknesses."

In many ways, religious interpretation comes closer to constitutional interpretation than that of other disciplines.[19] Most religions have sacred texts that carry a special authority seen as deriving largely from their source. Because social understandings change, problems arise over how to interpret ancient texts in modern times. As with constitutional law, one crucial question is how far to interpret in light of specific language as compared with more general themes. Particular examples of this for modern Jews, Christians, and Muslims is how now to read passages that seem to call for unequal treatment of women and that condemn gay sexual relations as sinful.

Two striking differences between religious and constitutional interpretation make it impossible to use the former to derive conclusions about the latter. Many religious persons believe the Bible was inspired by God, that it must be taken as presently controlling, that nothing in it can be discounted as misguided or mistaken. Other believers think some of what the Bible contains reflects misperceptions of human beings at the time of writing and carries no actual authority, or that, whatever the authority once was, it does not now apply. (The latter is the dominant Christian view about many specific behavioral requirements in the Old Testament.) The status of the constitutional text falls somewhat between these views; the enactors cannot reasonably be perceived to have had a perfect vision of life, yet the authority of particular provisions cannot simply be dismissed as based on error. As this book develops, matters are much more subtle.

Another difference between religious and legal understanding concerns individual reaction and generality of application. Many religious traditions do assume a kind of law that governs all humanity or at least all of those within a faith; but within some Protestant traditions, how an individual responds receives much more emphasis. On this view, as with music or poetry, there may be no problem if two people take passages in entirely different ways so long as their understanding brings them closer to God. By contrast, Justices resolving constitutional issues aim for a common understanding, and what they decide determines how provisions apply generally to officials and citizens.

I now turn to more general observations made in all three volumes. When one reflects on constitutional law and how it is understood, she can perceive an important illustration and confirmation about the limited practical significance of disagreements about the vague scope of what counts as "interpretation," about the boundaries of "the law," and about the relevance of political philosophy for difficult cases.

"Interpretation," which occupies a place in all areas of life, can be distinguished from application on the one hand and from construction or creativity that reaches beyond interpretation on the other. It is not a premise of these volumes that these distinctions are without substance. When Justices decide whether a clearly "cruel" penalty must also be "unusual" if it is to be unconstitutional, that is interpretation. If a terribly painful punishment is cruel and clearly meets the unusual standard, a court's resolution that it is unconstitutional can be regarded as application. But at the edges, there is no clear border. If Justices are determining whether a somewhat harsh and not very common penalty meets the standards of "cruel" and "unusual," interpretation slides into application. Similarly, if asking whether judges are interpreting a provision or creatively reaching beyond its genuine interpretation, one often can draw no clear line. This is particularly true with fairly creative and innovative treatments of broadly phrased constitutional provisions. A persistent claim of these books is that the focus needs to be on how judges should act, an answer that is not provided by a disputable labeling of what they do as application, genuine interpretation, or something beyond both. For this reason, all three books use the term "interpretation" broadly and in a way that is not designed to provide a full answer, or distinct limit, to how judges should perform.

A set of questions related to what is genuine interpretation is whether one can assume there is one real "meaning" and one "best answer" to each of the issues that arises. The first two volumes strongly suggest that in various nonlegal contexts, it is perfectly sensible to distinguish among various meanings, such as what the speaker intends to convey and how what he says would be taken by his actual audience or by most people.[20] Courts resolving legal disputes are settling what meaning will carry legal force. And they are seeking to arrive at the best answer they can. But even here, one needs to be careful about whether there is only one real meaning to authoritative language and one best answer to a legal problem. Volume II points out that when agencies are interpreting statutes, they may appropriately employ somewhat different approaches than courts; when this occurs, the best answer for an agency might differ from that for a court facing the issue on its own.[21] It follows that a court giving deference to any agency determination may reach a different answer than it would if facing the same issue without agency interpretation. This book presents a similar complexity. When the political branches agree about an allocation of power, the best judicial answer may involve significant deference and thus be different from how the branches themselves should see their constitutional limits, and how a court should see them absent the agreement.

When one recognizes that private citizens and groups appropriately adopt positions on constitutional issues, [22] a similar difference can arise. Although in claiming what "the constitution provides," private persons would be misguided if they completely disregarded everything the Supreme Court has decided throughout history, nonetheless, they might well give less weight to what they take as misguided precedents than do lower courts and even the Supreme Court itself.

Even if one focuses on a particular individual or collection of persons, such as a court, there is an interesting puzzle about what approach one seeking the best answer should take. Readers familiar with legal philosophy will be aware of Ronald Dworkin's suggestion that a judge should try to replicate how Hercules, a hypothetical person with perfect insight, would resolve an issue. This suggestion raises two basic questions about how a Supreme Court Hercules Justice would perceive his endeavor, and whether an actual Justice should try to behave as he would. In seeking the best answer, any Justice must take into account the imperfect competence of lower court judges, and likely successors on the Supreme Court, to administer various possible standards. She must also decide how far to compromise what she takes as the best possible positions in order to persuade others or join a needed majority opinion. To take a stark example, would Hercules have joined the far-from-theoretically-adequate opinion in *Brown v. Board of Education* if that was the only way to achieve what he felt was needed—unanimity?

The more complex question concerns an individual's recognition of her own limited competence. None of us are as able as Hercules. Should we try as hard as we can to replicate what he would do or settle for less? In ordinary life, that depends on what we are doing. If a person is in a sprinting race, she tries to come as close as she can to what the fastest person in the world would do. But on some moral issues, she may distrust her own judgment, believing that she does better mostly to follow simple standards than attempt to do what a person with perfect insight into the facts and moral values would do. Whether a Supreme Court Justice should actually try to replicate what a perfect Justice would do is actually doubtful; perhaps she should aim for approaches more susceptible to the capacities of actual human beings, even those as well trained and intelligent as Supreme Court Justices.

Tied to what is interpretation versus construction is the theoretical question of what are the limits of existing law. Are Supreme Court Justices doing their best to understand and apply "the law," or are they often "legislating" between the gaps or even rejecting existing law in favor of something they deem better? Of course, crucial to this inquiry is what counts as "the law." Here we may distinguish roughly among four positions—traditional natural law that basic moral norms are aspects of law; exclusive positivism that rejects the idea that the law can include any standards that are irreducibly moral; inclusive positivism that sees law as what is accepted as law, but does not rule out the possibility of its including some standards that are moral; and a more complex, limited version of "naturalism," associated with Ronald Dworkin, that needed moral judgments count as part of existing law.[23] In this last view, a Justice resolving a difficult case who must rely on a judgment of political morality not reached by existing legal sources is nonetheless answering what "the law" already requires, not acting in a legislative way. My own views about these positions include the belief that if the law specifically requires a moral judgment—and in a particular instance it is one as to which common morality and moral reflection leave no doubt—it makes sense, contrary to exclusive positivism, to say that "the law" provides the answer. But what really matters is not the exact limits of existing "law," but what judges should or should not take into account. Debates about the limits of existing law do not really have direct implications for how Justices should proceed in constitutional and other cases.

It is, of course, conceivable that how a Justice views this theoretical question *could* affect what she thinks should carry weight. But as Volume II explains, that influence could be different from what one might first assume. Is a Justice who thinks she is always "restrained" by the law likely to be less innovative than one who thinks he must occasionally legislate? Not necessarily. The Justice who accepts Dworkin's view that "the law" contains independent correct judgments of political morality not settled by existing legal sources might actually feel *more comfortable* relying on such judgments than a Justice who sees such a decision as "legislation," and would prefer to rely instead on what he takes as existing legal sources. But the major point here is that society's genuine concern is what judges should take into account—not whether all or only some of that counts as part of existing law. The jurisprudential debates about the exact borders of "the law" do not really help on the practical questions.

Closely connected to all of this are fundamental issues about the role of the Supreme Court and constitutional interpretation. A skeptic pointing to sharp divisions on the Court, how those typically reflect different political outlooks, and how approaches alter with changing membership, may urge that constitutional law really comes down to political preferences, not any objectively discernible content. A critic might similarly view many of the suggestions made in the last seven chapters of this book. What is often lost in the focus on the Supreme Court itself and the issues it addresses are that these are the hardest cases. When statutory or constitutional law is perfectly clear, no legal dispute may arise, and, if it does, it can be quickly settled by lower courts. In other words, a huge body of settled constitutional law may exist; that many Supreme Court decisions depend partly on judgments of political philosophy is precisely because the issues it addresses are not firmly settled by existing law. This is especially true if one sees decisions by a 5–4 majority with a particular political slant as not "settling" what is the law on that subject for decades to come. When one asks about interpretive strategies for the Supreme Court and lower courts in constitutional cases, one needs to reflect on how they will work not only in the most difficult cases but also across a range of cases. Although this book focuses mainly on controversial issues and notes that on some highly specific questions, such as the minimum age of the President, the constitutional text yields a clear answer, no single, apparently simple, interpretation strategy has worked for all constitutional questions now generally regarded as easy; many of these have been settled by the more nuanced, context-sensitive approaches to constitutional interpretation defended here.

Notes

Chapter 1

1. About most of the provisions protecting individual rights covered here, I have written myself. Since those articles and books were done over a span of years, they may not completely represent the positions taken in this book; but they could give an interested reader a more detailed explanation of many of my positions. For those interested, the relevant books are *Speech, Crime, and the Uses of Language* (New York, Oxford University Press, 1992); *Fighting Words* (Princeton: Princeton University Press, 1995); *Religion and the Constitution: Volume 1: Free Exercise and Fairness* (Princeton: Princeton University Press, 2006); *Religion and the Constitution: Volume 2: Establishment and Fairness* (Princeton: Princeton University Press, 2008); *Discrimination and Reverse Discrimination* (New York: Alfred A Knopf, 1983).

2. The modern understanding has been that Parliament may disregard what the "constitution" indicates, and that courts must accept what Parliament has done, but a view about constitutional norms can influence what legislators decide to do and how courts interpret unclear statutes. The role of courts in respect to Parliament has shifted with treaties and acts of the European Community, which courts may implement despite different approaches by Parliament. See generally Michael H. Lee, "Revolution, Evolution, Devolution: Confusion?: The Erosion of the 'Supremacy of Parliament' and the Expanding Powers of the Courts in the United Kingdom," 23 *Suffolk Transnational Law* Review 465 (2000). The history of the development of Parliamentary power and how it may now become more limited is analyzed in David Jenkins' "From Unwritten to Written: Transformation in the British Common-Law Constitution," 36 *Vanderbilt Journal of Transnational Law* 863 (2003).

3. However, there have been written constitutions about which it was understood that judges could not overturn what the political branches resolved. A modern example is the constitution of New Zealand, discussed in Jeremy Waldron, "The Core of the Case Against Judicial Review," 115 *Yale Law Journal* 1346 (2006). Some constitutions, including Canada's, provide for interpretive judicial decisions but allow legislatures to take special votes to override the effect of those decisions. See Canadian Charter of Rights and Freedoms, Part 1 of the Constitution Act, 1982, *being* Schedule B to the Canada Act 1982, c. 11 § 33 (UK); see also Nicholas Stephanopoulos, "The Case for the Legislative Override," Comment, 10 *UCLA Journal of International Law and Foreign Affairs* 250 (2005), listing Israel as the other country that has adopted the override.

4. See, e.g., Kevin M. Stack, "The Divergence of Constitutional and Statutory Interpretation," 75 *University of Colorado Law Review* 1 (2004).

5. These variations are also helpful in understanding the relation between this book and the previous two volumes. See Kent Greenawalt, *Statutory and Common Law Interpretation* (New York: Oxford University Press, 2013); *Legal Interpretation: Perspectives from Other Disciplines and Private Texts* (New York: Oxford University Press, 2010). Among other relations, the insights from nonlegal forms of interpretations generally have more relevance for open-ended constitutional standards than typical statutes or private texts. Id. at 5.

6. Common law courts were once free in the United States, as well as Great Britain, to develop new crimes, but constitutions and statutes have now abolished common law crimes for the federal government and many states. See 1 Wayne R. LaFave, *Substantive Criminal Law* § 2.1 (2d. ed. 2012). For an overview of the status of common law crimes in the states, see Paul H. Robinson, "Notice and Fair Adjudication: Two Kinds of Legality," 154 *University of Pennsylvania Law Review* 335, 339–40 (2005).

7. See David P. Currie, "Positive and Negative Constitutional Rights," 53 *University of Chicago Law Review* 864 (1986).

8. See Ann I. Park, Comment, "Human Rights and Basic Needs: Using International Human Rights Norms to Inform Constitutional Interpretation," 34 *UCLA Law Review* 1195, 1228–29 (1987).

9. See, e.g., Paul Nolette, "Lessons Learned from the South African Constitutional Court: Toward a Third Way of Judicial Enforcement of Socio-Economic Rights," 12 *Michigan State Journal of International Law* 91 (2003). On the value of positive rights, compare Susan Bandes, "The Negative Constitution: A Critique," 88 *Michigan Law Review* 2271 (1990), with Frank B. Cross, "The Error of Positive Rights," 48 *UCLA Law Review* 857 (2001). Constitutional assurances of minimal benefits are difficult for courts to enforce because it is very often hard to gauge what is feasible for the government. Insofar as the U.S. Constitution bars "cruel and unusual punishment," it may require minimally acceptable prison conditions, requiring judgments not so different from ones about minimal benefits. See, e.g., Brown v. Plata, 131 S. Ct. 1910, 563 U.S.   (2011).

10. U.S. Const. art. VI, cl. 2.

11. U.S. Const. art. III, § 2, cls. 1 & 2.

12. U.S. Const. art. I, § 3.

13. U.S. Const. art. I, § 5.

14. The word "apparently" is in this sentence because one may think that the original understanding reached only well-recognized specific examples *and* that courts should subsequently have gone no further. Later chapters take up this possible approach.

15. See Greenawalt, *Statutory and Common Law Interpretation*, supra note 5, at 112, 125, 225.

16. Michigan v. EPA, 213 F.3d 663 (D.C. Cir. 2000), discussed in Greenawalt, *Statutory and Common Law Interpretation*, supra note 5, at 150–51.

17. See, e.g., Alec Stone Sweet & Jud Mathews, "Proportionality Balancing and Global Constitutionalism," 47 *Columbia Journal of Transnational Law* 72 (2008). In Canada, for example, Section 1 of its constitution guarantees rights and freedoms "subject only to such reasonable limits prescribed by law as can be demonstrably justified in a free and democratic society." Canadian Charter of Rights and Freedoms, Part 1 of the Constitution Act, 1982, *being* Schedule B to the Canada Act, 1982, c. 11 § 1 (UK).

18. 554 U.S. 570, 635 (2008).
19. Id. at 634–35.
20. 494 U.S. 872 (1990).
21. See, e.g., Barry Friedman, "Dialogue and Judicial Review," 91 *Michigan Law Review* 577, 650 (1993); Terrance Sandalow, "Constitutional Interpretation," 79 *Michigan Law Review* 1033, 1045–46 (1981).
22. John O. McGinnis & Michael B. Rappaport, *Originalism and the Good Constitution* 73, 88, 201 (Cambridge, Mass.: Harvard University Press, 2013).
23. The alternative procedure specified in Article V has yet to be used.
24. Max Lerner, "Constitution and Court as Symbols," 46 *Yale Law Journal* 1290 (1937); Sanford Levinson, "The Constitution in American Civil Religion," 1979 *Supreme Court Review* 123.
25. An account along these lines that was once highly influential is James B. Thayer, "The Origin and Scope of the American Doctrine of Constitutional Law," 7 *Harvard Law Review* 129 (1893).
26. Frederick Schauer, "Neutrality and Judicial Review," 22 *Law and Philosophy* 217, 235–40 (2003).
27. See discussion in Chapters 3 and 4 of Greenawalt, *Statutory and Common Law Interpretation*, supra note 5.
28. See, e.g., David Strauss, *The Living Constitution* (New York: Oxford University Press, 2012); Michael C. Dorf, "The Undead Constitution," Book Review, 125 *Harvard Law Review* 2011 (2012).
29. See Peter J. Smith, "How Different Are Originalism and Non-Originalism?", 62 *Hastings Law Journal* 707 (2011).
30. See Chapters 3 and 4 of Greenawalt, *Statutory and Common Law Interpretation*, supra note 5, for analysis in regard to statutes.
31. I here pass over arguments that one cannot usefully combine subjective intentions or that actual intentions are too difficult to discern. See id.
32. Id.
33. This approach does not itself rule out the intentions of those at the ratifying conventions, whose deliberations were not secret but were not reported in detail.
34. Of course, for the Bill of Rights, enacted by an already specified amendment process, a person could argue that certain forms of expression during the process of enactment are precluded from consideration. That argument is unconvincing in respect to ordinary legislative history for statutes (see id., Chapters 3 and 4), and is even more so for the Bill of Rights.
35. This is a problem explored in Chapter 3.
36. One would need to include here any sense of delegation to others, such as committee members, about what obscure provisions entail. See Chapter 4 of Greenawalt, *Statutory and Common Law Interpretation*, supra note 5.
37. See id., Chapter 5.
38. See Dorf, supra note 28, at 2017–24 (distinguishing "expected-application" from "semantic" originalism).
39. See Smith, supra note 29.
40. See, e.g., Louis Henkin, "Is There a 'Political Question' Doctrine?," 85 *Yale Law Journal* 597 (1976).
41. One summary of the variety of underlying reasons for the doctrine is in *Baker v. Carr*, 369 U.S. 186, 217 (1962), in which the Court declined to follow the political question doctrine for issues of apportionment.

42. The issues of deference are especially important when courts consider the allocations of power among the political branches; these are treated in Chapters 7 and 8.

43. See, e.g., Richard H. Fallon, Jr., "Stare Decisis and the Constitution: An Essay on Constitutional Methodology," 76 *New York University Law Review* 570 (2001). For the role of precedent in statutory and common law, see Greenawalt, *Statutory and Common Law Interpretation*, supra note 5, at 125–27, 193–215.

44. Among the Supreme Court cases that are explicit on this point is *Rodriguez de Quijas v. Shearson/American Express, Inc.*, 490 U.S. 477, 489 (1989). A contrary view is developed by Evan H. Caminker, "Precedent and Prediction: The Forward-Looking Aspects of Inferior Court Decisionmaking," 73 *Texas Law Review* 1 (1994); C. Steven Bradford, "Following Dead Precedent: The Supreme Court's Ill-Advised Rejection of Anticipatory Overruling," 59 *Fordham Law Review* 39 (1990).

45. Greenawalt, *Statutory and Common Law Interpretation*, supra note 5, at 250–88, explores this question in respect to common law interpretation.

46. Ronald Dworkin, *Law's Empire* (Cambridge, Mass.: Harvard University Press, 1986).

47. Miranda v. Arizona, 384 U.S. 436 (1966).

48. U.S. Const. art. V.

49. The use of this rule and others of its kind (sometimes labeled "prophylactic rules") is persuasively defended in Yale Kamisar, "The Rise, Decline, and Fall of Miranda," 87 *Washington Law Review* 965, 1025–32 (2012); Frederick Schauer, "The Miranda Warning," 88 *Washington Law Review* 155, 158–60 (2013).

Chapter 2

1. In this respect, it is similar to illustrations used in the first two volumes, including the faculty committee report employed in the chapter on legislative intentions. See Kent Greenawalt, Chapter 3 of *Statutory and Common Law Interpretation* (New York: Oxford University Press, 2013). A chapter in Kent Greenawalt, *Legal Interpretation: Perspectives from Other Disciplines and Private Texts* (New York: Oxford University Press, 2010), explains informal instructions, at 181–214.

2. That failure to communicate might be used by David to disclaim a mutual understanding in a later encounter with Faith.

3. Conceivably, the omission of "lawyer" might be taken by David to conclude that Faith's wishes about that career were less clear or less intense. David could not assume there was no wish or preference simply because Faith did not focus on the precise choice. People can intend or wish a specific application of some generalized preference although they have not conceived that application. See discussion in Greenawalt, *Statutory and Common Law Interpretation*, supra note 1, at 70. But David might think that the inexplicit implications of a generalized attitude are less certain because the subject has not received direct attention or that, although certain, they somehow represent a lower level of intensity.

4. "Now, look, I think it is better for a guardian to make his own judgments. But I want to help out by taking care of Samuel. If you won't appoint me unless I agree to your terms, I will do so; but I shall regard myself as constrained only as to situations that are actually covered by the agreement." If David conveyed this

understanding, he may fairly conclude that Faith's failure to explicitly cover the lawyer-clerical choice leaves him free to decide what is best.

5. "I agree that you, as parent, should make the basic choices about Samuel's future, and I shall do everything I can to carry out those choices as they are revealed by your instructions." In this event, David could conclude that the agreement with Faith would strongly favor allowing Samuel to become a lawyer.

One might quibble about whether this latter undertaking merely binds David to other wishes of Faith's besides those in the agreement; but I think we can conclude that the very meaning of the agreement itself varies depending on the manner in which David has undertaken compliance with it, and that in the latter instance, the overall spirit of the terms takes on primary significance.

If David has indicated that he is to be constrained only by the terms of the instructions themselves, even Faith's explicit communication of an underlying purpose, "I want Samuel to get ahead as far as he can," may not require David to construe the agreement in favor of the legal career. But if David's undertaking has been more equivocal, the fact of communication may matter. An underlying purpose explicitly communicated may be thought to be more a part of an instruction than an underlying purpose that is mutually understood but never discussed.

6. David can fairly say that the meaning of the agreement does not include the unexpressed, unperceived purpose. The matter is trickier if he acknowledges that he would have signed on even if that preference had been conveyed to him; but even then, the breadth of his communicated commitment could matter to what he takes the instructions themselves to entail.

7. Suppose a general preference underlies a concrete wish, such as the desire of a child to go to a local amusement park with his family. The child has never heard of Disney World, which has better rides, food, and so forth. Linguistically, it may be awkward to say that the child "wishes" to go to Disney World, but the parents' taking her there can certainly be viewed by them as satisfying her general wish to visit an amusement park. In this sense, David could see allowing Samuel to become a lawyer as fulfilling Faith's wishes, so long as Faith wanted Samuel to occupy as high a position as possible.

8. If the guardian believes there is such a thing as an objective "best," of course, his own view about what will be the best is the closest he can come to discovering what is objectively best. Even if the guardian, as a convinced relativist, thinks his own view is ultimately an arbitrary preference, he still is in the position of having been given the responsibility to exercise his own judgment here.

9. Conversations with disinterested outsiders could have a similar effect. If David followed such advice, he would still be doing what he thought was probably best for Samuel (even though he might not understand why it was best).

10. Were Faith's instructions seen as not touching this choice at all, David might turn to the overall responsibilities of guardians, whether they are widely understood as partly representative of a larger community of concerned persons.

11. Such evidence could also clarify and enrich his own hazy recollections about what he could reasonably have assumed himself.

12. Most typically, such an inconclusive inquiry leads a person to find an answer he favors on other grounds, but an extremely insecure or guilt-ridden person might actually be led to conclude that his own independent assessment was at odds with the implications of the instructions.

13. This is my guess, not based on empirical studies.

14. This kind of conflict is not common. Most people have a psychological tendency not to find that the choices they prefer to make are at odds with unclear authoritative instructions.

15. In that event, David's reliance on Faith's more generalized preferences would be a claim of a justified deviation from the agreement itself, not an account about how he faithfully carried it out.

16. These points can be further illustrated by the term of the agreement that Samuel remains in a relative's home until age eighteen. A well-placed partner has offered to have Samuel live with his family. David believes that the home will provide a secure environment, that Samuel will have ample chance to keep close ties with his family, and that living with the partner would greatly enhance Samuel's career prospects. David could run through each of the approaches just discussed to warrant disregarding the *specific* terms of the agreement; but the stronger Faith's wish that Samuel live within the family, the less likely that she would have changed her mind if apprised of the present facts, and the stronger the reasons would have to be for permitting Samuel to live with the partner.

17. The only possible exception to this conclusion is if others—the relatives or Samuel himself—are justifiably relying on the faithful execution of these terms. It is difficult to see why the relatives should be able to count on the original agreement between Faith and David that neither wishes carried out in this particular respect, unless they have somehow put themselves out in reliance on the terms being fulfilled. Samuel may have a stronger argument. Whether or not he has acted differently because of his expectations, he has a legitimate interest in not having those expectations disturbed in a way he regards as detrimental. The strength of his interest depends partly on whether he has effectively been given a promise, one that carries considerable weight against a subsequent decision that the thing promised would actually be undesirable. If, on the other hand, David had indicated to Samuel an intent to act in a certain way, implicitly reserving the right to change his mind, Samuel would have a much weaker claim, one based only on his interest in not having expectations disturbed. That interest might be viewed simply as one aspect of what is best for the child.

18. Though the point may be debatable, we conceive of her as having that stake even if she predictably will never see Samuel again and even if she will never hear what has happened to him. Her present stake is even stronger if she will once again become a part of his life.

19. Many cultures have supposed that dead ancestors do somehow retain a legitimate concern in what their descendants do.

20. The spirit may be thought not to survive, or spirits may be thought to lose concern with what happens on this earth.

21. Thus, the practice of observing promises to the dead creates security in the living who wish to control events subsequent to their own deaths. This essentially utilitarian argument poses in sharp form questions about the relation of an underlying justification of a practice and the attitudes that underlie observance—most people feel honor bound to the person who has died to perform the promise, not that observance is owed to others who remain alive. The argument also raises the dilemma that reaches some other utilitarian arguments whether there is any ground for observance if nonobservance can be kept secret. I explore these familiar conundrums in Kent Greenawalt, *Conflicts of Law and Morality* (New York: Oxford University Press, Clarendon Series, 1987).

22. Michael C. Dorf, "Integrating Normative and Descriptive Constitutional Theory: The Case of Original Meaning," 85 *Georgetown Law Journal* 1765, 1786 (1997). See also Robert H. Bork, "Neutral Principles and Some First Amendment Problems," 47 *Indiana Law Review* 1 (1971).

23. Richard H. Fallon, Jr., "A Constructivist Coherence Theory of Constitutional Interpretation," 100 *Harvard Law Review* 1189 (1987).

24. See Dorf, supra note 22, at 1794, urging that Richard Fallon's hierarchy will not work because in some cases, "an argument in a lower rung legitimately trumps one on a higher rung."

25. See Lawrence H. Tribe, *American Constitutional Law* § 1-1, at 1–2 (2d ed. West Group, 2001).

26. One might or might not consider reversal by a higher court as a kind of setback or modest penalty for a lower court judge; this is a consequence most judges would prefer to avoid.

27. No penalty (other than political criticism) follows a failure to observe proper constraints, and only the complex process of constitutional amendment, or later overruling, can directly overturn standards on which the Supreme Court has settled.

28. See, e.g., Ronald Dworkin, *Law's Empire* (Cambridge, Mass.: Harvard University Press, 1986). On this approach, legal duty encompasses even the most debatable issues of interpretation, and every occasion on which a judge fails to reach the right answer, that is, every judge at some time or another, involves a failure to perform that duty. By contrast, one may believe that debates over controverted matters of interpretation are debates about what are desirable approaches, not about existing legal duties. An intermediate possibility is that some debatable choices are matters of legal duty, and others are not. This uncertain line might be drawn in terms of the degree of consensus over an issue, the ground on which a choice between outcomes should be made, or one's degree of confidence that a choice is correct. To take one illustration, a person like attorney and law professor Raoul Berger, who believed that the nature of written constitutions, democratic government, and judicial function clearly require judges to give dominance to Framers' intent, would be likely to describe that responsibility as a legal duty, though he recognized that his position was highly controversial. Someone who believes that in difficult cases the best way for judges to proceed is both complex and significantly uncertain is less likely to say that a failure to reach the best answer is always a breach of legal duty.

29. See, e.g., H.L.A. Hart, *The Concept of Law* (3d ed. Oxford: Clarendon Press, 2012).

30. Agostini v. Felton, 521 U.S. 203, 237 (1997).

31. The lower court may be less free to distinguish a case on a tenuous ground or to sharply restrict a previously elaborated principle. Though a lower court's function is more creative than simply trying to make its best guess about what the Supreme Court might decide, it is more hemmed in by existing authority.

32. Of course, a "category" can be defined in a way that makes it always wrong. If someone says, "A person should never commit murder," that is uncontroversial if "murder" is understood as wrongful killing. On that understanding, a person might react to the law's treatment of homicide as murder that she thinks is sometimes justified (e.g., assisting a terminally ill person in severe pain to die): "Well, despite the law, that's not really 'murder.'"

33. Some writers within the Roman Catholic tradition have urged that moral decisions are less straightforward than the dominant position the church now assumes. See Kent Greenawalt, "Religious Toleration and Claims of Conscience," 28 *Journal of Law and Politics*, 91, 122–25 (2013).

34. One concern is that without such criteria, people will overrate the significance of their own interests in comparison with those of others.

35. This illustration is developed somewhat more fully in Kent Greenawalt, "Fundamental Questions About the Religion Clauses: Reflections on Some Critiques," 47 *San Diego Law Review* 1131, 1135–36 (2010).

36. See H. Jefferson Powell, Constitutional Conscience: The Moral Dimension of Judicial Decisions (Chicago, Chicago University Press: 2008).

37. Understandings may not be treated equally if a contract is one of adherence (with one party having no choice about terms but simply whether to agree or not) or if one party is much more knowledgeable and powerful than the other. See Chapter 9 on Contracts in Kent Greenawalt, *Legal Interpretation: Perspectives from Other Disciplines and Private Texts* (New York: Oxford University Press, 2010).

38. On this score, it is troubling that federal judicial nominees, including those for the Supreme Court, now often cast their role during Senate hearings as much simpler than it really is and than they understand it to be. Were the formulations of responsibilities not so vague, one could well conceive this as being close to lying under oath.

39. See, e.g., John O. McGinnis & Michael B. Rappaport, *Originalism and the Good Constitution* 11–14 (Cambridge, Mass.: Harvard University Press, 2013) (connecting this premise to consequential considerations). Michael C. Dorf, Book Review, "The Undead Constitution," 125 *Harvard Law Review* 2011, 2015–16 (2012), explores a version of the premise about basic authority and why it is mistaken or contestable.

40. See McGinnis & Rappaport, supra note 39, at 14; Stephen E. Sachs, "Originalism as a Theory of Legal Change," *Harvard Journal of Law and Public Policy* 50–55 (forthcoming 2015).

41. A Justice might regard it as wise to move slowly toward what she perceives as the "best approach" to constitutional interpretation.

42. Dickerson v. United States, 530 U.S. 428, 443 (2000).

43. See, e.g., Henry Paul Monaghan, "Stare Decisis and Constitutional Adjudication," 88 *Columbia Law Review* 723, 772 (1988).

44. Alexander M. Bickel, *The Least Dangerous Branch* 39 (2d ed. Yale University Press: 1986).

45. Justice William J. Brennan, Jr., "The Constitution of the United States: Contemporary Ratification," 27 *South Texas Law Journal* 433, 438 (1986).

46. See Greenawalt, *Statutory and Common Law Interpretation*, supra note 1, at 13–15.

47. Greenawalt, *Legal Interpretation: Perspectives from Other Disciplines and Private Texts*, supra note 1, Chapters 8 and 10.

48. See Keith E. Whittington, "On Pluralism Within Originalism," *in* Grant Huscroft & Bradley W. Miller, *The Challenges of Originalism: Theories of Constitutional Interpretation* 20, 25 (Cambridge: Cambridge University Press, 2011) ("Constitutional construction is the process of elaborating constitutional meaning to supplement constitutional interpretation."); Keith E. Whittington, *Constitutional Construction: Divided Powers and Constitutional*

Meaning (Cambridge, Mass.: Harvard University Press 1999). I address the question of the possible boundaries of "interpretation" in the preceding two volumes. Greenawalt, *Legal Interpretation: Perspectives from Other Disciplines and Private Texts*, supra note 1, at 6–13; and Greenawalt, *Statutory and Common Law Interpretation*, supra note 1, at 5–7. For one defense of drawing a rather sharp line between "theories of interpretation" and theories of adjudication," see Gary Lawson, "On Reading Recipes ... and Constitutions," 15 *Georgetown Law Journal* 1823 (1997).

49. Of course, the label is not particularly difficult to apply if one uses "not genuine interpretation" to strengthen in a rhetorical way one's criticism of a competing view or of decisions to which one objects.

50. Richard A. Primus, "When Should Original Meaning Matter?," 107 *Michigan Law Review* 165, 181–82 (2008), describes division over what constitutes interpretation and its minimal practical significance per se.

51. As I have stressed in Chapter 1, the line between reader understanding and enactors' intent is far from sharp, given that readers take into account what they think those issuing authoritative instructions are trying to do. See also Greenawalt, *Statutory and Common Law Interpretation*, supra note 1, Chapters 3 and 4.

52. See An Act to Provide for the More Efficient Government of the Rebel States § 5, 14 Stat 428 (Mar. 2, 1867).

53. See Primus, supra note 50, at 167, 175.

54. Apparently, by that time, reliance on historical materials to reveal the subjective intentions of proposers and ratifiers was more widely accepted than when the Constitution and Bill of Rights were adopted, a matter that will be discussed in more detail in the next chapter. See Robert N. Clinton, "Original Understanding, Legal Realism, and the Interpretation of 'This Constitution,'" 72 *Iowa Law Review* 1177, 1195–96 (1987); Hans W. Baade, "'Original' Intent in Historical Perspective: Some Critical Glosses," 69 *Texas Law Review* 1001, 1019–21 (1991).

55. See, e.g., Akhil Reed Amar, *America's Constitution: A Biography* 323–26 (New York: Random House, 2005).

56. Professors McGinnis and Rappaport (supra note 39, at 126) urge that the text's defining itself as the "Supreme Law" conveys a reference to standard techniques of legal interpretation and that the linguistic practice of the community would have given priority to lawyers' understandings of legal documents.

57. Why is it that in the relevant sense, "intent" refers to understood coverage rather than wishes? The point is most easily seen with a compromise. *A*'s asking price for twenty books is $200. *B* offers to pay $100. *A* and *B* agree that *B* will pay $150 and draw up a document to that effect. Certainly their intent is that $150 be the price, although each would prefer a different price, and each might be happy if a court (mis)construes the agreement to provide a price closer to his preference. The political process is full of such compromises. This point is developed in Greenawalt, *Statutory and Common Law Interpretation*, supra note 1, Chapter 4.

58. The proposition that the Constitution went well beyond the Articles of Confederation is explained in The Federalist No. 23 (Alexander Hamilton).

59. See The Federalist Nos. 45–46 (James Madison).

60. The Federalist No. 78 (Alexander Hamilton).

61. For an overview of arguments and literature on point, see G. Edward White, "The Path of American Jurisprudence," 124 *University of Pennsylvania Law Review* 1212 (1976). See also Sachs, supra note 40.

62. For an overview, see William S. Jordan, III, "Legislative History and Statutory Interpretation," 29 *University of San Francisco Law Review* 1 (1994).

63. For a discussion of the contrasting views of William Eskridge and John Manning about equitable considerations, see Chapter 3 of *Statutory and Common Law Interpretation*, supra note 1.

64. For the latter point and an overview of the evolution of judicial review of state constitutions, see William F. Swindler, "Seedtime of An American Judiciary: From Independence to the Constitution," 17 *William & Mary Law Review* 503, 503–09 (1976), *reprinted in* Robert F. Williams, *State Constitutional Law: Cases and Materials* 690–92 (3d ed. Charlottesville: Lexis Law Publishing, 1999). For a history of state constitutions before the federal Constitution, see Williams at 1–74, especially 1–6 (noting the "first wave of state constitutions. . . . did not differ much from the colonial charters they replaced except in providing weakened executive power, and sometimes, including declarations of rights" and exploring the "second wave" of state constitution drafting.).

65. One might posit a sort of unceasing chain; each decision-maker owes it to the people of his time to be faithful to the ground rules then accepted, and since generations do not turn over all at one stage, the governing principles at any point could be traced back to the first generation. To illustrate, *A* takes office one year after the Constitution; he owes it to the adopters to follow their interpretive strategy and builds up legitimate expectations that others will do the same. *B* takes office fifteen years later, owing something to the adopters and something to persons like *A* in and out of office. C takes office fifteen years later and owes it to *B* and his like to carry out the same terms. The problem with this exercise is that it is too formal and rigid, given all the changes that do occur.

66. 554 U.S. 570, 574–75 (2008) (quoting D.C. Code § 7-2507.02).

67. "[T]he American people have considered the handgun to be the quintessential self-defense weapon." Id. at 629.

68. Id. at 636, 637 (Stevens, J., dissenting).

69. Id. at 681–82 (Breyer, J., dissenting).

70. U.S. Const. amend. II.

71. He concludes that although a prefatory clause may resolve an ambiguity in an operative clause, it does not limit or expand that clause grammatically. Id. at 577–78 (majority opinion).

72. Id. at 592. Justice Stevens notes the concern of the states at the time that the institution of their militia be protected. Id. at 655–60 (Stevens, J., dissenting).

73. Id. at 598 (majority opinion).

74. Id. at 595.

75. Although Justice Stevens' dissent stresses military use, he refers to state laws that required militia members to store arms in their homes and reads the Second Amendment as covering "a duty and a right to have arms available for military service. . . ." Id. at 651 (Stevens, J., dissenting).

76. Reviewing claims of continuing reliance on the ordinary uses of guns as preparation for the military, Justice Breyer notes that the District's law still allows people to use most standard weapons. Id. at 707–09 (Breyer, J., dissenting).

77. See Editorial, Gun Reform for a Generation, N.Y. Times, Jan. 17, 2013, at A26.

78. "In interpreting this text, we are guided by the principle that '[t]he Constitution was written to be understood by the voters; its words and phrases were used in their normal and ordinary as distinguished from technical meaning.'" Id. at 576 (quoting United States v. Sprague, 282 U.S. 716, 731 (1931)).

79. He writes that "the inherent right of self-defense has been central to the Second Amendment right." Id. at 628.

80. Id. at 582.

81. The *Heller* approach was extended to states in *McDonald v. City of Chicago*, 130 S. Ct. 3020, 561 U.S. (2010).

82. This basic argument, not including the point about effective judicial standards, is offered by Akhil Reed Amar, supra note 55.

83. Reva B. Siegel, "Dead or Alive: Originalism as Popular Constitutionalism in Heller," 122 *Harvard Law Review* 191, 192 (2008). She suggests that "mobilized citizens" are able "to contest and shape popular beliefs about the Constitution's original meaning and so confer upon courts the authority to enforce the nation's foundational commitments in new ways." Id. at 194. See also Jack M. Balkin, *Living Originalism* 120 (Cambridge, Mass.: Belknap Press of Harvard University Press, 2011), claiming that with arguments in both directions, original meaning was not really the basis for the Court's resolution.

84. Nicholas D. Kristof, "Lessons from Guns and a Goose," N.Y. Times, Jan. 17, 2013, at A27.

85. See Ben Dawson, Children's Defense Fund, *Protect Children Not Guns* (2012), *available at* http://issuu.com/cdfweb/docs/protect-children-not-guns-2012.

86. See District of Columbia v. Heller, 554 U.S. 696, 711–12 (2008) (Breyer, J., dissenting).

87. In April 2013, the Court declined to review a case sustaining New York's strict limit on carrying guns in public. Adam Liptak, "Justices Refuse Case on Gun Law in New York," N.Y. Times, Apr. 16, 2013, at A 13, col. 1.

88. Heller, 554 U.S. at 634–36 (majority opinion).

89. Id. at 719 (Breyer, J. dissenting).

90. Justice Breyer, referring to certain other constitutional issues, proposes a test here that does not involve a strong presumption in favor of legislation (a "rational basis" test) or a strong presumption against it (a "strict scrutiny" approach). Id. at 688–89 (Breyer, J., dissenting).

91. Gregory P. Magarian, "Speaking Truth to Firepower: How the First Amendment Destabilizes the Second," 91 *Texas Law Review* 49 (2012).

92. For a powerful illustration, see the analysis by Mitchell Berman that concludes that the eligibility of citizens born of American parents outside American states (such as John McCain) to run for President should not be determined by what the constitutional qualification that Presidents must be "natural born citizens" originally conveyed. Mitchell N. Berman, "Reflective Equilibrium and Constitutional Method: Lessons from John McCain and the Natural Born Citizenship Clause," *in* Huscroft and Miller, supra note 48, at 246.

93. Justice Scalia—in "Originalism: The Lesser Evil," 57 *University of Cincinnati Law Review* 849, 854 (1989)—has emphasized the value of originalism as providing clear answers and constraining judges' tendencies to implement their preferred values.

Chapter 3

1. See Kent Greenawalt, 2 *Statutory and Common Law Interpretation* Chapters 2 and 3 (New York: Oxford University Press, 2013).

2. These matters are explored in id.

3. See, e.g., Raoul Berger, *Government by Judiciary: The Transformation of the Fourteenth Amendment* 401–27 (Indianapolis: Liberty Fund, Inc., 1977). For one modern defense of this approach, see Larry Alexander, "Simple-Minded Originalism," *in The Challenge of Originalism: Theories of Constitutional Interpretation*, eds. Grant Huscroft & Bradley W. Miller (Cambridge, Mass.: Cambridge University Press, 2011), 87.

4. On the difference between linguistic meaning and expected application, see Mark Greenberg and Harry Litman, "The Meaning of Original Meaning," 86 *Georgetown Law Review* 569 (1998); Jack M. Balkin, "Original Meaning and Constitutional Redemption," 24 *Constitutional Comment* 427, 446 (2007). Michael Dorf suggests that although "new originalists," who include Justice Scalia, accept semantic originalism in theory, they often give great importance to expected applications. Michael C. Dorf, "The Undead Constitution," Book Review, 125 *Harvard Law Review* 2011, 2021–22 (2012).

5. Greenawalt, *Statutory and Common Law Interpretation*, supra note 1, Chapters 3 and 4. For skepticism about the sharpness of a distinction between meaning and application, see Brian H. Bix, "Constitutions, Originalism, and Meaning," *in* Huscroft & Miller, supra note 3, at 285, 288–91.

6. See, e.g., Lawrence B. Solum, "What Is Originalism? The Evolution of Contemporary Originalist Theory," *in* Huscroft & Miller, supra note 3, at 12, 35.

7. The Federalist No. 40 (James Madison).

8. See Jack N. Rakove, *Original Meanings: Politics and Ideas in the Making of the Constitution* 362 (New York: Alfred A. Knopf, 1996).

9. McCulloch v. Maryland, 17 U.S. (4 Wheat.) 316, 403–04 (1819).

10. See Robert N. Clinton, "Original Understanding, Legal Realism, and the Interpretation of 'This Constitution,'" 72 *Iowa Law Review* 1177, 1195–96 (1987).

11. In this respect, they were a bit like a President deciding whether to veto or not. Article VII of the Constitution on ratification was taken to preclude both ratification of some parts but not others and any approval made contingent on further provisions being adopted, such as guarantees of rights. See Rakove, supra note 8, at 105. For the controversies over conditional ratification, see Pauline Maier, *Ratification: The People Debate the Constitution* 149–50, 191–208, 379–82 (New York: Simon & Schuster, 2010).

12. The Federalist No. 22 (Alexander Hamilton).

13. When President George Washington rejected involvement of the House of Representatives in treaty-making partly on the basis of the position of the Convention, Madison urged that neither Congress nor the Supreme Court had relied on the sense of the Convention. See H. Jefferson Powell, "The Original Understanding of Original Intent," 98 *Harvard Law Review* 885, 921 (1985); Hans W. Baade, "'Original' Intent in Historical Perspective: Some Critical Glosses," 69 *Texas Law Review* 1001, 1019–21 (1991).

14. See references to the passage from *The Federalist* and later speech, supra note 7.

15. Linguists have noted that studies of vocabulary size based on dictionary sampling face many methodological problems. In an attempt to overcome

those problems, three linguists estimate a "average educated native speaker has a vocabulary of around 17,000 base words." Robin Goulden, Paul Nation & John Read, "How Large Can A Receptive Vocabulary Be?," 11 *Applied Linguistics* 341 (1990). The authors used the largest nonhistorical dictionary available to conclude that there were 58,000 base words and that the majority of those base words "are unknown to most native speakers of English." Id. at 356.

16. See Ilya Somin, "Originalism and Political Ignorance," 97 *Minnesota Law Review* 625 (2012).

17. Steven D. Smith, "That Old-Time Originalism," *in* Huscroft & Miller, supra note 3, at 223, 225. See, e.g., Gary Lawson & Guy Seidman, "Originalism as a Legal Enterprise," 23 *Constitutional Commentary* 47, 72–73 (2006); Smith, at 242, expresses doubt about whether greater theoretical sophistication has impaired originalism or improved it.

18. Solum, supra note 6, at 109.

19. When the right is not designed to protect and influence initial behavior, but to avoid unjust consequences after the fact, such as the ban on "cruel and unusual punishment," the analysis would be somewhat different. One might then treat what well-informed officials would grasp as more relevant than it is for rights on which people rely directly.

20. See Rakove, supra note 8, at 132–34, Introduction at x.

21. Id. at xv–xvi; Clinton, supra note 10, at 1215–19.

22. Cohens v. Virginia, 19 U.S. (6 Wheat.), 264, 418 (1821). Two years earlier (see McCulloch v. Maryland, supra note 9), Marshall had implied that the views of the Framers were not directly a basis for construing the Constitution.

23. However, Hans Baade (supra note 13, at 1008–12) indicates that when, in 1769, Justice Willes of the Court of Kings Bench in *Millar v. Taylor,* (1769) 4 Burr. 2303, 2332, 98 Eng. Rep. 201, 217 (K.B.), wrote that legislative history "was 'not known to the other house, or to the Sovereign,'" he was referring not to availability but to judicial relevance.

24. Powell, supra note 13, at 947.

25. Letter to Henry Lee (June 25, 1824), *in* 9 *The Writings of James Madison 1819–1836*, ed. Gailard Hunt (Whitefish, MT: Kessinger Publishing Co., 2010), 192. John O. McGinnis & Michael B. Rappaport, *Originalism and the Constitution* 1 (Cambridge, Mass.: Harvard University Press 2013), provide this quote at the beginning of their defense of an originalist approach.

26. The Federalist No. 37 (James Madison).

27. Rakove, supra note 8, at 160.

28. Gordon S. Wood, *The Creation of the American Republic* 1776–1787, at 296 (1969).

29. Powell, supra note 13, at 896 (quoting Prohibitions del Roy, 77 Eng. Rep. 1342, 1343 (1608)).

30. Powell, supra note 13, at 910. The Marshall Supreme Court employed this conventional view of statutory construction. Id. at 942–43.

31. Rakove, supra note 8, at xv.

32. In a letter of 1788, Edmund Pendleton remarked on the difficulty of listing individual rights because: "May we not in the progress of things discover some great and Important [right] which we don't now think of?" Edmund Pendleton, 2 *The Letters and Papers of Edmund Pendleton, 1734–1803*, ed. David John Mays (Charlottesville: University of Virginia Press, 1967), 533. Cf. Chester James Antieau, "Natural Rights and the Founding Fathers—the Virginians," 17 *Washington*

& *Lee Law Review* 43, 48–49 (1960) (noting that "[t]here is ample evidence that the Founding Fathers were aware of the ontological basis of our natural rights. It is because we are rational, intellectual, social, spiritual, and political beings that we naturally have rights to develop our intellect, to hear appeals made to reason that can make clearer the proper means to our ordained end, rights to assemble with our fellow men to discuss more effective political social groupings better suited for the development of our faculties and the protection of our basic rights. . . ."). For the proposition that the Framers thought inherent rights would be defended by courts beyond what the Constitution provided, see Daniel A. Farber, "The Originalism Debate: A Guide for the Perplexed," 49 *Ohio State Law Journal*, 1085, 1092–93 (1989). A contrary view is taken by John F. Hart, "Human Law, Higher Law, and Property Rights: Judicial Review in the Federal Courts, 1789–1835," 45 *San Diego Law Review* 823, 830–32 (2008).

33. The Federalist No. 40 (James Madison).

34. 17. U.S. (4 Wheat.) 316, 406–07, 415 (1819).

35. Rakove, supra note 8, at 6.

36. Gordon S. Wood, "Ideology and the Origins of Liberal America," 44 *William and Mary Quarterly* 628, 632 (1987).

37. See Dorf, supra note 4, at 2041.

38. A claim made by some that statutory interpretation should give extra weight to those whose acceptance is critical to passage has little relevance for constitutional interpretation. On the statutory issue, see Greenawalt, *Statutory and Common Law Interpretation*, supra note 1, at 71–72. The basic idea is that if some enactors might have voted the other way with different language (and the measure would then have lost), what the actual language entails should largely depend on their view. In the cited chapter, I find this view largely unpersuasive; and it is even more so for constitutional provisions. Most language in constitutional amendments is not tailored to win particular doubtful voters, and compromises in language are no longer possible when an amendment is up for ratification. Id. at 71. As with statutory interpretation, the understanding of those who vote against approval should not simply be written off. Individuals who vote against a measure may agree with much that a particular provision contains and may even have influenced its formation. Id. Their understanding should not be disregarded because they opposed another element strongly enough to vote against the complete package.

39. U.S. Const. art. I, § 3., cl. 1. This allocation cannot be altered by constitutional amendment without the state's consent.

40. We could imagine some disagreement over exactly what counts as a state—if the District of Columbia or Puerto Rico became essentially self-governing, without Congressional oversight, would each be a state even if not formally labeled as such? We could also imagine a dispute over what is valid state consent, if the federal government or larger states put intense pressure on smaller states to surrender equal representation. But the basic notion of a state's entitlement to equal representation is not a serious constitutional question.

41. U.S. Const., art. I, § 10, cl. 1.

42. For defenses of this position, see Paul Brest, "The Misconceived Quest for Original Understanding," 60 *Boston University Law Review* 204 (1980); Jack M. Balkin, *Living Originalism* 6 (Cambridge, Mass.: Belknap Press of Harvard University Press, 2011); David A. Strauss, *The Living Constitution* 13 (New York: Oxford University Press, 2010).

43. H. Jefferson Powell, *A Constitution Built on Words* 63–65 (Chicago: University of Chicago Press, 2002).

44. Id. at 65.

45. Katzenbach v. Morgan, 384 U.S. 641, 651, 651 n.10 (1966) ("Correctly viewed, § 5 is a positive grant of legislative power authorizing Congress to exercise its discretion in determining whether and what legislation is needed to secure the guarantees of the Fourteenth Amendment.... [It] does not grant Congress power to exercise discretion in the other direction....").

46. If one focused on original understanding rather than desirable development over time, one could posit such a one-sided development only by concluding that at the time of enactment, people recognized and approved development that was in one direction, say, toward greater equality or less severe punishments, but disapproved all backtracking. That is unlikely.

47. See, e.g., Home Bldg. & Loan Ass'n v. Blaisdell, 290 U.S. 398, 428 (1934) (acknowledging that the constitutional prohibition against impairment of obligation of contracts "is not an absolute one and is not to be read with literal exactness like a mathematical formula"). Against the possible claim that modern debtors were in peculiarly dire circumstances, Stephen E. Sachs, in "Originalism as a Theory of Legal Change," *Harvard Journal of Law and Public Policy* 20 (forthcoming 2015) has responded that conditions during the New Deal were not relatively so different from when the Constitution was adopted.

48. Since a state is involved, the understanding at the time of the adoption of the Fourteenth Amendment should matter more than that of 1791.

49. As Chapter 6 indicates, numerous Supreme Court cases embody that view.

50. The theory could be that it is now cruel and unusual or violates due process.

51. In that event, it would be hard to contend that forbidding capital punishment fit with what the enactors saw as acceptable applications of "cruel and unusual punishment."

52. 17 U.S. 316, 408. See supra note 34 and accompanying text. See also Gibbons v. Ogden, 22 U.S. (9 Wheat.) 1, 188–89 (1824).

53. See Greenawalt, *Statutory and Common Law Interpretation*, supra note 1, at 97–98.

54. However, compromise was the ground for the various treatments of slavery in the original document, and compromise also played a critical role in the equal state votes in the Senate.

55. The treatment, at the end of Chapter 2, of how the Second Amendment should be understood in relation to new weapons whose ordinary possession is unrelated to military needs, illustrates this point.

56. Evans v. Abney, 396 U.S. 435 (1970). This case is discussed in Chapter 10 of Kent Greenawalt, *Legal Interpretation: Perspectives from Other Disciplines and Private Texts* 305–06 (Oxford: Oxford University Press, 2010).

57. 330 U.S. 1 (1947).

58. Id. at 16.

59. Id. It does not follow that each of the other four Justices joining the opinion took the same view since Justices often accept language in majority opinions that does not reflect their precise views. Of course, the four dissenting Justices in *Everson* would also have regarded more substantial aid as forbidden.

60. See, e.g., Elk Grove Unified Sch. Dist. v. Newdow, 542 U.S. 1, 45–46 (2004) (Thomas, J., concurring).

61. See Gitlow v. New York, 268 U.S. 652 (1925); Cantwell v. Connecticut, 310 U.S. 296 (1940).

62. Those who did have such an intent probably conceived the Privileges and Immunities Clause, not the Due Process Clause, as doing the work, but that clause had earlier received a very narrow construction. See the Slaughter House Cases, 83 U.S. (1 Wall.) 36 (1872).

63. I consider these arguments in greater depth in Kent Greenawalt, 2 *Religion and the Constitution: Establishment and Fairness* 26–39 (Princeton: Princeton University Press, 2008).

64. See, e.g., Akhil Reed Amar, *The Bill of Rights: Creation and Reconstruction* 32–42 (New Haven: Yale University Press, 1998) ("The establishment clause did more than prohibit Congress from establishing a national church. Its mandate . . . also prohibited the national legislature from interfering with, or trying to *dis*establish, churches established by state and local governments."); Philip Hamburger, *Separation of Church and State* 101–07 (Cambridge, Mass.: Harvard University Press, 2002).

65. This response is developed in detail in Kent Greenawalt, "Common Sense About Original and Subsequent Understandings of the Religion Clauses," 8 *University of Pennsylvania Journal of Constitutional Law* 479 (2006), and is summarized in Greenawalt, 2 *Religion and the Constitution*, supra note 63, at 42–44.

66. Alexis de Tocqueville, 1 *Democracy in America* 308 (New York: George Adlard, 1839). No doubt, a country with an established religion can allow a substantial degree of free exercise, but "through the eighteenth century, most countries and principalities with established religions did not grant full privileges to nonadherents." Kent Greenawalt, "Some Reflections on Fundamental Questions about the Original Understanding of the Establishment Clause," *in No Establishment of Religion: America's Original Contribution to Religious Liberty*, eds. T. Jeremy Gunn & John Witte, Jr. (Oxford: Oxford University Press, 2012).

67. A disfavoring of someone's religion can easily be seen as an impediment to free exercise.

68. One can regard favoring by the government on the basis of religion as a kind of suspect classification.

69. For criticisms, see, e.g., Robert L. Cord, *Separation of Church and State: Historical Fact and Current Fiction* 120–22 (New York: Lambeth Press, 1982); David E. Steinberg, "The Myth of Church-State Separation," 59 *Cleveland State Law Review* 623, 640–41 (2011).

70. "Memorial and Remonstrance Against Religious Assessments, To The Honorable The General Assembly of the Commonwealth of Virginia from James Madison (1785)," *in* 2 *The Writings of James Madison*, ed. Gaillard Hunt (New York: G. P. Putnam's Sons, 1900–1910), 183. Dissenters in the *Everson* case included this historic essay in an appendix. 330 U.S. 1, 28, 63 (Rutledge, J., dissenting) (1947).

71. Letter from Thomas Jefferson to Nehemiah Dodge, Ephraim Robbins & Stephen S. Nelson, a committee of the Danbury Baptist Association in the state of Connecticut (Jan. 1, 1802).

72. See, e.g., David E. Steinberg, "Thomas Jefferson's Establishment Clause Federalism," 4 *Hastings Constitutional Law Quarterly* 277, 277–78 (2013) (arguing that "[t]he mainstream treatment of Jefferson's views on the

Establishment Clause is virtually the polar opposite of Jefferson's actual position.").

73. In reaching this conclusion, Donald L. Drakeman, "Everson v. Board of Education and the Quest for the Historical Establishment Clause," 49 *American Journal of Legal History* 119 (2007), refers to other relevant influences. For a balanced account of attitudes during the era of the Bill of Rights, see John Witte, Jr., *Religion and the American Constitutional Experiment* 21–105 (2d ed. Boulder, Colo.: Westview Press, 2005).

74. This judgment might be countered in one of two ways. Perhaps members of Congress and state legislators did advocate a very strict version of nonestablishment for the federal government within federal domains. As far as I am aware, there is virtually no evidence of precisely what kind of nonestablishment such legislators understood the Establishment Clause to enact.

The second type of countervailing evidence would be wide publicity that the Establishment Clause embraced the sense of nonestablishment that Jefferson and Madison favored. Regrettably, the Bill of Rights, as important to American liberties as it has become, was approved by Congress and ratified by state legislatures in a fairly cursory fashion. Since the precise language of "no law respecting an establishment of religion" was novel, not only in the United States but also in the world, it is hard to know what exactly a reasonable reader, whether legally trained or not, would have made of it, except to understand that at a minimum, a government church, along the lines of the Church of England, was forbidden. Witte, supra note 73, at 71–105, describes the origins of the religion clauses. Even a reader aware of the preceding Virginia controversy and Madison's position could not have been confident whether Madison's own opinions had succeeded within Congress or whether the differences between Madison and others had been compromised, or papered over without resolution. In short, whether one focuses on the subjective intent of most adopters, on how a reasonable adopter would have understood the language, or on what a reasonable reader would have understood, there is little basis simply to accept as decisive the favored positions of Madison and Jefferson.

75. Massachusetts was the last state to do so in 1833. See William H. Marnell, *The First Amendment: The History of Religious Freedom in America* 125 (1964).

76. Even if they did not assume this, those founders' views might have affected their judgments if they were asked hypothetically how the Establishment Clause should be understood if it were applicable to the states.

77. Public schools did not develop until early in the nineteenth century.

78. For some Justices and scholars, that is sufficient to condemn the present stricter approach. They may offer in its stead an interpretation of nonestablishment limited to a bar on preferences for particular churches, or at least a standard more flexible in regard to practices it allows.

79. See Letter from Thomas Jefferson to Nehemiah Dodge et al., supra note 71.

80. See Hamburger, supra note 64.

81. Zelman v. Simmons-Harris, 536 U.S. 639 (2002).

82. In fact, aid to other religious institutions besides schools that serve secular purposes, such as hospitals, adoption agencies, and social service providers, had been widely accepted before the Supreme Court's 2002 decision.

83. This broad subject is treated in Greenawalt, 2 *Religion and the Constitution: Establishment and Fairness*, supra note 63, at 57–121.

84. One exception is chaplains for military establishments and prisons, the idea being that in environments in which government controls all of life, it may appropriately provide opportunities to worship and receive ministerial assistance. Another exception is legislative chaplains, held to be justified because they were clearly accepted at the time of the Bill of Rights.

85. Justices have strained to explain that the words "In God We Trust" on coins and "under God" in the Pledge of Allegiance do not really have religious significance, but rather are understood as a reference to historical tradition. See Elk Grove Unified Sch. Dist. v. Newdow, 542 U.S. 1, 29–30 (2004). At least with respect to "under God," said by young children in school classrooms, such an explanation is wholly lacking in plausibility. A minority of Justices have proposed that it is entirely appropriate for governments to acknowledge a benign Supreme Being, a belief shared by Christians, Jews, and Muslims. See, e.g., Engel v. Vitale, 370 U.S. 421, 444 (1962) (Stewart, J., dissenting).

86. Hamburger, supra note 64.

87. See Kent Greenawalt, "History as Ideology: Philip Hamburger's Separation of Church and State," 93 *California Law Review* 367 (2005).

88. This illustration by itself proves almost nothing—it could be a peculiar anomaly in social and legal discourse—but it provides a sense of the distinction that is important.

89. In *Boyd v. United States*, 116 U.S. 616 (1886), the interaction did appear to significantly influence coverage, but that effect has diminished since then. See, e.g., Warden, Md. Penitentiary v. Hayden, 387 U.S. 294 (1967). This connection is treated in Chapter 11.

90. See Roe v. Wade, 410 U.S. 113 (1973); Lawrence v. Texas, 539 U.S. 558 (2003); Stanley v. Georgia, 394 U.S. 557 (1969).

91. To draw just two analogies, the ambits of freedom of speech and equal protection have undergone great adjustments without any substitution of a new terminology for the basic principles they embody.

92. At this stage in history, it is certainly possible that if the Supreme Court wholly abandons the separation metaphor, the abandonment will accompany greater permissiveness about what governments may do; but this need not be because of the differential implications of "separation" and "disestablishment."

93. Justice Thomas, in *Elk Grove*, said he would not apply the Establishment Clause against the states, but that is because he is persuaded it should not be regarded as incorporated. See Elk Grove Unified Sch. Dist. v. Newdow, 542 U.S. 1, 45 (2004).

94. The Supreme Court has refrained from developing two separate bodies of Bill of Rights law for the same sorts of reason that led it to conclude that the federal government could not maintain racially segregated schools once the states were forbidden to do so—although the original Bill of Rights had no Equal Protection Clause, and the founders, having accepted slavery in the original Constitution, had no objection to school segregation.

95. As we have seen, the idea that the most important understanding is that of those with authority to adopt a legal rule competes with the view that what is crucial is reader understanding. Reinforcing the focus on reader understanding is a concern that group intents do not exist (an implausible position in its most extreme form, since sometimes, virtually all members of a group do have

a common intent) or are rarely present and are nearly impossible to discern, and thus their "investigation" leads judges to implement their own opinions about what is right and just.

96. Chapter 3 of *Statutory and Common Law Interpretation*, supra note 1, suggests that this will not always be true.

97. In any event, for both the Bill of Rights and the Fourteenth Amendment, we have little basis to distinguish one from the other. There is slight evidence in the internal debates of the two Congresses about what provisions of the Bill of Rights meant. Although we do have alterations of wordings of the Establishment Clause, it is difficult to know exactly why changes were made. In any event, *half* of the process of adoption was ratification within the states. We have little basis to determine what state legislators thought the proposed clauses meant—if they thought about their meaning—apart from what reasonably well-informed people of the time would have understood. In short, the evidence for what those legislators intended would be essentially the same as the evidence we would need to comb were we to estimate reader understanding.

98. Of course, to some extent, one discerns abstract principles through conceived applications, and one discerns views about specific applications through a sense of the abstract principles thought to govern. But it still can matter greatly if later judges give their primary focus to understood applications or abstract principles, and to whether the adopters of the Establishment Clause believed a prohibition of blasphemy (limited to Christian blasphemy) was acceptable for the federal District of Columbia or whether such a prohibition does involve a significant promotion of one religion over others.

99. Religions dominant in Asia are bound to increase as our immigration laws continue not to impose the decisive discrimination that long favored residents of Europe.

100. See Torcaso v. Watkins, 367 U.S. 488 (1961). The original federal Constitution provided that no religious test could be imposed for federal office holders.

101. Very likely, any prohibition of blasphemy, however broad, would be thought to violate the Free Exercise and Free Speech Clauses.

102. A contrary argument, that judges have too much discretion when they depart from historically conceived applications, is not nearly strong enough to outweigh all the disadvantages of precluding changes of applications of general principles over time. And for many rights, the injunction to stick with understood applications of 1791 or 1868, if followed, would not greatly curb discretionary judgment because it is so hard now to figure out what were the historically understood applications.

103. Michael C. Dorf, "Integrating Normative and Deceptive Constitutional Theory: The Case of Original Meaning," 85 *Georgetown Law Review* 1765, 1800–01 (1997).

104. Sometimes judges are fully aware of their actual bases of judgment and decide not to reveal them. At other times, their rhetoric persuades themselves.

105. In the context of the common law itself, this means minimizing radical departures from previously decided cases. In the law of statutory interpretation, it entails following earlier decisions about statutory meaning.

106. Dorf, supra note 103, at 1803–05.

107. No doubt, one could conceive that virtually all members of society in the early republic had a wisdom we lack today, but that seems a highly implausible

hypothesis with respect to subjects of political organization and fundamental legal rights. Indeed, one core assumption at the Philadelphia Convention was that state governments under the Articles of Confederation were functioning poorly.

108. By extra weight, I mean beyond what a simple political authority version, which ascribes equal weight to all those with equal formal authority, would assign.

109. Richard A. Primas, "When Should Original Meanings Matter?," 107 *Michigan Law Review* 165 (2008), provides a powerful argument for diminished significance that leads him to afford even less weight to the original understanding of provisions adopted long ago than I have suggested here. He claims that in some cases, "consideration of original meaning should not be a factor in the content of constitutional decisions." Id. at 167.

Chapter 4

1. A minor qualification for courts is for a provision whose application is taken to be assigned exclusively to a different branch of government.

2. With respect to statutory interpretation, a number of states have formally adopted such an approach. See Abbe R. Gluck, "The States as Laboratories of Statutory Interpretation: Methodological Consensus and the New Modified Textualism," 119 *Yale Law Journal* 1750 (2010).

3. Richard H. Fallon, Jr., "A Constructivist Coherence Theory of Constitutional Interpretation," 100 *Harvard Law Review* 1189 (1987).

4. Id. at 1245. In "Legitimacy and the Constitution," 118 *Harvard Law Review* 1787 (2005), Fallon emphasizes the importance of settled precedents and defends their extension even if they are contrary to original understanding. His fuller account of the place of precedents is found in "Stare Decisis and the Constitution: An Essay on Constitutional Methodology," 76 *New York University Law Review* 570 (2001).

5. Kent Greenawalt, 2 *Statutory and Common Law Interpretation* (New York: Oxford University Press 2013), develops this theme in those two contexts.

6. In his well-known account of various methods, Philip Bobbitt refers to historical, textual, structural, prudential, and doctrinal arguments. *Constitutional Fate: Theory of the Constitution* (New York: Oxford University Press, 1982); see also Philip Bobbitt, *Constitutional Interpretation* (Oxford, UK: Blackwell Ltd., 1991).

7. See Chapters 3 and 6 of this volume.

8. As the prior chapter illustrates, it is hard to divorce any such inquiry from a judgment about what approach makes good sense.

9. A Justice who adopts such an approach might or might not think that the original understanding would in some respect endorse it.

10. This would constitute one form of aiming for "constructive coherence." See Fallon, supra note 3.

11. With respect to such a view about statutory interpretation, see Greenawalt, *Statutory and Common Law Interpretation*, supra note 5, at 64–67.

12. The place of precedents is explored in some depth in Greenawalt, *Statutory and Common Law Interpretation*, supra note 5, especially Chapter 8.

13. 347 U.S. 483 (1954).

14. What is meant here is more than the later court trying to discern how the preceding court saw things (which of course is unavoidable if the judgment of the prior court controls). The notion here is that the later court self-consciously may see the material facts differently. Thus, for example, the later court might treat the age of the plaintiff in the earlier case as relevant, although it did not matter to the first court.

15. Shawn J. Bayern, "Case Interpretation," 36 *Florida State University Law Review* 125 (2009), has urged that the force of prior cases could better be developed by a broader interpretive inquiry than the holding/dicta distinction suggests.

16. If lower court judges can identify clear approaches the Supreme Court uses, they might well feel constrained to follow them, even if dissenting Supreme Court Justices do not.

17. The very idea of Justices being constrained by settled interpretive strategies in constitutional cases might be resisted on the basis that each Justice should use the strategy he or she believes is called for by the Constitution. However, following "precedent" in this respect does not seem different from following precedents on more specific constitutional issues that a Justice believes are in tension with other standards of decision. And the Constitution, as best understood, *could* be seen as allowing enough flexibility about interpretive strategies so that settled approaches within a certain range should be followed.

18. These claims are explored in much more depth in Greenawalt, *Statutory and Common Law Interpretation*, supra note 5, Chapter 8.

19. See Kathryn A. Watts, "Constraining Certiorari Using Administrative Law Principles," 160 *University of Pennsylvania Law Review* 1 (2011) ("Various statutes enacted by Congress from 1891 to 1988 almost entirely eliminated the Court's obligatory jurisdiction and delegated to the Court the task of setting its agenda."). An exception to this broad discretion is for unconstitutional voter disenfranchisement. See 42 U.S.C. § 1973c(a) (2006).

20. One such need is raised by splits among lower courts over how issues should be resolved.

21. 384 U.S. 436 (1966).

22. See Greenawalt, *Statutory and Common Law Interpretation*, supra note 5, at 273–77.

23. For sharp criticism of the Supreme Court's present approach to precedents as not serving claimed policy justifications, see Michael Stokes Paulsen, "Does the Supreme Court's Current Doctrine of Stare Decisis Require Adherence to the Supreme Court's Current Doctrine of Stare Decisis?" 86 *North Carolina Law Review* 1165 (2008).

24. "*Expressio unius est exclusium alterius.*"

25. Antonin Scalia & Bryan A. Garner, *Reading Law: The Interpretation of Legal Texts* 69–239 (St. Paul, Minn.: Thomson/West, 2012). For a critical review, see William N. Eskridge, Jr., Book Review, "The New Textualism and Normative Cannons," 113 *Columbia Law Review* 531 (2013).

26. See Scalia & Garner, supra note 25.

27. Scalia & Garner, supra note 25, at 241. They divide these into Expected-Meaning, Government Structuring, Private-Right, and Stabilizing Canons. Id. at 243–336. Some of the canons they categorize as "contextual" could also be regarded as substantive. The canons in these categories that they

treat mainly concern statutory interpretation, but some are relevant for constitutional provisions.

28. See Scalia & Garner, supra note 25, at 59. They offer five "fundamental principles of interpretation" before they enumerate fifty-two canons. Id. at 53–68.

29. 494 U.S. 872 (1990). Congress attempted to reinstitute the previous Free Exercise approach by The Religious Freedom Restoration Act (RFRA), 42 U.S.C. § 2000 (1993), which was sustained in its application to federal laws but not state laws.

30. See Greenawalt, *Statutory and Common Law Interpretation*, supra note 5, Chapter 5.

31. John Hart Ely, *Democracy and Distrust: A Theory of Judicial Review* (Cambridge, Mass.: Harvard University Press, 1980).

32. I put aside here claims that some mandatory requirements for insurance violate the religious freedom of dissenting groups. Such claims could be seen as on behalf of group minorities. See Kent Greenawalt, "Religious Toleration and Claims of Conscience," 28 *Journal of Law & Politics* 91 (2013).

33. Charles Black, Jr., *Structure and Relationship in Constitutional Law* 7 (Woodbridge, CT: Ox Bow Press, 1969).

34. Though the idea that the force of other provisions *could* bear to a degree on how to interpret a particular provision was well established, Professor Black was proposing a greater reliance on the entire document.

35. See Greenawalt, *Statutory and Common Law Interpretation*, supra note 5, Chapter 6.

36. See id. at 120.

37. See Richard A. Posner, "Statutory Interpretation—In the Classroom and in the Courtroom," 50 *University of Chicago Law Review* 800, 816 (1983), and Earnest A. Young, "Constitutional Avoidance, Resistance Norms, and the Preservation of Judicial Review," 78 *Texas Law Review* 1549 (2000). For a helpful overview of relevant arguments, see Gillian E. Metzger & Trevor W. Morrison, "The Presumption of Constitutionality & the Individual Mandate, 81 *Fordham Law Review* 1715, 1717–20 (2013).

38. U.S. Const. art. III, § 2, cl. 1.

39. The exact stage at which a suit may be brought can itself be a subject of dispute, as it was with respect to the challenge to the healthcare legislation of the Obama administration. See Nat'l Fed'n of Indep. Bus. v. Sebelius, 132 S. Ct. 2566, 2582–85, 567 U.S. (2012).

40. See, e.g., Bennett v. Spear, 520 U.S. 154, 163–64 (1997) (explaining that "Congress legislates against the backdrop of our prudential standing doctrine, which applies unless it is expressly negated" and holding that the Endangered Species Act's citizen-suit provision "negates the zone of interest test (or, perhaps more accurately expands the zone of interests)." For a view that Congress cannot easily overcome prudential considerations, see Heather Elliott, "Congress's Inability to Solve Standing Problems," 91 *Boston University Law Review* 159 (2011).

41. See Louis Henkin, "Is There a 'Political Questions' Doctrine?," 85 *Yale Law Journal* 597, 601 (1976) (arguing that "[t]he cases which are supposed to have established the political question doctrine required no such extra-ordinary abstention from judicial review; they called only for the ordinary respect by the courts for the political domain.").

42. The language of the Constitution itself can arguably be seen as impliedly conferring this authority. See U.S. Const. art. V.

43. See, e.g., Rachel E. Barkow, "More Supreme Than Court? The Rise and Fall of the Political Question Doctrine and the Rise of Judicial Supremacy," 102 *Columbia Law Review* 237 (2002).

44. James B. Thayer, "The Origin and Scope of American Constitutional Law," 7 *Harvard Law Review* 129 (1893).

45. How far that premise seems persuasive may depend partly on the extent to which judicial decisions were initially seen to control what the political branches were bound to do. See William Michael Treanor, "Original Understanding and the Whether, Why, and How of Judicial Review," 116 *Yale Law Journal Pocket Part* 218 (2007).

46. This matter is explored in Chapter 8.

47. Thayer, supra note 44, at 154–55.

48. A useful overview of the term "living constitution" is provided in William H. Rehnquist, "The Notion of a Living Constitution," 54 *Texas Law Review* 693 (1976). For a strong defense of a living constitution, see David A. Strauss, *The Living Constitution* (New York: Oxford University Press, 2010).

49. As suggested earlier, one could easily see such a punishment as directly covered by the enactors' intentions.

50. See Terry v. Ohio, 392 U.S. 1 (1968); Sibron v. New York, 392 U.S. 40 (1968).

51. Changes in values are almost always tied to some shifts in external social facts. Thus, modern views of church and state are undoubtedly affected by the fact that a much higher percentage of the present population is not Protestant.

52. The proposal of John Hart Ely, supra note 31, is that the Supreme Court should limit its innovative judgments to protecting the place of minorities in the political process and correcting discrimination against minorities. As both the Equal Protection and Establishment Clause illustrations reflect, many particular judgments can be fitted into both of these broad approaches.

53. This change in value is undoubtedly related to the ability to preserve a high percentage of human lives over time.

54. See Roper v. Simmons, 543 U.S. 551 (2005).

55. See West Virginia State Bd. of Educ. v. Barnette, 319 U.S. 624, 646, 647 (1943) (Frankfurter, J., dissenting) (proclaiming, "[a]s a member of this Court, I am not justified in writing my private notions of policy into the Constitution, no matter how deeply I may cherish them or how mischievous I may deem their disregard.").

56. Citizens United v. Fed. Election Comm'n, 558 U.S. 310 (2010).

57. In a television interview, Justice Scalia made clear that he saw no problem whatsoever with all the "speech" that has resulted. *Piers Morgan Tonight: Interview with Antonin Scalia* (CNN television broadcast July 18, 2012).

58. An alternative conceptual way to put the same substantive conclusion is to say that the terms "activism" and "restraint" have significance only when there is genuine disagreement about what judges should do. This alternative has the disadvantage of introducing a kind of value judgment that the legitimacy of an action is at least debatable whenever these concepts are employed; but the alternative may well come closer to capturing ordinary understanding than use of the concepts with respect to undoubtedly correct exercises of judicial power. When those occur, people do not commonly speak of "activism" or "restraint."

59. Of course, in some cases, different political authorities are involved on opposite sides—Congress versus the President, state government versus federal government—but we shall pass over these sorts of cases because the simpler, more common situations pose the dilemmas of activism more clearly.

60. 410 U.S. 113 (1973).

61. 384 U.S. 436 (1966).

62. Issues of activism can arise in nonconstitutional contexts as well. A court may interpret a statute in a manner that reflects its own perceptions of a desirable outcome, but which is only weakly supported by statutory language and legislative purpose. See, e.g., Vance v. Ball State Univ., 133 S. Ct. 2434, 2454, 2465–66, 570 U.S. (2013) (Ginsburg, J. dissenting). Or a court may decide to develop a novel principle of common law in the face of arguments that the new step constitutes too sharp a break with the past and should be left to legislative action. Judicial institution of a standard of comparative negligence and elimination of immunities for charitable organizations fall into this category. These illustrations show how courts may be activist with respect to legislative powers and common law development in nonconstitutional settings. On occasion, trial judges consciously misfind the facts because they are appalled by the outcome that would result from application of the authoritative rule of law to the actual facts. In doing so, they are clearly being activist vis-à-vis the legislature or the higher courts, whichever is the source of the unwanted rule of law. When appellate courts reverse trial judges whom they distrust for reasons that are not revealed on the record, they may be described as being activist in relation to the functions of trial judges.

63. 377 U.S. 533 (1964).

64. Ironically, and probably not coincidentally, the very activist substantive standard that the Court laid down simplified the process of judicial oversight of reapportionment, necessitating less close involvement in, and review of, that process than might have resulted from a more flexible standard. Had the Supreme Court invalidated only unreasonable malapportionments, courts would have been thrown headlong into political thickets they have been able to avoid with the simple population-based test.

65. For a recent example of suggested deference to institutions, see *Fisher v. University of Texas at Austin*, 133 S. Ct. 2411, 2432, 570 U.S. (2013) (Ginsburg, J. dissenting).

66. I had the good fortune to serve as a law clerk to Justice Harlan. My thoughts about how his approach related to judicial activism are set forth in "Justice Harlan's Conservatism and Alternative Possibilities," 36 *New York Law School Law Review* 53 (1991).

67. Related to this point is an argument that the genius of federalism is impaired if federal courts do not pay enough respect to the states.

Chapter 5

1. Herbert Wechsler, "Toward Neutral Principles of Constitutional Law," 73 *Harvard Law Review* 1 (1959), *reprinted in* Herbert Wechsler, *Principles, Policies, and Fundamental Law: Selected Essays* 3 (Cambridge, Mass.: Harvard University Press, 1961). Subsequent citations are to the book's pages.

2. See, e.g., Arthur Selwyn Miller & Alan W. Scheflin, "The Power of the Supreme Court in the Age of the Positive State: A Preliminary Excursion Part

One: On Candor and the Court, Or, Why Bamboozle the Natives?," 1967 *Duke Law Journal* 273; Arthur S. Miller & Ronald F. Howell, "The Myth of Neutrality in Constitutional Adjudication," 27 *University of Chicago Law Review* 661 (1960).

3. See, e.g., Robert H. Bork, "Neutral Principles and Some First Amendment Problems," 47 *Indiana Law Journal* 1 (1971); Alexander M. Bickel, "The Supreme Court, 1960 Term—Foreword: The Passive Virtues," 75 *Harvard Law Review* 40 (1961).

4. On the other hand, one may take this inherent difficulty as a reason to recommend reliance on more particular moral standards rather than any subtle calculation of interests.

5. 349 U.S. 294 (1954).

6. Wechsler, supra note 1, at 30–31.

7. Id at 44–45. Wechsler wrote that such effects, as compared with those of being in racially integrated schools, would depend on the schools involved and the reactions of white students.

8. 334 U.S. 1 (1948).

9. See Kent Greenawalt, 2 *Statutory and Common Law Interpretation* Chapter 9 (New York: Oxford University Press, 2013).

10. As the chapter on analogy suggests (id. at 236–40), the line between no stated standard and one that simply lines up a variety of factors is extremely thin.

11. Burton v. Wilmington Parking Auth., 365 U.S. 715 (1961).

12. Mark V. Tushnet, "Following the Rules Laid Down: A Critique of Interpretivism and Neutral Principles," 96 *Harvard Law Review* 781, 814 (1983).

13. One imagines that at that stage of history, most members of "different races" (as then categorized, so that someone who was three-quarters white was considered to be black) who wished to marry would have preferred not to live in the South.

14. As Greenawalt, *Statutory and Common Law Interpretation*, supra note 9, explains, the aspiration for majority opinions is not shared in many common law courts in other countries.

15. This problem may have been particularly acute in *Brown v. Board of Education* because of the aim to achieve an opinion on which all nine Justices could agree.

16. Wechsler, supra note 1, at 24.

17. As the discussion in Chapters 3 and 5 of Greenawalt, *Statutory and Common Law Interpretation*, supra note 9, at 43, 131–32, indicates, some state courts have provided such an ordering for statutory interpretation.

18. Wechsler did not recommend that judges abandon this approach to opinion writing, although he did suggest that when they have different reasons for reaching a result, they should disclose these variations. Wechsler, supra note 1, at 30.

19. See Miller & Howell, supra note 2, at 664; Frederick Schauer, "Neutrality and Judicial Review," 22 *Law and Philosophy* 217, 232–33 (2003).

20. Cass R. Sunstein, "Neutrality in Constitutional Law (With Special Reference to Pornography, Abortion, and Surrogacy)," 92 *Columbia Law Review* 1, 6 (1992), suggests that "partisanship" inevitably depends on the baseline from which measurements are made.

21. As Chapter 12 explains, I support that conclusion on the basis of considerations that include, but reach beyond, original understanding.

22. My views on many of these topics are developed more fully in Kent Greenawalt, *Law and Objectivity* (New York: Oxford University Press, 1992).

23. Under most moral theories, not all morally desirable acts are morally required.

24. For one leading modern articulation of this position, see John Finnis, *Natural Law and Natural Rights* (New York: Oxford University Press, 1980).

25. It would probably be immoral to leave nothing to children with serious financial needs.

26. That is simplest to accept if one believes in a powerful beneficent God.

27. John Rawls, in *A Theory of Justice* (Cambridge, Mass.: Harvard University Press, 1971), urges implicitly that reason—based on original position analysis—can provide answers to basic political premises even for people who disagree about many other moral questions. He qualifies that claim in *Political Liberalism* (New York: Columbia University Press, 1993).

28. That is to say that people and judges should not be relying on simple intuitions or biblical sources.

29. For common law interpretation, the subjective intent of those joining the majority opinion that counts as the precedent matters less than it does according to a theory of statutory interpretation that credits original intentions. The reasons for this are the fuller explanations possible in judicial opinions themselves and the appropriateness of the later court revising in various ways what the precedent court has laid down as principles.

30. People might disagree about whether discerning what a general statement of value implies about specific situations is really a factual judgment, depending as it does on the significance of the broader principle.

31. Miller and Howell, supra note 2, at 664–71, summarize skeptical views about objectivity in even natural and social sciences.

32. On how complicated this can be, see Ilya Somin, "Originalism and Political Ignorance," 97 *Minnesota Law Review* 625 (2012).

33. Tushnet, supra 12, at 797–802.

34. Historians, unlike lawyers, often find ambiguity when they search for past attitudes and intentions. Id. at 793.

35. This can be true even if the new speech has some negative characteristic not present in the speech of the earlier cases, at least if the judges lack any solid basis to conclude that this negative aspect warrants a different approach.

36. Ronald Dworkin, *Law's Empire* 379–81 (Cambridge, Mass.: Harvard University Press, 1986). Dworkin is discussed in Chapter 10 of Greenawalt, *Statutory and Common Law Interpretation*, supra note 9, at 266–69.

Tara Smith has urged that when judges interpret terms like "equal protection" they should ask not what these terms were originally seen to cover but what the authors meant by the concepts. "Why Originalism Won't Die—Common Mistakes in Competing Theories of Judicial Interpretation," 2 *Duke Journal of Constitutional Law and Public Policy* 1259, 189–92 (2007).

37. See Larry Alexander, "Legal Objectivity and the Illusion of Legal Principles," *in Institutionalized Reason: The Jurisprudence of Robert Alexy*, ed. Matthias Klatt (New York: Oxford University Press, 2012), 115.

38. Jules L. Coleman & Brian Leiter, "Determinacy, Objectivity, and Authority," 142 *University of Pennsylvania Law Review* 549, 616–20 (1993), have suggested that law amounts to what it would seem to someone under "ideal epistemic conditions."

39. It is conceptually possible, however, that judges who self-consciously rely on their own judgments about justice, rather than trying to rest entirely on legal materials, could more often reach undesirable conclusions. Even if perfect judges would sometimes deviate from what a "neutral" evaluation of the compendium of legal materials would yield, actual judges, who might make too many mistakes if they consciously engaged in such deviations, might do better to stick to an attempted objective evaluation based on the existing law.

40. See Jan G. Deutsch, "Neutrality, Legitimacy, and the Supreme Court: Some Intersections Between Law and Political Science," 20 *Stanford Law Review* 169, 240 (1968).

41. E.g., Martin M. Shapiro, *Law and Politics in the Supreme Court: New Approaches to Political Jurisprudence* (New York: Free Press of Glencoe, 1964).

42. See Benjamin F. Wright, "The Supreme Court Cannot Be Neutral," 40 *Texas Law Review* 599, 613 (1962).

43. As explained in Chapter 4, one can think of activism with respect to original understanding, legislative decisions, and precedents. In general, the Warren Court was fairly activist in all three of these respects.

44. Schauer, supra note 19, at 235–40.

45. Tushnet, supra note 12, at 787, has noted the opposition of liberals in 1940–1970 to what he labels "interpretivism" as being too conservative.

46. These questions are also relevant, though less central, for statutory and common law interpretation.

47. See Tushnet, supra note 12, at 809–10.

48. Dan M. Kahan, "'Ideology in,' or 'Cultural Cognition of' Judging: What Difference Does It Make?," 92 *Marquette Law Review* 413 (2009).

49. H. Jefferson Powell has praised Justice Jackson's concurring opinion in *Youngstown Sheet Tube Co. v. Sawyer,* 343 U.S. 579 (1952), for revealing the complexities of difficult interpretation. H. Jefferson Powell, "Slow Reading and Living Speech: James Boyd White on What a Constitutional Law Opinion Is For," *in Living in a Law Transformed: Encounters with the Works of James Boyd White,* eds. Julen Etxabe & Gary Watts (Ann Arbor, Mich.: Michigan Publishing, 2014).

Chapter 6

1. If a judge could say that anyone who conceived of punishment *A* as "cruel and unusual" would indisputably also regard punishment *A1* in that way, it would be close to ridiculous to say that *A1* was not covered if *A* was.

2. See Anthony F. Granucci, "'Nor Cruel and Unusual Punishments Inflicted': The Original Meaning," 57 *California Law Review* 839, 852–60 (1969). Various positions of Supreme Court Justices on the significance of the English Bill of Rights are summarized in Deborah M. Forhan, Note, "Harmelin v. Michigan: Should the Existence of an Eighth Amendment Guarantee of Proportionate Prison Sentences Rest on the Fate of Titus Oates and the Dread Consequences of Overtime Parking?," 22 *Southwestern University Law Review* 1133, 1141–47 (1993).

3. Granucci, supra note 2, at 858.

4. 10 Journal of the House of Commons 247 (Aug. 2, 1689).

5. Id.

6. See Granucci, supra note 2, at 855–56.

7. See John F. Stinneford, "The Original Meaning of 'Unusual': The Eighth Amendment as a Bar to Cruel Innovation," 102 *Northwestern University Law Review* 1739, 1798–99 (2008).

8. Granucci, supra note 2, at 839, 860–65.

9. Stinneford, supra note 7, at 1766–71.

10. 463 U.S. 277, 288–89 (1983).

11. Granucci, supra note 2, at 843–44, 848–65.

12. One might argue, to the contrary, that the absence of comparable explicit proportional language means that "cruel" should be taken more narrowly. But given the implicit notion that what is "cruel" often involves a notion of disproportionate severity, this argument is not persuasive.

13. At that stage of history, the authority of Parliament in relation to courts was not entirely clear, and the fact that the House of Lords constituted the highest court somewhat undercut the difference between these branches. Stinneford, supra note 7, at 1771–92, discusses in some detail the influential views of Edward Coke, who regarded Parliamentary power as essentially limited, and William Blackstone, who conceived it having a broader authority.

14. This particular formulation first appeared in Chief Justice Warren's opinion for the Court in *Trop v. Dulles*, 356 U.S. 86, 101 (1958).

15. Granucci, supra note 2, at 854.

16. John D. Bessler, *Cruel and Unusual: The American Death Penalty and the Founders' Eighth Amendment* 188–89 (Boston: Northeastern University Press, 2012).

17. John F. Stinneford, "Rethinking Proportionality Under the Cruel and Unusual Punishments Clause," 97 *Virginia Law Review* 899, 942, 947–55 (2011).

18. Weems v. United States, 217 U.S. 349 (1910).

19. A counterargument made by Justice Scalia is that, given some state references to proportionality in punishment, the specific language of "excessive" fines does not carry over to coverage of the proportionality of other sentences. Harmelin v. Michigan, 501 U.S. 957, 976–84 (1991) (plurality opinion). This argument is not persuasive if, as Professor Stinneford contends, the phrase "cruel and unusual" was generally assumed to forbid excessive punishments as demonstrated by use of the phrase in other contexts and arguments made during the ratification debates. Stinneford, supra note 17, at 938–47.

20. Solem v. Helm, 463 U.S. 277, 288–89 (1983).

21. Stinneford, supra note 17, at 939–42.

22. 217 U.S. 349 (1910).

23. Id. at 367.

24. 408 U.S. 238 (1972).

25. Kennedy v. Louisiana, 554 U.S. 407, 437 (2008). The Court's opinion did not address crimes such as "treason, espionage, terrorism, and drug kingpin activity . . . ."

26. See, e.g., Roper v. Simmons, 543 U.S. 551 (2005); Ford v. Wainwright, 477 U.S. 399 (1986). In May of 2014, the Supreme Court held invalid Florida's rigid IQ test, which relied on whether a person scored above 70 or not. See Adam Liptak, "Justices Reject a Rigid I.Q. Rule for Executions," N.Y. Times, May 28, 2014, at A1, col. 2. In addition to who can receive capital punishment, the Court has also reviewed the way in which the death penalty is actually inflicted, assuming that if that were unnecessarily painful, it would be unconstitutional. See Baze v. Rees, 553 U.S. 35 (2008).

27. Graham v. Florida, 560 U.S. 48, 82 (2010).

28. See Tom Stacy, "Cleaning Up the Eighth Amendment Mess," 14 *William and Mary Bill of Rights Journal* 475, 502–505 (2005).

29. Not every novel punishment would necessarily be cruel; some could be obviously more humane than what they replaced.

30. As noted earlier, even if courts had to accept what Parliament specifically enacted regarding punishments, the protection against cruel and unusual punishment could also be seen as designed to restrain legislative choices.

31. Some early decisions of federal courts assumed that it did. See, e.g., United States v. Ravara, 27 F. Cas. 714 (C.C.D. Pa. 1794) (No. 16,122a) (upholding indictment of foreign consul for extortion); United States v. Smith, 27 F. Cas. 1147 (C.C.D. Mass. 1792) (No. 16,323) (upholding conviction for counterfeiting United States banknotes); Henfield's Case, 11 F. Cas. 1099 (C.C.D. Pa. 1793) (No. 6,360) (upholding charge of common law crime of violating neutrality).

32. United States v. Hudson & Goodwin, 11 U.S. (7 Cranch) 32, 32 (1812).

33. Cases involving prison conditions and modes of inflicting capital punishment do not necessarily involve legislative authorization, although modes of execution are frequently prescribed by state legislatures, and those condemned may be permitted to choose between authorized methods. See generally Tracy L. Snell, Bureau of Justice Statistics, NCJ 242185, "Capital Punishment, 2011—Statistical Tables" (2013).

34. 501 U.S. 957 (1991).

35. See Stinneford, supra notes 7 and 17. Using that standard does not bar legislative authorization of what definitely seems a more humane punishment than what is then prevailing.

36. Stinneford, supra note 7, at 1823. The case is *Coker v. Georgia*, 433 U.S. 584 (1972).

37. See U.S. General Accounting Office Report to the Senate and House Committees on the Judiciary, "Death Penalty Sentencing: Research Indicates Pattern of Racial Disparities" (Feb. 1990) (finding that killers of white victims are more likely to be sentenced to death than killers of black victims); Randall L. Kennedy, "McClesky v. Kemp: Race, Capital Punishment, and the Supreme Court," 101 *Harvard Law Review* 1388 (1988) (discussing equal protection concerns arising from racially driven disparities in criminal sentencing). Just how much race matters now in sentencing, and exactly how it matters when it does, is far from clear. See R. Richard Banks, Jennifer L. Eberhardt & Lee Ross, "Discrimination and Implicit Bias in A Racially Unequal Society," 94 *California Law Review* 1169 (2006) (reviewing literature on and discussing the impact of implicit bias); Shima Baradaran, "Race, Prediction, and Discretion," 81 *George Washington Law Review* 157 (2013) (arguing that judges detain white defendants for longer than similarly situated black defendants, and that many other aspects of conventional wisdom on racial disparities in criminal sentencing are inaccurate).

38. A very recent enactment of a novel punishment does not establish conformity with prior practice, and a practice that ended a century ago would no longer count (unless one uses an originalist approach).

39. 356 U.S. 86, 100–01 (1958).

40. 408 U.S. 238 (1972).

41. Id. at 242 (Douglas, J., concurring).

42. Id. at 309–10 (Stewart, J., concurring).
43. Id. at 312–13 (White, J., concurring).
44. Id. at 290–91 (Brennan, J., concurring).
45. Id. at 361 (Marshall, J., concurring).
46. 428 U.S. 153 (1976).
47. Id. at 179.
48. Roper v. Simmons, 543 U.S. 551 (2005).
49. Ford v. Wainwright, 477 U.S. 399 (1986).
50. Roberts v. Louisiana, 428 U.S. 325 (1976).
51. Woodson v. North Carolina 428 U.S. 280 (1976).
52. 543 U.S. 551 (2005).
53. See Bressler, supra note 16, at 12–14.
54. Thompson v. Oklahoma, 487 U.S. 815 (1988).
55. Stanford v. Kentucky, 492 U.S. 361 (1989).
56. 543 U.S. at 561.
57. 543 U.S. at 564.
58. 543 U.S. at 553, 575.
59. See Stinneford, supra note 17, at 974. Between 1973 (with the resumption of the death penalty in 1976 after *Furman v. Georgia*) and 2005, the year of *Roper*, only twenty-two juveniles had been executed in the United States. Carrie Martin, "Spare the Death Penalty, Spoil the Child: How the Execution of Juveniles Violates the Eighth Amendment's Ban on Cruel and Unusual Punishment, 46 *South Texas Law Review* 695, 698–99 (2005).
60. Penry v. Lynaugh, 492 U.S. 302 (1989).
61. Atkins v. Virginia, U.S. 304, 315–17 (2002).
62. 433 U.S. 584 (1977). At that time, Georgia was the only state authorizing that penalty for rape of adult women.
63. Kennedy v. Louisiana, 554 U.S. 407 (2008). Five states then had laws authorizing the death penalty for rape of a minor. That only eight states allowed the death penalty for participation in a crime in which an accomplice happened to commit murder bore on the Court's earlier resolution that this was unconstitutional. Enmund v. Florida, 458 U.S. 782 (1982).
64. See Richard C. Dieter, "Methods of Execution and Their Effect on the Use of the Death Penalty in the United States," 35 *Fordham Urban Law Journal* 789, 790–92 (2008).
65. Baze v. Rees, 553 U.S. 35 (2008).
66. DeShaney v. Winnebago Country Dep't Soc. Servs., 489 U.S. 189 (1989).
67. Hudson v. McMillian, 503 U.S. 1 (1992).
68. Brown v. Plata, 131 S. Ct. 1910, 563 U.S. (2011).
69. Robert A. Ferguson, *Inferno: An Anatomy of American Punishment* 138–69 (Cambridge, Mass.: Harvard University Press, 2014). For one critique of an unjustified overuse of solitary confinement, see Editorial, "New York Rethinks Solitary Confinement," N.Y. Times, Feb. 21, 2014, at A24, col. 1.
70. Farmer v. Brennan, 511 U.S. 825, 837, 847 (1994).
71. See Ferguson, supra note 69. Among the institutions in which deeply troubling practices have been employed is Rikers Island in New York City. See, e.g., Michael Weinrip & Michael Schwirtz, "Where Mental Illness Meets Brutality in Jail," N.Y. Times, July 14, 2014, at A1, col. 5; Benjamin Weiser & Michael Schwirtz, "U.S. Finds Excessive Force Against Youths at Rikers," N.Y. Times, Aug. 15, 2014, at A1, col. 5.

72. See Graham v. Florida, 560 U.S. 48 (2010) (nonhomicidal crimes); Miller v. Alabama, 132 S. Ct. 2455, 567 U.S. (2012) (homicide cases).

73. 463 U.S. 277 (1983).

74. 501 U.S. 957 (1991).

75. Id. at 1002–05 (Kennedy, J., concurring).

76. Ewing v. California, 538 U.S. 11 (2003).

77. See John Tierney, "For Lesser Crimes, Rethinking Life Behind Bars," N.Y. Times, Dec. 12, 2012, at A1.

78. See Richard S. Frase, "Limiting Excessive Prison Sentences Under Federal and State Constitutions," 11 *University of Pennsylvania Journal of Constitutional Law* 39, 64 (2008); Gregory S. Schneider, "Sentencing Proportionality in the States," 54 *Arizona Law Review* 241, 242–43 (2012).

79. Ferguson, supra note 69. "Reviving Clemency, Serving Justice," a N.Y. Times editorial from April 2, 2014, A30, col. 1, refers to "absurdly long mandatory minimum sentences that prosecutors have used to secure disproportionally harsh punishments for many low-level offenders." An interesting response to one variety of low-level offense, possession of small amounts of marijuana, has been a proposal by the Brooklyn District Attorney to stop prosecuting for that offense. See Stephanie Clifford, "Proposal to Limit Prosecutions of Marijuana Cases in Brooklyn," N.Y. Times, Apr. 23, 2014, at A22, col. 4.

80. Ferguson, supra note 69, at 16.

81. Speech by Justice Anthony M. Kennedy, American Bar Association Annual Meeting (Aug. 9, 2003).

82. Stinneford, supra note 17, at 961–68.

83. Id. at 968–69.

84. Bessler, supra note 16, at 223 (covering 1976 to 2012). For a detailed account that includes executions in all states authorizing capital punishment, see Death Penalty Information Center, "Number of Executions by State and Region Since 1976" (May 6, 2014), http://deathpenaltyinfo.org/number-executions-state-and-region-1976.

85. In *Graham v. Florida*, 560 U.S. 48 (2010), five Justices (Kennedy, Ginsburg, Breyer, Sotomayor, Kagan) joined an opinion giving weight to foreign practices with respect to the length of sentences for juveniles. Justice Thomas's dissent, joined by Justices Scalia and Alito, included a footnote criticizing the practice of using foreign law to interpret the Constitution. Chief Justice Roberts concurred in the result, but did not refer to international sources. See David A. Shapiro, "What's Beneath the Graham Cracker?: The Potential Impact of Comparative Law on the Future of Juvenile Justice Reform After Graham v. Florida," 24 *Pace International Law Review* 119, 130 n.66 (2012).

86. 370 U.S. 660 (1962).

87. 392 U.S. 514 (1968).

88. Id. at 517 (plurality opinion).

89. Id. at 521 (plurality opinion).

90. Id. at 526 (plurality opinion).

91. Id. at 569 (Fortas, J., dissenting).

92. Id. at 552–54. Since White had dissented in *Robinson v. California*, it is not clear whether he would have accepted Powell's basic argument if the outcome had depended on alcoholism as a status.

93. Id. at 559 n.2 (Fortas, J., dissenting).

94. Id. at 534 (plurality opinion).

95. Id. at 536 (plurality opinion).

96. Id. at 544 (Black., J., concurring).

97. M'Naghten's Case, 10 Clark & Fin. 200, 210 (1843).

98. Wayne R. LaFave, 1 *Substantive Criminal Law* § 7.2 n.7 (2d ed. 2003, database updated 2013).

99. 343 U.S. 790 (1952).

100. Id. at 800–01.

101. Ford v. Wainwright, 477 U.S. 399 (1986). The Court reached a similar conclusion when a prisoner suffered from severe "mental retardation." Atkins v. Virginia, 536 U.S. 304 (2002).

102. 477 U.S. at 399.

103. See People v. Young, 11 N.Y.2d 274 (1962) (per curiam) (discussed in "Intervener Held Liable for Assault Despite Reasonable Belief That His Conduct Protected Another from Unlawful Harm," 63 *Columbia Law Review* 160 (1963)).

104. See, e.g., United States v. Balint, 258 U.S. 250 (1922).

105. An individual in this situation could still be "negligent" if the standard for perceiving the risk was "objective"; objective meaning that of an average person.

Chapter 7

1. Rachel E. Barkow, "More Supreme than Court? The Fall of the Political Question Doctrine and the Rise of Judicial Supremacy," 102 *Columbia Law Review* 237, 325 (2002).

2. Someone who claims a right to judicial resolution about his behavior often includes an assertion about what fairness to individuals requires.

3. The status of the unwritten British constitution is more debatable.

4. See Canadian Charter of Rights and Freedoms, Part 1 of the Constitution Act, 1982, *being* Schedule B to the Canada Act 1982, c. 11 § 33 (UK).

5. One might calculate acceptance by a standard like H.L.A. Hart's rule of recognition, but the basic point here is true whether or not one is persuaded by Hart's approach. See H.L.A. Hart, *The Concept of Law* (3d ed. Oxford: Oxford University Press, 2012). My efforts to deal with ambiguities and oversimplifications in Hart's formulation are in "The Rule of Recognition and the Constitution," 85 *Michigan Law Review* 621 (1987), *reprinted in The Rule of Recognition and the U.S. Constitution*, eds. Matthew D. Adler & Kenneth Einar Himma (New York: Oxford University Press, 2009), at 1; and "How to Understand the Rule of Recognition and the American Constitution," *reprinted in* id. at 145.

6. See Lawrence Gene Sager, "Fair Measure: The Legal Status of Underenforced Constitutional Norms," 91 *Harvard Law Review* 1212 (1978).

7. It is worth mentioning an alternative kind of circumstance with much less significance for this chapter. The Supreme Court decides that the Constitution, ideally interpreted, would set certain restrictions, but given difficulties of judicial administration or needs of enforcement, it creates more severe limits. One might see *Miranda v. Arizona*, 384 U.S. 436 (1966), in this way. One could characterize the added restraints as not really imposed by the Constitution itself, but nevertheless applicable to officials and enforceable by courts. In other words, in practical effect, these are constitutional restraints on political officials, and they certainly have legal force. In *United States v. Dickerson*, 530 U.S. 428

(2000), the Court made clear that it considered *Miranda* a constitutional precedent that Congress could not overturn.

Although the Supreme Court acknowledges with some frequency that it is providing less than full enforcement, it rarely states that it is actually enforcing beyond what an ideal interpretation of the Constitution would suggest. The primary concern in this chapter is how far, and in what respects, political officials should interpret the Constitution to impose restraints that they understand courts will not, or are unlikely to, enforce.

8. See Curtis A. Bradley & Trevor W. Morrison, "Presidential Power, Historical Practice, and Legal Constraint," 113 *Columbia Law Review* 1097 (2013).

9. This term is used by Richard H. Fallon, Jr., "Judicially Manageable Standards and Constitutional Meaning," 119 *Harvard Law Review* 1274 (2006), but he does not dispute that officials may regard themselves as constrained beyond what courts will enforce; and even when they believe that, like a court's decision to under-enforce, they need not try to comply precisely with a constitutional norm, it can still stand in the background as a legal constraint on what they do. Id. at 1323–24.

10. Id.

11. Bruce Ackerman, *The Decline and Fall of the American Republic* 143–46 (Cambridge, Mass.: Belknap Press of Harvard University Press, 2010). In a more recent column, Professor Ackerman strongly criticized President Obama's authorization of continuing military force against ISIS as not justified by an earlier statute directed to al-Qaeda. He concludes that the President's "assault on the rule of law is a devastating setback for our constitutional order." Bruce Ackerman, "Obama's Betrayal of the Constitution," N.Y. Times, Sept. 12, 2014, at A31, col. 2. For a general view similar to Ackerman's—that the President is essentially unconstrained legally—see Eric A. Posner & Adrian Vermeule, *The Executive Unbound: After the Madisonian Republic* (New York: Oxford University Press, 2010). On whether a modern President is likely to rely on "prerogative" power that exceeds legal limits, see Jack Goldsmith, "The Irrelevance of Prerogative Power, and the Evils of Secret Legal Interpretation," *in Extra-Legal Power and Legitimacy: Perspectives on Prerogative*, eds. Clement Fatovic & Benjamin A. Kleinerman (New York: Oxford University Press, 2013), 214.

12. Trevor W. Morrison, "Constitutional Alarmism," Book Review, 124 *Harvard Law Review* 1688 (2011). Stephen M. Griffin, *Long Wars and the Constitution* (Cambridge, Mass.: Harvard University Press, 2013), is among others who also conclude that those in government believe they should respect the Constitution. For an emphasis on the importance of political officials reaching conclusions about constitutional power on the basis of reasons that regard legal constraints as compelling, see H. Jefferson Powell, *Constitutional Conscience: The Moral Dimension of Judicial Decision* (Chicago: University of Chicago Press, 2008).

13. Morrison, supra note 12, at 1717–20.

14. Id. at 1727–30.

15. Id. at 1713–14.

16. Id. at 1715–16.

17. Id. at 1709, 1719–24.

18. See, e.g., Larry D. Kramer, "The Supreme Court 2000 Term Forward: We the Court," 115 *Harvard Law Review* 4 (2001).

19. The Federalist No. 78, at 505–08 (Alexander Hamilton) (1788); Alexander M. Bickel, *The Least Dangerous Branch: The Supreme Court at the Bar of Politics* 15–16 (Indianapolis: Bobbs-Merrill Company, Inc., 1962); William E. Nelson, *Marbury v. Madison: The Origins and Legacy of Judicial Review* (Lawrence: University Press of Kansas, 2000).

20. 5 U.S. (1 Cranch) 137 (1803).

21. The Court declared that the refusal of the Jefferson administration to deliver formal commissions for appointment of justices of the peace made by the outgoing Adams administration was itself unconstitutional, but that contrary to a statutory authorization, the Supreme Court could not itself grant a remedy of mandate directing delivery.

22. *Marbury*, 5 U.S. at 170. See Barkow, supra note 1, at 239–40.

23. Louis Fisher, *Presidential War Power* 1 (Lawrence: University Press of Kansas, 1995) (quoting a passage from an encyclopedia).

24. See Griffin, supra note 12, at 248–55. It may be that, absent any congressional action, the President would have this power but that Congress may set limits on or forbid such responses.

25. For accounts of how the Framers broke ground that did not replicate precisely what existed or was previously conceived, see Henry P. Monaghan, "The Protective Power of the Presidency," 93 *Columbia Law Review* 1, 12–14 (1992); M. Elizabeth Magill, "The Real Separation in Separation of Powers Law," 86 *Virginia Law Review* 1127, 1162–67 (2000).

26. John F. Manning, "Separation of Powers as Ordinary Interpretation," 124 *Harvard Law Review* 1939, 2015–16 (2011). Manning himself is a formalist who refers to reader understanding, but one might think some language that reflected self-conscious compromises would have not been seen by readers as having clearly resolved certain matters that the adopters did intend to settle.

27. 542 U.S. 507 (2004).

28. Id. at 509 (plurality opinion of Justice O'Connor).

29. 343 U.S. 579 (1952). See especially the concurring opinion of Justice Jackson, id. at 635–38.

30. 132 S. Ct. 1421, 566 U.S. (2012).

31. Coleman v. Miller, 307 U.S. 433 (1939). Neither article V nor article VII actually explicitly provides this.

32. However, for a discussion of why the courts, not Congress, should consider whether an amendment has been ratified in a timely manner, see Stewart Dalzell & Eric J. Beste, "Is the Twenty-Seventh Amendment 200 Years Too Late?", 62 *George Washington Law Review* 501 (1994).

33. Barkow, supra note 1, at 242.

34. Id.

35. Luther v. Borden, 48 U.S. (7 How.) 1, 47 (1849) (concluding that interpretation rests with Congress). See also Pacific States Telephone & Telegraph Co. v. Oregon, 223 U.S. 118 (1912).

36. Colegrove v. Green, 328 U.S. 549, 552–56 (1946) (plurality opinion of Justice Frankfurter).

37. 369 U.S. 186 (1962).

38. Id. at 217.

39. Akhil Reed Amar, *America's Constitution: A Biography* 170–73 (New York: Random House, 2005).

40. See Stephen G. Calabresi, "The Political Question of Presidential Succession," 48 *Stanford Law Review* 155 (1995).

41. See The Presidential Succession Act of 1886, Act of Jan. 19, 1886, ch. 4, § 1, 24 Stat. 1 (repealed 1947).

42. 377 U.S. 533 (1964).

43. For a rich account of how judicially manageable standards can be conceived and how they may lead to a kind of over-enforcement as well as under-enforcement, see Fallon, supra note 9.

44. Powell v. McCormack, 395 U.S. 486 (1969).

45. Barkow, supra note 1, at 270–71, referring to cases including *New York v. United States*, 505 U.S. 144, 184–86 (1992), has raised the question whether the Court would adhere to its earlier Guarantee Clause avoidance.

46. Gilligan v. Morgan, 413 U.S. 1 (1973).

47. Nixon v. United States, 506 U.S. 224 (1993).

48. Bush v. Palm Beach Cnty. Canvassing Bd., 531 U.S. 70 (2000).

49. Barkow, supra note 1, at 273.

50. 132 S. Ct. 1421, 566 U.S. (2012).

51. Id. at 1427 (quoting Nixon v. United States, 506 U.S. 224, 228 (1993)).

52. After that court ruled that the statutory requirement violated the President's authority over recognition of foreign governments, the Supreme Court then granted certiorari and on November 3, 2014, heard arguments on the merits about the disputed powers. See Adam Liptak, N.Y. Times, Nov. 4, 2014, at A12, col. 5.

53. *Zivotofsky*, 132 S. Ct. at 1431–35 (concurring opinion of Justice Sotomayor).

54. However, one scholar has claimed that this would be a sensible conclusion. See Stephen G. Calabresi, "The Political Question of Presidential Succession," 48 *Stanford Law Review* 155 (1995).

55. Barkow, supra note 1, at 336.

56. The decision of June 8, 2015, was Zivotovsky v. Kerry, No. 13–628. For the political question discussion, see supra notes 50–52 and accompanying text.

57. Eric A. Posner & Adrian Vermeule, "Constitutional Showdowns," 156 *University of Pennsylvania Law Review* 991, 1016–17 (2008).

58. See Jack M. Beermann, "An Inductive Understanding of Separation of Powers," 63 *Administrative Law Review* 467, 470 (2011). However, *Free Enterprise Fund v. Public Company Accounting Oversight Board*, 561 U.S. 477 (2010), discussed below, does concern division of authority. In *Zivotofsky v. Clinton*, 132 S. Ct. 1421 (2012), in which the Court declared that the standards of decision were judicial and manageable and that the political question doctrine was inapplicable, the underlying issue, not yet resolved, also concerns that division.

59. [59] Manning, supra note 26, at 1971–93.

60. For a discussion of those values, see Powell, supra note 12, at 97–100, 109–10.

61. [61] Bruce Ackerman, *We the People, Vol. 1: Foundations* (Cambridge, Mass.: Belknap Press of Harvard University Press, 1991), and *Vol. 2: Transformations* (Cambridge, Mass.: Belknap Press of Harvard University Press, 1998).

62. I develop these views at some length in Greenawalt, "Dualism and Its Status," 104 *Ethics* 480 (1994). Professor Ackerman does contend that it is feasible to identify what count as the critical changes in the Constitution.

63. See Curtis A. Bradley & Trevor W. Morrison, "Historical Gloss and Separation of Powers," 126 *Harvard Law Review* 411, 426–28 (2012).

64. Magill, supra note 25.

65. Thomas W. Merrill, "The Constitutional Principle of Separation of Powers," 1991 *Supreme Court Review* 225.

66. Daryl J. Levinson & Richard H. Pildes, "Separation of Parties, Not Powers," 119 *Harvard Law Review* 2311 (2006).

67. See Bradley & Morrison, supra note 63.

68. See infra Section V.D ("Domestic Affairs").

69. See Peter L. Strauss, "The Place of Agencies in Government: Separation of Powers and the Fourth Branch," 84 *Columbia Law Review* 573, 582 (1984). For an overview of the first executive branch, see John Yoo, "George Washington and the Executive Power," 5 *University of St. Thomas Journal of Law and Public Policy* 1 (2010).

70. See U.S. Office of Personnel Management, Sizing Up the Executive Branch of the Federal Workforce: Fiscal Year 2013 (Apr. 2014), *available at* https://www.opm.gov/policy-data-oversight/data-analysis-documentation/federal-employment-reports/reports-publications/sizinguptheexecutivebranch.pdf.

71. Strauss, supra note 69, at 583.

72. See Panama Ref. Co. v. Ryan, 293 U.S. 388 (1935); A.L.A. Schechter Poultry Corp. v. United States, 295 U.S. 495 (1935).

73. 462 U.S. 919 (1983).

74. In practical terms, one might worry that single-house disapproval would impede government when the two houses are dominated by different political parties.

75. Regulations from the Executive in Need of Scrutiny Act (REINS Act), H.R. 367 (passed by the House Aug. 2, 2013). For the relationship of this bill to *Chadha*, see Jonathan H. Adler, "Placing 'Reins' on Regulation: Assessing the Proposed Reins Act," 16 *New York University Journal of Legislation and Public Policy* 1 (2013).

76. See Oona A. Hathaway, "Treaties' End: The Past, Present, and Future of International Lawmaking in the United States" 117 *Yale Law Journal* 1236, 1278–79 (2008).

77. Goldwater v. Carter, 444 U.S. 996 (1979) (vacating 617 F.2d 697 (D.C. Cir. 1979) and remanding to district court for dismissal of complaint). For competing views on this power, see David Gray Adler, *The Constitution and the Termination of Treaties* 149–206 (New York: Garland Publishing, Inc., 1986) (outlining a "checkered" historical evidence and concluding it does not support a unilateral authority), and Saikrishna B. Prakash & Michael D. Ramsey, "The Executive Power over Foreign Affairs," 111 *Yale Law Journal* 231 (2001) (President does have unilateral authority).

78. See Hathaway, supra note 76, at 1318–21 (arguing that if a treaty is self-executing, it is on equal footing with a federal statute, and the last-in-time rule will apply; but if it is not self-executing, to take effect, a treaty requires implementing legislation).

79. 252 U.S. 416 (1920).

80. Bond v. United States, 134 S. Ct. 2077, U.S. (2014).

81. One might hesitate to say that the Senate has relevantly "consented" to this if its approval of the agreements is by less than the two-thirds needed to accept a treaty.

82. Hathaway, supra note 76, at 1252–71.

83. See id. at 1298 (citing United States v. Belmont, 301 U.S. 324 (1937), and United States v. Pink, 351 U.S. 203 (1942), as evidence of "the Court's stamp of authority to the use of executive and congressional-executive agreements far from the trade arena").

84. Restatement (Third) of Foreign Relations Law of the United States § 303 cmt. e (1987) refers to "the prevailing view" of congressional-executive agreements as "an alternative to the treaty method in every instance." See also Louis Henkin, *Foreign Affairs and the United States Constitution* 217 (2d ed. New York: Oxford University Press, 1997). Bruce Ackerman & David Golove, "Is NAFTA Constitutional?," 108 *Harvard Law Review* 799, 805–07 (1995), support full interchangeability, employing Ackerman's theory that the Constitution has been amended by a non-formal democratic process. This view is rejected by Laurence H. Tribe, "Taking Text and Structure Seriously: Reflections on Free-Form Method in Constitutional Interpretation," 108 *Harvard Law Review* 1221, 1223–28 (1995). Oona Hathaway, supra note 76, at 1307–38, has suggested that historical practice does not support full interchangeability, but that given the absence of a principled division, a move in that direction would be desirable.

85. S. Exec. Rep. No. 102-22, at 81 (1991); Bradley & Morrison, supra note 63, at 474–75.

86. Bradley & Morrison, id., describe instances in which Presidents Clinton and George W. Bush were responsive to such views among Senators.

87. 299 U.S. 304 (1936).

88. 453 U.S. 654 (1981).

89. Based substantially on what he sees as the limited domain of treaties, which should not encroach on Congress's legislative authority, John C. Yoo, in "Laws as Treaties?: The Constitutionality of Congressional-Executive Agreements," 99 *Michigan Law Review* 757 (2001), has proposed a somewhat similar division, but one that would more sharply constrain the domains of Congress and executive agreements, as well as treaties.

90. 552 U.S. 491 (2008).

91. See Fisher, supra note 23; Jane E. Stromseth, Book Review, "Understanding Constitutional War Powers Today: Why Methodology Matters," 106 *Yale Law Journal* 845 (1996).

92. The Persian Gulf Crisis is an example of Congress not accepting the President's declaration in respect to war. See Jane E. Stromseth, "Rethinking War Powers: Congress, the President, and the United Nations," 81 *Georgetown Law Journal* 597, 673 (1993).

93. War Powers Resolution of 1973, 50 U.S.C. §§ 1541–1548.

94. Memorandum Opinion from Caroline D. Krass, Principal Deputy Assistant Attorney General, Office of Legal Counsel, to the Attorney General, Authority to Use Military Force in Libya (2011).

95. For a transcript of Obama's speech on August 31, 2013, in which he stated just that, see White House, Office of the Press Secretary, News Release, *Statement by the President on Syria*, Aug. 31, 2013, *available at* http://www.whitehouse.gov/the-press-office/2013/08/31/statement-president-syria.

96. Korematsu v. United States, 324 U.S. 885 (1945).

97. 542 U.S. 507, 519 (2004), relying on Pub. L. 107–40 § 2(a), 115 Stat. 234 (2001).

98. Youngstown Sheet & Tube Co. v. Sawyer, 343 U.S. 579, 610–11 (1952) (Frankfurter, J., concurring) and 635–38 (Jackson, J., concurring).

99. H. Jefferson Powell, "Slow Reading and Living Speech: James Boyd White on What a Constitutional Law Opinion Is For," in *Living in a Law Transformed: Encounters with the Works of James Boyd White*, eds. Julen Etxabe & Gary Watts (Ann Arbor, Mich.: Michigan Publishing, 2014).

100. *Youngstown*, 343 U.S. at 634.

101. Id.

102. 548 U.S. 557, 620–25 (2006).

103. David J. Barron & Martin S. Lederman, "The Commander in Chief at the Lowest Ebb—Framing the Problem, Doctrine, and Original Understanding," 121 *Harvard Law Review* 689 (2008); David J. Barron & Martin S. Lederman, "The Commander in Chief at the Lowest Ebb—A Constitutional History," 121 *Harvard Law Review* 941 (2008).

104. See Bas v. Tingy, 4 U.S. (4 Dall.) 37 (1800); Talbot v. Seeman, 5 U.S. (1 Cranch) 1 (1801); Little v. Barreme, 6 U.S. (2 Cranch) 170 (1804).

105. Pub. L. 107-40 § 2(a), 115 Stat. 224 (2001). On the issue of congressional non-involvement in the efforts against ISIS, see, e.g., Ackerman, supra note 11, and Editorial, "Legal Authority for Fighting ISIS," N.Y. Times, Sept. 12, 2014, at A 30, col. 1.

106. This issue is explored in much greater depth in a forthcoming book by Jefferson Powell, which will be entitled *The Limits of War and Law: Targeted Killing as a Constitutional Problem*.

107. See critique by Powell, id. (forthcoming).

108. Bradley & Morrison, supra note 8.

109. Such coherence was not present on many important issues when the Democratic Party dominated in all southern states; its representatives did not share views about civil rights held by Democrats from other states.

110. See Levinson & Pildes, supra note 66.

111. Bradley & Morrison, supra note 8.

112. Of course, such action might be restrained by the need for finances approved by Congress to carry out the conflict. For an account of how Congress might more effectively exercise its powers in various "soft" as well as "hard" ways, see Josh Chafetz, "Congress's Constitution," 160 *University of Pennsylvania Law Review* 715 (2012).

113. A different way to deal with the political party problem includes creating formal opposition rights and setting up voting rules that are open to changing viewpoints. See Levinson & Pildes, supra note 66, at 2368–84.

114. Panama Ref. Co. v. Ryan, 293 U.S. 388 (1935); A.L.A. Schechter Poultry Corp. v. United States, 295 U.S. 495 (1935).

115. See, e.g., Eric A. Posner & Adrian Vermeule, "Interring the Nondelegation Doctrine," 69 *University of Chicago Law Review* 1721, 1722–23 (2002).

116. Commodity Futures Trading Comm'n v. Schor, 478 U.S. 833 (1986); on the status of the Chief Judge of the Tax Court, see Freytag v. Comm'r, 501 U.S. 868 (1991).

117. Chevron, U.S.A., Inc. v. Natural Res. Def. Council, Inc., 467 U.S. 837 (1984). Judicial deference to agency statutory interpretations is discussed at length in Kent Greenawalt, *Statutory and Common Law Interpretation* Chapter 6 (New York: Oxford University Press, 2013).

118. FDA v. Brown & Williamson Tobacco Corp., 529 U.S. 120 (2000).

119. The power was substantially supported by the "Decision of 1789," in which Congress debated the President's power to remove the Secretary of Foreign Affairs. See Congressional Register (June 17, 1789), *reprinted in* "Debates in the House of Representatives, First Session, June–September 1789," *in* 11 *The Documentary History of the First Federal Congress of the United States of America, March 4, 1789–March 3, 1791*, eds. Charlene Bangs Bickford et al. (Baltimore: John Hopkins University Press, 1992).

120. 272 U.S. 52 (1926).

121. 295 U.S. 602, 623 (1935).

122. Morrison v. Olson, 487 U.S. 654, 691 (1988). Peter L. Strauss has described a functional approach in Strauss, supra note 69.

123. 130 S. Ct.. 3138 (2010).

124. Id. at 3153–55.

125. Peter L. Strauss, "On the Difficulties of Generalization—PCAOB in the Footsteps of *Myers, Humphrey's Executor, Morrison*, and *Freytag*," 32 *Cardozo Law Review* 2255, 2276 (2011). One wonders if the Court's logic should also reach all civil servants who cannot be dismissed at will, even though they can be removed from particular duties. The opinion of Chief Justice Roberts distinguishes them as not "officers" under Article II, and leaves open the decision's relevance for them. 130 S. Ct. at 3160.

126. Strauss, supra note 125, at 2274–75.

127. The difficulty of the needed assessments has led Aziz Huq to suggest that removal should be taken as a political question. Azia Z. Huq, "Removal as a Political Question," 65 *Stanford Law Review* 1 (2013).

128. See Ronald J. Krotoszynski, Jr., "Cooperative Federalism, the New Formalism, and the Separation of Powers Revisited: *Free Enterprise Fund* and the Problem of Presidential Oversight of State-Government Officers Enforcing Federal Law," 61 *Duke Law Journal* 1599 (2012).

129. 501 U.S. 252 (1991).

130. 424 U.S. 1 (1976).

131. 478 U.S. 714 (1986).

132. 462 U.S. 919 (1983).

133. Clinton v. City of New York, 524 U.S. 417 (1998).

134. See generally Magill, supra note 25.

135. 134 S. Ct. 2550, 573 U.S. (2014).

136. U.S. Const. art. II, § 2, cl. 3. For an account of legal issues involving the Clause and their history, see Vivian S. Chu, Cong. Research Serv., RL33009, Recess Appointments: A Legal Overview (2012), *available at* http://works.bepress.com/cgi/viewcontent.cgi?article=1320&context=seth_barrett_tillman.

137. 134 S. Ct., at 2560–62.

138. Id. at 2567.

139. Id. at 2564–66.

140. Id. at 2567–73.

141. Id. at 2563.

142. Id. at 2592.

143. Id. at 2617.

144. Id. at 2605–06.

145. Id. at 2606–07.

146. S. Res. 15, 113th Cong. (2013–2014), S. Res. 16, 113th Cong. (2013–2014).

Chapter 8

1. U.S. Const. art. IV, § 2(1).
2. Id., art. VI, § 2.
3. By 1800, the federal government employed around 3,000 employees in six departments: State, Treasury, War, the Post Office, the Navy, and the Office of the Attorney General. Congressional Budget Office, "The Federal Work Force: Its Size, Cost and Activities" (Mar. 1977). In 2012, the executive branch alone employed over 2.1 million employees, excluding the Postal Service. U.S. Office of Personnel Management, "Historical Federal Workforce Tables: Executive Branch Civilian Employment Since 1940" (last accessed June 22, 2014). Including personnel of the Postal Service, uniformed military, and the judicial and legislative branches, the federal government had over 4.3 million employees in 2012. U.S. Office of Personnel Management, "Historical Federal Workforce Tables: Total Government Employment Since 1962" (last accessed June 22, 2014).
4. See Heather K. Gerken, "Our Federalism(s)," 53 *William and Mary Law Review* 1549, 1553–54 (2012).
5. Id. at 1556–58.
6. Jessica Bulman-Pozen & Heather K. Gerken, "Uncooperative Federalism," 118 *Yale Law Journal* 1256 (2009).
7. U.S. Const. art. I, § 8(3).
8. Id. § 8(1).
9. Id.
10. 132 S. Ct. 2566, 567 U.S. (2012).
11. 22 U.S. (9 Wheat.) 1 (1824).
12. As Chief Justice Marshall pointed out, "the power of Congress . . . must be exercised within the territorial jurisdiction of the several States." Id. at 196.
13. Houston, East & West Tex. Ry. Co. v. United States, 234 U.S. 342 (1914).
14. 156 U.S. 1 (1895).
15. Id. at 33 (dissent of Justice Harlan).
16. 247 U.S. 251 (1918).
17. Id. at 273. Joined by three other Justices, Justice Holmes dissented on the ground that Congress may prohibit shipping across state lines goods produced in a manner it regards as evil and contrary to national welfare. Id. at 280 (Holmes, J., dissenting). The decision in the *Hammer* case was in serious tension with another decided fifteen years earlier that sustained a prohibition on the interstate transportation of foreign lottery tickets. Champion v. Ames, 188 U.S. 321 (1903).
18. A.L.A. Schecter Poultry Corp. v. United States, 295 U.S. 495 (1935).
19. Carter v. Carter Coal Co., 298 U.S. 238 (1936). Justice Cardozo concurred in the poultry case, rejecting "a view of causation that would obliterate the distinction between" national and local commerce and remarking that "the law is not indifferent to matters of degree." 295 U.S. at 554. In the coal case, he dissented, referring again to "considerations of degree," rather than accepting any crucial distinction between direct and indirect effects. 298 U.S. at 327–28.
20. Id. at 308.
21. 301 U.S. 1 (1937).
22. Id. at 36–37.
23. 312 U.S. 100 (1941).
24. 317 U.S. 111 (1942).

25. Heart of Atlanta Motel, Inc. v. United States, 379 U.S. 241, 246 (1964).
26. Katzenbach v. McClung, 379 U.S. 294 (1964).
27. U.S. Const. art. I, § 2(3), 9(4).
28. Id., amend. XVI (1913).
29. 249 U.S. 86 (1919).
30. Id. at 90, 93.
31. 259 U.S. 20 (1922).
32. Id. at 38.
33. United States v. Kahriger, 345 U.S. 22 (1953).
34. 297 U.S. 1 (1936).
35. Id. at 65. This view contrasted with that of James Madison.
36. It did so by imposing a loss of benefits so severe that it rendered the farmers' choice not voluntary and by requiring farmers to undertake a contractual obligation if they were to receive the federal grants.
37. Charles C. Steward Mach. Co. v. Davis, 301 U.S. 548, 586 (1937).
38. Id. at 590.
39. Perez v. United States, 402 U.S. 146 (1971).
40. 514 U.S. 549 (1995).
41. Id. at 619–20 (Breyer, J., dissenting).
42. Id. at 559.
43. Id. at 584–85 (Thomas, J., concurring).
44. Id. at 574–77, 583 (Kennedy, J. concurring).
45. 529 U.S. 598 (2000).
46. Robert D. Cooter & Neil S. Siegel, "Collective Action Federalism: A General Theory of Article I, Section 8," 63 *Stanford Law Review* 115 (2010). See also Donald H. Regan, "How to Think About the Federal Commerce Power and Incidentally Rewrite United States v. Lopez," 94 *Michigan Law Review* 554 (1995).
47. 17 U.S. (4 Wheat.) 316 (1819).
48. 426 U.S. 833, 851 (1976).
49. 469 U.S. 528 (1985).
50. Id. at 548.
51. 501 U.S. 452 (1991).
52. Id. at 460.
53. Justice White, concurring in part. Id. at 482.
54. Justice Blackmun, dissenting. Id. at 486.
55. In this respect, professors with tenure are in a somewhat similar situation. There must be a serious defect in performance and a less than simple process in order to dismiss them.
56. 505 U.S. 144 (1992).
57. 521 U.S. 898 (1997).
58. See generally Vicki C. Jackson, "Federalism and the Uses and Limits of Law: Printz and Principle?," 111 *Harvard Law Review* 2180 (1998).
59. Jessica Bulman-Pozen, "Partisan Federalism," 127 *Harvard Law Review* 1077 (2014).
60. The Federalist Papers No. 51 (James Madison).
61. John Manning, "Federalism and the Generality Problem in Constitutional Interpretation," 122 *Harvard Law Review* 2003, 2031, 2058 (2009).
62. For a critique of Manning's approach, see Gillian E. Metzger, "The Constitutional Legitimacy of Freestanding Federalism," 122 *Harvard Law Review Forum* 98 (2009).

63. Michael S. Greve, *The Upside-Down Constitution* (Cambridge, Mass.: Harvard University Press, 2012).

64. U.S. Const. art. I, § 10(3).

65. Greve, supra note 63, at 69

66. Ilya Somin, "Turning Federalism Right-Side Up," Review of *The Upside-Down Constitution* by Michael Greve, 28 *Constitutional Commentary* 303, 307 (2012).

67. Bulman-Pozen & Gerken, note 5 supra, at 1265–70.

68. Id. at 1274–76.

69. Id. at 1276–78.

70. Id. at 1278–86. On the general subject of state involvement in national security law and policy, see Matthew C. Waxman, "National Security Federalism in the Age of Terror," 64 *Stanford Law Review* 289 (2012).

71. Bulman-Pozen & Gerken, note 5 supra, at 1295–1302.

72. Id. at 1302–07. See also Roderick M. Hills, Jr., "Against Preemption: How Federalism Can Improve the National Legislature Process," 82 *New York University Law Review* I (2007).

73. See generally Julian N. Eule, "Laying the Dormant Commerce Clause to Rest," 91 *Yale Law Journal* 425 (1982).

74. Herbert Wechsler, *Principles, Politics and Fundamental Law* 49–82 (Cambridge, Mass.: Harvard University Press, 1961).

75. U.S. Const. amend. XVII (1913).

76. For a more recent emphasis on the need to rely on the political branches, see Larry Kramer, "Putting the Politics Back into the Political Safeguards of Federalism," 100 *Columbia Law Review* 215 (2000).

77. See generally John O. McGinnis & Ilya Somin, "Federalism v. State's Rights: A Defense of Judicial Review in a Federal System," 99 *Northwestern Law Review* 89 (2004).

78. One persuasive account of the nuanced role courts might best take is provided by Vicki C. Jackson, supra note 58, 2223–59.

79. Gillian E. Metzger, "Embracing Administrative Common Law," 80 *George Washington Law Review* 1293 (2012).

80. 132 S. Ct. 2566, 567 U.S. (2012).

81. 42 U.S.C. § 18091(2)(F).

82. 132 S. Ct. at 2604 (opinion of Roberts, C.J.).

83. 26 U.S.C. §7421(a)

84. 132 S. Ct. at 2586 (opinion of Roberts, C.J.).

85. Id. at 2587.

86. Id. at 2588–89.

87. Id. at 2593.

88. 17 U.S. 316, 411 (1819).

89. Andrew Koppelman, "'Necessary,' 'Proper,' and Health Care Reform," *The Health Care Case: The Supreme Court's Decision and Its Implications*, eds. Nathaniel Persily, Gillian Metzger & Trevor W. Manson (New York: Oxford University Press, 2013), 105, 115, challenges that part of the Roberts opinion and the "even murkier" joint dissent. Ilya Somin, "The Individual Mandate and the Proper Meaning of 'Proper,'" id. at 148, relying partly on original meaning, concludes to the contrary that an unlimited power to impose a mandate would be improper. For a critique of the Supreme Court's recent reliance on the Necessary and Proper Clause to curtail the scope of federal laws as unhelpful because

it fails to set adequately clear standards, see Alison L. La Croix, "The Shadow Powers of Article I," 123 *Yale Law Journal* 2044 (2014).

90. 132 S. Ct. at 2643 (Scalia, Kennedy, Thomas, Alito, JJ., dissenting).

91. Robert N. Weiner, "Much Ado: The Potential Impact of the Supreme Court Decision Upholding the Affordable Care Act," supra note 89, at 73–74, says it does not count as a holding, although the opinion of the Chief Justice assumes the contrary, 132 S. Ct. at 2593 (opinion of Roberts, C.J.).

92. See Kent Greenawalt, *Statutory and Common Law Interpretation* 185–87, 193–215 (New York: Oxford University Press, 2013).

93. 132 S. Ct. at 2609 (Ginsburg, J., concurring in part and dissenting in part).

94. Id. at 2612.

95. Id. at 2614.

96. Id. at 2615–18.

97. Id. at 2617–20.

98. Id. at 2618.

99. Abbe R. Gluck, "Federalism from Federal Statutes: Health Reform, Medicaid, and the Old-Fashioned Federalists' Gamble," *in The Health Care Case,* supra note 89, at 276.

100. 132 S. Ct. at 2650–55 (Scalia, Kennedy, Thomas, Alito, JJ., dissenting).

101. Id. at 2594 (opinion of Roberts, C.J.).

102. 259 U.S. 20 (1922).

103. 132 S. Ct.. at 2595–96 (majority opinion).

104. Id. at 2597.

105. Id. at 2599–600.

106. See Gillian E. Metzger & Trevor W. Morrison, "The Presumption of Constitutionality and the Individual Mandate," *in The Health Care Case,* supra note 89, at 124–41.

107. 501 U.S. 452 (1991).

108. See Metzger & Morrison, supra note 106, at 140–141.

109. 132 S. Ct. at 2582–84. See also Charles Fried, "The June Surprises: Balls, Strikes, and the Fog of War," *in The Health Care Case,* supra note 89, at 58, calling the distinction the Chief Justice drew "an act of interpretive jujitsu."

110. Adrian Vermule, "Saving Constructions," 15 *Georgetown Law Journal* 1945, 1949 (1996–1997) (citing Blodgett v. Holden, 275 U.S. 142, 148 (1927) (Holmes, J., concurring)).

111. For a view that this is how the Chief Justice should have proceeded, see Neil S. Siegel, "More Law Than Politics: The Chief, the 'Mandate,' Legality, and Statesmanship," *in The Health Care Case,* supra note 89, 199–200.

112. For a view that he should not have resolved the Commerce Clause question, see Gregory P. Magarian, "Chief Justice Roberts's Individual Mandate: The Lawless Medicine of NFIB v. Sebelius," 108 *Northwestern University Law Review Colloquy* 15 (2013).

113. See 132 S. Ct. at 2601 (opinion of Roberts, C.J.).

114. Id. at 2602 (citing 301 U.S. 548, 590 (1937)).

115. Id. at 2605.

116. Id. at 2605–06. That the Social Security Act with the original Medicaid provisions included a right to "alter, amend, or repeal," provisions did not, in Robert's view, include such a radical shift in coverage.

117. Id. at 2664 (Scalia, Kennedy, Thomas, Alito, JJ., dissenting).

118. Id. at 2662. As I have noted, these four Justices concluded that this coercive aspect was so closely related to the rest of the proposal to expand Medicaid that the whole program should have been held invalid.

119. Id. at 2629–41 (Ginsburg, J., concurring in part and dissenting in part).

120. Id. at 2641.

121. See Mitchell N. Berman, "Coercion, Compulsion, and the Medicaid Expansion: A Study in the Doctrine of Unconstitutional Conditions," 91 *Texas Law Review* 1283 (2013). See also Mitchell N. Berman, "Coercion Without Baselines: Unconstitutional Conditions in Three Dimensions," 90 *Georgetown Law Journal* 1 (2001).

122. 483 U.S. 203 (1987).

123. Id. at 211. Chief Justice Rehnquist's opinion for the Court did enumerate the following conditions on the spending power: (1) its exercise "must be in pursuit of 'the general welfare,'" and on this, courts should give Congress substantial deference; (2) "if Congress desires to condition the States' receipt of federal funds, it 'must do so unambiguously;'" (3) imposed conditions might be illegal if unrelated to national projects; and (4) conditions may be invalid if at odds with other constitutional provisions. Id. at 207–08.

124. Id. at 212 (O'Connor, J., dissenting).

125. This would distinguish plea bargaining on the basis that conferral of the benefit of a lighter sentence is related to what the accused forgoes.

126. Berman, "Coercion, Compulsion, and the Medicaid Expansion" supra note 121, at 1291–92.

127. Id. at 1302.

128. Id. at 1337.

129. Id. at 1344.

130. One might believe that the degree of judicial scrutiny should depend substantially on whether the form of possible discrimination is itself subject to strict scrutiny. Evan Tsen Lee, "The Trouble with *City of Boerne,* and Why It Matters for the Fifteenth Amendment as Well," 90 *Denver University Law Review* 483 (2012), argues that a court should be much more accepting of actions by Congress that respond to a strict scrutiny kind of discrimination.

Chapter 9

1. See, e.g., Duncan v. Louisiana, 391 U.S. 145 (1968); McDonald v. City of Chicago, 130 S. Ct. 3020, 561 U.S. (2010).

2. See, e.g., Twining v. New Jersey, 211 U.S. 78 (1908) (self-incrimination); Palko v. Connecticut, 302 U.S. 319 (1937) (double jeopardy).

3. See, e.g., Brown v. Mississippi, 297 U.S. 278 (1936); Rochin v. California, 342 U.S. 165 (1982).

4. Urging its incorporation, see Justice Black's dissent in *Adamson v. California*, 332 U.S. 46, 71–72 (1947). The language limiting to "citizens" may support the claim that it was really designed to make effective the clause with similar language in the original Constitution. Id.

5. Slaughter-House Cases, 83 U.S. (1 Wall.) 36 (1873).

6. See, e.g., John Harrison, "Reconstructing the Privileges or Immunities Clause," 101 *Yale Law Journal* 1385, 1418 (1992) (limited coverage); Michael Kent Curtis, *No State Shall Abridge: The Fourteenth Amendment and the Bill of Rights* 100 (Durham, N.C.: Duke University Press, 1986) (incorporates first

eight amendments); Akhil R. Amar, "The Bill of Rights and the Fourteenth Amendment," 101 *Yale Law Journal* 1193, 1194 (1992) (proposing a model of "refined incorporation" and describing the flaws in the three main approaches that the Fourteenth Amendment resulted in: (1) no incorporation, (2) total incorporation, or (3) selective incorporation of the Bill of Rights).

7. See Randy E. Barnett, "Whence Comes Section One? The Abolitionist Origins of the Fourteenth Amendment," 3 *Journal of Legal Analysis* 165 (2011).

8. See supra note 4.

9. See Barnett, supra note 7.

10. Jamal Greene, "Fourteenth Amendment Originalism," 71 *Maryland Law Review* 978 (2012).

11. See Akhil R. Amar, "The Bill of Rights and the Fourteenth Amendment," 101 *Yale Law Journal* 1193 (1992); Akhil Reed Amar, "Intratextualism," 112 *Harvard Law Review* 747, 827 (1999).

12. Ryan C. Williams, "The One and Only Substantive Due Process Clause," 120 *Yale Law Journal* 408, 500–09 (2010). Williams surveys various ways the Fifth and Fourteenth Amendment clauses could be seen as related to each other and examines arguments for competing alternatives.

13. 521 U.S. 507 (1997).

14. That assumption leaves open whether on issues not yet settled, the Court should give more deference to decisions by the national government.

15. See George Anastaplo, *The Constitutionalist: Notes on the First Amendment* 290 (Lanham, Md.: Rowman & Littlefield, 2005).

16. Geoffrey R. Stone, "Free Speech in the Twenty-First Century: Ten Lessons from the Twentieth Century," 36 *Pepperdine Law Review* 273, 274 (2009).

17. Frederick Schauer, "Towards an Institutional First Amendment," 89 *Minnesota Law Review* 1256, 1278 (2005).

18. Susan H. Williams, "Content Discrimination and the First Amendment," 139 *University of Pennsylvania Law Review* 615, 616 (1991). Joshua Davis and Joshua Rosenberg note these various comments as an introduction to their effort to provide a more systematic approach. See Joshua P. Davis & Joshua D. Rosenberg, "The Inherent Structure of Free Speech Law," 19 *William and Mary Bill of Rights Journal* 131, 131–34 (2010).

19. Akhil Reed Amar, *America's Unwritten Constitution* 32–38 (New York: Basic Books, 2012), suggests that the original Constitution implicitly barred the states from interfering with free expression, but that is a doubtful inference.

20. Fred Seaton Siebert, *Freedom of the Press in England, 1476–1776: The Rise and Decline of Government Controls* (Champaign, Ill.: University of Illinois Press, 1965). See also Jason McElligott, *Royalism, Print and Censorship in Revolutionary England* 183–85 (2007).

21. William Blackstone, *Commentaries on the Laws of England* 151–52 (4th ed. 1769).

22. Hugo Black, *A Constitutional Faith* 43–63 (New York: Alfred A. Knopf, 1968). The only plausible basis for this absolute reading is that needed interferences with speech were left to the states. But on that view, it would be hard to treat the Fourteenth Amendment as providing a similar restriction on the states.

23. Compare Zechariah Chafee, *Free Speech in the United States* 3–35, 497–516 (Cambridge, Mass.: Harvard University Press, 1942), with Leonard Levy, *Legacy of Suppression: Freedom of Speech and Press in Early American*

History (Cambridge, Mass.: Belknap Press of Harvard University Press, 1960). In his substantially revised and enlarged account, *The Emergence of a Free Press* (New York: Oxford University Press, 1985), Leonard Levy softens some of the judgments of his original book, but he remains convinced that the Framers did not mean to abolish the crime of seditious libel.

David Rabban has suggested that the Framers might have wished to provide significant protection for political expression without entirely eliminating the law of seditious libel. David Rabban, "The Ahistorical Historian: Leonard Levy on Freedom of Expression in Early American History," 37 *Stanford Law Review* 795, 800 (1985).

H. Jefferson Powell, *A Community Built on Words* 63–65 (Chicago: University of Chicago Press, 2002), has summarized a correspondence between William Cushing and John Adams that indicates that, given the basic value of free expression, truth should be a defense to seditious libel despite English law to the contrary. See Chapter 3, text accompanying notes 43 and 44.

24. J.F. Stephan, *A History of the Criminal Law of England* 353 (London: Macmillan and Co., 1883). See generally Philip Hamburger, "The Development of the Law of Seditious Libel and the Control of the Press," 37 *Stanford Law Review* 661 (1985).

25. See 17 Thomas B. Howell, *The Trial of Mr. John Peter Zenger, in* A Complete Collection of State Trials 675 (London: T.C. Hansard, 1735).

26. See an act in addition to the 1798 "Sedition Act," entitled "An Act for the Punishment of Certain Crimes against the United States," ch. 74, § 2, 1 Stat. 596 (1798). Leonard Levy, in The Emergence of a Free Press, supra note 23, at xi, writes that in comparison with prevailing English law the act was "truly libertarian" in adopting the approach of *Zenger.* The act was broader in its coverage than the Sedition Act of 1718.

27. Geoffrey R. Stone et al., *Constitutional Law* 1031 (7th ed. New York: Aspen Publishers, 2013). See also William W. Van Alstyne, *A Critical Guide to Marbury v. Madison, in* Kermit L. Hall ed., *Judicial Review and Judicial Power in the Supreme Court* 367 (New York and London: Garland Publishing, 2000).

28. New York Times Co. v. Sullivan, 376 U.S. 254, 276 (1964).

29. See Geoffrey R. Stone, *Perilous Times: Free Speech in Wartime from the Sedition Act of 1798 to the War on Terrorism* 79–134 (New York: W.W. Norton & Co., 2004); Michael Curtis, *Free Speech, "The People's Darling Privilege"* (New York: Duke University Press, 2000); David M. Rabban, *Free Speech in Its Forgotten Years* (New York: Cambridge University Press, 1997).

30. Patterson v. Colorado, 205 U.S. 454 (1907). Levy has indicated in *The Emergence of a Free Press,* supra note 23, at xi, that freedom of the press was perceived more broadly than this.

31. Espionage Act of 1917, ch. 30, tit. I, § 3, 40 Stat. 217 (1917).

32. Sedition Act of 1918, ch. 75, 40 Stat. 553, repealed by Act of Mar. 3, 1921, ch. 136, 41 Stat. 1359.

33. 249 U.S. 47 (1919).

34. See Thomas Healy, *The Great Dissent* 100–01 (New York: Metropolitan Books, 2013).

35. 249 U.S. at 52.

36. Id. at 51.

37. Frohwerk v. United States, 249 U.S. 204, 208 (1919).

38. Debs v. United States, 249 U.S. 211, 214 (1919).

39. See Healy, supra note 34.
40. Gitlow v. New York, 268 U.S. 652 (1925).
41. Healy, supra note 34, at 53–54.
42. Stewart Jay, "The Creation of the First Amendment Right to Free Expression: From the Eighteenth Century to the Mid-Twentieth Century," 34 *William Mitchell Law Review* 773, 877–91 (2008). Jay notes that between World War I and the Cold War, although the Espionage Act was still in effect, the Supreme Court upheld free expression claims in a variety of circumstances and only reviewed one conviction, in which the Court abandoned its earlier World War I era approach and set the defendant free. See Hartzel v. United States, 322 U.S. 680 (1944). Jay also notes that there were only a few prosecutions during World War II. Id. at 930. See also Robert J. Goldstein, *Political Repression in Modern America from 1870 to Present* 147 (Urbana and Chicago: University of Illinois Press, 1978). Geoffrey R. Stone, *Perilous Times: Free Speech in Wartime from the Sedition Act of 1798 to the War on Terrorism* (New York: W.W. Norton & Company, 2004). Neil S. Siegel, "A Prescription for Perilous Times Review of Perilous Times: Free Speech in Wartime from the Sedition Act of 1798 to the War on Terrorism, by Geoffrey R. Stone," 93 *Georgetown Law Journal* 1645, 1647 (2005).
43. Much fuller accounts of my views about this are in Kent Greenawalt, "Free Speech Justifications," 89 *Columbia Law Review* 119 (1989), and *Speech, Crime, and the Uses of Language* 9–39 (New York: Oxford University Press, 1989).
44. John Stuart Mill, *On Liberty*, ed. Elizabeth Rapaport (Indianapolis: Hackett Publishing Co., 1978).
45. Abrams v. United States, 250 U.S. 616 (1919) (Holmes, J., dissenting); Whitney v. California, 274 U.S. 357 (1927) (Brandeis, J., concurring). See also Vincent Blasi, "The First Amendment and the Ideal of Civic Courage: The Brandeis Opinion in *Whitney v. California*," 29 *William and Mary Law Review* 653 (1988).
46. Stanley Ingber, "The Marketplace of Ideas: A Legitimizing Myth," 1984 *Duke Law Journal* 1, 25 (1984).
47. See Vincent Blasi, "The Checking Value in First Amendment Theory," 2 *American Bar Foundation Research Journal* 921 (1977).
48. Vincent Blasi, "Free Speech and Good Character," 46 *University of California in Los Angeles Law Review* 1567, 1571 (1999).
49. Lee Bollinger, *The Tolerant Society* (New York: Oxford University Press, 1986).
50. See Alexander Meiklejohn, *Political Freedom: The Constitutional Powers of the People* (New York: Harper & Brothers, 1960); Robert Bork, "Neutral Principles and Some First Amendment Problems," 47 *Indiana Law Journal* 1 (1971). Bork's fairly narrow views about the range of constitutional protections were one reason his appointment to the Supreme Court was not confirmed (though his views about free speech were not the primary difficulty).
51. The restriction is particularly hard to defend given the protection of religious expression by the Free Exercise Clause.
52. Robert Post, "Reconciling Theory and Doctrine in First Amendment Jurisprudence," 88 *California Law Review* 2353 (2000).
53. Id. at 2367–71.

54. The suggestion that the lack of a distinctive value for freedom of speech is troubling has been made by Martin Redish, "The Value of Free Speech," 130 *University of Pennsylvania Law Review* 591 (1982). See also Frederick Schauer, "Free Speech and the Good Life," *in Free Speech: A Philosophical Enquiry* (Cambridge: Cambridge University Press, 1982). For a more extensive discussion in response to this concern, see Kent Greenawalt, *Speech, Crime, and the Uses of Language*, supra note 43.

55. Thomas Scanlon, "A Theory of Freedom of Expression," 1 *Philosophy and Public Affairs* 204, 206 (1972).

56. See Davis & Rosenberg, supra note 18, at 148–49, mentioning that burglary is a possible communication.

57. In *Speech, Crime, and the Uses of Language*, supra note 43, at 57–59, I explain why the term "situation-altering utterances" is preferable here to "performative utterances" discussed by J.L. Austin, *How to Do Things with Words*, 2nd ed., pp. 5–14 (Oxford: Oxford University Press, 1976). For an article that is critical of the force of my categorization, see Eugene Volokh, "Speech as Conduct: Generally Applicable Laws, Illegal Courses of Conduct, 'Situation-Altering Utterances,' and the Uncharted Zones," 90 *Cornell Law Review* 1277 (2005).

58. See text accompanying notes 33–35 supra.

59. 250 U.S. 616, 624–30 (1919) (Holmes, J., dissenting).

60. Id. at 627.

61. Post, supra note 52, at 2358–60.

62. Healy, supra note 34.

63. See supra note 40 and accompanying text.

64. 274 U.S. 357, 372 (1927).

65. Id. at 377.

66. I discuss the various possibilities and the language of relevant opinions in "'Clear and Present Danger' and Criminal Speech," *in Eternally Vigilant*, eds. Lee C. Bollinger & Geoffrey R. Stone (Chicago: University of Chicago Press, 2002), 97–119.

67. 274 U.S. at 376.

68. 301 U.S. 242 (1937).

69. 322 U.S. 680 (1944).

70. 310 U.S. 296 (1940).

71. 314 U.S. 252 (1941).

72. Id. at 263, 270, n.15.

73. 341 U.S. 494 (1951).

74. Id. at 510.

75. 367 U.S. 203 (1961).

76. 367 U.S. 290 (1965).

77. 395 U.S. 444 (1969).

78. Id. at 447.

79. Daniel A. Farber, "The Categorical Approach to Protecting Speech in American Constitutional Law," 84 *Indiana Law Journal* 917, 921 (2009), considers *Brandenberg* a "highly successful" categorical approach that protects speech and has "dried up" prosecutions for subversive speech.

80. 414 U.S. 105 (1973).

81. 458 U.S. 886 (1982).

82. United States v. Spock, 416 F.2d 165 (1st Cir. 1969).

83. 130 S. Ct. 2705, 561 U.S. (2010).

84. The dissenters in *Holder* rightly called for a stringent form of review in these circumstances. Id. at 2739. See generally David Cole, "The First Amendment's Borders: The Place of *Holder v. Humanitarian Law Project* in First Amendment Doctrine," 6 *Harvard Journal of Law and Policy Review* 147 (2012).

85. Pickering v. Bd. of Educ., 391 U.S. 563 (1968).

86. Garcetti v. Ceballos, 547 U.S. 410 (2006).

87. Elfbrandt v. Russell, 384 U.S. 11 (1966).

88. Barenblatt v. United States, 360 U.S. 109 (1959) (involving Communist Party membership). However, in *Gibson v. Florida Legislative Investigation Committee*, 372 U.S. 539 (1963), the Court ruled that the president of a local NAACP organization could not be held in contempt for refusing to answer whether individuals previously identified as Communists belonged to his organization.

89. 453 U.S. 280 (1981).

90. 444 U.S. 507 (1980).

91. See Julie Tate, "Bradley Manning Sentenced to 35 Years in WikiLeaks Case," *Washington Post*, Aug. 21, 2013, http://www.washingtonpost.com/world/national-security/judge-to-sentence-bradley-manning-today/2013/08/20/85bee184-09d0-11e3-b87c-476db8ac34cd_story.html. Manning was acquitted of aiding the enemy. See also Charlie Savage, "Manning Found Not Guilty of Aiding the Enemy," *N.Y. Times*, July 31, 2013, at A1, *available at* http://www.nytimes.com/2013/07/31/us/bradley-manning-verdict.html?_r = 0 (as "Manning Is Acquitted of Aiding the Enemy").

92. Gerry Mullany and Scott Shane, "U.S. Asks Hong Kong to Extradite N.S.A. Leaker," *N.Y. Times*, June 23, 2013, at A4, *available at* http://www.nytimes.com/2013/06/23/world/asia/arrest-of-nsa-leaker-seen-as-easier-than-transfer-to-us.html?pagewanted = all (as "U.S. Petitions for Extradition in N.S.A. Case").

93. 532 U.S. 514 (2001).

94. N.Y. Times Co. v. United States, 403 U.S. 713 (1971). After working in the Defense Department and the State Department, Ellsberg revealed a secret study of U.S. decision-making in Vietnam, which later came to be known as the Pentagon Papers. See http://www.ellsberg.net/bio.

95. Geoffrey R. Stone, "Government Secrecy vs. Freedom of the Press," 1 *Harvard Law and Policy Review* 185, 185–205 (2007).

96. 408 U.S. 665 (1972). As the Deputy Solicitor General for a year dealing with criminal cases, I played a modest role in reviewing the government's brief.

97. In *Zurcher v. Stanford Daily*, 436 U.S. 547 (1978), the Court rejected an argument of a student newspaper that a search of its offices should be under greater restrictions than are ordinary searches. Congress subsequently adopted a Privacy Protection Act of 1980, 42 U.S.C. § 2000 (2012), that did impose some restraint on searches of work products or documents to be published.

98. Richmond Newspapers, Inc. v. Virginia, 448 U.S. 555 (1980); Globe Newspaper Co. v. Superior Court, 457 U.S. 596 (1982); Press-Enterprise Co. v. Superior Court, 464 U.S. 501 (1984).

99. Minneapolis Star & Tribune Co. v. Minnesota Comm'r of Revenue, 460 U.S. 575 (1983).

100. Id. at 590 n.13.

101. Miami Herald Publ'g Co. v. Tornillo, 418 U.S. 241 (1974).

102. Red Lion Broad. Co. v. FCC, 395 U.S. 367 (1969). In 1987, the FCC repealed the fairness doctrine, claiming that it unconstitutionally "chilled" First Amendment rights.

103. Turner Broad. Sys., Inc. v. FCC, 512 U.S. 622 (1994).

104. Lee Bollinger, "Freedom of the Press and Public Access: Toward a Theory of Partial Regulation of the Mass Media," 75 *Michigan Law Review* 1, 26–36 (1976).

105. Model Penal Code § 5.02 (1).

106. This would be different if the possible commission of the crime was already a subject of broad public discussion, such as draft evasion during an unpopular war. One might think it would matter then that the recipient would obviously be presented with competing perspectives.

107. In a case involving the speaker's statement about his own intentions, the Supreme Court overturned a young man's conviction for threatening the life of the President by saying that if forced to carry a rifle, "the first man I want to get in my sights is L.B.J." Watts v. United States, 394 U.S. 705, 706 (1969). The Court concluded that this "political hyperbole" was not a genuine threat under the statute. Id. at 708.

108. 315 U.S. 568 (1942).

109. Id. at 572.

110. Id. at 574.

111. As I have noted, nonverbal behavior is often also partly expressive, and that is certainly true about most physical assaults undertaken in anger.

112. An interesting aspect of a culture is how the acceptability of forms of expression can vary over time. In my lifetime, the use of crude language has become increasingly accepted in general cultural settings.

113. A great deal depends on a person's facial expression and tone of voice as to whether words seem "fighting."

114. See Vincent Blasi & Seana Shiffrin, "The Story of West Virginia State Board of Education v. Barnette," *in Constitutional Law Stories*, ed. Michael Dorf (New York: Foundation Press, 2004), 433.

115. It may be that officials in certain categories are more inclined to fight back.

116. I put this point this way because, here, a person who is half or even three-quarters white may be regarded as an African American, President Obama and Tiger Woods being notable examples.

117. Mari Matsuda, "Public Response to Racist Speech: Considering the Victim's Story," 87 *Michigan Law Review* 2320, 2336 (1989).

118. 343 U.S. 250 (1952).

119. Id. at 252.

120. Id. at 258.

121. 403 U.S. 15 (1971).

122. See, e.g., Gooding v. Wilson, 405 U.S. 518 (1972); Lewis v. City of New Orleans, 415 U.S. 130 (1974).

123. Nat'l Socialist Party of Am. v. Village of Skokie, 432 U.S. 43 (1977).

124. 505 U.S. 377 (1992).

125. 538 U.S. 343 (2003).

126. Doe v. Univ. of Mich., 721 F. Supp. 852, 856 (E.D. Mich. 1989).

127. Id. My views about such codes are developed in Kent Greenawalt, *Fighting Words* 71–82 (Princeton: Princeton University Press, 1995).

128. Civil Rights Act of 1964, Title VII, 42 U.S.C. § 2000e-2(a)(1) (1991).
129. Harris v. Forklift Sys., Inc., 510 U.S. 17 (1993).
130. 132 S. Ct. 2537, 567 U.S. (2012).
131. Id. at 2546–47.
132. Id. at 2548.
133. Id. at 2552.
134. Id. at 2556.
135. 376 U.S. 254 (1964).
136. Id. at 279–80.
137. St. Amant v. Thompson, 390 U.S. 727 (1968).
138. Curtis Publ'g Co. v. Butts, 388 U.S. 130 (1967).
139. Dun & Bradstreet, Inc. v. Greenmoss Builders, Inc., 472 U.S. 749 (1985).
140. Cox Broad. Corp. v. Cohn, 420 U.S. 469 (1975).
141. This view is developed in *Speech, Crime, and the Uses of Language*, supra note 43, at 142.
142. 485 U.S. 46 (1988).
143. Snyder v. Phelps, 131 S. Ct. 1207, 562 U.S. (2011).
144. Id. at 1222.
145. One *might* resist my conclusion on the ground that drawing the line of when invasions on the sensibilities of those grieving are actionable would be too difficult. It is relevant that the federal Respect for American Fallen Heroes Act enacted in 2006 sharply limits demonstrations when funerals are at national cemeteries. See Christina Wells, "Privacy and Funeral Protests," 87 *North Carolina Law Review* 151 (2008). On the somewhat related question of the possible range of laws forbidding antiabortion protests close to abortion facilities, see, e.g., Benjamin Mueller, "Ruling Puts Focus on City's Abortion Protest Laws," *N.Y. Times*, July 31, 2014, at A19, col. 1.
146. This formulation is from the British case of *Regina v. Hicklin* (1868) L.R. 3 Q.B. 360.
147. Roth v. United States, 354 U.S. 476, 487 (1957).
148. Id. at 484.
149. Memoirs v. Attorney General of Mass., 383 U.S. 413, 418 (1966).
150. Miller v. California, 413 U.S. 15, 24 (1973). Subsequent cases indicated that although "social value" does not depend on *local* community standards, patent offensiveness does. Hamling v. United States, 418 U.S. 87 (1974); Pope v. Illinois, 481 U.S. 497 (1987).
151. See Frederick Schauer, *Free Speech: A Philosophical Enquiry* 181–89 (Cambridge: Cambridge University Press, 1982).
152. These possible bases are discussed in more detail in Greenawalt, *Fighting Words*, supra note 127, at 106–13. Those pages also consider the narrower claim that sexually violent material causes actual sexual violence.
153. New York v. Ferber, 458 U.S. 747 (1982).
154. Ashcroft v. Free Speech Coalition, 535 U.S. 234 (2002).
155. United States v. Stevens, 130 S. Ct. 1577, 559 U.S. 460 (2010).
156. See Valentine v. Chrestensen, 316 U.S. 52 (1942).
157. 425 U.S. 748 (1976).
158. Id. at 771 n.24.
159. Central Hudson Gas & Elec. Corp. v. Pub. Serv. Comm'n of N.Y., 447 U.S. 557 (1980).

160. Liquormart, Inc. v. Rhode Island, 517 U.S. 484 (1996).

161. Thompson v. Western States Med. Ctr., 535 U.S. 357 (2002).

162. See Friedman v. Rogers, 440 U.S. 1 (1979).

163. Zauderer v. Office of Disciplinary Counsel, 471 U.S. 626 (1985).

164. Metromedia, Inc. v. San Diego, 453 U.S. 490 (1981).

165. N.Y. Times Co. v. United States, 403 U.S. 713 (1971), discussed supra Section VI.

166. See Erwin Chemerinsky, "The First Amendment: When the Government Must Make Content-Based Choices," 42 *Cleveland State Law Review* 199 (1994); Farber, supra note 79.

167. Although, as Section VIII asserts, explicitly urging particular behavior is not exactly the same as an expression of one's sense of facts and values, it is close enough to put it within the domain of free speech if it poses no serious threat to others.

168. See Chemerinsky, supra note 166, at 204, on obscenity and a compelling interest.

169. See Farber, supra note 79, at 934.

170. See Post, supra note 52, at 2363–64. Just how far this regulation should, and can constitutionally, extend is itself a controversial question. See, e.g., Paul Sherman & Robert McNamara, "Practicing the Speech We Hate," N.Y. Times, Oct. 10, 2014, at A31, col. 2; Paul Sherman & Robert McNamara, "Censorship in Your Doctor's Office," N.Y. Times, Aug. 2, 2014, at 17, col. 2.

171. 505 U.S. 377 (1992).

172. See supra Section X.

173. The statute reviewed was explicitly broader than "fighting words," but Justice Scalia's opinion regards it as unconstitutional, even if limited to that scope.

174. This constraint may derive from the basic constitutional structure rather than the First Amendment.

175. See Chemerinsky, supra note 166.

176. Id. at 211–13.

177. 515 U.S. 819 (1995).

178. The majority considered the restriction viewpoint discrimination. Id. at 831. The four dissenters, in an opinion by Justice Souter, saw it as a subject matter classification. My analysis of why the truth lies somewhere between these two positions is in 2 *Religion and the Constitution: Establishment and Fairness* 200–05 (Princeton: Princeton University Press, 2008).

179. Boy Scouts of America v. Dale, 530 U.S. 640 (2000).

180. Christian Legal Society Chapter v. Martinez, 130 S. Ct. 2971, 561 U.S. (2010).

181. Id. at 3000.

182. Id. at 2984–86.

183. Kathleen M. Sullivan, "Two Concepts of Freedom of Speech," 124 *Harvard Law Review* 143, 165–66 (2010), notes that liberal Justices who generally favor free speech claims have been more accepting of less favorable treatment for religious practices and speech than conservative Justices, who, in other contexts, are less supportive of speech claims.

184. However, it is a problem that an organization unable to limit membership could be effectively "taken over" by people who oppose its basic purposes.

185. Buckley v. Valeo, 424 U.S. 1 (1976). However, the Supreme Court in 2014 held invalid overall limits on individual contributions to national party and federal candidate committees. McCutcheon v. General Election Comm'n, 134 S. Ct. 1434, 572 U.S. ___ (2014).

186. For a recent case assuming that such financing is acceptable, though striking down escalating matching funds, see *Arizona Free Enterprise Club's Freedom Club PAC v. Bennett*, 131 S. Ct. 2806, 564 U.S. ___ (2011).

187. Davis v. Federal Election Comm'n, 554 U.S. 724 (2008).

188. 558 U.S. 310 (2010).

189. Austin v. Mich. Chamber of Commerce, 494 U.S. 652 (1990).

190. Sullivan, supra note 183.

191. McCutcheon v. General Election Comm'n, 134 S. Ct. 1434, 572 U.S. (2014).

192. Id., slip op. at 10. *Buckley v. Valeo*, supra note 185, had used a "rigorous" review for which measures must be "closely drawn."

193. This is sometimes referred to as "corruption" in a broad sense that goes beyond direct exchanges of money for political favors. See dissenting opinion of Justice Breyer in *McCutcheon*, supra note 191, slip op. at 3–9. On the troubling reality that the supposed independence of "Super PACs" from the candidates' decisions about how to spend money is often blurred, see Editorial, "The Custom-Made Super PAC," N.Y. Times, Aug. 4, 2014, at A20, col. 1.

194. I add the words "about expression" because such laws need not be "content neutral" about forms of behavior.

195. 391 U.S. 367 (1968).

196. Id. at 376–77.

197. E.g., City of Erie v. Pap's A.M., 529 U.S. 277 (2000).

198. Employment Div. v. Smith, 494 U.S. 872 (1990). This case is treated in the following chapter.

199. Texas v. Johnson, 491 U.S 397 (1989).

200. United States v. Eichman, 496 U.S. 310 (1990).

201. Boy Scouts of America v. Dale, 530 U.S. 640 (2000).

202. Roberts v. United States Jaycees, 468 U.S. 609 (1984).

203. See Cox v. New Hampshire, 312 U.S. 569 (1941).

204. Police Dep't of Chicago v. Mosley, 408 U.S. 92 (1972).

205. Lehman v. City of Shaker Heights, 418 U.S. 298 (1974).

206. Geoffrey R. Stone, "Content Regulation and the First Amendment," 25 *William and Mary Law Review* 189, 190–93 (1983).

207. See Schad v. Borough of Mount Ephraim, 452 U.S. 61, 70 (1981); Stone, supra note 206, at 190–93. See Wilson R. Huhn, "Assessing the Constitutionality of Laws That Are Both Content-Based and Content-Neutral: The Emerging Constitutional Calculus," 79 *Indiana Law Journal* 801, 803 (2004) (proposing an assessment of the "extent to which the law suppresses particular ideas and/or restricts opportunities for expression," rather than determining whether the law is content-based or content-neutral); see also Jed Rubenfeld, "The First Amendment's Purpose," 53 *Stanford Law Review* 767, 769 (2001) (arguing that state purpose is dispositive and should be the primary ground for determining constitutionality, rather than the balancing approach).

208. Burt Neuborne, *Madison's Music: On Reading the First Amendment* (New York: The New Press 2015).

Chapter 10

1. 330 U.S. 1 (1947)

2. 1 *Religion and the Constitution: Free Exercise and Fairness* (Princeton: Princeton University Press, 2006); 2 *Religion and the Constitution: Establishment and Fairness* (Princeton: Princeton University Press, 2008); *Does God Belong in Public Schools?* (Princeton: Princeton University Press, 2005).

3. Supra note 1.

4. Id. at 44–45.

5. Id. at 18.

6. Id. at 15–16 (quoting Reynolds v. United States, 98 U.S. 145, 164 (1878)).

7. *Everson*, 330 U.S. at 15–16.

8. Id. at 16.

9. 392 U.S. 236 (1968).

10. 403 U.S. 602 (1971).

11. Id. at 612–13.

12. Id. at 614.

13. Id. at 612.

14. Id. at 622.

15. McCreary County, Ky. v. American Civil Liberties Union of Ky., 545 U.S. 844, 860–62 (2005).

16. Tilton v. Richardson, 403 U.S. 672 (1971). The Court did rule that the restriction on how the facilities were used could not end, as the statute provided, after twenty years.

17. Roemer v. Board of Pub. Works, 426 U.S. 736, 755 (1976).

18. What was permitted and not permitted during the 1970s is summarized with citations to the relevant cases, supra note 2, vol. 2, at 400–06.

19. 463 U.S. 388 (1983).

20. School Dist. of Grand Rapids v. Ball, 473 U.S. 373, 385 (1985); See also Aguilar v. Felton, 473 U.S. 402 (1985). New York City's program, reviewed in *Aguilar*, involved only public school teachers.

21. 473 U.S. at 390.

22. Witters v. Washington Dep't of Services for the Blind, 474 U.S. 481 (1986).

23. Zobrest v. Catalina Foothills Sch. Dist., 509 U.S. 1 (1993).

24. Agostini v. Felton, 521 U.S. 203 (1997).

25. 530 U.S. 793 (2000).

26. Meek v. Pittinger, 421 U.S. 349 (1975).

27. 530 U.S. at 837.

28. Justice Thomas gives no ground to treat financial aid differently from books and materials and does not treat direct aid as different from indirect aid.

29. Id. at 828–29.

30. Whether it could be used as a rough approximation to distinguish parochial schools from religion-related universities is a harder question.

31. 536 U.S. 639 (2002).

32. Id. at 644.

33. Id. at 645.

34. Id. at 649.

35. If schools charged tuition well over $2,500, they could accept students receiving the state funds only by giving them effective scholarships.

36. Justice Souter suggested that the anti-discrimination language might cover hiring as well as admissions. Id. at 712–13.

37. Id. at 718–20.

38. This is reproduced by the dissenting opinion in *Everson v. Board of Education*.

39. 397 U.S. 664 (1970).

40. Torcaso v. Watkins, 367 U.S. 488 (1961).

41. 370 U.S. 421 (1962).

42. 374 U.S. 203 (1963).

43. Id. at 222.

44. Lee v. Weisman, 505 U.S. 577 (1992).

45. Santa Fe Indep. Sch. Dist. v. Doe, 530 U.S. 290 (2000).

46. Any prayer that refers to God does not include those who do not believe in a single deity, and any broad prayer may trouble those who take a very specific narrow view of what is the proper recognition of the God in whom they believe.

47. Wallace v. Jaffree, 472 U.S. 38, 40 (1985).

48. Id. at 76, 73.

49. Some moments of silence are meant to help us reflect on something, such as what a person's life has meant.

50. 592 F.2d 197 (3d Cir. 1979) (per curiam).

51. Id. at 207–10.

52. 1 *Religion and the Constitution*, supra note 2, at 124–56.

53. 393 U.S. 97 (1968).

54. Edwards v. Aguillard, 482 U.S. 578 (1987).

55. A fairly extensive discussion is in 2 *Religion and the Constitution*, supra note 2, at 136–56. For an expression of concern about the number of Americans whose religious beliefs are at odds with clear scientific evidence of evolution, see Charles M. Blow, "Religious Constriction," N.Y. Times, June 9, 2014, at A19, col. 2.

56. 333 U.S. 203 (1948).

57. 343 U.S. 306 (1952).

58. Widmar v. Vincent, 454 U.S. 263 (1981).

59. Board of Educ. v. Mergens, 496 U.S. 226 (1990).

60. Good News Club v. Milford Cent. Sch., 533 U.S. 98 (2001).

61. Rosenberger v. Rector & Visitors of Univ. of Va., 515 U.S. 819 (1995).

62. Recently, nontheists have claimed a right to have military chaplains. See Anthony Barone Kulenc, "Not 'For God and Country': Atheist Military Chaplains and the Free Exercise Clause," 48 *University of San Francisco Law Review* 305 (2014).

63. Marsh v. Chambers, 463 U.S. 783 (1983); Town of Greece, N.Y. v. Galloway, 134 S.Ct. 18(2014).

64. 449 U.S. 39 (1980) (per curium).

65. Id. at 41.

66. McCreary County, Ky. v. American Civil Liberties Union of Ky., 545 U.S. 894 (2005).

67. Van Orden v. Perry, 545 U.S. 677 (2005).

68. Id. at 739.

69. Id. at 698–707.

70. 465 U.S. 668 (1984).

71. Id. at 688.

72. County of Allegheny v. American Civil Liberties Union, 492 U.S. 573 (1989).

73. Capitol Square Review & Advisory Bd. v. Pinette, 515 U.S. 753 (1995). For a forceful argument that a constitutional bar on endorsement covers various positions a government might take on nonreligious issues, such as support of a candidate or racial superiority, see Nelson Tebbe, "Government Nonendorsement," 98 *Minnesota Law Review* 648 (2013).

74. 555 U.S. 460 (2009).

75. See, e.g., Christopher C. Lund, "Keeping the Government's Religion Pure: *Pleasant Grove City v. Summum*," 104 *Northwestern University Law Review* 46 (2009); Mary Jean Dolan, "Government Identity Speech and Religious Establishment Clause Limits after *Summum*," 19 *William and Mary Bill of Rights Journal* 1 (2010); Ron Nell Anderson Jones, "Pick Your Poison: Private Speech, Government Speech, and the Special Problem of Religious Displays," 2010 *Brigham Young University Law Review* 2045.

76. 559 U.S. 700 (2010).

77. See Christopher Lund, "*Salazar v. Buono* and the Future of the Establishment Clause," 105 *Northwestern University Law Review* 60, 64–65 (2010). Lund sees a contrast with the Ten Commandments, which can have a secular meaning dissociated from a religious one. Although there are components of the Ten Commandments which could be taken as secular, its religious significance is so well established that the contrast is highly dubious.

78. Frederick Mark Gedicks, "Undoing Neutrality? From Church-State Separation to Judeo-Christian Tolerance," 46 *Willamette Law Review* 691, 692 (2010). See also Carolyn A. Deverich, "Establishment Clause Jurisprudence and the Free Exercise Dilemma: A Structural Unitary-Accommodationist Argument for the Constitutionality of God in the Public Square," 2006 *Brigham Young University Law Review* 211.

79. 465 U.S. 668, at 687 (1984).

80. Id. at 668.

81. 472 U.S. 38, at 76 (1985).

82. Capitol Square Review & Advisory Bd. v. Pinette, 515 U.S. 753, 779 (1995).

83. Elk Grove Unified Sch. Dist. v. Newdow, 542 U.S. 1, 25 (2004) (Rehnquist, C.J., concurring).

84. Id.

85. Id. at 31.

86. Id. at 37.

87. Id. at 36–37.

88. Mike Schaps has suggested that the general Establishment Clause standard could be seen as: "Government cannot favor one religion over another, or act to benefit religion over nonreligion, unless a government practice promotes nonsectarian religion only slightly and is so deeply woven into our national traditions that enjoining it would be highly divisive. "Vagueness as a Virtue: Why the Supreme Court Decided the Ten Commandments Cases Inexactly Right," 94 *California Law Review* 1243, 1244 (2006).

89. One troubling illustration has been the conflict between Sunni and Shiite Muslims in Iraq in 2014–15 and the brutal attacks by ISIS on non-Muslims (and, in some cases, Muslims).

90. 367 U.S. 488 (1961).

91. 319 U.S. 624 (1943).

92. Id. at 642.

93. 508 U.S. 520 (1993).

94. Id. at 533.

95. It is hard to imagine actual examples in which the law would restrict practices *because* of their religious motivation and also be serving a compelling interest.

96. Mark 16:17–18.

97. I defend this resolution in 1 *Religion and the Constitution*, supra note 2, at 39–42.

98. McDaniel v. Paty, 435 U.S. 618 (1978).

99. 456 U.S. 228 (1982).

100. Reynolds v. United States, 98 U.S. 145 (1878).

101. Id. at 164.

102. 310 U.S. 296 (1940).

103. Id. at 303–04 (footnote omitted).

104. Braunfeld v. Brown, 366 U.S. 599 (1961). The Court found a secular purpose in having one set day of freedom from work, and the opinions noted concerns about administrability, the risk of fraud, and possible economic advantage if one store was open when others were closed.

105. 374 U.S. 398 (1963).

106. Id. at 403.

107. United States v. Lee, 455 U.S. 252 (1982).

108. Welsh v. United States, 398 U.S. 333 (1970). Justice Harlan, concurring, thought Welsh was not making a religious claim but that it was unconstitutional to treat religious and nonreligious claims differently in this context. See also the preceding case of *United States v. Seeger*, 380 U.S. 163 (1965).

109. 450 U.S. 707 (1981).

110. Id. at 714.

111. 406 U.S. 205 (1972).

112. Id. at 212.

113. Id. at 221, 225. Given the subsequent decline of work that does not depend on machines, especially computers, one wonders how well the present skills of the Amish would fit in the broader society.

114. Id. at 225.

115. Brian Barry, *Culture and Equality: An Egalitarian Critique of Multiculturalism* 191–92, 242 (Cambridge, Mass.: Harvard University Press, 2001).

116. 406 U.S. at 216.

117. 494 U.S. 872 (1990).

118. However, Justice O'Connor, concurring, did conclude that the state could forbid use on the basis that ingesting the drug "is inherently harmful and dangerous." Id. at 905.

119. Id. at 878–79.

120. Id. at 888.

121. For a court of appeals case dismissing the hybrid language, see *Kissinger v. Board of Trustees of Ohio State University*, 5 F.3d 177, 180 (6th Cir. 1993). A very limited application was proposed in "Note, The Best of a Bad Lot: Compromise and Hybrid Religious Exemptions," 123 *Harvard Law Review* 1494 (2010). In a case in which parents sought to combine a free exercise claim with one about parental rights involving their children's education, the Tenth Circuit

declared that there must be at least "a colorable showing of infringement of recognized and specific constitutional rights, rather than the mere invocation of a general right. . . ." Swanson v. Guthrie Indep. Sch. Dist. No. 1-L, 135 F.3d 694, 700 (10th Cir. 1998).

122. Fraternal Order of Police v. City of Newark, 170 F. 3d 359 (3d Cir. 1999).

123. 42 U.S.C. §§ 2000bb–2000bb-4 (2004).

124. Goldman v. Weinberger, 475 U.S. 503 (1986) (rejecting a challenge by an Orthodox Jewish rabbi serving as a psychologist in a mental health clinic to the rule that he could not wear headgear, including his yarmulke, indoors.)

125. O'Lone v. Estate of Shabazz, 482 U.S. 342 (1987) (using a relaxed standard to review challenged applications of prison regulations).

126. 521 U.S. 507 (1997).

127. Id. at 508.

128. Id. at 533.

129. 546 U.S. 418 (2006).

130. 42 U.S.C. § 2000cc. (2004).

131. 544 U.S. 709 (2005).

132. Id. at 723.

133. Burwell v. Hobby Lobby Stores, 134 S. Ct. 2751, 573 U.S. (2014).

134. Justice O'Connor's concurring opinion in Corporation of the Presiding Bishop of the Church of Jesus Christ of Latter-Day Saints v. Amos, 483 U.S. 327, 348–49 (1987). Justice White's opinion for the Court treated permissible accommodations as a secular purpose to make up for disadvantages to religions.

135. 132 S. Ct. 694, 565 U.S. (2012).

136. 132 S. Ct. at 702.

137. Id. at 707–08.

138. Id. at 710.

139. Id. at 711–16.

140. Id. at 710. One presumes that the case does preclude a remedy for breach of contract that would require someone's reinstatement in a ministerial position.

141. Id. at 709.

142. 472 U.S. 703 (1985).

143. Id. at 710.

144. Id. at 711.

145. Id. at 712.

146. I discuss my thoughts on these topics in "Religious Toleration and Claims of Conscience," 28 *Journal of Law and Politics* 91 (2013).

147. Texas Monthly, Inc. v. Bullock, 489 U.S. 1 (1989).

148. Rosenberger v. Rector & Visitors of Univ. of Va., 515 U.S. 819 (1995).

149. I treat this issue in some detail in 1 *Religion and the Constitution*, supra note 2, at 246–60.

150. 540 U.S. 712 (2004).

151. 536 U.S. 639 (2002).

152. Locke, 540 U.S. at 718–19.

153. A fuller analysis of *Locke v. Davey* and its implications is in 2 *Religion and the Constitution*, supra note 2, at 424–32. Among other points, I claim that the Court's rejection of free speech concerns in the case is unconvincing. See also Laura S. Underkuffler, "*Davey* and the Limits of Equality," 40 *Tulsa Law Review* 267 (2004); Ira C. Lupa & Robert W. Tuttle, "*Zelman*'s Future: Vouchers,

Sectarian Providers and the Next Round of Constitutional Battles," 78 *Notre Dame Law Review* 917 (2003).

Chapter 11

1. 384 U.S. 436 (1966).
2. Sir William F. Stephen, 1 *A History of the Criminal Law of England* 262 (MacMillan 1883).
3. Id. at 424.
4. Treason Act of 1695, 2 and 8 W. 3, C. 3, S. 1.
5. Connecticut apparently had the most robust right, which included appointed counsel. See Christopher Collier, "The Common Law and Individual Rights in Connecticut Before the Federal Bill of Rights," 76 *Connecticut Bar Journal* 1 (2002). For an extensive examination of New York practices, see Julius Goebel, Jr. & T. Raymond Naughton, *Law Enforcement in Colonial New York: A Study in Criminal Procedure* (1664–1776) (Montclair, N.J.: Patterson Smith, 1970) (concluding that the scope of the right to counsel was no greater than in English common law. Id. at 574.).
6. William N. Beaney, *The Right to Counsel in American Courts* 25 (Ann Arbor: University of Michigan, 1955).
7. See, e.g., New Hampshire Constitution of 1784, Part I, Art. XV; South Carolina statute of 1731 remained in effect when its 1778 constitution required that criminal proceedings be in accord with the "law of the land," Para. XLI.
8. See Eben Moglen, "Taking the Fifth: Reconsidering the Origins of the Constitutional Privilege Against Self-Incrimination," 92 *Michigan Law Review* 1087, 1092, 1130 (1994).
9. 287 U.S. 45 (1932).
10. Johnson v. Zerbst, 304 U.S. 458 (1938).
11. 316 U.S. 455, 473 (1942).
12. 372 U.S. 335 (1963).
13. Alabama v. Shelton, 535 U.S. 654 (2002).
14. Scott v. Illinois, 440 U.S. 367 (1979).
15. See *Shelton*, 535 U.S. at 675 (Scalia, J., dissenting).
16. See Caroline Wolf Harlow, Bureau of Justice Statistics, U.S. Dep't of Justice, *Bureau of Justice Special Report: Defense Counsel in Criminal Cases* (2000), *available at* http://www.bjs.gov/content/pub/pdf/dccc.pdf (reporting that 82 percent of felony defendants in the seventy-five largest counties were represented by assigned counsel in 1996 and 68 percent of felony defendants in federal court were represented by assigned counsel in 1998).
17. See, e.g., Lee Silverstein, *Defense of the Poor in Criminal Cases in American State Courts: A Field Study and Report* 22–23 (1965); Lindsey Devers, Bureau of Justice Assistance, U.S. Dep't of Justice, *Pleas and Charge Bargaining: Research Summary* (2011), *available at* https://www.bja.gov/Publications/PleaBargainingResearchSummary.pdf. For a powerful critique of our present level and practices of criminal punishment, see Robert A. Ferguson, *Inferno: An Anatomy of American Punishment* (Cambridge, Mass.: Harvard University Press, 2014).
18. See, e.g., Reno, Marcus, Leary & Gist, Bureau of Justice Assistance, *Contracting for Indigent Defense Services: A Special Report* (2000), *available at* https://www.ncjrs.gov/pdffiles1/bja/181160.pdf. It turns out to be difficult to receive effective assistance of counsel in misdemeanor cases because of inadequate

funding and resources. Boruchowitz, Brink & Dimino, National Association of Criminal Defense Lawyers, *Minor Crimes, Massive Waste: The Terrible Toll of America's Misdemeanor Courts* (2009), *available at* http://www.opensociety-foundations.org/sites/default/files/misdemeanor_20090401.pdf.

19. 422 U.S. 806 (1975).

20. 422 U.S. at 844 (Burger, C.J., dissenting). The answer is that legislators might wish to make specific a right they think is probably, but not obviously, protected by a constitutional provision.

21. Godinez v. Moran, 509 U.S. 389 (1993).

22. 554 U.S. 164 (2008).

23. Justice Scalia dissented in *Edwards*, at 186, with the view that the crucial dignity involved was a person "being master of one's own fate. . . ."

24. Miranda v. Arizona, 384 U.S. 436 (1966).

25. Rothgeny v. Gillespie County, Texas, 554 U.S. 191 (2008).

26. Id. at 213.

27. Id. at 212 (from majority opinion).

28. United States v. Wade, 388 U.S. 218 (1967); Gilbert v. California, 388 U.S. 263 (1967).

29. Kirby v. Illinois, 406 U.S. 682 (1972).

30. United States v. Ash, 413 U.S . 300 (1973).

31. Manson v. Braithwaite, 432 U.S. 98 (1977).

32. McKane v. Durston, 153 U.S. 684 (1894); James v. Barnes, 463 U.S. 745 (1983).

33. Douglas v. California, 372 U.S. 353 (1963).

34. See, e.g., Ross v. Moffitt, 417 U.S. 353 (1963) (counsel does not need to be provided to a defendant seeking a discretionary, second-tier appeal to the North Carolina Supreme Court); Pennsylvania v. Finley, 481 U.S. 551, 554–55 (1997) (prisoners, state or federal, have no constitutional right to counsel to attack their convictions on collateral review); Murray vs. Giarratano, 492 U.S. 1 (1989) (applying *Finley* to capital cases). Thus, any right to counsel in these contexts must be derived from state or federal statutes.

For capital cases, Congress has conferred a right to appointed counsel on indigent prisoners attacking their capital sentences on federal collateral review. See 18 U.S.C. § 3599. Likewise, many states provide a right of counsel in state post-conviction proceedings in capital cases. See, e.g., Ariz. R. Crim. P. 32.4(c); Fla. Stat Ann. § 27.702 (2004); Nev. Rev. Stat. § 34.820(1)(a); Okla. Stat. Ann. tit. 22, § 1089 (2006).

In non-capital cases, an indigent prisoner's right to appointed counsel is governed by § 2254 of the Antiterrorism and Effective Death Penalty Act of 1996. Counsel must be appointed in two circumstances: when an evidentiary hearing is required, or counsel is necessary to utilize effective discovery. See Rule 8(c). The appointment of counsel is rare in non-capital habeas corpus proceedings, with about 95 percent of petitioners making claims pro se. See King, Cheesman, & Ostrom, *Final Technical Report: Habeas Litigation in U.S District Courts: An Empirical Study of Habeas Corpus Cases Filed by State Prisoners Under the Antiterrorism and Effective Death Penalty Act of 1996*, National Center for State Courts, 23 *available at* https://www.ncjrs.gov/pdffiles1/nij/grants/219559.pdf.

35. At the federal level, a statutory right to counsel exists for post-conviction capital cases and nearly all petitioners do take counsel. See id. at 23.

36. *Ross*, 417 U.S. at 608–09.

37. See Peter Westen, "The Empty Idea of Equality," 95 *Harvard Law Review* 137 (1982); Christopher J. Peters, "Equality Revisited," 110 *Harvard Law Review* 1210 (1997).

38. I analyze this topic in considerable detail in "How Empty is the Idea of Equality," 83 *Columbia Law Review* 167 (1983); "'Prescriptive Equality:' Two Steps Forward," 110 *Harvard Law Review* 1265 (1997).

39. A rather different question is whether a person can claim that counsel he hired proved inadequate, because the counsel has represented multiple defendants. See, e.g., Cuyler v. Sullivan, 446 U.S. 335 (1980); Wheat v. United States, 486 U.S. 153 (1988).

40. Most judicial responses to the structural inadequacies of indigent defense have come from state courts. See "Effectively Ineffective: The Failure of the Courts to Address Underfunded Indigent Defense Systems," 118 *Harvard Law Review* 1731 (2005) (examining State v. Pert, 621 So. 2d 780 (La. 1993), State v. Lynch 796 P.2d 1150 (Okla. 1990), and State v. Smith, 681 P.2d 1374 (Ariz. 1984)).

41. Strickland v. Washington, 466 U.S. 668 (1984). On the issue of whether counsel has been able to function effectively enough, see United States v. Cronic, 466 U.S. 648 (1984); Bell v. Cone, 535 U.S. 685 (2002).

42. *Strickland*, supra note 41.

43. Rompilla v. Beard, 545 U.S. 374 (2005).

44. Strickland, 466 U.S. at 711 (Marshall, J., dissenting). Making a claim's success turn on an effect on outcome would not itself be practically different from seeing the basic right as violated only if the conviction or sentence is likely affected.

45. See King, Cheesman & Ostrom, supra note 34, *available at* https://www.ncjrs.gov/pdffiles1/nij/grants/219559.pdf (reporting that of 2,300 randomly selected noncapital federal habeas corpus petitions filed since the passage of AEDPA in 1996, the success rate of noncapital cases was fewer than .03 percent, and no ineffective assistance of counsel claim was granted relief—although half of the petitions contained such a claim).

46. The Court has framed the relationship between state court deference and § 2254(d)(1) of AEDPA as the difference between standards and rules. See Yarborough v. Alvarado, 541 U.S. 652 (2004) (barring relief under § 2254(d)(1) for an alleged *Miranda* violation and observing that "applying a general standard to a specific case can demand a substantial element of judgment ... [t]he more general the rule, the more leeway the [state] courts have in reaching outcomes in case by case determinations"). Accordingly, the Court has extended the *Yarborough* principle to ineffective assistance of counsel claims. See Knowles v. Mirzayance, 556 U.S. 111 (2009) (concluding that when a federal court assesses an ineffective assistance of counsel claim under § 2254(d)(1), the petitioner faces "doubly deferential judicial review").

47. See King, Cheesman & Ostrom, supra note 34, at 28 (reporting that of the sample, 368 capital petitions in 2000–2002, 81 percent presented a claim of ineffective assistance of counsel, 14 percent of which were granted).

48. 8 John H. Wigmore, *Evidence in Criminal Trials at Common Law* § 2250, at 267–69 (McNaughton rev. ed. 1961).

49. See John H. Langbein, "The Historical Origin of the Privilege Against Self-Incrimination at Common Law," 92 *Michigan Law Review* 1047, 1072

(1994); R.H. Helmholz, "Origins of the Privilege Against Self Incrimination: The Rule of the European Ius Commune," 65 *New York University Law Review* 962, 967–89 (1990).

50. Langbein, supra note 49, at 1047–48; Eben Moglen, supra 8 supra, at 1087–1100.

51. Langbein, supra note 49, at 1051–53; Moglen, supra note 8, at 1092–96.

52. Moglen, supra note 8, at 1111–20.

53. Id. at 1121; John Fabian Witt, "Making the Fifth: The Constitutionalization of the American Self-Incrimination Doctrine, 1791–1903," 77 *Texas Law Review* 825, 828 (1999); Albert W. Alschuler, "A Peculiar Privilege in Historical Perspective: The Right to Remain Silent," 94 *Michigan Law Review* 2625, 2650–53 (1996).

54. Id. at 2625–26.

55. Langbein, supra note 49, at 1048.

56. Julius Goebel, Jr., & T. Raymond Naughton, *Law Enforcement in Colonial New York: A Study in Criminal Procedure 1664–1776* (1944).

57. See Witt, supra note 53; Moglen, supra note 8, at 1130.

58. Boyd v. United States, 116 U.S. 616 (1886); Witt, supra note 53, at 900–04.

59. United States v. Burr, 25 F. Cas. 38 (C.C.D. Va. 1807).

60. See Silas J. Wasserstom & Louis Michael Seidman, "The Fourth Amendment as Constitutional Theory," 77 *Georgetown Law Journal* 19, 82 (1988); William J. Stuntz, "The Substantive Origins of Criminal Procedure," 105 *Yale Law Journal* 393, 408 (1995). However, one might take the existence of police in 1868 as an indication that the privilege was, nonetheless, not taken as applicable to police investigations.

61. 384 U.S. 436 (1966). Even prior to that case, persons were not treated as punishable for declining to answer questions about their possible criminal behavior. See Thomas Y. Davies, "Farther and Farther from the Original Fifth Amendment: The Recharacterization of the Right Against Self-Incrimination as a 'Trial Right' in *Chavez v. Martinez*," 70 *Tennessee Law Review* 987, 998–1007 (2003) (arguing that the core of the right, as understood by the Framers, was that the government could not engage in compelled interrogation).

62. Allen, Stuntz, Hoffman, Livingston, Leipold, *Criminal Procedure: Investigation and Right to Counsel* 711 (2d ed. New York: Aspen Casebook Series, 2011).

63. For a survey of possible justifications for the privilege that rejects each as unpersuasive, see David Dolinko, "Is There a Rationale for the Privilege Against Self-Incrimination?," 33 *University of California Los Angeles Law Review* 1063 (1986).

64. See Brown v. Walker, 161 U.S. 591, 596–97 (1896). For a broad and detailed historical overview of this privilege, see Langbein, supra note 49, at 1047. Witt, supra note 53, at 829, indicates that "for almost three quarters of a century after the [Constitution's] enactment . . . , the law of self-incrimination was common law doctrine rather than constitutional law. . . ."

65. For a much more detailed analysis, see Kent Greenawalt, "Silence as a Moral and Constitutional Right," 23 *William and Mary Law Review* 15 (1981). For reflections on that by an author who has supported a shift in doctrine that would allow persuasion of accused persons to speak but bar improper methods of interrogation, see Alschuler, supra note 53, at 2640–72.

66. In urging that the privilege against self-incrimination lacks a rationale, David Delinko, supra note 63, at 1069–70, emphasizes the accumulation of evidence by a trial and the typical existence of evidence prior to stages of investigation.

67. For a proper invocation of the privilege, the risk of incrimination must be substantial. See Marchetti v. United States, 390 U.S. 39 (1968); Minor v. United States, 396 U.S. 87 (1969).

68. See United States v. Burr, 25 F. Cas. 38, 41 (C.C.D. Va. 1807).

69. See Griffin v. California, 380 U.S. 609 (1965).

70. See Carter v. Kentucky, 450 U.S. 288 (1981) (defendant's right to have instruction of no inference). In the recent case of *White v. Woodall*, 134 S. Ct. 1967 (2014), the Court ruled that a challenge to a state's death penalty failed because the Supreme Court has not established that a similar instruction is required about the relevance of a failure to testify at a sentencing hearing.

71. For my reaction to a proposal in Great Britain that would have relaxed the protection further than then existed, see Kent Greenawalt, "Perspectives on the Right to Silence," *in Crime, Criminology and Public Policy: Essays in Honor of Sir Leon Radzinowicz*, ed. R. Hood (London: Heinemann, 1974), 239.

72. Mitchell v. United States, 526 U.S. 314, 311 (1999) (dissenting opinion, joined by three other Justices).

73. Salinas v. Texas, 133 S. Ct. 2174, 2184 (2013) (concurring opinion). The plurality had relied on the suspect's silence as a failure to explicitly invoke the privilege, thus allowing an inference to be drawn.

74. Although there are few studies that examine defendants who testify, a summary of several studies from 1920–1992 leads one commentator to conclude that "the extent of refusal to testify varies from one-third to well over one-half in some jurisdictions." Gordon van Kessel, "Quieting the Guilty and Acquitting the Innocent: A Close Look at a New Twist on the Right to Silence," 35 *Indiana Law Review* 925, 950–51 (2002). Similarly, another report of a 1980s Philadelphia study finds that 49 percent of felony defendants and 57 percent of misdemeanor defendants chose to testify. Stephen Schulhofer, "Some Kind Words for the Privilege Against Self-Incrimination," 26 *Valparaiso University Law Review* 311, 329–30 (1991).

75. Brown v. Walker, 161 U.S. 591 (1896); Ullman v. United States, 350 U.S. 422 (1956).

76. Kastigar v. United States, 406 U.S. 411 (1972).

77. See United States. v. Hubbell, 530 U.S. 27, 40 (2000).

78. 116 U.S. 616 (1886).

79. See George Campbell Painting Corp. v. Reid, 392 U.S. 286, 288–89 (1968); Hale v. Henkel, 201 U.S. 43 (1906).

80. See Shapiro v. United States, 335 U.S. 1 (1948) (required records). But see the contrary result in *Marchetti v. United States*, 390 U.S. 39 (1968), involving registration requirements for professional gamblers—a criminal profession. An individual must disclose required records if the purpose of the requirement is regulatory, the party has customarily kept the records, and they have assumed a public aspect. See Grosso v. United States, 390 U.S. 62 (1968).

81. See United States v. Ward, 448 U.S. 242 (1980); Allen v. Illinois, 478 U.S. 364 (1986).

82. See Fischer v. United States, 425 U.S. 391 (1976); United States v. Hubbell, 530 U.S. 27 (2000); In re Grand Jury Subpoena Duces Tecum dated Mar. 25, 2011, 670 F.3d 1335 (11th Cir. 2012).

83. Id. at 1346. For the claim that the Fifth Amendment privilege should provide substantial protection against compelled decryption or production of a private key, see Aaron M. Clemens, "No Computer Exception to the Constitution: The Fifth Amendment Protects Against Compelled Production of an Encrypted Document or Private Key," 2004 *University of California of Los Angeles Journal of Law and Technology* 2.

84. United States v. Fricosu, 841 F. Supp. 2d. 1232 (D. Colo. 2012).

85. Nicholas Soares, "The Right to Remain Encrypted: The Self-Incrimination Doctrine in the Digital Age," 49 *American Criminal Law Review* 2001, 2016 (2012).

86. Bram v. United States, 168 U.S. 532 (1897).

87. Brown v. Mississippi, 297 U.S. 278 (1936).

88. Malloy v. Hogan, 378 U.S. 1 (1964).

89. 384 U.S. 436 (1966).

90. Id. at 472–73.

91. Id. at 477.

92. Id. at 467.

93. Id. at 476. Alschuler, note 53 supra, at 2629–30, raises the question of how the Supreme Court could require states to employ a remedy not constitutionally compelled, and suggests that its prescribed consequences are best seen as constitutionally required for prophylactic reasons.

94. Richard A. Leo has reported that about 80 percent of suspects routinely waive their *Miranda* rights. "The Impact of *Miranda* Revisited," 80 *Journal of Criminal Law and Criminology* 621, 653 (1996).

95. Thomas P. Sullivan, Northwestern University School of Law, Center on Wrongful Conviction, *Police Experiences with Recording Custodial Interrogations*, (Special Report, Summer 2004), at 4, *available at* http://mcadams.posc.mu.edu/Recording_Interrogations.pdf (reporting that 238 law enforcement agencies in 38 different states record custodial interrogations).

96. Welsh S. White, "Police Trickery in Inducing Confessions,"127 *University of Pennsylvania Law Review* 581, 614–17 (1979).

97. See, e.g., id. at 609–10 n.153 (citing State v. Braun, 509 P.2d 742 (Wash. 1973) (police told the accused that codefendant's confession asserting that accused was primarily responsible for the crime would be admissible against him if repeated in his presence)); Welsh S. White, "What Is an Involuntary Confession Now?," 50 *Rutgers Law Review* 2001, 2053–54 (1998) (false statements that the suspect's fingerprints or hair were found at the scene of the crime or that the suspect failed a polygraph test are more likely than false statements about eyewitness reports to lead to false confessions).

98. See, e.g., Illinois v. Perkins, 496 U.S. 292 (1990). For a treatment of unacceptable pressure—telling a father he needed to talk to save the life of a son (who was in fact already brain-dead)—see James C. McKinley, Jr., "Police Coercion Cited in Order for Retrial," N.Y. Times, Feb. 21, 2014, at A21, col. 3. The piece notes the obvious truth that no clear line distinguishes acceptable from unacceptable pressure.

99. The original development of the privilege did not concern deception, but it was focused on formal processes in which that was not a common element.

100. Harris v. New York, 401 U.S. 222 (1971).

101. Michigan v. Mosley, 423 U.S. 96 (1975). The Court has been stricter when the right to counsel has been asserted.

102. Berghuis v. Thompkins, 560 U.S. 370, 381 (2010).
103. Salinas v. Texas, 133 S. Ct. 2174, 2179, 570 U.S. (2013).
104. 133 S. Ct. at 2183.
105. Schmerber v. California, 384 U.S. 757 (1966).
106. See Doe v. United States, 487 U.S. 201 (1988); Pennsylvania v. Muniz, 496 U.S. 582 (1990).
107. Estelle v. Smith, 451 U.S. 454 (1981). Under Federal Rule of Criminal Procedure 12.2, the court may order a capital defendant who intends to introduce expert evidence relating to mental disease, defect, or condition at sentencing to submit to a mental evaluation, but the results of the evaluation are to remain sealed and undisclosed to the government and the defendant unless the defendant is found guilty and confirms his intent to offer expert evidence during sentencing proceedings.
108. Buchanan v. Kentucky, 483 U.S. 402 (1987).
109. See Nita A. Farahany, "Incriminating Thoughts," 64 *Stanford Law Review* 351 (2012); Sarah E. Stoller & Paul Root Wolpe, "Emerging Neurotechnologies for Lie Detection and the Fifth Amendment," 33 *American Journal of Law and Medicine* 359 (2007); Matthew Baptiste Holloway, "One Image, One Thousand Incriminating Words: Images of Brain Activity and the Privilege Against Self-Incrimination," 27 *Temple Journal of Science Technology and Environmental Law* 142 (2008).
110. Jenkins v. Anderson, 447 U.S. 231 (1980)
111. California v. Byers, 402 U.S. 424 (1971).
112. Baltimore City Dep't of Soc. Servs. v. Bournight, 493 U.S. 549 (1990).
113. New York v. Quarles, 407 U.S. 649 (1984).
114. Id. at 654–60.
115. See, e.g., Garrity v. New Jersey, 385 U.S. 493 (1967); Spevack v. Klein, 385 U.S. 511 (1967); Cohen v. Hurley, 366 U.S. 117 (1961); Slochower v. Bd. of Higher Educ., 350 U.S. 551 (1956). *Cohen* and *Spevack* involved disbarred lawyers; most of the Justices assumed that the principles applicable to public employment were irrelevant to disbarment.
116. See Lefkowitz v. Cunningham, 431 U.S. 801 (1977); Lefkowitz v. Turley, 414 U.S. 70 (1973); Gardner v. Broderick, 392 U.S. 273 (1968). *Cunningham* involved a political party official and *Turley* a contractor, but the Court decided that the principles relating to public employment were applicable.
117. I take the same view about revocation of the license to practice law, but I do not defend that view here or attempt to analyze which relationships with the government can properly be the basis for imposition of some adverse consequences based on failure to speak.
118. See Slochower v. Bd. of Higher Educ., 350 U.S. 551, 558 (1956). There may be a few positions—for example, police chief or United States Attorney—for which dismissal would be appropriate, even for exercises of privilege unrelated to the job. Most of these positions would be ones as to which a chief executive would have wide discretion over dismissal, so it is difficult to imagine litigation arising over the cause of dismissal.
119. See Lefkowitz v. Cunningham, 431 U.S. at 812 (Stevens, J., dissenting).
120. See, e.g., William J. Cuddihy, *The Fourth Amendment: Origins and Original Meaning* 602–1791 (New York: Oxford University Press, 2009).
121. M. H. Smith, *The Writs of Assistance Case* (Oakland: University of California Press, 1978).

122. See, e.g., Akhil Reed Amar, "Fourth Amendment First Principles," 107 *Harvard Law Review* 757 (1994); Fabio Areila, Jr., "The Death of Suspicion," 51 *William and Mary Law Review* 1275, 1294–95 (2010). Modern Supreme Court cases have adopted this assumption, although with different approaches regarding how to decide the issue of reasonableness.

123. Thomas Y. Davies, "The Supreme Court Giveth and the Supreme Court Taketh Away: The Century of Fourth Amendment 'Search and Seizure' Doctrine," 100 *Journal of Criminal Law and Criminology* 933, 941 (2010). See also Thomas Y. Davies, "Recovering the Original Fourth Amendment," 98 *Michigan Law Review* 547, 600–11 (1999).

124. See Davies, The Supreme Court, supra note 123, at 941.

125. Cuddihy, supra note 120, at 740–41, 748–49.

126. Id. at 771. Conflicting views about the relation of "reasonableness" to the warrant clause are summarized and analyzed in a review of the major book by William Cuddihy, cited supra note 120. Tracey Maclin & Julia Mirabella, "Framing the Fourth," 109 *Michigan Law Review* 1049 (2011).

127. Cuddihy, supra note 120, at 771 (concluding that despite developing over the centuries, probable cause had "never occasioned the intensity of depth of thought, adjudication, and legislation" as had general warrants).

128. See, e.g., H. Blaine Michael, "Reading the Fourth Amendment: Guidance from the Mischief That Gave It Birth," 85 *New York University Law Review* 905, 916–18 (2010).

129. Id. at 913–18; Davies, "The Supreme Court," supra note 123, at 556; Maclin & Mirabella, supra note 126, at 1075.

130. The development of Scalia's views is described in David A. Sklansky, "The Fourth Amendment and Common Law," 100 *Columbia Law Review* 1739, 1745–62 (2000).

131. See especially Wyoming v. Houghton, 526 U.S. 295 (1999).

132. For this position, it should not matter whether the original relevant clause was the Fifth Amendment's "due process" language." Judge Michael, supra note 128, at 913–14, criticizes this approach as "freez[ing] in place eighteenth-century rules without considering whether this method is practical or whether these old rules still make sense 200 years later." As Michael points out, the common law itself has been flexible over time.

133. Id. at 918–19; Davies, "The Supreme Court," supra note 123, at 1036, refers to its "gross inadequacy."

134. If I say, "Don't offend me and disappoint me," that could mean "don't either offend me or disappoint me," or "don't behave in a way that both offends me and disappoints me."

135. See G. M. Leasing Corp. v. United States, 429 U.S. 338 (1977) (holding that there is no Fourth Amendment deprivation when the government, in an attempt to collect taxes, does not enter the delinquent taxpayer's own premises).

136. 277 U.S. 438 (1928).

137. Id. at 471–85.

138. I put aside a situation in which a "search" is undertaken just to upset someone.

139. For instance, the National Security Agency's (NSA) PRISM program allegedly allows the government to collect foreign communications flowing through the Internet servers of United States service providers such as Yahoo, Google, and Microsoft. See, e.g., Glenn Greenwald & Ewen MacAskill,

"NSA Prism Program Taps In to User Data of Apple, Google and Others," *The Guardian*, June 7, 2013, *available at* http://www.theguardian.com/world/2013/jun/06/us-tech-giants-nsa-data; Barton Gellman & Laura Poitras, "U.S., British Intelligence Mining Data from Nine U.S. Internet Companies in Broad Secret Program," *Washington Post*, June 6, 2013, *available at* http://www.washingtonpost.com/investigations/us-intelligence-mining-data-from-nine-us-internet-companies-in-broad-secret-program/2013/06/06/3a0c0da8-cebf-11e2-8845-d970ccb04497_story.html.

In order to secure the information from a "targeted" individual, the Attorney General and Director of the Intelligence must obtain an order from Foreign Intelligence Surveillance Court by certifying that the target is reasonably believed to be located outside the United States and that a significant purpose of acquisition is to obtain foreign intelligence information. See generally 50 U.S.C. § 1881(a), (c). "Reasonable belief" is defined as 51 percent confidence. See "NSA Slides Explain the PRISM Data-Collection Program," *Washington Post*, June 10, 2013, *available at* http://www.washingtonpost.com/wp-srv/special/politics/prism-collection-documents/.

After obtaining authorization from the FISA Court, the government may direct an internet service provider to give them access to the information to carry out the targeting. See generally id. at (h). The service provider may challenge the directive with the FISA Court and then challenge any denial of such challenge with the Foreign Intelligence Surveillance Court of Review and then the Supreme Court. See generally, id. at (h)(4). Compliance with the request releases the company from any liability. Id. at §1881(h)(3). If the internet service provider refuses to comply with the directive, the government may request an enforcement order from the FISA Court, see § 1881 (h)(5), and if the service provider refuses to comply with the order, it can be held in contempt of court. See id. at (h)(4).

Once the government has obtained authorization, the NSA may perform as many as "three hops" through its data collection to find connections between the target and terrorist organizations. See Spencer Ackerman, "NSA Warned to Rein in Surveillance As Agency Reveals Even Greater Scope," *The Guardian*, June 17, 2013, *available at* http://www.theguardian.com/world/2013/jul/17/nsa-surveillance-house-hearing. "Hops" refers to the connections between people. For instance, for a Facebook user with 190 "friends," two hops—the friends of your friends—results in a network of 31,046 friends. Three hops results in a network larger than the population of Colorado. See Ewan MacAskill & Gabriel Dance, "The NSA Files: Decoded," Nov. 1, 2013, *available at* http://www.theguardian.com/world/interactive/2013/nov/01/snowden-nsa-files-surveillance-revelations-decoded#section/1.

The data-collection program, mostly authorized by the PATRIOT Act, temporarily expired on May 31, 2015, when Congress failed to renew the act over disagreements about this collection. (The Second Circuit had deemed the program unconstitutional in early May 2015, see *ACLU v. Clapper*, No. 14-42-cv [2d Cir May 7, 2014].) Two days later, Congress passed, and President Obama signed, the reformed USA Freedom Act, which revises these provisions. According to the House Judiciary Committee, the revised program prohibits bulk collection, including collection of all records from a certain state, city, or zip code, along with other changes. (See U.S. House of Rep. Judiciary Comm., H.R. 2048, The USA Freedom Act, http://judiciary.house.gov/index.cfm/usa-freedom-act

[accessed June 12, 2015].) Instead, the NSA and FBI now must obtain phone records from the telecommunications companies on an individual basis, with a FISA court order.

140. 116 U.S. 616 (1886).

141. Id. at 622.

142. Id. at 630. Davies, "The Supreme Court," supra note 123, at 955–56, regards Bradley as engaging in "fictional originalism" in order to serve the purpose of protecting business records.

143. 116 U.S. at 633. The fraud to import property illegally did carry the possibility of criminal charges.

144. The *Boyd* Court did qualify its ruling not to include property held by someone but to which the government was actually entitled.

145. *Boyd,* 116 U.S. at 635.

146. Gouled v. United States, 255 U.S. 208 (1921). See Stanton D. Krauss, "The Life and Times of *Boyd* v. *United States* (1886–1976)," 76 *Michigan Law Review* 184, 190 (1977).

147. Olmstead v. United States, 277 U.S. 438 (1928).

148. Id.

149. See Berger v. New York, 388 U.S. 41 (1967); Katz v. United States, 389 U.S. 347 (1967).

150. Warden, Maryland Penitentiary v. Hayden, 387 U.S. 294 (1967).

151. Fisher v. United States, 425 U.S. 391, 399 (1976).

152. Hale v. Henkel, 201 U.S. 43 (1906).

153. Andersen v. Maryland, 427 U.S. 391 (1967).

154. See United States v. Doe, 465 U.S. 605 (1984) (holding that the contents of a sole proprietor's voluntarily made business records were not privileged, but deferring to the district court's finding of fact that the act of producing the document would involve testimonial self-incrimination); Braswell v. United States, 487 U.S. 99 (1989) (holding that president and sole shareholder of a corporation had no act of production privilege under the Fifth Amendment regarding corporate documents).

155. See Fisher, 425 U.S. at 427 (arguing that "[p]apers in the nature of a personal diary are a fortiori protected under the privilege.") (Brennan. J., concurring); Doe, 465 U.S. at 619 (noting that business records implicate a lesser degree of concern than personal diaries) (Marshall, & Brennan, JJ., concurring); but see In re Grand Jury Subpoena Duces Tecum, 1 F.3d 87, 93 (2d Cir. 1993) (holding that the Fifth Amendment does not protect the contents of voluntarily prepared documents, either business or personal), cert. denied, 510 U.S. 1091 (1994).

156. This position was proposed by Telford Taylor, *Two Studies in Constitutional Interpretation* 23–50 (Columbus: Ohio State University Press, 1969). For a more recent historical account, see the two articles by Davies, supra note 123. Of course, if, as Davies claims, the original due process clause was meant to embody common law restrictions on criminal investigations, it might have effectively required warrants in some circumstances.

157. See, e.g., Johnson v. United States, 333 U.S. 10, 13–14 (1948).

158. See Administrative Office of the U.S. Courts, *Wire Tap Report 2012,* Table 7, Authorized Intercepts Granted Pursuant to 18 U.S.C. § 2519 as Reported in Wiretap Reports for Calendar Years 2002–2012, *available at* http://www.uscourts.gov/uscourts/statistics/wiretapreports/2012/Table7.pdf (showing that

from 2008 through 2012, only 5 of 13,593 Title III wiretap applications were denied).

159. Even Perez, "Secret Court's Oversight Gets Scrutiny," Wall St. Journal, June 9, 2013 (reporting that none of the 1,856 applications made by the Department of Justice in 2012 were denied).

160. William J. Stuntz, "Warrants and Fourth Amendment Remedies," 77 *Virginia Law Review* 881, 890–97 (1991).

161. Id. at 884, 942–43. Warrants can also protect the police against actions for damages. Id. at 941–92.

162. See Kent Greenawalt, "Privacy and Its Legal Protections," *The Hastings Center Studies* Vol. 2, No. 2 (1974). Recent national statistics do not indicate how many arrests were executed without warrants. See, e.g., Bureau of Justice Statistics, U.S. Department of Justice, Patterns and Trends: Arrests in the United States, 1980–2009, Table 1, *available at* http://www.bjs.gov/content/pub/pdf/aus8009.pdf; U.S. Census Bureau, U.S. Department of Commerce, Arrests by Sex and Age: 2009, Table 324, *available at* http://www.census.gov/compendia/statab/2012/tables/12s0324.pdf.

Similarly, recent statistics of New York arrests do not indicate how many arrests were executed without warrants. See New York State Division of Criminal Justice Services, New York City Adult Arrests 2004–2013, *available at* http://www.criminaljustice.ny.gov/crimnet/ojsa/arrests/NewYorkCity.pdf.

The lack of reliable statistics in this area has been long observed by commentators. See Wayne E. Logan, "Street Legal: The Court Afford Police Constitutional Carte Blanche," 77 *Indiana Law Journal* 419, 432 n.107 (2002) (citing articles by Caleb Foote and Jerome Hall from 1957 and 1936, respectively). However, many commentators have recognized that the overwhelming majority of arrests are executed without warrants. See, e.g., David A. Slanksy, "The Private Police, "46 *University of Los Angeles Law Review,* 1165, 1184 (1999).

163. See United States v. Watson, 423 U.S 411, 425 (1976) (concurring opinion of Powell, J.). Davies, "The Supreme Court," supra note 123, at 945–47, writes that nineteenth-century judges in the United States relaxed the standards required earlier at common law for warrantless arrests. But even Davies, who is critical of the Court's exposition of history in Fourth Amendment jurisprudence, appears to agree that at the time of framing, warrantless felony arrests were largely accepted by the common law. See also Thomas Y. Davies, "Correcting Search-and-Seizure History: Now-Forgotten Common-Law Warrantless Arrest Standards and the Original Meaning of "Due Process of Law," 77 *Mississippi Law Journal* 1 (2007).

164. Atwater v. Lago Vista, 532 U.S. 318 (2001).

165. Id. at 346–47. Four dissenting Justices considered the arrest constitutionally unreasonable. Id. at 360–73 (O'Connor, Stevens, Ginsburg, Breyer, JJ., dissenting).

166. Following the Court's decisions in *Watson* and *Atwater,* supra notes 163 and 164, it remains an open question whether an officer may make a warrantless arrest for a misdemeanor not occurring in her presence. However, the weight of authority holds that the common law "in the presence" rule is not part of the Fourth Amendment. See, e.g., Veach v. Bartels Lutheran Home 627 F.3d 1254, 1258 (8th Cir. 2010) (citing Woods v. City of Chicago, 234 F.3d 979, 995 (7th Cir. 2000) (collecting cases)); Welsh v. Wisconsin, 446 U.S. 740, 756 (1984) (White, J., dissenting). For an argument that warrantless arrests

for misdemeanors committed outside an officer's presence are contrary to the Fourth Amendment, see William A. Schroeder, "Warrantless Arrests and the Fourth Amendment," 58 *Missouri Law Review* 771 (1993).

167. Brinegar v. United States, 338 U.S. 160, 175–76 (1949).

168. Illinois v. Gates, 462 U.S. 213, 238 (1983).

169. Texas v. Brown, 460 U.S. 730 (1983). For an analysis of probable cause, see Joshua Dressler, *Understanding Criminal Procedure* 135 (6th ed. Lexis Nexis, 2013).

170. See Richard Van Duizend, L. Paul Sutton & Charlotte A. Carter, "The Search Warrant Process: Preconceptions, Perceptions, Practices," *National Center for State Courts* (1985) at Table 21 (recorded instances of seizures was 90 percent, but authors acknowledge this may be too high).

171. See Radley Balko, "Was the Police Response to the Boston Bombing Really Appropriate?," *Washington Post*, Apr. 22, 2014,, http://www.washingtonpost.com/news/the-watch/wp/2014/04/22/the-police-response-to-the-boston-marathon-bombing/. Judge Gould proposes that large-scale searches undertaken to prevent catastrophic harms may be constitutionally sound even when the search of each particular location does not have a fair probability or substantial chance of resulting in the object sought. See Ronald M. Gould & Simon Stern, "Catastrophic Threats and the Fourth Amendment," 77 *Southern California Law Review* 777 (2004).

172. Sherry F. Colb, "The Qualitative Dimension of Fourth Amendment 'Reasonableness,'" 98 *Columbia Law Review* 1642 (1998).

173. Spinelli v. United States, 393 U.S. 410 (1969). Thomas Davies, "The Supreme Court," supra note 123, at 943 suggests that when the Bill of Rights was adopted, under common law, felony arrests required proof that a felony had been committed and probable cause that an arrestee was the felon.

174. Illinoi v. Gates, 462 U.S. 213, 231(1983).

175. See Florida v. J.L., 529 U.S. 266 (2000).

176. See, e.g., *Gates*, 462 U.S. at 234 (observing that some anonymous tips have a higher degree of reliability because the details supplied by the informant are so specific or are of a nature that they establish the personal knowledge of the informant); Harris v. Virginia, 276 Va. 689, 695–96 (2010) (noting that anonymous tips have a relatively low degree of reliability, but "indicia" of reliability may be bolstered when the tipster provides more predictive information, which the police can use to test the tipster's basis of knowledge and credibility); Hall v. State, 74 S.W.3d 521, 525 n.1 (Tex. Ct. App. 2002) (reasoning that because the court has no way of evaluating the reliability of the information provided by the anonymous source, further indicia from which a police officer can reasonably conclude that the tip is reliable and justified—such as the license of the vehicle, the number of its occupants, or the year or make of the automobile—must be present).

177. See Judge Charles Burns & Michael Conte, "Terry Stops, Anonymous Tips, and Driving Under the Influence: A Study of Illinois Law," 45(4) *Loyola University Chicago Law Journal* 1144 (discussing the lower courts' struggles in determining how to apply the relevant standard, especially in the context of anonymous tips on possible drunk driving and concluding that, in light of the Court's recent decision in *Navarette v. California*, 134 S. Ct. 1683 (2014), courts should judge the propriety of stopping a driver based on an anonymous tip of drunk driving on a number of factors, including the degree to which the tip was

specific and truly anonymous, and the danger posed to the public by the conduct described in the tip).

178. Gates, 462 U.S. at 236–37 (1983).

179. California v. Ciraolo, 477 U.S. 227, 234–35 (1986).

180. Kyllo v. United States, 533 U.S. 27 (2001).

181. Id. at 34.

182. California v. Greenwood, 486 U.S. 35 (1988).

183. 488 U.S. 445 (1989).

184. Id. at 454.

185. Oliver v. United States, 466 U.S. 170 (1984).

186. United States v. Dunn, 480 U.S. 294 (1987).

187. In *City of Indianapolis v. Edmond*, 531 U.S. 32, 37–38 (2000), the Supreme Court outlined various "limited circumstances" in which individualized suspicion is not required.

188. New Jersey v. T.L.O., 469 U.S. 325 (1985).

189. United States v. Drayton, 536 U.S. 194 (2002). The issue in the case was whether voluntary consent had been given.

190. According to the National Safety Council, buses, trains, and airlines all have much lower death rates than automobiles when the risk is expressed as passenger deaths per passenger mile of travel. In 2011, the passenger death rate for automobiles was 0.48 deaths for every 100 million passenger miles, buses were at .06, trains at .03, and airlines at 0.00. See "Frequently Asked Questions," *National Safety Council, available at* http://www.nsc.org/news_resources/Resources/res_stats_services/Pages/FrequentlyAskedQuestions.aspx#question10.

191. See Charles J. Keeley III, "Subway Searches: Which Exception to the Warrant and Probable Cause Requirement Applies to Suspicionless Searches of Mass Transit Passengers to Prevent Terrorism?," 74 *Fordham Law Review* 3231, 3257–62 (2006).

192. Id.

193. See L. Rush Atkinson, "The Fourth Amendment's National Security Exception: Its History and Limits," 66 *Vanderbilt Law Review* 1343 (2013).

194. Wyoming v. Houghton, 526 U.S. 295, 299–300 (1999).

195. See Michael, supra note 128, at 918–19. The Court's use of balancing, which has mainly accepted government claims, has been called "blind" because based on insufficient facts, by Shima Baradaran, "Rebalancing the Fourth Amendment," 102 *Georgetown Law Journal* 1 (2013), who recommends greater reliance on broader statistical data and rights of the whole society.

196. Terry v. Ohio, 392 U.S. 1 (1968).

197. See United States v. Arvizu, 534 U.S. 226 (2002). The Court overruled a Ninth Circuit decision invalidating a border patrol agent's *Terry* stop of a minivan containing two adults, three children, and over 100 pounds of marijuana. The basis of the border patrol's reasonable suspicion were the following facts: the vehicle was a minivan of the sort the agent knew smugglers used, the minivan was driving along a dirt road used sometimes by smugglers and vacationers, the minivan was driving during the time the patrol agents' shift changed, the minivan slowed down when the driver saw the agent, the posture of the driver was stiff, the knees of the children at the back of the van appeared to be propped up on something, the children waived "abnormally," and the van was registered to an address near the Mexican border known for drug smuggling.

Indeed, some commentators argue the Court's "reasonable suspicion" requirement is no more than a directive to officers to behave reasonably under the circumstances. See, e.g., Silas J. Wasserstom, "The Court's Turn Toward a General Reasonableness Interpretation of the Fourth Amendment," 27 *American Criminal Law Review* 119, 129–30 (1989); Brian D. Walsh, "*Illinois v. Wardlow*: High Crime Areas, Flight, and the Fourth Amendment," 54 *Arkansas Law Review* 879, 908 (noting that "the judicial scrutiny applied in reasonable suspicion cases is a post facto determination of the reasonableness of an officer's actions").

198. Floyd v. City of New York, 959 F. Supp. 2d 540 (S.D.N.Y. 2013).

199. Id.

200. *Floyd*, 959 F. Supp. 2d at 668; Ligon v. City of New York, 736 F.3d 231 (2013).

201. Benjamin Weiser & Joseph Goldstein, "Mayor Says New York City Will Settle Suits on Stop-and-Frisk Tactics," *N.Y. Times*, Jan. 30, 2014, *available at* http://www.nytimes.com/2014/01/31/nyregion/de-blasio-stop-and-frisk.html.

202. *Floyd*, 959 F. Supp. 2d at 652.

203. *Floyd*, 959 F. Supp. 2d at 570.

204. Among the illuminating writings on the use of racial criteria are Bernard E. Harcourt, "Rethinking Racial Profiling: A Critique of the Economics, Civil Liberties, and Constitutional Literature, and of Criminal Profiling More Generally," 71 *University of Chicago Law Review* 1275 (2004) (treating the topic in depth); Samuel R. Gross & Debra Livingston, "Racial Profiling Under Attack," 102 *Columbia Law Review* 1413 (2002).

205. Id. at 587.

206. Id. at 560.

207. Women, of course, have the particular fear of rape, but any person could conceivably be sexually assaulted by someone else of the same gender.

208. Harcourt, supra note 204, at 1361–71, demonstrates such a discrepancy between actual criminal behavior and arrests in connection with the use of illegal drugs.

209. This was clearly revealed by President Obama's remarks after George Zimmerman was acquitted for shooting Trayvon Martin. See "White House, Office of the Press Secretary, News Release, *Remarks by the President on Trayvon Martin*, July 19, 2013, *available at* http://www.whitehouse.gov/the-press-office/2013/07/19/remarks-president-trayvon-martin.

210. See United States v. Bayless, 201 F.3d 116, 133 (2d Cir. 2000).

211. For the purposes of this exercise, I am assuming, unrealistically, that all individual movements are roughly comparable in their degree of creating suspicion.

212. That conclusion must rest on a refined evaluation of all the relevant considerations—*not* on any simple notion of what constitutes "discrimination" nor any assumption that a person's race could never affect objective probabilities. See Daniel Richman, "The Process of *Terry*-Lawmaking," 72 *St. John's Law Review* 1043 (1998).

213. Hudson v. Michigan, 547 U.S. 586 (2006) (four dissenters believed evidence obtained should have been excluded).

214. Wilson v. Arkansas, 514 U.S. 927 (1995); Richards v. Wisconsin, 520 U.S. 385 (1997); United States v. Ramirez, 523 U.S. 65 (1998).

215. See Marron v. United States, 275 U.S. 192, 196 (1927) (invalidating the search and seizure of ledgers and bills because they were not described in

a warrant which specified only that liquor was to be seized; noting that "[t]he the requirement that warrants shall particularly describe the things to be seized ... prevents the seizure of one thing under a warrant describing another. As to what is to be taken, nothing is left to the discretion of the officer executing the warrant.").

216. Arizona v. Hicks, 480 U.S. 321 (1987).

217. Schmerber v. California, 384 U.S. 757 (1966).

218. Id. at 768 (officer who arrived at the scene shortly after the automobile accident smelled liquor on the defendant's breath and noted other symptoms of intoxication had reason to order a blood alcohol test).

219. A police officer is free to ask a person for identification without implicating the Fourth Amendment. See INS v. Delgado, 446 U.S. 210, 216 (1984) (noting that police questioning relating to one's identity and requesting identification do not constitute a Fourth Amendment seizure). However, the Fourth Amendment itself does not require a suspect to answer questions. See Hibel v. Sixth Judicial Dist. Court of Nevada, Humbolt County, 542 U.S. 177, 187 (2004).

On the other hand, many states have "stop and identify" statutes which permit officers to require suspects to disclose their identity and arrest or detain them if the suspect refuses. See, e.g. Ari. Rev. Stat. Tit. 13, §2412; Fla Stat. § 901.151 and § 856.021(2); La. Code Crim. Proc. Ann. Art. 215.1(A) and La. Rev. Stat. 14:108(B)(1)(c); N.M. Stat. Ann. §30-22-3; Oh. Rev. Code § 2921.29; Vt. Stat. Ann. § 77-7-15. These statutes violate the Fourth Amendment if the initial stop is not based on specific, objective facts establishing reasonable suspicion to believe the suspect was involved in criminal activity. See Brown v. Texas, 443 U.S. 47, 52 (1979). In other words, the request for identification cannot be an effort "to obtain an arrest for failure to identify after a *Terry* stop yielded insufficient evidence." Hibel, at 189.

220. County of Riverside v. McLaughlin, 500 U.S. 44, 58 (1991).

221. Maryland v. King, 133 S. Ct. 1958, 569 U.S. (2013).

222. Id at 1977–80.

223. Id. at 1972–74.

224. Id. at 1980–89.

225. Id. at 1984–86.

226. Id. at 1989.

227. Id.

228. Schneckloth v. Bustamente, 412 U.S. 218 (1973).

229. Id. at 223.

230. Donald Sterling declared, under penalty of perjury, that the remarks were made during a "lovers' quarrel" and that he did not know he was being recorded. See Donald Sterling's Answer to Charge, *available at* http://i.usatoday.net/sports/!sterling/2014-05-27%20Secured%20DTS%20Answer%20to%20NBA%20Charge.pdf.

Stiviano claims that Sterling knew that she recorded their conversations to better assist him in light of his dementia. See Soraya Nadia Macdonald, "Report: Donald Sterling Will Fight the Sale of the L.A. Clippers," *Washington Post*, May 2014, *available at* http://www.washingtonpost.com/news/morning-mix/wp/2014/05/28/report-donald-sterling-will-fight-the-sale-of-team/.

231. See generally Kent Greenawalt, "The Consent Problem in Wiretapping and Eavesdropping: Surreptitious Monitoring with the Consent of a Participant in a Conversation," 68 *Columbia Law Review* 189, 212–40 (1968).

232. 401 U.S. 475 (1971).

233. See, e.g., Adam Liptar & Jeremy W. Peters, "Congress and the Courts Weigh New Attempts to Scale Back N.S. A. Spying," *N.Y. Times*, Nov. 19, 2013, at A16, col. 1; Charlie Savage & James Risen, "Latest Release of Documents on N.S.A. Includes 2004 Ruling on Email Surveillance," *N.Y. Times*, Nov. 19, 2013, at A16, col. 1.

234. Orin S. Kerr has written two important pieces on this topic. "Searches and Seizures in a Digital World," 119 *Harvard Law Review* 531 (2005); "Applying the Fourth Amendment to the Internet: A General Approach," 62 *Stanford Law Review* 1005 (2010). See also Michael, supra note 128, at 922–30; Nicole Friess, "When Rummaging Goes Digital: Fourth Amendment Particularity and Stored E-mail Surveillance," 90 *Nebraska Law Review* 971 (2012); Susan Freiwald, "First Principles of Communication Privacy," 2007 *Stanford Technical Law Review* 3 (2007).

235. Kerr, "Applying the Fourth Amendment," supra note 234, at 1008, 1025–28.

236. Katz v. United States, 389 U.S. 347 (1967).

237. Id. at 353. The relevance of the *Katz* principle for "cloud computing" is explored in Lon A. Berk, "After *Jones*, The Deluge: The Fourth Amendment's Treatment of Information, Big Data and the Cloud," XIV *Journal of High Technology Law* 1, 12–22 (2014).

238. Friess, supra note 234, at 982.

239. See Macwade v. Kelley, 460 F.3d 260, 272–75 (2d Cir. 2006) (upholding New York City's random, suspicionless container search program in the face of the threat of a terrorist attack).

240. See Friess, supra note 234, at 991–1003; Kerr, "Searches and Seizures," supra note 234, at 571–76, urges that ex ante restrictions on the way a computer search is carried out is not a good idea; he suggests nonapplication of the plain view doctrine as a way to conduct searches that are too extensive. Id. at 576–84.

241. Brad Leneis, Note, "Mapping a Way Out: Protecting Cellphone Location Information Without Starting Over on the Fourth Amendment," 50 *American Criminal Law Review* 499, 510–15 (2013). For a proposal that the Stranger Principle should not be used to end protection for information given to others, see Berk, supra note 237, at 30–31. For recent legislative concerns about these matters, see n. 139, supra.

242. Kerr, "Applying the Fourth Amendment," supra note 234, at 1040–43.

243. See supra note 139.

244. Apparently, when the Fourth Amendment was adopted, officials had much less authority to search and were subject to individual liability in damages for personal misconduct when they overstepped. See Davies, note 123, supra, at 554, 660–66; Michael, supra note 128, at 918.

245. 367 U.S. 643 (1961). For commentary discussing the exclusionary rule's lack of historical support, see, e.g., Akhil Reed Amar, supra note 122, at 786; Justice Potter Stewart, "The Road to *Mapp v. Ohio* and Beyond: The Origins, the Development and Future of the Exclusionary Rule in Search-and-Seizure Cases," 83 *Columbia Law Review* 1365, 1366–73(1983) (concluding "that the exclusionary rule seems a bit like a jerry-built roller coaster track constructed while the roller coaster sped along" because exclusion was not apparently contemplated by the Framers, yet by 1914, the rule had been established in three Court cases without ever acknowledging this

issue. According to Davies, supra note 123, at 938, the Court's decision, along with other cases, was partly directed at reducing racial inequality within some state systems.

246. The exclusionary rule has been strongly criticized by Akhil Amar, supra note 122, at 785–800. David Gray has suggested that the rule be conceived as partly a retributive response to an officer's wrongful behavior. "A Spectacular Non Sequitur: The Supreme Court's Contemporary Fourth Amendment Exclusionary Rule Jurisprudence," 50 *American Criminal Law Review* 1 (2013).

247. Prior to *Mapp*, the Warren Court itself had decided that the only persons who can have evidence excluded are those against whom searches were directed. See Jones v. United States, 362 U.S. 257 (1960). Genuine guests in homes are protected, but not everyone who happens to be in a dwelling at the time of a search. Minnesota v. Carter, 529 U.S. 83 (1998).

248. United States v. Haven, 446 U.S. 620 (1980).

249. See United States v. Leon, 468 U.S. 897 (1984). For a proposal that the exception should reach every type of reasonable official mistake, see Note, "Toward a General Good Faith Exception," 127 *Harvard Law Review* 773 (2013).

250. Herring v. United States, 555 U.S. 135 (2009).

251. See Kenneth Katkin, "Incorporation of the Criminal Procedure Amendments: The View from the States," 89 *Nebraska Law Review* 397, 420–22 (2005).

252. Carroll v. United States, 267 U.S. 132 (1925).

253. It would be possible to stop the car and detain it until a search warrant was obtained, but that would be a cumbersome waste of resources. Given the comparative ease of arrests without warrants, it would also be possible to say no warrant is needed for the arrest of the driver, and that much or all of the search follows from that; but that would not fairly reach every aspect of a search for materials.

254. Following *Soto v. State*, 734 A.2d 350 (N.J. Sup. Ct. Law Div. 1995) (holding that statistical evidence of disproportionate traffic stops against African Americans established a de facto policy of targeting blacks for selective enforcement and thus violated the equal protection and due process clauses), New Jersey entered into a consent decree with the Department of Justice to settle complaints filed against the state by the Civil Rights Division. The consent decree, which, among other things, appointed an outside monitor to the State Police, was lifted in 2009. See Associated Press, "Oversight of New Jersey State Police is Ended," *N.Y. Times*, Sept. 22, 2009, at A28, *available at* http://www.nytimes.com/2009/09/22/nyregion/22profile.html?_r = 0.

255. Whren v. United States, 517 U.S. 806, 813–819(1996). Justice Scalia assumed that intentional racial discrimination in enforcement would implicate the Equal Protection Clause, but implied that even that was not relevant for ordinary probable cause analysis.

256. See, e.g., Carroll v. United States, 267 U.S. 132, 153 (1925) (noting that "the guaranty of freedom from unreasonable searches a seizures by the Fourth Amendment has been construed ... [h]as recogniz[ed] a necessary difference between search of a store, dwelling house, or other structure in respect of which a proper official warrant readily may be obtained and a search of a ship, motor boat, wagon or automobile for contraband goods, where it is not practicable to secure a warrant, because the vehicle can be quickly moved out of the locality or jurisdiction in which the warrant must be sought"); Chambers v. Maroney, 399 U.S. 42 (1970) (affirming a warrantless search of an automobile stopped on

the highway because the automobile is movable, the occupants are alert, and the contents of the automobile may be lost if a warrant must be obtained); United States v. Ellis, 461 F.2d 962, 966 (1972) (upholding the warrantless search of an automobile because the officer "undoubtedly thought that the automobile contained evidence which might aid in the apprehension of the two criminals still at large and waiting for a warrant might enable them to evade capture").

257. Indianapolis v. Edmond, 531 U.S. 32, 47 (2000). Commentators observe that *Edmond*'s "quantum of individualized suspicion" standard creates a loophole allowing law enforcement to use "ruse" drug enforcement checkpoints to manufacture the required suspicion necessary for a search incident to arrest. See Kathryn Howard, "Stop in the Name of That Checkpoint: Sacrificing Our Fourth Amendment Right in Order to Prevent Criminal Activity," 68 *Missouri Law Review* 485 (2003); Allison M. Low, "Designing a Constitutional Drug Ruse Checkpoint: What Does the Fourth Amendment Really Protect?," 44 *University of San Francisco Law Review* 995 (2010).

Two commentators propose a different framework for evaluating *Terry* stops, but primarily from the perspective of stop and frisk itself. First, they argue that suspicion of a civil offense violation cannot justify the intrusiveness of a stop and frisk. Second, they argue there ought to be a rebuttable presumption that stop and frisks based on the suspicion of petty offense violations are presumptively invalid. See David Keenan & Tina M. Thomas, "An Offense Severity Model for Stop-and-Frisks," 123 *Yale Law Journal* 1448 (2014). Id. at 1454 n.26, suggests that the model should be extended to automobile stops, although the authors acknowledge that there may be reasons that such an extension might be inappropriate.

258. United States v. Martinez-Fuerte, 428 U.S. 543 (1976).

259. Michigan Dep't of State Police v. Sitz, 496 U.S. 444 (1990).

260. Illinois v. Lister, 540 U.S. 419 (2004).

261. Indianapolis v. Edmond, 531 U.S. 32 (2000). About 9 percent of the motorists stopped were arrested, slightly more than half of these for drug-related crimes.

262. Knowles v. Iowa, 525 U.S. 113 (1998) (invalidating a state statute allowing officers to conduct full searches of automobiles and drivers when they issue a citation instead of making a custodial arrest).

263. Chambers v. Maroney, 399 U.S. 42 (1970).

264. United States v. Chadwick, 433 U.S. 1 (1977).

265. Arkansas v. Sanders, 442 U.S. 753 (1979).

266. Robbins v. California, 435 U.S. 420 (1981).

267. United States v. Ross, 456 U.S. 798 (1982).

268. California v. Acevedo, 500 U.S. 565 (1991).

269. 526 U.S. 295 (1999).

270. Id. at 300–02.

271. See generally Davies, the Supreme Court, supra note 123; Katkin, supra note 251.

Chapter 12

1. U.S. Const. amend. XIV, § 1.

2. See, e.g., Michael Perry, "Modern Equal Protection: A Conceptualization and Appraisal," 79 *Columbia Law Review* 1023, 1025–28 (1979).

3. Relying partly on the sense of fundamental rights covered by the Privileges and Immunities Clause, Professor Perry, supra note 1, at 1027–28, explains that the rights seen to be covered included "physical security, freedom of movement, and capacity to contract and own property."

4. See Jamal Greene, "Fourteenth Amendment Originalism," 71 *Maryland Law Review* 978 (2012) for why originalists have concentrated on some aspects of the Fourteenth Amendment and written little about others.

5. See Randy E. Barnett, "Whence Comes Section One? The Abolitionist Origins of the Fourteenth Amendment," 3 *Journal of Legal Analysis* 165 (2011).

6. Id. at 246.

7. Id. at 251.

8. 60 U.S. (19 How.) 393 (1857).

9. See Barnett, supra note 5. Some abolitionists even urged that the text of the Constitution, which did not explicitly refer to slavery, allowed Congress to forbid slavery in Southern states. Id. at 194–95.

10. See Perry, supra note 2, at 1026–28. Professor Perry relies significantly on the work of Raoul Berger, *Government By Judiciary: The Transformation of the Fourteenth Amendment* (Liberty Fund, 1977).

11. Strauder v. West Virginia, 100 U.S. 303 (1879).

12. Yick Wo v. Hopkins, 118 U.S. 356 (1886).

13. 163 U.S. 537 (1896).

14. Id. at 551.

15. See, e.g., F. James Davis, *Who Is Black? One Nation's Definition* (University Park, Penn.: Pennsylvania State University Press, 1991); Neil Gotanda, "A Critique of 'Our Constitution is Color-Blind,'" 44 *Stanford Law Review* 1, 23–24, 35 (1991).

16. McCabe v. Atchison, Topeka, & Santa Fe R. Co., 235 U.S. 151 (1914).

17. Missouri ex rel. Gaines v. Canada, 305 U.S. 337 (1938).

18. Sweatt v. Painter, 339 U.S. 629 (1950).

19. 347 U.S. 483 (1954).

20. Id. at 494.

21. Herbert Wechsler, "Toward Neutral Principles of Constitutional Law," *Principles, Politics, and Fundamental Law: Selected Essays* 3, 45–46 (Cambridge, Mass.: Harvard University Press, 1961).

22. After *Brown*, the Supreme Court avoided ruling on the acceptability of a marriage ban (even though the case before it involved an appeal as of right). Naim v. Naim, 350 U.S. 985 (1956). Herbert Wechsler called the procedural grounds for that dismissal "wholly without basis in the law." Wechsler, supra note 21, at 47.

23. Bolling v. Sharpe, 347 U.S. 497 (1954).

24. This is a position notably defended by Akhil Reed Amar, *America's Unwritten Constitution* 211–18, 279–96 (New York: Basic Books, 2012).

25. Brown v. Bd. of Educ. of Topeka, Kan., 349 U.S. 294 (1955) (Brown II).

26. Id. at 299.

27. Id. at 301.

28. Cooper v. Aaron, 358 U.S. 1 (1958).

29. 42 U.S.C. § 2000 et seq.

30. Green v. County Sch. Bd., 391 U.S. 430 (1968).

31. 402 U.S. 1 (1971).

32. Id. at 22–31.

33. 388 U.S. 1, 11 (1967) (quoting Korematsu v. United States, 323 U.S. 214 (1944)).

34. One may view *Korematsu v. United States*, 323 U.S. 214 (1944) as involving a successful argument of this sort, but almost everyone agrees that the detention of most Japanese Americans was highly unjust, and few are inclined to defend the Supreme Court's acceptance of that.

35. See Lee v. Washington, 390 U.S. 333 (1968).

36. 323 U.S. 214, 216 (1944).

37. Hernandez v. Texas, 347 U.S. 475 (1954).

38. St. Francis College v. Al-Khazraji, 481 U.S. 604, 613 (1987).

39. See Gotanda, supra note 15, at 23–35.

40. 426 U.S. 229 (1976).

41. 429 U.S. 252 (1977).

42. Hernandez v. New York, 500 U.S. 352 (1991).

43. 403 U.S. 217 (1971).

44. See Charles R. Lawrence III, "The Id, the Ego, and Equal Protection: Reckoning with Unconscious Racism," 39 *Stanford Law Review* 317 (1987); Nicholas Kristof, "Is Everyone a Little Bit Racist?," N.Y. Times, Aug. 28, 2014, at A25, col. 5.

45. Charles Lawrence notes five different ways in which race could figure in a zoning determination: (1) wanting to deny housing to blacks, (2) believing that excluding blacks will be of economic or environmental benefit, (3) wanting to exclude poor people, but being affected by their race, (4) acceptance by poorer whites of rules they would have opposed if the rules did not have the racial effect, and (5) lack of consciousness about negative effects on blacks. Lawrence, supra note 44, at 348–49.

46. Id. at 355–81.

47. Id. at 365–76.

48. Batson v. Kentucky, 476 U.S. 79 (1986). But in *Hernandez v. New York*, 500 U.S. 352 (1991), supra note 42, the Court did accept excluding Latinos on the basis of language considerations.

49. McCleskey v. Kemp, 481 U.S. 279 (1987).

50. The section on searches and seizures in Chapter 11 explores the issue of "stop and frisk" in some detail.

51. United States v. Cruikshank, 92 U.S. 542 (1875).

52. The Civil Rights Cases, 109 U.S. 3 (1883).

53. 334 U.S. 1 (1948).

54. See Cong. Globe, 39th Cong., 1st Sess. 3840–41 (1866) (Statement of Senator Saulsbury).

55. See Greene, supra note 4, at 988–89.

56. See Kent Greenawalt, *Discrimination and Reverse Discrimination* (New York: Alfred A. Knopf, Inc., Borzoi Books, 1983), and the two previous essays cited therein.

57. Morton v. Mancari, 417 U.S. 535 (1974).

58. 416 U.S. 312 (1974).

59. Id. at 341, 343 (Douglas, J., dissenting).

60. 438 U.S. 265 (1978).

61. Id. at 412 (opinion of Justice Stevens).

62. Id. at 320 (opinion of Justice Powell); id. at 325–26 (opinion of Justice Brennan).

63. Id. at 284.

64. Id. at 357 (opinion of Justice Brennan) (quoting Califano v. Webster, 430 U.S. 313, 317 (1977) and Craig v. Boren 429 U.S. 190, 197 (1976)).

65. Id. at 303.

66. Id. at 314.

67. Id. at 312.

68. United Steelworkers of America, AFL-CIO-CLC v. Weber, 443 U.S. 193 (1979). See Kent Greenawalt, 2 *Statutory and Common Law Interpretation* 26 (New York: Oxford University Press, 2013), for a discussion of the case.

69. 42 U.S.C. § 2000e-2(a) (2).

70. 448 U.S. 448 (1980).

71. Id. at 517.

72. Id. at 463–67.

73. Id. at 496.

74. 488 U.S. 469 (1989).

75. Adarand Constructors, Inc. v. Pena, 515 U.S. 200 (1995).

76. Id. at 227.

77. See Gotanda, supra note 14, at 46–52.

78. Gratz v. Bollinger, 539 U.S. 244 (2003).

79. Grutter v. Bollinger, 539 U.S. 306 (2003).

80. Id. at 323.

81. Id. at 342–43.

82. Fisher v. University of Texas at Austin, 133 S. Ct. 2411, 570 U.S. (2013).

83. Id. at 2420.

84. Parents Involved in Community Schools v. Seattle Sch. Dist. No. 1, 551 U.S. 701 (2007).

85. 377 U.S. 533 (1964).

86. Harper v. Virginia State Bd. of Elections, 383 U.S. 663 (1966).

87. Kramer v. Union Free Sch. Dist. 395 U.S. 621 (1969); Cipriano v. City of Houma, 395 U.S. 701 (1969). For certain elections to government units with limited purposes related to water storage and use, the Court has permitted limiting voting to property owners. Salyer Land Co. v. Tulare Lake Basin Water Storage Dist., 410 U.S. 719 (1973); Ball v. James, 451 U.S. 355 (1981).

88. Gomillion v. Lightfoot, 364 U.S. 339 (1960).

89. Hunter v. Underwood, 471 U.S. 222 (1985).

90. Shaw v. Reno, 509 U.S. 630 (1993). For a more recent case in which the Supreme Court overturned lower court acceptance of Alabama's drawing of districts, see *Alabama Legislative Black Caucus et al. v. Alabama et al.* (Slip opinion March 25, 2015; sending the case back for further review).

91. Village of Arlington Heights v. Metropolitan Hous. Dev. Corp., 429 U.S. 252, 265–66 (1977). See Hunter v. Underwood, 471 U.S. 222 (1985).

92. Miller v. Johnson, 515 U.S. 900, 916 (1995); Bush v. Vera, 517 U.S. 952 (1996) (plurality opinion); Easley v. Cromartie, 532 U.S. 234 (2001).

93. 42 U.S.C. § 1973.

94. South Carolina v. Katzenbach, 383 U.S. 301 (1966).

95. League of United Latin American Citizens v. Perry, 548 U.S. 399, 475–76 n.12, 518 (2006) (opinion by Justice Stevens) (opinion by Justice Scalia).

96. Shelby County, Alabama v. Holder, 133 S. Ct. 2612, 570 U.S. (2013).

97. Id. at 2632–36.

98. 83 U.S. (16 Wall.) 36 (1873).
99. 83 U.S. (16 Wall.) 130 (1873).
100. Id. at 141.
101. Minor v. Happersett, 88 U.S. (21 Wall.) 162 (1874). Forty-six years later ,the Nineteenth Amendment guaranteeing that right was adopted.
102. Muller v. Oregon, 208 U.S. 412 (1908).
103. Goesaert v. Cleary, 335 U.S. 464 (1948).
104. 404 U.S. 71, 73 (1971).
105. Id. at 76.
106. 411 U.S. 677 (1973).
107. Id. at 688.
108. Id. at 691–92.
109. 429 U.S. 190 (1976).
110. Id. at 197.
111. Kahn v. Shevin, 416 U.S. 351 (1974).
112. Schlesinger v. Ballard, 419 U.S. 498 (1975).
113. 417 U.S. 484 (1974).
114. Id. at 501.
115. Coleman v. Court of Appeals of Maryland, 132 S. Ct. 1327, 1344–45, 566 U.S. (2012) (Ginsburg, J., dissenting).
116. Mississippi Univ. for Women v. Hogan, 458 U.S. 718 (1982).
117. 518 U.S. 515 (1996).
118. Rostker v. Goldberg, 453 U.S. 57 (1981).
119. Michael M. v. Superior Court of Sonoma County, 450 U.S. 464 (1981).
120. Parham v. Hughes, 441 U.S. 347 (1979).
121. Lehr v. Robertson, 463 U.S. 248 (1983).
122. Caban v. Mohammed, 441 U.S. 380 (1979).
123. 533 U.S. 53 (2001).
124. Flores-Villar v. United States, 131 S. Ct. 2312, 564 U.S. (2011).
125. Califano v. Goldfarb, 430 U.S. 199 (1977).
126. Id. at 219–20.
127. Califano v. Webster, 430 U.S. 313 (1977).
128. Id. at 318.
129. Obergefell v. Hodges, No. 14-556. Decided June 26, 2015.
130. 348 U.S. 483 (1955).
131. Id. at 489.
132. 449 U.S. 456 (1981).
133. 413 U.S. 634, 642–43 (1973).
134. Harper v. Virginia State Bd. of Elections, 383 U.S. 663 (1966).
135. 411 U.S. 1 (1973).
136. Id. at 68, 71–72 (White, J., dissenting) (Marshall, J., dissenting). Michael C. Dorf, "Equal Protection Incorporation," 88 *Virginia Law Review* 951, 962 n.35 (2002), has written, "*Rodriguez* does not explain why an implicit fundamental right to vote can be inferred from the Constitution's silence, while a right to education cannot. . . ."
137. 304 U.S. 144, 152 n.4 (1938).
138. 539 U.S. 558 (2003).
139. 478 U.S. 186 (1986).
140. *Lawrence*, 539 U.S. at 575.
141. 517 U.S. 620 (1996).

142. Id. at 624.
143. Id. at 636 (Scalia, J., dissenting).
144. Id. at 633.
145. Hollingsworth v. Perry, 133 S. Ct. 2652, 570 U.S. (2013).
146. Perry v. Brown, 671 F.3d 1052, 1076–95 (9th Cir. 2012).
147. 133 S. Ct. 2675, 570 U.S. (2013).
148. Windsor v. United States, 699 F.3d 169,181 (2d Cir. 2012).
149. *Windsor,* 133 S. Ct. at 2692.
150. Id. at 2693.
151. Id. at 2694.
152. 413 U.S. 528 (1973).
153. *Windsor,* 133 S. Ct. at 2693.
154. Id. at 2696, 2707, 2711 (Roberts, C.J., Scalia, Alioto, J., dissenting).
155. Greene, supra note 4, at 1002.
156. Writing about constitutional interpretation more generally, T. Alexander Aleinikoff, "Constitutional Law in the Age of Balancing," 96 *Yale Law Journal* 943, 1003 (1987), commented, "A unitary theory of constitutional interpretation may be elegant, but it is likely to be a distinctly unrealistic approach to the document."
157. See Andrew M. Siegel, "Equal Protection Unmodified: Justice John Paul Stevens and the Case for Unmediated Constitutional Interpretation," 74 *Fordham Law Review* 2339 (2006).
158. Aleinikoff, supra note 156, at 999.
159. William N. Eskridge Jr., "Some Effects of Identity-Based Social Movements on Constitutional Law in the Twentieth Century," 100 *Michigan Law Review* 2062 (2002).
160. Dorf, supra note 135.

Conclusion

1. The point about levels of purpose is explained in 2 *Statutory and Common Law Interpretation* 10–11.
2. An example in id. at 56–58 of a term about which people may have conflicting views is exactly what counts as "discrimination"—does a prohibition of it bar preferential treatment for disadvantaged minorities?
3. Id. at 19–75.
4. Id. at 181–82.
5. Id. at 217–44.
6. 1 *Legal Interpretation: Perspectives from Other Disciplines and Private Texts* 232–36.
7. Id. at 261–62.
8. Id. at 282–84.
9. National Labor Relations Board v. Noel Canning, 134 S. Ct. 2550 (2014).
10. Id. at 241–42.
11. Id. at 301–13. Judges sometimes treat similarly servitudes and easements in real property documents and terms of contracts that have become seriously impractical. Id. at 313–20.
12. Id. at 218–24.
13. Id. at 19–33.
14. Id. at 329–36.

15. Id. at 149–073.
16. Volume I, at 59–76.
17. Volume II, at 142.
18. Volume I, at 89–95.
19. See id., at 107–38.
20. Id. at 181–206.
21. Volume II, at 141–74.
22. This was a point emphasized by Robert Cover in his comparison of religious and legal interpretation. Volume I, at 117–18.
23. See id.

Cases

F

G

Index

C

P